REAL LIFE
DICTIONARY
OF
THE LAW

Taking The Mystery Out Of Legal Language

Gerald N. Hill
&
Kathleen Thompson Hill

GENERAL PUBLISHING GROUP
Los Angeles

Publisher: W. Quay Hays
Editor: Sarah Pirch
Design: Catherine Vo Bailey
Copy Editor: Peter Hoffman

For information:
General Publishing Group, Inc.
2701 Ocean Park Boulevard, Suite 140
Santa Monica, CA 90405

Hill, Gerald N.
    Real life dictionary of the law : taking the mystery out of legal
language / Gerald N. Hill & Kathleen Thompson Hill.
        p. cm.
        ISBN 1-57544-054-7
        1. Law--United States--Dictionaries.   2. Law--United States-
-Popular works.   I. Hill, Kathleen.   II. Title.
KF156.H55   1995
349.73 ' 03--dc20   95-12249
[347.3003]   CIP

Printed in the USA
10 9 8 7 6 5 4 3 2 1

General Publishing Group, Inc.
Los Angeles

The language of the law must not be foreign
to the ears of those who are to obey it.
—Judge Learned Hand

The language of laws should be simple;
directness is always better than elaborate wording.
—Charles Louis de Montesquieu

ACKNOWLEDGMENTS

In developing this project we benefitted greatly from the help of Mary Evelyn Arnold, who read the original manuscript and made numerous valuable suggestions, by the comments of attorneys Joel S. Coble, Melville Owen and Jerome Marks, by the encouragement of our agent, Mike Hamilburg, and by the care of our editors, Colby Allerton and Sarah Pirch.

Gerald N. Hill
Kathleen Thompson Hill

TABLE OF CONTENTS

FOREWORD

Legal proceedings have become the entertainment of the masses. If you doubt this, try to find a television station at dinner time in early 1995 that did not cover some aspect of the O.J. Simpson murder trial. Of course, observing trials is a very old sport in the western world. The difference now is that one need not scramble for room in the gallery; if you own a television set, you cannot escape the law.

But does the average viewer fully understand what he or she is viewing in the televised courtroom? While legal proceedings have become more accessible, the language of the law has become more arcane. Standard legal dictionaries (e.g., the venerable *Black's Law Dictionary*), packaged in imposing bound volumes and filled with ponderous definitions, are not helpful to the average non-lawyer. That is precisely where the Hills' *Real Life Dictionary of the Law* finds its niche. Such a reference work can be invaluable not only for watching and understanding televised legal proceedings about other people's problems, but also in better comprehending the legal language that daily confronts us all.

Gerald N. Hill, a Hastings graduate, and his co-author, Kathleen Thompson Hill, a political psychologist, have produced a book of great value for laymen and lawyers alike. As their subtitle suggests, the law should not be the mystery it has become.

Mary Kay Kane, Dean
Hastings College of the Law, University of California

INTRODUCTION

The language of law often appears to be much like the hieroglyphics of ancient Egypt devised by the priests to keep knowledge of the rites of the temple from the people. To an extent, that suspicion is true, since no one will pay for common knowledge. However, the fact that legal definitions are special, obscure and confusing is also due to historic accident, the multiplicity of their sources, and the increasing complexity of modern life. The people's need to comprehend legal meanings is far more than mere curiosity. In today's world it is a public necessity.

This dictionary intends to demystify and clarify the language of the law for all people. The definitions are put into real life context, so that they do not just stand alone on the printed page, unconnected to reality. Where necessary there are explanations beyond the mere definitions, with illustrations, examples, phonic pronunciation and internal definitions so that the reader need not search from one definition to another for meaning.

To remove the veil of mystery is not easy, but necessary in a democracy in which the law is constantly demanding attention, from an apartment lease to a permit for a street dance, a speeding ticket to a class action for victims of a faulty product. Since the invention of the photocopier (now followed by the FAX) this has become a paper-driven society, in which the public is flooded with documentation. The closing of a sale of a house involves agreements, acknowledgments and warranties in legal jargon worthy of a merger of two major corporations a generation ago.

Trials, particularly involving crime, are often high drama attracting great attention (hence the list of 30 leading legal films in the Appendix). Fictional law firms as well as actual high-profile cases are brought directly from courtroom to living room via television, with the lawyers and judges sparring under rules and in language which the public wants to understand.

The reliance on Latin, and occasionally French, lingers from the past as the special province of lawyers. While phrases like *ab initio* and *res ipsa loquitur* are handy shorthand for attorneys, they serve to isolate the public from understanding the meanings of the law. And in their wake comes the lingo of the tax expert which confounds all but the specially trained. Readily understood definitions in English can assist in breaking down these language barriers.

The present craving for simplicity, common sense and common knowledge of the meanings of legal language is not new. Thus the Greek playwright Aeschylus calls out from the fifth century before Christ that "wrong must not win on technicalities," and Montesquieu wrote in 1748 that "the language of laws should be simple."

The *Real Life Dictionary of the Law* fulfills the general public's right to understand legal language. It also provides the thousands of law students a ready reference to assist them in their formidable task of absorbing the lore of law. The same is true of the legion of paralegals and legal secretaries who make law offices effective. And every lawyer can benefit from this single-volume source of simply worded, self-contained legal definitions which do not require further research.

In sum, our contribution to legal understanding is based on Samuel Johnson's definition of the law as "the last result of human wisdom acting upon human experience for the benefit of the public."

Gerald N. Hill
Kathleen Thompson Hill

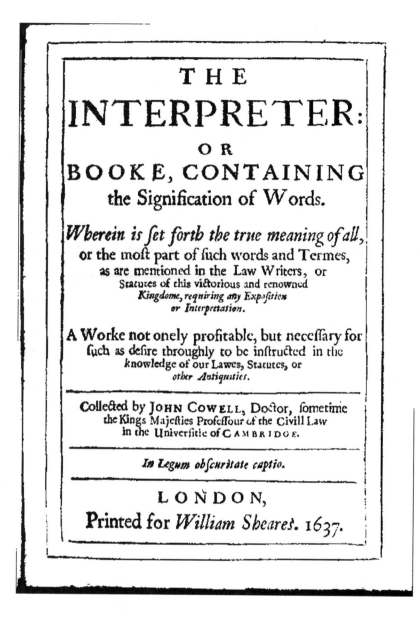

THE
INTERPRETER:
OR
BOOKE, CONTAINING
the Signification of Words.

Wherein is set forth the true meaning of all,
or the most part of such words and Termes,
as are mentioned in the Law Writers, or
Statutes of this victorious and renowned
*Kingdome, requiring any Exposition
or Interpretation.*

A Worke not onely profitable, but necessary for
such as desire throughly to be instructed in the
knowledge of our Lawes, Statutes, or
other Antiquities.

Collected by JOHN COWELL, Doctor, sometime
the Kings Majesties Professour of the Civill Law
in the Universitie of CAMBRIDGE.

In Legum obscuritate captio.

LONDON,
Printed for *William Sheares*. 1637.

The title page to one of the earliest legal dictionaries, Cowell's Interpreter, *which had a very rocky beginning. John Cowell, professor of law at Cambridge University, originally published this pioneer work in 1607. However, Parliament found the book politically incorrect since some of the definitions upheld the King's absolute power. So, in 1610, Parliament ordered* The Interpreter *"suppressed" and all copies burned. Dr. Cowell lost his professorship and the next year he died. His dictionary was not reprinted until 1637.*

To the memory of our fathers

RAYMOND TEAL HILL
and
GEORGE EDWARD THOMPSON

DEFINITIONS

A – Z

abandon: v. to intentionally and permanently give up, surrender, leave, desert or relinquish all interest or ownership in property, a home or other premises, a right of way, and even a spouse, family, or children. The word is often used in situations to determine whether a tenant has left his/her apartment and the property inside and does not intend to come back. Thus, a landlord can take over an apparently abandoned residence, but must store anything a tenant leaves behind and give notice to the tenant before selling the possessions which are left. To abandon children can mean to have no contact and give no support for a year or more. (See: **abandoned property, abandonment**)

abandoned property: n. property left behind (often by a tenant) intentionally and permanently when it appears that the former owner (or tenant) does not intend to come back, pick it up, or use it. Examples may include possessions left in a house after the tenant has moved out or autos left beside a road for a long period of time, or patent rights of an inventor who does not apply for a patent and lets others use his invention without protest. One may have abandoned the property of contract rights by not doing what is required by the contract. However, an easement and other land rights are not abandoned property just because of non-use. (See: **abandon, abandonment**)

abandonment: n. the act of intentionally and permanently giving up, surrendering, deserting or relinquishing property, premises, a right of way, a ship, contract rights, a spouse and/or children. Abandonment of a spouse means intent at permanent separation, and with children a lengthy period of neither contact nor any support. In maritime law abandonment has a special meaning: when an owner surrenders a ship and its contents to a trustee for the benefit of claimants, particularly after a wreck. If one invents something and does not get a patent but allows others to use the invention or dedicates it to public use, the right to patent is probably abandoned. Confusion arises over abandonment of water rights, mining rights, or rights of way, since mere non-use is not sufficient to show abandonment. (See: **abandon, abandoned property, patent**)

abate: v. to do away with a problem, such as a public or private nuisance or some structure built contrary to public policy. This can include dikes which illegally direct water onto a neighbor's property, high volume noise from a rock band or a factory, an improvement constructed in violation of building and safety codes, or seepage from a faulty septic tank. (See: **abatement**)

abatement: n. 1) the removal of a problem which is against public or private policy, or endangers others, including nuisances such as weeds that might catch fire on an otherwise empty lot; 2) an equal reduction of recovery of debts by all creditors when there are not enough funds or assets to pay the full amount; 3) an equal reduction of benefits to beneficiaries (heirs) when an estate is not large enough to pay each beneficiary in full. (See: **abate**)

abduction: n. the criminal taking away of a person by persuasion (convincing someone—particularly a minor or a woman—he/she is better off leaving with the persuader), by fraud (telling the person he/she is needed, or that the mother or father wants him/her to come with the abductor), or by open force or violence. Originally abduction applied only to protect women and children as victims. Currently in most states it can also apply to an adult male. In fact, in some states like New York abduction meant the unlawful taking or detention of any female for purposes of "marriage, concubinage or prostitution." Kidnapping is more limited, requiring force, threat of force upon an adult or the taking of children. (See: **kidnapping**)

> *There are not enough jails, not enough policemen, not enough courts to enforce a law not supported by the people.*
> *—Senator and Vice President Hubert H. Humphrey*

abet: v. to help someone commit a crime, including helping them escape from police or plan the crime. (See: **aid and abet**)

abeyance: 1) n. when the ownership of property has not been determined. Examples include title to real property in the estate of a person who has died and there is no obvious party to receive title or there appears to be no legal owner of the property, a shipwreck while it is being determined who has the right to salvage the ship and its cargo, or a bankrupt person's property before the bankruptcy court has decided what property is available to creditors or alleged heirs. 2) legal jargon for "undetermined."

ab initio: prep. lawyer Latin for "from the start," as "it was legal *ab initio*."

able-bodied: adj. physically capable of working at a job or in the military. It is often used to describe a person as capable of earning a living and, therefore, of paying alimony or child support.

abortion: n. the termination of pregnancy by various means, including medical surgery, before the fetus is able to sustain independent life. Until 1973 abortion was considered a crime (by the mother and the doctor) unless performed by physicians to protect the life of the mother, a phrase often broadly interpreted. Untrained persons performed thousands of abortions each year in the U.S. using hasty, unsanitary and dangerous means, resulting in maiming, permanent damage of organs, and death of many women. The Supreme Court ruled in the case of Roe v. Wade (1973) that a woman had the right to choose abortion to end a pregnancy through the first trimester (three months) of gestation. In the latter stages of pregnancy, danger to the life of the mother could still justify a legal abortion. Political struggles followed over legalized abortions. Some state legislatures passed limitations such as requiring teenage girls to obtain their parents' consent in order to get an abortion. Despite appointment of anti-abortion justices by Presidents Reagan and Bush, the Supreme Court has not over-turned the basic Wade case rule. President Bill Clinton's appointments are expected to make legalized abortion continue in the future.

abrogate: v. to annul or repeal a law or pass legislation that contradicts the prior law. Abrogate also applies to revoking or withdrawing conditions of a contract. (See: **repeal**)

Avoid litigation
—Abraham Lincoln

abscond: v. 1) traditionally to leave a jurisdiction (where the court, a process server or law enforcement can find one) to avoid being served with legal papers or being arrested. 2) a surprise leaving with funds or goods that have been stolen, as in "he absconded with the loot."

absolute: adj. complete, and without condition.

abstention doctrine: n. when the Supreme Court refuses to exercise its federal constitutional jurisdiction or declines to consider a question of state law arising from a case being appealed from a state court.

abstract: n. in general, a summary of a record or document, such as an abstract of judgment or abstract of title to real property. (See: **abstract of judgment, abstract of title**)

abstract of judgment: n. a written summary of a judgment which states how much money the losing party owes to the person who won the lawsuit (judgment creditor), the rate of interest to be paid on the judgment amount, court costs, and any specific orders that the losing party (judgment debtor) must obey, which abstract is acknowledged and stamped so that it can be recorded at the county recorder. The purpose of an abstract of judgment is to create a public record and create a lien or claim if necessary on any real estate owned or later acquired by the loser located in the county in which the abstract of judgment is recorded. If the loser does not pay the judgment voluntarily then the winner can force a sheriff's sale of any property to collect. There are several problems: a) to find the county where the loser owns real estate; b) the probability that there are secured loans, tax liens and/or other judgments that come ahead of the judgment lien; c) the possibility that the loser/debtor may go bankrupt and avoid paying the debt. (See: **levy, lien**)

abstract of title: n. the written report on a title search which shows the history of every change of ownership on a piece of real estate, and any claims against the property, such as easements on the property, loans against it, deeds of trust, mortgages, liens, judgments, and real property taxes. Some abstracts only go back in history to the last change in title. In some places the abstract of title is prepared by a title company, and in other places by an individual who is called an abstractor. Most buyers and all lenders require the title report with an abstract. The information in the abstract is up to the moment, comes from the local county recorder's office, and usually requires an expert search. (See: **chain of title, title report**)

abuse of discretion: n. a polite way of saying a trial judge has made such a bad mistake ("clearly against reason and evidence" or against established law) during a trial or on ruling on a motion that a person did not get a fair trial. A court of appeals will use a finding of this abuse as a reason to reverse the trial court judgment. Examples of "abuse of discretion" or judges' mistakes include not allowing an important witness to testify, making improper comments that might influence a jury, showing bias, or making rulings on evidence that deny a person a chance to tell his or her side of the matter. This does not mean a trial or the judge has to be perfect, but it does mean that the judge's actions were so far out of bounds that someone truly did not get a fair trial. Sometimes the appeals courts admit the judge was wrong, but not wrong enough to have influenced the outcome of the trial, often to the annoyance of the losing party. In criminal cases abuse of discretion can include sentences that are grossly too harsh. In a divorce action, it includes awarding alimony way beyond the established formula or the spouse's or life partner's realistic ability to pay.

abuse of process: n. the use of legal process by illegal, malicious, or perverted means. Examples include serving (officially giving) a complaint to someone when it has not actually been filed, just to intimidate an enemy; filing a false declaration of service (filing a paper untruthfully stating a lie that someone has officially given a notice to another person, filing a lawsuit which has no basis at law, but is intended to get information, force payment through fear of legal entanglement or gain an unfair or illegal advantage. Some people think they are clever by abusing the process this way. A few unscrupulous lawyers do so intentionally and can be subject to discipline and punishment. Sometimes a lawyer will abuse the process accidentally; an honest one will promptly correct the error and apologize.

abut: v. when two parcels of real property touch each other.

acceleration: n. 1) speeding up the time when there is vesting (absolute ownership) of an interest in an estate, when the interest in front of it is terminated earlier than expected; 2) in a contract or promissory note, when the payment of debt is moved up to the present time due to some event like non-payment of an installment or sale of the property which secures the debt. (See: **acceleration clause, vest**)

acceleration clause: n. a provision in a contract or promissory note that if some specified event (like not making payments on time) occurs then the entire amount is due or other requirements are due now, pronto. This clause is most often found in promissory notes with installment payments for purchase of real property and requires that if the property is sold then the entire amount of the note is due immediately (the so-called "due on sale clause"). Some states prohibit "due on sale" and always allow the new property owner to assume the debt. (See: **acceleration, assumption)**

accept: v. to receive something with approval and intention to keep it. This use often arises on the question of accepting a payment which is late or not complete or accepting the "service" (delivery) of legal papers.

acceptance: n. 1) receiving something from another with the intent to keep it, and showing that this was based on a previous agreement. 2) agreeing verbally or in writing to the terms of a contract, which is one of the requirements to show there was a contract (an offer and an acceptance of that offer). A written offer can be accepted only in writing. 3) receiving goods with the intention of paying for them if a sale has been agreed to. 4) agreement to pay a bill of exchange, which can be an "absolute acceptance" (to pay as the bill is written) or "conditional acceptance" (to pay only when some condition actually occurs such as the shipment or delivery of certain goods). "Acceptance" is most often used in the factual determination of whether a contract was entered into. (See: **contract, offer**)

acceptance of service: n. agreement by a defendant (or his/her attorney) in a legal action to accept a complaint or other petition (like divorce papers) without having the sheriff or process server show up at the door. The agreement of "acceptance of service" must be in writing or there is no proof that it happened. In most jurisdictions there is a form entitled "receipt and acknowledgment of acceptance of service" or similar language which must be signed, dated and sent back to the attorney who sent the complaint or petition. Attorneys must be careful that they have legal authority from a client to act on his/her behalf, because a client may deny later that he/she gave authority to accept service. (See: **service**)

access: n. 1) in real estate the right and ability to get to the property. 2) when a husband has the opportunity to make love to his wife, it is said he has access. This rather vulgar use of "access" has been important because if a husband "had access" to his wife during the time when she became pregnant, it is presumed he is the father. Modern use of blood tests and DNA studies may show the father to be someone other than the husband whether the husband "had access" or not. (See: **DNA, egress, paternity suit**)

accessory: n. a second-string player who helps in the commission of a crime by driving the getaway car, providing the weapons, assisting in the planning, providing an alibi, or hiding the principal offender after the crime. Usually the accessory is not immediately present during the crime, but must be aware that the crime is going to be committed or has been committed. Usually an accessory's punishment is less than that of the main perpetrator, but a tough jury or judge may find the accessory just as responsible. (See: **aid and abet**)

accommodation: n. 1) a favor done without compensation (pay or consideration), such as a signature guaranteeing payment of a debt, sometimes called an accommodation endorsement. Such accommodation is not the smartest business practice, since the holder of the note can go after the accommodator rather than the debtor and will do so if the accommodator has lots of money or is easier to locate than the debtor. 2) giving in to an adversary on a point to make a deal work. (See: **guarantor**)

accomplice: n. someone who assists in the commission of a crime and, unlike a mere accessory, is usually present or directly aids in the crime (like holding a gun on the bank guard while the vault is looted, or holding a victim of assault and battery). Also unlike an accessory who can claim being only a subordinate figure, the accomplice may share in the same charge and punishment as the principal criminal. (See: **accessory**)

accord and satisfaction: n. an agreement to accept less than is legally due in order to wrap up the matter. Once the accord and satisfaction is made and the amount paid (even though it is less than owed) the debt is wiped out since the new agreement (accord) and payment (the satisfaction) replaces the original obligation. It is often used by creditors as "a bird in the hand is worth two in the bush" practicality. (See: **novation**)

account stated: n. a statement between a creditor or the person to whom money is owed and a debtor (the person who owes) that a particular amount is owed to the seller as of a certain date. Often the account stated is a bill, invoice or a summary of invoices, signed by the customer or sent to the customer who pays part or all of it without protest. This is important when a frustrated businessman sues for "account stated" which sets both the debtor's liability and the exact amount the debtor must pay, which is less complicated than claiming a debt is due and payable. An account stated may carry a longer statute of limitations (time to file suit) than some other forms of debt depending on the state. (See: **debt**)

accounts payable: n. bills that are owed. (See: **debt**)

accounts receivable: n. the amounts of money due or owed to a business or professional by customers or clients. Generally, accounts receivable refers to the total amount due and is considered in calculating the value of a business or the business's problems in paying its own debts. Evaluation of the chances of collecting based on history of customers' payments, quality of customers and age of the accounts receivable and debts is important. A big mistake made by people overly eager to buy a business is to give too high a value to the accounts receivable without considering the chances of collection.

America is the paradise of lawyers.
—Justice David J. Brewer

accretion: n. 1) in real estate, the increase of the actual land on a stream, lake or sea by the action of water which deposits soil upon the shoreline. Accretion is Mother Nature's little gift to a landowner. 2) in estates, when a beneficiary of the person who died gets more of the estate than he/she was meant to because another beneficiary or heir dies or rejects the gift. Example: if a brother and sister were supposed to divide a share of Dad's estate, but brother doesn't want it, then sister's share grows by accretion. 3) in trusts, accretion occurs when a beneficiary gets a surprising increase in benefits due to an unexpected event. (See: **probate, trust**)

accrue: v. 1) growing or adding to, such as interest on a debt or investment which continues to accumulate. 2) the coming into being of the right to bring a lawsuit. For example, the right to sue on a contract only accrues when the contract is breached (not on mere suspicion that it might be breached) or when the other party repudiates the contract (anticipatory breach).

accusation: n. 1) in legal terms accusation means officially charging someone with a crime either by indictment by a Grand Jury or filing charges by a District Attorney. 2) in lay terms any claim of wrongdoing by another person.

accused: n. a person charged with a crime.

acknowledge: v. 1) generally to admit something, whether bad, good or indifferent. 2) to verify to a notary public or other officer (such as a County Clerk) that the signer executed (wrote, signed) the document like a deed, lease, or power of attorney, to make it certified as legal and suitable for recording. (See: **acknowledgment**)

acknowledgment: n. the section at the end of a document where a notary public verifies that the signer of the document states he/she actually signed it. Typical language is: "State of Texas, County of Deaf Smith: (signed and sealed) On July 1, 1994, before me, a notary public for said state, personally appeared James Fifield, personally known to me, or proved to be said person by proper proof, and acknowledged that he executed the above Deed." Then the notary signs the acknowledgment and puts on his/her seal, which is usually a rubber stamp, although some still use a metal seal. The person acknowledging that he/she signed must be ready to produce a driver's license or other proof of existence, and must sign the notary's journal. The acknowledgment is vital for any document which must be recorded by the County Recorder or Recorder of Deeds, including deeds, deeds of trust, mortgages, powers of attorney that may involve real estate, some leases and various other papers.

acquit: v. what a jury or judge sitting without a jury does at the end of a criminal trial if the jury or judge finds the accused defendant not guilty. (See: **verdict**)

acquittal: n. what an accused criminal defendant receives if he/she is found not guilty. It is a verdict (a judgment in a criminal case) of not guilty. (See: **acquit**)

act: 1) n. in general, any action by a person. 2) n. a statutory plan passed by

Congress or any legislature which is a "bill" until enacted and becomes law. 3) v. for a court to make a decision and rule on a motion or petition, as in "the court will act on your motion for a new trial."

action: n. a lawsuit in which one party (or parties) sues another. (See: **cause of action, lawsuit**)

actionable: adj. when enough facts or circumstances exist to meet the legal requirements to file a legitimate lawsuit. If the facts required to prove a case cannot be alleged in the complaint, the case is not "actionable" and the client and his/her attorney should not file a suit. Of course, whether many cases are actionable is a matter of judgment and interpretation of the facts and/or law, resulting in many lawsuits that clog the courts. Incidentally, if a case is filed which is clearly not actionable, it may result in a lawsuit against the filer of the original suit for malicious prosecution by the defendant after he/she has won the original suit. (See: **cause of action, lawsuit, malicious prosecution**)

act of God: n. a natural catastrophe which no one can prevent such as an earthquake, a tidal wave, a volcanic eruption, a hurricane or a tornado. Acts of God are significant for two reasons: 1) for the havoc and damage they wreak, and 2) because often contracts state that "acts of God" are an excuse for delay or failure to fulfill a commitment or to complete a construction project. Many insurance policies exempt coverage for damage caused by acts of God, which is one time an insurance company gets religion. At times disputes arise as to whether a violent storm or other disaster was an act of God (and therefore exempt from a claim) or a foreseeable natural event. God knows the answer!

actual controversy: n. a true legal dispute which leads to a genuine lawsuit rather than merely a "cooked up" legal action filed to get a court to give the equivalent of an advisory opinion. Federal courts, including the U.S. Supreme Court, will only consider an "actual controversy", on appeal, since they will not give advisory (informal) opinions or make judgments on "friendly suits" filed to test the potential outcome. (See: **friendly suit**)

actual notice: n. having been informed directly of something or having seen it occur, as distinguished from constructive notice (e.g. a notice was mailed but not received, published in a newspaper, or placed in official records). (See: **notice**)

addendum: n. an addition to a completed written document. Most commonly this is a proposed change or explanation (such as a list of goods to be included) in a contract, or some point that has been the subject of negotiation after the contract was originally proposed by one party. Real property sales agreements often have addenda (plural of addendum) as the buyer and seller negotiate fine points (how payments will be made, what appliances will be included, date of transfer of title, the terms of financing by the seller and the like). Although often they are not, addenda should be signed separately and attached to the original agreement so that there will be no confusion as to what is included or intended. Unsigned addenda could be confused with rough drafts or unaccepted proposals or included fraudulently.

adeem: v. to revoke a gift made in a will by destroying, selling or giving away the gift item during the lifetime of the testator (writer of the will). Example: a person writes in his/her will, "I leave my son my 1988 Cadillac automobile" and then Dad totals or sells the car. Nasty legal fights can arise if the supposed adeemed gift is not clearly identified, as in "I give Robert my family car." Then the giver sells the Cadillac and buys a Jeep. Better will language would be: "To Johnny any (or the newest) automobile of which I shall be possessed at the time of my death." (See: **ademption**)

ademption: n. the act of adeeming, which is revoking (getting rid of) a gift mentioned in a will by destruction, or selling or giving away the gift before death. (See: **adeem**)

adequate remedy: n. a remedy (money or performance) awarded by a court or through private action (including compromise) which affords "complete" satisfaction, and is "practical, efficient and appropriate" in the circumstances. In part this depends on what relief (like an order granting one an easement over a neighbor's property or an order keeping the drunken husband away from the complaining wife) a party is seeking. A court is a bit self-congratulatory and subjectively judgmental when it announces that the remedy granted is "adequate" when it has done the best it can in the circumstances. Example: a "stay away" order telling an abusive husband to keep his distance from his wife but not putting him in jail. The order is only a piece of paper until he violates it, giving cause for his arrest.

adhesion contract (contract of adhesion): n. a contract (often a signed form) so imbalanced in favor of one party over the other that there is a strong implication it was not freely bargained. Example: a rich landlord dealing with a poor tenant who has no choice and must accept all terms of a lease, no matter how restrictive or burdensome, since the tenant cannot afford to move. An adhesion contract can give the little guy the opportunity to claim in court that the contract with the big shot is invalid. This doctrine should be used and applied more often, but the same big guy-little guy inequity may apply in the ability to afford a trial or find and pay a resourceful lawyer. (See: **contract**)

ad hoc: adj. Latin shorthand meaning "for this purpose only." Thus, an *ad hoc* committee is formed for a specific purpose, usually appointed to solve a particular problem. An *ad hoc* attorney is one hired to handle one problem only and often is a specialist in a particular area or considered especially able to argue a key point.

adjourn: v. the final closing of a meeting, such as a convention, a meeting of the board of directors, or any official gathering. It should not be confused with a recess, meaning the meeting will break and then continue at a later time. (See: **recess, session**)

adjudication: n. the act of giving a judicial ruling such as a judgment or decree. The term is used particularly in bankruptcy proceedings, in which the order declaring a debtor bankrupt is called an adjudication. (See: **bankruptcy**)

adjusted basis: n. in accounting, the original cost of an asset adjusted for costs of improvements, depreciation, damage and other events which may have affected its value during the period of ownership. This is important in calculating capital gains for income tax purposes since the adjusted basis is generally higher than the original price and will lower capital gains taxes. (See: **basis, income tax**)

> *A lawyer has no business with the justice or injustice of the cause which he undertakes, unless his client asks his opinion, and then he is bound to give it honestly. The justice or injustice of the cause is to be decided by the judge.*
> *—Samuel Johnson*

adjuster: n. an employee (usually a non-lawyer) of an insurance company or an adjustment firm employed by an insurance company to negotiate an early settlement of a claim for damages against a person, a business or public body (like a city). While a fair and responsible adjuster can serve a real purpose in getting information and evaluating the case for the insurance company, some adjusters try to make a settlement before the injured person has retained an attorney ("don't worry, we'll pay your bills. You don't need an attorney. He'll only confuse things."), get a statement from the injured without counsel, or delay the payout with the promise he/she will negotiate any reasonable demand, and then making an offer of payment that is absurdly low. Some insurance companies try to make the attorney deal with the adjuster, which is cheaper than sending the case to defense attorneys. Adjusters also represent the company in approving settlements.

ad litem adj. legal Latin meaning "for the purposes of the legal action only." Most often the term applies to a parent who files a lawsuit for his or her minor child as "guardian at litem" (guardian just for the purposes of the lawsuit) or for a person who is incompetent. Either at the time the lawsuit is filed or shortly thereafter, the parent petitions the court to allow him/her to be guardian *ad litem*, which is brought ex parte (without a noticed hearing) and is almost always granted. A person acting *ad litem* has the responsibility to pursue the lawsuit and to account for the money recovered for damages. If a child in such a lawsuit reaches majority (18 in most states) while the suit is pending, the *ad litem* guardianship terminates and the "new" adult can run his/her own lawsuit. Some courts require an order terminating the guardianship *ad litem* upon proof of coming of age. (See: **guardian *ad litem***)

administer: v. 1) to conduct the duties of a job or position. 2) particularly, to manage the affairs of the estate of a person who has died under supervision of the local court. 3) to give an oath, as in "administer the oath." (See: **administrator, executor, probate**)

administrative hearing: n. a hearing before any governmental agency or before an administrative law judge. Such hearings can range from simple arguments to what amounts to a trial. There is no jury, but the agency or the administrative law judge will make a ruling. (See: **administrative law, hearing**)

administrative law: n. the procedures created by administrative agencies (governmental bodies of the city, county, state or federal government) involving rules, regulations, applications, licenses, permits, available information, hearings, appeals and decision-making. Federal agency procedures are governed by the Administrative Procedure Act, and many states have adopted similar procedural formats either by law or regulation. It is important to consider two vital factors in dealing with administrative agencies: 1) the rules and regulations are often special for each agency and are not usually found in the statutes but in those regulations; 2) a member of the public must "exhaust his/her administrative remedies" (take every step, including appeals) with the agency and its system before he/she can challenge the administrative ruling with a lawsuit in court. There are exceptions (such as emergency or obvious futility) to exhausting one's remedies, but those are rare. Administrative law can be a technical jungle, and many lawyers make lots of money from knowing how to hack their way through it on behalf of their clients. (See: **administrative law judge, Administrative Procedure Act**)

administrative law judge: n. a professional hearing officer who works for the government to preside over hearings and appeals involving governmental agencies. They are generally experienced in the particular subject matter of the agency involved or of several agencies. Formerly called "hearing officers," they discovered that there was more prestige and higher pay in being called "judge."

Administrative Procedure Act: n. the federal act which established the rules and regulations for applications, claims, hearings and appeals involving governmental agencies. There are similar acts in many states which spell out the rules for dealing with state government agencies. (See: **administrative hearing, administrative law**)

administrator: n. the person appointed by the court to handle the estate of someone who died without a will, with a will but no nominated executor, or the executor named in the will has died, has been removed from the case or does not desire to serve. If there is a will but no available executor, the administrator is called an "administrator with will annexed." The procedure is that if an estate must be probated (filed and approved by a court) then someone (usually a relative or close friend) petitions the court in the appropriate county (usually where the late lamented last lived) for appointment of a particular person as administrator. If an estate requires attention and no one has come forward to administer the estate, then the county Public Administrator may do so. In most cases state law requires that the administrator post a bond ordered by the court to protect the estate from mishandling or malfeasance. If the will includes real property in another state then the administrator or executor must find someone in the other state to handle the change of title and paying of local taxes, and that person is called an "ancillary administrator." (See: **administer, ancillary administrator, executor, probate**)

admiralty: n. concerning activities which occur at sea, including on small boats and ships in navigable bays. Admiralty law (maritime law) includes accidents and injuries at sea, maritime contracts and commerce, alleged violations of rules of the sea over shipping lanes and rights-of-way, and mutiny and other crimes on shipboard. Jurisdiction over all these matters rests in the federal courts, which do not use juries in admiralty cases. There are other special rules in processing maritime cases, which are often handled by admiralty law specialists. Lawyers appearing in admiralty cases are called "proctors." (See: **maritime law**)

admissible evidence: n. evidence which the trial judge finds is useful in helping the trier of fact (a jury if there is a jury, otherwise the judge), and which cannot be objected to on the basis that it is irrelevant, immaterial, or violates the rules against hearsay and other objections. Sometimes the evidence which a person tries to introduce has little relevant value (usually called probative value) in determining some fact, or prejudice from the

jury's shock at gory details may outweigh that probative value. In criminal cases the courts tend to be more restrictive on letting the jury hear such details for fear they will result in "undue prejudice." Thus, the jury may only hear a sanitized version of the facts in prosecutions involving violence. (See: **evidence, objections**)

admission: n. a statement made by a party to a lawsuit or a criminal defendant, usually prior to trial, that certain facts are true. An admission is not to be confused with a confession of blame or guilt, but admits only some facts. In civil cases, each party is permitted to submit a written list of alleged facts and request the other party to admit or deny whether each is true or correct. Failure to respond in writing is an admission of the alleged facts and may be used in trial. (See: **admission against interest, confession**)

admission against interest: n. an admission of the truth of a fact by any person, but especially by the parties to a lawsuit, when a statement obviously would do that person harm, be embarrassing, or be against his/her personal or business interests. Another party can quote in court an admission against interest even though it is only hearsay. (See: **admission, hearsay**)

admission of evidence: n. a judge's acceptance of evidence in a trial. (See: **evidence**)

admission of guilt: n. a statement by someone accused of a crime that he/she committed the offense. If the admission is made outside court to a police officer it may be introduced as evidence if the defendant was given the proper warnings as to his/her rights ("Miranda warning") before talking. (See: **admission, confession, guilty, Miranda warning, rights**)

admission to bail: n. an order of a court in a criminal case allowing an accused defendant to be freed pending trial if he/she posts bail (deposits either cash or a bond) in an amount set by the court. Theoretically the posting of bail is intended to guarantee the appearance of the defendant in court when required. In minor routine cases (e.g. petty theft or drunk driving) a judge automatically sets bail based on a rate schedule which can be obtained and put up quickly. Otherwise bail is set at the first court appearance (arraignment). Although the U.S. Constitution guarantees the right to bail, in extreme cases (murder, treason, mayhem) the court is not required to admit a prisoner to bail of any amount due to the likelihood of the defendent fleeing the area, or causing further harm. Bail bondsmen are usually readily available near larger courthouses and jails, charge ten percent of the amount of the court-required bond, and often demand collateral for the amount posted. If the defendant fails to show up in court or flees ("jumps bail"), the defendant may have to give up his/her deposit (bail). When the case is concluded, the bail is "exonerated" (released) and returned to the bail bond company or to whoever put up the cash. If a bail bondsman has good reason to believe his client is attempting to flee he may bring him/her in to jail, revoke the bond, and surrender the client. (See: **bail, bail bondsman**)

admit: v. 1) to state something is true in answering a complaint filed in a lawsuit. The defendant will admit or deny each allegation in his or her answer filed with the court. If he or she agrees and states that he/she did what he/she is accused of, then the allegation need not be proved in trial. 2) in criminal law, to agree a fact is true or confess guilt. 3) to allow as evidence in a trial, as the judge says: "Exhibit D, the letter, is admitted." (See: **admission, evidence**)

adopt: v. 1) to take on the relationship of parent to child of another person, particularly (but not necessarily) a minor, by official legal action. 2) to accept or make use of, such as to adopt another party's argument in a lawsuit. (See: **adoption**)

adoption: n. the taking of a child into one's family, creating a parent to child relationship, and giving him or her all the rights and privileges of one's own child, including the right to inherit as if the child were the adopter's natural child. The adoption procedure varies depending on whether the child comes through an agency which handles adoptions or comes from a stranger or a relative, and on the age of the child and the adoptive parent or parents. The hopeful adoptive parent must file a petition, which may be handled by the adoption agency. Natural parents must either give binding written permission for the adoption or have abandoned the child for a lengthy period of time. An investigation will be made by a county office (probation or family services) as to the future parents' suitability to adoption, their relationship status, their home situation, and their health, as well as the best interests of the child. If the child is old enough to understand the procedure he or she may have a say in the adoption. Finally there is a hearing before a local court judge (called "surrogate" in some states) and an adoption order made. In many states a new birth certificate can be issued, with the adoptive parents listed as the parents. If there is an adoption of an adult, the adopting adult usually must be several years older, based on the state law. In recent years, there has been much controversy over adoption by single parents, including gays and lesbians, with the tendency toward allowing such adoptions, provided all other criteria beneficial to the child are met. (See: **adopt**)

ad seriatim (add sear-ee-ah-tim): adj. Latin for "one after another". (See: *seriatim*)

adultery: n. consensual sexual relations when one of the participants is legally married to another. In some states it is still a crime and and in many states it is grounds for divorce for the spouse of the married adulterer. The criminal charges are almost never brought, and in those states in which there is no-fault divorce (or dissolution), adultery is legally not relevant. Until the 1970s, in community property states adultery was grounds for giving the person cheated upon most of the couple's property, often resulting in lurid and long trials and grist for scandal newspapers.

ad valorem: adj. Latin for "based on value," which applies to property taxes based on a percentage of the county's assessment of the property's value. The assessed value is the standard basis for local real property taxes, although some place "caps" (maximums) on the percentage of value (as under Proposition 13 in California) or "parcel taxes" which establish a flat rate per parcel. (See: **property tax**)

advance: n. a payment which is made before it is legally due, such as before shipment is made, a sale is completed, a book is completed by the author, or a note is due to be paid.

advancement: n. a gift made by a person to one of his or her children or heirs (a presumptive heir since an heir is only determined on the date of death) in anticipation of a gift from the still-living parent's potential estate as an advance on one's inheritance. Example: John Richguy is going to leave his son $100,000 under his will or a percentage of the estate on John's death. John gives the son $50,000 with the intention that it would be deducted from the inheritance. The main problem is one of proof that the advanced sum was against the projected inheritance. A person making an advancement should leave a written statement about the advancement or get a signed receipt. Such gifts made shortly before death are more readily treated as an advancement than one made several years earlier. (See: **beneficiary, estate, gift in contemplation of death**)

adverse: adj. clearly contrary, such as an adverse party being the one suing

31

you. An adverse interest in real property is a claim against the property, such as an easement.

adverse interest: n. a right or concern that is contrary to the interest or claim of another.

adverse party: n. the opposite side in a lawsuit. Sometimes when there are numerous parties and cross-complaints, parties may be adverse to each other on some issues and in agreement on other matters. Two beneficiaries of a person who has died may join together to claim a will was valid, but fight each other over the assets of the dead person's estate if the court rules the will was legal.

adverse possession: n. a means to acquire title to land through obvious occupancy of the land, while claiming ownership for the period of years set by the law of the state where the property exists. This can arise when a rancher fences in a parcel contending he was to get title from some prior owner, and then grazes cattle on the property for many years without objection by the title holder. Payment of real property taxes and making improvements (such as paving or fencing) for the statutory period (varies by state) are evidence of adverse possession but cannot be used by a land grabber with no claim to title other than possession. (See: **possession, prescriptive easement**)

adverse witness: n. a witness in a trial who is found by the judge to be adverse to the position of the party whose attorney is questioning the witness, even though the attorney called the witness to testify on behalf of his/her client. When the attorney calling the witness finds that answers are contrary to the legal position of his/her client or the witness becomes openly antagonistic, the attorney may request the judge to declare the witness to be "adverse" or "hostile." If the judge declares the witness to be adverse (i.e. hostile) then the attorney may ask "leading" questions which suggest answers or are challenging to the testimony just as on cross examination of a witness who has testified for the opposition. (See: **witness, cross examination, leading hostile witness**)

advisory opinion: n. an opinion stated by a judge or a court upon the request of a legislative body or government agency. An advisory opinion has no force of law but is given as a matter of courtesy. A private citizen cannot get an advisory ruling from a court and can only get rulings in an actual lawsuit. State attorneys general also give advisory opinions at the request of government officials. These opinions are often cited as the probable correct law on the subject but are not binding. (See: **actual controversy, friendly suit**)

affiant: n. a person who signs an affidavit and swears to its truth before a notary public or some person authorized to take oaths, like a County Clerk. (See: **affidavit, declarant**)

affidavit: n. 1) any written document in which the signer swears under oath before a notary public or someone authorized to take oaths (like a County Clerk), that the statements in the document are true. 2) in many states a declaration under penalty of perjury, which does not require the oath-taking before a notary, is the equivalent of an affidavit. (See: **declaration**)

affirm: v. what an appeals court does if it agrees with and confirms a lower court's decision.

affirmative action: n. the process of a business or governmental agency in which it gives special rights of hiring or advancement to ethnic minorities to make up for past discrimination against that minority. Affirmative action has been the subject of legal battles on the basis that it is reverse discrimination against Caucasians, but in most challenges to affirmative action the programs have been upheld. In 1995 there was substantial political agitation to repeal or modify federal and state affirmative action laws.

affirmative defense: n. part of an answer to a charge or complaint in which a defendant takes the offense and responds to the allegations with his/her own charges, which are called "affirmative defenses." These defenses can contain allegations, take the initiative against statements of facts contrary to those stated in the original complaint against them, and include various defenses based on legal principles. Many of these defenses fall into the "boilerplate" (stated in routine, non-specific language) category, but one or more of the defenses may help the defendant. (See: **defense**)

affix: v. 1) to attach something to

real estate in a permanent way, including planting trees and shrubs, constructing a building, or adding to existing improvements. The key is that affixed items are permanent and cannot be picked up and moved away like a washing machine. 2) to sign or seal, as affix a signature or a seal.

a fortiori (ah-for-she-ory) prep. Latin for "with even stronger reason," which applies to a situation in which if one thing is true then it can be inferred that a second thing is even more certainly true. Thus, if Abel is too young to serve as administrator, then his younger brother Cain certainly is too young.

after-acquired property: n. 1) personal or real property acquired by a debtor after he/she has agreed that all his/her property secures a debt. Thus, the new property also becomes security for the debt. This includes improvements to real property which is security on a deed of trust or mortgage and personal property pledged in a security agreement (UCC-1). 2) in bankruptcy, property acquired by the bankrupt person after he/she has filed papers to be declared bankrupt. This after-acquired property is not included in the assets which may be used to pay any debts which existed at the time of bankruptcy filing. (See: **bankruptcy, secured transaction**)

after-acquired title: n. title to property acquired after the owner attempts to sell or transfer the title to another person before he/she actually got legal title. When the title is acquired by the seller in this paper shuffle, title automatically goes to the person to whom it was sold, passing through the person who acquired title "like a dose of salts" on its way to the new purchaser. Example: John signs, acknowledges, and records a deed of the ranch to Sam, but John has not yet received title from the estate of his late father. When John gets title from his father's estate and records it, the after-acquired title goes automatically to Sam. (See: **title**)

after-discovered evidence: n. evidence found by a losing party after a trial has been completed and judgment (or criminal conviction) given, also called newly-discovered evidence. If the evidence absolutely could not have been discovered at the time of trial, it may be considered on a motion for a new trial. (See: **evidence, writ of** *coram nobis*)

age discrimination: n. an employer's unfair treatment of a current or potential employee up to age 70, which is made illegal by the Age Discrimination Unemployment Act, first adopted in 1967. The claimant's problem is proof of age discrimination, but employers should beware. Even flight attendants in their late 30s have proved that there was age discrimination in replacing them with younger, "more attractive" women. (See: **wrongful termination**)

agency: n. the relationship of a person (called the agent) who acts on behalf of another person, company, or government, known as the principal. "Agency" may arise when an employer (principal) and employee (agent) ask someone to make a delivery or name someone as an agent in a contract. The basic rule

is that the principal becomes responsible for the acts of the agent, and the agent's acts are like those of the principal (Latin: *respondeat superior*). Factual questions arise such as: was the agent in the scope of employment when he/she ran down the little child, got drunk and punched someone, or sold impure wheat? There is also the problem of whether the principal acted in such a way as to make others believe someone was his agent—this is known as "apparent" or "ostensible" authority. When someone who is or is not an employee uses company business cards, finance documents, or a truck with the company logo, such use gives apparent authority as an agent. (See: **agent, authority,** *respondeat superior*, **scope of employment**)

agent: n. a person who is authorized to act for another (the agent's principal) through employment, by contract or apparent authority. The importance is that the agent can bind the principal by contract or create liability if he/she causes injury while in the scope of the agency. Who is an agent and what is his/her authority are often difficult and crucial factual issues. (See: **agency, authority**)

agent for acceptance of service: n. states require that a corporation name an actual person (usually in the articles of incorporation or other filing with the Secretary of State) who is authorized to accept service of any lawsuit or claim against the corporation. Many larger corporations, particularly those which operate in several states, name a professional agent which represents many corporations. (See: **corporation**)

age of consent: n. (See: **legal age, majority**)

aggravated assault: n. the crime of physically attacking another person which results in serious bodily harm and/or is made with a deadly or dangerous weapon such as a gun, knife, sword, ax or blunt instrument. Aggravated assault is usually a felony punishable by a term in state prison. (See: **assault**)

agreed statement: n. occasionally the two parties on opposite sides of a lawsuit or on an appeal from a trial judgment will agree upon certain facts and sign a statement to be used in court for that purpose. Agreed statements are only used when the only remaining dispute boils down to a question of law and legal argument and not of the actual facts.

agreement: 1) n. any meeting of the minds, even without legal obligation. 2) in law, another name for a contract including all the elements of a legal contract: offer, acceptance, and consideration (payment or performance), based on specific terms. (See: **contract**)

aid and abet: v. help commit a crime. A lawyer redundancy since abet means aid, which lends credence to the old rumor that lawyers used to be paid by the word. (See: **abet**)

a.k.a.: prep. abbreviation for "also known as" when someone uses different initials, a nickname, a maiden or married name. Example: Harold G. Snodgrass, a.k.a. Harry Snodgrass, a.k.a. H. G. Snodgrass, a.k.a. "Snuffy the Snod."

aleatory: adj. uncertain; usually applied to insurance contracts in which payment is dependent on the occurrence of a contingent event, such as injury to the insured person in an accident or fire damage to his insured building.

alias: n. 1) a name used other than the given name of a person or reference to that other name, which may not be an attempt to hide his/her identity (such as Harry for Harold, initials or a maiden name). (See: **a.k.a.**)

alibi: n. an excuse used by a person accused or suspected of a crime. In the original Latin it means "in another place," which has to be the ultimate alibi.

alien: 1) n. a person who is not a citizen of the country. 2) in the United States any person born in another country to parents who are not American and who has not become a naturalized citizen. There are resident aliens officially permitted to live in the country and illegal aliens who have sneaked into the country or stayed beyond the time allowed on a visa. 3) v. to convey title to property.

alienation: n. the transfer of title to real property, voluntarily and completely. It does not apply to interests other than title, such as a mortgage. (See: **alien**)

alienation of affections: n. convincing a wife to leave her husband, often for another man, causing the husband to lose conjugal relations. This is primarily of historic interest, since alienation of affections was a civil wrong for which a deprived husband could sue the party convincing the wife to leave, but the right to sue has been abolished in almost all states.

alimony: n. support paid by one ex-spouse to the other as ordered by a court in a divorce (dissolution) case. Alimony is also called "spousal support" in California and some other states. Usually it is paid by the male to his ex, but in some cases a wealthy woman may have to pay her husband, or, in same-sex relationships the "breadwinner" may pay to support his/her stay-at-home former partner. Many counties and states have adopted formulas for alimony based on the income of each party. Payment of alimony is usually limited in time based on the number of years of marriage. Lengthy marriages may result in a lifetime of payments. A substantial change in circumstance, such as illness, retirement, or loss of income, can be grounds for the court to grant a modification or termination of the payment. Failure to pay ordered alimony can result in contempt of court citations and even jail time. The level of alimony can be determined by written agreement and submitted to the court for a stipulated order. Income tax-wise, alimony is deductible as an expense for the payer and charged as income to the recipient. Child support is not alimony. (See: **child support, dissolution of marriage, divorce, spousal support**)

aliquot: (al-ee-kwoh) adj. a definite fractional share, usually applied when dividing and distributing a dead person's estate or trust assets. (See: **share**)

allegation: n. a statement of claimed fact contained in a complaint (a written pleading filed to begin a lawsuit), a criminal charge, or an affirmative defense (part of the written answer to a complaint). Until each statement is proved it is only an allegation. Some allegations are made "on information and belief" if the person making the statement is not sure of a fact. (See: **complaint**)

allege: v. to claim a fact is true, commonly in a complaint which is filed to commence a lawsuit, in an "affirmative defense" to a complaint, in a criminal charge of the commission of a crime or any claim. (See: **allegation**)

all the estate I own: n. a phrase from a poorly drafted will which means the possessions owned by the deceased at the moment of death, not when the will was written. (See: **will**)

alluvion: n. an increase in one's land from soil deposited on the shoreline by natural action of a stream, river, bay or ocean. (See: **accretion**)

alter ego: n. a corporation, organization or other entity set up to provide a legal shield for the person actually controlling the operation. Proving that such an organization is a cover or alter ego for the real defendant breaks down that protection, but it can be difficult to prove complete control by an individual. In the case of corporations, proving one is an alter ego is one way of "piercing the corporate veil." In a lawsuit complaint, it might be stated (pleaded) that "the Hotshot Corporation was the alter ego of Joseph Snakeoil." (See: **pierce the corporate veil**)

Facts are stubborn things; and whatever may be our wishes, our inclinations, or the dictates of our passions, they cannot alter the state of facts and evidence.
—John Adams, while defending soldiers accused of the Boston Massacre

alternative pleading: n. a legal fiction in which a party to a lawsuit or a defendant charged with a crime can plead two ways which are inconsistent with each other. Examples: a) someone hurt in an accident can plead that the other party was negligent or ran into him intentionally. b) "not guilty" and "not guilty by reason of insanity" (in which there is the implied admission that the defendant committed the act).

ambiguity: n. when language has more than one meaning. If the ambiguity is obvious it is called "patent," and if there is a hidden ambiguity it is called "latent." If there is an ambiguity, and the original writer cannot effectively explain it, then the ambiguity will be decided in the light most favorable to the other party.

amend: v. to alter or change by adding, subtracting, or substituting. One can amend a statute, a contract or a written pleading filed in a law - suit. The change is usually called an amendment. The legislature will amend a statute, the parties to a contract can amend it, and a party to a lawsuit can amend his or her own pleading. A contract can be amended only by the parties participating in the contract. If the contract is written, it can be amended only in writing (although, curiously, an oral contract can be amended orally or in writing). A pleading can be amended before it is served on the other party, by stipulation or agreement in court between the parties (actually usually between their attorneys), or upon order of the court. (See: **amended complaint, amended pleading, statute, stipulation**)

amended complaint: n. what results when the party suing (plaintiff or petitioner) changes the complaint he/she has filed. It must be in writing, and can be done before the complaint is served on any defendant, by agreement between the parties (usually their lawyers), or upon order of the court. Complaints are amended to correct facts, add new causes of action (bases for the lawsuit), substitute discovered names for persons sued as "Does," or to properly plead a cause of action (the legal basis for suing) after the court has found the complaint inadequate. (See: **amend, cause of action, complaint, demurrer**)

amended pleading: n. a changed written pleading in a lawsuit, including complaint or answer to a complaint. Pleadings are amended for various reasons, including correcting facts, adding causes of action (legal bases for a suit), adding affirmative defenses, or responding to a court's finding that a pleading is inadequate as a matter of law. Amendments cannot be made willy-nilly, but only prior to being served, upon stipulation by the parties or order of the court. (See: **amend, amended complaint, demurrer**)

American Bar Association: n. the largest organization of American lawyers, which has no official standing, but is prestigious in formulating guidelines for the practice of law, giving direction to legislation, lobbying for the law profession, and evaluating federal judges. Less then one-third of attorneys belong to the A.B.A., and it is often dominated by the larger urban law firms and those who are interested in bar association politics. Nevertheless the A.B.A., its leaders, and its legal opinions are highly respected, and thus it is an important bellwether in legal circles. It publishes the monthly ABA Journal, books, specialized reports, and law office management manuals. The ABA holds a large annual national convention. Annual dues run as high as $225 (for attorneys with 10 years experience). Address: 750 North Lake Shore Drive, Chicago, IL 60611; tel.: (312) 988-5522.

American Civil Liberties Union: n. a membership organization founded in 1920 to defend and protect "the rights of man set forth in the Declaration of Independence and the Constitution." The ACLU researches the legalities of public policies and actions and defends clients in court when civil liberties are in question, without charge and often as *amicus curiae* (friend of the court). It has committees on academic freedom, state issues, media rights, free speech and association, due process, equal rights, labor/management relations and privacy. It also finances projects on voting rights, reproductive freedom, women's rights, and lesbian and gay rights. While some people consider it to be extremely liberal, the ACLU has defended ex-Ku Klux Klan leader David Duke's right to be on the ballot and the Ku Klux Klan's right to obtain parade permits. Address: 132 West 43rd Street, New York, NY 10036; tel.: (212) 944-9800.

American Depository Receipt: n. called in the banking trade an ADR, it is a receipt issued by American banks to Americans as a substitute for actual ownership of shares of foreign stocks. ADRs are traded on American stock exchanges and over-the-counter easily without the necessity of trading the foreign shares themselves.

amicus curiae: n. Latin for "friend of the court," a party or an organization interested in an issue which files a brief or participates in the argument in a case in which that party or organization is not one of the litigants. For example, the American Civil Liberties Union often files briefs on behalf of a party who contends his constitutional rights have been violated, even though the claimant has his own attorney. Friends of the Earth or the Sierra Club may file a supporting *amicus curiae* brief in an environmental action in which they are not actually parties. Usually the court must give permission for the brief to be filed and arguments may only be made with the agreement of the party the *amicus curiae* is supporting, and that argument comes out of the time allowed for that party's presentation to the court.

amnesty: n. a blanket abolition of an offense by the government, with the legal result that those charged or convicted have the charge or conviction wiped out. Examples: a) the amnesty given to Confederate officials and soldiers after the Civil War, or b) President Jimmy Carter's granting amnesty (under certain conditions) to those who violated the Selective Service Act in evading the draft during the Vietnam War. The basis for amnesty is generally because the war or other conditions that made the acts criminal no longer exist or have faded in importance. Amnesty is not a pardon as some believe, since a pardon implies forgiveness, and amnesty indicates a reason to overlook or forget the offenses. (See: **pardon**)

amortization: n. a periodic payment plan to pay a debt in which the interest and a portion of the principal are included in each payment by an established mathematical formula. Most commonly it is used on a real property loan or financing of an automobile or other purchase. By figuring the interest on the declining principal and the number of years of the loan, the monthly payments are averaged and determined. Since the main portion of the early payments is interest, the principal does not decline rapidly until the latter stages of the loan term. If the amortization leaves a principal balance at the close of the time for repayment, this final lump sum is called a "balloon" payment. (See: **promissory note**)

ancillary administration: n. administration of an estate's assets in another state. An "ancillary administrator" is chosen by the executor or administrator of an estate to handle the property (primarily real estate) of the deceased's estate in a state other than the one in which the estate is probated. Example: John Dunn dies in Montana where he had been living and leaves a parcel of land in downtown Columbus, Ohio. There must be ancillary administration in Ohio to obtain Ohio court approval and tax agency clearance. Technically ancillary means "aiding" or "subordinate." (See: **administration, probate**)

ancillary jurisdiction: n. a term used in federal courts when the court decides matters not normally under federal jurisdiction so that it can give a judgment on the entire controversy, when the main issue is a federal matter which it is authorized by law to determine. (See: **pendent jurisdiction**)

and: conj. this little word is important in law, particularly when compared to or. Most commonly it determines if one or both owners have to sign documents. Example: when an automobile registration reads that the title is for Barney and Sarah Oldfield, then both must sign off upon sale, but if it says "or" then only one will have to sign; if Barney dies then the title is automatically in Sarah's name if it reads "or," but not if it reads "and."

annuity: n. 1) an annual sum paid from a policy or gift. 2) short for a purchased annuity policy which will pay dividends to the owner regularly for years or for life.

answer: n. in law, a written pleading filed by a defendant to respond to a complaint in a lawsuit filed and served upon that defendant. An answer generally responds to each allegation in the complaint by denying or admitting it, or admitting in part and denying in part. The answer may also comprise "affirmative defenses" including allegations which contradict the complaint or contain legal theories (like "unclean hands," "contributory negligence" or "anticipatory breach") which are intended to derail the claims in the complaint. Sometimes the answer is in the form of a "general denial," denying everything. The answer must be in typed form, follow specific rules of pleading established by law and the courts, and be filed with the court and served on the defendant within a specific statutory time (e.g. 20 or 30 days after service of the complaint). If the complaint is verified as under penalty of perjury, the answer must be also. There is a fairly steep filing fee for each defendant filing an answer. In short, if served a complaint, one should see a lawyer as soon as possible to prevent a default judgment. (See: **complaint, demurrer, general denial, verification**)

antenuptial (prenuptial) agreement: n. a written contract between two people who are about to marry, setting out the terms of possession of assets, treatment of future earnings, control of the property of each, and potential division if the marriage is later dissolved. These are fairly common if either or both parties have substantial assets, children from a previous marriage, potential large inheritances, high incomes, or have been "taken" by a prior spouse.

anticipatory breach: n. when a party to a contract repudiates (reneges on) his/her obligations under that contract before fully performing those obligations. This can be by word ("I won't deliver the rest of the goods" or "I can't make any more payments") or by action (not showing up with goods or stopping payments). The result is that the other party does not have to perform his/her obligations and cannot be liable for not doing so. This is often a defense to a lawsuit for payment or performance on a contract. One cannot repudiate his obligations and demand that the other person perform. (See: **breach, contract**)

antitrust laws: n. acts adopted by Congress to outlaw or restrict business practices considered to be monopolistic or which restrain interstate commerce. The Sherman Antitrust Act of 1890 declared illegal "every contract, combination...or conspiracy in restraint of trade or commerce" between states or foreign countries. The Clayton Antitrust Act of 1914, amended by the Robinson-Patman Act of 1936, prohibits discrimination among customers through pricing and disallows mergers, acquisitions or takeovers of one firm by another if the effect will "substantially lessen competition." Interstate commerce includes commerce within a state which affects the flow of that commerce, thus making it pretty broad. There are also some state laws against restraint of trade. The Antitrust Division of the U.S. Department of Justice enforces for the federal government, but private lawsuits to halt antitrust activities have become increasingly popular, particularly since attorney's fees are awarded to the winning party. This is a legal specialty which has kept some industries relatively honest and made some lawyers wealthy. (See: **price fixing, restraint of trade**)

apparent authority: n. the appearance of being the agent of another (employer or principal) with the power to act for the principal. Since under the law of agency the employer (the principal) is liable for the acts of his employee (agent), if a person who is not an agent appears to an outsider (a customer) to have been given authority by the principal, then the principal is stuck for the acts of anyone he allows to appear to have authority. This "apparent authority" can be given by providing Joe Slobovia (who has no authority to contract) with materials, stationery, forms, a truck with a company logo, or letting him work out of the company office, so that a reasonable person would think Joe had authority to act for the company. Then the contract or the price quote given by Joe and accepted by a third party is binding on the company. Apparent authority may also arise when Joe works for the company, has no authority to contract, but appears to have been given that authority. Beware of the salesman who exceeds his authority or the hanger-on who claims to work for the boss. (See: **agency, ostensible authority**)

appeal: 1) v. to ask a higher court to reverse the decision of a trial court after final judgment or other legal ruling. After the lower court judgment is entered into the record, the losing party (appellant) must file a notice of appeal, request transcripts or other records of the trial court (or agree with the other party on an "agreed-upon statement"), file briefs with the appeals court citing legal reasons for overturning the ruling, and show how those reasons (usually other appeal decisions called "precedents") relate to the facts in the case. No new evidence is admitted on appeal, for it is strictly a legal argument. The other party (Respondent or appellee) usually files a responsive brief countering these arguments. The appellant then can counter that response with a final brief. If desired by either party, they will then argue the case before the appeals court, which may sustain the original ruling, reverse it, send it back to the trial court, or reverse in part and confirm in part. For state cases there are Supreme Courts (called Courts of Appeal in New York and Maryland) which are the highest appeals courts, and most states have lower appeals courts as well. For Federal cases there are Federal Courts of Appeal in ten different "circuits," and above them is the Supreme Court, which selectively hears only a few appeals at the highest level. 2) n. the name for the process of appealing, as in "he has filed an appeal." (See: **courts, appendix on courts**)

appear: v. for a party or an attorney to show up in court. (See: **appearance**)

appearance: n. the act of a party or an attorney showing up in court. Once it is established that an attorney represents the person (by filing a notice of appearance or representation or actually appearing), the lawyer may make an appearance for the client on some matters without the client being present. An attorney makes a "special appearance" when he/she is appearing only for the purpose of what is before the court that day—such as arraignment of one charged with a crime. If an attorney makes a "general appearance" he or she is telling the court that the client is definitely his or hers and the court can proceed. In the future that attorney will be required to represent the client. Some appearances are voluntary, but most are compulsory and are by notice to the party or, if represented, to his/her attorney. There are variations on appearance rules in states, federal courts, local court procedures, and according to the desires of particular judges. (See: **appear, general appearance, special appearance**)

appellant: n. the party who appeals a trial court decision he/she/it has lost. (See: **appeal**)

appellate court: n. a court of appeals which hears appeals from lower court decisions. The term is often used in legal briefs to describe a court of appeals. (See: **appeal**)

appellee: n. in some jurisdictions the name used for the party who has won at the trial court level, but the loser (appellant) has appealed the decision to a higher court. Thus the appellee has to file a response to the legal brief filed by the appellant. In many jurisdictions the appellee is called the "respondent." (See: **appeal, respondent**)

appraise: v. to professionally evaluate the value of property including real estate, jewelry, antique furniture, securities, or in certain cases the loss of value (or cost of replacement) due to damage. This may be necessary in determining the value of the estate of someone who has died, particularly when the items must be divided among the beneficiaries, to determine the value of assets for insurance coverage, to divide partnership assets, set a sales price, determine taxes, or make insurance claims. (See: **appraiser**)

appraiser: n. a professional who makes appraisals of the value of property. Some specialize in real property, and others in other types of assets from rugs to rings. A careful, well-trained and practical appraiser may be more important than any other professional in a transaction, since one who grossly undervalues or overvalues property (or has no knowledge of true value) can wreak havoc. Where possible, a person should ask for a profile of other clients and training, and ask whether the appraiser is "MAI" (Member, Appraisal Institute). (See: **appraise**)

appreciate: v. to increase in value over a period of time through the natural course of events, including inflation, greater rarity, or public acceptance. This can include real property, jewelry, rare books, art works or securities. (See: **appreciation**)

appreciation: n. the increase in value through the natural course of events as distinguished from improvements or additions. (See: **appreciate**)

approach: v. short for "approach the bench," as in "may I approach, your honor," or "will counsel approach?" (See: **approach the bench**)

approach the bench: v. an attorney's movement from the counsel table to the front of the bench (the large desk at which the judge sits) in order to speak to the judge off the record and/or out of earshot of the jury. Since the bench area is the sacred territory of the judge the attorney must ask permission as "may I approach the bench," or simply, "may I approach." If the judge consents, then opposing counsel must be allowed to come forward and participate in the conversation. The purpose can range from explaining the order of witnesses, a technical problem or the need to take a recess to go to the restroom.

approach the witness: v. a request by an attorney to the judge for permission to go up to a witness on the witness stand to show the witness a document or exhibit. "May I approach the witness?" is the typical request, and it is almost always granted.

appurtenant: adj. pertaining to something that attaches. In real property law this describes any right or restriction which goes with that property, such as an easement to gain access across the neighbor's parcel, or a covenant (agreement) against blocking the neighbor's view. Thus, there are references to appurtenant easement or appurtenant covenant. (See: **real property, easement**)

a priori **assumption**: (ah-pree-ory) n. from Latin, an assumption that is true without further proof or need to prove it. It is assumed the sun will come up tomorrow. However, it has a negative side: an *a priori* assumption made without question on the basis that no analysis or study is necessary, can be mental laziness when the reality is not so certain.

arbiter: n. in some jurisdictions the name for a referee appointed by the court to decide a question and report back to the court, which must confirm the arbiter's finding before it is binding on the parties.

arbitrary: adj. not supported by fair or substantial cause or reason. Most often it is used in reference to a judge's ruling.

arbitration: n. a mini-trial, which may be for a lawsuit ready to go to trial, held in an attempt to avoid a court trial and conducted by a person or a panel of people who are not judges. The arbitration may be agreed to by the parties, may be required by a provision in a contract for settling disputes, or may be provided for under statute. To avoid clogged court calendars the parties often agree to have the matter determined by a panel such as one provided by the American Arbitration Association (which has a specific set of rules), a retired judge, some other respected lawyer, or some organization that provides these services. Usually contract-required arbitration may be converted into a legal judgment on petition to the court, unless some party has protested that there has been a gross injustice, collusion or fraud. Many states provide for mandatory arbitration of cases on a non-binding basis in the hope that these "mini-trials" (proceedings) conducted by experienced attorneys will give the parties a clearer picture of the probable result and lead to acceptance of the arbitrator's decision. (See: **arbitrator**)

arbitrator: n. one who conducts an arbitration, and serves as a judge who conducts a "mini-trial," somewhat less formally than a court trial. In most cases the arbitrator is an attorney, either alone or as part of a panel. Most court jurisdictions now have lists of attorneys who serve as arbitrators. Other arbitrators come from arbitration services which provide lists from which the parties can agree on an arbitrator (many of whom are retired judges—even "People's Court" Judge Wapner is on such a panel in Los Angeles County). There is also the American Arbitration Association which usually has a panel of attorneys chosen by the association. Professional arbitration services are paid well to move cases along. There are also arbitrators who are experts on everything from construction to maritime damage. In some contracts there is a provision for such an expert-type arbitrator named by each side with a third chosen by the other two. (See: **arbitration**)

arguendo: prep. Latin meaning "for the sake of argument," used by lawyers in the context of "assuming arguendo" that the facts were as the other party contends, but the law prevents the other side from prevailing. Example: "assuming arguendo" that the court finds our client, the defendant, was negligent, the other party (plaintiff) was so contributorily negligent he cannot recover damages. In short, the lawyer is not admitting anything, but wants to make a legal argument only. The word appears most commonly in appeals briefs.

argumentative: adj. the characterization of a question asked by the opposing attorney which does not really seek information but challenges the truthfulness or credibility of the witness. Since such a question is not allowable, often it is the basis of an objection before the question is answered, much like irrelevant, immaterial or hearsay. The definition of argumentative is somewhat vague, and different judges hear it differently. A simple example would be "Do you believe you should pay your mistress' rent before catching up with delinquent child support?" or "Do you think that bloody glove just walked over there?"

arm's length: adj. the description of an agreement made by two parties freely and independently of each other, and without some special relationship, such as being a relative, having another deal on the side or one party having complete control of the other. It becomes important to determine if an agreement was freely entered into to show that the price, requirements, and other conditions were fair and real. Example: if a man sells property to his son the value set may not be the true value since it may not have been an "arm's length" transaction. (See: **contract**)

arraign: v. to bring a criminal defendant before the court, at which time the charges are presented to him/her, the opportunity to enter a plea (or ask for a continuance to plead) is given, a determination of whether the party has a lawyer is made (or whether a lawyer needs to be appointed), if necessary setting the amount of bail, and future appearances are scheduled. (See: **appearance, arraignment**)

arraignment: n. the hearing in which a person charged with a crime is arraigned in his or her first appearance before a judge. This is the initial appearance of a criminal defendant (unless continued from an earlier time) in which all the preliminaries are taken care of. (See: **arraign**)

arrears: n. money not paid when due, usually the sum of a series of unpaid amounts, such as rent, installments on an account or promissory note, or monthly child support. Sometimes these are called "arrearages."

arrest: v. 1) to take or hold a suspected criminal with legal authority, as by a law enforcement officer. An arrest may be made legally based on a warrant issued by a court after receiving a sworn statement of probable cause to believe there has been a crime committed by this person, for an apparent crime committed in the presence of the arresting officer, or upon probable cause to believe a crime has been committed by that person. Once the arrest has been made, the officer must give the arrestee his/her rights ("Miranda rights") at the first practical moment, and either cite the person to appear in court or bring him/her in to jail. A person arrested must be brought before a judge for arraignment in a short time (e.g. within two business days), and have his/her bail set. A private "security guard" cannot actually arrest someone except by cit-izen's arrest, but can hold someone briefly until a law officer is summoned. A "citizen's arrest" can be made by any person when a crime has been committed in his/her presence. However, such self-help arrests can lead to lawsuits for "false arrest" if proved to be mistaken, unjustified or involving unnecessary holding. 2) to delay the enforcement of a judgment by a judge while errors in the record are corrected. (See: **arrest warrant, false arrest, Miranda warning, probable cause, warrant**)

arrest warrant: n. a judge's order to law enforcement officers to arrest and bring to jail a person charged with a crime, also called a warrant of arrest. The warrant is issued upon a sworn declaration by the district attorney, a police officer or an alleged victim that the accused person committed a crime. (See: **warrant**)

arson: n. the felony crime of intentionally burning a house or other building. The perpetrators range from mentally ill pyromaniacs to store owners hoping to get insurance proceeds. Historically, arson meant just the burning of a house, but now covers any structure. A death resulting from arson is murder.

article: n. a paragraph or section of any writing such as each portion of a will, corporate charter (articles of incorporation), or different sections of a statute.

articles of impeachment: n. the charges brought (filed) to impeach a public official. In regard to the President, Vice President and federal judges, the articles are prepared and voted upon by the House of Representatives, and if it votes to charge the official with a crime, the trial is held by the Senate. (See: **impeachment**)

articles of incorporation: n. the basic charter of a corporation which spells out the name, basic purpose, incorporators, amount and types of stock which may be issued, and any special characteristics such as being non-profit. Each state has its own system of approval of articles, prohibits names which are confusingly similar to those of existing corporations (so an incorporator can test the name by applying to reserve the name), sets specific requirements for non-profits (charitable, religious, educational, public benefit, and so forth), and regulates the issuance of shares of stock. Articles must be signed by the incorporating person or persons or by the first board of directors. Major stock issuances require application to the Securities and Exchange Commission. The starting point for filing and approval of articles of incorporation is usually the state's Secretary of State. There will be a fee and, often, a deposit of an estimated first year's taxes. (See: **corporation**)

as is: adj. description of a condition in a sales contract in which the buyer agrees to take the property (e.g. house, horse, auto, or appliance) without the right to complain if it is faulty. However, the buyer must have had the right to reasonable inspection, so that he/she has a chance to find any obvious deficiency. Intentionally hiding a known defect will make a seller liable for fraud and serves to cancel the "as is" provision.

> *It is not desirable to cultivate a respect for the law, so much as for the right.*
> *—Henry David Thoreau*

assault: 1) v. the threat or attempt to strike another, whether successful or not, provided the target is aware of the danger. The assaulter must be reasonably capable of carrying through the attack. In some states if the assault is with a deadly weapon (such as sniping with a rifle), the intended victim does not need to know of the peril. Other state laws distinguish between different degrees (first or second) of assault depending on whether there is actual hitting, injury or just a threat. "Aggravated assault" is an attack connected with the commission of another crime, such as beating a clerk during a robbery or a particularly vicious attack. 2) n. the act of committing an assault, as in "there was an assault down on Third Avenue." Assault is both a criminal wrong, for which one may be charged and tried, and civil wrong for which the target may sue for damages due to the assault, including for mental distress.

assault and battery: n. the combination of the two crimes of threat (assault) and actual beating (battery). They are both also intentional civil wrongs for which the party attacked may file a suit for damages. (See: **assault, battery**)

assess: v. to set a value on property, usually for the purpose of calculating real property taxes. The assessed value is multiplied by the tax rate to determine the annual tax bill. This function is usually performed by employees of the County Assessor. In California, under Proposition 13, the new assessment can only take place upon sale of real property.

asset: n. generally any item of property that has monetary value, including articles with only sentimental value (particularly in the estates of the dead). Assets are shown in balance sheets of businesses and inventories of probate estates. There are current assets (which includes accounts receivable), fixed assets (basic equipment and structures), and such intangibles as business good will and rights to market a product.

assign: 1) v. to transfer to another person any asset such as real property or a valuable right such as a contract or promissory note. 2) n. the person (assignee) who receives a piece of property by purchase, gift or by will. The word often shows up in contracts and wills.

assigned risk: n. a person whose official driving record (accidents and tickets) is so poor that he/she cannot purchase commercial auto insurance, and must be assigned to a state operated or designated insurance program at high rates.

assignee: n. a person to whom property is transferred by sale or gift, particularly real property. (See: **assign**)

assignment: n. the act of transferring an interest in property or some right (such as contract benefits) to another. It is used commonly by lawyers, accountants, business people, title companies and others dealing with property. (See: **assign**)

assignment for benefit of creditors: n. a method used for a debtor to work out a payment schedule to his/her creditors through a trustee who receives directly a portion of the debtor's income on a regular basis to pay the debtor's bills.

Associate Justice: n. a member of the U.S. Supreme Court appointed by the President and confirmed by the U.S. Senate. There are eight Associate Justices and one Chief Justice. They serve for life or until voluntary retirement or removal after being convicted after impeachment. (Only one was ever charged (1805) and he was acquitted.) (See: **Supreme Court**)

association: n. any group of people who have joined together for a particular purpose, ranging from social to business, and usually meant to be a continuing organization. It can be formal, with rules and/or bylaws, membership requirements and other trappings of an organization, or it can be a collection of people without structure. An association is not a legally established corporation or a partnership. To make this distinction the term "unincorporated association" is often used, although technically redundant.

assume: v. to take over the liability for a debt on a promissory note, which is often done by the buyer of real property which has a secured debt upon it. Example: Bob Buyer pays part of the price of a piece of real property by taking over the debt that Sally Seller had on the property. However, usually the original owner to whom Sally owes the debt must agree to the assumption. (See: **assumption**)

assumption: n. the act of taking over a debt as part of payment for property which secures that debt. (See: **assume**)

assumption of risk: n. 1) taking a chance in a potentially dangerous situation. This is a typical affirmative defense in a negligence case, in which the defendant claims that the situation (taking a ski-lift, climbing a steep cliff, riding in an old crowded car, working on the girders of a sky-scraper) was so inherently or obviously hazardous that the injured plaintiff should have known there was danger and took the chance that he/she could be injured. 2) the act of contracting to take over the risk, such as buying the right to a shipment and accepting the danger that it could be damaged or prove unprofitable. (See: **affirmative defense**)

assured: n. the person or entity that is insured, often found in insurance contracts. (See: **insurance**)

attached: adj. 1) referring to two buildings which are connected, or equipment which is solidly incorporated into a structure such as bolted to the floor or wired to the ceiling (and not capable of being removed without damage to the structure). If an item is so attached it probably has become a part of the real property, except for "trade fixtures," which can be detached. 2) referring to money or an object which is taken by court order based on a sworn claim by a plaintiff (person suing) that the owner-defendant being sued may soon depart to avoid payment of the debt. (See: **attachment, fixture, trade fixture**)

attachment: n. the seizing of money or property prior to getting a judgment in court, in contemplation that the plaintiff will win at trial (usually in simple cases of money owed) and will require the money or property to cover (satisfy) the judgment. The Supreme Court has ruled that an attachment may be made only after a hearing before a judge in which both sides can argue the danger that the party being sued (defendant) is likely to leave the area or otherwise avoid probable payment. A temporary attachment may be allowed by court order without both parties being present based on a declaration of the party wanting the attachment that there is clear proof that the defendant is going to flee. The court must also require a bond to cover damages to the defendant if the attachment proves not to have been necessary. Before the hearing requirement, pre-judgment attachments were common in which automobiles and bank accounts were held by the sheriff merely upon the plaintiff seeking the attachment getting a writ of attachment, posting a bond. (See: **writ of attachment**)

attempt: v. and n. to actually try to commit a crime and have the ability to do so. This means more than just thinking about doing a criminal act or planning it without overt action. It also requires the opportunity and ability. Attempts can include attempted murder, attempted robbery, attempted rape, attempted forgery, attempted arson, and a host of other crimes. The person accused cannot attempt to commit murder with an unloaded gun or attempt rape over the telephone. The attempt becomes a crime in itself, and usually means one really tried to commit the crime, but failed through no fault of himself or herself. Example: if a husband laces his wife's cocktail with cyanide, it is no defense that by chance the intended victim decided not to drink the deadly potion. One defendant claimed he could not attempt rape in an old Model A coupe because it was too cramped to make the act possible. The court threw out this defense. Sometimes a criminal defendant is accused of both the crime (e.g. robbery) and the attempt in case the jury felt he tried but did not succeed.

attest: v. 1) to confirm (usually in writing) that a document is genuine. 2) to bear witness that someone actually signed a document, such as a will. All states require at least two witnesses (three in Vermont) to attest that a will was signed and declared to be a will (except a will written in one's own handwriting in some states). (See: **holographic will, will, witness**)

attestation: n. the act of witnessing a signature for the purpose of declaring that a document (like a will) was properly signed and declared by the signer to be his or her signature. (See: **attest**)

attorney: n. 1) an agent or someone authorized to act for another. 2) a person who has been qualified by a state or federal court to provide legal services, including appearing in court. Each state has a bar examination which is a qualifying test to practice law. The examinations vary in difficulty, but cannot be taken until the applicant is a graduate of an accredited law school (with a three-year minimum course of study) or in seven states has fulfilled extensive other training. Passage of the bar examination qualifies the attorney for that state only and for the federal courts located in that state (and other federal courts upon request). Some states will accept attorneys from other states, but many will not grant this "reciprocity" and require at least a basic test for out-of-state attorneys. Attorneys from other states may practice in a limited way, but cannot appear (except on a single case with court permission) in state courts (but in federal courts). Graduation from law school does not make one an attorney. There are also patent attorneys who can practice in federal patent courts only and have both legal and engineering training. Most patent attorneys today are regular attorneys who specialize. (See: **attorney at law, court, reciprocity**)

attorney at law (or attorney-at-law): n. a slightly fancier way of saying attorney or lawyer.

Th' supreme court follows the illiction returns.
—Finley Peter Dunne, Mr. Dooley's Opinions

attorney's advertising: n. the commercials which appear on television or crowd the yellow pages of the telephone book. Until the Supreme Court ruled (1977) that any restriction on lawyer advertising was an abridgement of free speech, advertising by lawyers was illegal and cause for discipline or disbarment. One problem is that the size and cleverness of the ads are no indication of the quality of the talent, experience, integrity, or level of personal attention by the lawyers. It has been said that "the bigger the ad, the worse the attorney," but that is an exaggeration. Advertising has led to a "chain store" approach to law representation and the use of paralegals and green attorneys at low wages to handle high volume practices.

attorney-client privilege: n. the requirement that an attorney may not reveal communications, conversations and letters between himself/herself and his/her client, under the theory that a person should be able to speak freely and honestly with his/her attorney without fear of future revelation. In a trial, deposition, and written questions (interrogatories), the attorney is required and the client is entitled to refuse to answer any question or produce any document which was part of the attorney-client contact. The problem sometimes arises as to whether the conversation was in an attorney-client relationship. If a man tells his neighbor who happens to be an attorney that he embezzled funds, is he doing so while seeking legal advice or just chatting over the fence (which is the test)? If a document was prepared as part of the legal preparation for a client, it usually is a "work product" and is also privileged. Similar privileges exist between pastor and parishioner and doctor and patient. (See: **attorney's work product, privileged communication, work product**)

Attorney General: n. in each state and the federal government the highest ranking legal officer of the government. The federal Attorney General is chief of the Department of Justice appointed by the President with confirmation required by the Senate, and a member of the Cabinet. He or she is in charge of federal prosecutions (including overseeing the numerous regional U.S. Attorneys), and numerous cases and matters in which the federal government has a legal interest, particularly when the federal government is a party or federal regulations are at issue. The Attorney General also has oversight of the Federal Bureau of Investigation and other law enforcement operations of the Justice Department. Although elected, state Attorneys General have similar functions within their states, although the supervision of local prosecutions is seldom exercised unless there is some gross mismanagement. Different legislatures have assigned varying functions to the state departments of justice, including consumer protection, environmental law, supervision of trusts and non-profit corporations, and other issues in which the state government may have a particular interest in protecting the citizenry. (See: **Solicitor General**)

attorney-in-fact: n. someone specifically named by another through a written "power of attorney" to act for that person in the conduct of the appointer's business. In a "general power of attorney" the attorney-in-fact can conduct all business or sign any document, and in a "special power of attorney" he/she can only sign documents or act in relation to special identified matters. Too often people sign themselves as attorney-in-fact for relatives or associates without any power of attorney. If someone claims to be able to sign for another, a demand to see the written power of attorney is reasonable and necessary. In real estate matters the power of attorney must be formally acknowledged before a notary public so that it can be recorded along with the real estate deed, deed of trust, mortgage, or other document. (See: **power of attorney**)

> *It is far better to have less learning and more moral character in the practice of the law than it is to have great learning and no morals.*
> *—Vice President Thomas R. Marshall*

attorney of record: n. the attorney who has appeared in court and/or signed pleadings or other forms on behalf of a client. The lawyer remains the attorney of record until some other attorney or the client substitutes for him/her, he/she is allowed by the court to withdraw, or after the case is closed. Sometimes lawyers find themselves still on the record in cases (such as divorces) which they believe have long since been completed.

attorney's fee: n. the payment for legal services. It can take several forms: 1) hourly charge, 2) flat fee for the performance of a particular service (like $250 to write a will), 3) contingent fee (such as one-third of the gross recovery, and nothing if there is no recovery), 4) statutory fees (such as percentages of an estate for representing the estate), 5) court-approved fees (such as in

bankruptcy or guardianships), 6) some mixture of hourly and contingent fee or other combination. It is wise (and often mandatory) for the attorney and the client to have a signed contract for any extensive legal work, particularly in contingent fee cases. Most attorneys keep records of time spent on cases to justify fees (and keep track of when actions were taken), even when the work is not on an hourly basis. A "retainer" is a down payment on fees, often required by the attorney in order to make sure he or she is not left holding the bag for work performed, or at least as a good faith indication that the client is serious and can afford the services. On the other hand, contingent fees require limits (often one-third) to protect the unwary client. Attorney fee disputes can be decided by arbitration, often operated by the local bar association. Attorney's fees are not awarded to the winning party in a lawsuit except where there is a provision in a contract for the fees or there is a statute which provides for an award of fees in the particular type of case.

attorney's work product: n. written materials, charts, notes of conversations and investigations, and other materials directed toward preparation of a case or other legal representation. Their importance is that they cannot be required to be introduced in court or otherwise revealed to the other side. Sometimes there is a question as to whether documents were prepared by the attorney and/or the client for their use in the case preparation or are documents which are independent and legitimate evidence. (See: **attorney-client privilege, privileged communication, work product**)

attractive nuisance doctrine: n. a legal doctrine which makes a person negligent for leaving a piece of equipment or other condition on property which would be both attractive and dangerous to curious children. These have included tractors, unguarded swimming pools, open pits, and abandoned refrigerators. Liability could be placed on the people owning or controlling the premises even when the child was a trespasser who sneaked on the property. Basically the doctrine was intended to make people careful about what dangerous conditions they left untended. Some jurisdictions (including California) have abolished the attractive nuisance doctrine and replaced it with specific conditions (e.g. open pit and refrigerators) and would make property owners liable only by applying rules of foreseeable danger which make negligence harder to prove.

"at will" employment: n. a provision found in many employment contracts which suggest the employee works at the will of the employer, and which the employers insert in order to avoid claims of termination in breach of contract, breach of the covenant of good faith and fair dealing, or discrimination. Inclusion of such a term puts the burden on the discharged employee to show that he or she had reasons to believe the employment was permanent. The employer uses the "at will" provision to claim: We could fire the employee at any time, no matter what the reasons. (See: **wrongful termination**)

audit: n. an examination by a trained accountant of the financial records of a business or governmental entity, including noting improper or careless practices, recommendations for improvements, and a balancing of the books. An audit performed by employees is called "internal audit," and one done by an independent (outside) accountant is an "independent audit." Even an independent audit may be limited in that the financial information is given to the auditor without an examination of all supporting documents. Auditors will note that the audit was based on such limited information and will refuse to sign the audit as a guarantee of the accuracy of the information provided. (See: **auditor**)

auditor: n. an accountant who conducts an audit to verify the accuracy of the financial records and accounting practices of a business or government. A proper audit will point out deficiencies in accounting and other financial operations. Many counties have an appointed or elected auditor to make independent audits of all governmental agencies in the county government. The term "auditor" is often misused as meaning any accountant. (See: **audit**)

authorities: n. 1) previous decisions by courts of appeal which provide legal guidance to a court on questions in a current lawsuit, which are called "precedents." Legal briefs (written arguments) are often called "points and authorities." Thus, a lawyer "cites" the previously decided cases as "authorities" for his/her legal positions. 2) a common term for law enforcement, as in "I'm going to call the authorities" (i.e. police). (See: **brief, cite, decision, precedent**)

authority: n. permission, a right coupled with the power to do an act or order others to act. Often one person gives another authority to act, as an employer to an employee, a principal to an agent, a corporation to its officers, or governmental empowerment to perform certain functions. There are different types of authority, including "apparent authority" when a principal gives an agent various signs of authority to make others believe he or she has authority; "express authority" or "limited authority," which spells out exactly what authority is granted (usually a written set of instructions) "implied authority," which flows from the position one holds and "general authority," which is the broad power to act for another. (See: **agency, agent, apparent authority, authorize, ostensible authority, principal**)

authorize: v. to officially empower someone to act. (See: **authority**)

avulsion: n. the change in the border of two properties due to a sudden change in the natural course of a stream or river, when the border is defined by the channel of the waterway. The most famous American case is the Mississippi River's change which put Vicksburg on the other side of the river.

award: 1) n. the decision of an arbitrator or commissioner (or any non-judicial arbiter) of a controversy. 2) v. to give a judgment of money to a party to a lawsuit, arbitration, or administrative claim. Example: "Plaintiff is awarded $27,000." (See: **judgment**)

Bachelor of Laws: n. the degree in law from a law school, abbreviated to LLB, which means that the recipient has successfully completed three years of law studies in addition to at least three undergraduate years on any subject. Since the early 1960s most accredited law schools grant a Juris Doctor (JD) degree instead of the LLB. Law schools which made the switch allowed the prior holders of the LLB to claim the JD retroactively. (See: **Juris Doctor**)

> *Laws grind the poor, and rich men rule the law.*
> *—Oliver Goldsmith*

back-to-back life sentences: n. slang for consecutive life terms imposed by a judge when there were two crimes committed by the defendant, both of which can result in punishment of a life term, such as two murders, or a murder and a rape involving aggravated assault. The purpose of making the sentences subsequent ("back-to-back") and not "concurrent" (served at the same time) is to lessen the chance of parole, since if parole were permissible after 25 years, the defendant would then begin the second "life" sentence and would wait another 25 years for a parole hearing. (See: **concurrent sentence**)

bad debt: n. an uncollectible debt. The problem is to determine when a debt is realistically dead, which means there must be some evidence of uncollectibility or a lengthy passage of time. Discharge in bankruptcy, the running of the statute of limitations to bring a lawsuit, disappearance of the debtor, a pattern of avoiding debts or the destruction of the collateral security can all make a debt "bad." For income tax deduction purposes such a debt in business is deductible against ordinary income (found in federal income tax Form 1040 Schedule C) and such a personal debt is deductible against short-term capital gains. A debt due for services rendered is not a bad debt for tax purposes, since there is just no income on which to be taxed.

bad faith: 1) n. intentional dishonest act by not fulfilling legal or contractual obligations, misleading another, entering into an agreement without the intention or means to fulfill it, or violating basic standards of honesty in dealing with others. Most states recognize what is called "implied covenant of good faith and fair dealing" which is breached by acts of bad faith, for which a lawsuit may be brought (filed) for the breach (just as one might sue for breach of contract). The question of bad faith may be raised as a defense to a suit on a contract. 2) adj. when there is bad faith then a transaction is called a "bad faith" contract or "bad faith" offer. (See: **clean hands doctrine, fraud, good faith**)

bail: 1) n. the money or bond put up to secure the release of a person who has been charged with a crime. For minor crimes bail is usually set by a schedule which will show the amount to be paid before any court appearance (arraignment). For more serious crimes the amount of bail is set by the judge at the suspect's first court appearance. The theory is that bail guarantees the appearance of the defendant in court when required. While the Constitution guarantees the right to reasonable bail, a court may deny bail in cases charging murder or treason, or when there is a danger that the defendant will flee or commit mayhem. In some traffic matters the defendant may forfeit the bail by non-appearance since the bail is equivalent to the fine. 2) v. to post money or bond to secure an accused defendant's release. This is generally called "bailing out" a prisoner. (See: **bail bond, bail bondsman, own recognizance**)

bail bond: n. a bond provided by an insurance company through a bail bondsman acting as agent for the company, to secure the release from jail of an accused defendant pending trial. Usually there is a charge of 10 percent of the amount of the bond (e.g. $100 for a $1,000 bond) and often the defendant must put up some collateral like a second deed of trust or mortgage on one's house. Upon acquittal, conviction, or other conclusion of the case, the bail bond is "exonerated" and returned to the insurance company. If the person who has been bailed out disappears and does not appear in court, the bond funds will be forfeited unless the defendant is found and returned. (See: **bail, bail bondsman**)

bail bondsman: n. a professional agent for an insurance company who specializes in providing bail bonds for people charged with crimes and awaiting trial in order to have them released. The offices of a bail bondsman (or woman) are usually found close to the local courthouse and jail, his/her advertising is found in the yellow pages, and some make "house calls" to the jail or hand out cards in court. Bail bondsmen usually charge the suspect a fee of 10 percent of the amount of the bond. If a bail bondsman has reason to believe a person he bailed out is about to flee, he may revoke the bond and surrender his client to jail. (See: **bail, bail bond**)

bailee: n. a person, also called a custodian, with whom some article is left, usually pursuant to a contract (called a "contract of bailment"), who is responsible for the safe return of the article to the owner when the contract is fulfilled. These can include banks holding bonds, storage companies where furniture or files are deposited, a parking garage, or a kennel or horse ranch where an animal is boarded. Leaving goods in a sealed rented box, like a safe deposit box, is not a bailment, and the holder is not a bailee since he cannot handle or control the goods. (See: **bailment, bailor**)

bailiff: n. 1) a court official, usually a deputy sheriff, who keeps order in the courtroom and handles various errands for the judge and clerk. 2) in some jurisdictions, a person appointed by the court to handle the affairs of an incompetent person or to be a "keeper" of goods or money pending further order of the court. "Bailiff" has its origin in Old French and Middle English for custodian, and in the Middle Ages was a significant position in the

English court system. The word "bailiwick" originally meant the jurisdictional territory of a bailiff.

bailment: n. 1) the act of placing property in the custody and control of another, usually by agreement in which the holder (bailee) is responsible for the safekeeping and return of the property. Examples: bonds left with the bank, autos parked in a garage, animals lodged with a kennel, or a storage facility (as long as the goods can be moved and are under the control of the custodian). While most are "bailments for hire" in which the custodian (bailee) is paid, there is also "constructive bailment" when the circumstances create an obligation upon the custodian to protect the goods, and "gratuitous bailment" in which there is no payment, but the bailee is still responsible, such as when a finder of a lost diamond ring places it with a custodian pending finding the owner. 2) the goods themselves which are held by a bailee. Thus, the "bailor" (owner) leaves the "bailment" (goods) with the "bailee" (custodian), and the entire transaction is a "bailment." (See: **bailee, bailor**)

bailor: n. a person who leaves goods in the custody of another, usually under a "contract of bailment," in which the custodian ("bailee") is responsible for the safekeeping and return of the property. Sometimes the bailor is not the owner but a person who is a servant of the owner or a finder (say, of jewelry) who places the goods with the bailee until the owner is found. (See: **bailee, bailment**)

bait and switch: n. a dishonest sales practice in which a business advertises a bargain price for an item in order to draw customers into the store and then tells the prospective buyer that the advertised item is of poor quality or no longer available and attempts to switch the customer to a more expensive product. Electronic items such as stereos, televisions, or telephones are favorites, but there are also loan interest rates which turn out to be only for short term or low maximums, and then the switch is to a more expensive loan. In most states this practice is a crime and can also be the basis for a personal lawsuit if damages can be proved. The business using "bait and switch" is an apt target for a class action since there are many customers but each transaction scarcely warrants the costs of a separate suit.

balance due: n. the amount of a debt still owed on an account or the principal owed on a promissory note. In the case of a promissory note, the balance due is not the sum of installments due, since these include amortized interest, but may be the principal due without further interest.

balance sheet: n. the statement of the assets and the liabilities (amounts owed) of a business at a particular time usually prepared each month, quarter of a year, annually, or upon sale of the business. It is intended to show the overall condition of the business. A balance sheet should not be confused with a profit and loss statement, which is an indicator of the current activity and health of the business.

bank: n. 1) an officially chartered institution empowered to receive deposits, make loans, and provide checking and savings account services, all at a profit. In the United States banks must be organized under strict requirements by either the federal or a state government. Banks receive funds for loans from the Federal Reserve System provided they meet safe standards of operation and have sufficient financial reserves. Bank accounts are insured up to $100,000 per account by the Federal Deposit Insurance Corporation. Most banks are so-called "commercial" banks with broad powers. In the east and midwest there are some "savings" banks which are basically mutual banks owned by the depositors, concentrate on savings accounts, and place their funds in such safe investments as government bonds. Savings and loan associations have been allowed to perform some banking services under so-called deregulation in 1981, but are not full-service commercial banks and lack strict regulation. Mortgage loan brokers and thrift institutions (often industrial loan companies) are not banks and do not have insurance and governmental control. Severe losses to customers of these institutions have occurred in times of economic contraction or due to insider profiteering or outright fraud. Credit unions are not banks, but are fairly safe since they are operated by the members of the industry, union or profession of the depositors and borrowers. 2) a group of judges sitting together as an appeals court, referred to as "in bank" or "en banc."

bankruptcy: n. a federal system of statutes and courts which permits persons and businesses which are insolvent (debtors) or (in some cases) face potential insolvency, to place his/her/its financial affairs under the control of the bankruptcy court. The procedure is that when the debtor's debts exceed his/her/its assets or ability to pay, the debtor can file a petition with the bankruptcy court for voluntary bankruptcy or the debtor's unpaid creditors can file an "involuntary" petition to force the debtor into bankruptcy, although voluntary bankruptcy is far more common. The most common petition is under Chapter 7, in which a trustee is appointed by the court, the current assets are counted up by the trustee (with many of them exempt from bankruptcy), who pays debts to the extent possible with priority for taxes, then secured debts (mortgages or some judgments), and finally unsecured debts. Then the court adjudicates (officially declares) the debtor a bankrupt and discharges the unpayable debts, to the loss of the creditors. Exempt from sale to pay debts are a portion of the value of a home (equal to a homestead), secured notes that can be kept current, an automobile, tools of the trade, furniture, and some other items. The concept is to give someone a fresh start, but it has often led to careless, profligate business operations and casual running up bills with those giving credit being badly hurt by bankruptcies. Not dischargeable in bankruptcy are alimony and child support, taxes, and fraudulent transactions.

Filing a bankruptcy petition automatically suspends all existing legal actions (even on the eve of trial or judgment, or on the day of foreclosure on real property), and is often used to forestall foreclosure or imposition of judgment. After 45 or more days a creditor with a debt secured by real or personal property can petition the court to have the "automatic stay" of legal rights removed and a foreclosure to proceed. Upon adjudication (officially declared) as a bankrupt a party cannot file for bankruptcy again for seven years.

Chapter 11 bankruptcy allows a business to reorganize and refinance to be able to prevent final insolvency. Often there is no trustee, but a "debtor in possession," and considerable time to present a plan of reorganization. Sometimes this works, but often it is just a bottomless pit of more debt and delay. The final plan often requires creditors to take only a small percentage of the debts due (what is owed them) or to take payment over a long period of time. Chapter 13 is similar to Chapter 11, but is for individuals to work out payment schedules, which is more likely to be worthwhile.

Bankruptcy law has become a specialty due to complex regulation as well as administration. Initial fees must be paid up front by the petitioner or the creditors, but much of the assets may be eaten up by the court-approved fees of the trustees and attorneys (although often the attorneys find no assets available for payment).

There are some limited state bankruptcy laws to aid debtors, but they are seldom employed, except to create creditors' committees, which can be developed voluntarily. (See: **bankruptcy court, bankruptcy proceedings, trustee in bankruptcy**)

bankruptcy court: n. the specialized federal court in which bankruptcy matters under the Federal Bankruptcy Act are conducted. There are several bankruptcy courts in each state, and each one's territory covers several counties. The office of a court clerk, where petitions can be filed, is located next to each court. (See: **bankruptcy, bankruptcy proceedings**)

bankruptcy proceedings: n. the bankruptcy procedure is: a) filing a petition (voluntary or involuntary) to declare a debtor person or business bankrupt, under Chapter 7, Chapter 11, or Chapter 13, to allow reorganization or refinancing under a plan to meet the debts of the party unable to meet his/her/its obligations. The petition is supposed to include a schedule of debts, assets and income potential. b) A hearing called "first meeting of creditors" with notice to all known creditors. This is often brief and usually results in the judge assigning the matter to a professional trustee. c) Later the trustee reports and there is a determination of what debts are dischargeable, what assets are exempt, and what payments are possible. d) If there are assets available then the creditors are requested in writing to file a "creditor's claim." e) There may be other hearings, reports, proposals, hearings on claims of fraudulent debts, petitions for removing the stay on foreclosures and other matters. f) Debts secured by property or by judgment lien are paid up to the amount of assets and funds available. g) The final step is a hearing on discharge of the bankrupt, which wipes out unsecured debts (or a pro rata share of them).

Under Chapter 11 and 13 proceedings, the process will be more drawn out and can go on for years as plans are proposed, possibilities of refinancing are considered and, in effect, the debtor tries either to legitimately get out from under his/her/its financial woes or delay while current profits are made and prayers for economic salvation are made. (See: **bankruptcy, bankruptcy court, claim in bankruptcy**)

bar: 1) n. collectively all attorneys, as "the bar," which comes from the bar or railing which separates the general spectator area of the courtroom from the area reserved for judges, attorneys, parties and court officials. A party to a case or criminal defendant is "before the bar" when he/she is inside the railing. 2) v. to prevent some legal maneuver, as in "barring" a lawsuit due to the running out of the time to file. 3) to prohibit and keep someone from entering a room, building, or real property.

I would pray, O Lord, never to diminish my passion for a client's cause, for from it springs the flame which leaps across the jury box and sets fire to the conviction of the jurors.
—Louis Nizer, A Lawyer's Prayer

bar association: n. an organization of lawyers. There are two types, one of which is official and usually called an "integrated bar," which is qualified by the particular state's highest court to establish rules for admission and conduct. There are also local bar associations by city or county which are unofficial and voluntary, but do conduct the business of attorneys, such as settling fee disputes and working with the local courts on rules. There is also the American Bar Association, a national voluntary organization of attorneys. (See: **appendix State Bar Associations**)

bar examination: n. the examination given in each state by either the highest court or, if an "integrated" bar, by the state bar association (subject to appeal to the State Supreme Court) for admission as an attorney. The examinations vary in difficulty, but most include up to three days of questions, many of which are essay type posing factual situations which call upon an ability to identify and analyze the legal "issues" and to demonstrate substantial knowledge of various areas of the law. Usually there are some multiple choice or true and false questions, depending on the state. The pass/fail rate varies from state to state and year to year. Some states, like California, have a pass rate of below 60 percent of applicants, but do allow several tries. Other states pass 90 percent. To qualify one must have received a law degree (LLB or JD) from an established law school or, in seven states, prove that he/she studied for several years in law school and/or with an attorney. Very few graduates ever pass the examination. Some states require a special bar examination for attorneys from other states, while others recognize out-of-state attorneys if they have established local residence. Passing a state's bar examination will automatically qualify the attorney to practice in the federal courts in that district. (See: **attorney**)

bargain: n. 1) a mutual agreement or contract between two parties which is voluntary and involves the exchange of consideration (money, goods, services, or a promise for a promise). 2) a supposed good deal. (See: **agreement, consideration, contract**)

barratry: n. creating legal business by stirring up disputes and quarrels, generally for the benefit of the lawyer who sees fees in the matter. Barratry is illegal in all states and subject to criminal punishment and/or discipline by the state bar, but there must be a showing that the resulting lawsuit was totally groundless. There is a lot of border-line barratry in which attorneys, in the name of being tough or protecting the client, fail to seek avenues for settlement of disputes or will not tell the client he/she has no legitimate claim.

barrister: n. in the United States a fancy name for a lawyer or attorney. In Great Britain, there is a two-tier bar made up of solicitors, who perform all legal tasks except appearance in court, and barristers, who try cases. Some solicitors will "take the silk" (quaint expression) and become barristers. (See: **solicitor**)

basis: n. the original cost of an asset to be used to determine the amount of capital gain tax upon its sale. An "adjusted basis" includes improvements, expenses, and damages between the time the original basis (price) is established and transfer (sale) of the asset. "Stepped up basis" means that the original basis of an asset (especially real property) will be stepped up to current value at the time of the death of the owner, and thus keep down capital gain taxes if the beneficiary of the dead person sells the asset. Exam-ple: Daniel Oldboy buys a house for $30,000, and when he dies the place is worth $250,000. When his son and heir receives the property, the son can sell it for $250,000 with no capital gains tax, but if Dad had sold it before his death there would have been capital gains on $220,000. It can be more complicated than this simple example with assets jointly held with a spouse, exchanges of property, and other variations which require professional assistance. (See: **adjusted basis**)

battery: n. the actual intentional striking of someone, with intent to harm, or in a "rude and insolent manner" even if the injury is slight. Negligent or careless unintentional contact is not battery no matter how great the harm. Battery is a crime and also the basis for a lawsuit as a civil wrong if there is damage. It is often coupled with "assault" (which does not require actual touching) in "assault and battery." (See: **assault, assault and battery**)

beach bum trust provision: n. a requirement in a trust that a beneficiary can only receive profit from the trust equal to the amount he/she earns. This provision is intended to encourage the beneficiary to work, and not just lie around the beach and live off the trust. (See: **trust**)

bearer: n. anyone holding something, such as a check, promissory note, bank draft, or bond. This becomes important when the document (generally called a "negotiable instrument") states it is "payable to bearer," which means whoever holds this paper can receive the funds due on it. (See: **bearer paper, negotiable instrument**)

bearer paper: n. negotiable instrument (e.g. a bond) which is payable to whoever has possession (the bearer). (See: **bearer**)

belief: n. convinced of the truth of a statement or allegation. In a common phrase "upon information and belief," the so-called belief is based only on unconfirmed information, so the person declaring the belief is hedging his/her bet as to whether the belief is correct. (See: **information and belief**)

bench: n. 1) general term for all judges, as in "the bench," or for the particular judge or panel of judges, as in an order coming from the "bench." 2) the large, usually long and wide desk raised above the level of the rest of the courtroom, at which the judge or panel of judges sit. (See: **approach the bench, court, judge, sidebar, witness stand**)

bench warrant: n. a warrant issued by a judge, often to command someone to appear before the judge, with a setting of an amount of bail to be posted. Often a bench warrant is used in lesser matters to encourage the party to appear in court. (See: **warrant**)

beneficial interest: n. the right of a party to some profit, distribution, or benefit from a contract or trust. A beneficial interest is distinguished from the rights of someone like a trustee or official who has responsibility to perform and/or title to the assets but does not share in the benefits. (See: **contract, trust**)

beneficial use: n. the right to enjoy the use of something (particularly such pleasant qualities as light, air, view, access, water in a stream) even though the title to the property in which the use exists is held by another. (See: **use**)

beneficiary: n. a broad definition for any person or entity (like a charity) who is to receive assets or profits from an estate, a trust, an insurance policy or any instrument in which there is distribution. There is also an "incidental beneficiary" or a "third party beneficiary" who gets a benefit although not specifically named, such as someone who will make a profit if a piece of property is distributed to another. (See: **incidental beneficiary, third-party beneficiary**)

benefit: 1) n. any profit or acquired right or privilege, primarily through a contract. 2) in worker's compensation the term "benefit" is the insurance payment resulting from a fatal accident on the job, while "compensation" is for injury without death. 3) in income taxation, anything that brings economic gain. 4) "fringe benefits" may be part of the compensation for employment other than salary or wages, and may include health or disability insurance. 5) v. to gain something, as "This sale will benefit Ken Murray." (See: **contract, Workers' Compensation Act**)

benefit of counsel: n. having the opportunity to have an attorney and legal advice in any legal matter, but particularly while appearing in court. If someone makes an appearance or agrees to a contract without benefit of counsel, when a lawyer would be either essential or at least quite valuable, he/she may challenge the court rulings or the contract terms, usually without success since failure to have an attorney is the person's own fault.

bequeath: v. to give personal property under provisions of a will (as distinct from "devise," which is to give real estate). 2) the act of giving any asset by the terms of a will. (See: **bequest, will**)

bequest: n. the gift of personal property under the terms of a will. Bequests are not always outright, but may be "conditional" upon the happening or non-happening of an event (such as marriage), or "executory" in which the gift is contingent upon a future event. Bequest can be of specific assets or of the "residue" (what is left after specific gifts have been made). (See: **legacy, will**)

best evidence rule: n. the legal doctrine that an original piece of evidence, particularly a document, is superior to a copy. If the original is available, a copy will not be allowed as evidence in a trial. (See: **evidence**)

bestiality: n. copulation by a human with an animal, which is a crime in all states as a "crime against nature." (See: **crime against nature**)

beyond a reasonable doubt: adj. part of jury instructions in all criminal trials, in which the jurors are told that they can only find the defendant guilty if they are convinced "beyond a reasonable doubt" of his or her guilt.

Sometimes referred to as "to a moral certainty," the phrase is fraught with uncertainty as to meaning, but try: "you better be damned sure." By comparison it is meant to be a tougher standard than "preponderance of the evidence," used as a test to give judgment to a plaintiff in a civil (non-criminal) case. (See: **conviction, moral certainty, reasonable doubt**)

BFP: n. slang for bona fide purchaser, which means someone who purchased something (e.g. a bond, a promissory note, or jewelry) with no reason to be suspicious that it was stolen, belonged to someone else, or was subject to another party's claim. The BFP must have paid a full and fair price and have received the item in the normal course of business, otherwise he/she might have some doubts ("wanta buy a watch, cheap?" from a character on a street corner). (See: bona fide **purchaser**)

bias: n. the predisposition of a judge, arbitrator, prospective juror, or anyone making a judicial decision, against or in favor of one of the parties or a class of persons. This can be shown by remarks, decisions contrary to fact, reason or law, or other unfair conduct. Bias can be toward an ethnic group, homosexuals, women or men, defendants or plaintiffs, large corporations, or local parties. Getting a "hometown" decision is a form of bias which is the bane of the out-of-town lawyer. There is also the subtle bias of some male judges in favor of pretty women. Obvious bias is a ground for reversal on appeal, but it is hard to prove, since judges are usually careful to display apparent fairness in their comments.

The possibility of juror bias is explored in questioning at the beginning of trial in a questioning process called *voir dire*. (See: **hometowned**, *voir dire*)

bid: n. an offer to purchase with a specific price stated. It includes offers during an auction in which people compete by raising the bid until there is no more bidding, or contractors offer to contract to build a project or sell goods or services at a given price, with usually the lowest bidder getting the job. (See: **contract**)

[The legal profession is] ever illustrating the obvious, explaining the evident, expatiating the commonplace.
—Prime Minister Benjamin Disraeli

bifurcate: v. the order or ruling of a judge that one issue in a case can be tried to a conclusion or a judgment given on one phase of the case without trying all aspects of the matter. A typical example is when the judge will grant a divorce judgment without hearing evidence or making a ruling on such issues as division of marital property, child custody or spousal support (alimony). Thus the parties can be free of each other promptly while still fighting over other issues at their leisure. In a negligence case when the question of responsibility (liability) is clearly in doubt or rests on some legal technicality, the court may bifurcate the issues and hear evidence on the defendant's liability and decide that issue before going ahead with a trial

on the amount of damages. If the court rules there is no liability, then the amount of damages is meaningless and further trial is necessary. (See: **bifurcation**)

bifurcation: n. the act of a judge in dividing issues before a trial so that one issue will be ruled upon before hearing evidence on the other issue. (See **bifurcate**)

bigamy: n. the condition of having two wives or two husbands at the same time. A marriage in which one of the parties is already legally married is bigamous, void, and ground for annulment. The one who knowingly enters into a bigamous marriage is guilty of the crime of bigamy, but it is seldom prosecuted unless it is part of a fraudulent scheme to get another's property or some other felony. Occasionally people commit bigamy accidentally, usually in the belief that a prior marriage had been dissolved. The most famous case in the United States was that of Andrew Jackson and his wife Rachel Robards. Ms. Robards' husband had applied for a divorce, but it had not been granted (it required legislative approval) at the time of her second marriage. She completed the divorce and then the Jacksons remarried. Jackson was embarrassed for life over his carelessness (he was a lawyer and a judge), which had hurt his wife's reputation. Having several wives at the same time is called polygamy and being married to several husbands is polyandry.

bilateral contract: n. an agreement in which the parties exchange promises for each to do something in the future.

"Susette Seller promises to sell her house to Bobby Buyer and Buyer promises to pay Seller $100,000 for it." This is distinct from a "unilateral contract," in which there is a promise to pay if the other party chooses to do something. "I'll pay you $1,000 if you'll stop smoking." These are basically academic differences which are only important in the rare instance in which one person has acted in anticipation that the other will have obligations as well. (See: **contract, unilateral contract**)

bill: n. 1) what is commonly called a "check" by which the signer requires the bank to pay a third party a sum of money. This is a holdover from the days when a person would draw up a "bill of exchange." 2) a statement of what is owed. 3) any paper money. 4) a legislative proposal for enactment of a law. It is called a bill until it is passed and signed, at which time it is a law (statute) and is no longer referred to as a bill. 5) an old-fashioned term for various filed documents in lawsuits or criminal prosecutions, which is falling into disuse.

bill of attainder: n. a legislative act which declares a named person guilty of a crime, particularly treason. Such bills are prohibited by Article I, Section 9 of the Constitution.

bill of exchange: n. a writing by a party (maker or drawer) ordering another (payor) to pay a certain amount to a third party (payee). It is the same as a draft. A bill of exchange drawn on a bank account is a "check."

bill of lading: n. a receipt obtained by the shipper of goods from the carrier (trucking company, railroad, ship or air freighter) for shipment to a particular buyer. It is a contract protecting the shipper by guaranteeing payment and satisfies the carrier that the recipient has proof of the right to the goods. The bill of lading is then sent to the buyer by the shipper upon payment for the goods, and is thus proof that the recipient is entitled to the goods when received. Thus, if there is no bill of lading, there is no delivery.

bill of particulars: n. a written itemization of claims which a defendant in a lawsuit can demand of the plaintiff to find out what are the details of the claims. Thus, a general claim that defendant owes plaintiff $50,000 for goods delivered or damaged must be broken down so the defendant can understand and defend. In criminal cases it can give an accused person notice of the factual bases for the charges.

Bill of Rights: n. the first ten amendments to the federal Constitution demanded by several states in return for ratifying the Constitution, since the failure to protect these rights was a glaring omission in the Constitution as adopted in convention in 1787. Adopted and ratified in 1791, the Bill of Rights are:
First: Prohibits laws establishing a religion (separation of church and state), and bans laws which would restrict freedom of religion, speech, press (now interpreted as covering all media), right to peaceably assemble and petition the government.
Second: A "well regulated Militia, being necessary to the security of a

free state, the right of the people to keep and bear Arms, shall not be infringed." This is often claimed as giving the unfettered right of individuals to own guns, but is actually limited to the right of "the" people, meaning the body politic or the public as a group, to bear arms as militiamen.

Third: No quartering of soldiers in private homes without the owner's consent.

Fourth: No unreasonable search and seizures, no warrants without probable cause, and such warrants must be upon "oath or affirmation" and describe the place to be searched or the person or things to be taken.

Fifth: Prohibits criminal charges for death penalty ("capital punishment") or any other "infamous" crime (felony) without indictment by a Grand Jury except under martial law in the time of war or "public danger"; no person may be tried twice for the same offense; no one may be compelled to be a witness against himself ("taking the Fifth"), no one can be deprived of life, liberty or property without "due process of law"; no taking of property for public use (eminent domain) without just compensation. These rights have become applicable to states through the 14th Amendment as well as state constitutions.

Sixth: Rights of criminal defendants to a speedy and public trial, impartial local jury, information on the nature and cause of accusation, confront witnesses against him, right to subpena witnesses, and have counsel.

Seventh: Juries may be demanded in civil cases (over $20) and the jury shall be trier of the fact in such cases as required by Common Law.

Eighth: No excessive bail, excessive fines or "cruel and unusual punishment." Note that denial of bail in murder cases or when the accused may flee is not "excessive," and capital punishment (like the gas chamber) may be cruel but not necessarily unusual.

Ninth: Stating these rights shall not be construed to deny that other rights are retained by the people.

Tenth: Powers given to the United States (central government) and not prohibited to the states, are reserved to the states or to the people.

> *In colonial America Esq. seems to have been confined to justices of the peace, who acquired thereby the informal title of Squire, but inasmuch as every lawyer of any dignity became a justice almost automatically it was eventually applied to most members of the bar.*
> *—H. L. Mencken*

bill of sale: n. a written statement attesting to the transfer (sale) of goods, possessions, or a business to a buyer. It is useful to show that the buyer now has ownership and to detail what was actually purchased. A bill of sale may accompany an agreement which states the agreed-upon terms of sale, including the date of transfer, the price, timing of payment and other provisions. (See: **contract**)

binder: n. a written statement of the key terms of an agreement, in particular insurance policies, so that the insured as well as lenders can be assured there is valid and adequate insurance coverage. (See: **insurance**)

blackmail: n. the crime of threatening to reveal embarrassing, disgraceful or damaging facts (or rumors) about a person to the public, family, spouse or associates unless paid off to not carry out the threat. It is one form of extortion (which may include other threats such as physical harm or damage to property). (See: **extortion**)

blank endorsement: n. endorsement of a check or other negotiable paper without naming the person to whom it would be paid. (See: **negotiable instrument**)

blue laws: n. state or local laws which prohibit certain activities, particularly entertainment, sports or drinking on Sunday, to honor the Christian Sabbath. They were employed in the New England colonies controlled by the puritans who kept the Sabbath sacred. "Blue" was slang for puritanical. In most cases blue laws have been repealed, but vestiges remain at least informally.

blue ribbon jury: n. a jury selected from prominent, well-educated citizens, sometimes to investigate a particular problem such as civic corruption. Use of blue ribbon juries in criminal cases violates the right to have a jury of one's peers.

blue sky laws: n. laws intended to protect the public from purchasing stock in fraudulent companies that lack substance, such as those selling swamp land, non-existent gold strikes and dry oil wells, or who have no assets besides a post office box. Blue sky laws require that corporations advertising and selling shares to the public must get approval from the state corporations commissioner and/or the Securities and Exchange Commission after providing details on financing and management. The term comes from the intent to prevent the existence of corporations that have nothing behind them but "blue sky." (See: **corporation, shares, stock**)

board of directors: n. the policy managers of a corporation or organization elected by the shareholders or members. The board in turn chooses the officers of the corporation, sets basic policy, and is responsible to the shareholders. In small corporations there are usually only three directors. In larger corporations board members provide illustrious names, but the company is often run by the officers and middle-management who have the expertise. (See: **corporation**)

boilerplate: n., adj. slang for provisions in a contract, form or legal pleading which are apparently routine and often preprinted. The term comes from an old method of printing. Today "boilerplate" is commonly stored in computer memory to be retrieved and copied when needed. A layperson should beware that the party supplying the boilerplate form usually has developed supposedly "standard" terms (some of which may not apply to every situation) to favor and/or protect the provider.

boiler room: n. a telephone bank operation in which fast-talking telemarketers or campaigners attempt to sell stock, services, goods, or candidates and act as if they are calling from an established company or brokerage. Often the telemarketers are totally fraudulent and in violation of security laws.

bona fide: adj. Latin for "good faith," it signifies honesty, the "real thing" and, in the case of a party claiming title as bona fide purchaser or holder, it indicates innocence or lack of knowledge of any fact that would cast doubt on the right to hold title.

***bona fide* purchaser**: n. commonly called BFP in legal and banking circles; a person who has purchased an asset (including a promissory note, bond or other negotiable instrument) for stated value, innocent of any fact which would cast doubt on the right of the seller to have sold it in good faith. This is vital if the true owner shows up to claim title, since the BFP will be able to keep the asset, and the real owner will have to look to the fraudulent seller for recompense. (See: **BFP, holder in due course**)

bond: n. 1) written evidence of debt issued by a company with the terms of payment spelled out. A bond differs from corporate shares of stock since bond payments are pre-determined and provide a final payoff date, while stock dividends vary depending on profitability and corporate decisions to distribute. There are two types of such bonds: "registered," in which the name of the owner is recorded by the company and "bearer," in which interest payments are made to whomever is holding the bond. 2) written guaranty or pledge which is purchased from a bonding company (usually an insurance firm) or by an individual as security (called a "bondsman") to guarantee some form of performance, including showing up in court ("bail bond"), properly complete construction or other contract terms ("performance bond"), that the bonded party will not steal or mismanage funds, that a purchased article is the real thing, or that title is good. If there is a failure then the bonding company will make good up to the amount of the bond.

bondsman: n. 1) someone who sells bail bonds. 2) a surety (guarantor or insurance company, who/which provides bonds for performance. (See: **bail bond, bail bondsman, bond**)

booby trap: n. a device set up to be triggered to harm or kill anyone entering the trap, such as a shotgun which will go off if a room is entered, or dynamite which will explode if the ignition key on an auto is turned. If a person sets up such a trap to protect his/her property, he/she will be liable for any injury or death even to an unwanted intruder such as a burglar. Setting a booby trap to even protect one's property is a crime.

book account: n. an account of a customer kept in a business ledger of debits and credits (charges and payments), which shows the amount due at any given time. This can provide a clear basis for suing for a debt. (See: **account stated**)

book value: n. a determination of the value of a corporation's stock by adding up the stated value of corporate assets as shown on the books (records) of a corporation and deducting all the liabilities (debts) of the corporation. This may not be the true value of the corporation or its shares since the assets may be under- or over-valued.

bottomry: n. a mortgage contract in which a ship and/or its freight is pledged as security for a loan for equipment, repair, or use of a vessel. The contract is generally called a "bottomry bond." If the loan is not paid back, the lender can sell the ship and/or its freight.

boycott: n. organized refusal to purchase products or patronize a store to damage the producer or merchant monetarily, to influence its policy, and/or to attract attention to a social cause. Labor unions and their sympathizers have boycotted lettuce and grapes not picked by union farm workers, and civil rights activists have boycotted stores and restaurants that had "white only" hiring policies. The term is named for Captain Charles C. Boycott, a notorious land agent whose neighbors ostracized him during Ireland's Land League rent wars in the 1880's. Boycotts are not illegal in themselves, unless there are threats of violence involved. A "secondary" boycott, which boycotts those who do business with the primary target of the boycotters, is an unfair labor practice under federal and state laws. (See: **secondary boycott**)

breach: 1) n. literally, a break. A breach may be a failure to perform a contract (breaking its terms), failure to do one's duty (breach of duty, or breach of trust), causing a disturbance, threatening, or other violent acts which break public tranquility (breach of peace), illegally entering property (breach of close), not telling the truth—knowingly or innocently—about title to property (breach of warranty), or, in past times, refusal to honor a promise to marry (breach of promise). 2) v. the act of failing to perform one's agreement, breaking one's word, or otherwise actively violating one's duty to other. (See: **breach of contract, breach of the peace, breach of promise, breach of trust, breach of warranty**)

breach of contract: n. failing to perform any term of a contract, written or oral, without a legitimate legal excuse. This may include not completing a job, not paying in full or on time, failure to deliver all the goods, substituting inferior or significantly different goods, not providing a bond when required, being late without excuse, or any act which shows the party will not complete the work ("anticipatory breach"). Breach of contract is one of the most common causes of law suits for damages and/or court-ordered "specific performance" of the contract. (See: **anticipatory breach, breach, specific performance**)

breach of the peace: n. any act which disturbs the public or even one person. It can include almost any criminal act causing fear or attempting intimidation, such as displaying a pistol or shouting inappropriately. (See: **breach**)

> *I do not believe in the law of hate. I may not be true to my ideals always, but I believe in the law of love, and I believe you can do nothing with hatred.*
> —*Clarence Darrow*

breach of promise: n. historically, the dumping of a female fiancee by her intended husband after he had proposed marriage and she had accepted. She was entitled to file a suit for damages for the embarrassment of the broken engagement. Such lawsuits were gradually outlawed in various states and no longer exist. (See: **breach**)

breach of trust: n. 1) any act which is in violation of the duties of a trustee or of the terms of a trust. Such a breach need not be intentional or with malice, but can be due to negligence. 2) breaking a promise or confidence. (See: **breach**)

breach of warranty: n. determination that a statement as to title of property, including real property or any goods, is proved to be untrue, whether intended as a falsehood or not. It can also apply to an assurance of quality of a product or item sold. The party making the warranty is liable to the party to whom the guarantee was made. In modern law the warranty need not be expressed in so many words, but may be implied from the circumstances or surrounding language at the time of sale. (See: **implied warranty, warranty**)

breaking and entering: n. 1) the criminal act of entering a residence or other enclosed property through the slightest amount of force (even pushing open a door), without authorization. If there is intent to commit a crime, this is burglary. If there is no such intent, the breaking and entering alone is probably at least illegal trespass, which is a misdemeanor crime. 2) the criminal charge for the above. (See: **burglary, trespass**)

bribery: n. the crime of giving or taking money or some other valuable item in order to influence a public official (any governmental employee) in the performance of his/her duties. Bribery includes paying to get government contracts (cutting in the roads commissioner for a secret percentage of the profit), giving a bottle of liquor to a building inspector to ignore a violation or grant a permit, or selling stock to a Congressman at a cut-rate price. Example: Governor (later Vice President) Spiro T. Agnew received five cents from the concessionaire for each pack of cigarettes sold in the Maryland capitol building. The definition has been expanded to include bribes given to corporate officials to obtain contracts or other advantages which are against company policy.

brief: 1) n. a written legal argument, usually in a format prescribed by the courts, stating the legal reasons for the suit based on statutes, regulations, case precedents, legal texts, and reasoning applied to facts in the particular situation. A brief is submitted to lay out the argument for various petitions and motions before the court (sometimes called "points and authorities"), to counter the arguments of opposing lawyers, and to provide the judge or judges with reasons to rule in favor of the party represented by the brief writer. Occasionally on minor or follow-up legal issues, the judge will specify that a letter or memorandum brief will be sufficient. On appeals and certain other major arguments, the brief is bound with color-coded covers stipulated in state and/or federal court rules. Ironically, although the term was originally intended to mean a brief or summary argument (shorter than an oral presentation), legal briefs are quite often notoriously long. 2) v. to summarize a precedent case or lay out in writing a legal argument. Attentive law students "brief" each case in their casebooks, which means extracting the rule of law, the reasoning (rationale), the essential facts, and the outcome. 3) v. to give a summary of important information to another person. (See: **precedent**)

broker: n. in general, a person who arranges contracts between a buyer and seller for a commission (a percentage of the sales price). These include real estate brokers (who have responsibility over an agency and its sales agents as well as their own conduct), insurance brokers (handling more than one company rather than being an agent for just a single carrier), and stockbrokers, who are the upper-level of stock salespersons and/or the operators of brokerage houses. Brokers in the more technical fields (as above) are regulated and licensed by each state and have a "fiduciary" duty to act in the best interests of the customer. Consumers should investigate whether the broker is representing the customer's best interest or just wants to make a sale. A "pawnbroker" is a lender for items left for security ("hocked") at high rates.

brought to trial: v. the act of actually beginning a trial, usually signaled by swearing in the first witness (not the impanelling of the jury or beginning opening statements).

bucket shop: n. an unofficial and usually illegal betting operation in which the prices of stocks and commodities are posted and the customers bet on the rise and fall of prices without actually buying stock, commodities, or commodity futures. Bucket shops are seldom seen today since there are many opportunities to gamble legally on the stock and commodities markets.

building and loan: n. another name for savings and loan association. As the name implies, originally these institutions were meant to provide loans for building a house after the depositor had saved enough for a down payment. (See: **savings and loan**)

bulk sale: n. the sale of all or a large part of a merchant's stock as well as equipment. This generally applies to retailers, restaurants, and other businesses with inventories. (See: **bulk sales acts**)

bulk sales acts: n. state laws (spelled out in the Uniform Commercial Code adopted generally throughout the country) which require a seller of the business including his/her inventory to a) publish notice of the sale, b) give written notice to all creditors, and c) set up an escrow of the funds realized from the sale upon which the creditors can make a claim for a brief period of time. These statutes are intended to prevent a merchant from quietly selling his/her business inventory and disappearing without paying current creditors.

bulk transfer: (See: **bulk sale**)

burden: n. anything that results in a restrictive load upon something. This is not meant in a tangible sense, but includes a "burden" on interstate commerce (which is any matter which limits, restricts or is onerous such as a license or fee for passage), and "burdens" on land such as zoning restrictions or the right of a neighbor to pass over the property to reach his home (easement).

burden of proof: n. the requirement that the plaintiff (the party bringing a civil lawsuit) show by a "preponderance of evidence" or "weight of evidence" that all the facts necessary to win a judgment are presented and are probably true. In a criminal trial the burden of proof required of the prosecutor is to prove the guilt of the accused "beyond a reasonable doubt," a much more difficult task. Unless there is a complete failure to present substantial evidence of a vital fact (usually called an "element of the cause of action"), the ultimate decision as to whether the plaintiff has met his/her burden of proof rests

with the jury or the judge if there is no jury. However, the burden of proof is not always on the plaintiff. In some issues it may shift to the defendant if he/she raises a factual issue in defense, such as a claim that he/she was not the registered owner of the car that hit the plaintiff, so the defendant has the burden to prove that defense. If at the close of the plaintiff's presentation he/she has not produced any evidence on a necessary fact (e.g. any evidence of damage) then the case may be dismissed without the defendant having to put on any evidence. (See: **beyond a reasonable doubt, preponderance of the evidence,** *prima facie*, **weight of evidence**)

In a democracy the law says that it is just for the poor to have no more advantage than the rich; and that neither should be masters, but both equal.
—Aristotle, Politics

burglary: n. the crime of breaking and entering into a structure for the purpose of committing a crime. No great force is needed (pushing open a door or slipping through an open window is sufficient) if the entry is unauthorized. Contrary to common belief, a burglary is not necessarily for theft. It can apply to any crime, such as assault or sexual harassment, whether the intended criminal act is committed or not. Originally under English common law burglary was limited to entry in residences at night, but it has been expanded to all criminal entries into any building, or even into a vehicle. (See: **breaking and entering**)

business: n. any activity or enterprise entered into for profit. It does not mean it is a company, a corporation, partnership, or has any such formal organization, but it can range from a street peddler to General Motors. It is sometimes significant to determine if an accident, visit, travel, meal or other activity was part of "business" or for pleasure or no particular purpose.

business invitee: n. a person entering commercial premises for the purpose of doing business, rather than just taking a short cut to the next street. It is important since a business is liable to a business invitee for injury caused by dangerous conditions such as bad floors or oil on the linoleum. There is a presumption that anyone entering a retail store or restaurant in which one may browse is a business invitee unless there is evidence to the contrary. (See: **invitee**)

"but for" rule: n. one of several tests to determine if a defendant is responsible for a particular happening. In this test, was there any other cause, or would it have occurred "but for" the defendant's actions? Example: "But for" defendant Drivewild's speeding, the car would not have gone out of control, and therefore the defendant is responsible. This is shorthand for whether the action was the "proximate cause" of the damage. (See: **proximate cause**)

buy-sell agreement: n. a contract among the owners of a business which provides terms for their purchase of a withdrawing part- ner's or stockholder's interest in the enterprise.

bylaws: n. the written rules for conduct of a corporation, association, partnership or any organization. They should not be confused with the articles of incorporation, which only state the basic outline of the company, including stock structure. Bylaws generally provide for meetings, elections of a board of directors and officers, filling vacancies, notices, types and duties of officers, committees, assessments and other routine conduct. Bylaws are in effect a contract among members and must be formally adopted and/or amended. (See: **corporation**)

calendar: 1) n. the list of cases to be called for trial before a particular court; 2) v. to set and give a date and time for a case, petition or motion to be heard by a court. Usually a judge, a trial setting commissioner, or the clerk of the court calendars cases.

calendar call: n. the hearing at which a case is set for trial.

call: n. the demand by a corporation that a stockholder pay an installment or assessment on shares already owned.

> *Laws are sand, customs are rock.*
> *—Mark Twain*

calumny: n. the intentional and generally vicious false accusation of a crime or other offense designed to damage one's reputation. (See: **defamation**)

cancel: v. to cross out, annul, destroy, void and/or rescind a document. Cancelling can be done in several ways: tear up the document or mark on its face that it is cancelled, void, or terminated if the debt for which it stood has been paid. It is important that the document (like a promissory note) itself become no longer operative either by destruction or marking, so that it cannot be used again.

cancellation: (See: **cancel**)

caning: n. a punishment for crimes employed in certain Asian countries (notably Singapore) even for misdemeanors (lesser crimes) in which the convicted defendant receives several lashes with a flexible "cane" meted out by a husky and skilled whipper. Such corporal punishment as a specific punishment or sentence so far is unknown in the last century in the United States.

canon law: n. laws and regulations over ecclesiastical (church) matters developed between circa 1100 and 1500 and used by the Roman Catholic Church in reference to personal morality, status and powers of the clergy, administration of the sacraments and church and personal discipline. Canon law comprises ordinances of general councils of the church, decrees, bulls and epistles of the Popes, and the scriptures and writings of the early fathers of the church. Canon law has no legal force except within the Vatican in Rome, Italy, and in those nations in which the Catholic Church is the "official" church and where it prevails in religious matters which may affect all citizens (such as abortion and divorce). In Great Britain there is also a body of canon law dating back to pre-reformation in the 16th Century, which is used by the Anglican (Episcopal) Church. Canon law is not to be confused with professional canons, which are rules of conduct with no religious connection.

cap: n. slang for maximum, as the most interest that can be charged on an "adjustable rate" promissory note.

capital: 1) n. from Latin for *caput*, meaning "head," the basic assets of a business (particularly corporations or partnerships) or of an individual, including actual funds, equipment and property as distinguished from stock in trade, inventory, payroll, maintenance and services. 2) adj. related to the basic assets or activities of a business or individual, such as capital account, capital assets, capital expenditure, and capital gain or loss. 3) n. an amount of money a person owns, as in "how much capital do you have to put into this investment?" as distinguished from the amount which must be financed. (See: **capital account, capital assets, capital gains or losses, stock in trade**)

capital account: n. the record which lists all basic assets of a business, not including inventory or the alleged value of good will.

capital assets: n. equipment, property, and funds owned by a business. (See: **capital, capital account**)

capital expenditure: n. payment by a business for basic assets such as property, fixtures, or machinery, but not for day-to-day operations such as payroll, inventory, maintenance and advertising. Capital expenditures supposedly increase the value of company assets and are usually intended to improve productivity.

capital gains: n. the difference between the sales price and the original cost (plus improvements) of property. Capital gains taxes can be a terrible financial shock to individuals who bought a house or business many years ago for the going price and now find it is highly valued, greatly due to inflation. Example: a couple buy a house in 1950 for $20,000 (then a high price) and upon retirement want to sell it for $400,000. There is a potential of tax on a $360,000 gain. There are some statutory cushions to ease this blow, such as a one-time $125,000 deduction from the gain (profit) on sale of real property if the seller is over 55, deferred (temporarily put off) tax if investment property is "exchanged" (profits are invested in other property) under strict rules, making lifetime gifts to children or charity, or buying another home. Another escape is death, which gives the property to heirs at the value on the day of the owner's death without capital gains tax ("stepped up basis"). Reduction of capital gains tax rates has been resisted by a majority of Congress, partly because lowering the rate generally would become a tax break for the wealthy. (See: **basis, delayed exchange, exchange**)

capital investment: (See: **capital expenditure**)

capital offense: n. any criminal charge which is punishable by the death penalty, called "capital" since the defendant could lose his/her head (Latin for *caput*). Crimes punishable by death vary from state to state and country to country. In 38 American states these offenses may include first degree murder (premeditated), murder with special circumstances (such as intentional, multiple, involved with another crime, with guns, of a police officer, or a repeat offense), and rape with additional bodily harm, and the federal crime of treason. A charge of a capital offense usually means no bail will be allowed. (See: **bail, capital punishment**)

capital punishment: n. execution (death) for a capital offense. The U.S. Supreme Court has vacillated on the application of capital punishment, ruling in the *Furman* decision (1972) that capital punishment was a violation of the Eighth Amendment's prohibition against "cruel and unusual punishment" in certain cases, and then reinstated it in 1976. New York, which once led the nation in executions, abolished capital punishment but reinstated it in 1995. There is no capital punishment in Alaska, Hawaii, Iowa, Kansas, Massachusetts, Maine, Minnesota, Michigan, North Dakota, Rhode Island, Vermont, West Virginia and the District of Columbia. There have been no federal executions in more than 30 years. Texas, Florida, Louisiana, Georgia, Virginia, and Alabama have held the most executions in recent years. Means of capital punishment used in the United States include lethal injection, electrocution, gas chamber, hanging, and firing squad. All capital offenses require automatic appeals, which means that approximately 2,500 men and women are presently on "death row" awaiting their appeals or death. (See: **capital offense, Appendix on capital punishment**)

capitalization: n. 1) the act of counting anticipated earnings and expenses as capital assets (property, equipment, fixtures) for accounting purposes. 2) the amount of anticipated net earnings which

hypothetically can be used for conversion into capital assets.

For where no law is, there is no transgression.
—The Bible, Romans IV.15

capitalized value: n. anticipated earnings which are discounted (given a lower value) so that they represent a more realistic current value since projected earnings do not always turn out as favorably as expected or hoped.

capital stock: n. the original amount paid by investors into a corporation for its issued stock. Capital stock bears no direct relationship to the present value of stock, which can fluctuate after the initial issue or first stock offering. Capital stock also does not reflect the value of corporate assets, which can go up or down based on profits, losses, or purchases of equipment. Capital stock remains as a ledger entry at the original price. (See: **stock, corporation**)

capricious: adv., adj. unpredictable and subject to whim, often used to refer to judges and judicial decisions which do not follow the law, logic or proper trial procedure. A semi-polite way of saying a judge is inconsistent or erratic.

caption: n. the first section of any written legal pleading (papers) to be filed, which contains the name, address, telephone number of the attorney, the person or persons the attorney represents, the court name, the title of the case, the number of the case, and the title of the documents (complaint, accusation, answer, motion, etc.). Each jurisdiction has its own rules as to the exact format of the caption.

care: n. in law, to be attentive, prudent and vigilant. Essentially, care (and careful) means that a person does everything he/she is supposed to do (to prevent an accident). It is the opposite of negligence (and negligent), which makes the responsible person liable for damages to persons injured. If a person "exercises care," a court cannot find him/her responsible for damages from an accident in which he/she is involved. (See: **careless**)

careless: adj., adv. 1) negligent. 2) the opposite of careful. A careless act can result in liability for damages to others. (See: **care, negligence, negligent**)

carnal knowledge: n. from Latin *carnalis* for "fleshly:" sexual intercourse between a male and female in which there is at least some slight penetration of the woman's vagina by the man's penis. It is legally significant in that it is a necessary legal characteristic or element of rape, child molestation, or consensual sexual relations with a female below the age of consent ("statutory rape"). Age of consent varies from 14 to 18, depending upon the state. (See: **rape, statutory rape**)

carrier: n. in general, any person or business which transports property or people by any means of conveyance (truck, auto, taxi, bus, airplane, railroad, ship), almost always for a charge. The carrier is the transportation system and not the owner or operator of the system.

There are two types of carriers: common carrier (in the regular business or a public utility of transportation) and a private carrier (a party not in the business, which agrees to make a delivery or carry a passenger in a specific instance). Common carriers are regulated by states and by the Interstate Commerce Commission if they cross state lines. (See: **common carrier, private carrier**)

carryback: n. in taxation accounting, using a current tax year's deductions, business losses or credits to refigure and amend a previously filed tax return to reduce the tax liability. (See: **carryover**)

carrying for hire: n. the act of transporting goods or individuals for a fee. It is important to determine if the carrier has liability for safe delivery or is subject to regulation. (See: **carrier, common carrier, private carrier**).

carrying on business: v. pursuing a particular occupation on a continuous and substantial basis. There need not be a physical or visible business "entity" as such.

carryover: n. in taxation accounting, using a tax year's deductions, business losses or credits to apply to the following year's tax return to reduce the tax liability. (See: **carryback**)

cartel: n. 1) an arrangement among supposedly independent corporations or national monopolies in the same industrial or resource development field organized to control distribution, set prices, reduce competition, and sometimes share technical expertise. Often the participants are multinational corporations which operate across numerous borders and have little or no loyalty to any home country, and great loyalty to profits. The most prominent cartel is OPEC (Organization of Petroleum Exporting Countries), which represents all of the oil producing countries in the Middle East, North Africa and Venezuela. Many cartels operate behind a veil of secrecy, particularly since under American antitrust laws (the Sherman and Clayton Acts) they are illegal. 2) a criminal syndicate like the international drug cartel headquartered in Colombia. (See: **antitrust laws,**)

case: n. short for a cause of action, lawsuit, or the right to sue (as in "does he have a case against Jones?"). It is also shorthand for the reported decisions (appeals, certain decisions of federal courts and special courts such as the tax court) which can be cited as precedents. Thus, "in the case of *Malarkey v. Hogwash Printing Company*, the court stated the rule as...."

case law: n. reported decisions of appeals courts and other courts which make new interpretations of the law and, therefore, can be cited as precedents. These interpretations are distinguished from "statutory law," which is the statutes and codes (laws) enacted by legislative bodies; "regulatory law," which is regulations required by agencies based on statutes; and in some states, the common law, which is the generally accepted law carried down from England. The rulings in trials and hearings which are not appealed and not reported are not case law and, therefore, not precedent or new interpretations. Law students principally study case law to understand the application of law to facts and learn the courts' subsequent interpretations of statutes. (See: **case system, precedent**)

case of first impression: n. a case in which a question of interpretation of law is presented which has never arisen before in any reported case. Sometimes, it is only of first impression in the particular state or jurisdiction, so decisions from other states or the federal courts may be examined as a guideline.

case system: n. the method of studying law generally used in American law schools, in which the students read, outline (brief), discuss and hear lectures about the cases. Each case presented stands for a particular rule of law in the subject matter covered and is contained in "casebooks" on particular topics (contracts, torts, criminal law, constitutional law, agency, etc.). The system is useful since it relates the law to real and factual situations which assist students in memorization and encourages deductive reasoning. The case system is reinforced by textbooks and outlines on the subject matter, which were formerly the principal sources of learning. The method was introduced first at Harvard in 1869 by professor Christopher C. Langdell and soon became standard.

cashier's check: n. a check issued by a bank on its own account for the amount paid to the bank by the purchaser with a named payee, and stating the name of the party purchasing the check (the remitter). The check is received as cash since it is guaranteed by the bank and does not depend on the account of a private individual or business. Cashiers' checks are commonly used when payment must be credited immediately upon receipt for business, real estate transfers, tax payments and the like.

casual: adj. defining something that happens by chance, without being foreseen, or informally. This includes "casual" labor or employment, which is someone hired to do a task just because he/she was available at the moment. "Casual laborer" carries the implication that the laborer does not belong to a union and that the employer and the laborer will not pay appropriate taxes on the wages paid.

casualty: n. 1) an accident which could not have been foreseen or guarded against, such as a shipwreck caused by storm or fire caused by lightning. 2) the loss, as of life, from such an unavoidable accident. The courts remain inconsistent on the exact definition. (See: **casualty loss**)

casualty loss: n. in taxation, loss due to damage which qualifies for a casualty loss tax deduction. It must be caused by a sudden, unexpected or unusual occurrence such as a storm, flood, fire, shipwreck, earthquake or act of God, but would not include gradual damage from water seepage or erosion.

cause: from Latin *causa*: 1) v. to make something happen. 2) n. the reason something happens. A cause

implies what is called a "causal connection" as distinguished from events which may occur but do not have any effect on later events. Example: While driving his convertible, Johnny Youngblood begins to stare at pretty Sally Golightly, who is standing on the sidewalk. While so distracted he veers into a car parked at the curb. Johnny's inattention (negligence) is the cause of the accident, and neither Sally nor her beauty is the cause. 3) n. short for cause of action. (See: **cause of action, proximate cause**)

The fine for peering into your neighbor's house without permission is one cow.
—Irish Laws, collected by Mary Dowling Daley

cause of action: n. the basis of a lawsuit founded on legal grounds and alleged facts which, if proved, would constitute all the "elements" required by statute. Examples: to have a cause of action for breach of contract there must have been an offer of acceptance; for a tort (civil wrong) there must have been negligence or intentional wrongdoing and failure to perform; for libel there must have been an untruth published which is particularly harmful; and in all cases there must be a connection between the acts of the defendant and damages. In many lawsuits there are several causes of action stated separately, such as fraud, breach of contract, and debt, or negligence and intentional destruction of property. (See: **element, lawsuit**)

caveat: n. (kah-vee-ott) from Latin *caveat* for "let him beware." 1) a warning or caution. 2) a popular term used by lawyers to point out that there may be a hidden problem or defect. In effect, "I just want to warn you that...."

caveat emptor: (kah-vee-ott emptor) Latin for "let the buyer beware." The basic premise that the buyer buys at his/her own risk and therefore should examine and test a product himself/herself for obvious defects and imperfections. *Caveat emptor* still applies even if the purchase is "as is" or when a defect is obvious upon reasonable inspection before purchase. Since implied warranties (assumed quality of goods) and consumer protections have come upon the legal landscape, the seller is held to a higher standard of disclosure than "buyer beware" and has responsibility for defects which could not be noted by casual inspection (particularly since modern devices cannot be tested except by use and many products are pre-packaged). (See: **consumer protection laws**)

cease and desist order: n. an order of a court or government agency to a person, business or organization to stop doing something upon a strong showing that the activity is harmful and/or contrary to law. The order may be permanent or hold until a final judicial determination of legality occurs. In many instances the activity is believed to cause irreparable damage such as receipt of funds illegally, felling of timber contrary to regulation, selling of shares of stock without a proper permit, or oil drilling which would damage the ecology.

certificate of deposit (CD): n. a document issued by a bank in return for a deposit of money which pays a fixed interest rate for a specified period (from a month to several years). Interest rates on CD's are usually higher than savings accounts because banking institutions require a commitment to leave money in the CD for a fixed period of time. Often there is a financial penalty (fee) for cashing in a CD before the pledged time runs out.

certificate of incorporation: n. document which some states issue to prove a corporation's existence upon the filing of articles of incorporation. In most states the articles are sufficient proof.

certificate of title: n. generally, the title document for a motor vehicle issued by the state in which it is registered, describing the vehicle by type and engine number, as well as the name and address of the registered owner and the lienholder (financial institution that loaned money to buy the car). Since in some states these documents are usually pink, the certificate of title is sometimes called a "pink slip." (See: **pink slip**)

certified check: n. a check issued by a bank which certifies that the maker of the check has enough money in his/her account to cover the amount to be paid. The bank sets aside the funds so that the check will remain good even if other checks are written on the particular account. Like a cashier's check, a certified check guarantees that it is immediately good since it is guaranteed by the bank and the recipient does not have to wait until it "clears." (See: **cashier's check**)

certiorari: n. (sersh-oh-rare-ee) a writ (order) of a higher court to a lower court to send all the documents in a case to it so the higher court can review the lower court's decision. *Certiorari* is most commonly used by the U.S. Supreme Court, which is selective about which cases it will hear on appeal. To appeal to the Supreme Court one applies to the Supreme Court for a writ of *certiorari*, which it grants at its discretion and only when at least three members believe that the case involves a sufficiently significant federal question in the public interest. By denying such a writ the Supreme Court says it will let the lower court decision stand, particularly if it conforms to accepted precedents (previously decided cases).

cestui que trust: n. (properly pronounced ses-tee kay, but lawyers popularly pronounce it setty kay) from old French. 1) an old-fashioned expression for the beneficiary of a trust. 2) "the one who trusts" or the person who will benefit from the trust and will receive payments or a future distribution from the trust's assets. (See: **beneficiary**)

cestui que use: (pronounced ses-tee kay use or setty kay use) n. an old-fashioned term for a person who benefits from assets held in a trust for the beneficiary's use. The term "beneficiary" is now used instead. (See: **beneficiary,** *cestui que* **trust, trust**)

chain of title: n. the succession of title ownership to real property from the present owner back to the original owner at some distant time. Chains of title include notations of deeds, judgments of distribution from estates, certificates of death of a joint tenant, foreclosures, judgments of quiet title (lawsuit to prove one's right to property title) and other recorded transfers (conveyances) of title to real property. Usually title companies or abstractors are the professionals who search out the chain of title and provide a report so that a purchaser will be sure the title is clear of any claims. (See: **abstract of title, conveyance, foreclosure, quiet title actions, title**)

challenge: n. the right of each attorney in a jury trial to request that a juror be excused. There may be a "challenge for cause" on the basis the juror had admitted prejudice or shows some obvious conflict of interest (e.g. the juror used to work for the defendant or was once charged with the same type of crime) which the judge must resolve. If the juror is excused (removed) "for cause," then the challenge does not count against the limited number of challenges allowed each side. More common is the "peremptory challenge," which is a request that a juror be excused without stating a reason. An attorney might say: "Juror number eight may be excused." Only six or eight peremptory challenges are normally allowed each side. Systematic peremptory challenges of all blacks or all women may be examples and proof that a defendant has been deprived of a jury of his/her peers and result in an appeal based on lack of due process. (See: **peremptory challenge**)

challenge for cause: n. a request that a prospective juror be dismissed because there is a specific and forceful reason to believe the person cannot be fair, unbiased or capable of serving as a juror. Causes include acquaintanceship with either of the parties, one of the attorneys or a witness, the potential juror's expression during *voir dire* (questioning of the prospective jurors) of inability to be unbiased due to prior experience in a similar case (having been convicted of drunk driving, being a battered wife, etc.), any obvious prejudice, or inability to serve (such as being mentally disturbed). The judge determines if the person shall be dismissed. Challenges and dismissal for cause differ from peremptory challenges, which each side may use to dismiss potential jurors without stating any reason. (See: **juror, jury, panel, peremptory challenge,** *venire, voir dire*)

chambers: n. the private office of a judge, usually close to the courtroom so that the judge can enter the court from behind the bench and not encounter people on the way. Judges hear some motions, discuss formal legal problems like jury instructions, or conduct hearings on sensitive matters such as adoptions "in chambers." (See: **in camera, in chambers**)

champerty: n. an agreement between the party suing in a lawsuit (plaintiff) and another person, usually an attorney, who agrees to finance and carry the lawsuit in return for a percentage of the recovery (money won and paid). In common law this was illegal on the theory that it encouraged lawsuits. Today it is legal and often part of a "contingent fee" agreement between

lawyer and client. It is not the same as barratry, which is active encouragement of lawsuits. (See: **barratry, contingent fee**)

chancellor: n. from the old English legal system, a chancellor is a judge who sits in what is called a chancery (equity) court with the power to order something be done (as distinguished from just paying damages). Almost all states now combine chancery (equity) functions and law in the same courts. (See: **equity**)

chancery: n. a court that can order acts performed. Today chancery courts are merged with law courts in most states. (See: **equity**)

> *True law is right reason in agreement with nature; it is of universal application, unchanging and everlasting; it summons to duty by its commands, and averts from wrong doing by its prohibitions.*
> —*Cicero*

change of circumstances: n. the principal reason for a court modifying (amending) an existing order for the payment of alimony and/or child support. The change may be an increase or decrease in the income of either the party obligated to pay or the ex-spouse receiving payment, or the health, the employment, or needs of either party. Thus, if an ex-husband's income is substantially increased or the ex-wife becomes ill and cannot work, the judge may order the ex-husband to pay her more. Remarriage of a spouse who is receiving alimony automatically terminates the alimony order, unless there is a special provision that it continue, which is rare. (See: **alimony, child support, dissolution of marriage, divorce, spousal support**)

character witness: n. a person who testifies in a trial on behalf of a person (usually a criminal defendant) as to that person's good ethical qualities and morality both by the personal knowledge of the witness and the person's reputation in the community. Such testimony is primarily relevant when the party's honesty or morality is an issue, particularly in most criminal cases and civil cases such as fraud.

charge: n. 1) in a criminal case, the specific statement of what crime the party is accused (charged with) contained in the indictment or criminal complaint. 2) in jury trials, the oral instructions by the judge to the jurors just before the jury begins deliberations. This charge is based on jury instructions submitted by attorneys on both sides and agreed upon by the trial judge. 3) a fee for services.

charitable contribution: n. in taxation, a contribution to an organization which is officially created for charitable, religious, educational, scientific, artistic, literary, or other good works. Such contributions are deductible from gross income, and thus lower the taxes paid. (See: **charitable remainder trust, charity**)

charitable remainder trust (Charitable Remainder Irrevocable Unitrust): n. a form of trust in which the donor (trustor or settlor) places substantial funds or assets into an irrevocable trust (a trust in which the basic terms cannot be changed or the gift withdrawn) with an independent trustee, in which the assets are to go to charity on the death of the donor, but the donor (or specific beneficiaries) will receive regular profits from the trust during the donor's lifetime. The IRS will allow a large deduction in the year the funds or assets are donated to the trust, and the tax savings can be used to buy an insurance policy on the life of the donor which will pay his/her children the proceeds upon the donor's death. Thus, the donor (trustor) can make the gift to charity, receive a return on his/her money and still arrange to make a large gift at death to his/her heirs. The disadvantage is that the assets are permanently tied up or committed. (See: **trust**)

charity: n. 1) in general the sentiment of benevolence, doing good works, assisting the less fortunate, philanthropy and contributing to the general public. 2) an organization which exists to help those in need or provide educational, scientific, religious and artistic assistance to members of the public. Charities are usually corporations established under state guidelines and require IRS approval in order for contributions to them to be deductible from gross income by donors. (See: **charitable contribution**)

charter: n. the name for articles of incorporation in some states, as in a corporate charter. (See: **corporation**)

chattel: n. an item of personal property

which is movable, as distinguished from real property (land and improvements). (See: **personal property**)

chattel mortgage: n. an outmoded written document which made a chattel (tangible personal asset) security for a loan of a certain amount. It has been replaced in most states by a security agreement, the form of which is designated in a Uniform Commercial Code as UCC-1. UCC-1 security agreements must be filed with a specific public agency (e.g. a state Secretary of State) to protect buyers of the personal property and lenders making loans secured by the property. (See: **UCC-1**)

check: n. a draft upon a particular account in a bank, in which the drawer or maker (the person who has the account and signs the check) directs the bank to pay a certain amount to the payee (which may include the drawer, "cash," or someone else). Other checks include cashier's checks issued by the bank for a sum paid to the bank, and certified checks in which the bank sets aside an amount from the maker's bank account and then guarantees the check can be cashed immediately. (See: **cashier's check, certified check, negotiable instrument**)

Chief Justice: n. the presiding judge of any State Supreme Court and the U.S. Supreme Court. The Chief Justice of the U.S. Supreme Court is appointed by the President and then must be confirmed by the U.S. Senate. The Chief Justice sets the tone for the court, assigns the writing of majority opinions to fellow justices or to himself/herself, and oversees the management of the court and its staff. Since U.S. Supreme Court justices serve for life or until voluntary retirement, they can have long-term influence. There have been only 16 U.S. Supreme Court Chief Justices in over 200 years. All but two were appointed from outside the ranks of existing Associate Justices.

child: n. 1) a person's natural offspring. 2) a person 14 years and under. A "child" should be distinguished from a "minor" who is anyone under 18 in almost all states. (See: **minor**)

child custody: n. a court's determination of which parent, relative or other adult should have physical and/or legal control and responsibility for a minor (child) under 18. Child custody can be decided by a local court in a divorce or if a child, relative, close friend or state agency questions whether one or both parents is unfit, absent, dead, in prison or dangerous to the child's well-being. In such cases custody can be awarded to a grandparent or other relative, a foster parent or an orphanage or other organization or institution. While a divorce is pending the court may grant temporary custody to one of the parents, require conferences or investigation (in some states, if the parents cannot agree, custody is automatically referred to a mediator, commissioner or social worker) before making a final ruling. There is a difference between physical custody, which designates where the child will actually live, and legal custody, which gives the custodial person(s) the right to make decisions for the child's welfare. If the parents agree, the court can award joint custody, physical and/or legal. Joint legal custody is becoming increasingly common. The basic consideration on custody matters is supposed to be the best interests of the child or children. In most cases the non-custodial parent is given visitation rights, which may include weekends, parts of vacations and other occasions. The court can always change custody if circumstances warrant. (See: **child support, custody, dissolution of marriage, divorce, joint custody**)

child support: n. court-ordered funds to be paid by one parent to the custodial parent of a minor child after divorce (dissolution) or separation. Usually the dollar amounts are based on the income of both parents, the number of children, the expenses of the custodial parent, and any special needs of the child. In many states or locales the amount is determined by a chart which factors in all these figures. It may also include health plan coverage, school tuition or other expenses, and may be reduced during periods of extended visitation such as summer vacations. Child support generally continues until the child reaches 18 years, graduates from high school, is emancipated (no longer lives with either parent), or, in some cases, for an extended period such as college attendance. The amount and continuation of support may be changed by the court upon application of either party depending on a proved change of circumstance of the parents or child. Child support should not be confused with alimony (spousal support) which is for the ex-spouse's support. Child support is not deductible from gross income for tax purposes (but may allow a dependent exemption) nor is it taxed as income, unlike alimony, which is deductible by the payer and taxed as the adult recipient's income. (See: **alimony, child custody, dissolution of marriage, divorce, spousal support, change of circumstances**)

churning: n. the unethical and usually illegal practice of excessive buying and selling of shares of stock for a customer by a stockbroker or sales agent for the purpose of obtaining high sales commissions.

C.I.F.: n. the total of cost, insurance and freight charges to be paid on goods purchased and shipped.

circuit courts: n. a movable court in which the judge holds court sessions at several different locations for pre-specified periods of time. In effect, the judge "rides the circuit" from town to town and takes the "court" with him/her. Formerly, the Federal District Courts of Appeal were called the Circuit Courts of Appeal.

circumstantial evidence: n. evidence in a trial which is not directly from an eyewitness or participant and requires some reasoning to prove a fact. There is a public perception that such evidence is weak ("all they have is circumstantial evidence"), but the probable conclusion from the circumstances may be so strong that there can be little doubt as to a vital fact ("beyond a reasonable doubt" in a criminal case, and "a preponderance of the evidence" in a civil case). Particularly in criminal cases, "eyewitness" ("I saw Frankie shoot Johnny") type evidence is often lacking and may be unreliable, so circumstantial evidence becomes essential. Prior threats to the victim, fingerprints found at the scene of the crime, ownership of the murder weapon, and the accused being seen in the neighborhood, certainly point to the suspect as being the killer, but each bit of evidence is circumstantial. (See: **evidence**)

citation: n. 1) a notice to appear in court due to the probable commission of a minor crime such as a traffic violation, drinking liquor in a park where prohibited, letting a dog loose without a leash, and in some states for possession of a small amount of marijuana. Failure to appear can result in a warrant for the citee's arrest. 2) a notice to appear in court in a civil matter in which the presence of a party appears necessary, usually required by statute, such as a person whose relatives wish to place him/her under a conservatorship (take over and manage his/her affairs). 3) the act of referring to (citing) a statute, precedent-setting case or legal textbook, in a brief (written legal court statement) or argument in court, called "citation of authority." 4) the section of the statute or the name of the case as well as the volume number, the report series and the page number of a case referred to in a brief, points and authorities, or other legal argument. Example: *United States vs. Wong Kim Ark*, (1898) 169 U.S. 649, which is the name of the case, the year when decided, with the decision found at volume 169 of the United States [Supreme Court] Reporter at page 649. A citation

also refers to the case itself, as in "counsel's citation of the *Wong* case is not in point." (See: **cite**)

cite: v. 1) to make reference to a decision in another case to make a legal point in argument. 2) to give notice of being charged with a minor crime and a date for appearance in court to answer the charge rather than being arrested (usually given by a police officer). (See: **citation**)

citizen: n. person who by place of birth, nationality of one or both parents, or by going through the naturalization process has sworn loyalty to a nation. The United States has traditionally taken the position that an American citizen is subject to losing his/her citizenship if he/she commits acts showing loyalty to another country, including serving in armed forces potentially unfriendly to the United States, or voting in a foreign country. However, if the foreign nation recognizes dual citizenship (Canada, Israel, and Ireland are common examples) the U.S. will overlook this duality of nationalities.

civil: adj. 1) that part of the law that encompasses business, contracts, estates, domestic (family) relations, accidents, negligence and everything related to legal issues, statutes and lawsuits, that is not criminal law. In a few areas civil and criminal law may overlap or coincide. For example, a person may be liable under a civil lawsuit for negligently killing a pedestrian with his auto by running over the person and be charged with the crime of vehicular homicide due to his/her reckless driving. Assault may bring about arrest by the police under criminal law and a lawsuit by the party attacked under civil law. 2) referring to one's basic rights guaranteed under the Constitution (and the interpretations and statutes intended to implement the enforcement of those rights) such as voting, equitable taxation, freedom of speech, press, religion and assembly. Generally these are referred to as "civil rights," which have required constant diligence and struggle to ensure and expand, as in the Civil Rights movement between 1950 and 1980. Violation of one's civil rights may be a crime under federal and/or state statutes. Civil rights include civil liberties. Civil liberties emphasize protection from infringement upon basic freedoms, while statutory rights are based on laws passed by Congress or state legislatures. (See: **civil liberties, civil rights**)

Delay works always for the man with the longest purse.
—William Howard Taft

civil action: n. any lawsuit relating to civil matters and not criminal prosecution. (See: **lawsuit**)

civil calendar: n. the list of lawsuits (cases) that are approaching trial in any court. Attorneys and/or parties whose cases are coming to the top of the list receive notice of the "calling" of the civil calendar on a particular day for setting a trial date. Unfortunately, some courts are so clogged with pending lawsuits that one case may be called on several civil calendars, possibly months apart, before being finally sent to trial. (See: **calendar**)

civil code: n. in many states, the name for the collection of statutes and laws which deal with business and negligence lawsuits and practices.

civil law: n. 1) a body of laws and legal concepts which come down from old Roman laws established by Emperor Justinian, and which differ from Englishcommon law, which is the framework of most state legal systems. In the United States only Louisiana (relying on the French Napoleonic Code) has a legal structure based on civil law. 2) generic term for non-criminal law.

civil liability: n. potential responsibility for payment of damages or other court-enforcement in a lawsuit, as distinguished from criminal liability, which means open to punishment for a crime.

civil liberties: n. rights or freedoms given to the people by the First Amendment to the Constitution, by Common Law, or legislation, allowing the individual to be free to speak, think, assemble, organize, worship, or petition without government (or even private) interference or restraints. These liberties are protective in nature, while civil rights form a broader concept and include positive elements such as the right to use facilities, the right to an equal education, or the right to participate in government. (See: **civil, civil rights**)

civil penalties: n. fines or surcharges imposed by a governmental agency to enforce regulations such as late payment of taxes, failure to obtain a permit, etc.

civil procedure: n. the complex and often confusing body of rules and regulations set out in both state (usually Code of Civil Procedure) and federal (Federal Code of Procedure) laws which establish the format under which civil lawsuits are filed, pursued and tried. Civil procedure refers only to form and procedure, and not to the substantive law which gives people the right to sue or defend a lawsuit. (See: **civil, civil action, civil code, civil law**)

civil rights: n. those rights guaranteed by the Bill of Rights, the 13th and 14th Amendments to the Constitution, including the right to due process, equal treatment under the law of all people regarding enjoyment of life, liberty, property, and protection. Positive civil rights include the right to vote, the opportunity to enjoy the benefits of a democratic society, such as equal access to public schools, recreation, transportation, public facilities, and housing, and equal and fair treatment by law enforcement and the courts. (See: **Bill of Rights, civil, civil liberties**)

claim: 1) v. to make a demand for money, for property, or for enforcement of a right provided by law. 2) n. the making of a demand (asserting a claim) for money due, for property, from damages or for enforcement of a right. If such a demand is not honored, it may result in a lawsuit. In order to enforce a right against a government agency (ranging for damages from a negligent bus driver to a shortage in payroll) a claim must be filed first. If rejected or ignored by the government, it is lawsuit time.

claim in bankruptcy: n. the written claim filed by persons or businesses owed money (creditors) by a party who files for bankruptcy (debtor) to benefit from the distribution if money becomes available. The known creditors receive written notice of the bankruptcy and will receive a creditor's claim form. They may also receive notice that the bankrupt party has no assets to distribute and that they should not file a claim until further notice (this is bad news for the creditor). (See: **bankruptcy, bankruptcy proceedings**)

claim against an estate: n. upon the death of a person and beginning of probate (filing of will, etc.), a person believing he/she is owed money should file a written claim (statement) promptly with the executor or administrator of the estate, who will then approve it, in whole or in part, or deny the claim. If the claim is not approved the claimant can demand a hearing to have the court determine his/her rights. The period for filing a claim begins upon publication of a death notice or a date specified by state law and continues for a few months (four in California, for example). If there is no probate the claim should be made to the heirs. (See: **probate**)

claim against a governmental agency: n. any time one believes he/she has a right to payment for damages from the government or on an unpaid contract with a government agency (including city, county, state, school district) the first step is to file a written claim according to state laws which vary considerably. Usually the time to file a claim is relatively brief. If the claim is rejected or ignored and the claimant wants to try again, the claimant must file a lawsuit within a time period usually shorter than other types of lawsuits.

class: n. in legal (not sociological) terms, all those persons in the same category, level of rights (e.g. heirs of dead person who are related by the same degree), or who have suffered from the same incident. Whether a person is part of a class is often crucial in determining who can sue on behalf of the people who have been similarly damaged or collect his/her share if a class action judgment is given. (See: **class action**)

class action: n. a lawsuit filed by one or more people on behalf of themselves and a larger group of people "who are similarly situated." Examples might include: all women who have suffered from defective contraceptive devices or breast implants, all those overcharged by a public utility during a particular period, or all those who were underpaid by an employer in violation of the Fair Labor Standards Act. If a class action is successful, a period of time is given for those who can prove they fit the class to file claims to participate in the judgment amount. Class actions are difficult and expensive to file and follow through, but the results can be helpful to people who could not afford to carry a suit alone. They can force businesses that have caused broad damage or have a "public be damned" attitude to change their practices and/or pay for damages. They often result in high fees for the winning attorneys,

although often attorneys do not collect a fee at the beginning of a class action suit but might charge a contingent fee (such as one-third of the final judgment), which, occasionally, can be millions of dollars. Such fees usually require court approval.

clean hands doctrine: n. a rule of law that a person coming to court with a lawsuit or petition for a court order must be free from unfair conduct (have "clean hands" or not have done anything wrong) in regard to the subject matter of his/her claim. His/her activities not involved in the legal action can be abominable because they are considered irrelevant. As an affirmative defense (positive response) a defendant might claim the plaintiff (party suing him/her) has a "lack of clean hands" or "violates the clean hands doctrine" because the plaintiff has misled the defendant or has done something wrong regarding the matter under consideration. Example: A former partner sues on a claim that he was owed money on a consulting contract with the partnership when he left, but the defense states that the plaintiff (party suing) has tried to get customers from the partnership by spreading untrue stories about the remaining partner's business practices. (See: **affirmative defense**)

clear and convincing evidence: n. evidence that proves a matter by the "preponderance of evidence" required in civil cases and beyond the "reasonable doubt" needed to convict in a criminal case. (See: **beyond a reasonable doubt, preponderance of evidence**)

clear and present danger: n. the doctrine established in an opinion written by Oliver Wendell Holmes, Jr. in *Schenk vs. United States* (1919) which is used to determine if a situation creates a threat to the public, individual citizens or to the nation. If so, limits can be placed on First Amendment freedoms of speech, press or assembly. His famous example was that no one should shout "fire" in a crowded theater (speech), but other cases have included the printing of a list of the names and addresses of CIA agents (press) or the gathering together of a lynch mob (assembly).

clear title: n. holding ownership of real property without any claims by others on the owner's title and no history of past claims which might affect the ownership. (See: **cloud on title**)

clerk: n. 1) an official or employee who handles the business of a court or a system of courts, maintains files of each case, and issues routine documents. Almost every county has a clerk of the courts or County Clerk who fulfills those functions, and most courtrooms have a clerk to keep records and assist the judge in the management of the court. 2) a young lawyer who assists a judge or a senior attorney in research and drafting of documents, usually for a year or two, and benefits in at least two ways: learning from the judge or attorney and enjoying association with them. Law clerks for judges, particularly on the Courts of Appeal and the Supreme Court, are chosen from among the top students graduating from law school.

3) a person who works in an office or a store who performs physical work such as filing, stocking shelves, or counter sales.

close corporation: n. a corporation which is permitted by state law to operate more informally than most corporations (allowing decisions without meetings of the board of directors) and has only a limited number of shareholders. Usually a close corporation's shareholders are involved in the actual operation of the business and often are family members. (See: **corporation**)

closed shop: n. a business that will hire only union members by choice or by agreement with the unions, although the Labor-Management Relations Act prohibits closed shop practices which require employees to be union members. A "union shop" is a business in which a majority of the workers have voted to name a union as their certified bargaining agent.

closing: n. the final step in the sale and purchase of real estate in which a deed of title, financing documents, title insurance policies, and remaining funds due are exchanged. Some of the final documents, including the deed and mortgage or deed of trust, are then delivered to the county recorder to be recorded. Depending on local practice, the closing is handled by a title company, escrow holder or attorney.

closing argument: n. the final argument by an attorney on behalf of his/her client after all evidence has been produced for both sides. The lawyer for the plaintiff or prosecution (in a criminal case) makes the first closing argument, followed by counsel for the defendant, and then the plaintiff's attorney can respond to the defense argument. Unlike the "opening statement," which is limited to what is going to be proved, the "closing argument" may include opinions on the law, comment on the opposing party's evidence, and usually requests a judgment or verdict (jury's decision) favorable to the client. (See: **opening statement, trial**)

cloud on title (cloud): n. an actual or apparent outstanding claim on the title to real property. "Clouds" can include an old mortgage or deed of trust with no recording showing the secured debt was paid off, a failure to properly transfer all interests in the real property (such as mineral rights) to a former owner, a previous deed which was improperly written or signed, an unresolved legal debt or levy by a creditor or a taxing authority, or some other doubtful link in the chain of title. Often the "cloud" can be removed by a quiet title action, by finding a person to create or execute a document to prove a debt had been paid or corrected. Title companies will refuse to insure title to be transferred with a "cloud," or they will insure ownership except for ("insure around") the "cloud." (See: **chain of title, deed of trust, mortgage, quiet title action, reconveyance, title, title report**)

code: n. a collection of written laws gathered together, usually covering specific subject matter. Thus, a state may have a civil code, corporations code, education code, evidence code, health and safety codes, insurance code, labor code, motor vehicle code, penal code, revenue and taxation code, and so forth. Federal statutes which deal with legal matters are grouped together in codes. There are also statutes which are not codified. Despite their apparent permanence, codes are constantly being amended by legislative bodies. Some codes are administrative and have the force of law even though they were created and adopted by regulatory agencies and are not actually statutes or laws. (See: **law, statute**)

codefendant: n. when more than one person or entity is sued in one lawsuit, each party sued is called a codefendant.

Code of Professional Responsibility: n. a set of rules governing the ethical conduct of attorneys in the practice of the law. It covers such topics as conflicts of interest, honesty with clients, confidentiality and conduct toward other attorneys and the courts. First developed and pushed by the American Bar Association, the code has been adopted by most states.

codicil: n. a written amendment to a person's will, which must be dated, signed and witnessed just as a will would be, and must make some reference to the will it amends. A codicil can add to, subtract from or modify the terms of the original will. When the person dies, both the original will and the codicil are submitted for approval by the court (probate) and form the basis for administration of the estate and distribution of the belongings of the writer. (See: **probate, will**)

codify: v. to arrange and label a system of laws.

cohabitation: n. living together in the same residence, generally either as husband and wife or for an extended period of time as if the parties were married. Cohabitation implies that the parties are having sexual intercourse while living together, but the definition would not apply to a casual sexual encounter. Legal disputes have arisen as to whether cohabitation would refer to same sex partners, which is important to those involved since "cohabitation" is the basis of certain rights and privileges under various laws, regulations and contracts. The findings of the courts vary on this question, but the trend is to include long-standing homosexual relationships as cohabitation.

coinsurance: n. an insurance policy in which the insurance company insures only a partial value of the property owned by the insured owner. Essentially the owner and the insurance company share the risk.

collateral: 1) n. property pledged to secure a loan or debt, usually funds or personal property as distinguished from real property (but technically collateral can include real estate). 2) adj. referring to something that is going on at the same time parallel to the main issue in a lawsuit or controversy which may affect the outcome of the case, such as adoption of a new federal regulation or a criminal trial of one of the parties. Example: John has filed a lawsuit in New Mexico, where he lives, to establish that he is not the father of Betty's child, while Betty has filed for divorce in Colorado asking that John pay child support for the child. The New Mexico paternity suit is collateral to the Colorado divorce action.

collateral attack: n. a legal action to challenge a ruling in another case. For example, Joe Parenti has been ordered to pay child support in a divorce case, but he then files another lawsuit trying to prove a claim that he is not the father of the child. A "direct attack" would have been to raise the issue of paternity in the divorce action.

collateral descendant: n. a relative descended from a brother or sister of an ancestor, and thus a cousin, niece, nephew, aunt or uncle. (See: **descent and distribution**)

collateral estoppel: n. the situation in which a judgment in one case prevents (estops) a party to that suit from trying to litigate the issue in another legal action. In effect, once decided, the parties are permanently bound by that ruling. (See: **estoppel**, *res judicata*)

collusion: n. where two persons (or business entities through their officers or other employees) enter into a deceitful agreement, usually secret, to defraud and/or gain an unfair advantage over a third party, competitors, consumers or those with whom they are negotiating. Collusion can include secret price or wage fixing, secret rebates, or pretending to be independent of each other when actually conspiring together for their joint ends. It can range from small-town shopkeepers or heirs to a grandma's estate, to

91

gigantic electronics companies or big league baseball team owners. (See: **fraud**)

collusive action: n. a lawsuit brought by parties pretending to be adversaries in order to obtain by subterfuge an advisory opinion or precedent-setting decision from the court. If a judge determines the action does not involve a true controversy he/she will dismiss it. (See: **advisory opinion, collusion, controversy, precedent**)

color of law: n. the appearance of an act being performed based upon legal right or enforcement of statute, when in reality no such right exists. An outstanding example is found in the civil rights acts which penalize law enforcement officers for violating civil rights by making arrests "under color of law" of peaceful protesters or to disrupt voter registration. It could apply to phony traffic arrests in order to raise revenue from fines or extort payoffs to forget the ticket.

color of title: n. the appearance of having title to personal or real property by some evidence, but in reality there is either no title or a vital defect in the title. One might show a title document to real property, but in reality he/she may have deeded the property to another; a patent to an invention may have passed to the inventor's widow, who sells the rights to one party and then, using the original patent documents, sells the patent to a second party based on this "color of title."

comaker: n. when two or more people sign a check or a promissory note, each is a comaker, and each is liable for the entire amount to be paid. (See: **maker**)

The income tax has made more liars out of the American people than golf has.
—Will Rogers

comity: n. when one court defers to the jurisdiction of another in a case in which both would have the right to handle the case. Usually this is applied to a federal court allowing a state court to try a criminal case (either exclusively or first) in which both a state and federal crime has apparently been committed. Murder which also violates civil rights, kidnapping across state borders, murder of a federal official, fraud involving violations of both federal and state laws are examples of cases to which comity may apply.

commencement of action: n. an action (a lawsuit) commences (begins officially) when the party suing files a written complaint or petition with the clerk of the court. Under a unique New York statute a plaintiff may prepare a summons and get a case number before filing a complaint. (See: **summons complaint, petition**)

comment: n. a statement made by a judge or an attorney during a trial which is based on an alleged fact, but not a proven fact. If a comment is made in the presence of the jury, the jurors should be reminded it is not evidence and should not be considered. But how can a juror forget? The old adage: "a bell once rung, cannot be unrung," applies.

commercial frustration: n. an unforeseen uncontrollable event which occurs after a written or oral contract is entered into between parties, and makes it impossible for one of the parties to fulfill his/her duties under the contract. This circumstance allows the frustrated party to rescind the contract without penalty. Such frustration (called frustration of purpose) could include the destruction by fire of the goods to be purchased, the denial of a permit to construct a building by a potential buyer, or denial of an application for a zoning variance to allow expansion by a contractor. (See: **contract, frustration of purpose, impossibility**)

commercial law: n. all the law which applies to the rights, relations and conduct of persons and businesses engaged in commerce, merchandising, trade and sales. In recent years this body of law has been codified in the Uniform Commercial Code, which has been almost universally adopted by the states. (See: **Uniform Commercial Code**)

commingling: n. the act of mixing the funds belonging to one party with those of another party, or, most importantly with funds held in trust for another. Spouses or business partners may commingle without a problem, except that a spouse may thus risk turning separate property into community property (transmutation), and a business partner may have to account to the other. However, trustees, guardians or lawyers holding client funds must be careful not to commingle those funds with their own, since commingling is generally prohibited as a conflict of interest. Use of commingled funds for an investment, even though it might benefit both the trustee and the beneficiary, is still improper. Inadvertent commingling or temporary commingling (say, upon receipt of a settlement check in which both the client and attorney have an interest) requires prompt separation of funds and accounting to the client or beneficiary. To avoid commingling, trustees, lawyers, guardians and those responsible for another's funds set up trust accounts for funds of another.

commission: n. 1) a fee paid based on a percentage of the sale made by an employee or agent, as distinguished from regular payments of wages or salary. 2) a group appointed pursuant to law to conduct certain government business, especially regulation. These range from the local planning or zoning commission to the Securities and Exchange Commission or the Federal Trade Commission.

commitment: n. a judge's order sending someone to jail or prison, upon conviction or before trial, or directing that a mentally unstable person be confined to a mental institution. Technically the judge orders law enforcement personnel to take the prisoner or patient to such places.

common area: n. in condominium and some cooperative housing projects, the areas not owned by an individual owner of the condominium or cooperative residence, but shared by all owners, either by percentage interest or owned by the management organization. Common areas may include recreation facilities, outdoor space, parking, landscaping, fences, laundry rooms and all other jointly used space. Management is by a homeowners' association or cooperative board, which collects assessments from the owners and pays for upkeep, some insurance, maintenance and reserves for replacement of improvements in the common area. This can also refer to the area in a shopping center or mall outside of the individual stores, for which each business pays a share of maintenance based on percentage of total store space occupied.

common carrier: n. an individual, a company or a public utility (like municipal buses) which is in the regular business of transporting people and/or freight. This is distinguished from a private carrier, which only transports occasionally or as a one-time-only event. (See: **carrier**)

common counts: n. claims for debt alleged in a lawsuit (included in the complaint) which are general and alleged together so that the defendant cannot squirm out of liability on some technicality on one of the counts. Common counts may include claims of debt for goods sold and delivered, for work performed, for money loaned or advanced, for money paid requiring repayment, for money received on behalf of the plaintiff, or for money due on an account stated or on an open book account. (See: **cause of action, complaint, count**)

common law: n. the traditional un-written law of England, based on custom and usage, which began to develop over a thousand years before the founding of the United States. The best of the pre-Saxon compendiums of the common law was reportedly written by a woman, Queen Martia, wife of a king of a small English kingdom. Together with a book on the "law of the monarchy" by a Duke of Cornwall, Queen Martia's work was translated into the emerging English language by King Alfred (849-899 A.D.). When William the Conqueror invaded England in 1066, he combined the best of this Anglo-Saxon law with Norman law, which resulted in the English common law, much of which was by custom and precedent rather than by written code. By the 14th century legal decisions and commentaries on the common law began providing precedents for the courts and lawyers to follow. It did not include the so-called law of equity (chancery), which came from the royal power to order or prohibit specific acts. The common law became the basic law of most states due to the *Commentaries on the Laws of England,* completed by Sir William Blackstone in 1769, which became every American lawyer's bible. Today almost all common law has been enacted into statutes with modern variations by all the states except Louisiana, which is still influenced by the Napoleonic Code. In some states the principles of Common Law are so basic they are applied without reference to statute.

common-law marriage: n. an agreement between a man and woman to live together as husband and wife without any legal formalities, followed and/or preceded by cohabitation on a regular basis (usually for seven years). Common-law marriage is legal in Alabama, Colorado, Georgia, Idaho, Iowa, Kansas, Montana, Ohio, Oklahoma, Pennsylvania, Rhode Island, South Carolina, Texas and Utah, thereby recognizing a marriage for purposes of giving the other party the rights of a spouse, including inheritance or employee benefits. Such informal partnerships are recognized by some local governments for purposes of the rights of a spouse under employment contracts and pension rights even where the state does not recognize this as a marriage. (See: **cohabitation**)

common property: n. 1) real property owned by "tenants in common," who each have an "undivided interest" in the entire property. 2) property managed by a homeowners' association in a condominium project or a subdivision development, which all owners may use and each owns a percentage interest in. 3) lands owned by the government for public (common) use, like parks and national forests. (See: **tenancys in common**)

> *The only thing that saves us from bureaucracy is inefficiency. An efficient bureaucracy is the greatest threat to liberty.*
> *—Senator Eugene J. McCarthy*

common stock: n. stock in a corporation in which dividends (payouts) are calculated upon a percentage of net profits, with distribution determined by the board of directors. Usually holders of common stock have voting rights. These are distinguished from preferred stock in which the profits are a predetermined percentage and are paid before the common shareholders who gamble on higher profits, and collectively have voting control of the corporation. (See: **corporation, preferred stock, share, stock**)

community property: n. property and profits received by a husband and wife during the marriage, with the exception of inheritances, specific gifts to one of the spouses, and property and profits clearly traceable to property owned before marriage, all of which is separate property. Community property is a concept which began in Spain to protect rich women from losing everything to profligate husbands, and is only officially recognized in some states which were once under or influenced by Spanish or Mexican control, including California, Arizona, New Mexico, Texas, Nevada, Idaho, Washington and Louisiana. Community property recognizes the equal contribution of both parties to the marriage even though one or the other may earn more income through employment. By agreement or action the married couple can turn (transmute) separate property into community property, including by commingling community and separate funds in one account. Community property is recognized based on fact or agreement of the parties, rather than holding of title. The state courts have wavered on what constitutes proof of community property, including the issue of whether joint tenancy is evidence of community property or not. Upon divorce community property is divided equally without regard to fault. Upon the death of one spouse all the community property goes to the other except in Texas surviving children get one half and in obvious sexual discrimination Nevada and New Mexico allow the husband to will a half to someone other than his wife. (See: **descent, descent and distribution, separate property**)

commutation: n. the act of reducing a criminal sentence resulting from a criminal conviction by the executive clemency of the Governor of the state, or President of the United States in the case of federal crimes. This is not the same as a pardon, which wipes out the conviction or the actual or potential charge (as when President Gerald R. Ford pardoned ex-President Richard M. Nixon even without charges having been officially made—a rare instance). A pardon implies either that the conviction was wrong, that there has been complete rehabilitation of the party, or that he/she has lived an exemplary life for many years and deserves to have his/her name cleared in old age. Commutation implies the penalty was excessive or there has been rehabilitation, reform or other circumstances such as good conduct or community service. Commutation is sometimes used when there is evidence that the defendant was not guilty, but it would prove embarrassing to admit an outright error by the courts. (See: **executive clemency, pardon**)

commute a sentence: v. (See: **commutation**)

company: n. any formal business

entity for profit, which may be a corporation, a partnership, association or individual proprietorship. Often people think the term "company" means the business is incorporated, but that is not true. In fact, a corporation usually must use some term in its name such as "corporation," "incorporated," "corp." or "inc." to show it is a corporation. (See: **business**)

comparative negligence: n. a rule of law applied in accident cases to determine responsibility and damages based on the negligence of every party directly involved in the accident. For a simple example, Eddie Leadfoot, the driver of one automobile, is speeding and Rudy Airhead, the driver of an oncoming car, has failed to signal and starts to turn left, incorrectly judging Leadfoot's speed. A crash ensues in which Airhead is hurt. Airhead's damage recovery will be reduced by the percentage his failure to judge Leadfoot's speed contributed to or caused the accident. Most cases are not as simple, and the formulas to figure out, attribute and compare negligence often make assessment of damages problematic, difficult, and possibly totally subjective. Not all states use comparative negligence (California is a fairly recent convert), and some states still use contributory negligence which denies recovery to any party whose negligence has added to the cause of the accident in any way. Contributory negligence is often so unfair that juries tend to ignore it. (See: **contributory negligence, damages, negligence**)

compensation: n. 1) payment for work performed, by salary, wages, commission or otherwise. It can include giving goods rather than money. 2) the amount received to "make one whole" (or at least better) after an injury or loss, particularly that paid by an insurance company either of the party causing the damage or by one's own insurer.

compensatory damages: n. damages recovered in payment for actual injury or economic loss, which does not include punitive damages (as added damages due to malicious or grossly negligent action). (See: **damages, general damages, punitive damages, special damages**)

competent: adj. 1) in general, able to act in the circumstances, including the ability to perform a job or occupation, or to reason or make decisions. 2) in wills, trusts and contracts, sufficiently mentally able to understand and execute a document. To be competent to make a will a person must understand what a will is, what he/she owns (although forgetting a few items among many does not show incompetency), and who are relatives who would normally inherit ("the natural objects of his/her bounty") such as children and spouse (although forgetting a child in a will is not automatic proof of lack of competency, since it may be intentional or the child has been long gone). 3) in criminal law, sufficiently mentally able to stand trial, if he/she understands the proceedings and can rationally deal with his/her lawyer. This is often broadly interpreted by psychiatrists whose testimony may persuade a court that a party is too psychotic to be tried. If the court finds

incompetency then the defendant may be sent to a state mental facility until such time as he/she regains sanity. At that time a trial may be held, but this is rare. 4) in evidence, "competent" means "relevant" and/or "material." Lawyers often make the objection to evidence: "incompetent, irrelevant and immaterial" to cover all bases. (See: **evidence, will**)

complainant: n. a person or entity who begins a lawsuit by filing a complaint and is usually called the plaintiff, or in some cases the petitioner. (See: **complaint, petitioner, plaintiff**)

complaint: n. the first document filed with the court (actually with the County Clerk or Clerk of the Court) by a person or entity claiming legal rights against another. The party filing the complaint is usually called the plaintiff and the party against whom the complaint is filed is called the defendant or defendants. Complaints are pleadings and must be drafted carefully (usually by an attorney) to properly state the factual as well as legal basis for the claim, although some states have approved complaint forms which can be filled in by an individual. A complaint also must follow statutory requirements as to form. For example, a complaint must be typed on a specific type of paper or on forms approved by the courts, name both the party making the claim and all defendants, and should state what damages or performance is demanded (the prayer). When the complaint is filed, the court clerk will issue a summons, which gives the name and file number of the lawsuit and the address of the attorney filing the complaint, and instructs the defendant that he/she/it has a specific time to file an answer or other response. A copy of the complaint and the summons must be served on a defendant before a response is required. Under a unique statute, New York allows a summons to be served without a complaint. A complaint filing must be accompanied by a filing fee payable to the court clerk, unless a waiver based on poverty is obtained. (See: **answer, caption,** *in forma pauperis***, pleading, prayer, service of process, summons**)

compos mentis: n. (com-pose-men-tis) Latin for "having a sound mind." (See: *non compos mentis*)

compounding a felony: n. when a person injured by a felony (being shot, having one's business trashed, being robbed) reaches an agreement with the one causing the harm that the injured party (victim) will not prosecute (complain to law authorities or testify) the apparent felon in return for money payment, reparations, return of stolen goods or other recompense. Since it smacks of a bribe, in most jurisdictions it is a crime.

compound interest: n. payment of interest upon principal and previously accumulated interest, which increases the amount paid for money use above simple interest. Thus, it can increase more rapidly if compounded daily, monthly or quarterly. The genius physicist Albert Einstein called compound interest man's "greatest invention." Most lenders agree. (See: **interest, promissory note**)

compound question: n. the combination of more than one question into what seems to be a single question asked of a witness during a trial or deposition. A compound question can be objected to by opposing counsel since it is confusing to the witness, who is entitled to answer each question separately. If the objection is sustained the question must be withdrawn and asked in a series of separate questions. (See: **objection**)

compromise: 1) n. an agreement between opposing parties to settle a dispute or reach a settlement in which each gives some ground, rather than continue the dispute or go to trial. Judges encourage compromise and settlement, which is often economically sensible, since it avoids mounting attorneys' fees and costs. 2) v. to reach a settlement in which each party gives up some demands. (See: **settlement**)

compromise verdict: n. a decision made by a jury in which the jurors split the difference between the high amount of damages which one group of jurors feel is justified and the low amount other jurors favor. Since this is a "chance" verdict not computed on a careful determination of the damages, it may do an injustice to one party or the other, and is thus misconduct, which can result in an appeals court overturning the verdict. (See: **verdict**)

The law is a causeway upon which so long as he keeps to it a citizen may walk safely.
—Robert Bolt, A Man for All Seasons

concealed weapon: n. a weapon, particularly a handgun, which is kept hidden on one's person, or under one's control (in a glove compartment or under a car seat). Carrying a concealed weapon is a crime in most states unless the party with the weapon is a law enforcement officer or has a permit to carry a concealed weapon. A permit is usually issued by local law enforcement under guidelines of need—such as being a carrier of large amounts of cash in business—and having a record free of convictions, arrests or improper activity.

concealment: n. fraudulent failure to reveal information which someone knows and is aware that in good faith he/she should communicate to another. Examples include failure to disclose defects in goods sold (the horse has been sick, the car has been in an accident), leaving out significant liabilities in a credit application, or omitting assets from a bankruptcy schedule to keep them from being available for distribution to creditors. Such concealment at minimum can be a cause for rescission (cancellation) of a contract by the misled party or basis for a civil lawsuit for fraud. (See: **fraud**)

conclusion: n. 1) in general, the end. 2) in a trial, when all evidence has been introduced and final arguments made, so nothing more can be presented, even if a lawyer thinks of something new or forgotten. 3) in a trial or court hearing, a final determination of the facts by the trier of fact (jury or judge) and/or a judge's decision on the law. (See: **conclusion of fact, conclusion of law**)

conclusion of fact: n. in a trial, the final result of an analysis of the facts presented in evidence, made by the trier of fact (a jury or by the judge if there is no jury). When a judge is the trier of fact he/she will present orally in open court or in a written judgment his/her findings of fact to support his/her decision. In most cases either party is entitled to written conclusion of facts if requested. (See: **finding, judgment**)

conclusion of law: n. a judge's final decision on a question of law which has been raised in a trial or a court hearing, particularly those issues which are vital to reaching a statement. These may be presented orally by the judge in open court, but are often contained in a written judgment in support of his/her judgment such as an award of damages or denial of a petition. In most cases either party is entitled to written conclusions of law if requested. (See: **judgment**)

concurrent sentences: n. sentences for more than one crime which are to be served at one time. When a criminal defendant is convicted of two or more crimes, a judge sentences him/her to a certain period of time for each crime. Then out of compassion, leniency, plea bargaining or the fact that the several crimes are interrelated, the judge will rule that the sentences may all be served at the same time, with the longest period controlling.

condemn: v. 1) for a public agency to determine that a building is unsafe or unfit for habitation and must be torn down or rebuilt to meet building and health code requirements. 2) for a governmental agency to take private property for public use under the right of eminent domain, but constitutionally the property owner must receive just compensation. If an agreement cannot be reached then the owner is entitled to a court determination of value in a condemnation action (lawsuit), but the public body can take the property immediately upon deposit of the estimated value. 3) to sentence a convicted defendant to death. 4) send to prison. (See: **capital punishment, condemnation action, eminent domain**)

condemnation: n. the legal process by which a governmental body exercises its right of "eminent domain" to acquire private property for public uses (highways, schools, redevelopment, etc.). Condemnation includes a resolution of public need, an offer to purchase, and, if a negotiated purchase is not possible, then a condemnation suit. The government may take the property at the time of suit if it deposits money with the court in the amount of the government's appraisal. (See: **condemnation action, eminent domain, inverse condemnation**)

condemnation action: n. a lawsuit brought by a public agency to acquire private property for public purposes (schools, highways, parks, hospitals, redevelopment, civic buildings, for example), and a determination of the value to be paid. While the government has the right to acquire the private property (eminent domain), the owner is entitled under the Constitution to receive just compensation to be determined by a court. (See: **condemnation, eminent domain**)

condition: n. a term or requirement stated in a contract, which must be met for the other party to have the duty to fulfill his/her obligations. (See: **condition precedent, condition subsequent**)

conditional bequest: n. in a will, a gift which will take place only if a particular event has occurred by the time the maker of the will dies. Example: Ruth's will provides that "Griselda will receive the nursery furniture if she has children at the time of my death." This is slightly different from an executory bequest, which could provide for a gift to a beneficiary upon the happening of a specified event. Example of an executory bequest: a trust provides "Betty shall receive the house held in trust when she marries." (See: **bequest, executory**)

conditional sale: n. a sale of property or goods which will be completed if certain conditions are met (as agreed) by one or both parties to the transaction. Example: Hotrod agrees to buy Tappit's 1939 LaSalle for $1,000 cash if Tappit can get the car running by September 1st. (See: **sale**)

condition precedent: n. 1) in a contract, an event which must take place before a party to a contract must perform or do their part. 2) in a deed to real property, an event which has to occur before the title (or other right) to the property will actually be in the name of the party receiving title. Examples: if the ship makes it to port, the buyer agrees to pay for the freight on the ship and unload it; when daughter Gracella marries she shall then have full title to the property. (See: **condition**)

condition subsequent: n. 1) in a contract, a happening which terminates the duty of a party to perform or do his/her part. 2) in a deed to real property, an event which terminates a person's interest in the property. Examples: if the Dingbat Company closes its business, a supplier will not be required to fulfill its contract and deliver gidgets to the company and the contract will terminate; if daughter-in-law Beatrice terminates her marriage to Reggie Fauntleroy, her interest in the real property will terminate and revert to the grantors, Mom and Dad Fauntleroy. (See: **condition**)

condominium: n. title to a unit of real property which, in reality, is the airspace which an apartment, office or store occupies. An increasingly common form of property title in a multi-unit project, condominiums actually date back to ancient Rome, hence the Latin name. The owner of the condominium also owns a common tenancy with owners of other units in the common area, which includes all the driveways, parking, elevators, outside hallways, recreation and landscaped areas, which are managed by a homeowners' or tenant's association. If the condominium unit is destroyed by fire or other disaster, the owner has the right to rebuild in his/her airspace. Most states have adopted statutes to cover special issues involving development, construction, management and taxation of condominium projects. (See: **common area**)

condone: v. 1) to forgive, support, and/or overlook moral or legal failures of another without protest, with the result that it appears that such breaches of moral or legal duties are acceptable. An employer may overlook an employee overcharging customers or a police officer may look the other way when a party uses violent self-help to solve a problem. 2) to forgive the marital infidelity of one's spouse and resume marital sexual relations on the condition that the sin is not repeated.

confess: v. in criminal law, to voluntarily state that one is guilty of a criminal offense. This admission may be made to a law enforcement officer or in court either prior to or upon arrest, or after the person is charged with a specific crime. A confession must be truly voluntary (not forced by threat, torture, or trickery) and cannot be admitted in trial unless the defendant has been given the so-called Miranda warnings at the time of arrest or when it is clear he/she is the prime suspect, all based on the Fifth Amendment prohibition against self-incrimination. The Miranda warnings are: the right to remain silent, the right to have an attorney present and that one can be appointed, and that his/her statements may be used against the defendant in court. (See: **Bill of Rights, confession, Miranda warning, self-incrimination**)

confession: n. the statement of one charged with a crime that he/she committed the crime. Such an admission is generally put in writing (by the confessor, law enforcement officers or their stenographer) and then read and signed by the defendant. If the defendant cannot read English, he/she has the right to have his/her confession read aloud or translated. It can be used against the defendant in trial (and his/her codefendants) if it is truly voluntary. (See: **Bill of Rights, confess, Miranda warning, self-incrimination**)

confession and avoidance: n. when a defendant admits the allegations in a complaint against him/her in a lawsuit or accusations in a criminal case but alleges other facts (affirmative defenses) to show that the original allegations do not prove a case against him/her. Often this means the defendant confesses to the accuracy of the stated facts and tries to avoid their legal impact.

confession of judgment: n. a written agreement in which the defendant in a lawsuit admits liability and accepts the amount of agreed-upon damages he/she must pay to plaintiff (person suing him/her), and agrees that the statement may be filed as a court judgment against him/her if he/she does not pay or perform as agreed. This avoids further legal proceedings and may prevent a legal judgment being entered (filed) if the terms are fulfilled by the defendant.

confidence game: n. the obtaining of money from others through trick or swindle, generally by gaining the victim's trust and confidence. (See: **swindle**)

confidential communication: n. certain written communications which can be kept confidential and need not be disclosed in court as evidence, answered by a witness either in depositions or trial, or provided to the parties to a lawsuit or their attorneys. This is based on the inherent private relationship between the person communicating and the confidant's occupation or relationship to him/her. They include communications between husband and wife, lawyer and client, physician or other medical person (most therapists) and patient, minister or priest and parishioner (or anyone seeking spiritual help), and journalist and source in some states. Moral conflicts may arise when a murderer or child molester confesses to his/her priest, who is pledged to silence and confidentiality by his priestly vows and cannot reveal the confession in legal cases. (See: **attorney-client privilege, privileged communication**)

confidential relation: n. a relationship in which one person has confidence in and relies on another because of some combination of a history of trust, older age, family connection and/or superior training and knowledge, to a point where the party relied upon dominates the situation, for good or bad. While it may include attorney and client, stockbroker and customer, real estate agent and buyer, a senior family member and an unsophisticated relative, the relationship is defined on a case-by-case basis, with reliance and dominance the key factors. In this situation, the trusting party does not have to be as vigilant or suspicious as with strangers or people who are not relied upon. The time clock (statute of limitations) to bring a lawsuit against a crook who is in a confidential relationship may not start to run until the misdeeds become extremely obvious. (See: **fiduciary**)

confiscate: v. to take one's goods or property without legal right, although there may appear to be some lawful basis. In the case of a government seizing property, it may include taking without the just compensation as guaranteed by the Constitution. There are some acts of legal confiscation, such as taking an automobile used in illegal drug traffic. (See: **condemnation, theft**)

conflict of interest: n. a situation in which a person has a duty to more than one person or organization, but cannot do justice to the actual or potentially adverse interests of both parties. This includes when an individual's personal interests or concerns are inconsistent with the best for a customer, or when a public official's personal interests are contrary to his/her loyalty to public business. An attorney, an accountant, a business adviser or realtor cannot represent two parties in a dispute and must avoid even the appearance of conflict. He/she may not join with a client in business without making full disclosure of his/her potential conflicts, he/she must avoid commingling funds with the client, and never, never take a position adverse to the customer.

conflict of law: n. a situation in which both state and federal laws or courts, or laws of more than one state, are applicable to a potential lawsuit or interpretation of a document and seem to be inconsistent or in conflict. The plaintiff's attorney's first problem is to decide in what state or federal court the lawsuit should be filed. This can apply to a dead person's estate with property in several states, when people earn income in several states, are involved in business in several states, or violate both state and federal laws in one scheme. Also to be considered is the issue of federal preemption, which may dictate that the federal statutes have been given a monopoly on the subject (pre-empted the field) and that a federal court must try the case, but that it will apply the laws of the state where the controversy arose. (See: **forum, preemption**)

confrontation: n. 1) fight or argument. 2) the right of a criminal defendant "to be confronted with the witnesses against him" (Sixth Amendment to the Constitution). Confrontation includes the right to object to the witness against him/her (sometimes depending on whether the witness can identify the defendant) and to cross-examine that witness. (See: **Bill of Rights, witness**)

confusingly similar: adj. in the law of trademarks, when a trademark, logo or business name is so close to that of a pre-existing trademark, logo or name that the public might misidentify the new one with the old trademark, logo or name. Such confusion may not be found if the products or businesses are clearly not in the actual or potential product markets or geographic area of the other. (See: **trademark**)

conjugal rights: n. a spouse's so-called "rights" to the comforts and companionship from his/her mate, meaning sexual relations. Some states allow prisoners to have "conjugal visits" so that they may have private visits and sexual relations with their spouse (or "significant other") in a special room or apartment.

conscientious objector: n. a person who refuses to serve in the military due to religious or strong philosophical views against war or killing. Refusing to answer a draft call is a federal felony, but when a person's religious beliefs are long-standing and consistent (as with the Quakers) then the objection to service is excused. Conscientious objectors may be required to perform some non-violent work like driving an ambulance. During the Vietnam War some conscientious objectors fled to Canada to avoid any service. However, heavyweight boxing champion Muhammad Ali refused induction during the Vietnam War (1967) on the basis of his Black Muslim religious beliefs against war and other philosophical reasons, but was charged with draft evasion anyway. Ali was convicted and sentenced to five years in prison. On June 28, 1971, the Supreme Court overturned Ali's conviction. Those who do not agree with these objectors sometimes call them "draft dodgers."

> *Woe unto you, lawyers, for ye have taken away the key of knowledge.*
> *—The Bible, Luke XI.52*

conscious parallelism: n. an undiscussed imitation by a business of a competitor's action, such as changing prices up or down without the active conspiracy between business rivals, which would make this coincidental activity a violation of anti-trust laws. Example: a) Air Chance Airline offers a two-for-one special for all flights over 1,000 miles, and, within a week, several other airlines offer the same bargain. b) Rumble Oil Company stations set gasoline prices at $1.38 for premium and the next day all gas stations in the Rumble market area set their pumps at $1.38. Coincidence? No, conscious parallelism.

consent: 1) n. a voluntary agreement to another's proposition. 2) v. to voluntarily agree to an act or proposal of another, which may range from contracts to sexual relations.

consent decree: n. an order of a judge based upon an agreement, almost always put in writing, between the parties to a lawsuit instead of continuing the case through trial or hearing. It cannot be appealed unless it was based upon fraud by one of the parties (he lied about the situation), mutual mistake (both parties misunderstood the situation) or if the court does not have jurisdiction over the case or the parties. Obviously, such a decree is almost always final and non-appealable since the parties worked it out. A consent decree is a common practice when the government has sued to make a person or corporation comply with the law (improper securities practices, pollution, restraints of trade, conspiracy) or the defendant agrees to the consent decree (often not to repeat the offense) in return for the government not pursuing criminal penalties. In general a consent decree and a consent judgment are the same. (See: **consent judgment**)

consent judgment: n. a judgment

issued by a judge based on an agreement between the parties to a lawsuit to settle the matter, aimed at ending the litigation with a judgment that is enforceable. (See: **consent decree**)

consequential damages: n. damages claimed and/or awarded in a lawsuit which were caused as a direct foreseeable result of wrongdoing. (See: **damages, foreseeable risk**)

conservatee: n. a person whom a court has determined because of physical or mental limitations or just plain old age requires a conservator to handle his/her financial affairs, and/or his/her actual personal activities such as arranging a residence, health care and the like. (See: **conservator**)

conservator: n. a guardian and protector appointed by a judge to protect and manage the financial affairs and/or the person's daily life due to physical or mental limitations or old age. The conservator may be only of the "estate" (meaning financial affairs), but may be also of the "person," when he/she takes charge of overseeing the daily activities, such as health care or living arrangements of the conservatee. The process is that a relative or friend petitions the appropriate local court for appointment of a specific conservator, with written notice served on the potential conservatee. The object of this concern is interviewed by a court-appointed investigator to determine need, desire and understanding of the potential conservatee as well as the suitability of the proposed conservator. An open hearing is held before the appointment is made. The conservator is required to make regular accountings which must be approved by the court. The conservator may be removed by order of the court if no longer needed, upon the petition of the conservatee or relatives, or for failure to perform his/her duties. (See: **conservatee, guardian**)

consideration: n. 1) payment or money. 2) a vital element in the law of contracts, consideration is a benefit which must be bargained for between the parties, and is the essential reason for a party entering into a contract. Consideration must be of value (at least to the parties), and is exchanged for the performance or promise of performance by the other party (such performance itself is consideration). In a contract, one consideration (thing given) is exchanged for another consideration. Not doing an act (forbearance) can be consideration, such as "I will pay you $1,000 not to build a road next to my fence." Sometimes consideration is "nominal," meaning it is stated for form only, such as "$10 as consideration for conveyance of title," which is used to hide the true amount being paid. Contracts may become unenforceable or rescindable (undone by rescission) for "failure of consideration" when the intended consideration is found to be worth less than expected, is damaged or destroyed, or performance is not made properly (as when the mechanic does not make the car run properly). Acts which are illegal or so immoral that they are against established public policy cannot serve as consideration for enforceable contracts. Examples:

prostitution, gambling where outlawed, hiring someone to break a skater's knee or inducing someone to breach an agreement (talk someone into backing out of a promise). (See: **contract**)

consign: v. 1) to deliver goods to a merchant to sell on behalf of the party delivering the items, as distinguished from transferring to a retailer at a wholesale price for resale. Example: leaving one's auto at a dealer to sell and split the profit. 2) to deliver to a carrier to be taken to an agent of the sender. 3) when a debtor has belongings but no money to pay his/her creditors and deposits his/her goods with a trustee who will sell them to raise money to pay the owner's debts and creditors. This is done by agreement between a debtor and his/her creditors or by order of a bankruptcy judge.

consignee: n. a person or business holding another's goods for sale or for delivery to a designated agent. (See: **consign**)

consignment: n. the act of consigning goods to one who will sell them for the owner or transport them for the owner. (See: **consign, consignee**)

consortium: n. 1) a group of separate businesses or business people joining together and cooperating to complete a project, work together to perform a contract or conduct an on-going business. For example, six companies, including Bechtel and Kaiser, joined together in a consortium to build Boulder (now Hoover) Dam, with each providing different expertise or components. 2) the marital relationship, particularly sexual intimacies, between husband and wife. Consortium arises in a lawsuit as a claim of "loss of consortium." Often it means that due to one spouse's injuries or emotional distress he/she cannot have sexual relations for a period of time or permanently, which is a loss to the mate for which he/she should be awarded damages. How loss of consortium is valued in money terms is a difficult question.

conspiracy: n. when people work together by agreement to commit an illegal act. A conspiracy may exist when the parties use legal means to accomplish an illegal result, or to use illegal means to achieve something that in itself is lawful. To prove a conspiracy those involved must have agreed to the plan before all the actions have been taken, or it is just a series of independent illegal acts. A conspiracy can be criminal for planning and carrying out illegal activities, or give rise to a civil lawsuit for damages by someone injured by the conspiracy. Thus, a scheme by a group of salesmen to sell used automobiles as new, could be prosecuted as a crime of fraud and conspiracy, and also allow a purchaser of an auto to sue for damages for the fraud and conspiracy. (See: **conspirator**)

conspirator: n. a person or entity who enters into a plot with one or more other people or entities to commit illegal acts, legal acts with an illegal object, or using illegal methods, to the harm of others. Conspirators may range from small-time bootleggers to electronics companies meeting to fix prices in violation of antitrust laws. (See **conspiracy**)

constable: n. a law officer for a particular area such as a rural township, much like a sheriff (who serves a county) and usually elected, who is responsible for such duties as serving summonses, complaints, subpenas, and court orders, assisting the local court, as well as "keeping the peace." In England this was an exalted position as law enforcement chief for an extensive area, but in the United States the office of constable is a dying breed, like Justice of the Peace. (See: **sheriff**)

constitution: n. the fundamental, underlying document which establishes the government of a nation or state. The U.S. Constitution, originally adopted in convention on September 17, 1787, ratified by the states in 1788, and thereafter amended 27 times, is the prime example of such a document. It is the basis for all decisions by the U.S. Supreme Court (and federal and state courts) on constitutionality. The case of *Marbury v. Madison* (1803) firmly established the power of the Supreme Court to strike down federal statutes it found unconstitutional, making the Supreme Court the final arbiter of constitutional interpretation. The "equal rights" provision of the 14th Amendment established that the rights in the first ten amendments ("Bill of Rights") applied to state governments. Unfortunately, state constitutions have gathered tremendous amounts of baggage of detail by amendment over the years, and it is more difficult to "fine tune" state constitutions by further amendment than it is to enact statutes (pass new laws). However, state courts are bound by their state's constitution on fundamental issues. The so-called English constitution is an unwritten body of legal customs and rights developed by practice and court decisions from the 11th to the 18th Century. (See: **Bill of Rights, common law, constitutional rights**)

constitutional rights: n. rights given or reserved to the people by the U.S. Constitution, and in particular, the Bill of Rights (first ten amendments). These rights include: writ of habeas corpus, no bill of attainder, no duties or taxes on transporting goods from one state to another (Article I, Section 9); jury trials (Article III, Section 1); freedom of religion, speech, press (which includes all media), assembly and petition (First Amendment); state militia to bear arms (Second Amendment); no quartering of troops in homes (Third Amendment); no unreasonable search and seizure (Fourth Amendment); major ("capital and infamous") crimes require indictment, no double jeopardy (more than one prosecution) for the same crime, no self-incrimination, right to due process, right to just compensation for property taken by eminent domain (Fifth Amendment); in criminal law, right to a speedy trial, to confront witnesses against one, and to counsel (Sixth Amendment); trial by jury (Seventh Amendment); right to bail, no excessive fines, and no cruel and unusual punishments (Eighth Amendment); unenumerated rights are reserved to the people (Ninth Amendment); equal protection of the laws (14th Amendment); no racial bars to voting (15th

Amendment); no sex bar to voting (19th Amendment); and no poll tax (24th Amendment). Constitutional interpretation has expanded and added nuances to these rights. (See: **Bill of Rights, constitution**)

construction: n. the act of a lawyer or court in interpreting and giving meaning to a statute or the language of a document such as a contract or will when there is some ambiguity or question about its meaning. In constitutional law, there is a distinction between liberal construction (broad construction) and strict construction (narrow construction). Liberal construction adds modern and societal meanings to the language, while strict construction adheres closely to the original language and intent without interpretation. (See: **strict construction**)

constructive: adj. a legal fiction for treating a situation as if it were actually so. Some examples help to clarify this term: a) although Jeremiah Gotrocks does not have the jewelry in his possession, he has the key to the safe deposit box and the right to enter so he has "constructive possession"; b) although there is no written trust document, George Holder has picked up $10,000 in bearer bonds from the post office box of his niece Tess Truehart, who gave him her post office box combination while she was traveling in Europe—this makes Holder her "constructive trustee." (See: **constructive eviction, constructive fraud, constructive notice, constructive possession, constructive trust**)

constructive eviction: n. when the landlord does not go through a legal eviction of a tenant but takes steps which keep the tenant from continuing to live in the premises. This could include changing the locks, turning off the drinking water, blocking the driveway, yelling at the tenant all the time or nailing the door shut. (See: **constructive**)

constructive fraud: n. when the circumstances show that someone's actions give him/her an unfair advantage over another by unfair means (lying or not telling a buyer about defects in a product, for example), the court may decide from the methods used and the result that it should treat the situation as if there was actual fraud even if all the technical elements of fraud have not been proven. (See: **constructive**)

constructive notice: n. a fiction that a person got notice even though actual notice was not personally delivered to him/her. The law may provide that a public notice put on the courthouse bulletin board is a substitute for actual notice. A prime example is allowing service by publication when a spouse has left the state to avoid service (legal delivery of a legal notice) in a divorce action. The legal advertisement of the summons in an approved newspaper is treated as constructive notice, just as if the summons and petition had been served personally. (See: **constructive**)

constructive possession: n. when a person does not have actual possession, but has the power to control an asset, he/she has constructive possession. Having the key to a safe deposit box, for example, gives one constructive possession. (See: **constructive**)

constructive trust: n. when a person has title to property and/or takes possession of it under circumstances in which he/she is holding it for another, even though there is no formal trust document or agreement. The court may determine that the holder of the title holds it as constructive trustee for the benefit of the intended owner. This may occur through fraud, breach of faith, ignorance or inadvertence. (See: **constructive, trust**)

construe: v. to determine the meaning of the words of a written document, statute or legal decision, based upon rules of legal interpretation as well as normal, widely accepted meanings.

consumer protection laws: n. almost all states and the federal government have enacted laws and set up agencies to protect the consumer (the retail purchasers of goods and services) from inferior, adulterated, hazardous or deceptively advertised products, and deceptive or fraudulent sales practices. Federal statutes and regulations govern mail fraud, wholesome poultry and meat, misbranding and adulteration of food and cosmetics, truth in lending, false advertising, the soundness of banks, securities sales, standards of housing materials, flammable fabrics, and various business practices. The Magnuson-Moss Act (1973) sets minimum standards for product warranties, makes a company that financed the sale responsible for product defects, and creates liability (financial responsibility) for "implied" warranties (when the circumstances show that a warranty of lack of defects was intended) as well as express (specific) warranties. Mail fraud may include fake contests, "low-ball" price traps (bait and switch), supposed credit for referrals of your friends, phoney home improvement loans with huge final payments, and swamp land sales. Some states' laws regulate and give some protection against high-pressure door-to-door sales, false labeling, unsolicited merchandise, abusive collection practices, misleading advertising and referral and promotional sales. Almost all states have agencies set up to actively protect the consumer. (See: **bait and switch, fraud, implied warranty, product liability, securities**)

contemplation of death: n. the anticipation of death in a relatively short time due to age, illness, injury or great danger, which causes a person to make a gift, transfer property or take some other dramatic action. (Lawyers who like Latin call this *causa mortis*.) It can be important since such a gift or transfer can be subject to federal estate taxes. (See: **unified estate and gift tax**)

contempt of court: n. there are essentially two types of contempt: a) being rude, disrespectful to the judge or other attorneys or causing a disturbance in the courtroom, particularly after being warned by the judge; b) willful failure to obey an order of the court. This latter can include failure to pay child support or alimony. The court's power to punish for contempt (called "citing" one for contempt) includes fines and/or jail time (called "imposing sanctions").

109

Incarceration is generally just a threat and if imposed, usually brief. Since the judge has discretion to control the courtroom, contempt citations are generally not appealable unless the amount of fine or jail time is excessive. "Criminal contempt" involves contempt with the aim of obstruction of justice, such as threatening a judge or witness or disobeying an order to produce evidence. (See: **sanction**)

contiguous: adj. connected or "next to", usually meaning adjoining pieces of real estate.

contingency: n. an event that might not occur.

contingent: adj. possible, but not certain. (See: **contingent beneficiary, contingent fee, contingent interest**)

contingent beneficiary: n. a person or entity named to receive a gift under the terms of a will, trust or insurance policy, who will only receive that gift if a certain event occurs or a certain set of circumstances happen. Examples: surviving another beneficiary, still being married to the same spouse, having completed college, or being certified as having shaken his/her drug habit. (See: **contingent, contingent interest**)

contingent fee: n. a fee to a lawyer which will be due and payable only if there is a successful conclusion of the legal work, usually winning or settling a lawsuit in favor of the client (particularly in negligence cases), or collecting funds due with or without filing a lawsuit. In many states, such agreements must be in writing and signed by attorney and client. The fee is generally a percentage of the recovery (money won), but may be partly a fee for time worked and partly a percentage. Although fees are negotiable, a standard contingent fee in accident cases is one-third of the money won, unless particular difficulties exist with the case, making the attorney believe he/she has the right to ask for more. States vary but some put a cap on the amount of fee for cases handled for minors even if the parent as guardian *ad litem* agrees to more. Contingent fee agreements in criminal cases which depend on the outcome are unethical.

contingent interest: n. an interest in real property which, according to the deed (or a will or trust), a party will receive only if a certain event occurs or certain circumstances happen. Examples: surviving a person who had a life estate (the right to use the property for his/her life), or having children at the time such a life estate ends. (See: **contingent, contingent remainder, future interest**)

contingent remainder: n. an interest, particularly in real estate property, which will go to a person or entity only upon a certain set of circumstances existing at the time the title-holder dies. Examples of those potential circumstances include surviving one's brother or still operating the family farm next door. (See: **contingent, contingent interest, future interest**)

continuance: n. a postponement of a date of a trial, hearing or other court appearance to a later fixed date by order of the court, or upon a stipulation (legal agreement) by the attorneys and approved by the court or (where local rules permit) by the clerk of the court. In general courts frown on too many continuances and will not allow them unless there is a legitimate reason. Some states demand payment of fees for continuances to discourage delays.

> *It cannot be helped, it is as it should be, that the law is behind the times.*
> *—Justice Oliver Wendell Holmes, Jr.*

continuing objection: n. an objection to certain questions or testimony during a trial which has been "overruled" by the judge, but the attorney who made the objection announces he/she is "continuing" the objection to all other questions on the same topic or with the same legal impropriety in the opinion of the attorney. Thus a "continuing" objection does not require an objection every time the same question or same subject is introduced. Example: the attorney for the plaintiff (the person suing) begins asking questions about emotional distress, which the defendant's attorney objects to as "immaterial," but the judge allows the first questions. The defense attorney states he has a "continuing" objection to all questions about the emotional distress. (See: **objection**)

continuing trespass: n. the repeated unauthorized use of another's real property, as compared to an occasional illegal entry. (See: **trespass**)

contra: adj. Latin for "against" or "opposite to". This usage is usually found in legal writing in statements like: "The decision in the case of *Hammerhead v. Nail* is *contra* to the rule stated in *Keeler v. Beach.*"

contract: 1) n. an agreement with specific terms between two or more persons or entities in which there is a promise to do something in return for a valuable benefit known as consideration. Since the law of contracts is at the heart of most business dealings, it is one of the three or four most significant areas of legal concern and can involve variations on circumstances and complexities. The existence of a contract requires finding the following factual elements: a) an offer; b) an acceptance of that offer which results in a meeting of the minds; c) a promise to perform; d) a valuable consideration (which can be a promise or payment in some form); e) a time or event when performance must be made (meet commitments); f) terms and conditions for performance, including fulfilling promises; g) performance, if the contract is "unilateral". A unilateral contract is one in which there is a promise to pay or give other consideration in return for actual performance. (I will pay you $500 to fix my car by Thursday; the performance is fixing the car by that date.) A bilateral contract is one in which a promise is exchanged for a promise. (I promise to fix your car by Thursday and you promise to pay $500 on Thursday.) Contracts can be either written or oral, but oral contracts are more difficult to prove and in most jurisdictions the time to sue on the contract is shorter (such as two years for oral compared to four years for written). In some cases a contract can consist of several documents, such as a series of letters, orders, offers and counteroffers. There are a variety of types of contracts: "conditional" on an event occurring; "joint and several," in which several parties make a joint promise to perform, but each is responsible; "implied," in which the courts will determine there is a contract based on the circumstances. Parties can contract to supply all of another's requirements, buy all the products made, or enter into an option to renew a contract. The variations are almost limitless. Contracts for illegal purposes are not enforceable at law. 2) v. to enter into an agreement. (See: **adhesion contract, bilateral contract, consideration, oral contract, unilateral contract**)

contract of adhesion: n. (See: **adhesion contract**)

contractor: n. 1) a person or entity that enters into a contract. 2) commonly, a person or entity that agrees to construct a building or to provide or install specialized portions of the construction. The party responsible for the overall job is a "general contractor," and those he/she/it hires to construct or install certain parts (electrical, plumbing, roofing, tile-laying, etc.) are "subcontractors," who are responsible to the general contractor and not to the property owner. An owner must be sure that the subcontractors are paid by the general contractor by demanding and receiving proof of payment, or the subcontractor will be entitled to payment from the owner based on a

mechanic's lien against the property. 3) a person who performs services but is not an employee, often called an "independent contractor." (See: **contract, independent contractor, mechanic's lien, subcontractor**)

contribution: n. 1) donation to a charity or political campaign. 2) the sharing of a loss by each of several persons who may have been jointly responsible for injury to a third party, who entered into a business which lost money or who owe a debt jointly. Quite often this arises when one responsible party pays more than his share and then demands contribution from the others in proportion to their share of the obligation. Example: three partners own equal shares in a building from which a cornice falls and injures Bobby Hardhat. One partner pays the demand of $9,000 for Hardhat's injury; he is entitled to a contribution of $3,000 from each of his partners.

contributory negligence: n. a doctrine of common law that if a person was injured in part due to his/her own negligence (his/her negligence "contributed" to the accident), the injured party would not be entitled to collect any damages (money) from another party who supposedly caused the accident. Under this rule, a badly injured person who was only slightly negligent could not win in court against a very negligent defendant. If Joe Tosspot was driving drunk and speeding and Angela Comfort was going 25 m.p.h. but six inches over the centerline, most likely Angela would be precluded from any recovery (receiving any money for injuries or damages) from a car crash. The possible unfair results have led some juries to ignore the rule and, in the past few decades, most states have adopted a comparative negligence test in which the relative percentages of negligence by each person are used to determine damage recovery (how much money would be paid to the injured person). (See: **comparative negligence, negligence**)

control: 1) n. the power to direct, manage, oversee and/or restrict the affairs, business or assets of a person or entity. 2) v. to exercise the power of control.

controlled substance: n. a drug which has been declared by federal or state law to be illegal for sale or use, but may be dispensed under a physician's prescription. The basis for control and regulation is the danger of addiction, abuse, physical and mental harm (including death), the trafficking by illegal means, and the dangers from actions of those who have used the substances.

controlling law: n. the laws of the state which will be relied upon in interpreting or judging disputes involving a contract, trust or other documents. Quite often an agreement will state as one of its provisions that the controlling law will be that of a particular state.

controversy: n. 1) disagreement, argument or quarrel. 2) a dispute, which must be an actual contested issue between parties in order to be heard by a court. The U.S. Supreme Court particularly requires an "actual controversy" and avoids giving "what if" advisory opinions. (See: **advisory opinion**)

conversion: n. a civil wrong (tort) in which one converts another's property to his/her own use, which is a fancy way of saying "steals." Conversion includes treating another's goods as one's own, holding onto such property which accidentally comes into the convertor's (taker's) hands, or purposely giving the impression the assets belong to him/her. This gives the true owner the right to sue for his/her own property or the value and loss of use of it, as well as going to law enforcement authorities since conversion usually includes the crime of theft. (See: **theft**)

convey: v. to transfer title (official ownership) to real property (or an interest in real property) from one (grantor) to another (grantee) by a written deed (or an equivalent document such as a judgment of distribution which conveys real property from an estate). This is completed by recording the document with the County Recorder or Recorder of Deeds. It only applies to real property. (See: **alienation, conveyance, deed, grantor, grantee, quit claim deed**)

conveyance: n. a generic term for any written document which transfers (conveys) real property or real property interests from one party to another. A conveyance must be acknowledged before a notary (or if a court judgment be certified as the same as the document on file) and recorded with the County Recorder or Recorder of Deeds. (See: **deed**)

convict: 1) v. to find guilty of a crime after a trial. 2) n. a person who has been convicted of a felony and sent to prison.

conviction: n. the result of a criminal trial in which the defendant has been found guilty of a crime.

cooperative: n. an association of individual businesses, farmers, ranchers or manufacturers with similar interests, intending to cooperate in marketing, shipping and related activities (sometimes under a single brand name) to sell their products efficiently, and then share the profits based on the production, capital or effort of each. "Sunkist" oranges is an example of a large cooperative. Cooperatives include dairy milk producers, cotton gins and thousands of other enterprises of all sizes. There are also cooperatives in which consumers form retail outlets like grocery stores and share the profits based on the amount of patronage of each member, but they have found it difficult to compete with the giant supermarket chains. Some cooperatives exist to operate housing complexes. (See: **cooperative housing**)

cooperative housing: n. an arrangement in which an association or corporation owns a group of housing units and the common areas for the use of all the residents. The individual participants own a share in the cooperative which entitles them to occupy an apartment (or town house) as if they were owners, to have equal access to the common areas and to vote for members of the board of directors which manages the cooperative. A cooperative differs from a condominium project in that the owners of the condominium units actually own their airspace and a percentage interest in the common area. In a cooperative there are often restrictions on transfer of shares such as giving priority to other members, limits on income or maximum sales price. (See: **common area, condominium, cooperative**)

cop a plea: n. slang for a "plea bargain" in which an accused defendant in a criminal case agrees to plead guilty or "no contest" to a crime in return for a promise of a recommendation of leniency in sentencing to be made by the prosecutor to the judge and/or an agreement by the prosecutor to drop some of the charges. Often the judge agrees to the recommendation before the plea is entered (becomes final). (See: **plea bargain**)

copartner: n. one who is a member of a partnership. The prefix "co" is a redundancy, since a partner is a member of a partnership. The same is true of the term "copartnership." (See: **partner, partnership**)

copyright: 1) n. the exclusive right of the author or creator of a literary or artistic property (such as a book, movie or musical composition) to print, copy, sell, license, distribute, transform to another medium, translate, record or perform or otherwise use (or not use) and to give it to another by will. As soon as a work is created and is in a tangible form (such as writing or taping) the work automatically has federal copyright protection. On any distributed and/or published work a notice should be affixed stating the word copyright, copy or ©, with the name of the creator and the date of copyright (which is the year of first publication). The notice should be on the title page or the page immediately following and for graphic arts on a clearly visible or accessible place. A work should be registered with the U.S. Copyright Office by submitting a registration form and two copies of the work with a fee which a) establishes proof of earliest creation and publication, b) is required to file a lawsuit for infringement of copyright, c) if filed within three months of publication, establishes a right to attorneys' fees in an infringement suit. Copyrights cover the following: literary, musical and dramatic works, periodicals, maps, works of art (including models), art reproductions, sculptural works, technical drawings, photographs, prints (including labels), movies and other audiovisual works, computer programs, compilations of works and derivative works, and architectural drawings. Not subject to copyright are short phrases, titles, extemporaneous speeches or live unrecorded performances, common information, government publications, mere ideas, and seditious, obscene, libelous and fraudulent work. For any work created from 1978 to date, a copyright is good for the author's life, plus 50 years, with a few exceptions such as work "for hire" which is owned by the one commissioning the work for a period of 75 years from publication. After that it falls into the public domain. Many, but not all, countries recognize international copyrights under the "Universal Copyright Convention," to which the United States is a party. (See: **infringement, plagiarism, public domain, trademark**)

> *Law is a bottomless pit.*
> *—John Arbuthnot*

coroner: n. a county official with the responsibility to determine the cause of death of anyone who dies violently (by attack or accident), suddenly, or suspiciously. The coroner or one of his/her staff must examine the body at the scene of such a death and make a report. If the cause is not obvious or certified by an attending physician, then the coroner may order a "coroner's inquest" which requires an autopsy (postmortem). If that is not conclusive, the coroner may hold a hearing as part of the inquest, although this is rare due to scientific advances in pathology. (See: **forensic medicine, postmortem**)

corporate opportunity: n. a business opportunity which becomes known to a corporate official, particularly a director or other upper management, due to his/her position within the corporation. In essence, the opportunity or knowledge belongs to the corporation, and the officials owe a duty (a fiduciary duty) not to use that opportunity or knowledge for their own benefit. The corporation may have the right to damages (to be paid off) for such improper appropriation (use) of the opportunity on the theory that the official holds it in "constructive trust" for the corporation. The corporation may obtain an injunction (court order) to prevent someone's use of the knowledge or opportunity. In such cases angry stockholders may bring their own legal action for their benefit in what is called a derivative action. Such insider misappropriation (inappropriate use of information) may also be criminal theft, or be violative of federal or state securities laws. (See: **conflict of interest, conversion, derivative action, fiduciary relationship**)

corporation: n. an organization formed with state governmental approval to act as an artificial person to carry on business (or other activities), which can sue or be sued, and (unless it is non-profit) can issue shares of stock to raise funds with which to start a business or increase its capital. One benefit is that a corporation's liability for damages or debts is limited to its assets, so the shareholders and officers are protected from personal claims, unless they commit fraud. For private business corporations the articles of incorporation filed with the Secretary of State of the incorporating state must include certain information, including the name of the responsible party or parties (incorporators and agent for acceptance of service), the amount of stock it will be authorized to issue, and its purpose. In some states the purpose may be a general statement of any purpose allowed by law, while others require greater specificity. Corporation shareholders elect a board of directors, which in turn adopts bylaws, chooses the officers and hires top management (which in smaller corporations are often the directors and/or shareholders). Annual meetings are required of both the shareholders and the board, and major policy decisions must be made by resolution of the board (which often delegates much authority to officers and commit-

tees). Issuance of stock of less than $300,000, with no public solicitation and relatively few shareholders, is either automatically approved by the state commissioner of corporations or requires a petition outlining the financing. Some states are considered lax in supervision, have low filing fees and corporate taxes and are popular incorporation states, but corporations must register with Secretaries of State of other states where they do substantial business as a "foreign" corporation. Larger stock offerings and/or those offered to the general public require approval by the Securities and Exchange Commission after close scrutiny and approval of a public "prospectus" which details the entire operation of the corporation. There are also non-profit (or not for profit) corporations organized for religious, educational, charitable or public service purposes. Public corporations are those formed by a municipal, state or federal government for public purposes such as operating a dam and utility project. A close corporation is made up of a handful of shareholders with a working or familial connection which is permitted to operate informally without resolutions and regular board meetings. A *de jure* corporation is one that is formally operated under the law, while a *de facto* corporation is one which operates as if it were legal, but without the articles of incorporation being valid. Corporations can range from the Corner Mini-Mart to General Electric. (See: **articles of incorporation, board of directors, bylaws, close corporation, *de facto* corporation, *de jure* corporation, non-profit corporation, public** corporation, securities, share-holder, stock)

corpus: n. 1) Latin for body. 2) the principal (usually money, securities and other assets) of a trust or estate as distinguished from interest or profits.

corpus delicti: n. (corpus dee-lick-tie) Latin for the substantial fact that a crime has been committed, and in popular crime jargon, the body of the murder victim.

corpus juris: n. the body of the law, meaning a compendium of all laws, cases and the varied interpretations of them. There are several encyclopedias of the law which fit this definition, the most famous of which is *Corpus Juris Secundum.* Several states have such series of books covering explanations of the law of that state.

corroborate: v. to confirm and sometimes add substantiating (reinforcing) testimony to the testimony of another witness or a party in a trial. (See: **corroborating evidence**)

corroborating evidence: n. evidence which strengthens, adds to, or confirms already existing evidence.

cosign: v. to sign a promissory note or other obligation in order to share liability for the obligation.

cost bill: n. a list of claimed court costs submitted by the prevailing (winning) party in a lawsuit after the judge states his/her judgment formally called a "memorandum of costs." Statutes limit what can be included in these costs. (See: **court costs, prevailing party**)

cost of completion: n. the amount of money (damages) required to complete performance (finish the job) when a contract has been breached by the failure to perform. Example: when a general contractor breaches by not completing a house, the cost of completion is the actual cost of bringing in a new builder to finish what is left to do. The actual costs become the measure of damages rather than an estimate of cost based on percentage of work to be done.

costs: n. shorthand for court costs. (See: **court costs**)

cotenancy: n. the situation when more than one person has an interest in real property at the same time, which may include tenancy in common, joint tenancy or tenancy by the entirety. (See: **community property, cotenant, joint tenancy, tenancy by the entirety, tenancy in common**)

cotenant: n. one who holds an interest in real property together with one or more others. (See: **cotenancy**)

co-trustee: n. a trustee of a trust when there is more than one trustee serving at the same time, usually with the same powers and obligations. Occasionally a co-trustee may be a temporary fill-in, as when the original trustee is ill but recovers. The co-trustee must act in consultation with the other trustee(s), unless the language of the trust allows one co-trustee to act alone. (See: **trust, trustee**)

counsel: 1) n. a lawyer, attorney, attorney-at-law, counsellor, counsellor-at-law, solicitor, barrister, advocate or proctor (a lawyer in admiralty court), licensed to practice law. In the United States they all mean the same thing. 2) v. to give legal advice. 3) v. in some jurisdictions, to urge someone to commit a crime, which in itself is a crime. (See: **attorney**)

counsellor: n. a licensed attorney. (See: **counsel**)

count: n. each separate statement in a complaint which states a cause of action which, standing alone, would give rise to a lawsuit, or each separate charge in a criminal action. For example, the complaint in a civil (non-criminal) lawsuit might state: First Count (or cause of action) for negligence, and then state the detailed allegations; Second Count for breach of contract; Third Count for debt and so forth. In a criminal case each count would be a statement of a different alleged crime. There are also so-called common counts which cover various types of debt. (See: **cause of action, common counts**)

Legal process is an essential part of the democratic process. —Justice Felix Frankfurter

counterclaim: n. a retaliatory claim by a defendant against a plaintiff in a lawsuit included in the defendant's answer and intending to offset and/or reduce the amount of the plaintiff's original claim against the defendant. For example, Hotdog Products sues Barbecue Bill's Eatery for $40,000 for meat delivered to Bill's but not paid for, and Bill counterclaims that Hotdog owes him $20,000 for a load of bad chicken livers, so Hotdog is only entitled to $20,000. In many states the counterclaim is no longer allowed, in which case a cross-complaint, which is a separate complaint, must be filed by the defendant, but as part of the same lawsuit. On the other hand, in federal cases, if the defendant believes he/she/it has a legitimate counterclaim to reduce damages it must be alleged (stated) in the answer or it is barred from being considered. (See: **answer, cross-complaint**)

counterfeit: 1) adj. describing a document, particularly money, which is forged or created to look real and intended to pass for real. 2) v. to criminally forge or print a false copy of money, bonds, or other valuable documents, intending to profit from the falsity. 3) n. shorthand for phoney money passed for real. (See: **forgery, utter**)

counter offer: n. an offer made in response to a previous offer by the other party during negotiations for a final contract. Making a counter offer automatically rejects the prior offer, and requires an acceptance under the terms of the counter offer or there is no contract. Example: Susan Seller offers to sell her house for $150,000, to be paid in 60 days; Bruce Buyer receives the offer and gives Seller a counter offer of $140,000, payable in 45 days. The original offer is dead, despite the shorter time for payment since the price is lower. Seller then can choose to accept at $140,000, counter again at some compromise price, reject the counter offer, or let it expire. (See: **contract, offer**)

counterpart: n. in the law of contracts, a written paper which is one of several documents which constitute a contract, such as a written offer and a written acceptance. Often a contract is in several counterparts which are the same but each paper is signed by a different party, particularly if they are in different localities. (See: **contract**)

course: n. in the midst of or actively involved in at that time, as "in the course of business, course of employment, course of trade."

course of employment: adj. actively involved in a person's employment at a particular time, most likely when an accident occurred, which is required to make a claim for work-related injury under state Worker's Compensation Acts. (See: **scope of employment**)

court: n. 1) the judge, as in "The court rules in favor of the plaintiff." 2) any official tribunal (court) presided over by a judge or judges in which legal issues and claims are heard and determined. In the United States there are essentially two systems: federal courts and state courts. The basic federal court system has jurisdiction over cases involving federal statutes, constitutional questions, actions between citizens of different states, and certain other types of cases. Its trial courts are District Courts in one or more districts per state, over which there are District Courts of Appeal (usually three-judge panels) to hear appeals from judgments of the District Courts within the "circuit." There are 10 geographic circuits throughout the nation. Appeals on constitutional questions and other significant cases are heard by the Supreme Court, but only if that court agrees to hear the case. There are also special federal courts such as bankruptcy and tax courts with appeals directed to the District Courts.

Each state has local trial courts, which include courts for misdemeanors (non-penitentiary crimes), smaller demand civil actions (called municipal, city, justice or some other designation), and then courts, usually set up in each county (variously called Superior, District, County, Common Pleas courts and called Supreme Court in New York) to hear felonies (crimes punished by state prison terms), estates, divorces and major lawsuits. The highest state court is called the State Supreme Court, except in New York and Maryland, which call them Court of Appeals. Some 29 states have intermediate appeals courts which hear appeals from trial courts which will result in final decisions unless the State Supreme Court chooses to consider the matter. Some states have speciality courts such as family, surrogate and domestic relations. Small claims courts are an adjunct of the lowest courts handling lesser disputes (although California's limit is $5,000) with no representation by attorneys and short and somewhat informal trials conducted by judges, commissioners or lawyers.

The great number of law cases and lawyers' procedural maneuvers has clogged courts' calendars and has induced many states or local courts to set up mediation, arbitration, mandatory settlement conferences and other formats to encourage settlement or early judgments without the cost and wait of full court trials. (See: appendix on **courts**)

court calendar: n. the list of matters to be heard or set for trial or hearing by a court. (See: **calendar**)

court costs: n. fees for expenses that the courts pass on to attorneys, who then pass them on to their clients or to the losing party. Court costs usually include: filing fees, charges for serving summons and subpenas, court reporter charges for depositions (which can be very expensive), court transcripts and copying papers and exhibits. The prevailing party in a lawsuit is usually awarded court costs. Attorneys' fees can be included as court costs only if there is a statute providing for attorneys' fee awards in a particular type of case, or if the case involved a contract which had an attorneys' fee clause (commonly found in promissory notes, mortgages and deeds of trust). If a losing party does not agree with the claimed court costs (included in a filed cost bill) he/she/it may move (ask) the judge to "tax costs" (meaning reduce or disallow the cost), resulting in a hearing at which the court determines which costs to allow and in what amount (how much). (See: **cost bill, prevailing party**)

court docket: n. (See: **docket**)

court-martial: 1) n. a military court for trying offenses in violation of army, navy or other armed service rules and regulations, made up of military officers, who act as both finders of fact (in effect, a jury) and as arbiters (judges) of the law applying to the case. A general court-martial is conducted by a military legal officer (Judge Advocate) and at least five officers for major offenses, including those requiring the death penalty. A special court-martial is generally for lesser offenses and is conducted by three officers, who may order dismissal, hard labor or lengthy confinement. Minor offenses are conducted by a single officer in a summary court-martial. 2) v. to charge a member of the military with an offense against military law or to find him/her guilty of such a violation. A court-martial conviction can be appealed to the U.S. Court of Military Appeals.

court of appeals: n. any court (state or federal) which hears appeals from judgments and rulings of trial courts or lower appeals courts. (See: **appeal, court**)

Court of Customs and Patent Appeals: n. a federal court established (1929) to hear appeals from decisions by the U.S. Patent Office and from the U.S. Customs Court. It sits in Washington, D. C. and is composed of five judges. (See: **Customs Court, patent, trademark**)

court of equity: n. originally in English common law and in several states there were separate courts (often called chancery courts) which handled lawsuits and petitions requesting remedies other than damages, such as writs, injunctions and specific performance. Gradually the courts of equity have merged with courts of law. Federal bankruptcy courts are the one example of courts which operate as courts of equity. (See: **chancery, court of law, equity**)

court of law: n. any tribunal within a judicial system. Under English common law and in some states it was a court which heard only lawsuits in which damages were sought, as distinguished from a court of equity which could grant special remedies. That distinction has dissolved and every court (with the exception of federal bankruptcy courts) is a court of law. (See: **court, chancery, equity**)

court trial ("non-jury trial"): a trial with a judge but no jury.

covenant: 1) n. a promise in a written contract or a deed of real property. The term is used only for certain types of promises such as a covenant of warranty, which is a promise to guarantee the title (clear ownership) to property, a promise agreeing to joint use of an easement for access to real property, or a covenant not to compete, which is commonly included in promises made by a seller of a business for a certain period of time. Mutual covenants among members of a homeowners association are promises to respect the rules of conduct or restrictions on use of property to insure peaceful use, limitations on intrusive construction, etc., which are usually part of the recorded covenants, conditions and restrictions which govern a development or condominium project. Covenants which run with the land, such as permanent easement of access or restrictions on use, are binding on future title holders of the property. Covenants can be concurrent (mutu-al promises to be performed at the same time), dependent (one promise need be performed if the other party performs his/hers), or independent (a promise to be honored without reference to any other promise). Until 1949 many deeds contained restrictive covenants which limited transfer of the property to the Caucasian race. These blatantly racist covenants were then declared unconstitutional. 2) v. to promise. (See: **contract, covenant not to compete, covenants that runs with the land, covenants, conditions and restrictions, deed, restrictive covenant**)

covenants, conditions and restrictions: n. commonly called "CC and Rs," these are written rules, limitations and restrictions on use, mutually agreed to by all owners of homes in a subdivision or condominium complex. CC and Rs may limit size and placement of homes, exterior colors, pets, ages of residents, use of barbecues and other conduct to protect the quiet enjoyment of the various residents. CC and Rs are enforced by the homeowners association or by individual owners who can bring lawsuits against violators and are permanent or "run with the land" so future owners are bound to the same rules. Most state laws require that a copy of the CC and Rs be recorded with the County Recorder and be provided to any prospective purchaser. (See: **covenant**)

covenant not to compete: n. a common provision in a contract for sale of a business in which the seller agrees not to compete in the same business for a period of years or in the geographic area. This covenant is usually allocated (given) a value in the sales price. (See: **covenant**)

covenant that runs with the land: n. a promise contained in a deed to land or real estate which is binding upon the current owner and all future owners. (See: **covenant**)

credibility: n. whether testimony is worthy of belief, based on competence of the witness and likelihood that it is true. Unless the testimony is contrary to other known facts or is extremely unlikely based on human experience, the test of credibility is purely subjective. (See: **credible witness**)

credible witness: n. a witness whose testimony is more than likely to be true based on his/her experience, knowledge, training and appearance of honesty and forthrightness, as well as common human experience. This is subjective in that the trier of fact (judge or jury) may be influenced by the demeanor of the witness or other factors. (See: **credibility**)

> *I cannot agree that it should be the declared public policy of Illinois that a cat visiting a neighbor's yard or crossing the highway is a public nuisance.*
> *—Adlai E. Stevenson, vetoing a bill requiring that cats be restrained from leaving their owners' property.*

creditor: n. a person or entity to whom a debt is owed.

creditor's claim: n. a claim required to be filed in writing, in a proper form by a person or entity owed money by a debtor who has filed a petition in bankruptcy court (or had a petition filed to declare the debtor bankrupt), or is owed money by a person who has died. Notice of the need to file a creditor's claim in the estate of a person who has died must be printed in a legal advertisement giving notice of death. Then a creditor has only a few months to file the claim, and it must be in a form approved by the courts. (See: **claim in bankruptcy, probate**)

creditor's rights: n. the field of law dealing with the legal means and procedures to collect debts and judgments. (See: **creditor, debt, debtor, judgment**)

crime: n. a violation of a law in which there is injury to the public or a member of the public and a term in jail or prison, and/or a fine as possible penalties. There is some sentiment for excluding from the "crime" category crimes without victims, such as consensual acts, or violations in which only the perpetrator is hurt or involved such as personal use of illegal drugs. (See: **felony, misdemeanor**)

crime against nature: n. an oldfashioned term for sodomy (anal sexual intercourse), which has been a crime in most states. Several states have removed consensual anal intercourse between consenting adults from the crime. However, in Indiana an ex-wife insisted on a criminal charge of sodomy being filed against her former husband, even though the act was consensual and during their marriage; he was convicted. The term is also applied to sexual intercourse between a human and an animal (bestiality), which is a crime in most states. (See: **bestiality, sodomy**)

crime of passion: n. a defendant's excuse for committing a crime due to sudden anger or heartbreak, in order to eliminate the element of "premeditation." This usually arises in murder or attempted murder cases, when a spouse or sweetheart finds his/her "beloved" having sexual intercourse with another and shoots or stabs one or both of the coupled pair. To make this claim the defendant must have acted immediately upon the rise of passion, without the time for contemplation or allowing for "a cooling of the blood." It is sometimes called the "Law of Texas" since juries in that state are supposedly lenient to cuckolded lovers who wreak their own vengeance. The benefit of eliminating premeditation is to lessen the provable homicide to manslaughter with no death penalty and limited prison terms. An emotionally charged jury may even acquit the impassioned defendant. (See: **manslaughter, murder**)

criminal: 1) n. a popular term for anyone who has committed a crime, whether convicted of the offense or not. More properly it should apply only to those actually convicted of a crime. Repeat offenders are sometimes called habitual criminals. 2) adj. describing certain acts or people involved in or relating to a crime. Examples of uses include "criminal taking," "criminal conspiracy," a "criminal gang." (See: **convict, felon, habitual criminal**)

criminal attorney: n. a popular term for an attorney who specializes in defending people charged with crimes. Many lawyers handle criminal defense but also have other clientele. However, some states will certify a lawyer as a "criminal law specialist" based on experience and extra training in that field. (See: **crime, felon, misdemeanor**)

criminal calendar: n. the list of criminal cases to be called in court on a particular time and date. The parties charged and their attorneys are given a written notice of the time and place to appear. The criminal calendar may list arraignments, bail settings, cases continued (put off) awaiting a plea of guilt or innocence, changes of pleas, setting of hearing or trial dates, motions brought by attorneys, pronouncing sentences, hearing reports of probation officers, appointment of public defenders or other attorneys, and other business concerning criminal cases. (See: **arraignment, bail, crime, plea, plea bargaining, preliminary hearing, sentence**)

criminal justice: n. a generic term for the procedure by which criminal conduct is investigated, evidence gathered, arrests made, charges brought, defenses raised, trials conducted, sentences rendered and punishment carried out.

criminal law: n. those statutes dealing with crimes against the public and members of the public, with penalties and all the procedures connected with charging, trying, sentencing and imprisoning defendants convicted of crimes. (See: **crime, felony, misdemeanor**)

cross-complaint: n. after a complaint has been filed against a defendant for damages or other orders of the court, the defendant may file a written complaint against the party suing him/her or against a third party as long as the subject matter is related to the original complaint. The defendant's filing of a complaint is called a cross-complaint, and the defendant is then called a cross-complainant and the party he/she sues is called a cross-defendant. The defendant must still file an answer or other response to the original complaint. If the cross-complaint is against the original plaintiff (original suer) then it can be served on the plaintiff's attorney by mail, but a third party must be served in person with the cross-complaint and a new summons issued by the clerk of the court. The cross-defendants must then file answers or other responses. These are called pleadings and must be carefully drafted (usually by an attorney) to properly state the factual as well as legal basis for the claim and contain a prayer for damages or other relief. (See: **answer, complaint, demurrer, pleading, prayer, service of process, summons**)

cross-examination: n. the opportunity for the attorney (or an unrepresented party) to ask questions in court of a witness who has testified in a trial on behalf of the opposing party. The questions on cross-examination are limited to the subjects covered in the direct examination of the witness, but importantly, the attorney may ask leading questions, in which he/she is allowed to suggest answers or put words in the witness's mouth. (For example, "Isn't it true that you told Mrs. Jones she had done nothing wrong?" which is leading, as compared to "Did you say anything to Mrs. Jones?") A strong cross-examination (often called just "cross" by lawyers and judges) can force contradictions, expressions of doubts or even complete obliteration of a witness's prior carefully rehearsed testimony. On the other hand, repetition of a witness' s story, vehemently defended, can strengthen his/her credibility. (See: **credibility, direct examination, testimony, trial, witness**)

cruel and unusual punishment: n. governmental penalties against convicted criminal defendants which are barbaric, involve torture and/or shock the public morality. They are specifically prohibited under the Eighth Amendment to the U.S. Constitution. However, nowhere are they specifically defined. Tortures like the rack (stretching the body inch by inch) or the thumbscrew, dismemberment, breaking bones, maiming, actions involving deep or long-lasting pain are all banned. But solitary confinement, enforced silence, necessary force to prevent injury to fellow prisoners or guards, psychological humiliation and bad food are generally allowed. In short, there is a large gray area, in which "cruel and unusual" is definitely subjective based on individual sensitivities and moral outlook. The U.S. Supreme Court has waffled on the death penalty, declaring that some forms of the penalty were cruel and prohibited under the *Furman* case (1972), which halted executions for several years, but later relaxed the prohibition. The question remains if the gas chamber, hanging or electrocution are cruel and unusual. For instance, hanging is certainly cruel but was not unusual at the time the Bill of Rights was adopted. (See: **capital punishment,**)

cruelty: n. the intentional and malicious infliction of physical or psychological pain on another. In most states various forms of "cruelty," "extreme cruelty," and/or "mental cruelty" used to be grounds for divorce if proved. This brought about a lot of unnecessary (and sometimes exaggerated or false) derogatory (nasty) testimony about the other party. There was little standardization of what constituted sufficient "cruelty" to prove a divorce should be granted. Starting in the 1960s "no fault" divorce (sometimes now called "dissolution") began to replace contentious divorces in most states, so that incompatibility became good enough grounds for granting a divorce. (See: **cruel and unusual punishment, dissolution of marriage, divorce**)

cruelty to animals: n. the crime of inflicting physical pain, suffering or death on an animal, usually a tame one, beyond necessity for normal discipline. It can include neglect that is so monstrous (withholding food and water) that the animal has suffered, died or been put in imminent danger of death. (See: **cruelty**)

culpability: (See: **culpable**)

culpable: adj. sufficiently responsible for criminal acts or negligence

to be at fault and liable for the conduct. Sometimes culpability rests on whether the person realized the wrongful nature of his/her actions and thus should take the blame.

Justice delayed is justice denied.
—Anonymous, often quoted

cumis counsel: n. an attorney employed by a defendant in a lawsuit when there is an insurance policy supposedly covering the claim, but there is a conflict of interest between the insurance company and the insured defendant. Such a conflict might arise if the insurance company is denying full coverage. In some states (notably California) the defendant can demand that the insurance company pay the fees of his/her own attorney rather than use an insurance company lawyer. Often the insurance company will require that the attorney for the defendant be approved by the company.

cumulative sentence: n. when a criminal defendant has been found guilty of more than one offense, the judge may sentence him/her to prison for successive terms for each crime (e.g. five years for burglary, three years for possession of stolen property, which add up and accumulate to eight years). The other choice would be to sentence the defendant to a concurrent sentence, in which the lesser term would be merged with the longer, they would run at the same time, and thus result in a five-year term in the example. (See: **concurrent sentence, successive terms**)

cumulative voting: n. in corporations, a system of voting by shareholders for directors in which the shareholder can multiply his voting shares by the number of candidates and vote them all for one person for director. This is intended to give minority shareholders a chance to elect at least one director whom they favor. For example, there are five directors to be elected, and 10,000 shares issued, a shareholder with 1,000 shares could vote 5,000 for his candidate rather than being limited to 1,000 for each of five candidates, always outvoted by shareholders with 1,001 or more shares.

curtesy: n. in old common law, the right of a surviving husband to a life estate in the lands of his deceased wife, if they had a surviving child or children who would inherit the land. A few states still recognize this charming anachronism. (See: **community property, dower, life estate**)

custody: n. 1) holding property under one's control. 2) law enforcement officials' act of holding an accused or convicted person in criminal proceedings, beginning with the arrest of that person. 3) in domestic relations (divorce, dissolution) a court's determination of which parent (or other appropriate party) should have physical and/or legal control and responsibility for a minor child. (See: **child custody**)

Customs Court: n. a federal court established (1926) to hear appeals from decisions of customs officials on classification of merchandise, duty rates and interpretation of customs laws. In turn its decisions can be appealed to the Court of Customs and Patent Appeals. (See: **Court of Customs and Patent Appeals**)

cut a check: v. to write (prepare) and sign a check.

cy pres **doctrine**: n. (see-pray doctrine) from French, meaning "as close as possible." When a gift is made by will or trust (usually for charitable or educational purposes), and the named recipient of the gift does not exist, has dissolved or no longer conducts the activity for which the gift is made, then the estate or trustee must make the gift to an organization which comes closest to fulfilling the purpose of the gift. Sometimes this results in heated court disputes in which a judge must determine the appropriate substitute to receive the gift. Example: dozens of local Societies for Protection of Cruelty to Animals contested for a gift which was made without designating which chapter would receive the benefits. The judge wisely divided up the money among several S.P.C.A. chapters.

D

D.A.: n. slang for District Attorney. (See: **District Attorney**)

damages: n. the amount of money which a plaintiff (the person suing) may be awarded in a lawsuit. There are many types of damages. Special damages are those which actually were caused by the injury and include medical and hospital bills, ambulance charges, loss of wages, property repair or replacement costs or loss of money due on a contract. The second basic area of damages are general damages, which are presumed to be a result of the other party's actions, but are subjective both in nature and determination of value of damages. These include pain and suffering, future problems and crippling effect of an injury, loss of ability to perform various acts, shortening of life span, mental anguish, loss of companionship, loss of reputation (in a libel suit, for example), humiliation from scars, loss of anticipated business and other harm. The third major form of damage is exemplary (or punitive) damages, which combines punishment and the setting of public example. Exemplary damages may be awarded when the defendant acted in a malicious, violent, oppressive, fraudulent, wanton or grossly reckless way in causing the special and general damages to the plaintiff. On occasion punitive damages can be greater than the actual damages, as, for example, in a sexual harassment case or fraudulent schemes. Although often asked for, they are seldom awarded. Nominal damages are those given when the actual harm is minor and an award is warranted under the circumstances. The most famous case was when Winston Churchill was awarded a shilling (about 25 cents) against author Louis Adamic, who had written that the British Prime Minister had been drunk at a dinner at the White House. Liquidated damages are those pre-set by the parties in a contract to be awarded in case one party defaults as in breach of contract. (See: **consequential damages, exemplary damages, general damages, judgment, liquidated damages, special damages**)

dangerous: adj. unsafe, hazardous, fraught with risk. It can be negligence for which a lawsuit can be brought if damage results from creating or leaving unguarded a dangerous condition which can cause harm to others, a dangerous instrumentality (any device which can cause harm, including explosives and poisonous substances) or dangerous weapon which is inherently hazardous to anyone handling it or within the weapon's range. (See: **negligence**)

dangerous weapon: n. any gun, knife, sword, crossbow, slingshot or other weapon which can cause bodily harm to people (even though used for target shooting). If a person is harmed by such a weapon that is left unguarded, improperly used, or causes harm even to a person who plays with it without permission, the victim or his/her survivors can sue for negligence and possibly win a judgment.

date rape: n. forcible sexual intercourse by a male acquaintance of a woman, during a voluntary social engagement in which the woman did not intend to submit to the sexual advances and resisted the acts by verbal refusals, denials or pleas to stop, and/or physical resistance. The fact that the parties knew each other or that the woman willingly accompanied the man are not legal defenses to a charge of rape, although one Pennsylvania decision ruled that there had to be some actual physical resistance. (See: **rape**)

day in court: n. popular term for everyone's opportunity to bring a lawsuit or use the court system if he/she thinks he/she has a gripe which can be resolved in court. Example: "John finally got his day in court to protest his speeding ticket."

d.b.a.: n. short for "doing business as," when a person or entity uses a business name instead of his/her/its own. All states have requirements for filing a certificate of "doing business under a fictitious name" either with the County Clerk, the state Secretary of State or some other official to inform the public as to the real person or entity behind a business name. It is not necessary if the business includes the name of the true owner and is not to be confused with the use of a corporation name, since that is registered with the state.

deadly weapon: n. any weapon which can kill. This includes not only weapons which are intended to do harm like a gun or knife, but also blunt instruments like clubs, baseball bats, monkey wrenches, an automobile or any object which actually causes death. This becomes important when trying to prove criminal charges brought for assault with a deadly weapon. In a few 1990s cases courts have found rocks and even penises of AIDS sufferers as "deadly weapons." (See: **assault, dangerous weapon**)

> *Good men must not obey the laws too well.*
> *—Ralph Waldo Emerson*

dealer: n. anyone who buys goods or property for the purpose of selling as a business. It is important to distinguish a dealer from someone who occasionally buys and occasionally sells, since dealers may need to obtain business licenses, register with the sales tax authorities, and may not defer capital gains taxes by buying other property.

death penalty: n. the sentence of execution for murder and some other capital crimes. (See: **capital punishment, appendix on capital punishment**)

death row: n. nickname for that portion of a prison in which prisoners are housed who are under death sentences and are awaiting appeals and/or potential execution. (See: **capital punishment, death penalty, appendix on capital punishment**)

debenture: n. a form of bond certificate issued by a corporation to show funds invested, repayment of which is guaranteed by the overall capital value of the company under certain specific terms. Thus, it is more secure than shares of stock or general bonds.

debt: n. 1) a sum of money due to another. 2) obligation to deliver particular goods or perform certain acts according to an agreement, such as returning a favor. 3) a cause of action in a lawsuit for a particular amount owed. (See: **common counts**)

debtor: n. 1) a person or entity that owes an amount of money or favor to another. 2) in bankruptcy, the party whose affairs are the subject of the proceedings is called the "debtor." (See: **bankruptcy**)

debtor in possession: n. in bankruptcy proceedings when a debtor has filed for the right to submit a plan for reorganization or refinancing under Chapter 11, and the debtor is allowed to continue to manage his/her/its business without an appointed trustee, that debtor is called a "debtor in possession." (See: **bankruptcy**)

deceased: 1) adj. dead. 2) n. the person who has died, as used in the handling of his/her estate, probate of will and other proceedings after death, or in reference to the victim of a homicide (as: "The deceased had been shot three times.") In probate law the more genteel word is the "decedent."

decedent: n. the person who has died, sometimes referred to as the "deceased." (See: **deceased**)

deceit: n. dishonesty, fraudulent conduct, false statements made knowing them to be untrue, by which the liar intends to deceive a party receiving the statements and expects the party to believe and rely on them. This is a civil wrong (tort) giving rise to the right of a person to sue the deceiver if he/she reasonably relied on such dishonesty to the point of his/her injury. (See: **fraud, misrepresentation**)

deception: n. the act of misleading another through intentionally false statements or fraudulent actions. (See: **deceit, fraud**)

decide: v. for a judge, arbitrator, court of appeals or other magistrate or tribunal to reach a determination (decision) by choosing what is right and wrong according to the law as he/she sees it.

decision: n. judgment, decree or determination of findings of fact and/or of law by a judge, arbitrator, court, governmental agency or other official tribunal (court). (See: **decree, judgment**)

declarant: n. the person making a statement, usually written and signed by that person, under "penalty of perjury" pursuant to the laws of the state in which the statement, called a declaration, is made. The declaration is more commonly used than the affidavit, which is similar to a declaration but requires taking an oath to swear to the truth attested to (certified in writing) by a notary public. In theory, a declarant who knowingly does not tell the truth would be subject to the criminal charge of perjury. Such violations are seldom pursued. (See: **affiant, affidavit, declaration**)

declaration: n. 1) any statement made,

particularly in writing. 2) a written statement made "under penalty of perjury" and signed by the declarant, which is the modern substitute for the more cumbersome affidavit, which requires swearing to its truth before a notary public. (See: **affidavit, declarant**)

declaration of mailing: n. a form stating that a particular document has been mailed to a particular person or persons (such as opposing attorneys or the clerk of the court) and declaring the truth of that fact "under penalty of perjury," and signed by the person in the law office responsible for mailing it. This is almost always required to be attached to filed documents so that the court is assured it has been sent to the other party. (See: **declaration**)

declaration of trust: n. the document signed by a trustor (settlor) creating a trust into which assets are placed, a trustee is appointed to manage the trust (who may be the party who created the trust), the powers and duties of management of the principal and profits of the trust are stated, and distribution of profits and principal is spelled out. (See: **settlor, trust, trustee, trustor**)

declaratory judgment: n. a judgment of a court which determines the rights of parties without ordering anything be done or awarding damages. While this borders on the prohibited "advisory opinion," it is allowed to nip controversies in the bud. Examples: a party to a contract may seek the legal interpretation of a contract to determine the parties' rights, or a corporation may ask a court to decide whether a new tax is truly applicable to that business before it pays it. (See: **declaratory relief**)

declaratory relief: n. a judge's determination (called a "declaratory judgment") of the parties' rights under a contract or a statute often requested (prayed for) in a lawsuit over a contract. The theory is that an early resolution of legal rights will resolve some or all of the other issues in the matter. (See: **declaratory judgment**)

The law was not made for a righteous man, but for the lawless and disobedient.
—The Bible, St. Paul in Timothy I.9

decree: n. in general, synonymous with judgment. However, in some areas of the law, the term decree is either more common or preferred as in probates of estates, domestic relations (divorce), admiralty law and in equity (court rulings ordering or prohibiting certain acts). Thus, there may be references to a final or interlocutory decree of divorce, final decree of distribution of a dead person's estate, etc. (See: **judgment**)

decriminalization: n. the repeal or amendment of statutes which made certain acts criminal, so that those acts no longer are crimes subject to prosecution. Many states have decriminalized certain sexual practices between consenting adults, "loitering" (hanging out without any criminal activity), or outmoded racist laws against miscegenation (marriage or cohabitation between people of different races). Currently, there is a considerable movement toward decriminalization of the use of some narcotics (particularly marijuana) by adults, on various grounds, including individual rights and contention that decriminalization would take the profit out of the drug trade by making drugs available through clinics and other legal sources.

dedication: n. the giving of land by a private person or entity to the government, typically for a street, park or school site, as part of and a condition of a real estate development. The local county or city (or other public body) must accept the dedication before it is complete. In many cases there are "dedicated" streets on old subdivision maps which were never officially accepted and, in effect, belong to no one. The adjoining property owners can sue for a judgment to give them the title to the unclaimed (unowned) street or property by a quiet title action or request abandonment by the government which did not accept the street or other property. (See: **quiet title action**)

deduction: n. an expenditure which an income tax payer may subtract from gross (total) income to determine taxable income. This is not the same as an exemption, which is for one's marital status, age over 65, blindness and number of dependents (e.g. children), which, added together, reduce the tax owed.

deed: 1) n. the written document which transfers title (ownership) or an interest in real property to another person. The deed must describe the real property, name the party transferring the property (grantor), the party receiving the property (grantee) and be signed by the grantor, who must then acknowledge before a notary public that he/she/it executed the deed. To complete the transfer (conveyance) the deed must be recorded in the office of the County Recorder or Recorder of Deeds. There are two basic types of deeds: a warranty deed, which guarantees that the grantor owns title, and the quitclaim deed, which transfers only that interest in the real property which the grantor actually has. The quitclaim is often used among family members or from one joint owner to the other when there is little question about existing ownership, or just to clear the title. This is not to be confused with a deed of trust, which is a form of mortgage. 2) v. to transfer title by a written deed. (See: **conveyance, deed of trust, quitclaim deed, warranty deed**)

deed of trust: n. a document which pledges real property to secure a loan, used instead of a mortgage in Alaska, Arizona, California, Colorado, Georgia, Idaho, Illinois, Mississippi, Missouri, Montana, North Carolina, Texas, Virginia and West Virginia. The property is deeded by the title holder (trustor) to a trustee (often a title or escrow company) which holds the title in trust for the beneficiary (the lender of the money). When the loan is fully paid, the trustor requests the trustee to return the title by reconveyance. If the loan becomes delinquent the beneficiary can file a notice of default and, if the loan is not brought current, can demand that the trustee begin foreclosure on the property so that the beneficiary may either be paid or obtain title. (See: **foreclosure, mortgage, reconveyance**)

de facto: adj. Latin for "in fact." Often used in place of "actual" to show that the court will treat as a fact authority being exercised or an entity acting as if it had authority, even though the legal requirements have not been met. (See: *de facto, de jure*)

de facto **corporation**: n. a company which operates as if it were a corporation although it has not completed the legal steps to become incorporated (has not filed its articles, for example) or has been dissolved or suspended but continues to function. The court temporarily treats the corporation as if it were legal in order to avoid unfairness to people who thought the corporation was legal. (See: *de facto, de jure, ultra vires*)

defalcation: v. from Latin for "deduction," withholding or misappropriating funds held for another, particularly by a public official, or failing to make a proper accounting.

defamation: n. the act of making untrue statements about another which damages his/her reputation. If the defamatory statement is printed or broadcast over the media it is libel and, if only oral, it is slander. Public figures, including officeholders and candidates, have to show that the defamation was made with malicious intent and was not just fair comment. Damages for slander may be limited to actual (special) damages unless there is malice. Some statements such as an

accusation of having committed a crime, having a feared disease or being unable to perform one's occupation are called libel per se or slander per se and can more easily lead to large money awards in court and even punitive damage recovery by the person harmed. Most states provide for a demand for a printed retraction of defamation and only allow a lawsuit if there is no such admission of error. (See: **fair comment, libel, public figure, slander**)

default: 1) n. failure to respond to a summons and complaint served on a party in the time required by law. If a legal answer or other response is not filed, the suing party (plaintiff) can request a default be entered in the record, which terminates the rights of the defaulting party to defend the case. Under a unique New York statute a default can be taken by failure to respond to a summons served without a complaint. 2) the failure to make a payment when due, which can lead to a notice of default and the start of foreclosure proceedings if the debt is secured by a mortgage or deed of trust. 3) v. to fail to file an answer or other response to a summons and complaint, or fail to make a payment when due. (See: **default judgment, notice of default**)

default judgment: n. if a defendant in a lawsuit fails to respond to a complaint in the time set by law (commonly 20 or 30 days), then the plaintiff (suer) can request that the default (failure) be entered into the court record by the clerk, which gives the plaintiff the right to get a default judgment. If the complaint was for a specific amount of money owed on a note, other money due, or a specific contract price (or if the amount due is easy to calculate) then the clerk of the court can enter a default judgment. If proof of damages or other relief is necessary, a hearing will be held in which the judge determines terms of the default judgment. In either case the defendant cannot speak for himself/herself. A defendant who fails to file an answer or other legal response when it is due can request that the default be set aside, but must show a legitimate excuse and a good defense to the lawsuit. (See: **complaint, default, summons**)

defeasance: n. an antiquated word for a document which terminates the effect of an existing writing such as a deed, bond or contract if some event occurs.

defect: n. an imperfection, quite often so great that the machinery or written document cannot be used. A car that will not run or has faulty brakes has a defect, and so does a deed in which a party who signed the deed to give over property did not have title to the property described. There are also minor defects, like scratches that only lessen value but do not make an object useless. (See: **defective, defective title**)

defective: adj. not being capable of fulfilling its function, ranging from a deed of land to a piece of equipment. (See: **defect, defective title**)

defective title: n. an apparent title to real property which fails because a claimed prior holder of the title did not have title, or there is a faulty description of the property or some other "cloud" over it, which may or may not be apparent from reading the deed. (See: **chain of title, defect, defective**)

defendant: n. 1) the party sued in a civil lawsuit or the party charged with a crime in a criminal prosecution. In some types of cases (such as divorce) a defendant may be called a respondent. (See: **codefendant, plaintiff**)

defense: n. 1) a general term for the effort of an attorney representing a defendant during trial and in pre-trial maneuvers to defeat the party suing or the prosecution in a criminal case. 2) a response to a complaint, called an affirmative defense, to counter, defeat or remove all or a part of the contentions of the plaintiff. (See: **affirmative defense**)

defense attorney: n. 1) the attorney representing the defendant in a lawsuit or criminal prosecution. 2) a lawyer who regularly represents defendants who have insurance and who is chosen by the insurance company. 3) a lawyer who regularly represents criminal defendants. Attorneys who regularly represent clients in actions for damages are often called "plaintiff's attorneys." (See: **defendant, plaintiff's attorney**)

deficiency judgment: n. a judgment for an amount not covered by the value of security put up for a loan or installment payments. In most states the party owed money can only get a deficiency judgment if he/she chooses to file a suit for judicial foreclosure instead of just foreclosing on real property. However, some states allow a lawsuit for a deficiency after foreclosure on the mortgage or deed of trust. The right to a deficiency judgment is often written into a lease or installment contract on a vehicle. There is a danger that the sale of a repossessed vehicle will be at a wholesale price or to a friend at a sheriff's sale or auction, leaving the debtor holding the bag for the difference between the sale price and remainder due on the lease or contract. (See: **foreclosure, judicial foreclosure**)

deficit: n. a shortage, less than is due, or in the case of a business or government budget, more expenditures than income. Unbalanced budgets with a planned year-end deficit are prohibited at every level of government except the federal.

defraud: v. to use deceit, falsehoods or trickery to obtain money, an object, rights or anything of value belonging to another. (See: **fraud**)

degree of kinship: n. the level of relationship between two persons related by blood, such as parent to child, one sibling to another, grandparent to grandchild or uncle to nephew, first cousins, etc., calculated as one degree for each step from a common ancestor. This may become important when determining the heirs of an estate when there is no will. (See: **descent**)

de jure: adj. Latin for "lawful," as distinguished from *de facto* (actual). (See: *de facto, de jure* **corporation**)

de jure **corporation**: n. a corporation in good standing under the law, as compared to a *de facto* corporation which is acting while not fulfilling legal requirements. (See: *de facto* **corporation,** *de jure*)

delayed exchange: n. an exchange of property to put off capital gain taxes, in which the funds are placed in a binding trust for up to 180 days while the seller acquires an "exchanged" (another similar) property, pursuant to IRS Code sec. 1031. It is sometimes called a "Starker" after the man who first used this method and survived an IRS lawsuit.

delegate: 1) v. to assign authority to another. 2) n. a person chosen to attend a convention, conference or meeting on behalf of an organization, constituency, interest group or business.

deleterious: adj. harmful.

deliberate: 1) adj. (dee-lib-er-et) done with care and intention or premeditated. 2) v. (dee-lib-er-ate) to consider the facts, the laws and/or other matters, particularly by members of a jury, a panel of judges or by any group including a legislature.

deliberation: n. the act of considering, discussing and, hopefully, reaching a conclusion, such as a jury's discussions, voting and decision-making.

The law is only a memorandum.
—Ralph Waldo Emerson

delinquent: 1) adj. not paid in full

amount or on time. 2) n. short for an underage violator of the law as in juvenile delinquent. (See: **youthful offender**)

deliver: v. to actually hand an object, money or document to another.

delivery: n. the actual handing to another of an object, money or document (such as a deed) to complete a transaction. The delivery of a deed transfers title (provided it is then recorded), and the delivery of goods makes a sale complete and final if payment has been made. Symbolic or constructive delivery (depositing something with an agent or third person) falls short of completion unless agreed to by the parties. (See: **contract, deed, sale**)

demand: 1) v. to claim as a need, requirement or entitlement, as in to demand payment or performance under a contract. In a lawsuit for payment of a debt or performance of an act, the party suing (plaintiff) should allege that he/she/it demanded payment or performance. 2) n. a claim, such as an unqualified request for payment or other action. 3) the amount requested by a plaintiff (usually in writing) during negotiations to settle a lawsuit. 4) adj. referring to a note payable at any time a request to pay is made. (See: **demand note**)

demand note: n. a promissory note which is payable any time the holder of the note makes a request. This is different from a note due at a specific time, upon occurrence of an event, or by installments. (See: **promissory note**)

de minimis: adj. (dee-minnie-miss) Latin for "of minimum importance" or "trifling." Essentially it refers to something or a difference that is so little, small, minuscule or tiny that the law does not refer to it and will not consider it. In a million dollar deal, a $10 mistake is *de minimis*.

demise: 1) v. an old-fashioned expression meaning to lease or transfer (convey) real property for years or life, but not beyond that. 2) n. the deed that conveys real property only for years or life. 3) n. death. 4) n. failure.

demonstrative evidence: n. actual objects, pictures, models and other devices which are supposedly intended to clarify the facts for the judge and jury: how an accident occurred, actual damages, medical problems, or methods used in committing an alleged crime. Many of these are not supposed to be actual evidence, but "aids" to understanding. A model of a knee or a photograph of an accident scene obviously helps, but color photos of an operation in progress or a bullet-riddled body can excite the passions of a jury. The borderline balance between legitimate aids and evidence intended to inflame a juror's emotions is in the hands of the trial judge. (See: **evidence**)

demurrer: n. (dee-muhr-ur) a written response to a complaint filed in a lawsuit which, in effect, pleads for dismissal on the point that even if the facts alleged in the complaint were true, there is no legal basis for a lawsuit. A hearing before a judge (on the law and motion calendar) will then be held to determine the validity of the demurrer. Some causes of action may be defeated by a demurrer while others may survive. Some demurrers contend that the complaint is unclear or omits an essential element of fact. If the judge finds these errors, he/she will usually sustain the demurrer (state it is valid), but "with leave to amend" in order to allow changes to make the original complaint good. An amendment to the complaint cannot always overcome a demurrer, as in a case filed after the time allowed by law to bring a suit. If after amendment the complaint is still not legally good, a demurrer will be granted sustained. In rare occasions, a demurrer can be used to attack an answer to a complaint. Some states have substituted a motion to dismiss for failure to state a cause of action for the demurrer. (See: **motion, pleading**)

denial: n. a statement in the defendant's answer to a complaint in a lawsuit that an allegation (claim of fact) is not true. If a defendant denies all allegations it is called a general denial. In answering, the defendant is limited to admitting, denying or denying on the basis he/she/it has no information to affirm or deny. The defendant may also state affirmative defenses. (See: **admission, affirmative defense, answer, general denial**)

de novo: adj. Latin for "anew," which means starting over, as in a trial *de novo*. For example, a decision in a small claims case may be appealed to a local trial court, which may try the case again, *de novo*. (See: **trial *de novo***)

dependent: 1) n. a person receiving support from another person (such as a parent), which may qualify the party supporting the dependent for an exemption to reduce his/her income taxes. 2) adj. requiring an event to occur, as the fulfillment of a contract is dependent on the expert being available.

depletion: n. when a natural resource (particularly oil) is being used up. The annual amount of depletion may, ironically, provide a tax deduction for the company exploiting the resource because if the resource they are exploiting runs out, they will no longer be able to make money from it.

deponent: n. a person testifying (stating answers in response to questions) at a deposition. (See: **depose, deposition**)

deportation: n. the act of expelling a foreigner from a country, usually because he/she has a criminal record, committed a crime, lied on his/her entry documents, is in the country illegally or his/her presence is deemed by the Immigration and Naturalization Service, FBI or State Department officials to be against the best interests of the nation. Deportation is usually to the country of origin.

depose: v. 1) to ask questions of a witness or a party to a lawsuit at a deposition (testimony outside of the courtroom before trial). 2) to testify at a deposition. (See: **deponent, deposition**)

deposition: n. the taking and recording of testimony of a witness under oath before a court reporter in a place away from the courtroom before trial. A deposition is part of permitted pre-trial discovery (investigation), set up by an attorney for one of the parties to a lawsuit demanding the sworn testimony of the opposing party (defendant or plaintiff), a witness to an event, or an expert intended to be called at trial by the opposition. If the person requested to testify (deponent) is a party to the lawsuit or someone who works for an involved party, notice of time and place of the deposition can be given to the other side's attorney, but if the witness is an independent third party, a subpena must be served on him/her if he/she is reluctant to testify. The testimony is taken down by the court reporter, who will prepare a transcript if requested and paid for, which assists in trial preparation and can be used in trial either to contradict (impeach) or refresh the memory of the witness, or be read into the record if the witness is not available. (See: **deponent, depose, discovery**)

depreciate: v. in accounting, to reduce the value of an asset each year theoretically on the basis that the assets (such as equipment, vehicles or structures) will eventually become obsolete, worn out and of little value. (See: **depreciation**)

depreciation: n. the actual or theoretical gradual loss of value of an asset (particularly business equipment or buildings) through increasing age, natural wear and tear, or deterioration, even though the item may retain or even increase its replacement value due to inflation. Depreciation may be used as a business deduction for income tax reduction, spread out over the expect-ed useful life of the asset (straight line) or at a higher rate in the early years of use (accelerated).

depreciation reserve: n. a business fund in which the probable replacement cost of equipment is accumulated each year over the life of the asset, so it can be replaced readily when it becomes obsolete and totally depreciated.

derelict: n. something or someone who is abandoned, such as a ship left to drift at sea or a homeless person ignored by family and society. (See: **abandon, dereliction**)

dereliction: n. 1) abandoning possession, which is sometimes used in the phrase "dereliction of duty." It includes abandoning a ship, which then becomes a "derelict" which salvagers can board. 2) an old expression for increase of land due to gradual lowering of a tide line (which means the land is building up). (See: **derelict**)

derivative action: n. a lawsuit brought by a corporation shareholder against the directors, management and/or other shareholders of the corporation, for a failure by management. In effect, the suing shareholder claims to be acting on behalf of the corporation, because the directors and management are failing to exercise their authority for the benefit of the company and all of its shareholders. This type of suit often arises when there is fraud, mismanagement, self-dealing and/or dishonesty which are being ignored by officers and the board of directors of a corporation. (See: **corporation, director, shareholder, stockholder**)

descent: n. the rules of inheritance established by law in cases in which there is no will naming the persons to receive the possessions of a person who has died. The rules of descent vary somewhat from state to state and will usually be governed by the law of the state in which the deceased party lived. Depending on which relatives survive, the estate may go all or in part to the surviving spouse, and down the line from a parent to children (or if none survive, to grandchildren), or up to surviving parents, or collaterally to brothers and sisters. If there are no survivors among those relatives, then aunts, uncles, cousins, nieces and nephews may inherit, depending on their degree of kinship (closeness of family relationship), state laws of descent and distribution, or whether the deceased person lived in a community property state, in which the wife has a survivorship right to community property. (See: **community property, degree of kinship, descent and distribution, inheritance, intestate succession**)

descent and distribution: n. the system of laws which determine who will inherit and divide the possessions of a person who has died without a will (intestate). (See: **degree of kinship, descent, inheritance, intestate succession**)

desert: v. to intentionally abandon a person or thing.

desertion: n. the act of abandoning, particularly leaving one's spouse and/or children without an intent to return. In desertion cases it is often expected that a deserter who is the family breadwinner may not intend to support the family he/she left. Such conduct is less significant legally in the present era of no-fault divorce and standardized rights to child support and alimony (spousal support). Desertion can influence a court in determining visitation, custody and other post-marital issues.

determinable: adj. defining something which may be terminated upon the occurrence of a particular event, used primarily to describe an interest in real property, such as a fee simple determinable, in which property is deeded to another, but may revert to the giver or go to a third person if, as examples, the receiver (grantee) marries, divorces or no longer lives in the house.

"deuce": n. slang term for a drunk driving conviction. The term originated in California, where the offense was once governed by Section 502 of the California Vehicle Code.

devise: 1) v. an old-fashioned word for giving real property by a will, as distinguished from words for giving personal property. 2) n. the gift of real property by will. (See: **bequest, gift, legacy, remise, will**)

devisee: n. a person who receives a gift of real property by a will. The distinction between gifts of real property and personal property is actually blurred, so terms like beneficiary or legatee cover those receiving any gift by a will. (See: **beneficiary, legatee**)

devolution: n. the transfer of rights, powers or an office (public or private) from one person or government to another. (See: **devolve**)

devolve: v. when property is automatically transferred from one party to another by operation of law, without any act required of either past or present owner. The most common example is passing of title to the natural heir of a person upon his/her death. 2) passing of authority to a vice president on the death of a president. 3) to give a territory sovereign rights to run itself.

devolution: n. 1) the transfer of title to real property by the automatic operation of law. 2) the giving away of power. (See: **devolve**)

"No, no," said the Queen. "Sentence first, verdict afterwards."
—Lewis Carroll, Alice in Wonderland

dicta: n. the plural of *dictum*.

dictum: n. Latin for "remark," a comment by a judge in a decision or ruling which is not required to reach the decision, but may state a related legal principle as the judge understands it. While it may be cited in legal argument, it does not have the full force of a precedent (previous court decisions or interpretations) since the comment was not part of the legal basis for judgment. The standard counter argument is: "it is only *dictum* (or *dicta*)." (See: *dicta*, *obiter dicta*)

diligence: n. reasonable care or attention to a matter, which is good enough to avoid a claim of negligence, or is a fair attempt (as in due diligence in a process server's attempt to locate someone).

diminished capacity: n. essentially a psychological term which has found its way into criminal trials. A contention of diminished capacity means that although the accused was not insane, due to emotional distress, physical condition or other factors he/she could not fully comprehend the nature of the criminal act he/she is accused of committing, particularly murder or attempted murder. It is raised by the defense in attempts to remove the element of premeditation or criminal intent and thus obtain a conviction for a lesser crime, such as manslaughter instead of murder. While the theory has some legitimacy, at times juries have been overly impressed by psychiatric testimony. The most notorious case was in *People v. Dan White*, the admitted killer of San Francisco Mayor George Moscone and Supervisor Harvey Milk, who got only a manslaughter conviction on the basis that his capacity was diminished by the sugar content of his blood due to eating "Twinkies." (See: **insanity, M'Naughten Rule, Twinky defense**)

diminution in value: n. in the event of a breach of contract, the decrease in value of property due to the failure to construct something exactly as specified in the contract.

direct and proximate cause: n. the immediate reason damage was caused by an act or omission (negligence); the negligence must have caused the damages, without intervention of another party, and cannot be remote in time or place. Example (in a complaint): "Defendant's negligent acts (speeding and losing control of his vehicle) directly and proximately caused plaintiff's injuries." (See: **cause, complaint, proximate cause**)

directed verdict: n. a verdict by a jury based on the specific direction by a trial judge that they must bring in that verdict because one of the parties has not proved his/her/its case as a matter of law (failed to present credible testimony on some key element of the claim or of the defense). A judge in a criminal case may direct a verdict of acquittal on the basis that the prosecution has not proved its case, but the judge may not direct a verdict of guilty, since that would deprive the accused of the constitutional right to a jury trial. (See: **acquittal, element, judgment, jury trial, verdict**)

direct evidence: n. real, tangible or clear evidence of a fact, happening or thing that requires no thinking or consideration to prove its existence, as compared to circumstantial evidence. (See: **circumstantial evidence, evidence**)

direct examination: n. the first questioning of a witness during a trial or deposition (testimony out of court), as distinguished from cross-examination by opposing attorneys and redirect examination when the witness is again questioned by the original attorney. (See: **cross-examination, deposition, testimony, witness**)

director: n. a member of the governing board of a corporation or association elected or re-elected at annual meetings of the shareholders or members. As a group the directors are responsible for the policy mak-ing, but not day-to-day operation, which is handled by officers and other managers. In some cases, a director may also be an officer, but need not be a shareholder. Most states require a minimum of three directors on corporate boards. Often lay people dealing with corporations confuse directors with officers. Officers are employees hired by the board of directors to manage the business. (See: **board of directors, corporation**)

disability: n. 1) a condition which prevents one from performing all usual physical or mental functions. This usually means a permanent state, like blindness, but in some cases is temporary. In recent times society and the law have dictated that people with disabilities should be accommodated and encouraged to operate to their maximum potential and have the right to participate in societal and governmental activity without impediments. Hence, access by ramps, elevators, special parking places and other special arrangements have become required in many states. 2) a legal impediment, including being a minor who cannot make a contract, or being insane or incompetent.

disbar: v. to remove an attorney from the list of practicing attorneys for improper conduct. This penalty is usually invoked by the State Bar Association (if so empowered) or the highest state court, and will automatically prohibit the attorney from practicing law before the courts in that state or from giving advice for a fee to clients. The causes of permanent disbarment include conviction of a felony involving "moral turpitude," forgery, fraud, a history of dishonesty, consistent lack of attention to clients, abandoning several clients, alcoholism or drug abuse which affect the attorney's ability to practice, theft of funds, or any pattern of violation of the professional code of ethics. Singular incidents (other than felony conviction) will generally result in reprimand, suspension and/or a requirement that the lawyer correct his/her conduct, show remorse and/or pass a test on legal ethics. (See **moral turpitude**)

disbarment: n. the ultimate discipline of an attorney, which is taking away his/her license to practice law, often for life. Disbarment only comes after investigation and opportunities for the attorney to explain his/her improper conduct. Sometimes an attorney may be reinstated upon a showing of rehabilitation and/or cure. (See: **disbar**)

discharge: v. 1) to perform one's duties. 2) to dismiss someone from a job. 3) to pay one's debts or obligations. 4) in bankruptcy, to issue an order of the court that all debts (with certain statutory exceptions) are forgiven and need not be paid. (See: **bankruptcy**)

discharge in bankruptcy: n. an order given by the bankruptcy judge, at the conclusion of all legal steps in processing a bankrupt person's assets and debts, which forgives those remaining debts which cannot be paid, with certain exceptions. Debts for fraudulent or illegal actions, alimony and child support and taxes are not dischargeable and remain owed (but

often not collectible if the bankrupt person has nothing). A discharge in bankruptcy is bad news for unsecured creditors. (See: **bankruptcy**)

disclaimer: n. 1) denial or renunciation by someone of his/her title to property. 2) denial of responsibility for another's claim, such as an insurance company's refusal to admit coverage under an insurance policy. 3) statement of non-responsibility, as is made when dissolving a partnership or business.

discount: n. the payment of less than the full amount due on a promissory note or price for goods or services. Usually a discount is by agreement and includes the common situation in which a holder of a long-term promissory note or material goods will sell it/them for less than face value in order to get cash now—the difference is the discount.

discovery: n. the entire efforts of a party to a lawsuit and his/her/its attorneys to obtain information before trial through demands for production of documents, depositions of parties and potential witnesses, written interrogatories (questions and answers written under oath), written requests for admissions of fact, examination of the scene and the petitions and motions employed to enforce discovery rights. The theory of broad rights of discovery is that all parties will go to trial with as much knowledge as possible and that neither party should be able to keep secrets from the other (except for constitutional protection against self-incrimination). Often much of the fight between the two sides in a suit takes place during the discovery period. (See: **deposition, interrogatories**)

discretion: n. the power of a judge, public official or a private party (under authority given by contract, trust or will) to make decisions on various matters based on his/her opinion within general legal guidelines. Examples: a) a judge may have discretion as to the amount of a fine or whether to grant a continuance of a trial; b) a trustee or executor of an estate may have discretion to divide assets among the beneficiaries so long as the value to each is approximately equal; c) a District Attorney may have discretion to charge a crime as a misdemeanor (maximum term of one year) or felony; d) a Governor may have discretion to grant a pardon; or e) a planning commission may use its discretion to grant or not to grant a variance to a zoning ordinance.

discrimination: n. unequal treatment of persons, for a reason which has nothing to do with legal rights or ability. Federal and state laws prohibit discrimination in employment, availability of housing, rates of pay, right to promotion, educational opportunity, civil rights, and use of facilities based on race, nationality, creed, color, age, sex or sexual orientation. The rights to protest discrimination or enforce one's rights to equal treatment are provided in various federal and state laws, which allow for private lawsuits with the right to damages. There are also federal and state commissions to investigate and enforce equal rights. (See: **civil rights**)

disfigure: v. to cause permanent change in a person's body, particularly by leaving visible scars which affect a person's appearance. In lawsuits or claims due to injuries caused by another's negligence or intentional actions, such scarring can add considerably to general damages. (See: **damages, general damages**)

dishonor: v. to refuse to pay the face amount of a check or the amount due on a promissory note.

disinherit: v. to intentionally take actions to guarantee that a person who would normally inherit upon a party's death (wife, child or closest relative) would get nothing. Usually this is done by a provision in a will or codicil (amendment) to a will which states that a specific person is not to take anything ("my son, Robert Hands, shall receive nothing," "no descendant of my hated brother shall take anything on account of my death."). It is not enough to merely ignore or not mention a child in a will since he/she may become a "pretermitted heir" (a child apparently forgotten). A spouse can be disinherited only to the extent that the state law allows. A writer of a will can also disinherit anyone who challenges the validity of the will in what is called an *"in terrorem"* clause, which might say "I leave anyone who challenges this will or any part of it one dollar." (See: **codicil, descent, descent and distribution, heir, *in terrorem* clause, pretermitted heir, will**)

disinheritance: n. the act of disinheriting. (See: **disinherit**)

disjunctive allegations: n. the

attempt to claim in a civil lawsuit that one thing "or" another occurred, and in criminal charges that the accused committed one crime "or" another. Such complaints are disallowed because the defendant is entitled to know what he/she must defend. (See: **cause of action, charge, complaint**)

dismiss: v. the ruling by a judge that all or a portion (one or more of the causes of action) of the plaintiff's lawsuit is terminated (thrown out) at that point without further evidence or testimony. This judgment may be made before, during or at the end of a trial, when the judge becomes convinced that the plaintiff has not and cannot prove his/her/its case. This can be based on the complaint failing to allege a cause of action, on a motion for summary judgment, plaintiff's opening statement of what will be proved, or on some development in the evidence by either side which bars judgment for the plaintiff. The judge may dismiss on his own or upon motion by the defendant. The plaintiff may voluntarily dismiss a cause of action before or during trial if the case is settled, if it is not provable or trial strategy dictates getting rid of a weak claim. A defendant may be "dismissed" from a lawsuit, meaning the suit is dropped against that party. (See: **dismissal**)

dismissal: n. 1) the act of voluntarily terminating a criminal prosecution or a lawsuit or one of its causes of action by one of the parties. 2) a judge's ruling that a lawsuit or criminal charge is terminated. 3) an appeals court's act of dismissing an appeal, letting the lower court decision stand. 4) the act of a plaintiff dismissing a lawsuit upon settling the case. Such a dismissal may be dismissal with prejudice, meaning it can never be filed again, or dismissal without prejudice, leaving open the possibility of bringing the suit again if the defendant does not follow through on the terms of the settlement. (See: **dismiss**)

dismissal with prejudice: n. (See: **dismissal**)

dismissal without prejudice: n. (See: **dismissal**)

disorderly conduct: n. 1) actions that disturb others. 2) minor criminal offenses, such as public drunkenness, loitering, disturbing the peace, and loud threats or parties.

disorderly house: n. 1) polite term for house of prostitution. 2) place of illegal gambling.

disposing mind and memory: n. the mental ability to understand in general what one possesses and the persons who are the "natural objects of bounty" (wife and/or children), at the time of making a will. (See: **competent, will**)

disposition: n. the court's final determination of a lawsuit or criminal charge.

dispossess: v. to eject someone from real property, either legally or by self-help.

dissent: n. 1) the opinion of a judge of a court of appeals, including the U.S. Supreme Court, which disagrees with the majority opinion. Sometimes a dissent may eventually prevail as the law or society evolves. Prime examples include the many dissenting opinions of Oliver Wendell Holmes, Associate Justice of the U.S. Supreme Court (1902–1932), which were widely quoted and often formed the basis for later majority decisions. 2) stated disagreement with prevailing thought.

dissenting opinion: n. (See: **dissent**)

dissolution of corporation: n. termination of a corporation, either a) voluntarily by resolution, paying debts, distributing assets and filing dissolution documents with the Secretary of State; or b) by state suspension for not paying corporate taxes or some other action of the government. (See: **corporation**)

dissolution: n. modern, gentler sounding, term for divorce, officially used in California since 1970 and symbolic of the no-fault, non-confrontational approach to dissolving a marriage. (See: **divorce**)

distinguish: v. to argue that the rule in one appeals court decision does not apply to a particular case although there is an apparent similarity (i.e. it is "distinguished").

distress: 1) n. the self-help taking of another's possessions in order to force payment of a claim, which is generally illegal without a court order. 2) adj. at lowest price due to negative circumstances.

distribute: v. 1) the dividing up of those assets of an estate or trust when someone has died according to the terms of the deceased's will or trust, or in absence of a will, according to the laws of descent and distribution. 2) division of profits or assets of a corporation or business. (See: **corporation, descent and distribution, probate, trust, will**)

distribution: n. the act of dividing up the assets of an estate or trust, or paying out profits or assets of a corporation or business according to the ownership percentages. (See: **distribute**)

District Attorney (D.A.): n. an elected official of a county or a designated district with the responsibility for prosecuting crimes. The duties include managing the prosecutor's office, investigating alleged crimes in cooperation with law enforcement, and filing criminal charges or bringing evidence before the Grand Jury that may lead to an indictment for a crime. In some states a District Attorney is officially entitled County Attorney or State's Attorney. U.S. Attorneys are also called Federal District Attorneys and are prosecutors for districts (there are several in larger states) within the Department of Justice, are appointed by the President and serve at his/her pleasure.

district court: n. 1) in the federal court system, a trial court for federal cases in a court district, which is all or a portion of a state. 2) a local court in some states. (See: **court**)

disturbing the peace: n. upsetting the quiet and good order particularly through loud noise, by fighting or other unsocial behavior which frightens or upsets people. It is a misdemeanor, punishable by fine or brief term in jail.

diversion: n. in criminal procedure, a system for giving a chance for a first-time criminal defendant in lesser crimes to perform community service, make restitution for damage due to the crime, obtain treatment for alcohol or drug problems and/or counselling for antisocial or mentally unstable conduct. If the defendant cooperates and the diversion results in progress, the charges eventually may be dismissed. Usually diversion may not be granted for a second offense. (See: **probation**)

diversity of citizenship: n. when opposing parties in a lawsuit are citizens of different states (including corporations incorporated or doing business in different states) or a citizen of a foreign country, which places the case under federal court jurisdiction, pursuant to Article III, section 2 of the U.S. Constitution, and the federal Judicial Code, if the amount in controversy exceeds $10,000.

divestiture: n. the court-ordered or voluntary giving up of a possession or right, which is a common result in an antitrust action to prevent monopoly or other restraint of trade.

divestment: n. the act of stripping one's investment from an entity.

dividend: n. a portion of profit, usually based on the number of shares of stock in a corporation and the rate of distribution approved by the board of directors or management, that is paid to shareholders for each share they own. Dividends are not always paid in money, but can be paid in shares of stock, known as a stock dividend. (See: **corporation, shareholder**)

divorce: 1) n. the termination of a marriage by legal action, requiring a petition or complaint for divorce (or dissolution in some states, including California) by one party. Some states still require at least a minimal showing of fault, but no-fault divorce is now the rule in which "incompatibility" is sufficient to grant a divorce. The substantive issues in divorces are division of property, child custody and support, alimony (spousal support), child visitation and attorney's fees. Only state courts have jurisdiction over divorces, so the petitioning or complaining party can only file in the state in which he/she is and has been a resident for a period of time (as little as six weeks in Nevada). In most states the period from original filing for divorce, serving the petition on the other party and final judgment (or decree) takes several months to allow for a chance to reconcile. (See: **alimony, child custody, child support, community property, dissolution of marriage, incompatibility, separate property, spousal support**)

DNA: n. scientifically, deoxyribonucleic acid, a chromosomal double chain (the famous "double helix") in the nucleus of each living cell, the combination of which determines each individual's hereditary characteristics. In law, the importance is the discovery that each person's DNA is different and is found in each living cell, so blood, hair, skin or any part of the body can be used to identify and distinguish an individual from all other people. DNA testing can result in proof of one's involvement or lack of involvement in a crime scene.

While recent DNA tests have proved a convicted killer on death row did not commit a crime and resulted in his release, current debate concerns whether DNA evidence is scientifically certain enough to be admitted in trials. The trend is strongly in favor of admission.

docket: 1) n. the cases on a court calendar. 2) n. brief notes, usually written by the court clerk, stating what action was taken that day in court. 3) v. to write down the name of a case to be put on calendar or make notes on action in court.

document: n. a popular generic word among lawyers for any paper with writing on it. Technically it could include a piece of wood with a will or message scratched on it. (See: **documentary evidence**)

documentary evidence: n. any document (paper) which is presented and allowed as evidence in a trial or hearing, as distinguished from oral testimony. However, the opposing attorney may object to its being admitted. In the first place, it must be proved by other evidence from a witness that the paper is genuine (called "laying a foundation"), as well as pass muster over the usual objections such as relevancy. (See: **document, evidence, a foundation**)

doing business: v. carrying on the normal activities of a corporation on a regular basis or with substantial contacts—not just an occasional shipment. This is important to determine if an out-of-state corporation is "doing business" in a state so that it can be served with a complaint, is subject to certain state taxes and/or must register as a "foreign" (out-of-state) corporation operating within the state.

domestic partners: n. unmarried couples, including homosexuals, living together in long-standing relationships, who may be entitled to some of the same benefits as married people, such as job-related health plans.

domestic relations: n. a polite term for the legal field of divorce, dissolution, annulment, child custody, child support and alimony. (See: **divorce**)

The Constitution of the United States forms a government, not a league.
—Andrew Jackson

domestic violence: n. the continuing crime and problem of the physical beating of a wife, girlfriend or children, usually by the woman's male partner (although it can also be female violence against a male). It is now recognized as an antisocial mental illness. Sometimes a woman's dependence, low self-esteem and fear of leaving cause her to endure this conduct or fail to protect a child. Prosecutors and police often face the problem that a battered woman will not press charges or testify due to fear, intimidation and misplaced "love." Increasingly domestic violence is attracting the sympathetic attention of law enforcement, the courts and community services, including shelters and protection for those in danger. (See: **aggravated assault, assault and battery**)

domicile: n. the place where a person has his/her permanent principal home to which he/she returns or intends to return. This becomes significant in determining in what state a probate of a dead person's estate is filed, what state can assess income or inheritance taxes, where a party can begin divorce proceedings, or whether there is "diversity of citizenship" between two parties which may give federal courts jurisdiction over a lawsuit. Where a person has several "residences" it may be a matter of proof as to which is the state of domicile. A business has its domicile in the state where its headquarters is located.

dominant estate: n. in real estate law, the property retained when the owner splits off and conveys part of the property to another party but retains some rights such as an easement for access (a driveway) or utilities. The property sold off upon which there is the easement is called the servient estate. These are also called dominant tenement and servient tenement, respectively. (See: **easement, servient estate, servient tenement**)

dominant tenement: n. (See: **dominant estate**)

donation: n. gift. If made to a qualified non-profit charitable, religious, educational or public service organization, it may be deductible as a contribution in calculating income tax.

donative intent: n. conscious desire to make a gift, as distinguished from giving something for nothing by mistake or under pressure.

donee: n. a person or entity receiving an outright gift or donation.

donor: n. a person or entity making a gift or donation.

double jeopardy: n. placing someone on trial a second time for an offense for which he/she has been previously acquitted, even when new incriminating evidence has been unearthed. This is specifically prohibited by the Fifth Amendment to the U.S. Constitution, which states: "...nor shall any person be subject for the same offence [sic] to be twice put in jeopardy of life or limb..." However, in rare instances a person may be tried for a different crime based on some of the same facts which were used to try him/her when he/she was acquitted. A prime example is the use of the Federal Civil Rights Act to charge a person with violation of another's civil rights by killing him, after a state murder case had resulted in an acquittal, as happened in the 1994 trials for the deaths of civil rights activists and freedom riders Andrew Goldman, Michael Schwerner, James Chaney and Viola Liuzzo, that occurred thirty years earlier.

double taxation: n. taxation of the same property for the same purpose twice in one year. This is generally prohibited if it occurs through such circumstances as transfer of property which has been taxed once and then the tax is imposed on a new owner. However, if all property in a jurisdiction is taxed twice in the same year, it is legal since it is not discriminatory or unfair.

dower: n. an old English common law right of a widow to one-third of her late husband's estate, which is still the law in a few states. In those states the surviving wife can choose either the dower rights or, if more generous, accept the terms of her husband's will in what is called a widow's election. In an obvious sexist imbalance, a surviving husband's equivalent right (called curtesy) is to the wife's entire estate, or if there are living children, to a life estate in everything. (See: **curtesy, descent and distribution, widow's election**)

dowry: n. from the days when a groom expected to profit from a marriage, the money and personal property which a bride brings to her new husband which becomes his alone. Dowry still exists in the Civil Code of Louisiana.

draft: 1) n. a bill of exchange or check in which one party (including a bank) is directed by the party drafting (writing) the bill or check to take money from the drafter's (writer's) bank account and pay it to another person or entity. 2) v. to prepare and sign a bill of exchange or check. 3) n. a less than final document, which is ready for discussion, rewriting and/or editing, such as a book, a proposal, or a legislative bill. 4) n. compulsory enrollment of non-volunteers for military service by lottery, as existed under the Selective Service System during World War I, from 1940 as World War II threatened to involve the United States, through the Korean and Vietnam conflicts until 1973. Since 1980 all men are required to register at 18, but there is no draft or call-ups. (See: **bill of exchange, check**)

dram shop rule: n. a statute (Dram Shop Act) or case law in 38 states which makes a business which sells alcoholic drinks or a host who serves liquor to a drinker who is obviously intoxicated or close to it, strictly liable to anyone injured by the drunken patron or guest. To the contrary, California recently passed legislation specifically banning such strict liability. It is often hard to prove that the liquor bought or served was the specific cause of an accident (such as an automobile crash while driving home), since there is always an intervening cause, namely, the drunk.

draw: v. 1) to prepare any document. 2) specifically to have prepared and signed a bill of exchange or check.

drawee: n. the party who is to be paid on a bill of exchange or check. (See: **bill of exchange**)

drawer: n. the person who signs a bill of exchange. (See: **bill of exchange**)

driving under the influence (DUI): n. commonly called "drunk driving," it refers to operating a motor vehicle while one's blood alcohol content is above the legal limit set by statute, which supposedly is the level at which a person cannot drive safely. State statutes vary as to what that level is, but it ranges from .08 to .10 for adults, which means a 8/100ths to one-tenth of one percent by weight of alcohol to the weight of blood. This is translated into grams of alcohol per 100 milliliters of blood in tests of blood or urine sample, or grams of alcohol per

210 liters of air in a "breathalizer" test. A combination of the use of alchol and narcotics can also be "under the influence" based on erratic driving. Driving on private property such as a parking lot is no defense, but sitting in a non-moving vehicle without the ignition on probably is (sometimes resulting in a charge of "drunk in and about a vehicle"). This is a misdemeanor and is variously referred to as DUI, driving while intoxicated (DWI), drunk driving, or a "deuce".

driving while intoxicated: n. (See: **driving under the influence**)

drop dead date: n. a provision in a contract or a court order which sets the last date an event must take place (such as payment) or otherwise certain consequences will automatically follow, such as cancelling the contract, taking property or entering a judgment.

due: n. and adj. owed as of a specific date. A popular legal redundancy is that a debt is "due, owing and unpaid." Unpaid does not necessarily mean that a debt is due.

due care: n. the conduct that a reasonable man or woman will exercise in a particular situation, in looking out for the safety of others. If one uses due care then an injured party cannot prove negligence. This is one of those nebulous standards by which negligence is tested. Each juror has to determine what a "reasonable" man or woman would do.

due and owing: adj. (See: **due**)

due, owing and unpaid: adj. (See: **due**)

due process of law: n. a fundamental principle of fairness in all legal matters, both civil and criminal, especially in the courts. All legal procedures set by statute and court practice, including notice of rights, must be followed for each individual so that no prejudicial or unequal treatment will result. While somewhat indefinite, the term can be gauged by its aim to safeguard both private and public rights against unfairness. The universal guarantee of due process is in the Fifth Amendment to the U.S. Constitution, which provides "No person shall...be deprived of life, liberty, or property, without due process of law," and is applied to all states by the 14th Amendment. From this basic principle flows many legal decisions determining both procedural and substantive rights.

> *Injustice anywhere is a threat to justice everywhere.*
> *—Martin Luther King, Jr.*

D.U.I.: n. short for driving under the influence of alcohol. (See: **driving under the influence**)

duress: n. the use of force, false imprisonment or threats (and possibly psychological torture or "brainwashing") to compel someone to act contrary to his/her wishes or interests. If duress is used to get someone to sign an agreement or execute a will, a court may find the document null and void. A defendant in a criminal prosecution may raise the defense that others used duress to force him/her to take part in an alleged crime. The most famous case is that of publishing heiress Patty Hearst, who was kidnapped, raped, imprisoned and psychologically tortured until she joined her captors in a bank holdup and issued statements justifying her actions. She was later convicted of the bank robbery, but was eventually pardoned by President Jimmy Carter.

duty: n. 1) a legal obligation, the breach of which can result in liability. In a lawsuit a plaintiff must claim and prove that there was a duty by defendant to plaintiff. This can be a duty of care in a negligence case or a duty to perform in a contract case. 2) a tax on imports. (See: **duty of care**)

duty of care: n. a requirement that a person act toward others and the public with the watchfulness, attention, caution and prudence that a reasonable person in the circumstances would use. If a person's actions do not meet this standard of care, then the acts are considered negligent, and any damages resulting may be claimed in a lawsuit for negligence. (See: **negligence, standard of care**)

D.W.I.: n. 1) short for driving while intoxicated. 2) abbreviation for dying without issue (children). (See: **driving under the influence**)

dying declaration: n. the statement of a mortally injured person who is aware he/she is about to die, telling who caused the injury and possibly the circumstances ("Frankie shot me"). Although hearsay since the dead person cannot testify in person, it is admissible on the theory that a dying person has no reason not to tell the truth.

earnest payment: n. a deposit paid to demonstrate commitment and to bind a contract, with the remainder due at a particular time. If the contract is breached by failure to pay, then the earnest payment is kept by the recipient as pre-determined (liquidated) or committed damages.

easement: n. the right to use the real property of another for a specific purpose. The easement is itself a real property interest, but legal title to the underlying land is retained by the original owner for all other purposes. Typical easements are for access to another property (often redundantly stated "access and egress," since entry and exit are over the same path), for utility or sewer lines both under and above ground, use of spring water, entry to make repairs on a fence or slide area, drive cattle across and other uses. Easements can be created by a deed to be recorded just like any real property interest, by continuous and open use by the non-owner against the rights of the property owner for a statutory number of years, typically five ("prescriptive easement"), or to do equity (fairness), including giving access to a "land-locked" piece of property (sometimes called an "easement of necessity"). Easements may be specifically described by boundaries ("24 feet wide along the northern line for a distance of 180 feet"), somewhat indefinite ("along the trail to the northern boundary") or just for a purpose ("to provide access to the Jones property" or "access to the spring") sometimes called a "floating easement." There is also a "negative easement" such as a prohibition against building a structure which blocks a view. Title reports and title abstracts will usually describe all existing easements upon a parcel of real property. Issues of maintenance, joint use, locking gates, damage to easement and other conflicts clog the judicial system, mostly due to misunderstandings at the time of creation.

> *The Constitution is either a superior paramount law, unchangeable by ordinary means, or it is on a level with ordinary legislative acts.*
> *—Chief Justice John Marshall, in Marbury v. Madison*

egress: n. way of departure. A word usually used in conjunction with "access" or "ingress."

EIR: n. popular acronym for environmental impact report, required by many states as part of the application to a county or city for approval of a land development or project. (See: **environmental impact report**)

ejectment: n. a lawsuit brought to remove a party who is occupying real property. This is not the same as an unlawful detainer (eviction) suit against a non-paying or unsatisfactory tenant. It is against someone who has tried to claim title to the property. Example: George Grabby lives on a ranch which he claims he has inherited from his great uncle, but Betty Benefield sues for ejectment on the basis that, in fact, she was entitled to the property through her parents.

ejusdem generis: (eh-youse-dem generous) adj. Latin for "of the same kind," used to interpret loosely written statutes. Where a law lists specific classes of persons or things and then refers to them in general, the general statements only apply to the same kind of persons or things specifically listed. Example: if a law refers to automobiles, trucks, tractors, motorcycles and other motor-powered vehicles, "vehicles" would not include airplanes, since the list was of land-based transportation.

elder law: n. a newly coined vague term covering estate planning, wills, trusts and the problems of older people. Essentially it is a sales gimmick to attract older clientele.

election of remedies: n. an outmoded requirement that if a plaintiff (party filing suit) asks for two remedies based on legal theories which are inconsistent (a judge can grant only one or the other), the plaintiff must decide which one is the most provable and which one he/she really wants to pursue, usually just before the trial begins. Example: suing someone for both breach of contract and for fraud (a secret plan not to fulfill the contract when it was made). Fraud might bring punitive damages, but proof of fraud might be more difficult than of breach of contract. Increasingly, the courts have dispensed with the election of remedies as unfair to the plaintiff since the evidence has not been fully presented.

election under the will: n. in those states which have statutes which give a widow a particular percentage of the late husband's estate (such as dower), the surviving wife may elect to take that percentage instead of any lesser amount (or assets with unacceptable conditions such as an estate which will be cancelled if she remarries) left to her under his will.

eleemosynary: (eh-luh-moss-uh-nary) adj. charitable, as applied to a purpose or institution.

element: n. 1) an essential requirement to a cause of action (the right to bring a lawsuit to enforce a particular right). Each cause of action (negligence, breach of contract, trespass, assault, etc.) is made up of a basic set of elements which must be alleged and proved. Each charge of a criminal offense requires allegation and proof of its elements. 2) essential requirement of a zoning general plan. (See: **cause of action, crime, general plan, zoning**)

emancipation: n. freeing a minor child from the control of parents and allowing the minor to live on his/her own or under the control of others. It usually applies to adolescents who leave the parents' household by agreement or demand. Emancipation may also end the responsibility of a parent for the acts of a child, including debts, negligence or criminal acts. Sometimes it is one of the events which cuts off the obligation of a divorced parent to pay child support.

embezzlement: n. the crime of stealing the funds or property of an employer, company or government or misappropriating money or assets held in trust. (See: **embezzler, theft**)

embezzler: n. a person who commits the crime of embezzlement by fraudulently taking funds or property of an employer or trust.

emblements: n. crops to which a tenant who cultivated the land is entitled by agreement with the owner. If the tenant dies before harvest the crop will become the property of his/her estate.

emergency: n. a sudden, unforeseen happening which requires action to correct or to protect lives and/or property.

eminent domain: n. the power of a governmental entity (federal, state, county or city government, school district, hospital district or other agencies) to take private real estate for public use, with or without the permission of the owner. The Fifth Amendment to the Constitution provides that "private property [may not] be taken for public use without just compensation." The Fourteenth Amendment added the requirement of just compensation to state and local government takings. The usual process includes passage of a resolution by the acquiring agency to take the property (condemnation), including a declaration of public need, followed by an appraisal, an offer, and then negotiation. If the owner is not satisfied, he/she may sue the government agency for a court's determination of just compensation. The government, however, becomes owner while a trial is pending if the amount of the offer is deposited in a trust account. Public uses include schools, streets and highways, parks, airports, dams, reservoirs, redevelopment, public housing, hospitals and public buildings. (See: **condemn, condemnation**)

emolument: n. salary, wages and benefits paid for employment or an office held.

emotional distress: n. an increasingly popular basis for a claim of damages in lawsuits for injury due to the negligence or intentional acts of another. Originally damages for emotional distress were only awardable in conjunction with damages for actual physical harm. Recently courts in many states, including New York and California, have recognized a right to an award of money damages for emotional distress without physical injury or contact. In sexual harassment claims, emotional distress can be the major, or even only, harmful result. In most jurisdictions, emotional distress cannot be claimed for breach of contract or other business activity, but can be alleged in cases of libel and slander. Evidentiary problems include the fact that such distress is easily feigned or exaggerated, and professional testimony by a therapist or psychiatrist may be required to validate the existence and depth of the distress and place a dollar value upon it. (See: **damages**)

employee: n. a person who is hired for a wage, salary, fee or payment to perform work for an employer. In agency law the employee is called an agent and the employer is called the principal. This is important to determine if one is acting as employee when injured (for worker's compensation) or when he/she causes damage to another, thereby making the employer liable for damages to the injured party. (See: **agency, employer, principal,** *respondeat superior*, **scope of employment**)

employer: n. a person or entity which hires the services of another called a principal in the law of agency. (See: **employee, principal**)

employment: n. the hiring of a person for compensation. It is important to determine if acts occurred in the "scope of employment" to establish the possible responsibility of the employer to the employee for injuries on the job or to the public for acts of the employee. (See: **agency, employee,** *respondeat superior*, **scope of employment, Workers' Compensation Acts**)

enabling clause: n. a provision in a new statute which empowers a particular public official (Governor, State Treasurer) to put it into effect, including making expenditures.

en banc: (on bonk) French for "in the bench," it signifies a decision by the full court of all the appeals judges in jurisdictions where there is more than one three- or four-judge panel. The larger number sit in judgment when the court feels there is a particularly significant issue at stake or when requested by one or both parties to the case and agreed to by the court.

enclosure (inclosure): n. land bounded by a fence, wall, hedge, ditch or other physical evidence of boundary. Unfortunately, too often these creations are not included among the actual legally described boundaries and cause legal problems.

encroach: v. to build a structure which is in whole or in part across the property line of another's real property. This may occur due to incorrect surveys, guesses or miscalculations by builders and/or owners when erecting a building. The solutions vary from giving the encroaching party an easement or lease (for a price, usually) for the lifetime of the building, or if the structure is small, actually moving it onto the owner's own property. (See: **encroachment**)

encroachment: n. the act of building a structure which is in whole or in part on a neighbor's property. (See: **encroach**)

encumbrance (incumbrance): n. a general term for any claim or lien on a parcel of real property. These include: mortgages, deeds of trust, recorded abstracts of judgment, unpaid real property taxes, tax liens, mechanic's liens, easements and water or timber rights. While the owner has title, any encumbrance is usually on record (with the County Recorder or Recorder of Deeds) and must be paid for at some point.

endorse (indorse): v. 1) to sign one's name to the back of a check, bill of exchange or other negotiable instrument with the intention of making it cashable or transferable. 2) to pledge support to a program, proposal or candidate. (See: **endorsement**)

endorsement (indorsement): n. 1) the act of the owner or payee signing his/her name to the back of a check, bill of exchange or other negotiable instrument so as to make it payable to another or cashable by any person. An endorsement may be made after a specific direction ("pay to Dolly Madison" or "for deposit only"), called a qualified endorsement, or with no qualifying language, thereby making it payable to the holder, called a blank endorsement. There are also other forms of endorsement which may give credit or restrict the use of the check. 2) the act of pledging or committing support to a program, proposal or candidate. (See: **negotiable instrument**)

endowment: n. the creation of a fund, often by gift or bequest from a dead person's estate, for the maintenance of a public institution, particularly a college, university or scholarship.

enjoin: v. for a court to order that someone either do a specific act, cease a course of conduct or be prohibited from committing a certain act. To obtain such an order, called an injunction, a private party or public agency has to file a petition for a writ of injunction, serve it on the party he/she/it hopes to be enjoined, allowing time for a written response. Then a court hearing is held in which the judge will consider evidence, both written and oral, listen to the arguments and then either grant the writ or deny it. If granted the court will issue a final or permanent injunction. A preliminary injunction or temporary injunction is an order made by the court while the matter is being processed and considered, based on the petition and any accompanying declarations, either of which is intended to keep matters in status quo (as they are) or prevent possible irreparable harm (like cutting trees, poisoning a stream or moving out of the country with a child or money) until a final decision is made. (See: **injunction, temporary injunction**)

enjoyment: n. 1) to exercise a right. 2) pleasure. 3) the use of funds or occupancy of property. Sometimes this is used in the phrase "quiet enjoyment" which means one is entitled to be free of noise or interference.

enter a judgment: v. to officially record a judgment on the "judgment roll," which entry is normally performed by the court clerk once the exact wording of the judgment has been prepared or approved and signed by the trial judge. All times for appeal and other post-judgment actions are based on the date of the entry of judgment and not the date when the judgment is announced. (See: **entry of judgment**)

entity: n. a general term for any institution, company, corporation, partnership, government agency, university or any other organization which is distinguished from individuals.

entrapment: n. in criminal law, the act of law enforcement officers or government agents inducing or encouraging a person to commit a crime when the potential criminal expresses a desire not to go ahead. The key to entrapment is whether the idea for the commission or encouragement of the criminal act originated with the police or government agents instead of with the "criminal." Entrapment, if proved, is a defense to a criminal prosecution. The accused often claims entrapment in so-called "stings" in which undercover agents buy or sell narcotics, prostitutes' services or arrange to purchase goods believed to be stolen. The factual question is: Would Johnny Begood have purchased the drugs if not pressed by the narc?

entry of judgment: n. the placement of a judgment on the official roll of judgments.

environmental impact report: n. a study of all the factors which a land development or construction project would have on the environment in the area, including population, traffic, schools, fire protection, endangered species, archeological artifacts and community beauty. Many states require such reports be submitted to local governments before the development or project can be approved, unless the governmental body finds there is no possible impact, which finding is called a "negative declaration." (See: **EIR, negative declaration**)

environmental law: n. a body of state and federal statutes intended to protect the environment, wildlife, land and beauty, prevent pollution or over-cutting of forests, save endangered species, conserve water, develop and follow general plans and prevent damaging practices. These laws often give individuals and groups the right to bring legal actions or seek court orders to enforce the protections or demand revisions of private and public activity which may have detrimental effects on the environment.

equal opportunity: 1) n. a right supposedly guaranteed by both federal and many state laws against any discrimination in employment, education, housing or credit rights due to a person's race, color, sex (or sometimes sexual orientation), religion, national origin, age or handicap. A person who believes he/she has not been granted equal opportunity or has been outright sexually harassed or discriminated against may bring a lawsuit under federal and most state laws, or file a complaint with the federal Equal Opportunity Employment Commission or a state equal opportunity agency. 2) adj. a term applied to employers, lenders and landlords, who advertise that they are "equal opportunity employers," subtly suggesting all others are not, even though they are required by law to be so. (See: **affirmative action**)

equal protection of the law: n. the right of all persons to have the same access to the law and courts and to be treated equally by the law and courts, both in procedures and in the substance of the law. It is akin to the right to due process of law, but in particular applies to equal treatment as an element of fundamental fairness. The most famous case on the subject is *Brown v. Board of Education of Topeka* (1954) in which Chief Justice Earl Warren, for a unanimous Supreme Court, ruled that "separate but equal" educational facilities for blacks were inherently unequal and unconstitutional since the segregated school system did not give all students equal rights under the law. It will also apply to other inequalities such as differentials in pay for the same work or unequal taxation. The principle is stated in the 14th Amendment to the Constitution: "No State shall...deny to any person within its jurisdiction the equal protection of the laws." (See: **due process of law**)

equitable: adj. 1) just, based on fairness and not legal technicalities. 2) refers to positive remedies (orders to do something, not money damages) employed by the courts to solve disputes or give relief. (See: **equity**)

equitable estoppel: n. where a court will not grant a judgment or other legal relief to a party who has not acted fairly; for example, by having made false representations or concealing material facts from the other party. This illustrates the legal maxim: "he who seeks equity, must do equity." Example: Larry Landlord rents space to Dora Dressmaker in his shopping center but falsely tells her a Sears store will be a tenant and will draw customers to the project. He does not tell her a new freeway is going to divert traffic from the center. When she fails to pay her rent due to lack of business, Landlord sues her for breach of lease. Dressmaker may claim he is equitably estopped. (See: **clean hands doctrine, estoppel**)

equitable lien: n. a lien on property imposed by a court in order to achieve fairness, particularly when someone has possession of property which he/she holds for another. (See: **constructive trust, equity, lien**)

equity: n. 1) a venerable group of rights and procedures to provide fairness, unhampered by the narrow strictures of the old common law or other technical requirements of the law. In essence courts do the fair thing by court orders such as correction of property lines, taking possession of assets, imposing a lien, dividing assets, or injunctive relief (ordering a person to do something) to prevent irreparable damage. The rules of equity arose in England where the strict limitations of common law would not solve all problems, so the King set up courts of chancery (equity) to provide remedies through the royal power. Most eastern states had courts of equity or chancery separate from courts of law, and others had parallel systems of law and equity with different procedural rules. Now most states combine law and equity and treat both under "one cause of action." 2) the net value of real property, determined by subtracting the amount of unpaid debts secured by (against) the property from the appraised value of the property. (See: **chancery, enjoin, equitable, injunction, writ**)

equity of redemption: n. the right of a mortgagor (person owing on a loan or debt against their real property), after commencement of foreclosure proceedings, to "cure" his/her default by making delinquent payments. The mortgagor also must pay all accumulated costs as well as the delinquency to keep the property. (See: **foreclosure, mortgage, redemption**)

equivalent: n., adj. equal in value, force or meaning.

ergo: (air-go) conj. Latin for "therefore,"

157

often used in legal writings. Its most famous use was in *Cogito, ergo sum*: "I think, therefore I am" principle by French philosopher Rene Descartes (1596-1650).

erroneous: adj. 1) in error, wrong. 2) not according to established law, particularly in a legal decision or court ruling.

error: n. a mistake by a judge in procedure or in substantive law, during a hearing, upon petitions or motions, denial of rights, during the conduct of a trial (either granting or denying objections), on approving or denying jury instructions, on a judgment not supported by facts or applicable law or any other step in the judicial process. If a majority of an appeals court finds an error or errors which affect the result, or a denial of fundamental rights such as due process, the higher court will reverse the lower court's error in whole or in part (the entire judgment or a part of it), and remand (send it back) with instructions to the lower court. Appeals courts often find errors which have no prejudicial effect on the rights of a party and are thus harmless error. (See: **harmless error, remand**)

errors and omissions: n. short hand for malpractice insurance which gives physicians, attorneys, architects, accountants and other professionals coverage for claims by patients and clients for alleged professional errors and omissions which amount to negligence.

escalator clause: n. a provision in a lease or other agreement in which rent, installment payments or alimony, for example, will increase from time to time when the cost of living index (or a similar gauge) goes up. Often there is a maximum amount of increase ("cap") and seldom is there a provision for reduction if the cost of living goes down or for deflation instead of inflation. (See: **cap**)

escape clause: n. a provision in a contract which allows one of the parties to be relieved from (get out of) any obligation if a certain event occurs.

escheat: n. from old French *eschete*, which meant "that which falls to one," the forfeit of all property (including bank accounts) to the state treasury if it appears certain that there are no heirs, descendants or named beneficiaries to take the property upon the death of the last known owner.

escrow: 1) n. a form of account held by an "escrow agent" (an individual, escrow company or title company) into which is deposited the documents and funds in a transfer of real property, including the money, a mortgage or deed of trust, an existing promissory note secured by the real property, escrow "instructions" from both parties, an accounting of the funds and other documents necessary to complete the transaction by a date ("closing") agreed to by the buyer and seller. When the funding is complete and the deed is clear, the escrow agent will then record the deed to the buyer and deliver funds to the seller. The escrow agent or officer is an independent holder and agent for both parties who receives a fee for his/her/its services. 2) n. originally escrow meant the deed held by the escrow agent. 3) n.

colloquially, the escrow agent is called an "escrow," while actually the escrow is the account and not a person. 4) v. to place the documents and funds in an escrow account, as in: "we will escrow the deal." (See: **escrow agent**)

escrow agent: n. a person or entity holding documents and funds in a transfer of real property, acting for both parties pursuant to instructions. Typically the agent is a person (commonly an attorney), escrow company or title company, depending on local practice. (See: **escrow**)

escrow instructions: n. the written instructions by buyer and seller of real estate given to a title company, escrow company or individual escrow in "closing" a real estate transaction. These instructions are generally prepared by the escrow holder and then approved by the parties and their agents. (See: closing, escrow, escrow company, title company)

espionage: n. the crime of spying on the federal government and/or transferring state secrets on behalf of a foreign country. The other country need not be an "enemy," so espionage may not be treason, which involves aiding an enemy. (See: **sedition, treason**)

esquire: n. a form of address showing that someone is an attorney, usually written Albert Pettifog, Esquire, or simply Esq. Originally in England an Esquire was a rank just above "gentleman" and below "knight." It became a title for barristers, sheriffs and judges.

estate: n. 1) all that one owns in real estate and other assets. 2) commonly, all the possessions of one who has died and are subject to probate (administration supervised by the court) and distribution to heirs and beneficiaries, all the possessions which a guardian manages for a ward (young person requiring protection and administration of affairs), or assets a conservator manages for a conservatee (a person whose physical or mental lack of competence requires administration of his/her affairs). 3) an alternative term for real property interest which is used in conjunction with another defining word, like "life estate," "estate for years," or "real estate." (See: **conservator, guardian, life estate, real estate, probate, will**)

estate by entirety: n. (See: **tenancy by the entirety**)

estate tax: n. generally a federal tax on the transfer of a dead person's assets to his heirs and beneficiaries. Although a transfer tax, it is based on the amount in the decedent's estate (including distribution from a trust at the death) and can include insurance proceeds. Currently such federal taxation applies to the amount of an estate above $600,000, or as much as double that amount if the estate is distributed to a spouse. Some states have an estate tax, more commonly called an inheritance tax.

estop: v. to halt, bar or prevent. (See: **estoppel**)

estoppel: n. a bar or impediment (obstruction) which precludes a person from asserting a fact or a right or prevents one from denying a fact. Such a hindrance is due to a person's actions, conduct, statements, admissions, failure to act or judgment against the person in an identical legal case. Estoppel includes being barred by false representation or concealment (equitable estoppel), failure to take legal action until the other party is prejudiced by the delay (estoppel by laches), and a court ruling against the party on the same matter in a different case (collateral estoppel). (See: **collateral estoppel, equitable estoppel, estop, laches**)

et al.: n. abbreviation for the Latin phrase *et alii* meaning "and others." This is commonly used in shortening the name of a case, as in *"Pat Murgatroyd v. Sally Sherman, et al."*

et seq.: (et seek) n. abbreviation for the Latin phrase *et sequentes* meaning "and the following." It is commonly used by lawyers to include numbered lists, pages or sections after the first number is stated, as in "the rules of the road are found in Vehicle Code Section 1204, *et seq.*"

Lawyer: one who is willing to go to court and spend your last cent to prove he's right.
—Evan Esar, Esar's Comic Dictionary

et ux.: *(et uhks)* n. abbreviation for the Latin words *et uxor* meaning "and wife." It is usually found in deeds, tax assessment rolls and other documents in the form "John Alden *et ux.*," to show that the wife as well as the husband own property. The connotation that somehow the wife is merely an adjunct to her husband, as well as the modern concepts of joint tenancy, tenancy in common, community property where applicable and equal rights of the sexes have combined to make the expression a chauvinistic anachronism.

evasion of tax: n. the intentional attempt to avoid paying taxes through fraudulent means, as distinguished from late payment, using legal "loopholes" or errors. (See: **estate tax, income tax**)

eviction: n. a generic word for the act of expelling (kicking out) someone from real property either by legal action (suit for unlawful detainer), a claim of superior (actual) title to the property, or actions which prevent the tenant from continuing in possession (constructive eviction). Most frequently eviction consists of ousting a tenant who has breached the terms of a lease or rental agreement by not paying rent or a tenant who has stayed (held over) after the term of the lease has expired or only had a month-to-month tenancy. (See: **adverse possession, constructive eviction, lease, unlawful detainer**)

evidence: n. every type of proof legally presented at trial (allowed by the judge) which is intended to convince the judge and/or jury of alleged facts material to the case. It can include oral testimony of witnesses, including experts on technical matters, documents, public records, objects, photographs and depositions (testimony under oath taken before trial). It also includes socalled "circumstantial evidence" which is intended to create belief by showing surrounding circumstances which logically lead to a conclusion of fact.

Comments and arguments by the attorneys, statements by the judge and answers to questions which the judge has ruled objectionable are not evidence. Charts, maps and models which are used to demonstrate or explain matters are not evidence themselves, but testimony based upon such items and marks on such material may be evidence. Evidence must survive objections of opposing attorneys that it is irrelevant, immaterial or violates rules against "hearsay" (statements by a party not in court), and/or other technicalities. (See: **circumstantial evidence, competency, demonstrative evidence, deposition, hearsay, material, object, objection, relevant**)

examination: n. 1) the questioning of a witness by an attorney. Direct examination is interrogation by the attorney who called the witness, and cross-examination is questioning by the opposing attorney. A principal difference is that an attorney putting questions to his own witness cannot ask "leading" questions, which put words in the mouth of the witness or suggest the answer, while on cross-examination he/she can pose a question that seems to contain an answer or suggest language for the witness to use or agree to. 2) in bankruptcy, the questions asked of a debtor by the judge, trustee in bankruptcy, attorneys or even creditors, to determine the state of the debtor's affairs. 3) in criminal law, a preliminary examination is a hearing before a judge or other magistrate to determine whether a defendant charged with a felony should be held for trial. Usu-

ally this is held by a lower court and if there is any substantial evidence to show a felony has been committed by the defendant he/she is bound over to the appropriate court for trial, but otherwise the charge will be dismissed by the judge. (See: **bankruptcy, cross-examination, direct examination, testimony, witness**)

exception: n. 1) a formal objection during trial ("We take exception, or simply, "exception")" to the ruling of a judge on any matter, including rulings on objections to evidence, to show to a higher court that the lawyer did not agree with the ruling. In modern practice, it is not necessary "to take exception" to a judge's adverse ruling, since it is now assumed that the attorney against whom the ruling is made objects. This also keeps the transcribed record from being cluttered with shouts of "exception." 2) in contracts, statutes or deeds, a statement that some matter is not included. (See: **exception in deed**)

exception in deed: n. a notation in a deed of title to real property which states that certain interests, such as easements, mineral rights or a life estate, are not included in the transfer (conveyance) of title.

excessive bail: n. an amount of bail ordered posted by an accused defendant which is much more than necessary or usual to assure he/she will make court appearances, particularly in relation to minor crimes. If excessive bail is claimed, the defendant can make a motion for reduction of bail, and if it is not granted, he/she can then apply directly to a court of appeal for reduction. (See: **bail**)

exchange: 1) v. to trade or barter property, goods and/or services for other property, goods and/or services, unlike a sale or employment in which money is paid for the property, goods or services. 2) n. the act of making a trade or barter. An exchange of "equivalent" property, including real estate, can defer capital gains taxation until the acquired property is sold. 3) n. short for "Starker" exchange of investment real property to defer capital gains tax. (See: **delayed exchange**)

excise: n. a tax upon manufacture, sale or for a business license or charter, as distinguished from a tax on real property, income or estates. Sometimes it is redundantly called an excise tax.

exclusionary rule: n. the rule that evidence secured by illegal means and in bad faith cannot be introduced in a criminal trial. The technical term is that it is "excluded" upon a motion to suppress made by the lawyer for the accused. It is based on the constitutional requirement that "...no [person] can be deprived of life, liberty, or property, without due process of law" (Fifth Amendment to the Constitution, applied to the states by 14th Amendment). A technical error in a search warrant made in good faith will not cause exclusion of the evidence obtained under that warrant. In 1995 the U. S. Supreme Court ruled that evidence obtained with a warrant that had been cancelled could be admitted if the law enforcement officer believed it was still in force. However, evidence which was uncovered as a result of obtaining other evidence illegally will be excluded, under the "fruit of the poisonous tree doctrine." Thus, if an illegal wire tap reveals the location of other evidence, both the transcript of the wire tap conversation and the evidence to which the listeners were directed will be excluded. (See: **due process of law, fruit of the poisonous tree, motion to suppress**)

exculpatory: adj. applied to evidence which may justify or excuse an accused defendant's actions and which will tend to show the defendant is not guilty or has no criminal intent.

excusable neglect: n. a legitimate excuse for the failure of a party or his/her lawyer to take required action (like filing an answer to a complaint) on time. This is usually claimed to set aside a default judgment for failure to answer (or otherwise respond) in the period set by law. Illness, press of business by the lawyer (but not necessarily the defendant), or an understandable oversight by the lawyer's staff ("just blame the secretary") are common excuses which the courts will often accept. However, if the defendant loses the complaint or fails to call his/her attorney the courts will be less lenient. In any event, the defendant must also show he/she had some worthwhile defense. (See: **default, default judgment**)

ex delicto: (ex dee-lick-toe) adj. Latin for a reference to something that arises out of a fault or wrong, but not out of contracts. Of only academic interest today, it identified actions which were civil wrongs (torts).

execute: v. 1) to finish, complete or

perform as required, as in fulfilling one's obligations under a contract or a court order. 2) to sign and otherwise complete a document, such as acknowledging the signature if required to make the document valid. 3) to seize property under court order. 4) to put to death pursuant to a sentence rendered by a court. (See: **capital punishment, contract, executed, execution**)

executed: 1) adj. to have been completed. (Example: "it is an executed contract") 2) v. to have completed or fully performed. (Example: "he executed all the promises made in the contract") 3) v. completed and formally signed a document, such as a deed, contract or lease. 4) v. to have been put to death for a crime pursuant to a death sentence. (See: **execute**)

execution: n. 1) the act of getting an officer of the court to take possession of the property of a losing party in a lawsuit (judgment debtor) on behalf of the winner (judgment creditor), sell it and use the proceeds to pay the judgment. The procedure is to take the judgment to the clerk of the court and have a writ of execution issued which is taken to the sheriff (or marshal, constable or other authorized official) with instructions on what property to execute upon. In the case of real property the official must first levy (place a lien on the title), and then execute upon it (seize it). However, the judgment debtor (loser in the lawsuit) may pay the judgment and costs before sale to redeem real estate. 2) carrying out a death sentence. (See: **death penalty, writ of execution**)

executive clemency: n. the power of a President in federal criminal cases, and the Governor in state convictions, to pardon a person convicted of a crime, commute the sentence (shorten it, often to time already served) or reduce it from death to another lesser sentence. There are many reasons for exercising this power, including real doubts about the guilt of the party, apparent excessive sentence, humanitarian reasons such as illness of an aged inmate, to clear the record of someone who has demonstrated rehabilitation or public service, or because the party is a political or personal friend of the Governor. (See: **commutation, pardon**)

executive order: n. a President's or Governor's declaration which has the force of law, usually based on existing statutory powers, and requiring no action by the Congress or state legislature.

executive privilege: n. a claim by the President or another high official of the executive branch that he/she need not answer a request (including a subpena issued by a court or Congress) for confidential government or personal communications, on the ground that such revelations would hamper effective governmental operations and decision-making. The rationale is that such a demand would violate the principle of separation of powers among the executive, legislative and judicial branches. If there is a potential criminal charge, executive privilege will be denied, as Richard Nixon discovered when he attempted to use executive privilege to deny Congress, the courts and the Department of Justice access to tapes and documents in the Watergate scandal (1973–1974).

executor: n. the person appointed to administer the estate of a person who has died leaving a will which nominates that person. Unless there is a valid objection, the judge will appoint the person named in the will to be executor. The executor must insure that the person's desires expressed in the will are carried out. Practical responsibilities include gathering up and protecting the assets of the estate, obtaining information in regard to all beneficiaries named in the will and any other potential heirs, collecting and arranging for payment of debts of the estate, approving or disapproving creditor's claims, making sure estate taxes are calculated, forms filed and tax payments made, and in all ways assisting the attorney for the estate (which the executor can select). (See: **deceased, decedent, executrix, probate, will**)

executory: adj. something not yet performed or done. Examples: an executory contract is one in which all or part of the required performance has not been done; an executory bequest is a gift under a will which has not been distributed to the beneficiary.

executory interest: n. an interest in property (particularly real estate) which will only pass to another in the future, or never, if certain events occur.

executrix: (pl. executrices) n. Latin for female executor. However, the

term executor is now unisex. (See: **executor**)

exemplary damages: n. often called punitive damages, these are damages requested and/or awarded in a lawsuit when the defendant's willful acts were malicious, violent, oppressive, fraudulent, wanton or grossly reckless. Examples of acts warranting exemplary damages: publishing that someone had committed murders when the publisher knew it was not true but hated the person; an ex-husband trashes his former wife's auto and threatens further property damage; a stockbroker buys and sells a widow's stocks to generate commissions resulting in her losing all her capital (money). These damages are awarded both as a punishment and to set a public example. They reward the plaintiff for the horrible nature of what she/he went through or suffered. Although often requested, exemplary damages are seldom awarded. There have been major awards in egregious (remarkable or outstanding) cases, such as fraud schemes, sexual harassment or other intentional and vicious actions even when the provable actual damages were not extensive. (See: **damages, punitive damages**)

exemption: n. 1) in income taxation, a credit given for each dependent, blindness or other disability, and age over 65, which result in a downward calculation in tax levels. These are not to be confused with deductions, which reduce gross income upon which taxes are paid. 2) a right to be excluded from, such as not being subject to attachment of one's wages if one is in a low-income bracket, or not being subject to the military draft if one is employed in essential industry, has several children or is a college student.

exhibit: n. 1) a document or object (including a photograph) introduced as evidence during a trial. These are subject to objections by opposing attorneys just like any evidence. 2) a copy of a paper attached to a pleading (any legal paper filed in a lawsuit), declaration, affidavit or other document, which is referred to and incorporated into the main document.

ex officio: (ex oh-fish-ee-oh) adj. Latin for "from the office," to describe someone who has a right because of an office held, such as being allowed to sit on a committee simply because one is president of the corporation.

ex parte: (ex par-tay, but popularly, ex party) adj. Latin meaning "for one party," referring to motions, hearings or orders granted on the request of and for the benefit of one party only. This is an exception to the basic rule of court procedure that both parties must be present at any argument before a judge, and to the otherwise strict rule that an attorney may not notify a judge without previously notifying the opposition. *Ex parte* matters are usually temporary orders (like a restraining order or temporary custody) pending a formal hearing or an emergency request for a continuance. Most jurisdictions require at least a diligent attempt to contact the other party's lawyer of the time and place of any *ex parte* hearing.

expectancy: n. a possibility of future enjoyment of something one counts on receiving, usually referring to real property or the estate of a deceased person, such as a remainder, reversion, or distribution after the death of someone who has use for life. (See: **distribution, remainder, reversion**)

expense: n. in business accounting and business taxation, any current cost of operation, such as rent, utilities and payroll, as distinguished from capital expenditure for long-term property and equipment. (See: **capital expenditure**)

expert testimony: n. opinions stated during trial or deposition (testimony under oath before trial) by a specialist qualified as an expert on a subject relevant to a lawsuit or a criminal case. (See: **expert witness**)

expert witness: n. a person who is a specialist in a subject, often technical, who may present his/her expert opinion without having been a witness to any occurrence relating to the lawsuit or criminal case. It is an exception to the rule against giving an opinion in trial, provided that the expert is qualified by evidence of his/her expertise, training and special knowledge. If the expertise is challenged, the attorney for the party calling the "expert" must make a showing of the necessary background through questions in court, and the trial judge has discretion to qualify the witness or rule he/she is not an expert, or is an expert on limited subjects. Experts are usually paid handsomely for their services and may be asked by the opposition the amount they are receiving for their work on the case. In most jurisdictions, both sides must exchange the names and addresses of proposed experts to allow pre-trial depositions. (See: **expert testimony**)

ex post facto: adj. Latin for "after the fact," which refers to laws adopted after an act is committed making it illegal although it was legal when done, or increasing the penalty for a crime after it is committed. Such laws are specifically prohibited by the U.S. Constitution, Article I, Section 9. Therefore, if a state legislature or Congress enacts new rules of proof or longer sentences, those new rules or sentences do not apply to crimes committed before the new law was adopted.

express: adj. direct, unambiguous, distinct language, particularly in a contract, which does not require thought, guessing, inference or implication to determine the meaning.

express contract: n. a contract in which all elements are specifically stated (offer, acceptance, consideration), and the terms are stated, as compared to an "implied" contract in which the existence of the contract is assumed by the circumstances. (See: **contract**)

expropriation: n. a taking of property or rights by governmental authority such as eminent domain, possibly including an emergency situation, such as taking a person's truck or bulldozer to build a levee during a flood. In such a case just compensation eventually must be paid to the owner, who can make a claim against the taker. (See: **eminent domain**)

ex rel.: conj. abbreviation for Latin *ex relatione*, meaning "upon being related" or "upon information," used in the title of a legal proceeding filed by a state Attorney General (or the federal Department of Justice) on behalf of the government, on the instigation of a private person, who needs the state to enforce the rights of himself/herself and the public. For example, the caption would read: *The State of Tennessee ex rel. Archie Johnson v. Hardy Products*.

extension: n. granting of a specific amount of extra time to make a payment, file a legal document after the date due or continue a lease after the original expiration of the term.

extenuating circumstances: n. surrounding factors (sometimes called mitigation) which make a crime appear less serious, less aggravated or without criminal intent, and thus warranting a more lenient punishment or lesser charge (manslaughter rather than murder, for example). (See: **mitigating circumstances**)

extinguishment: n. the cancellation or destruction of a right, quite often because the time for enforcement has passed. Example: waiting more than four years after the due date to make a demand for payment on a promissory note wipes out the person's right to collect the money owed to him/her. It can also occur by fulfilling the obligation so no further money or performance is due.

extortion: n. obtaining money or property by threat to a victim's property or loved ones, intimidation, or false claim of a right (such as pretending to be an IRS agent). It is a felony in all states, except that a direct threat to harm the victim is usually treated as the crime of robbery. Blackmail is a form of extortion in which the threat is to expose embarrassing, damaging information to family, friends or the public. (See: **blackmail, robbery, theft**)

extradition: n. the surrender by one state or country of a person charged with a crime in another state or country. Formally, the request of the state (usually through the Governor's office) claiming the right to prosecute is made to the Governor of the state in which the accused is present. Occasionally a Governor will refuse to extradite (send the person back) if he/she is satisfied that the prosecution is not warranted, despite a constitutional mandate that "on demand of the Executive authority of the State from which [a fugitive from justice] fled, be delivered up, to be removed to the State having jurisdiction of the crime." The defendant may "waive extradition" and allow himself/herself to be taken into custody and returned to the state where charges are pending.

International extradition is more difficult and is governed in many cases by treaty. While most countries will extradite persons charged with serious crimes, some will not, others refuse to extradite for certain crimes, set up legal roadblocks, or, as in Canada's case, will not extradite if the accused may get the death penalty. (See: **fugitive from justice**)

extrajudicial: adj. referring to ac-

tions outside the judicial (court) system, such as an extralegal confession, which, if brought in as evidence, may be recognized by the judge during a trial.

extraordinary fees: n. attorneys' fees claimed, usually in the administration of a dead person's estate, for work beyond the normal, including filing collection suits, preparing tax returns or requiring unusual effort beneficial to the estate. This claim is in addition to the usual statutory or court-approved legal fees. The attorney must submit proof of time, effort and benefit to justify the claim, and the final determination is at the judge's discretion. (See: **attorney's fee, probate**)

extreme cruelty: n. an archaic requirement to show infliction of physical or mental harm by one of the parties to his/her spouse to support a judgment of divorce or an unequal division of the couple's property. All states except Illinois and South Dakota recognize "no fault" divorces, but in some states evidence of cruelty may result in division of property favoring the suffering spouse (victim).

*A man's home is his castle.
—Sir Edward Coke, Comments on Littleton*

extrinsic fraud: n. fraudulent acts which keep a person from obtaining information about his/her rights to enforce a contract or getting evidence to defend against a lawsuit. This could include destroying evidence or misleading an ignorant person about the right to sue. Extrinsic fraud is distinguished from "intrinsic fraud," which is the fraud that is the subject of a lawsuit. (See: **fraud, intrinsic fraud**)

eyewitness: n. a person who has actually seen an event and can so testify in court.

face amount: n. the original amount due on a promissory note or insurance policy as stated therein, without calculating interest.

face value: n. in shares of stock, the original cost of the stock shown on the certificate, or "par value."

fact: n. an actual thing or happening, which must be proved at trial by presentation of evidence and which is evaluated by the finder of fact (a jury in a jury trial, or by the judge if he/she sits without a jury).

fact finder (finder of fact): n. in a trial of a lawsuit or criminal prosecution, the jury or judge (if there is no jury) who decides if facts have been proven. Occasionally a judge may appoint a "special master" to investigate and report on the existence of certain facts. (See: **question of fact**)

factor: n. 1) a salesman who sells in his/her own name on behalf of others, taking a commission for services. 2) something that contributes to the result.

failure of consideration: n. not delivering goods or services when promised in a contract. When goods a party had bargained for have become damaged or worthless, failure of consideration (to deliver promised goods) makes the expectant recipient justified to withhold payment, demand performance or take legal action. (See: **consideration, contract**)

failure of issue: n. when someone dies leaving no children or other direct descendants.

fair comment: n. a statement of opinion (no matter how ludicrous) based on facts which are correctly stated and which does not allege dishonorable motives on the part of the target of the comment. The U.S. Supreme Court has ruled that to protect free speech, statements made about a public person (politician, officeholder, movie star, author, etc.), even though untrue and harmful, are fair comment unless the victim can prove the opinions were stated maliciously—with hate, dislike, intent and/or desire to harm. Thus, a public figure may not sue for defamation based on published opinions or alleged information which would be the basis of a lawsuit if said or published about a private person not worthy of opinion or comment. This is a crucial defense against libel suits put up by members of the media. (See: **defamation, libel, public figure, slander**)

fair market value: n. the amount for which property would sell on the open market if put up for sale. This is distinguished from "replacement value," which is the cost of duplicating the property. Real estate appraisers will use "comparable" sales of similar property in the area to determine market value, adding or deducting amounts based on differences in quality and size of the property. (See: **appraise, appraiser, market value**)

fair trade laws: n. state laws which permit manufacturers or producers to set minimum rates for resale of the product. They have been repealed or found violative of state constitutions in many states.

fair use: n. the non-competitive right to use of copyrighted material without giving the author the right to compensation or to sue for infringement of copyright. With the growing use of copy machines, teachers and businesses copy articles, pages of texts, charts and excerpts for classroom use, advice to employees or to assist in research without violating the copyright. For example, Professor Elmer Smedley makes 100 copies of a photograph from *Time* magazine of starving Somalians to illustrate to his students the deprivations in Africa (which is fair use), but then Smedley publishes a book *Africa on the Brink*, and uses the photograph in a chapter on starvation (not fair use), and is responsible to the photographer for a royalty. (See: **copyright**)

false arrest: n. physically detaining someone without the legal right to do so. Quite often this involves private security people or other owners or employees of retail establishments who hold someone without having seen a crime committed in their presence or pretend that they are police officers. While they may be entitled to make a "citizen's arrest" they had better be sure that they have a person who has committed a crime, and they must call law enforcement officers to take over at the first opportunity. Other common false arrest situations include an arrest by a police officer of the wrong person or without probable cause to believe a crime has been committed and/or without a warrant. Only when the arresting party knowingly holds someone who has not committed a crime, is the false arrest itself a crime. However, probable false arrest can be the basis of a lawsuit for damages, including mental distress and embarrassment. (See: **false imprisonment**)

false imprisonment: n. depriving someone of freedom of movement by holding a person in a confined space or by physical restraint including being locked in a car, driven about without opportunity to get out, being tied to a chair or locked in a closet. It may be the follow-up to a false arrest (holding someone in the office of a department store, for example), but more often it resembles a kidnapping with no belief or claim of a legal right to hold the person. Therefore, false imprisonment is often a crime and if proved is almost always the basis of a lawsuit for damages. (See: **false arrest**)

false pretenses: n. the crime of knowingly making untrue statements for the purpose of obtaining money or property fraudulently. This can range from claiming zircons are diamonds and turning back the odometer on a car, to falsely stating that a mine has been producing gold when it has not. It is one form of theft. (See: **fraud, theft**)

family: n. 1) husband, wife and children. 2) all blood relations. 3) all who live in the same household including servants and relatives, with some person or persons directing this economic and social unit.

> *We come now to analyze a law. In the first place, it is declaratory; in the second it is directory; in the third, it is remedial; and in the fourth, it is vindicatory.*
> —*Gilbert Abbott A Beckett, The Comic Blackstone*

family purpose doctrine: n. a rule of law that the registered owner of an automobile is responsible for damages to anyone injured when the auto is driven by a member of the family with or without the owner's permission. The theory of this liability is that the vehicle is owned for family purposes. This doctrine is the law in some states instead of making a registered owner liable for damages caused by anyone driving his/her car with permission.

federal courts: n. the court system which handles civil and criminal cases based on jurisdictions enumerated in the Constitution and federal statutes. They include federal district courts which are trial courts, district courts of appeals and the U.S. Supreme Court, as well as specialized courts such as bankruptcy, tax, claims (against the government) and veterans' appeals. (See: **bankruptcy, appendix on courts**)

federal question: n. one basis for filing a lawsuit in federal district court is that it is based on subjects enumerated in the U.S. Constitution or when a federal statute is involved. Thus, existence of such a federal question gives the federal court jurisdiction.

Federal Tort Claims Act: n. a statute (1948) which removed the power of the federal government to claim immunity from a lawsuit for damages due to negligent or intentional injury by a federal employee in the scope of his/her work for the government. It also established a set of regulations and format for making claims, giving jurisdiction to federal district courts.

fee: n. 1) absolute title in land, from old French, *fief*, for "payment," since lands were originally given by lords to those who served them. It often appears in deeds which transfer title as "Mary Jo Rock grants to Howard Takitall in fee..." or similar phrasing. The word "fee" can be modified to show that the title was "conditional" on some occurrence or could be terminated ("determinable") upon a future event. 2) a charge for services. (See: **attorney's fee, fee simple**)

fee simple: n. absolute title to land, free of any other claims against the title, which one can sell or pass to another by will or inheritance. This is a redundant form of "fee," but is used to show the fee (absolute title) is not a "conditional fee," or "determinable fee," or "fee tail." Like "fee" it is often used in deeds transferring title, as in "Harry Hadit grants to Robert Gotit title in fee simple..." or similar words. (See: **fee**)

fee tail: n. an old feudal expression for a title to real property which can only be passed to one's heirs "of his body" or certain heirs who are blood relatives. If the blood line ran out (no children) then the title would revert to the descendants of the lord who originally gave the land to the title-holding family. Thus, it could not be transferred to anyone outside the family. The intention was to keep lands within a family line and not subdivided. In 16th century England, trusts were established to get around this "restraint on alienation" so the land could be held in trust for another person to use. Fee tail is of historic and academic interest only. (See: **fee, fee simple, uses**)

felon: n. a person who has been convicted of a felony, which is a crime punishable by death or a term in state or federal prison. (See: **felony**)

felonious: adj. referring to an act done with criminal intent. The term is used to distinguish between a wrong which was not malicious, and an intentional crime, as in "felonious assault," which is an attack meant to do real harm.

felony: n. 1) a crime sufficiently serious to be punishable by death or a term in state or federal prison, as distinguished from a misdemeanor which is only punishable by confinement to county or local jail and/or a fine. 2) a crime carrying a minimum term of one year or more in state prison, since a year or less can be served in county jail. However, a sentence upon conviction for a felony may sometimes be less than one year at the discretion of the judge and within limits set by statute. Felonies are sometimes referred to as "high crimes" as described in the U.S. Constitution. (See: **misdemeanor, sentence**)

felony murder doctrine: n. a rule of criminal statutes that any death which occurs during the commission of a felony is first degree murder, and all participants in that felony or attempted felony can be charged with and found guilty of murder. A typical example is a robbery involving more than one criminal, in which one of them shoots, beats to death or runs over a store clerk, killing the clerk. Even if the death were accidental, all of the participants can be found guilty of felony murder, including those who did no harm, had no gun, and/or did not intend to hurt anyone. In a bizarre situation, if one of the holdup men or women is killed, his/her fellow robbers can be charged with murder. (See: **murder**)

fertile octogenarian: n. an unrealistic notion that any person (male or female) is capable of having a child no matter at what age, infirmity or physical deficiency. Thus, if property title could not pass to one's child as long as he or she might have or acquire a sibling, then he/she must wait until mother and dad have actually died, unnecessarily tying up the property. Most states have passed laws to cure this anomaly.

fictitious defendants: n. when a party suing (plaintiff) is not sure if he/she knows if there are unknown persons involved in the incident or the business being sued, there are named fictitious persons, usually designated Doe I, Doe II, and so forth, or "Green and Red Company," with an allegation in the complaint that if and when the true names are discovered they will be inserted in the complaint by amendment. Naming fictitious defendants stops the statute of limitations (the time in which a party has to file a lawsuit) from running out even though the true name is not yet known. Sometimes during the investigation or discovery (taking depositions or asking written questions under oath) new information about a potential defendant is found and the real name substituted. Then that person is served with a summons and complaint. If no substitution of a real name for a Doe has been made by the time of trial, usually the fictitious defendants are then dismissed from the case since they never existed in the first place, and the case continues against the named defendants. Fictitious defendants are not permitted in federal cases.

> *Death and taxes are inevitable, but death does not get worse every time Congress meets.*
> *—Anonymous*

fiduciary: 1) n. from the Latin *fiducia*, meaning "trust," a person (or a business like a bank or stock brokerage) who has the power and obligation to act for another (often called the beneficiary) under circumstances which require total trust, good faith and honesty. The most common is a trustee of a trust, but fiduciaries can include business advisers, attorneys, guardians, administrators of estates, real estate agents, bankers, stockbrokers, title companies or anyone who undertakes to assist someone who places complete confidence and trust in that person or company. Characteristically, the fiduciary has greater knowledge and expertise about the matters being handled. A fiduciary is held to a standard of conduct and trust above that of a stranger or of a casual business person. He/she/it must avoid "self-dealing" or "conflicts of interests" in which the potential benefit to the fiduciary is in conflict with what is best for the person who trusts him/her/it. For example, a stockbroker must consider the best investment for the client and not buy or sell on the basis of what brings him/her the highest commission. While a fiduciary and the beneficiary may join together in a business venture or a purchase of property, the best interest of the beneficiary must be primary, and absolute candor is required of the fiduciary. 2) adj. defining a situation or relationship in which a person is acting as a fiduciary for another. (See: **confidential relation, fiduciary relationship, trust**)

fiduciary relationship: n. where one person places complete confidence in another in regard to a particular transaction or one's general affairs or business. The relationship is not necessarily formally or legally established as in a declaration of trust, but can be one of moral or personal responsibility, due to the superior knowledge and training of the fiduciary as compared to the one whose affairs the fiduciary is handling. (See: **fiduciary, trust**)

fighting words: n. words intentionally directed toward another person which are so nasty and full of malice as to cause the hearer to suffer emotional distress or incite him/her to immediately retaliate physically (hit, stab, shoot, etc.). While such words are not an excuse or defense for a retaliatory assault and battery, if they are threatening they can form the basis for a lawsuit for assault.

file: 1) v. to deposit with the clerk of the court a written complaint or petition which is the opening step in a lawsuit and subsequent documents, including an answer, demurrer, motions, petitions and orders. All of these are placed in a case file which has a specific number assigned to it which must be stated on every document. The term is used: "When are you going to file the complaint," or "The answer will be filed tomorrow." 2) n. the master folder of a lawsuit kept by the clerk of the court, including all legal pleadings (documents) filed by both sides. Each document in the file must have a stamp showing the date it was received and the name of the clerk who received it. Any document which is filed must be served on the opposing attorney, usually by mail, except that the first paper filed (summons complaint, petition, motion) must be served on all defendants personally (hand delivered by a process server). 3) n. the record an attorney keeps on a case, containing all papers deposited with the clerk, as well as all correspondence and notes on the case.

final decree: n. another name for a final judgment. In states where there are interlocutory decrees of divorce (in the hope that a further wait may lead to reconciliation), followed several months later by the actual divorce, the second order is called a final decree, issued after the filing of a declaration that the couple is still asunder (can not get back together). (See: **final judgment**)

final judgment: n. the written determination of a lawsuit by the judge who presided at trial (or heard a successful motion to dismiss or a stipulation for judgment), which renders (makes) rulings on all issues and completes the case unless it is appealed to a higher court. It is also called a final decree or final decision. (See: **final decree, interlocutory decree**)

final settlement: n. an agreement reached by the parties to a lawsuit, usually in writing and/or read into the record in court, settling all issues. Usually there are elements of compromise, waiver of any right to reopen or appeal the matter even if there is information found later which would change matters (such as recurrence of a problem with an injury), mutual release of any further claim by each party, a statement that neither side is admitting fault, and some action or payment by one or both sides. In short, the case is over, provided the parties do what they are supposed to do according to the final settlement's terms. With the glut of cases crowding court calendars and overwhelming the system and delays in getting to trial (due to three factors: increased criminal case load, increased litigious nature of society and an insufficient number of judges), judges encourage attempts to settle, including mandatory settlement conferences with judges or experienced settlement attorneys present. (See: **settlement**)

finding: n. the determination of a factual question vital (contributing) to a decision in a case by the trier of fact (jury or judge sitting without a jury) after a trial of a lawsuit, often referred to as findings of fact. A finding of fact is distinguished from a conclusion of law which is determined by the judge as the sole legal expert. Findings of fact and conclusions of law, need not be made if waived or not requested by the trial attorneys, leaving just the bare judgment in the case. (See: **conclusion of law**)

findings of fact: n. (See: **finding**)

firm offer: n. in contract law, an offer (usually in writing) which states it may not be withdrawn, revoked or amended for a specific period of time. If the offer is accepted without a change during that period, there is a firm, enforceable contract. (See: **acceptance, contract, counter offer, offer**)

first degree murder: n. although it varies from state to state, it is generally a killing which is deliberate and premeditated (planned, after lying in wait, by poison or as part of a scheme), in conjunction with felonies such as rape, burglary, arson, or involving multiple deaths, the killing of certain types of people (such as a child, a police officer, a prison guard, a fellow prisoner), or certain weapons, particularly a gun. The specific criteria for first degree murder, are established by statute in each state and by the U.S. Code in federal prosecutions. It is distinguished from second degree murder in which premeditation is usually absent, and from manslaughter, which lacks premeditation and suggests that at most there was intent to harm rather than to kill. (See: **felony murder doctrine, manslaughter, murder, second degree murder**)

first impression: adj. referring to a legal issue which has never been decided by an appeals court and, therefore, there is no precedent for the court to follow. To reach a decision the court must use its own logic, analogies from prior rulings by appeals courts and refer to commentaries and articles by legal scholars. In such cases the trial judge usually asks for legal briefs by attorneys for both sides to assist him/her.

fixture: n. a piece of equipment which has been attached to real estate in such a way as to be part of the premises and its removal would do harm to the building or land. Thus, a fixture is transformed from a movable asset to an integral part of the real property. Essentially a question of fact, it often arises when a tenant has installed a lighting fixture, a heater, window box or other item which is bolted, nailed, screwed or wired into the wall, ceiling or floor. Trade fixtures are those which a merchant would normally use to operate the business and display goods and may be removed at the merchant's expense for any necessary repair. (See: **trade fixture**)

flight: n. running away or hiding by a person officially accused of a crime with the apparent intent of avoiding arrest or prosecution.

floating easement: n. an easement (a right to use another's property for a particular purpose) which allows access and/or egress but does not spell out the exact dimensions and location of the easement. (See: **easement**)

FOB: 1) adj. short for free on board, meaning shipped to a specific place without cost. 2) Friend of Bill (Clinton). (See: **free on board**)

forbearance: n. an intentional delay in collecting a debt or demanding performance on a contract, usually for a specific period of time. Forbearance is often consideration for a promise by the debtor to pay an added amount.

forced sale: n. a sale of goods seized by the sheriff to satisfy (pay) a judgment. (See: **execution**)

forcible entry: n. the crime of taking possession of a house or other structure or land by the use of physical force or serious threats against the occupants. This can include breaking windows or doors or using terror to gain entry, as well as forcing the occupants out by threat or violence after having come in peacefully.

foreclosure: n. the system by which a party who has loaned money secured by a mortgage or deed of trust on real property (or has an unpaid judgment), requires sale of the real property to recover the money due, unpaid interest, plus the costs of foreclosure, when the debtor fails to make payment. After the payments on the promissory note (which is evidence of the loan) have become delinquent for several months (time varies from state to state), the lender can have a notice of default served on the debtor (borrower) stating the amount due and the amount necessary to "cure" the default. If the delinquency and costs of foreclosure are not paid within a specified period, then the lender (or the trustee in states using deeds of trust) will set a foreclosure date, after which the property may be sold at public sale. Up to the time of foreclosure (or even afterwards in some states) the defaulting borrower can pay all delinquencies and costs (which are then greater due to foreclosure costs) and "redeem" the property. Upon sale of the property the amount due is paid to the creditor (lender or owner of the judgment) and the remainder of the money received from the sale, if any, is paid to the lender. There is also judicial foreclosure in which the lender can bring suit for foreclosure against the defaulting borrower for the delinquency and force a sale. This is used in several states with the mortgage system or in deed of trust states when it appears that the amount due is greater than the equity value of the real property, and the lender wishes to get a deficiency judgment for the amount still due after sale. This is not necessary in those states which give deficiency judgments without filing a lawsuit when the foreclosure is upon the mortgage or deed of trust. (See: **deed of trust, execution, forced sale, mortgage, notice of default**)

foreclosure sale: n. the actual forced sale of real property at a public auction (often on the courthouse steps following public notice posted at the courthouse and published in a local newspaper) after foreclosure on that property as security under a mortgage or deed of trust for a loan that is substantially delinquent. The lender who has not been paid may bid for the property, using his/her/its own unpaid note toward payment, which can result in a bargain purchase. (See: **deed of trust, execution, forced sale, foreclosure, judicial sale, mortgage, sheriff's sale**)

> *A government of laws and not of men.*
> *—Constitution of the Commonwealth of Massachusetts, written by John Adams*

foreign corporation: n. a corporation which is incorporated under the laws of a different state or nation. A "foreign" corporation must file a notice of doing business in any state in which it does substantial regular business. It must name an "agent for acceptance of service" in that state, or the Secretary of State in some jurisdictions will automatically be that agent so people doing business with a foreign corporation will be able to bring legal actions locally if necessary. Example: the Whoopee Widget Corporation is incorporated in Delaware. It has a sales office in Arizona, which does not make a guaranteed refund to Jack Jones of Arizona. Jones can sue Whoopee in Arizona and serve the Arizona Secretary of State or Whoopee's designated agent.

forensic: 1) adj. from Latin *forensis* for "belonging to the forum," ancient Rome's site for public debate and currently meaning pertaining to the courts. Thus, forensic testimony or forensic medicine are used to assist the court or the attorneys in legal matters, including trials.

forensics: n. public speaking or argumentation.

forensic medicine: n. research, reports and testimony in court by experts in medical science to assist in determining a legal question. Cause of death is a common issue determined by pathologists who may be coroners or medical examiners. (See: **forensic**)

forensic testimony: n. any testimony of expert scientific, engineering, economic or other specialized nature used to assist the court and the lawyers in a lawsuit or prosecution. (See: **forensic, forensic medicine**)

foreseeable risk: n. a danger which a reasonable person should anticipate as the result from his/her actions. Foreseeable risk is a common affirmative defense put up as a response by defendants in lawsuits for negligence. A skier hits a bump on a ski run, falls and breaks his leg. This is a foreseeable risk of skiing. A mother is severely injured while accompanying her child on a roller coaster when the car jumps the track and comes loose. While there is potential risk, she had the right to anticipate that the roller coaster was properly maintained and did not assume the risk that it would come apart. Signs that warn "use at your own risk" do not bar lawsuits for risks that are not foreseeable. (See: **affirmative defenses, foreseeability**)

foreseeability: n. reasonable anticipation of the possible results of an action, such as what may happen if one is negligent or consequential damages resulting from breach of a contract. (See: **foreseeable risk, negligence**)

forfeit: v. to lose property or rights involuntarily as a penalty for violation of law. Example: the government can take automobiles or houses which are used for illegal drug trafficking or manufacture. A drug pusher may forfeit his/her car (property) if caught carrying drugs in it and found guilty. A parent may have to forfeit his/her house if his/her daughter is selling drugs from the house, even though the parent had nothing to do with and no knowledge of the drugs. One may have to forfeit one's driver's license or lose driving privileges due to multiple traffic violations or drunk driving. (See: **forfeiture**)

forfeiture: n. loss of property due to a violation of law. (See: **forfeit**)

forger: n. a person who commits the crime of forgery, by making false documents or signatures. (See: **forgery**)

forgery: n. 1) the crime of creating a false document, altering a document, or writing a false signature for the illegal benefit of the person making the forgery. This includes improperly filling in a blank document, like an automobile purchase contract, over a buyer's signature, with the terms different from those agreed. It does not include such innocent representation as a staff member autographing photos of politicians or movie stars. While similar to forgery, counterfeiting refers to the creation of phoney money, stock certificates or bonds which are negotiable for cash. 2) a document or signature falsely created or altered. (See: **counterfeit, forger, fraud**)

fornication: n. sexual intercourse between a man and woman who are not married to each other. This usage comes from Latin *fornicari*, meaning vaulted, which became the nickname for brothel, because prostitutes operated in a vaulted underground cavern in Rome. Fornication is still a misdemeanor in some states, as is adultery (sexual intercourse by a married person with someone not his/her spouse), but is virtually never prosecuted. If such anachronistic laws were enforced, the jails of America would have no room for robbers, murderers and drug dealers.

forthwith: adv. a term found in contracts, court orders and statutes, meaning as soon as it can be reasonably done. It implies immediacy, with no excuses for delay.

forum: n. a court which has jurisdiction to hold a trial of a particular lawsuit or petition.

forum non conveniens: (for-uhm nahn cahn-vee-nee-ehns) n. Latin for a forum which is not convenient. This doctrine is employed when the court chosen by the plaintiff (the party suing) is inconvenient for witnesses or poses an undue hardship on the defendants, who must petition the court for an order transferring the case to a more convenient court. A typical example is a lawsuit arising from an accident involving an out-of-state resident who files the complaint in his/her home state (or in the defendant driver's home state), when the witnesses and doctors who treated the plaintiff are in the state where the accident occurred, which makes the latter state the most convenient location for trial.

for value received: prep. a phrase used in a promissory note, a bill of exchange or a deed to show that some consideration (value) has been given without stating what that payment was.

foster child: n. a child without parental support and protection, placed with a person or family to be cared for, usually by local welfare services or by court order. The foster parent(s) do not have custody, nor is there an adoption, but they are expected to treat the foster child as they would their own in regard to food, housing, clothing and education. Most foster parents are paid by the local government or a state agency.

four corners of an instrument: n. the term for studying an entire document to understand its meaning, without reference to anything outside of the document ("extrinsic evidence"), such as the circumstances surrounding its writing or the history of the party signing it. If possible a document should be construed based on what lies within its four corners, unless such examination cannot solve an ambiguity in its language.

franchise: 1) n. a right granted by the government to a person or corporation, such as a taxi permit, bus route, an airline's use of a public airport, business license or corporate existence. 2) n. the right to vote in a public election. 3) v. to grant (for a periodic fee or share of profits) the right to operate a business or sell goods or services under a brand or chain name. Well-known franchise operations include McDonald's, Holiday Inns, Ace Hardware, Rexall Drug Stores, and Amway Distributors. 4) n. the right one has to operate a store or sell goods or services under a franchise agreement, as in "we have the Taco Bell franchise in our town." 5) adj. referring to a "franchise tax" which is placed on businesses (especially corporations) for the right to conduct business, as distinguished from a tax on property, income or profits tax.

> *Laws too gentle are seldom obeyed; too severe, seldom executed.*
> *—Benjamin Franklin*

franchise tax: n. a state tax on corporations or businesses. (See: **corporation, tax**)

fraud: n. the intentional use of deceit, a trick or some dishonest means to deprive another of his/her/its money, property or a legal right. A party who has lost something due to fraud is entitled to file a lawsuit for damages against the party acting fraudulently, and the damages may include punitive damages as a punishment or public example due to the malicious nature of the fraud. Quite often there are several persons involved in a scheme to commit fraud and each and all may be liable for the total damages. Inherent in fraud is an unjust advantage over another which injures that person or entity. It includes failing to point out a known mistake in a contract or other writing (such as a deed), or not revealing a fact which he/she has a duty to communicate, such as a survey which shows there are only 10 acres of land being purchased and not 20 as originally understood. Constructive fraud can be proved by a showing of breach of legal duty (like using the trust funds held for another in an investment in one's own business) without direct proof of fraud or fraudulent intent. Extrinsic fraud occurs when deceit is employed to keep someone from exercising a right, such as a fair trial, by hiding evidence or misleading the opposing party in a lawsuit. Since fraud is intended to employ dishonesty to deprive another of money, property or a right, it can also be a crime for which the fraudulent person(s) can be charged, tried and convicted. Borderline overreaching or taking advantage of another's naiveté involving smaller amounts is often overlooked by law enforcement, which suggests the victim seek a "civil remedy" (i.e., sue). However, increasingly fraud, which has victimized a large segment of the public (even in individually small amounts), has become the target of consumer fraud divisions in the offices of district attorneys and attorneys general. (See: **constructive fraud, exemplary damages, extrinsic fraud, fraud in the inducement, fraudulent conveyance, intrinsic fraud**)

fraud in the inducement: n. the use of deceit or trick to cause someone to act to his/her disadvantage, such as signing an agreement or deeding away real property. The heart of this type of fraud is misleading the other party as to the facts upon which he/she will base his/her decision to act. Example: "there will be tax advantages to you if you let me take title to your property," or "you don't have to read the rest of the contract—it is just routine legal language" but actually includes a balloon payment. (See: **extrinsic fraud, fraud**)

fraudulent conveyance: n. the transfer (conveyance) of title to real property for the express purpose of putting it beyond the reach of a known creditor. In such a case the creditor may bring a lawsuit to void the transfer. However, if the transfer was made without knowledge of the claim (or before a debt has matured), for other legitimate reasons, and/or in the normal course of business, then the creditor's attempt to obtain a judgment setting aside the conveyance will probably fail.

free and clear: adj. referring to the ownership of real property upon which there is no lien, encumbrance, recorded judgment or the right of anyone to make a claim against the property. The term is used in contracts for sale of real property and deeds, to state that the title has no claim against it.

freehold: n. any interest in real property which is a life estate or of uncertain or undetermined duration (having no stated end), as distinguished from a leasehold which may have declining value toward the end of a long-term lease (such as the 99-year variety). (See: **leasehold**)

free on board (FOB): adj. referring to purchased goods shipped without transportation charge to a specific place. Free on board at the place of manufacture shows there is a charge for delivery. Example: if an automaker in Detroit sells a car "FOB Detroit," then there will be a shipping charge if delivery is taken anywhere else. If the contract reads "FOB New Orleans," then the auto will be shipped to that city without charge, but with charge for delivery from New Orleans to somewhere else. (See: **FOB**)

fresh pursuit: n. immediate chase of a suspected criminal by a law enforcement officer, in which situation the officer may arrest the suspect without a warrant. It can also refer to chasing a suspect or escaped felon into a neighboring jurisdiction in an emergency, as distinguished from entering another jurisdiction with time to alert law enforcement people in that area. Example: when a deputy sheriff from Montgomery County pursues a car driven by a suspected bank robber into Baltimore County (in which he normally has no power to enforce the law), the doctrine of fresh pursuit allows him/her to make the arrest. It is also called hot pursuit. (See: **hot pursuit**)

friendly suit: n. a lawsuit filed in order to obtain a court order when the parties to the suit agree on the expected outcome. Such a legal action will be dismissed if it is an attempt to get an advisory opinion, is collusive (deceitfully planned) to get a judgment to set a legal precedent or where there is no real controversy. However, such suits are allowed in situations in which the statutes require a court ruling to achieve a "reasonable result," such as reform-

ing (correcting) a trust or agreement in which there was an error.

frisk: v. quickly patting down the clothes of a possible criminal suspect to determine if there is a concealed weapon. This police action is generally considered legal (constitutional) without a search warrant. Generally it is preferred that women officers frisk women and men officers frisk men.

frivolous: adj. referring to a legal move in a lawsuit clearly intended merely to harass, delay or embarrass the opposition. Frivolous acts can include filing the lawsuit itself, a baseless motion for a legal ruling, an answer of a defendant to a complaint which does not deny, contest, prove or controvert anything, or an appeal which contains not a single arguable basis (by any stretch of the imagination) for the appeal. A frivolous lawsuit, motion or appeal can result in a successful claim by the other party for payment by the frivolous suer of their attorneys' fees for defending the case. Judges are reluctant to find an action frivolous, based on the desire not to discourage people from using the courts to resolve disputes.

fruit of the poisonous tree: n. in criminal law, the doctrine that evidence discovered due to information found through illegal search or other unconstitutional means (such as a forced confession) may not be introduced by a prosecutor. The theory is that the tree (original illegal evidence) is poisoned and thus taints what grows from it. For example, as part of a coerced admission made without giving a prime suspect the so-called

"Miranda warnings" (statement of rights, including the right to remain silent and what he/she says will be used against them), the suspect tells the police the location of stolen property. Since the admission cannot be introduced as evidence in trial, neither can the stolen property. (See: **Miranda warning**)

frustration of purpose: n. sometimes called commercial frustration, when unexpected events arise which make a contract impossible to be performed, entitling the frustrated party to rescind the contract without paying damages. Example: Jack Appleseller contracts to buy a commercial building to rent out, and, while the sale is pending, the building is condemned by the city as unsafe for any use. Mr. Appleseller can back out of the purchase without obligation. (See: **commercial frustration**)

fugitive from justice: n. a person convicted or accused of a crime who hides from law enforcement in the state or flees across state lines to avoid arrest or punishment. Under Article IV, Section 2 of the U.S. Constitution, Governors are required to "deliver up" and return any fugitives from justice to the state where they allegedly committed the crime, a process called extradition. (See: **extradition**)

fungible things: n. sometimes merely called "fungibles," goods which are interchangeable, often sold or delivered in bulk, since any one of them is as good as another. Grain or gravel are fungibles, as are securities which are identical.

full faith and credit: n. the provision in Article IV, Section 1 of the U.S. Constitution which states: "Full faith and credit shall be given in each State to the public acts, records and judicial proceedings of every other state." Thus, a judgment in a lawsuit or a criminal conviction rendered in one state shall be recognized and enforced in any other state, so long as the original judgment was reached by due process of law. Each state has a process for obtaining an enforceable judgment based on a "foreign" (out-of-state) judgment.

full disclosure: n. the need in business transactions to tell the "whole truth" about any matter which the other party should know in deciding to buy or contract. In real estate sales in many states there is a full disclosure form which must be filled out and signed under penalty of perjury for knowingly falsifying or concealing any significant fact. (See: *caveat emptor*)

future interest: n. a right to receive either real property or personal property some time in the future, either upon a particular date or upon the occurrence of an event. Typical examples are getting title upon the death of the person having present use, outliving another beneficiary, reaching maturity (age 18) or upon marriage.

G

gag order: n. a judge's order prohibiting the attorneys and the parties to a pending lawsuit or criminal prosecution from talking to the media or the public about the case. The supposed intent is to prevent prejudice due to pre-trial publicity which would influence potential jurors. A gag order has the secondary purpose of preventing the lawyers from trying the case in the press and on television, and thus creating a public mood (which could get ugly) in favor of one party or the other. Based on the "freedom of the press" provision of the First Amendment, the court cannot constitutionally restrict the media from printing or broadcasting information about the case, so the only way is to put a gag on the participants under the court's control. In Canada, however, the media can be restricted, as in a famous case in which American newspapers were smuggled across the border to report on a particularly lurid sex-murder case in which a second accused person was yet to be tried. A gag order can also be made by an executive agency such as when President George Bush issued a gag order which forbade federally funded health clinics from giving out information about abortions, a gag order which President Bill Clinton rescinded on his first day in office, January 22, 1993.

garnish: v. to obtain a court order directing a party holding funds (such as a bank) or about to pay wages (such as an employer) to an alleged debtor to set that money aside until the court determines (decides) how much the debtor owes to the creditor. Garnishing funds is also a warning to the party holding the funds (garnishee) not to pay them, and to inform the court as to how much money is being held. If the garnishee (such as a bank or employer) should mistakenly give the money to the account owner or employee, the garnishee will be liable to pay the creditor what he/she/it has coming. Garnishing wages is a typical means used to collect late child support and alimony payments or money judgments. Often the order will be to pay installment payments to the sheriff until the debt is collected. Then the sheriff pays the whole amount or payments to the person to whom the money is owed. (See: **garnishee, garnishment**)

garnishee: n. a person or entity, quite often a bank or employer, which receives a court order not to release funds held for or owed to a customer or employee, pending further order of the court. (See: **garnish, garnishment**)

> *Desertion: The poor man's method of divorce.*
> *—Evan Esar, Esar's Comic Dictionary*

garnishment: n. the entire process of petitioning for and getting a court order directing a person or entity (garnishee) to hold funds they owe to someone who allegedly is in debt to another person, often after a judgment has

183

been rendered. Usually the actual amounts owed have not been figured out or are to be paid by installments directly or through the sheriff. (See: **garnish, garnishee**)

gender bias: n. unequal treatment in employment opportunity (such as promotion, pay, benefits and privileges), and expectations due to attitudes based on the sex of an employee or group of employees. Gender bias can be a legitimate basis for a lawsuit under anti-discrimination statutes. (See: **discrimination**)

general appearance: n. an attorney's representation of a client in court for all purposes connected with a pending lawsuit or prosecution. After "appearing" in court, the attorney is then responsible for all future appearances in court unless officially relieved by court order or substitution of another attorney. A lawyer may be leery of making a general appearance unless all details of representation (such as the amount and payment of his/her fees) have been worked out with the client. This is distinguished from a special appearance, which is only for a particular purpose or court session and does not make the attorney responsible for future conduct of the case. (See: **special appearance**)

general counsel: n. the chief attorney for a corporation, who is paid usually full time for legal services. Attorneys who work only for one business are "house counsel." (See: **house counsel**)

general damages: n. monetary recovery (money won) in a lawsuit for injuries suffered (such as pain, suffering, inability to perform certain functions) or breach of contract for which there is no exact dollar value which can be calculated. They are distinguished from special damages, which are for specific costs, and from punitive (exemplary) damages for punishment and to set an example when malice, intent or gross negligence was a factor. (See: **damages, exemplary damages, special damages**)

> *Wrong must not win by technicalities.*
> *—Aeschylus, The Uemenides*

general denial: n. a statement in an answer to a lawsuit or claim by a defendant in a lawsuit, in which the defendant denies everything alleged in the complaint without specifically denying any allegation. It reads: "Defendant denies each and every allegation contained in the complaint on file herein," or similar inclusive language. (See: **answer, complaint**)

general partner: n. 1) usually one of the owners and operators of a partnership, which is a joint business entered into for profit, in which responsibility for management, profits and, most importantly, the liability for debts is shared by the general partners. Anyone entering into a general partnership (the most common business organization involving more than one owner) must remember that *each* general partner is liable for *all* the debts of the partnership. Furthermore, any partner alone can bind the partnership on contracts. Example: Joe Doright and Sam Sleazeball are partners in a retail store. Sleazeball runs up a large

American Express card bill in the name of the company while on a toot in Las Vegas, contracts for purchase of $30,000 worth of dresses which are out of fashion, and then takes off with a girlfriend for Tahiti. Doright is responsible for the entire debt. 2) in the 40 states which recognize limited partnerships, the managing partner or partners operate the partnership and are liable for its debts beyond the value of the investments by limited partners. The general partners usually receive a management fee and share in profits. Limited partners are prohibited by law from participating in management, can lose more than their investments, and get less than the general partners from unusually high profits. (See: **limited partnership, partner, partnership**)

> *Mercy bears richer fruits than strict justice.*
> *—Abraham Lincoln*

general plan: n. a plan of a city, county or area which establishes zones for different types of development, uses, traffic patterns and future development. (See: **zoning**)

generation skipping: adj., adv. referring to gifts made through trusts by a grandparent to a grandchild, skipping one's child (the grandchild's parent). Originally intended to avoid or defer federal gift or estate taxes if paid through a "generation skipping trust," it is now subject to a generation skipping tax, and if made directly without a trust, the gift is as taxable as any large gift. In other words, although generation skipping no longer works to avoid taxes, a grandparent can still give or leave gifts under $10,000 a year to a grandchild without a gift tax.

gift: n. the voluntary transfer of property (including money) to another person completely free of payment or strings while both the giver and the recipient are still alive. Large gifts are subject to the federal gift tax, and in some states, to a state gift tax. (See: **gift tax, unified estate and gift tax**)

> *In respect of civil rights, common to all citizens, the Constitution of the United States does not, I think, permit any public authority to know the race of those entitled to be protected in the enjoyment of such rights.*
> *—Justice John M. Harlan, dissent in Plessy v. Ferguson*

gift in contemplation of death: n. (called a gift *causa mortis* by lawyers showing off their Latin), a gift of personal property (not real estate) by a person expecting to die soon due to ill health or age. Federal tax law will recognize this reason for a gift if the giver dies within three years of the gift. Treating the gift as made in contemplation of death has the benefit of including the gift in the value of the estate, rather than making the gift subject to a separate federal gift tax charged the giver. If the giver gets over an apparently mortal illness, the gift is treated like any other gift for tax purposes. (See: **gift tax, unified estate and gift tax**)

gift tax: n. federal tax on large gifts. Gifts to members of a family may be up to $10,000 a year to each plus an additional $30,000 accumulation of gifts is allowed tax-free. Several states also impose gift taxes. As with all tax questions, professional assistance in gift tax planning is vital.

go bail: v. slang for putting up the bail money to get an accused defendant out of jail after an arrest or pending trial or appeal.

good cause: n. a legally sufficient reason for a ruling or other action by a judge. The language is commonly: "There being good cause shown, the court orders...."

good faith: n. honest intent to act without taking an unfair advantage over another person or to fulfill a promise to act, even when some legal technicality is not fulfilled. The term is applied to all kinds of transactions.

goods: n. items held for sale in the regular course of business, as in a retail store.

Good Samaritan rule: n. from a Biblical story, if a volunteer comes to the aid of an injured or ill person who is a stranger, the person giving the aid owes the stranger a duty of being reasonably careful. In some circumstances negligence could result in a claim of negligent care if the injuries or illness were made worse by the volunteer's negligence. Thus, if Jack Goodguy sees a man lying by the road, a victim of a hit and run accident, and moves the injured man, resulting in a worsening of the injury or a new injury, instead of calling for an ambulance, Goodguy may find

himself on the wrong end of a lawsuit for millions of dollars.

good title: n. ownership of real property which is totally free of claims against it and therefore can be sold, transferred or put up as security (placing a mortgage or deed of trust on the property).

goodwill: n. the benefit of a business having a good reputation under its name and regular patronage. Goodwill is not tangible like equipment, right to lease the premises or inventory of goods. It becomes important when a business is sold, since there can be an allocation in the sales price for the value of the goodwill, which is always a subjective estimate. Included in goodwill upon sale may be the right to do business without competition by the seller in the area and/or for a specified period of time. Sellers like the allocation to goodwill to be high since it is not subject to capital gains tax, while buyers prefer it to be low, because it cannot be depreciated for tax purposes like tangible assets. Goodwill also may be overestimated by a proud seller and believed by an unknowing buyer. (See: **sale**)

governmental immunity: n. the doctrine from English common law that no governmental body can be sued unless it gives permission. This protection resulted in terrible injustices, since public hospitals, government drivers and other employees could be negligent with impunity (free) from judgment. The Federal Tort Claims Act and state waivers of immunity (with specific claims systems) have negated this rule, which stemmed from the days when kings set prerogatives. (See: **Federal Tort Claims Act, immunity**)

grace period: n. a time stated in a contract in which a late payment or performance may be made without penalty. Often after the grace period ends without payment or performance by the person who is supposed to pay, the contract is suspended. Example: if a person does not pay his/her insurance payment (premium) by the stated deadline, he/she usually has a few days extra to pay before the *absolute* deadline. If the person does not pay by then, the insurance company cancels the contract, i.e. your insurance.

grandfather clause: n. 1) a clause in a statute or zoning ordinance (particularly a city ordinance) which permits the operator of a business or a land owner to be exempt from restrictions on use if the business or property continues to be used as it was when the law was adopted. Upon passage of the statute or regulation, the specific property may be referred to as "grandfathered in." Example: the city passes an ordinance which does not permit retail businesses in a particular zone, but any existing store can continue to function in the area, even with new owners. However, if the premises stop being a retail outlet then the grandfather clause will lapse. 2) among the state constitutional amendments passed by southern states in the late 1800s to keep blacks from voting, "grandfather clauses" denied voter registration to people who were illiterate, who did not own property or could not pass a test on citizenship obligations, unless their grandfathers had served in the Confederate Army. Such laws are now unconstitutional.

grandfathered in: adj. refers to continued allowed use of property as it was when restrictions or zoning ordinances were adopted.

Grand Jury: n. a jury in each county or federal court district which serves for a term of a year and is usually selected from a list of nominees offered by the judges in the county or district. The traditional 23 members may be appointed or have their names drawn from those nominated. A Grand Jury has two responsibilities: 1) to hear evidence of criminal accusations in possible felonies (major crimes) presented by the District Attorney and decide whether the accused should be indicted and tried for a crime. Since many felony charges are filed by the District Attorney in a municipal or other lower court which holds a preliminary hearing to determine if there is just cause for trial instead of having the Grand Jury hear the matter, this function is of minor importance in many jurisdictions. 2) to hear evidence of potential public wrongdoing by city and county officials, including acts which may not be crimes but are imprudent, ineffective or inefficient, and make recommendations to the county and cities involved. Example: a Grand Jury may recommend that a new jail is needed, find that there is evidence of favoritism in the sheriff's office, that some city council members are profiting by overlooking drug dealing by city staffers, or that judges are not carrying a full load of cases to be tried. (See: **charge, indictment, preliminary hearing**)

grand larceny: n. the crime of theft of another's property (including money) over a certain value (for example, $500), as distinguished from petty (or petit) larceny in which the value is below the grand larceny limit. Some states only recognize the crime of larceny, but draw the line between a felony (punishable by state prison time) and a misdemeanor (local jail and/or fine) based on the value of the loot. (See: **larceny, theft**)

grand theft: n. (See: **grand larceny**)

grant: v. to transfer real property from a title holder (grantor) or holders to another (grantee) with or without payment. However, there is an important difference between the types of deeds used. A grant deed warrants (guarantees) that the grantor (seller) has full right and title to the property, while a quitclaim deed only grants whatever the grantor owns (which may be nothing) and guarantees nothing. (See: **grant deed, grantee, grantor, quitclaim deed**)

grant deed: n. the document which transfers title to real property or a real property interest from one party (grantor) to another (grantee). It must describe the property by legal description of boundaries and/or parcel numbers, be signed by all people transferring the property, and be acknowledged before a notary public. The

transfer is finalized by recording with the County Recorder or Recorder of Deeds. Importantly, a grant deed warrants that the grantor actually owned the title to transfer, which a quitclaim deed would not, since it only transfers what the grantor owned, if anything. (See: **grant, grantee, grantor, quitclaim deed**)

grantee: n. the party who receives title to real property (buyer, recipient, donee) from the seller (grantor) by a document called a grant deed or quitclaim deed. (See: **grant**)

grantor: n. the party who transfers title in real property (seller, giver) to another (buyer, recipient, donee) by grant deed or quitclaim deed. (See: **grant**)

grantor-grantee index: n. a set of books and/or computerized lists found in the office of every County Recorder or Recorder of Deeds which lists all recorded transfers of title by deed (as well as liens, mortgages, deeds of trust and other documents affecting title). Each yearly index is usually alphabetized by the last names of grantors (the party transferring title) and grantee (the recipients of title). The listing includes the date of transfer, and cross-references to the book and page or document number where a copy of the document (often on microfilm) was recorded and can be examined. This is a key instrument in tracking a chain of title.

gratuitous: adj. or adv. voluntary or free.

gravamen: n. Latin for "to weigh down," the basic gist of every claim (cause of action) or charge in a complaint filed to begin a lawsuit. Example: in an accident case, the *gravamen* may be the negligence of the defendant, and in a contract case, it may be the breach of the defendant. (See: **cause of action, charge, complaint**)

gross negligence: n. carelessness which is in reckless disregard for the safety or lives of others, and is so great it appears to be a conscious violation of other people's rights to safety. It is more than simple inadvertence, but it is just shy of being intentionally evil. If one has borrowed or contracted to take care of another's property, then gross negligence is the failure to actively take the care one would of his/her own property. If gross negligence is found by the trier of fact (judge or jury), it can result in the award of punitive damages on top of general and special damages. (See: **damages, exemplary damages, negligence, punitive damages**)

gross income: n. in calculating income tax, the income of an individual or business from all sources before deducting allowable expenses, which will result in net income. (See: **income tax**)

guarantee: 1) v. to pledge or agree to be responsible for another's debt or contractual performance if that other person does not pay or perform. Usually, the party receiving the guarantee will first try to collect or obtain performance from the debtor before trying to collect from the one making the guarantee (guarantor). 2) the promise to pay another's debt or fulfill contract obligations if that party fails to pay or perform. 3) n. occasionally, the person to whom the guarantee is made. 4) a promise to make a product good if it has some defect. (See: **guarantor**)

guarantor: n. a person or entity that agrees to be responsible for another's debt or performance under a contract if the other fails to pay or perform. (See: **guarantee**)

guaranty: v. and n. an older spelling of guarantee, which the renowned Oxford etymologist Dr. Walter Skeat called a "better spelling" (1882). (See: **guarantee**)

guardian: n. a person who has been appointed by a judge to take care of a minor child or incompetent adult (both called "ward") personally and/or manage that person's affairs. To become a guardian of a child either the party intending to be the guardian or another family member, a close friend or a local official responsible for a minor's welfare will petition the court to appoint the guardian. In the case of a minor, the guardianship remains under court supervision until the child reaches majority at 18. Naming someone in a will as guardian of one's child in case of the death of the parent is merely a nomination. The judge does not have to honor that request, although he/she usually does. Sadly, often a parent must petition to become the guardian of his/her child's "estate" if the child inherits or receives a gift of substantial assets, including the situation in which a parent gives his/her own child an interest in real property or stocks. Therefore, that type of gift should be avoided and a trust created instead.

While the term "guardian" may refer to someone who is appointed to care for and/or handle the affairs of a person who is incompetent or incapable of administering his/her affairs, this is more often called a "conservator" under a conservatorship. (See: **conservator, ward**)

guardian *ad litem*: n. a person appointed by the court only to take legal action on behalf of a minor or an adult not able to handle his/her own affairs. Duties may include filing a lawsuit for an injured child, defending a lawsuit or filing a claim against an estate. Usually a parent will file a petition to be appointed the guardian *ad litem* of a child hurt in an accident at the same time the lawsuit is filed. (See: *ad litem*)

guest: n. 1) in general, a person paying to stay in a hotel, motel or inn for a short time. 2) a person staying at another's residence without charge, called a "social guest." An important distinction is that a non-paying guest is not owed the duty of being provided a safe boarding space, as is a paying customer. Thus if a social guest trips on a slippery rug, he/she has no right to sue for negligence, but a paying guest might. 3) an "automobile" guest is one who is a passenger without paying, as distinguished from a taxi fare, bus rider or one who has paid a friend to drive. However, the so-called "guest statute" may give a non-paying passenger the right to sue. An automobile guest is somewhat (but not entirely) analogous to the "social guest" in a residence. (See: **guest statute, invitee**)

guest statute: n. a state law which sets standards of care by the driver of a car to a non-paying passenger. Although state laws vary, the basic concept is that the social passenger can bring suit for negligence against the driver for gross negligence only if the driver could have foreseen that his/her actions or car could put the rider in great peril. Examples: driving while drunk, going far over the speed limit, playing "chicken," taking chances, driving a car knowing the brakes are faulty, or particularly continuing the reckless driving after the passenger has asked the driver to stop or asked to be let out. (See: **guest**)

guilty: adj. having been convicted of a crime or having admitted the commission of a crime by pleading "guilty" (saying you did it). A defendant may also be found guilty by a judge after a plea of "no contest," or in Latin *nolo contendere*. The term "guilty" is also sometimes applied to persons against whom a judgment has been found in a lawsuit for a civil wrong, such as negligence or some intentional act like assault or fraud, but that is a confusing misuse of the word since it should only apply to a criminal charge. (See: **admission of guilt, cop a plea, plea bargain**)

habeas corpus: (hay-bee-us core-puss) n. Latin for "you have the body," it is a writ (court order) which directs the law enforcement officials (prison administrators, police or sheriff) who have custody of a prisoner to appear in court with the prisoner to help the judge determine whether the prisoner is lawfully in prison or jail. The writ is obtained by petition to a judge in the county or district where the prisoner is incarcerated, and the judge sets a hearing on whether there is a legal basis for holding the prisoner. *Habeas corpus* is a protection against illegal confinement, such as holding a person without charges, when due process obviously has been denied, bail is excessive, parole has been granted, an accused has been improperly surrendered by the bail bondsman or probation has been summarily terminated without cause. Historically called "the great writ," the renowned scholar of the Common Law, William Blackstone, called it the "most celebrated writ in English law." It may also be used as a means to contest child custody and deportation proceedings in court. The writ of *habeas corpus* can be employed procedurally in federal district courts to challenge the constitutionality of a state court conviction.

habitable: adj. referring to a residence that is safe and can be occupied in reasonable comfort. Although standards vary by region, the premises should be closed in against the weather, provide running water, access to decent toilets and bathing facilities, heating, and electricity. Particularly in multi-dwelling buildings freedom from noxious smells, noise and garbage are included in the standard. This can become important in landlord–tenant disputes or government actions to force a landlord to make the premises livable (abatement of deficiencies). Example: if the roof begins to leak, the water goes off, the electricity shorts out or the toilet breaks, in most states the landlord has a duty to make repairs when requested or the tenant may order the repairs and deduct the cost from the rent. (See: **landlord and tenant**)

> *The first thing we do, let's kill all the lawyers.*
> *—William Shakespeare, Henry VI, Part II*

habitual criminal: n. under the statutes of many states, a person who has been convicted of either two or three felonies (or of numerous misdemeanors), a fact which may increase punishment for any further criminal convictions. (See: **three strikes, you're out**)

half blood: 1) adj. sharing one parent only. 2) n. a half brother or half sister. "Half blood" should not be confused with "half breed," which was a pejorative expression for a person born of parents of two races, particularly Native American and white.

harass: (either harris or huh-rass) v. systematic and/or continual unwanted and annoying pestering, which often includes threats and demands. This can include lewd or offensive remarks, sexual advances, threatening telephone calls from collection agencies, hassling by police officers or bringing criminal charges without cause. (See: **harassment, sexual harassment**)

In hearing cases I am like everyone else. The important thing, however, is to see to it that there are no cases.
—Confucius

harassment: (either harris-meant or huh-rass-meant) n. the act of systematic and/or continued unwanted and annoying actions of one party or a group, including threats and demands. The purposes may vary, including racial prejudice, personal malice, an attempt to force someone to quit a job or grant sexual favors, apply illegal pressure to collect a bill or merely gain sadistic pleasure from making someone anxious or fearful. Such activities may be the basis for a lawsuit if due to discrimination based on race or sex, a violation on the statutory limitations on collection agencies, involve revenge by an ex-spouse, or be shown to be a form of blackmail ("I'll stop bothering you if you'll go to bed with me"). The victim may file a petition for a "stay away" (restraining) order, intended to prevent contact by the offensive party. A systematic pattern of harassment by an employee against another worker may subject the employer to a lawsuit for failure to protect the worker. (See: **harass, sexual harassment**)

harmless error: n. an error by a judge in the conduct of a trial which an appellate court finds is not sufficient for it to reverse or modify the lower court's judgment at trial. Harmless error would include: a technical error which has no bearing on the outcome of the trial, an error that was corrected (such as allowing testimony and then ordering it stricken and admonishing the jury to ignore it), the issue affected by the error was found in the appellant's favor (such as hearsay evidence on premeditation, but the jury found no premeditation), and the appeals court's view that even though there were errors the appealing party could not have won in trial in any event. This last gives the appeals court broad latitude to rule that errors were not significant. It is frustrating to appealing parties and their attorneys for the appeals court to rule that there were indeed several errors, and then say: "However, they appear to be harmless." (See: **error**)

headnote: n. the summary of the key legal points determined by an appeals court, which appears just above each decision in published reports of cases. Headnotes are useful for a quick scan of the judgment, but they are the editor's remarks and not the court's. (See: **reports**)

head of household: n. 1) in federal income tax law, the person filing a tax return who manages the household which has dependents such as children and/or other dependent relatives living in the home, but does not file on a joint return with a spouse. The calculation of taxes is somewhat more favorable to a head of household than to a person filing singly. 2) anyone who manages the affairs of the family living in a household, who need not be the husband/father or wife/mother, but could be a grandparent, uncle, aunt, son or daughter. 3) "head of family."

hearing: n. any proceeding before a judge or other magistrate (such as a hearing officer or court commissioner) without a jury in which evidence and/or argument is presented to determine some issue of fact or both issues of fact and law. While technically a trial with a judge sitting without a jury fits the definition, a hearing usually refers to brief sessions involving a specific question at some time prior to the trial itself, or such specialized proceedings as administrative hearings. In criminal law, a "preliminary hearing" is held before a judge to determine whether the prosecutor has presented sufficient evidence that the accused has committed a crime to hold him/her for trial. (See: **administrative hearing, preliminary hearing, trial**)

hearsay: n. 1) second-hand evidence in which the witness is not telling what he/she knows personally, but what others have said to him/her. 2) a common objection made by the opposing lawyer to testimony when it appears the witness has violated the hearsay rule. 3) scuttlebutt or gossip. (See: **hearsay rule**)

hearsay rule: n. the basic rule that testimony or documents which quote persons not in court are not admissible. Because the person who supposedly knew the facts is not in court to state his/her exact words, the trier of fact cannot judge the demeanor and credibility of the alleged first-hand witness, and the other party's lawyer cannot cross-examine (ask questions of) him or her. However, as significant as the hearsay rule itself are the exceptions to the rule which allow hearsay testimony such as: a) a statement by the opposing party in the lawsuit which is inconsistent with what he/she has said in court (called an "admission against interest"); b) business entries made in the regular course of business, when a qualified witness can identify the records and tell how they were kept; c) official government records which can be shown to be properly kept; d) a writing about an event made close to the time it occurred, which may be used during trial to refresh a witness's memory about the event; e) a "learned treatise" which means historical works, scientific books, published art works, maps and charts; f) judgments in other cases; g) a spontaneous excited or startled utterance ("oh, God, the bus hit the little girl"); h) contemporaneous statement which explains the meaning of conduct if the conduct was ambiguous; i) a statement which explains a person's state of mind at the time of an event; j) a statement which explains a person's future intentions ("I plan to....") if that person's state of mind is in question; k) prior testimony, such as in deposition (taken under oath outside of court), or at a hearing, if the witness is not available (including being dead); l) a declaration by the opposing party in the lawsuit which was contrary to his/her best interest if the party is not available at trial (this differs from an admission against interest, which is admissible in trial if it differs from testimony at trial); m) a dying declaration by a person believing he/she is dying; n) a statement made about one's mental set, feeling, pain or health, if the person is not available—most often applied if the declarant is dead ("my back hurts horribly," and then dies); o) a statement about one's own will when the person is not available; p) other exceptions based on a judge's discretion that the hearsay testimony in the circumstances must be reliable. (See: **admission against interest, dying declaration, hearsay**)

heat of passion: n. in a criminal case, when the accused was in an uncontrollable rage at the time of commission of the alleged crime. If so, it may reduce the charge, indictment or judgment down from murder to manslaughter, since the passion precluded the defendant having premeditation or being fully mentally capable of knowing what he/she was doing. (See: **manslaughter, murder**)

heir: n. one who acquires property upon the death of another, based on the rules of descent and distribution, namely, being the child, descendant or other closest relative of the dear departed. It also has come to mean anyone who "takes" (receives something) by the terms of the will. An heir cannot be determined until the moment of death of the person leaving the property, since a supposed beneficiary (heir apparent) might die first. A presumptive heir is someone who would receive benefits unless a child was later born to the current owner of the property the presumptive heir hopes to get someday. A legally adopted child gains the chance to be an heir upon adoption as if he/she were the natural child of the adoptive parent or parents and is called an adoptive heir. A collateral heir is a relative who is not a direct descendant, but a brother, sister, uncle, aunt, cousin, nephew, niece or a parent. It is noteworthy that a spouse is not an heir unless specifically mentioned in the will. He/She may, however, receive an inheritance through marital property or community property laws. A child not mentioned in a will can claim to be a pretermitted heir, i.e. inadvertently or accidentally omitted from the will, and can claim he/she would (should) have received as an heir. (See: **descent and distribution, heir apparent, heirs of the body, pretermitted heir, succession, will**)

heir apparent: n. the person who is expected to receive a share of the estate of a family member if he/she lives longer, or is not specifically disinherited by will. (See: **heir**)

heiress: n. feminine heir, often used to denote a woman who has received a large amount upon the death of a rich relative, as in the "department store heiress."

heirs of the body: n. descendants of one's bloodline, such as children or grandchildren until such time as there are no direct descendants. If the bloodline runs out, the property will "revert" to the nearest relative traced back to the original owner. (See: **heir, reversion**)

held: v. decided or ruled, as "the court

held that the contract was valid." (See: **decision, judgment, ruling**)

hereditament: n. any kind of property which can be inherited. This is old-fashioned language still found in some wills and deeds.

hidden asset: n. an item of value which does not show on the books of a business, often excluded for some improper purpose such as escaping taxation or hiding it from a bankruptcy trustee. However, there may be a legitimate business reason for not including all assets on a profit and loss statement.

highway: n. any public street, road, turnpike or canal which any member of the public has the right to use, provided he/she/it follows the laws governing its use, such as having a driver's license if operating a vehicle. Thus, the use is really a privilege and not an absolute right.

hit and run: n. the crime of a driver of a vehicle who is involved in a collision with another vehicle, property or human being, who knowingly fails to stop to give his/her name, license number and other information as required by statute to the injured party, a witness or law enforcement officers. If there is only property damage and no other person is present, leaving the information attached to the damaged property may be sufficient, provided the person causing the accident makes a report to the police. Hit and run statutes vary from state to state. It is not a violation of the constitutional protection against self-incrimination to be required to stop and give this information since it is a report and not an admission of guilt. Some hit and run cases are difficult to determine, such as the driver leaves the accident scene to go a block to his/her house or the neighborhood repair garage, and then walks back to the scene.

hobby loss: n. in income tax, a loss from a business activity engaged in more for enjoyment than for profit, which can be deducted against annual income only.

holder: n. a general term for anyone in possession of property, but usually referring to anyone holding a promissory note, check, bond or other paper, either handed to the holder (delivery) or signed over by endorsement, for which he/she/it is entitled to receive payment as stated in the document. (See: **bill of exchange,** *bona fide* **purchaser, check, endorsement, holder in due course, promissory note**)

holder in due course: n. one holding a check or promissory note, received for value (he/she paid for it) in good faith and with no suspicion that it might be no good, claimed by another, overdue or previously dishonored (a bank had refused to pay since the account was overdrawn). Such a holder is entitled to payment by the maker of the check or note. (See: *bona fide* **purchaser**)

holding: 1) n. any ruling or decision of a court. 2) n. any real property to which one has title. 3) n. investment in a business. 4) v. keeping in one's possession.

holding company: n. a company, usually a corporation, which is created to own the stock of other corporations, thereby often controlling the management and policies of all of them.

holdover tenancy: n. the situation when a tenant of real estate continues to occupy the premises without the owner's agreement after the original lease or rental agreement between the owner (landlord) and the tenant has expired. The tenant is responsible for payment of the monthly rental at the existing rate and terms, which the landlord may accept without admitting the legality of the occupancy. A holdover tenant is subject to a notice to quit (get out) and, if he/she does not leave, to a lawsuit for unlawful detainer.

hold harmless: n. a promise to pay any costs or claims which may result from an agreement. Quite often this is part of a settlement agreement, in which one party is concerned that there might be unknown lawsuits or claims stemming from the situation, so the other party agrees to cover them.

holographic will: n. a will entirely handwritten, dated and signed by the testator (the person making the will), but not signed by required witnesses. Under those conditions it is valid in about half the states despite the lack of witnesses. A letter which has all the elements of a will can be a holographic will, as can a will scratched in the dust of an automobile hood of a person dying while lost in the desert. (See: **will**)

home rule: n. the power of a local city or county to set up its own system of governing and local ordinances without receiving a charter from the state which comes with certain requirements and limitations. The concept has become popular with so-called libertarians, survivalists and others who would like to divorce local government from as much state regulation as possible. However, few cities and counties have chosen this route. For example, in California, there is one small county (Colusa) out of the 58 which has chosen "home rule." This does not mean they will not take state funds for local improvements.

homestead: 1) n. the house and lot of a homeowner which the head of the household (usually either spouse) can declare in writing to be the principal dwelling of the family, record that declaration of homestead with the County Recorder or Recorder of Deeds and thereby exempt part of its value (based on state statutes) from judgment creditors. A similar exemption is available in bankruptcy without filing a declaration of homestead. 2) v. jargon for filing a declaration of homestead, as in "he homesteaded the property."

hometowned: adv. legalese for a lawyer or client suffering discrimination by a local judge who seems to favor local parties and/or attorneys over those from out of town.

homicide: n. the killing of a human being due to the act or omission of another. Included among homicides are murder and manslaughter, but not all homicides are a crime, particularly when there is a lack of criminal intent. Non-criminal homicides include killing in self-defense, a misadventure like a hunting accident or automobile wreck without a violation of law like reckless driving, or legal (government) execution. Suicide is a homicide, but in most cases there is no one to prosecute if the suicide is successful. Assisting or attempting suicide can be a crime. (See: **justifiable homicide, manslaughter, murder, self-defense, suicide**)

hornbook law: n. lawyer lingo for a fundamental and well-accepted legal principle that does not require any further explanation, since a hornbook is a primer of basics.

hostile possession: n. occupancy of a piece of real property coupled with a claim of ownership (which may be implied by actions, such as putting in a fence) over anyone, including the holder of recorded title. It may be an element of gaining title through long-term adverse possession or claiming real estate which has no known owner. (See: **adverse possession, quiet title action**)

hostile witness: n. technically an "adverse witness" in a trial who is found by the judge to be hostile (adverse) to the position of the party whose attorney is questioning the witness, even though the attorney called the witness to testify on behalf of his/her client. When the attorney calling the witness finds that the answers are contrary to the legal position of his/her client or the witness becomes openly antagonistic, the attorney may request the judge to declare the witness to be "hostile" or "adverse." If the judge declares the witness to be hostile (i.e. adverse), the attorney may ask "leading" questions which suggest answers or are challenging to the testimony just as on cross examination of

a witness who has testified for the opposition. (See: **witness, cross examination, leading, adverse witness**)

hotchpot: n. the putting together, blending or mixing of various properties in order to achieve equal division among beneficiaries or heirs. There may be cash, securities, personal belongings, and even real estate which are part of the residue of an estate to be given to "my children, share and share alike." To make such distribution possible, all of the items are put in the hotchpot and then divided.

hot pursuit: n. when a law enforcement officer is so close behind the alleged criminal that he/she may continue the chase into another jurisdiction without stopping or seeking a warrant for an arrest in the other county or state. It is equivalent to fresh pursuit. (See: **fresh pursuit**)

house counsel: n. any attorney who works only for a particular business. (See: **general counsel**)

No man is above the law, and none is below it.
—Theodore Roosevelt

household: n. a family living together, all of whom need not be related.

hung jury: n. slang for a hopelessly deadlocked jury in a criminal case, in which neither side is able to prevail. Usually it means there is no unanimous verdict (although in Oregon and Louisiana 10 of 12 jurors can convict or acquit). If the jury is hung the trial judge will declare a mistrial. A new trial from scratch, with a new jury panel, is required. The prosecutor can decide not to re-try the case, particularly if a majority of the jury favored acquittal. (See: **dismissal, jury, mistrial, trial**)

hypothecate: v. from Greek for "pledge," a generic term for using property to secure payment of a loan, which includes mortgages, pledges and putting up collateral, while the borrower retains possession. (See: **secured transaction**)

i.e.: prep. abbreviation for *id est,* which is Latin for "that is" or "that is to say." It is used to expand or explain a general term as in "his children (i.e. Matthew, Mark, Luke and Joan)." It should not be confused with "e.g.," which means "for example."

illegal: 1) adj. in violation of statute, regulation or ordinance, which may be criminal or merely not in conformity. Thus, an armed robbery is illegal, and so is an access road which is narrower than the county allows, but the violation is not criminal. 2) status of a person residing in a country of which he/she is not a citizen and who has no official permission to be there. (See: **alien, illegal immigrant**)

illegal immigrant: n. an alien (noncitizen) who has entered the United States without government permission or stayed beyond the termination date of a visa. (See: **alien**)

illusory promise: n. an agreement to do something that is so indefinite one cannot tell what is to be done or the performance is optional (usually because it is just a gesture and not a true agreement). Therefore, the other party need not perform or pay since he/she got nothing in what he/she may have thought was a contract.

immaterial: adj. a commonly heard objection to introducing evidence in a trial on the ground that it had nothing substantial to do with the case or any issue in the case. It can also apply to any matter (such as an argument or complaint) in a lawsuit which has no bearing on the issues to be decided in a trial. The public is often surprised at what is immaterial, such as references to a person's character or bad deeds in other situations. (See: **irrelevant, objection**)

immediately: adv. 1) at once. 2) in orders of the court or in contracts it means "as soon as can be done" without excuse.

immunity: n. exemption from penalties, payments or legal requirements, granted by authorities or statutes. Generally there are three types of immunity at law: a) a promise not to prosecute for a crime in exchange for information or testimony in a criminal matter, granted by the prosecutors, a judge, a grand jury or an investigating legislative committee; b) public officials' protection from liability for their decisions (like a city manager or member of a public hospital board); c) governmental (or sovereign) immunity, which protects government agencies from lawsuits unless the government agreed to be sued; d) diplomatic immunity which excuses foreign ambassadors from most U.S. criminal laws. (See: **governmental immunity**)

impanel: v. to select and install a jury. (See: **impaneling, jury**)

impaneling: n. the act of selecting a jury from the list of potential jurors, called the "panel" or *venire*." The steps are: 1) drawing names at random from a large number of jurors called; 2) seating 12 tentative jurors (or fewer where agreed to); 3) hearing individual juror requests for being excused, to be determined by the judge; 4) questions from judge and lawyers for both sides, called "*voir dire*"; 5) challenges of tentative jurors either for cause (decided by the judge) or peremptory (no reason given) by the lawyers; 6) swearing in the jurors who survive this process. (See: **challenge, juror, jury, panel,** *venire, voir dire*)

impeach: v. 1) to discredit the testimony of a witness by proving that he/she has not told the truth or has been inconsistent, by introducing contrary evidence, including statements made outside of the courtroom in depositions or in statements of the witness heard by another. 2) to charge a public official with a public crime for which the punishment is removal from office. One President, Andrew Johnson in 1868, was charged with violation of federal laws in a politically motivated impeachment, but was acquitted by the margin of one vote in a trial held by the Senate. President Richard Nixon resigned in 1974 rather than face impending impeachment charges brought by the House of Representatives in the Watergate affair, in which he was accused of obstructing the investigation and lying to Congress about his participation. Several federal judges have been impeached and nine have been found guilty by the Senate.

impeachment: n. 1) discrediting a witness by showing that he/she is not telling the truth or does not have the knowledge to testify as he/she did. 2) the trying of a public official for charges of illegal acts committed in the performance of public duty. It is not the conviction for the alleged crime nor the removal from office. It is only the trial itself. (See: **impeach**)

impleader: n. a procedural device before trial in which a party brings a third party into the lawsuit because that third party is the one who owes money to an original defendant, which money will be available to pay the original plaintiff. The theory is that two cases may be decided together and justice may be done more efficiently than having two suits in a series.

implied: adj., adv. referring to circumstances, conduct or statements of one or both parties which substitute for explicit language to prove authority to act, warranty, promise, trust, agreement, consent or easement, among other things. Thus circumstances "imply" something rather than spell it out. (See: **consideration, contract, covenant, easement, implied consent, implied warranty**)

implied consent: n. consent when surrounding circumstances exist which would lead a reasonable person to believe that this consent had been given, although no direct, express or explicit words of agreement had been uttered. Examples: a) a "contract" based on the fact that one person has been doing a particular thing and the other person expects him/her to continue; b) the defense in a "date rape" case in which there is a claim of assumed consent due to absence of protest or a belief that "no" really meant "yes," "maybe" or "later." (See: **implied**)

implied contract: n. an agreement which is found to exist based on the circumstances when to deny a contract would be unfair and/or result in unjust enrichment to one of the parties. An implied contract is distinguished from an "express contract." (See: **contract, express contract, implied**)

implied covenant of good faith and fair dealing: n. a general assumption of the law of contracts, that people will act in good faith and deal fairly without breaking their word, using shifty means to avoid obligations or denying what the other party obviously understood. A lawsuit (or one of the causes of action in a lawsuit) based on the breach of this covenant is often brought when the other party has been claiming technical excuses for breaching the contract or using the specific words of the contract to refuse to perform when the surrounding circumstances or apparent understanding of the parties were to the contrary. Example: an employer fires a long-time employee without cause and says it can fire at whim because the employment contract states the employment is "at will." However, the employee was encouraged to join the company on the basis of retirement plans and other conduct which led him/her to believe the job was permanent barring misconduct or financial downturn. Thus, there could be a breach of the implied covenant, since the surrounding circumstances implied that there would be career-long employment. (See: **implied**)

implied warranty: n. an assumption at law that products are "merchantable," meaning they work and are useable as normally expected by consumers, unless there is a warning that they are sold "as is" or second-hand without any warranty. A grant deed of real property carries the implied warranty of good title, meaning the grantor (seller) had a title (ownership) to transfer. (See: *caveat emptor*, **implied**)

impossibility: n. when an act cannot be performed due to nature, physical impediments or unforeseen events. It can be a legitimate basis to rescind (mutually cancel) a contract. (See: **contract**)

impotence: n. the male's inability to copulate. Impotence can be grounds for annulment of a marriage if the condition existed at the time of the marriage and grounds for divorce whenever it occurs under the laws of 26 states. It should not be confused with sterility, which means inability to produce children.

impound: v. 1) to collect funds, in addition to installment payments, from a person who owes a debt secured by property, and place them in a special account to pay property taxes and insurance when due. This protects the lender or seller from the borrower's possible failure to keep up the insurance or a mounting tax bill which is a lien on the property. 2) to take away records, money or property, such as an automobile or building, by government action pending the outcome of a criminal prosecution. The records may be essential evidence, or the money or property may be forfeit to the state as in illegal drug cases. (See: **forfeit, forfeiture**)

improvement: n. any permanent structure on real property, or any work on the property (such as planting trees) which increases its value.

impute: v. 1) to attach to a person responsibility (and therefore financial liability) for acts or injuries to another, because of a particular relationship, such as mother to child, guardian to ward, employer to employee or business associates. Example: a 16-year-old boy drives his father's car without a license and runs someone down. The child's negligence may be imputed to the parent, or, in the reverse, a mother drives her car and collides with a truck driven over the speed limit, and her baby in the front seat of the car is badly injured, in part due to not being put in a safety seat with a seat belt. The mother's negligence can be imputed to the child in any claim on behalf of the child against the truck driver. 2) to attribute knowledge and/or notice to a person only because of his/her relationship to the one actually possessing the information. Example: if a partner in a business is informed of something, that knowledge is imputed to his/her partner, and the partner is expected to have the information also. (See: **vicarious liability**)

in absentia: (in ab-sensh-ee-ah) adj. or adv. phrase. Latin for "in absence," or more fully, in one's absence. Occasionally a criminal trial is conducted without the defendant being present when he/she walks out or escapes after the trial has begun, since the accused has thus waived the constitutional right to face one's accusers. During the war crimes trials following World War II, it was employed against Nazis who had committed atrocities and then disappeared, the most famous being Martin Bormann, Hitler's closest aide.

in camera: adj. or adv. phrase. Latin for "in chambers." This refers to a hearing or discussions with the judge in the privacy of his chambers (office rooms) or when spectators and jurors have been excluded from the courtroom. (See: **in chambers**)

incapacity: adj. 1) not being able to perform any gainful employment due to congenital disability, illness (including mental), physical injury, advanced age or intellectual deficiency. This is significant in claims for worker's compensation, disability insurance, or Social Security claims under "SSI." 2) lacking the ability to understand one's actions in making a will, executing some other document or entering into an agreement. A challenge to the validity of a will often turns on a claim that the person (now dead and unable to testify) lacked the capacity to understand what he/she owned, who were the "natural objects of his/her bounty" (close relatives primarily), that no one was able to dominate the testator's (will writer's) judgment so as to exert "undue influence." Mental weakness may show lack of capacity to make a will, as can fear, intimidation or persistent drunkenness. Example: an old lady is kept well supplied with whiskey for several months by her greedy sisters, who finally convince her to change the will from benefitting her children to benefitting them when she is drunk and fearful they will cut off her supply. A court would probably find she had lacked capacity to decide to make the latest version of the will. (See: **incompetent**)

incest: n. sexual intercourse between close blood relatives, including brothers and sisters, parents and children, grandparents and grandchildren, or aunts or uncles with nephews or nieces. It is a crime in all states, even if consensual by both parties. However, it is often co-existent with sexual abuse since usually the younger person is a victim of the predatory sexual activities of an older relative. Recently, it has drawn more attention as people began talking about the "silent crime," which is often covered up by a wife fearful of losing a husband, or the memory has been suppressed by the youthful victims. One problem is that on the surface the family may appear to be "All-American" while abusive incest continues. In 18 states incest also includes copulation or cohabitation between first cousins, but the majority of jurisdictions permit marriage between such cousins. The rationale for prohibition of first cousin marriages is not so much moral as the fear of proliferation of mental or physical weakness due to the joining of recessive family genes carrying such weaknesses.

in chambers: adj. referring to discussions or hearings held in the judge's office, called his chambers. It is also called "*in camera*." (See: *in camera*)

inchoate: adj. or adv. referring to something which has begun but has not been completed, either an activity or some object which is incomplete. It may define a potential crime like a conspiracy which has been started but not perfected or finished (buying the explosives, but not yet blowing up the bank safe), a right contingent on an event (receiving property if one outlives the grantor of the property) or a decision or idea which has been only partially considered, such as a contract which has not been formalized.

incidental beneficiary: n. someone who obtains a benefit as the result of the main purpose of the trust. Example: the co-owner of property with a named beneficiary may benefit from moneys provided to improve the building they jointly own, or a grandchild might benefit from his/her parent receiving a gift which could be used by the entire family, or which he/she may inherit from the parent. (See: **beneficiary, trust**)

income: n. money, goods or other economic benefit received. Under income tax laws, income can be "active" through one's efforts or work (including management) or "passive" from rentals, stock dividends, investments and interest on deposits in which there is neither physical effort nor management. For tax purposes, income does not include gifts and inheritances received. Taxes are collected based on income by the federal government and most state governments.

income tax: n. a tax on an individual's net income, after deductions for various expenses and payments such as charitable gifts, calculated on a formula which takes into consideration whether it is paid jointly by a married couple, the number of dependents of the taxpayers, special breaks for ages over 65, disabilities and other factors. Federal income taxes have been collected since 1913 when they were authorized by the 16th Amendment to the Constitution. Most states also assess income taxes, but at a substantially lower rate than that of the federal government. (See: **income, tax**)

incompatible: adj. 1) inconsistent. 2) unmatching. 3) unable to live together as husband and wife due to irreconcilable differences. In no-fault divorce states, if one of the spouses desires to end the marriage, that fact proves incompatibility, and a divorce (dissolution) will be granted even though the other spouse does not want a divorce. The term also has the general meaning that two people do not get along with each other. (See: **incompatibility**)

incompatibility: n. the state of a marriage in which the spouses no longer have the mutual desire to live together and/or stay married, and is thus a ground for divorce (dissolution) in most states even though one spouse may disagree. (See: **incompatible, irreconcilable differences**)

incompetency: n. the condition of lacking the ability to handle one's affairs due to mental or physical incapacity. Before a condition of incompetency is officially declared by a court, a hearing must be held with the person who is involved interviewed by a court investigator; the person must be present

and/or represented by an attorney. (See: **incompetent**).

incompetent: adj. 1) referring to a person who is not able to manage his/her affairs due to mental deficiency (low I.Q., deterioration, illness or psychosis) or sometimes physical disability. Being incompetent can be the basis for appointment of a guardian or conservator (after a hearing in which the party who may be found to be incompetent has been interviewed by a court investigator and is present and/or represented by an attorney) to handle his/her person and/or affairs (often called "estate"). 2) in criminal law, the inability to understand the nature of a trial. In these cases the defendant is usually institutionalized until such time as he/she regains sanity and can be tried. 3) a generalized reference to evidence which cannot be introduced because it violates various rules against being allowed, particularly because it has no bearing on the case. It may be irrelevant (not sufficiently significant) or immaterial (does not matter to the issues). (See: **conservatee, conservator, guardian, incompetency, incompetent evidence**)

incompetent evidence: n. testimony, documents or things which one side attempts to present as evidence during trial, which the court finds (usually after objection by the opposition) are not admissible because they are irrelevant or immaterial to the issues in the lawsuit. Thus, trial lawyers often object with: "incompetent, irrelevant and immaterial," figuring that covers the waterfront of most objections. (See: **incompetent, objection**)

incontrovertible evidence: n. evidence introduced to prove a fact in a trial which is so conclusive, that by no stretch of the imagination can there be any other truth as to that matter. Examples: a fingerprint which shows someone had been present in a room, or a blood test which scientifically proves that a person is not the parent of a child.

incorporate: v. 1) to obtain an official charter or articles of incorporation from the state for an organization, which may be a profit-making business, a professional business such as a law office or medical office or a non-profit entity which operates for charitable, social, religious, civic or other public service purposes. The process includes having one or more incorporators (most states require a minimum of three for profit-making companies) choose a name not currently used by (nor confusingly similar to) any corporation, prepare articles, determine who will be responsible for accepting service of process, decide on the stock structure, adopt a set of by-laws, file the articles with the Secretary of State of the state of incorporation, and hold a first meeting of incorporators to launch the enterprise. Other steps follow such as electing a board of directors, selecting officers, issuing stock according to state laws and, if there is going to be a stock offering to the public, following the regulations of the Securities and Exchange Commission and/or the State Corporations Commissioner. If the corporation is non-profit, it will have to apply for non-profit status with the home state, and may, if desired, also apply to the Internal Revenue Service for federal non-profit recognition, both of which require detailed explanations of the intended operation of the organization. 2) to include into a unit. (See: **corporation, incorporate by reference, incorporation, stock**)

incorporate by reference: v. to include language from another document or elsewhere in a document by reference rather than repeat it. Typical language: "Plaintiff incorporates by reference all of the allegations contained in the First and Second Causes of Action hereinabove stated."

incorporation: n. the act of incorporating an organization. (See: **corporation, incorporate**)

incorporeal: adj. referring to a thing which is not physical, such as a right. This is distinguished from tangible.

The law is the last result of human wisdom acting upon human experience for the benefit of the public.
—Samuel Johnson

incriminate: v. to make a statement in which one admits that he/she has committed a crime or gives information that another named person has committed a crime. Under the Fifth Amendment to the Constitution, a person cannot be forced to give any information which would tend to incriminate himself/herself. Thus, he/she can refuse to answer any question which he/she feels might be a self-accusation or lead to information which would be so.

incumbrance: n. (See: **encumbrance**)

indecent exposure: n. the crime of displaying one's genitalia to one or more other people in a public place, usually with the apparent intent to shock the unsuspecting viewer and give the exposer a sexual charge.

indefeasible: adj. cannot be altered or voided, usually in reference to an interest in real property.

indemnify: v. to guarantee against any loss which another might suffer. Example: two parties settle a dispute over a contract, and one of them may agree to pay any claims which may arise from the contract, holding the other harmless. (See: **hold harmless**)

indemnity: n. the act of making someone "whole" (give equal to what they have lost) or protected from (insured against) any losses which have occurred or will occur. (See: **indemnify**)

indenture: n. a type of real property deed in which two parties agree to continuing mutual obligations. One party may agree to maintain the property, while the other agrees to make periodic payments. 2) a contract binding one person to work for another. 3) v. to bind a person to work for another.

independent contractor: n. a person or business which performs services for another person or entity under a contract between them, with the terms spelled out such as duties, pay, the amount and type of work and other matters. An independent contractor is distinguished from an employee, who works regularly for an employer. The exact nature of the independent contractor's relationship with the party hiring him/her/it has become vital since an independent contractor pays his/her/its own Social Security, income taxes without payroll deduction, has no retirement or health plan rights, and often is not entitled to worker's compensation coverage. Public agencies, particularly the Internal Revenue Service, look hard at independent contractor agreements when it appears the contractor is much like an employee. An independent contractor must be able to determine when and where work is performed, be able to work for others, provide own equipment and other factors which are indicative of true independence. (See: **employee**)

indeterminate sentence: n. the prison term imposed after conviction for a crime which does not state a specific period of time or release date, but just a range of time, such as "five-to-ten years." It is one side of a continuing debate as to whether it is better to make sentences absolute (subject to reduction for good behavior) without reference to potential rehabilitation, modification or review in the future. (See: **sentence**)

indicia: n. (in-dish-yah) from Latin for "signs," circumstances which tend to show or indicate that something is probable. It is used in the form of "*indicia* of title," or "*indicia* of partnership," particularly when the "signs" are items like letters, certificates or other things that one would not have unless the facts were as the possessor claimed. (See: **circumstantial evidence**)

indictable offense: n. a crime (offense) for which a Grand Jury rules that there is enough evidence to charge a defendant with a felony (a crime punishable by death or a term in the state penitentiary). These crimes include murder, manslaughter, rape, kidnapping, grand theft, robbery, burglary, arson, conspiracy, fraud and other major crimes, as well as attempts to commit them. (See: **indictment**)

indictment: n. a charge of a felony (serious crime) voted by a Grand Jury based upon a proposed charge, witnesses' testimony and other evidence presented by the public prosecutor (District Attorney). To bring an indictment the Grand Jury will not find guilt, but only the probability that a crime was committed, that the accused person did it and that he/she should be tried. District Attorneys often only introduce key facts sufficient to show the probability, both to save time and to avoid revealing all the evidence. The Fifth Amendment to the U.S. Constitution provides that "No person shall be held to answer for a capital, or otherwise infamous crime, unless on presentment of a Grand Jury...." However, while grand juries are common in charging federal crimes, many states use grand juries sparingly and use the criminal complaint, followed by a "preliminary hearing" held by a lower court judge or other magistrate, who will determine whether or not the prosecutor has presented sufficient evidence that the accused has committed a felony. If the judge finds there is enough evidence, he/she will order the case sent to the appropriate court for trial. (See: **felony, Grand Jury, indictable offense, preliminary hearing**)

indigent: 1) n. a person so poor and needy that he/she cannot provide the necessities of life (food, clothing, decent shelter) for himself/herself. 2) n. one without sufficient income to afford a lawyer for defense in a criminal case. If the court finds a person is an indigent, the court must appoint a public defender or other attorney to represent him/her. This constitutional right of counsel for the indigent was determined by *Gideon v. Wainright* in 1963, when a penciled letter from a prisoner came to the attention of prominent Washington attorney Abe Fortas, who carried the case to the Supreme Court for free. Fortas later became an Associate Justice of the Supreme Court. 3) adj. referring to a person who is very poor and needy.

indispensable party: n. a person or entity which must be included in a lawsuit so that the court can make a final judgment or order that will conclude the controversy. Example: Ned Neighbor brings an action to enforce his claimed right to cross the property of Oliver and Olivia Owner, but only names Oliver as a defendant. To make it possible for the court to order the property owners to honor Ned's easement, Olivia as a co-owner is an indispensable party. The procedural solution is for Neighbor to amend his complaint or petition to join Olivia as a defendant.

indorse: v. (See: **endorse**)

indorsement: n. (See: **endorsement**)

in extremis: (in ex-tree-miss) adj. from Latin, facing imminent death.

infancy: n. although the popular use of the word means the early years of age up to seven, in law, it is underage or minority. Historically this meant under 21 years, but statutes adopted in almost all states end minority and infancy at 18. An "infant" cannot file a lawsuit without a "guardian *ad litem*" (one-purpose guardian) acting for him/her, in most states cannot marry without parental permission, and cannot enter into a contract that is enforceable during his/her minority. (See: *ad litem*, **minority**)

in fee simple: adj. referring to holding clear title to real property. (See: **fee, fee simple**)

inference: n. a rule of logic applied to evidence in a trial, in which a fact is "proved" by presenting other "facts" which lead to only one reasonable conclusion—that if A and B are true, then C is. The process is called "deduction" or "deductive reasoning" and is a persuasive form of circumstantial evidence. (See: **circumstantial evidence**)

in forma pauperis: (in form-ah paw-purr-iss) adj. or adv. Latin for "in the form of a pauper," referring to a party to a lawsuit who gets filing fees waived by filing a declaration of lack of funds (has no money to pay). These declarations are most often found in divorces by young marrieds or poor defendants who have been sued.

information: n. an accusation or criminal charge brought by the public prosecutor (District Attorney) without a Grand Jury indictment. This "information" must state the alleged crimes in writing and must be delivered to the defendant at the first court appearance (arraignment). If the accusation is for a felony, there must be a preliminary hearing within a short period (such as five days) in which the prosecution is required to present enough evidence to convince the judge holding the hearing that the crime or crimes charged were committed and the defendant is likely to have committed them. If the judge becomes convinced, the defendant must face trial, and if the judge does not, the case against the defendant is dismissed. Sometimes it is a mixed bag, in that some of the charges in the information are sufficient for trial and the case is sent (remanded) to the appropriate court, and some are dismissed. (See: **accusation, charge, felony, Grand Jury, indictment, preliminary hearing**)

information and belief: n. a phrase often used in legal pleadings (complaints and answers in a lawsuit), declarations under penalty of perjury, and affidavits under oath, in which the person making the statement or allegation qualifies it. In effect, he/she says: "I am only stating what I have been told, and I believe it." This makes clear about which statements he/she does not have sure-fire, personal knowledge (perhaps it is just hearsay or surmise) and protects the maker of the statement from claims of outright falsehood or perjury. The typical phraseology is: "Plaintiff is informed and believes, and upon such information and belief, alleges that defendant diverted the funds to his own use." (See: **affidavit, answer, complaint, declaration, perjury**)

informed consent: n. agreement to do something or to allow something to happen only after all the relevant facts are known. In contracts, an agreement may be reached only if there has been full disclosure by both parties of everything each party knows which is significant to the agreement. A patient's consent to a medical procedure must be based on his/her having been told all the possible consequences, except in emergency cases when such consent cannot be obtained. A physician or dentist who does not tell all the possible bad news as well as the good, operates at his/her peril of a lawsuit if anything goes wrong. In criminal law, a person accused or even suspected of a crime cannot give up his/her legal rights such as remaining silent or having an attorney, unless he/she has been fully informed of his/her rights. (See: **consent, Miranda warning**)

infra: prep. Latin for "below," this is legal shorthand to indicate that the details or citation of a case will come later on in the brief. *Infra* is distinguished from *supra*, which shows that a case has already been cited "above." The typical language is *Jones v. McLaughlin, infra*, meaning the exact citation of the case, including volume and page number, will follow later in the document. (See: **citation, cite**)

infringement: n. 1) a trespassing or illegal entering. 2) in the law of patents (protected inventions) and copyrights (protected writings or graphics), the improper use of a patent, writing, graphic or trademark without permission, without notice, and especially without contracting for payment of a royalty. Even though the infringement may be accidental (an inventor thinks he is the first to develop the widget although someone else has a patent), the party infringing is responsible to pay the original patent or copyright owner substantial damages, which can be the normal royalty or as much as the infringers' accumulated gross profits. (See: **copyright, patent, plagiarism, royalty, trademark**)

ingress: 1) n. entrance. 2) n. the right to enter. 3) v. the act of entering. Often used in the combination "ingress and egress," which means entering and leaving, to describe one's rights to come and go under an easement over another's property. (See: **easement, egress**)

in haec verba: (in hike verb-ah) prep. Latin for "in these words," which refers to stating the exact language of an agreement in a complaint or other pleading rather than attaching a copy of the agreement as an exhibit incorporated into the pleading. (See: **complaint, pleading**)

inherit: v. to receive all or a portion of the estate of an ancestor upon his/her death, usually from a parent or other close relative pursuant to the laws of descent. Technically, one would "inherit" only if there is no will, but popularly it means any taking from the estate of a relative, including a wife or husband, by will or not. (See: **descent and distribution,**

heir, heiress, intestacy, intestate succession, will)

inheritance: n. whatever one receives upon the death of a relative due to the laws of descent and distribution, when there is no will. However, inheritance has come to mean anything received from the estate of a person who has died, whether by the laws of descent or as a beneficiary of a will or trust. (See: **descent and distribution, heir, heiress, inherit, intestacy, intestate succession, will**)

injunction: n. a writ (order) issued by a court ordering someone to do something or prohibiting some act after a court hearing. The procedure is for someone who has been or is in danger of being harmed, or needs some help (relief) or his/her attorney, to a) petition for the injunction to protect his/her rights; to b) get an "order to show cause" from the judge telling the other party to show why the injunction should not be issued; c) serve (personally delivered) the order to show cause on the party whom he/she wishes to have ordered to act or be restrained ("enjoined"); partake in a hearing in which both sides attempt to convince the judge why the injunction should or should not be granted. If there is danger of immediate irreparable harm at the time the petition is filed, a judge may issue a temporary injunction which goes into effect upon it being served (deliver or have delivered) to the other party. This temporary injunction will stay in force until the hearing or sometimes until the outcome of a lawsuit is decided in which an injunction is one of the parts of the plaintiff's demands (in the "prayer"). A final and continuing injunction is called a permanent injunction. Examples of injunctions include prohibitions against cutting trees, creating nuisances, polluting a stream, picketing which goes beyond the bounds of free speech and assembly, or removing funds from a bank account pending determination of ownership. So-called "mandatory" injunctions which require acts to be performed, may include return of property, keeping a gate to a road unlocked, clearing off tree limbs from a right-of-way, turning on electricity or heat in an apartment building, or depositing disputed funds with the court. (See: **injunctive relief, writ**)

injunctive relief: n. a court-ordered act or prohibition against an act or condition which has been requested, and sometimes granted, in a petition to the court for an injunction. Such an act is the use of judicial (court) authority to handle a problem and is not a judgment for money. Whether the relief will be granted is usually argued by both sides in a hearing rather than in a full-scale trial, although sometimes it is part of a lawsuit for damages and/or contract performance. Historically, the power to grant injunctive relief stems from English equity courts rather than damages from law courts. (See: **equity, injunction, permanent injunction, restraining order, writ**)

injury: n. any harm done to a person by the acts or omissions of another. Injury may include physical hurt as well as damage to reputation or dignity, loss of a legal right or breach of contract. If the party causing the injury was either willful (intentionally causing harm) or negligent then he/she is responsible (liable) for payment of damages for the harm caused. Theoretically, potential or continuing injury may be prevented by an order of the court upon a petition for an injunction. (See: **damages, injunction, injunctive relief, negligence**)

in kind: adj. referring to payment, distribution or substitution of things in lieu of money, a combination of goods and money, or money instead of an article. It is an expression often found in wills and trusts, which empowers the executor or trustee to make distribution to beneficiaries "in kind" according to his/her discretion as long as the value is equivalent to the value intended to be given to each beneficiary. This is important since it allows distribution of furniture, heirlooms, stocks and bonds, automobiles or even real property (as well as money) among the beneficiaries without selling assets to get cash. Example: Edward Doright dies with a will that leaves his estate equally to his two daughters and a son. He has a house worth $150,000, cash of $100,000, art works valued at $50,000, two cars at $10,000 each, $150,000 in stocks, and jewelry appraised at $25,000. Since the total value is $495,000, the executor can thus divide this up by giving each child things and money valued at $165,000. The one taking the house would then get a car and $5,000 cash, etc. In this way gifts can be distributed most appropriately to the needs of the recipients. The "in kind" provision may avoid the potential low value returns from estate sales and the cost of real estate commissions. (See: **distribution, trust, will**)

in lieu: prep. instead. "In lieu taxes" are use taxes paid instead of sales tax. A "deed in lieu of foreclosure" occurs when a debtor just deeds the property securing the loan to the lender rather than go through the foreclosure process.

in limine: (in lim-in-ay) from Latin for "at the threshold," referring to a motion before a trial begins. A motion to suppress illegally obtained evidence is such a motion. (See: **motion to suppress**)

in loco parentis: prep. (in loh-coh pah-rent-iss) Latin for "instead of a parent" or "in place of a parent," this phrase identifies a foster parent, a county custodial agency or a boarding school which is taking care of a minor, including protecting his/her rights. Thus, Boys' Town is legally *in loco parentis* to Johnny Boarder, aged 15, if and when he needs legal help.

innocent: adj. without guilt (not guilty). Usually the plea which an accused criminal defendant gives to the court at the time of his/her first appearance (or after a continued appearance). Such pleas often disturb the public in cases in which guilt seems obvious from the start. However, everyone is entitled to a fair trial, and the innocent plea gives defense lawyers an opportunity to investigate, find extenuating circumstances, develop reasons punishment should be lenient, bargain with the District

Attorney, and let the memories of witnesses fade. (See: **arraignment, guilt, plea, plea bargain**)

innuendo: n. from Latin *innuere*, "to nod toward." In law it means "an indirect hint." "Innuendo" is used in lawsuits for defamation (libel or slander), usually to show that the party suing was the person about whom the nasty statements were made or why the comments were defamatory. Example: "the former Mayor is a crook," and Joe Alabaster is the only living ex-Mayor, thus by innuendo Alabaster is the target of the statement; or "Joe Alabaster was paid $100,000 by the Hot Springs Water Company," when it was known that Hot Springs was bucking for a contract with the city. The innuendo is that Alabaster took a bribe. (See: **defamation, libel, slander**)

in pari delicto: adv. (in pah-ree dee-lick-toe) Latin for "in equal fault," which means that two (or more) people are all at fault or are all guilty of a crime. In contract law, if the fault is more or less equal then neither party can claim breach of the contract by the other; in an accident, neither can collect damages, unless the fault is more on one than the other under the rule of "comparative negligence"; in defense of a criminal charge, one defendant will have a difficult time blaming the other for inducing him or her into the criminal acts if the proof is that both were involved.

in perpetuity: adj. forever, as in one's right to keep the profits from the land in perpetuity.

in personam: adj. (in purr-soh-nam) from Latin for "directed toward a particular person." In a lawsuit in which the case is against a specific individual, that person must be served with a summons and complaint to give the court jurisdiction to try the case, and the judgment applies to that person and is called an "in personam judgment." *In personam* is distinguished from *in rem,* which applies to property or "all the world" instead of a specific person. This technical distinction is important to determine where to file a lawsuit and how to serve a defendant. *In personam* means that a judgment can be enforceable against the person wherever he/she is. On the other hand, if the lawsuit is to determine title to property *(in rem)* then the action must be filed where the property exists and is only enforceable there. (See: **in rem, jurisdiction**)

in pro per: adj. short for in *propria persona*. (See: **in propria persona**)

in propria persona: adj. from Latin "for one's self," acting on one's own behalf, generally used to identify a person who is acting as his/her own attorney in a lawsuit. The popular abbreviation is "in pro per." In the filed legal documents (pleadings), the party's name, address and telephone number are written where the name, address and telephone number of the attorney would normally be stated. The words "in propria persona" or "in pro per" are typed where normally it would say "attorney for plaintiff." Judges sometimes warn a party "in propria persona" of the old adage that "anyone who represents himself in court has a fool for a client and an ass for an attorney."

Two skillful lawyers are like two experts at any game of skill or endurance, and the result is, that the clearest case becomes at least somewhat doubtful, and the event quite problematical.
—*Irving Brown, Legal Recreations*

inquest: n. 1) an investigation and/or a hearing held by the coroner (a county official) when there is a violent death either by accident or homicide, the cause of death is not immediately clear, there are mysterious circumstances surrounding the death, or the deceased was a prisoner. Usually an autopsy by a qualified medical examiner from the coroner's office is a key part of the inquest. In rare cases a jury may be used to determine the cause of death. 2) a term used in New York for a hearing on the validity of a will by a surrogate judge. (See: **coroner**)

in re: prep. short for "in regard to" or concerning. Often "in re" is found near the top of lawyers' letters to identify the subject matter, as "*In re Matheson v. Roth*," or "*In re Estate of Ruth Bentley*." It is also used in naming legal actions in which there is only one party, the petitioning party, as in "*In re Adoption of Marcus McGillicuddy*."

in rem: adj. from Latin "against or about a thing," referring to a lawsuit or other legal action directed toward property, rather than toward a particular person. Thus, if title to property is the issue, the action is "*in rem*." The term is important since the location of the property determines which court has jurisdiction and enforcement of a judgment must be upon the property and does not follow a person. "*In rem*" is different from "*in personam*," which is directed toward a particular person. (See: *in personam*)

insanity: n. mental illness of such a severe nature that a person cannot distinguish fantasy from reality, cannot conduct her/his affairs due to psychosis, or is subject to uncontrollable impulsive behavior. Insanity is distinguished from low intelligence or mental deficiency due to age or injury. If a complaint is made to law enforcement, to the District Attorney or to medical personnel that a person is evidencing psychotic behavior, he/she may be confined to a medical facility long enough (typically 72 hours) to be examined by psychiatrists who submit written reports to the local superior/county/district court. A hearing is then held before a judge, with the person in question entitled to legal representation, to determine if she/he should be placed in an institution or special facility. The person ordered institutionalized at the hearing may request a trial to determine sanity. Particularly since the original hearings are often routine with the psychiatric findings accepted by the judge. In criminal cases, a plea of "not guilty by reason of insanity" will require a trial on the issue of the defendant's insanity (or sanity) at the time the crime was committed. In these cases the defendant usually claims "temporary insanity" (crazy then, but okay now). The traditional test of insanity in criminal cases is whether the accused knew "the difference between right and wrong," following the "M'Naughten rule" from

19th century England. Most states require more sophisticated tests based on psychiatric and/or psychological testimony evaluated by a jury of laypersons or a judge without psychiatric training. A claim by a criminal defendant of his/her insanity at the time of trial requires a separate hearing to determine if a defendant is sufficiently sane to understand the nature of a trial and participate in his/her own defense. If found to be insane, the defendant will be ordered to a mental facility, and the trial will be held only if sanity returns. Sex offenders may be found to be sane for all purposes except the compulsive dangerous and/or antisocial behavior. They are usually sentenced to special facilities for sex offenders, supposedly with counseling available. However, there are often maximum terms related to the type of crime, so that parole and release may occur with no proof of cure of the compulsive desire to commit sex crimes. (See: **insanity defense, M'Naughten rule, temporary insanity**)

insanity defense: n. the claim of a defendant in a criminal prosecution that he/she was insane when the crime was committed, usually only temporarily. (See: **insanity, temporary insanity**)

insertion: n. the addition of language at a place within an existing typed or written document, which is always suspect unless initialled by all parties.

insider: n. someone who has a position in a business or stock brokerage, which allows him/her to be privy to confidential information (such as future changes in management, upcoming profit and loss reports, secret sales figures and merger negotiations) which will affect the value of stocks or bonds. While there is nothing wrong with being an insider, use of the confidential information unavailable to the investing public in order to profit through sale or purchase of stocks or bonds is unethical and a crime under the Securities and Exchange Act. (See: **insider trading**)

> *Decency, security and liberty alike demand that government officials shall be subjected to the same rules of conduct that are commands to the citizen.*
> *—Justice Louis D. Brandeis*

insider trading: n. the use of confidential information about a business gained through employment in a company or a stock brokerage, to buy and/or sell stocks and bonds based on the private knowledge that the value will go up or down. The victims are the unsuspecting investing public. It is a crime under the Securities and Exchange Act, for which Ivan Boesky and others have been sentenced to prison for relatively short terms and only small fines, considering the percentage impact on their accumulated wealth. Joseph P. Kennedy, father of President John F. Kennedy, made much of his fortune in the 1920s by insider trading before it was a crime. When the Securities and Exchange Commission was created in the early days of the New Deal (1933), President Franklin D. Roosevelt appointed Kennedy to the Commission on the theory that it took an insider to catch insiders. (See: **insider**)

insolvency: n. 1) the condition of having more debts (liabilities) than total assets which might be available to pay them, even if the assets were mortgaged or sold. 2) a determination by a bankruptcy court that a person or business cannot raise the funds to pay all of his/her debts. The court will then "discharge" (forgive) some or all of the debts, leaving those creditors holding the bag and not getting what is owed them. The supposedly insolvent individual debtor, even though found to be bankrupt, is allowed certain exemptions, which permit him/her to retain a car, business equipment, personal property and often a home as long as he/she continues to make payments on a loan secured by the property. (See: **bankruptcy**)

inspection of documents: n. the right to examine and copy the opposing party's papers in a lawsuit which are relevant to the case. A demand (legal request) may be made, but the categories of documents must be stated so that the other party can know what he/she must produce. If the opposition either refuses to produce some documents or appears to hold back, the party wanting to see the documents can bring a "motion to produce" requesting a court order to produce and a penalty (sanctions) to be paid for failure to honor the demand. A party may also use a subpena *duces tecum* to obtain specific documents if they are known to exist. All of these procedures are part of the discovery process, intended to give both sides extensive pre-trial information. Such exchanges of documents can lead to settlement, minimize surprises at trial and keep one side from hiding material, thus preventing the other from being able to introduce relevant material at trial. However, it is well known that many law firms obfuscate, delay, pretend to misunderstand requests and fail to be forthcoming. (See: **discovery, evidence, subpena** *duces tecum*, **trial**)

installment contract: n. an agreement in which payments of money, delivery of goods or performance of services are to be made in a series of payments, deliveries or performances, usually on specific dates or upon certain happenings. One significance is that failure to pay an installment when due is a breach in which damages can be assessed based on the portion which has not been paid, and is an excuse for the other party not to perform further. In many installment contracts, failure to make a payment gives the seller of an article the right to repossess (take it back). (See: **anticipatory breach, breach, consideration, contract, failure of consideration**)

instruction: n. an explanation of the law governing a case which the judge gives orally to the jury after the attorneys have presented all the evidence and have made final arguments, but before the jury begins deliberations.

instrument: n. 1) a written legal document such as a contract, lease, deed, will or bond. 2) an object used to perform some task or action, ranging from a surgeon's scalpel to any hard thing used in an assault (a blunt instrument).

insufficient evidence: n. a finding (decision) by a trial judge or an appeals court that the prosecution in a criminal case or a plaintiff in a lawsuit has not proved the case because the attorney did not present enough convincing evidence. Insufficient evidence usually results in dismissal of the case after the prosecution or the plaintiff has completed his/her introduction of evidence or, if on appeal, reversal of the judgment by the trial court. (See: **evidence, finding**)

insurance: n. a contract (insurance policy) in which the insurer (insurance company) agrees for a fee (insurance premiums) to pay the insured party all or a portion of any loss suffered by accident or death. The losses covered by the policy may include property damage or loss from accident, fire, theft or intentional harm; medical costs and/or lost earnings due to physical injury; long-term or permanent loss of physical capacity; claims by others due to the insured's alleged negligence (e.g. public liability auto insurance); loss of a ship and/or cargo; finding a defect in title to real property; dishonest employees; or the loss of someone's life. Life insurance may be on the life of a spouse, a child, one of several business partners or an especially important manager ("key man" insurance), all of which is intended to provide for survivors or to ease the burden created by the loss of a financial contributor. So-called "mortgage" insurance is life insurance which will pay off the remaining amount due on a home loan on the death of the husband or wife. Life insurance proceeds are usually not included in the probate of a dead person's estate, but the funds may be counted by the Internal Revenue Service in calculating estate tax. Insurance companies may refuse to pay a claim by a third party against an insured, but at the same time may be required to assume the legal defense (pay attorney's fees or provide an attorney) under the doctrine of "reservation of rights." (See: **insured, insurer, reservation, uninsured motorist clause, Workers' Compensation Acts**)

insured: n. 1) the person or entity who will be compensated for loss by an insurer under the terms of a contract called an insurance policy. 2) the person whose life is insured by life insurance, after whose death the benefits go to others. (See: **insurance**)

insurer: n. an insurance company which agrees to pay someone who pays them for insurance for losses suffered pursuant to the terms of an insurance policy. For this benefit the customer pays the company a fee, called a premium. (See: **insurance**)

intangible property: n. items such as stock in a company which represent value but are not actual, tangible objects.

integration: n. 1) adopting a writing as part of an agreement, e.g. "the parties agree that Robert's Rules of Order shall be the procedural rules employed during negotiations." 2) removing barriers to schooling, housing and employment which formerly segregated races, particularly blacks and sometimes Hispanics, from the general society, dominated by whites in the United States. Integration includes encouragement of free and equal association, equal access to public facilities and housing in any neighborhood, equitable employment, promotions and pay levels, as well as racial mix in schools.

intent: n. mental desire and will to act in a particular way, including wishing not to participate. Intent is a crucial element in determining if certain acts were criminal. Occasionally a judge or jury may find that "there was no criminal intent." Example: lack of intent may reduce a charge of manslaughter to a finding of reckless homicide or other lesser crime.

inter alia: (in-tur eh-lee-ah) prep. Latin for "among other things." This phrase is often found in legal pleadings and writings to specify one example out of many possibilities. Example: "The judge said, *inter alia*, that the time to file the action had passed."

interest: n. 1) any and all, partial or total right to property or for the use of property, including an easement to pass over a neighboring parcel of land, the right to drill for oil, a possibility of acquiring title upon the happening of some event, or outright title. While most often referring to real property, one may have an interest in a business, a bank account or any article. 2) the financial amount (money) paid by someone else for the use of a person's money, as on a loan or debt, on a savings account in a bank, on a certificate of deposit, promissory note or the amount due on a judgment. Inter-

est is usually stated in writing at the time the money is loaned. There are variable rates of interest, particularly on savings accounts which depend on funding from the Federal Reserve or other banks and are controlled by the prevailing interest rates on those funds. Maximum interest rates on loans made by individuals are controlled by statute. To charge more than that rate is usury, the penalty for which may be the inability of a creditor to collect through the courts. The interest rates demanded by lending institutions are not so restricted. The maximum legal interest often granted by the courts on judgments is set by the law of the state. Simple interest is the annual rate charged for a loan, and compound interest includes interest upon interest during the year. 3) one's involvement in business, activities or with an individual which is sufficient to create doubt about a witness being objective— damaging his/her credibility. 4) one's involvement in business, activities or with an individual which is sufficient connection to give a person "standing" (the right based on interest in the outcome of the lawsuit or petition) to bring a lawsuit on a particular matter or act on behalf of other people. (See: **compound interest, easement, future interest, personal property, real property, standing**)

interim order: n. a temporary order of the court pending a hearing, trial, a final order or while awaiting an act by one of the parties. (See: **interlocutory decree, restraining order**)

interlineation: n. the act of writing between the lines of a document, usually to add something that was omitted or thought of later. The issue (debated question) is whether both parties to a document (a contract, for example) had agreed upon the addition or whether the new words were part of the document (like a will) when it was signed. Good practice is either to have all parties initial the change at the point of the writing or have the document re-typed and then signed.

interlocutory: adj. provisional and not intended to be final. This usually refers to court orders which are temporary. (See: **interlocutory decree**)

interlocutory decree: n. a court judgment which is temporary and not intended to be final until either a) other matters come before the judge, or b) there is a specified passage of time to determine if the interlocutory decree (judgment) is "working" (becomes accepted by both parties) and should become final. Interlocutory decrees were most commonly used in divorce actions, in which the terms of the divorce were stated in an interlocutory decree, which would be in force until a final decree could be granted after a period of time (such as one year after serving the divorce petition). The theory was that this would provide for a period in which reconciliation might be possible and would also test the efficacy of the original order which might be changed upon a motion of either party. Interlocutory decrees of divorce have been abandoned as a procedure in most states, because they seldom had the desired effect and appeared to waste the parties' time.

international law: n. treaties between countries; multi-lateral agreements; some commissions covering particular subjects, such as whaling or copyrights; procedures and precedents of the International Court of Justice ("World Court") which only has jurisdiction when countries agree to appear; the United Nations Charter; and custom. However, there is no specific body of law which governs the interaction of all nations. (See: **World Court**)

interpleader: n. the procedure when two parties are involved in a lawsuit over the right to collect a debt from a third party, who admits the money is owed but does not know which person to pay. The debtor deposits the funds with the court ("interpleads"), asks the court to dismiss him/her/it from the lawsuit and lets the claimants fight over it in court.

interrogation: n. questioning of a suspect or witness by law enforcement authorities. Once a person being questioned is arrested (is a "prime" suspect), he/she is entitled to be informed of his/her legal rights, and in no case may the interrogation violate rules of due process. (See: **due process, fruit of the poisonous tree, Miranda warning**)

interrogatories: n. a set of written questions to a party to a lawsuit asked by the opposing party as part of the pre-trial discovery process. These questions must be answered in writing under oath or under penalty of perjury within a specified time (such as 30 days). Several states ask basic "form" interrogatories on a printed form, with an allowance for "supplemental" interrogatories specifically relevant to the lawsuit. Normal practice is for the lawyers to prepare the questions and for the answering party to have help from his/her/its attorney in understanding the meaning (sometimes hidden) of the questions and to avoid wording in his/her answers which could be interpreted against the party answering. Objections as to relevancy or clarity may be raised either at the time the interrogatories are answered or when they are used in trial. Most states limit the number of interrogatories that may be asked without the court's permission to keep the questions from being a means of oppression rather than a source of information. While useful in getting basic information, they are much easier to ask than answer and are often intentionally burdensome. In addition the parties may request depositions (pre-trial questioning in front of a court reporter) or send "requests for admissions" which must be answered in writing. (See: **admissions, deposition, discovery**)

in terrorem **clause**: (in tehr-roar-em) n. from Latin for "in fear," a provision in a will which threatens that if anyone challenges the legality of the will or any part of it, then that person will be cut off or given only a dollar, instead of getting the full gift provided in the will. The clause is intended to discourage beneficiaries from causing a legal ruckus after the will writer is gone. However, if the will is challenged and found to be invalid (due to lack of mental capacity, undue influence or failure to have it properly executed), then such a clause also fails. So a prospective challenger takes his/her chances. The courts have ruled that merely putting in a claim for moneys due from the estate is not a legal challenge to the will itself and is permissible without losing the gift. (See: **will, will contest**)

inter se: (in-tur say) prep. Latin for "among themselves," meaning that, for instance, certain corporate rights are limited only to the shareholders or only to the trustees as a group.

interstate commerce: n. commercial trade, business, movement of goods or money, or transportation from one state to another, regulated by the federal government according to powers spelled out in Article I of the Constitution. The federal government can also regulate commerce within a state when it may impact interstate movement of goods and services and may strike down state actions which are barriers to such movement under Chief Justice John Marshall's decision in Gibbons v. Ogden (1824). Theoretically commerce is regulated by the Interstate Commerce Commission (I.C.C.) under authority granted by the Interstate Commerce Act, first enacted by Congress in 1887. This authority has been diffused among various federal agencies, and the I.C.C. may soon be history.

intervene: v. to obtain the court's permission to enter into a lawsuit which has already started between other parties and to file a complaint stating the basis for a claim in the existing lawsuit. Such intervention will be allowed only if the party wanting to enter into the case has some right or interest in the suit and will not unduly prejudice the ability of the original parties to the lawsuit to conduct their case. Example: Little Buttercup Butter Co. has been sued by Market Bag Grocers for selling below standard butter. Better Buy Market has also been buying Buttercup's butter and wishes to intervene (join in the lawsuit) to avoid either a loss by Market Bag which would affect Better Buy's possible claim, and also to avoid two separate suits. Or another butter company might want to join the suit on Buttercup's side in order to put up a united front with Buttercup against the markets. (See: **intervention, joinder, multiplicity of suits**)

intervening cause: n. an event which occurs between the original improper or dangerous action and the damage itself. Thus, the "causal connection" between the wrong and damages is broken by the intervening cause. This is a "but for" situation, in which the intervention becomes the real reason harm resulted. The result is that the person who started the chain of events is no longer responsible and will not be found liable for damages to the injured person. Example: Fred Flameout negligently starts a wildfire by welding on his hay bailer next to a row of haystacks, some hay catches fire, and the fire spreads, heading toward the next-door ranch. However, just as the county fire department has the fire nearly contained, Peter Petrol drives his oil truck through the fireline against a fire fighter's orders and stops on the road between Flameout's property and Richard Rancher's. Sparks from

the fire cause Petrol's truck to explode, sending the fire on the way to Rancher's barns and home, which burn down. Petrol's negligence is an intervening cause which gets Flameout off the liability hook. Sometimes this is called supervening cause or superseding. (See: **cause, negligence, superseding cause**)

intervention: n. the procedure under which a third party may join an ongoing lawsuit, providing the facts and the law issues apply to the intervenor as much as to one of the existing contestants. The determination to allow intervention is made by a judge after a petition to intervene and a hearing on the issue. Intervention must take place fairly early in the lawsuit, shortly after a complaint and answer have been filed and not just before trial since that could prejudice one or both parties who have prepared for trial on the basis of the original litigants. Intervention is not to be confused with joinder, which involves requiring all parties who have similar claims to join in the same lawsuit to prevent needless repetitious trials based on the same facts and legal questions, called multiplicity of actions. (See: **intervene, joinder, multiplicity of suits**)

inter vivos: (in-tur veye-vohs) adj. Latin for "among the living," usually referring to the transfer of property by agreement between living persons and not by a gift through a will. It can also refer to a trust (*inter vivos* trust) which commences during the lifetime of the person (trustor or settlor) creating the trust as distinguished from a trust created by a will (testamentary trust), which comes into existence upon the death of the writer of the will. (See: *inter vivos* **trust**)

inter vivos **trust**: n. a trust created by a writing (declaration of trust) which commences at that time, while the creator (called a trustor or settlor) is alive, sometimes called a "living trust." The property is then placed in trust with a trustee (often the trustor during his/her lifetime) and distribution will take place according to the terms of the trust—possibly both during the trustor's lifetime and then upon the trustor's death. This is different from a testamentary trust, which is created by the terms of a will and places some assets from the dead person's estate in a trust to exist from the date of death and until fully distributed. (See: **declaration of trust,** *inter vivos,* **testamentary trust, trust**)

intestacy: n. the condition of having died without a valid will. In such a case if the dead party has property it will be distributed according to statutes, primarily by the law of descent and distribution and others dealing with marital property and community property. In probate the administration of the estate of a person without a will is handled by an administrator (usually a close relative, the spouse, a close associate) or a public administrator if there is no one willing to act, since there is no executor named in a will. In most states an administrator must petition the court to be appointed and must post a bond from an insurance company guaranteeing that it will pay the value of the assets he/she/it may steal or misuse.

(See: **distribution and descent, intestate, probate, will**)

intestate: adj. referring to a situation where a person dies without leaving a valid will. This usually is voiced as "he died intestate," "intestate estate," or "intestate succession." (See: **intestacy, intestate succession**)

intestate succession: n. the distribution when a person dies without leaving a valid will and the spouse and heirs will take (receive the possessions) by the laws of descent and distribution and marital rights in the estate which may apply to a surviving spouse. Collectively these are called the laws of intestate succession. (See: **intestacy, intestate**)

in toto: (in toe-toe) adj. Latin for "completely" or "in total," referring to the entire thing, as in "the goods were destroyed *in toto*," or "the case was dismissed *in toto*."

intoxication: n. 1) the condition of being drunk as the result of drinking alcoholic beverages and/or use of narcotics. In the eyes of the law this definition may differ depending on the situation to which it is applied. 2) as it applies to drunk driving (DUI, DWI) the standard of intoxication varies by state between .08 and .10 alcohol in the bloodstream, or a combination of alcohol and narcotics which would produce the same effect even though the amount of alcohol is below the minimum. 3) as it applies to public drunkenness the standard is subjective, meaning the person must be unable to care for himself, be dangerous to himself or others, be causing a disturbance or refuse to leave or move along when requested. 4) a defense in a criminal case in which the claim is made by the defendant that he/she was too intoxicated to form an intent to commit the crime or to know what he/she was doing, where the amount of intoxication is subjective but higher than for drunk driving. There is also the question if the intoxication was an intentional aforethought to the crime ("I wanted to get drunk so I had the nerve to kill her"). Unintentional intoxication can show lack of capacity to form an intent and thus reduce the possible level of conviction and punishment, as from voluntary (intentional) manslaughter down to involuntary (unintentional but through a wrongful act) manslaughter. However, in vehicular manslaughter, the intoxication is an element in the crime, whether getting drunk was intentional or not, since criminal intent was not a factor. (See: **driving under the influence, vehicular manslaughter**)

intrinsic fraud: n. an intentionally false representation (lie) which is part of the fraud and can be considered in determining general and punitive damages. This is distinguished from extrinsic fraud (collateral fraud) which was a deceptive means to keeping one from enforcing his/her legal rights. (See: **extrinsic fraud, fraud**)

inure: v. result in. Commonly used in legal terminology in the phrase: "to inure to the benefit of Janet Jones."

invasion of privacy: n. the intrusion into the personal life of another, without just cause, which can give the person whose privacy has been invaded a right to bring a lawsuit for damages against the person or entity that intruded. However, public personages are not protected in most situations, since they have placed themselves already within the public eye, and their activities (even personal and sometimes intimate) are considered newsworthy, i.e. of legitimate public interest. However, an otherwise non-public individual has a right to privacy from: a) intrusion on one's solitude or into one's private affairs; b) public disclosure of embarrassing private information; c) publicity which puts him/her in a false light to the public; d) appropriation of one's name or picture for personal or commercial advantage. Lawsuits have arisen from magazine articles on obscure geniuses, use of a wife's name on a hospital insurance form to obtain insurance payment for delivery of a mistress's baby, unauthorized use of a girl's photo to advertise a photographer, and "tabloid" journalism treatment of people as freaks. There are also numerous instances of governmental invasion of privacy such as the Federal Bureau of Investigation compiling files on people considered as political opponents, partially corrected by the passage of the Freedom of Information Act in 1966. The right to privacy originated with an article in the *Harvard Law Review* in the 1890s written by lawyers "Bull" Warren and future Supreme Court Justice Louis D. Brandeis. (See: **right to privacy**)

inverse condemnation: n. the taking of property by a government agency which so greatly damages the use of a parcel of real property that it is the equivalent of condemnation of the entire property. Thus the owner claims he/she is entitled to payment for the loss of the property (in whole or in part) under the constitutional right to compensation for condemnation of property under the government's eminent domain right. Example: the city of Los Angeles widens a boulevard and thereby takes the entire parking lot of Bennison's Busy Bee Market. The city offers to pay for the lot, but Bennison claims the market has lost all its business since no one can park and wants the value of the entire parcel, including the market building. (See: **condemnation, eminent domain**)

invest: v. to put money into a business or buy property or securities for the purpose of eventually obtaining a profit. This is distinguished from a gift or a loan made merely to accommodate a friend or taking a complete gamble. (See: **investment**)

investment: n. the money put into use for profit, or the property or business interest purchased for profit. (See: **invest**)

invitee: n. a person who comes onto another's property, premises or business establishment upon invitation. The invitation may be direct and express or "implied," as when a shop is open and the public is expected to enter to inspect, purchase or otherwise do business on the premises. It may be legally important, because an invitee is entitled to assume safe conditions on the property or premises, so the owner or proprietor might be liable for any injury suffered by the invitee while on the property due to an unsafe condition which is not obvious to the invitee (a latent defect) and not due to the invitee's own negligence. An invitee is distinguished from a trespasser who cuts across the owner's vacant lot, a person who comes into the store to use the bathroom (although a clever lawyer will claim this is a goodwill aspect to the business in which the public is implicitly invited), or a burglar who falls through a faulty skylight. Examples of failures unexpected by an invitee: a person falls through a covered-over well, faulty stairs, weak floors, slippery floors on rainy days (a favorite), spills of jam which are not promptly cleaned up although known to the management, lack of adequate security guards to protect against muggers, and various careless acts of retail employees. (See: **negligence**)

involuntary: adj. or adv. without intent, will or choice. Participation in a crime is involuntary if forced by immediate threat to life or health of oneself or one's loved ones and will result in dismissal or acquittal.

ipse dixit: (ip-sah dicks-it) v. Latin for "he himself said it," meaning the only proof we have of the fact is that this person said it.

ipso facto: (ip-soh fact-toe) prep. Latin for "by the fact itself." An expression more popular with comedians imitating lawyers than with lawyers themselves. A simple example: "a blind person, *ipso facto*, is not entitled to a driver's license."

irreconcilable differences: n. the usual basis for granting a divorce (dissolution) in no-fault divorce states. If one party says the marriage is irretrievable and refuses to reconcile then such differences are proved to exist. (See: **dissolution of marriage, divorce, no fault divorce**)

irrelevant: adj. not important, pertinent, or germane to the matter at hand or to any issue before the court. This is the most common objection raised by attorneys to questions asked or to answers given during testimony in a trial. The objection is made as soon as an alert attorney believes the opposition is going into matters which are not concerned with the facts or outside the issues of the lawsuit. It is often stated in the trio: "Irrelevant, immaterial and incompetent" to cover the bases. The judge must then rule on the relevancy of the question. If the question has been answered before the lawyer could say "objection," the judge may order that answer stricken from the record. Blotting it from a jury's memory or conscience, though, is impossible. (See: **evidence, immaterial, incompetent, objection**)

irreparable damage or injury: n. the type of harm which no monetary compensation can cure or put conditions back the way they were, such as cutting down shade trees, polluting a stream, not giving a child needed medication, not supporting an excavation which may cause collapse of a building, tearing down a structure, or a host of other actions or omissions. The phrase must be used to claim that

a judge should order an injunction, writ, temporary restraining order or other judicial assistance, generally known as equitable relief. Such relief is a court order of positive action, such as prohibiting pollution or requiring the shoring up of a defective wall. (See: **equity, injunction, remedy, writ**)

issue: 1) n. a person's children or other lineal descendants such as grandchildren and great-grandchildren. It does not mean all heirs, but only the direct bloodline. Occasionally, there is a problem in determining whether a writer of a will or deed meant issue to include descendants beyond his or her immediate children. While a child or children are alive, issue refers only to them, but if they are deceased then it will apply to the next living generation unless there is language in the document which shows it specifically does not apply to them. 2) n. any matter of dispute in a legal controversy or lawsuit, very commonly used in such phrases as "the legal issues are," "the factual issues are," "this is an issue which the judge must decide," or "please, counsel, let us know what issues you have agreed upon." 3) v. to send out, promulgate, publish or make the original distribution, such as a corporation selling and distributing shares of stock to its initial investors. 4) n. the shares of stock or bonds of a corporation which have been sold and distributed. (See: **bond, corporation, heirs of the body, incorporation, share, stock**)

J: n. abbreviation for Judge, as in the Hon. William B. Boone, J.

jaywalking: n. walking across a street outside of marked crosswalks, and not at a corner, and/or against a signal light. If there is vehicle traffic or clear markings of a place to cross, this is a traffic misdemeanor subject to fine, and may be (but not conclusively) contributory negligence in the event of injury to the jaywalker by a vehicle.

Jane Doe: n. 1) a fictitious name used for a possible female defendant who is unknown at the time a complaint is filed to start a lawsuit. 2) the temporary fictitious name given to an unidentified hospitalized or dead woman. (See: **fictitious defendants, John Doe**)

JD: n. short for Juris Doctor, identifying the holder as having received that law degree. (See: **Juris Doctor**)

jeopardy: n. peril, particularly danger of being charged with or convicted of a particular crime. The U.S. Constitution guarantees in the Fifth Amendment that no one can "be twice put in jeopardy of life or limb" for the same offense. Thus, once a person has been acquitted, he/she may not be charged again for that crime. However, if there was a mistrial, hung jury or reversal of conviction on appeal (but the defendant was not declared innocent in the ruling), the defendant may be charged with the crime again and tried again. In a few situations, a defendant is not in double jeopardy when being tried for a violation of a similar (but different) federal criminal (penal) statute based on some of the same circumstances as a state prosecution, such as violation of a murder victim's civil rights, as was done in the case against the killer of civil rights leader Medgar Evers. (See: **double jeopardy**)

jobber: n. a merchant who buys products (usually in bulk or lots) and then sells them to various retailers. This middleman generally specializes in specific types of products, such as auto parts, electrical and plumbing materials, or petroleum. A jobber differs from a broker or agent, who buys and acts for specific clients.

John Doe: n. 1) a fictitious name used for a possible male defendant who is unknown at the time a complaint is filed to start a lawsuit. 2) the temporary fictitious name given to an unidentified hospitalized or dead man. (See: **fictitious defendants, Jane Doe**)

joinder: n. the joining together of several lawsuits or several parties all in one lawsuit, provided that the legal issues and the factual situation are the same for all plaintiffs and defendants. Joinder requires a) that one of the parties to one of the lawsuits make a motion to join the suits and the parties in a single case; b) notice must be made to all parties; c) there must be a hearing before a judge to show why joinder will not cause prejudice (hurt) to any of the parties to the existing lawsuits; and d) an order of the judge permitting joinder. Joinder may be mandatory if a person necessary to a fair result was not included in the original lawsuit, or it may be permissive if joining the cases together is only a matter of convenience or economy. (See: **mandatory joinder, misjoinder, multiplicity of suits**)

joinder of issue: n. that point in a lawsuit when the defendant has challenged (denied) some or all of plaintiff's allegations of facts, and/or when it is known which legal questions are in dispute. This is stated in the expression: "the issue is joined," in the same manner as a military man would say: "the battle has been joined," meaning the fight is underway. Thus, the pre-trial legal underbrush has been cleared away, the motions made, and the pre-trial discovery (depositions, requests for documents, written questions and answers, and other demands for information) sufficiently completed, all of which makes clear what matters are to be decided by trial.

joint: adj., adv. referring to property, rights or obligations which are united, undivided and shared by two or more persons or entities. Thus, a joint property held by both cannot be effectively transferred unless all owners join in the transaction. If a creditor sues to collect a joint debt, he/she must include all the debtors in the lawsuit, unless the debt is specifically "joint *and*

several," meaning any one of the debtors may be individually liable. Therefore, care must be taken in drafting deeds, sales agreements, promissory notes, joint venture agreements and other documents. A joint tenancy is treated specially, since it includes the right of the survivor to get the entire property when the other dies (right of survivorship). (See: **joint and several,, joint tenancy, joint venture, tenancy in common**)

joint adventure: n. when two or more people go together on a trip or some other action, not necessarily for profit, which may make them all liable for an accident or debt arising out of the activity. (See: **joint venture**)

joint and several: adj. referring to a debt or a judgment for negligence, in which each debtor (one who owes) or each judgment defendant (one who has a judgment against him/her) is responsible (liable) for the entire amount of the debt or judgment. Thus, in drafting a promissory note for a debt, it is important to state that if there is more than one person owing the funds to be paid, the debt is joint *and* several, since then the person owed money (creditor, promisee) can collect the entire amount from any of the joint signers of the note, and not be limited to a share from each debtor. If a party injured in an accident sues several parties for causing his/her damages, the court may find that several people were "jointly" negligent and contributed to the damages. The entire judgment may be collected from any of the defendants found responsible, unless the court finds different amounts of negligence of each defendant contributed to the injury. Defense attorneys should require the trier of fact (jury or judge sitting without a jury) to break down the amount of negligence of each defendant and the plaintiff if there is contributory negligence. Often the court will refuse to do so, allowing the plaintiff to collect from whichever defendant has the "deep pocket" (lots of money), and letting the defendant who pays demand contributions from the other defendants. (See: **comparative negligence, contribution, contributory negligence, joint, joint and several**)

joint custody: n. in divorce actions, a decision by the court (often upon agreement of the parents) that the parents will share custody of a child. There are two types of custody, physical and legal. Joint physical custody (instead of one parent having custody with the other having visitation), does not mean exact division of time with each parent, but can be based on reasonable time with each parent either specifically spelled out (certain days, weeks, holidays, alternative periods) or based on stated guidelines and shared payment of costs of raising the child. Joint legal custody means that both parents can make decisions for the child, including medical treatment, but where possible they should consult the other. Upon the death or disability of either parent, legal custody will go to the remaining parent and will give the active parent the sole ability to act as parent for the child without fur-

ther order of the court. The primary affect of this is a psychological benefit for the parent and the child, so that a child can be told that both parents cared for the child, even though the child had to live most of the time with one of them. (See: **child custody, dissolution of marriage, divorce**)

joint enterprise: n. a generic term for an activity of two or more people, usually (but not necessarily) for profit, which may include partnership, joint venture or any business in which more than one person invests, works, has equal management control and/or is otherwise involved for an agreed upon goal or purpose. One significant factor is that if a court finds that two or more people are involved in a joint enterprise and there is negligent damage to an outside party by any one of the enterprisers, or breach of a contract made by the joint enterprise, each of those who are part of the enterprise will be liable for all the damages to the party. However, not all joint enterprises are partnerships or joint ventures, although the terms are often used improperly as if they were synonymous. (See: **joint, joint adventure, joint and several, joint liability, joint venture, partnership**)

joint liability: n. when two or more persons are both responsible for a debt, claim or judgment. It can be important to the person making the claim, as well as to a person who is sued, who can demand that anyone with joint liability for the alleged debt or claim for damages be joined in (brought into) the lawsuit. (See: **joinder, joint and several**)

joint powers agreement: n. a contract between a city, a county and/or a special district in which the city or county agrees to perform services, cooperate with, or lend its powers to the special district or other government entity.

> *The law must be stable, but it cannot stand still.*
> *—Roscoe Pound, The Philosophy of Law*

joint tenancy: n. a crucial relationship in the ownership of real property, which provides that each party owns an undivided interest in the entire parcel, with both having the right to use all of it *and* the right of survivorship, which means that upon the death of one joint tenant, the other has title to it all. Procedurally, on the death of one joint tenant, title in the survivor is completed by recording an "affidavit of death of joint tenant," describing the property and the deceased tenant, with a death certificate attached, all of which is sworn to by the surviving joint tenant. This process avoids probate of the property, but may have some tax consequences which should be explored with an accountant at the time of recording the original deed. If the owners do not want full title to the property to pass to the survivor, then joint tenancy should not be used. Joint tenancy (as well as any other common ownership) between a parent and a minor child should be avoided since the property cannot be transferred in the future without the parent becoming appointed a guardian of the child's estate by court order, and the property and the proceeds therefrom will be under court control until the child is 18. In community property states, some courts have found that joint tenancy presumes that the property is *not* community property (which could result in loss of estate tax limitation on the death of the first spouse to die), but proof of community interests can be established. A bank account held in joint tenancy also presumes a right of survivorship, but this presumption can be overcome by evidence that the account was really the property of only one, and the joint tenancy was for convenience. (See: **community property, tenancy in common, title**)

joint tortfeasors: n. two or more persons whose negligence in a single accident or event causes damages to another person. In many cases the joint tortfeasors are jointly and severally liable for the damages, meaning that any of them can be responsible to pay the entire amount, no matter how unequal the negligence of each party was. Example: Harry Hotrod is doing 90 miles an hour along a two-lane road in the early evening, Adele Aimster has stopped her car to study a map with her car sticking out into the lane by six inches. Hotrod swings out a couple of feet to miss Aimster's vehicle, never touches the brake, and hits Victor Victim, driving from the other direction, killing him. While Hotrod is grossly negligent for the high speed and failure to slow down, Aimster is also negligent for her car's slight intrusion into the lane. As a joint tortfeasor she may have to pay all the damages, particularly if Hotrod has no money or insurance. However, comparative negligence rules by statute or case law in most jurisdictions will apportion the liability by percentages of negligence among the tortfeasors (wrongdoers) and the injured parties. (See: **comparative negligence, negligence**)

joint venture: n. an enterprise entered into by two or more people for profit, for a limited purpose, such as purchase, improvement and sale or leasing of real estate. A joint venture has most of the elements of a partnership, such as shared management, the power of each venturer to bind the others in the business, division of profits and joint responsibility for losses. However, unlike a partnership, a joint venture anticipates a specific area of activity and/or period of operation, so after the purpose is completed, bills are paid, profits (or losses) are divided, and the joint venture is terminated. (See: **partnership**)

Jones Act: n., adj. a federal law which covers injuries to crewmen at sea, gives jurisdiction to the federal courts and sets up various rules for conduct of these cases under maritime law. A claim for recompense (payment) for damages at sea is called a "Jones Act case." (See: **admiralty, maritime law**)

judge: 1) n. an official with the authority and responsibility to preside in a court, try lawsuits and make legal rulings. Judges are almost always attorneys. In some states, "justices of the peace" may need only to pass a test, and federal and state "administrative law judges" are often lawyer or non-lawyer hearing officers specializing in the subject matter upon which they are asked to rule. The word "court" often refers to the judge, as in the phrase "the court found the defendant at fault," or "may it please the court," when addressing the judge. The word "bench" also refers to the judge or judges in general. Judges on appeals courts are usually called "justices." Judges of courts established by a state at the county, district, city or township level, gain office by election, by appointment by the Governor or by some judicial selection process in case of a vacancy. Federal judges are appointed for life by the President of the United States with confirmation by the U.S. Senate. A senator of the same party as the President has considerable clout in recommending Federal judges from his/her home state. 2) v. to rule on a legal matter, including determining the result in a trial if there is no jury. (See: **administrative law judge, bench, court, jurist, justice, justice of the peace, magistrate**)

judge advocate: n. a military officer with legal training who has the mixed duties of giving advice on legal matters to the group of officers sitting as a court-martial (both judge and jury) and acting as the prosecutor of the accused serviceman or woman. A judge advocate holds responsibility to protect the accused from procedural improprieties such as questions from the members of the court which might incriminate the accused in violation of the

Constitution. The accused person also has a military officer as counsel, who may not be an attorney. (See: **court-martial, judge advocate general**)

judge advocate general (J.A.G.): n. a military officer who advises the government on courts-martial and administers the conduct of courts-martial. The officers who are judge advocates and counsel assigned to the accused come from the office of the judge advocate general or are appointed by it to work on certain courts-martial. (See: **court-martial, judge advocate**)

judgment: n. the final decision by a court in a lawsuit, criminal prosecution or appeal from a lower court's judgment, except for an "interlocutory judgment," which is tentative until a final judgment is made. The word "decree" is sometimes used as synonymous with judgment. (See: **decree**)

judgment by default: n. (See: **default judgment**)

judgment creditor: n. the winning plaintiff in a lawsuit to whom the court decides the defendant owes money. A judgment creditor can use various means to collect the judgment. The judgment is good for a specified number of years and then may be renewed by a filed request. If the defendant debtor files for bankruptcy, the judgment creditor will have priority (the right to share in assets) ahead of general creditors who are not secured by mortgages or deeds of trust and do not have judgments. However, if

the bankrupt person has no assets, this becomes an empty advantage. (See: **creditor's rights, judgment, prevailing party**)

judgment debt: n. the amount of money in a judgment award to the winning party, which is owed to the winner by the losing party. (See: **judgment, judgment creditor**)

judgment debtor: n. the losing defendant in a lawsuit who owes the amount of the judgment to the winner. (See: **judgment creditor**)

judgment notwithstanding the verdict (N.O.V.): n. reversal of a jury's verdict by the trial judge when the judge believes there was no factual basis for the verdict or it was contrary to law. The judge will then enter a different verdict as "a matter of law." Essentially the judge should have required a "directed verdict" (instruction to the jury to return with a particular verdict since the facts allowed no other conclusion), and when the jury "went wrong," the judge uses the power to reverse the verdict instead of approving it, to prevent injustice. This process is commonly called "judgment N.O.V." or simply "N.O.V.," for Latin *non obstante veredicto*. (See: **N.O.V., verdict**)

judicial: adj., adv. 1) referring to a judge, court or the court system. 2) fair.

judicial discretion: n. the power of the judge to make decisions on some matters without being bound by precedent or strict rules established by statutes. On appeal a higher court will usually accept and confirm decisions of trial judges when exercising permitted discretion, unless capricious, showing a pattern of bias, or exercising discretion beyond his/her authority.

judicial foreclosure: n. a judgment by a court in favor of foreclosure of a mortgage or deed of trust, which orders that the real property which secured the debt be sold under foreclosure proceedings to pay the debt. The party suing probably has chosen to seek a judicial foreclosure rather than use the foreclosure provisions of the mortgage or deed of trust. Usually this move is made to get a "deficiency judgment" for any amount still owed after the foreclosure sale. In many states (such as California) a foreclosure on the deed of trust limits the recovery to the amount of sale proceeds (sales price minus other debts), so a lawsuit for judicial foreclosure may help the party recover the total money owed to him/her if it was secured by the debtor's real property. (See: **deed of trust, foreclosure, mortgage, deficiency judgement**)

judicial notice: n. the authority of a judge to accept as facts certain matters which are of common knowledge from sources which guarantee accuracy or are a matter of official record, without the need for evidence establishing the fact. Examples of matters given judicial notice are public and court records, tides, times of sunset and sunrise, government rainfall and temperature records, known historic events or the fact that ice melts in the sun. (See: **evidence**)

judicial proceedings: n. any action by a judge re: trials, hearings, petitions or other matters formally before the court. (See: **judicial**)

judicial sale: n. a sale of goods by an official (keeper, trustee or sheriff) appointed by the court and ordered by a court, usually to satisfy a judgment or implement another order of the court. Such sales require public notice of time, place and a description of the goods to be sold. (See: **sheriff's sale**)

jump bail: v. to fail to appear for a court appearance after depositing (posting) bail with the intention of avoiding prosecution, sentencing or going to jail. Posting bail guarantees that the accused person will give up the money if he/she does not show up in court. It allows the accused person to remain free pending the final decision on his/her criminal case. In some circumstances a criminal defendant can be declared to have jumped bail even before missing an appearance in court, if it is discovered he/she has left the state, the country, disappeared or made plans to flee. At that point the court can revoke the bail and issue a warrant for the defendant's arrest. It is also called "skipping" bail. (See: **bail, bail bond, bail bondsman**)

No person ought to be punished simply for being drunk; but a soldier or a policeman should be punished for being drunk on duty.
—John Stuart Mill, On Liberty

jurat: (jur-at) n. Latin for "been sworn," the portion of an affidavit in which a person has sworn that the contents of his/her written statement are true, filled in by the notary public with the date, name of the person swearing, sometimes the place where sworn, and the name of the person before whom the oath was made. It reads generally: "Sworn to this 12th day of October, 1994, by Martha J. Milner, before me, a notary public for said state and county. Barbara A. Stenerson, Notary Public." A *jurat* is not to be confused with an "acknowledgment" in which the signer of a document such as a deed to real property has sworn to the notary public that he/she executed the document, and the notary signs and seals the document to that effect. (See: **acknowledgment, declaration, notary public**)

jurisdiction: n. the authority given by law to a court to try cases and rule on legal matters within a particular geographic area and/or over certain types of legal cases. It is vital to determine before a lawsuit is filed which court has jurisdiction. State courts have jurisdiction over matters within that state, and different levels of courts have jurisdiction over lawsuits involving different amounts of money. For example, Superior Courts (called District or County Courts in several states) generally have sole control of lawsuits for larger sums of money, domestic relations (divorces), probate of estates of deceased persons, guardianships, conservatorships and trials of felonies. In some states (like New York) probate and certain other matters are within the jurisdiction of so-called Surrogate Courts. Municipal courts (or other local courts) have jurisdiction over cases involving lesser amounts of money, misdemeanors (crimes not punishable by state prison), traffic matters and preliminary hearings on felony charges to determine if there is sufficient evidence to warrant a trial by the Superior Court. Some states have police courts to handle misdemeanors. Jurisdiction in the courts of a particular state may be determined by the location of real property in a state (*in rem* jurisdiction), or whether the parties are located within the state (*in personam* jurisdiction). Thus, a probate of Marsha Blackwood's estate would be in Idaho where she lived and died, but jurisdiction over her title to real estate in Utah will be under the jurisdiction of the Utah courts. Federal courts have jurisdiction over lawsuits between citizens of different states, cases based on federal statutes such as fair labor standards and antitrust violations, charges of federal crimes, appeals from bankruptcy proceedings, maritime cases or legal actions involving federal constitutional questions. Sometimes regulatory agencies have the initial jurisdiction before any legal action may be filed in court. More than one court may have concurrent jurisdiction, such as both state and federal courts, and the lawyer filing the lawsuit may have to make a tactical decision as to which jurisdiction is more favorable or useful to his/her cause, including time to get to trial, the potential pool of jurors or other considerations. Appellate jurisdiction is given by statute to appeals courts to hear appeals about the judgment of the lower court that tried a case, and to order reversal or other correction if error is found. State appeals are under the jurisdiction of the state appellate courts, while appeals from federal district courts are within the jurisdiction of the courts of appeal and eventually the Supreme Court. Jurisdiction is not to be confused with "venue," which means the best place to try a case. Thus, any state court may have jurisdiction over a matter, but the "venue" is in a particular county. (See: **district court, municipal court, police court, Superior Court, Supreme Court, venue**)

jurisdictional amount: n. the range between the minimum and maximum amount of money or value in dispute in a lawsuit (generally based on the amount demanded in the lawsuit), which determines which court has jurisdiction to try the case. Example: in California, municipal courts have jurisdiction up to $25,000, superior courts have jurisdiction over that sum, and small claims courts (an alternative to formal municipal court filing) have a maximum jurisdictional amount of $5,000. Federal jurisdiction commences at the $10,000 level, if the lawsuit fits other federal requirements. (See: **jurisdiction**)

jurisprudence: n. the entire subject of law, the study of law and legal questions.

Juris Doctor (J.D.): n. the law degree granted upon graduation by many university law schools with accepted high standards of admission and grading. This often super-

sedes the Bachelor of Laws in recognition that the law curriculum entitles a person to a graduate degree.

jurist: n. although it means any attorney or legal scholar, jurist popularly refers to a judge.

juror: n. any person who actually serves on a jury. Lists of potential jurors are chosen from various sources such as registered voters, automobile registration or telephone directories. The names are drawn by lot (more often by computer random selection) and requested to appear for possible service. Before a trial begins the names of jurors are assigned to a trial court, and a further selection process is made. Acceptable excuses from service are determined by state law or by the judge before or during the final selection process. If chosen, a juror receives a small amount of pay per day of service and payment for automobile mileage from home to court. A member of a Grand Jury is called a grand juror. (See: **Grand Jury, jury, jury panel, *venire***)

jury: n. one of the remarkable innovations of the English common law (from the Angles and Saxons, but also employed in Normandy prior to the Norman Conquest in 1066), it is a group of citizens called to hear a trial of a criminal prosecution or a lawsuit, decide the factual questions of guilt or innocence or determine the prevailing party (winner) in a lawsuit and the amount to be paid, if any, by the loser. Once selected, the jury is sworn to give an honest and fair decision. The legal questions are determined by the judge presiding at the trial, who explains those issues to the members of the jury (jurors) in "jury instructions." The common number of jurors is 12 (dating back a thousand years), but some states allow a smaller number (six or eight) if the parties agree. For a plaintiff (the party suing) to win a lawsuit with a jury, three-quarters of the jurors must favor the claim. Guilt or innocence in a criminal trial requires a unanimous decision of the jury, except two states (Oregon and Louisiana) allow a conviction with 10 of 12 jurors. Juries have greatly changed in recent decades, as the term "impartial jury" in the Fifth Amendment to the Constitution requires that the pool of jurors must include all races, ethnic groups and women as well as men in percentages relative to the general population. Any failure to achieve that balance or systematic challenges to those of the same ethnicity of the accused, may result in a claim on appeal that the jury was not fair—in popular jargon, not "a jury of one's peers." This does not mean that a Samoan male must be tried by other Samoan males, but it does mean that the potential jurors must come from a balanced group. Members of the jury are supposed to be free of bias, have no specific knowledge of the case and have no connection with any of the parties or witnesses. Questions are asked by the judge and attorneys (called *"voir dire"*) during jury selection to weed out those whom they may challenge on those grounds (challenge for cause). Some potential jurors are challenged (peremptory challenge) because the attorney for one side or the other feels there is some hidden bias. In well-financed cases this has led to the hiring of jury "specialists" and psychologists by attorneys to aid in jury selection. In a high-profile criminal case in which the jury might be influenced by public comment or media coverage during trial, the court may order the jury be sequestered (kept in a hotel away from family, friends, radio, television and newspapers.) (See: **challenge for cause, juror, jury panel, jury trial, peremptory challenge, sequester,** *venire, voir dire*)

jury box: n. the enclosed area in which the jury sits in assigned seats during a jury trial. (See: **juror, jury**)

jury fees: n. the rather minimal amount paid each day to jurors, plus payment for mileage from home to court. In criminal trials this amount is paid by the government (usually county government in state cases), but in civil lawsuits the jury fees are paid by the parties to the lawsuit in equal amounts. It is important for a party requesting a jury trial to deposit ("post") the first day's jury fees with the clerk of the court a set time in advance of the trial date, or the right to a jury trial may be lost on the basis that he/she/it has "waived" the right to a jury. The winner of the lawsuit (prevailing party) is usually entitled to reimbursement (payment by the loser) of jury fees as a court cost. (See: **jury**)

jury of one's peers: n. a guaranteed right of criminal defendants, in which "peer" means an "equal." This has been interpreted by courts to mean that the available jurors include a broad spectrum of the population, particularly of race, national origin and gender. Jury selection may include no process which excludes those of a particular race or intentionally narrows the spectrum of possible jurors. It does not mean that women are to be tried by women, Asians by Asians, or African Americans by African Americans. (See: **jury**)

jury panel: n. the list from which jurors for a particular trial may be chosen. (See: **juror, jury**)

jury selection: n. the means by which a jury is chosen, with a panel of potential jurors called, questioning of the jury by the judge and attorneys (*voir dire*), dismissal for cause, peremptory challenges by the attorneys without stating a cause and finally impaneling of the jury. (See: **impaneling, jury, panel, peremptory challenge,** *venire*)

jury stress: n. a form of mental, emotional, psychological, physical and sexual tension found to affect juries in long trials due to exhaustion, sequestration, the mountain of evidence and the desire to do the right thing. (See: **jury**)

jury tampering: n. the crime of attempting to influence a jury through any means other than presenting evidence and argument in court, including conversations about the case outside the court, offering bribes, making threats or asking acquaintances to intercede with a juror. (See: **jury, subornation of perjury**)

jury trial: n. a trial of a lawsuit or criminal prosecution in which the case is presented to a jury and the factual questions and the final judgment are determined by a jury. This is distinguished from a "court trial" in which the judge decides factual as well as legal questions, and makes the final judgment. (See: **jury**)

just compensation: n. 1) in general a fair and reasonable amount of money to be paid for work performed or to make one "whole" after loss due to damages. 2) the full value to be paid for property taken by the government for public purposes guaranteed by the Fifth Amendment to the U.S. Constitution, which states: "...nor shall private property be taken for public use without just compensation." If the amount offered by the governmental agency taking the property is not considered sufficient, the property owner may demand a trial to determine just compensation. (See: **condemnation, eminent domain, inverse condemnation, make one whole,** *quantum meruit*)

justice: n. 1) fairness. 2) moral rightness. 3) a scheme or system of law in which every person receives his/her/its due from the system, including all rights, both natural and legal. One problem is that attorneys, judges and legislatures often get caught up more in procedure than in achieving justice for all. Example: the adage "justice delayed is justice denied," applies to the burdensome procedures, lack of sufficient courts, the clogging of the system with meritless cases and the use of the courts to settle matters which could be resolved by negotiation. The imbalance between court privileges obtained by attorneys for the wealthy and for the person of modest means, the use of delay and "blizzards" of unnecessary paper by large law firms, and judges who fail to cut through the underbrush of procedure all erode justice. 4) an appellate judge, the Chief Justice and Associate Justices of the U.S. Supreme Court, a member of a Federal Court of Appeal and judges of any of the various state appellate courts. (See: **court**)

justice of the peace (JP): n. a judge who handles minor legal matters such as misdemeanors, small claims actions and traffic matters in "justice courts." Dating back to early English common law, "JPs" were very common up to the 1950s, but they now exist primarily in rural "justice districts" from which it is unreasonable for the public to travel to the county seat for trials of minor matters. In Nevada justices of the peace are lucrative jobs since they perform many of the marriages of elopers from other states, as Nevada has no waiting period from license to wedding. A justice of the peace is usually an attorney, but some states still allow laypersons to qualify by taking a test.

justiciable: n. referring to a matter which is capable of being decided by a court. Usually it is combined in such terms as: "justiciable issue," "justiciable cause of action" or "justiciable case."

> *The execution of laws is more important than the making of them.*
> *—Thomas Jefferson*

justifiable homicide: n. a killing without evil or criminal intent, for which there can be no blame, such as self-defense to protect oneself or to protect another or the shooting by a law enforcement officer in fulfilling his/her duties. This is not to be confused with a crime of passion or claim of diminished capacity, which refer to defenses aimed at reducing the penalty or degree of crime. (See: **homicide, self-defense**)

juvenile court: n. a special court or department of a trial court which deals with under-age defendants charged with crimes or who are neglected or out of the control of their parents. The normal age of these defendants is under 18, but juvenile court does not have jurisdiction in cases in which minors are charged as adults. The procedure in juvenile court is not always adversarial (although the minor is entitled to legal representation by a lawyer). It can be an attempt to involve parents or social workers and probation officers in the process to achieve positive results and save the minor from involvement in future crimes. However, serious crimes and repeated offenses can result in sentencing juvenile offenders to prison, with transfer to state prison upon reaching adulthood with limited maximum sentences. Where parental neglect or loss of control is a problem, the juvenile court may seek out foster homes for the juvenile, treating the child as a ward of the court. (See: **court, juvenile delinquent**)

juvenile delinquent: n. a person who is under age (usually below 18), who is found to have committed a crime in states which have declared by law that a minor lacks responsibility and thus may not be sentenced as an adult. However, the legislatures of several states have reduced the age of criminal responsibility for serious crimes or for repeat offenders to as low as 14. (See: **juvenile court**)

K: n. the shorthand symbol for "contract" used almost universally by lawyers and law students.

kangaroo court: n. 1) a mock court set up without legal basis, such as a fraternity, sports team or army squad might set up to punish minor violations of organizational decorum. 2) slang for a court of law in which the violations of procedure, precedents, and due process are so gross that fundamental justice is denied. It usually means that the judge is incompetent or obviously biased. (See: **star chamber proceedings**)

The law is a jealous mistress.
—Justice Joseph Story

kidnapping (also spelled kidnaping): n. the taking of a person against his/her will (or from the control of a parent or guardian) from one place to another under circumstances in which the person so taken does not have freedom of movement, will, or decision through violence, force, threat or intimidation. Although it is not necessary that the purpose be criminal (since all kidnapping is a criminal felony) the capture usually involves some related criminal act such as holding the person for ransom, sexual and/or sadistic abuse, or rape. It includes taking due to irresistible impulse and a parent taking and hiding a child in violation of court order. An includ-ed crime is false imprisonment. Any harm to the victim coupled with kidnapping can raise the degree of felony for the injury and can result in a capital (death penalty) offense in some states, even though the victim survives. Originally it meant the stealing of children, since "kid" is child in Scandinavian languages, but now applies to adults as well.

kin: n. blood relative. (See: **next of kin**)

labor and materials (time and materials): n. what some builders or repair people contract to provide and be paid for, rather than a fixed price or a percentage of the costs. In many states, if the person performing the work is not a licensed contractor, he/she is limited to labor and materials in any lawsuit for contract payment, and may not receive a profit above that amount. Consumers who believe they will get a better deal from someone working for labor or time and materials should beware and watch receipts and keep track of actual labor hours worked.

laches: n. the legal doctrine that a legal right or claim will not be enforced or allowed if a long delay in asserting the right or claim has prejudiced the adverse party (hurt the opponent) as a sort of "legal ambush." Examples: a) knowing the correct property line, Oliver Owner fails to bring a lawsuit to establish title to a portion of real estate until Nat Neighbor has built a house which encroaches on the property in which Owner has title; b) Tommy Traveler learns that his father has died, but waits four years to come forward until the entire estate has been distributed on the belief that Tommy was dead; c) Susan Smart has a legitimate claim against her old firm for sexual harassment, but waits three years to come forward and file a lawsuit, after the employee who caused the problem has died, and the witnesses have all left the company and scattered around the country. The defense of laches is often raised in the list of "affirmative defenses" in answers filed by defendants, but is seldom applied by the courts. Laches is not to be confused with the "statute of limitations," which sets specific periods to file a lawsuit for types of claims (negligence, breach of contract, fraud, etc.).

land: n. real property, real estate (and all that grows thereon), and the right to minerals underneath and the airspace over it. It may include improvements like buildings, but not necessarily. The owner of the land may give a long-term (like 99 years) lease to another with the right to build on it. The improvement is a "leasehold" for ownership of the right to use—without ownership of—the underlying land. The right to use the air above a parcel of land is subject to height limitations by local ordinance, state or federal law. (See: **real estate, real property**)

landlady: n. female of landlord or owner of real property from whom one rents or leases. (See: **landlord**)

landlocked: adj. referring to a parcel of real property which has no access or egress (entry or exit) to a public street and cannot be reached except by crossing another's property. In such a case there is an "implied easement" over the adjoining lot from which it was created (carved out).

landlord: n. a person who owns real property and rents or leases it to another, called a "tenant." (See: **lease, lessee, lessor, rent, tenant**)

landlord's lien: n. the right of a landlord to sell abandoned personal property left on rented or leased premises by a former tenant to cover unpaid rent or damages to the property. However, to exercise this lien the landlord must carefully follow procedures which differ in each state, but generally require written notice to the ex-tenant and a public sale.

In any country, regardless of what its laws may say, wherever people act upon the principle that the disadvantage of one man is the good of another, slavery exists.
—Booker T. Washington

landlord and tenant: n. the name for the area of law concerning renting and leasing property and the rights of both the owner and the renter or lessee. (See: **landlady, landlord, lease, lessee, lessor, rent, tenant**)

lapse: 1) v. to fail to occur, particularly a gift made in a will. 2) v. to become non-operative. 3) n. the termination of a gift made by will or for future distribution from a trust, caused by the death of the person to whom the gift was intended (the beneficiary, legatee, devisee) prior to the death of the person making the will or creating the trust (the testator, trustor or settlor). (See: **beneficiary, devisee, legatee, trust, will**)

larceny: n. the crime of taking the goods of another person without permission (usually secretly), with the intent of keeping them. It is one form of theft. Some states differentiate between grand larceny and petty larceny based on the value of the stolen goods. Grand larceny is a felony with a state prison sentence as a punishment and petty larceny is usually limited to county jail time. (See: **grand larceny, petty larceny, theft**)

last antecedent rule: n. a doctrine of interpretation (construction) of statutes that any qualifying words or phrases refer to the language immediately preceding the qualifier, unless common sense shows that it was meant to apply to something more distant or less obvious. Example: "The commercial vehicular license shall not apply to boats, tractors, and trucks, with only four wheels and under three tons...," the qualifier "only four wheels and under three tons" applies only to trucks and not boats or tractors.

last clear chance: n. a rule of law in determining responsibility for damages caused by negligence, which provides that if the plaintiff (the party suing for damages) is negligent, that will not matter if the defendant (the party being sued for damages caused by his/her negligence) could have still avoided the accident by reasonable care in the final moments (no matter how slight) before the accident. The theory is that although the plaintiff may have been negligent, his/her negligence no longer was the cause of the accident because the defendant could have prevented the accident. Most commonly applied to auto accidents, a typical case of last clear chance would be when one driver drifts over the center line, and this action was noted by an oncoming driver who proceeds without taking simple evasive action, crashes into the first driver and is thus liable for the injuries to the first driver who was over the line. In the few states which apply the strict "contributory negligence" rule which keeps a negligent plaintiff from recovering damages from a negligent defendant, "last clear chance" can save the careless plaintiff's lawsuit. (See: **comparative negligence, contributory negligence, negligence**)

last will and testament: n. a fancy and redundant way of saying "will." Lawyers and clients like the formal resonance of the language. Will and testament mean the same thing. A document will be the "last" will if the maker of it dies before writing another one. (See: **will**)

latent defect: n. a hidden flaw, weakness or imperfection in an article which a seller knows about, but the buyer cannot discover by reasonable inspection. It includes a hidden defect in the title to land, such as an incorrect property description. Generally, this entitles the purchaser to get his/her money back (rescind the deal) or get a replacement without a defect on the basis of "implied" warranty of quality that a buyer could expect ("merchantability"). Even an "as is" purchase could be rescinded if it could be shown the seller knew of the flaw. (See: **implied warranty, product liability, rescision, warranty**)

lateral support: n. the right of a landowner to assurance that his/her neighbor's land will provide support against any slippage, cave-in or landslide. Should the adjoining owner excavate into the soil for any reason (foundation, basement, leveling) then there must be a retaining wall constructed (or other protective engineering) to prevent a collapse. A classic example: a developer excavated into a hill along both the western and southern lines to create a pad for an apartment building and delayed putting in the retaining wall. Cracks appeared in the buildings next to the digging site, and the owners filed a lawsuit asking for an injunction to require the developer to build a wall. The judge so ordered, but the cave-in occurred anyway, the neighboring buildings toppled into the hole, and, in the subsequent lawsuit by the owners of the neighboring fallen buildings, the developer had to pay the entire value of the buildings which were destroyed. Most lateral support problems are less dramatic.

law: n. 1) any system of regulations to govern the conduct of the people of a community, society or nation, in response to the need for regularity, consistency and justice based upon collective human experience. Custom or conduct governed by the force of the local king were replaced by laws almost as soon as man learned to write. The earliest lawbook was written about 2100 B.C. for Ur-Nammu, king of Ur, a Middle Eastern city-state. Within three centuries Hammurabi, king of Babylonia, had enumerated laws of private conduct, business and legal precedents, of which 282 articles have survived. The term "eye for an eye" (or the equivalent value) is found there, as is drowning as punishment for adultery by a wife (while a husband could have slave concubines), and unequal treatment of the rich and the poor was codified here first. It took another thousand years before written law codes developed among the Greek city-states (particularly Athens) and Israel. China developed similar rules of conduct, as did Egypt. The first law system which has a direct influence on the American legal system was the codification of all classic law ordered by the Roman Emperor Justinian in 528 and completed by 534, becoming the law of the Roman empire. This is known as the Justinian Code, upon which most of the legal systems of most European nations are based to this day. The principal source of American law is the common law, which had its roots about the same time as Justinian, among Angles, Britons and later Saxons in Britain. William the Conqueror arrived in 1066 and combined the best of this Anglo-Saxon law with Norman law, which resulted in the English common law, much of which was by custom and precedent rather than by written code. The American colonies followed the English Common Law with minor variations, and the four-volume *Commentaries on the Laws of England* by Sir William Blackstone (completed in 1769) was the legal "bible" for all American frontier lawyers and influenced the development of state codes of law. To a great extent common law has been replaced by written statutes, and a gigantic body of such statutes have been enacted by federal and state legislatures supposedly in response to the greater complexity of modern life. 2) n. a statute, ordinance or regulation enacted by the legislative branch of a government and signed into law, or in some nations created by decree without any democratic process. This is distinguished from "natural law," which is not based on statute, but on alleged common understanding of what is right and proper (often based on moral and religious precepts as well as common understanding of fairness and justice). 3) n. a generic term for any body of regulations for conduct, including specialized rules (military law), moral conduct under various religions and for organizations, usually called "bylaws." (See: **bylaws, code, common law, courts,** *malum in se, malum prohibitum,* **maritime law, natural law, statute**)

law and motion calendar: n. a court calendar in which only motions and special legal arguments are heard.

law book: n. any of numerous volumes dealing with law, including statutes, reports of cases, digests of cases, commentaries on particular topics, encyclopedias, textbooks, summaries of the law, dictionaries, legal forms and various combinations of these such as case reports with commentaries. Statutes of every state and the Federal Code are published, usually with comments, "annotations" and brief statements of decisions which contribute to the interpretations of each particular statute. The written reports of appellate cases are collected for every state, the federal government, England and many other countries. Collections of digests (brief summaries) of case decisions divided by topics are available for each state as well as federal rulings. There are books on almost every legal subject. Almost all collections of statutes, digests, form books and commentaries are regularly updated with the latest decisions, legislative enactments and recent comments, often with loose-leaf "pocket parts" added each year, and completely new volumes when numerous changes have accumulated. Many of the books are now being replaced or supplemented by computer disks or computer modem services. The earliest known law book was written in 2100 B.C. for the king of Ur. (See: **common law, law, Shepardize, statute**)

law of admiralty: n. statutes, customs and treaties dealing with actions on navigable waters. It is synonymous with maritime law. (See: **Jones Act, maritime law**)

law of the case: n. once a judge has decided a legal question during the conduct of a lawsuit, he/she is unlikely to change his/her views and will respond that the ruling is the "law of the case."

law of the land: n. a slang term for existing laws.

lawsuit: n. a common term for a legal action by one person or entity against another person or entity, to be decided in a court of law, sometimes just called a "suit." The legal claims within a lawsuit are called "causes of action." (See: **case, cause of action, suit**)

lay a foundation: v. in evidence, to provide to the judge the qualification of a witness (particularly an expert witness) or a document or other piece of evidence which assures the court of the talent and experience of a witness or the authenticity of the document or article. Example: a medical report cannot be introduced unless the physician who wrote it testifies that he wrote it, or a photograph must be authenticated by the photographer or by testimony that it truly reflects a particular place or event. An expert witness is qualified by testimony as to experience and training. (See: **evidence**)

leading: 1) v. short for "leading the witness," in which the attorney during a trial or deposition asks questions in a form in which he/she puts words in the mouth of the witness or suggests the answer. Leading is improper if the attorney is questioning a witness called by that attorney and presumably friendly to the attorney's side of the case. Thus, the opposing attorney will object that a question is "leading," and if so the judge will sustain (uphold) the objection and prohibit the question in that form. However, leading questions are permissible in cross-examination of a witness called by the other party or if the witness is found to be hostile or adverse to the position of the attorney conducting the questioning. 2) adj. referring to a question asked of a witness which suggests the answer. (See: **leading the witness, objection, adverse witness, hostile witness, cross-examination**)

leading question: n. a question asked of a witness by an attorney during a trial or a deposition (questioning under oath outside of court), suggesting an answer or putting words in the mouth of the witness. Such a question is often objected to, usually with the simple objection: "leading." A leading question is allowable only when directed to the opposing party to the lawsuit or to an "adverse witness" during cross-examination (the chance to question after direct testimony) on the basis that such a witness can readily deny the proposed wording. Typical improper leading question: "Didn't the defendant appear to you to be going too fast in the limited visibility?" The proper question would be: "How fast do you estimate the defendant was going?" followed by "What was the visibility?" and "How far could you see?" (See: **cross-examination, objection**)

leading the witness: n. asking a question during a trial or deposition which puts words in the mouth of the witness or suggests the answer, which is improper questioning of a witness called by that attorney, but is proper in cross-examination or allowed if a witness is declared by the judge to be a hostile or adverse witness. (See: **leading, objection, adverse witness, hostile witness, cross-examination**)

lease: 1) n. a written agreement in which the owner of property (either real estate or some object like an automobile) allows use of the property for a specified period of time (term) for specific periodic payments (rent), and other terms and conditions. Leases of real property describe the premises (often by address); penalties for late payments, termination upon default of payment or breach of any significant conditions; increases in rent based on cost of living or some other standard; inclusion or exclusion of property taxes and insurance in rent; limitations on use (for a butcher shop, a residence for the family only, no pets); charges for staying on beyond the term (holding over); any right to renew the lease for another period; and/or a requirement for payment of attorneys' fees and costs in case of the need to enforce the lease (including eviction). A lease is distinguished from a mere renting of the premises on a month-to-month basis and cannot exceed a year unless agreed to in writing. A "triple net" lease includes both taxes and insurance in the rent. 2) v. to rent out real property or an object pursuant to a written agreement. (See: **holding over tenancy, lease, leasehold, real property, rent, statute of frauds, triple net lease, unlawful detainer**)

leasehold: n. the real estate which is the subject of a lease (a written rental agreement for an extended period of time). The term is commonly used to describe improvements on real property when the improvements are built on land owned by one party which is leased for a long term (such as 99 years) to the owner of the building. For example, the Pacific Land Company owns a lot and leases it for 99 years to the Highrise Development Corporation, which builds a 20-story apartment building and sells each apartment to individual owners as condominiums. At the end of the 99 years the building has to be moved (impossible), torn down, sold to Pacific (which need not pay much since the building is old and Highrise has no choice), or a new lease negotiated. Obviously, toward the end of the 99 years the individual condominiums will go down in value, partly from fear of lessened resale potential. This is generally theoretical (except to lending companies because the security does not include the land) since there are few buildings with less than 50 or 60 years to go on the leases or their expected lifetimes, although there are some commercial buildings which are within 20 years of termination of such leases. In most cases the buildings are obsolete by the end of the leasehold. (See: **condominium, lease**)

legacy: n. a gift of personal property or money to a beneficiary (legatee) of a will. While technically legacy does not include real property (which is a "devise"), legacy usually refers to any gift from the estate of one who has died. It is synonymous with the word "bequest." (See: **beneficiary, bequest, legatee, will**)

legal: adj., adv. according to law, not in violation of law or anything related to the law.

legal action: n. any lawsuit, petition or prosecution.

legal advertising: n. 1) notices of probate sales and other documents required by law to be published in court-approved local newspapers of general circulation. 2) commercials for the legal services of lawyers and law firms, which may range from television spots with actors to garish ads in telephone books' yellow pages. Such advertising would have been cause for disbarment for illegal solicitation of legal services until the U.S. Supreme Court ruled in 1977 that restrictions on advertising professional services were unconstitutional abridgments of free speech. While legal advertising may have the benefit of announcing specialties like worker's compensation or bankruptcy, the size, frequency and message bear little relationship to the quality of the lawyers advertising. (See: **attorney advertising**)

legal age: n. the age at which a person is responsible for his/her own actions (including the capacity to enter into a contract which is enforceable by the other party), for damages for negligence or intentional wrongs without a parent being liable and for punishment as an adult for a crime. In almost all states the basic legal age is 18, which is the universal American voting age under the 26th Amendment to the Constitution, ratified in 1971. The national legal age for drinking or buying alcoholic beverages is 21. Marriage with or without parental consent, driving, prosecution for crimes, the right to choose an abortion and liability for damages vary from state to state. (See: **infancy, juvenile court, minority**)

legal aid society: n. an organization formed to assist persons who have limited or no financial means but need legal help, usually sponsored by the local bar association's donations, sometimes with some local governmental financial support. Such societies examine the assets and income of the applicant, decide if the person has a legitimate need for legal services, give counselling, provide mediation, prepare simple documents, and if absolutely necessary give free legal assistance from a panel of volunteer attorneys. Originally most prevalent in larger cities, legal aid societies exist throughout the country. They do not usually provide assistance in criminal cases because indigent defendants are constitutionally entitled to representation by a public defender or appointed private counsel paid by the government. Some societies provide referral services to help a person find a suitable attorney, but normally referral is made by the local bar association. (See: ***pro bono***)

legal duty: n. the responsibility to others to act according to the law. Proving the duty (such as not to be negligent, to keep premises safe, or to drive within the speed limit) and then showing that the duty was breached are required elements of any lawsuit for damages due to negligence or intentional injuries. (See: **duty of care**)

legalese: n. slang for the sometimes arcane, convoluted and specialized jargon of lawyers and legal scholars.

legal fiction: n. a presumption of fact assumed by a court for convenience, consistency or to achieve justice. There is an old adage: "Fictions arise from the law, and not law from fictions."

legal separation: n. a court-decreed right to live apart, with the rights and obligations of divorced persons, but without divorce. The parties are still married and cannot remarry. A spouse may petition for a legal separation usually on the same basis as for a divorce, and include requests for child custody, alimony, child support and division of property. For people who want to avoid the supposed stigma of divorce, who hold strong religious objections to divorce or who hope to save a marriage, legal separation is an apparent solution. With more states allowing no-fault divorce, the use of separation agreements and informal separation, legal separation is rarely used. (See: **divorce**)

legal services: n. the work performed by a lawyer for a client.

legal tender: n. all money issued by the government.

legatee: n. a person or organization receiving a gift of an object or money under the terms of the will of a person who has died. Although technically a legatee does not receive real property (a devisee), "legatee" is often used to designate a person who takes anything pursuant (according) to the terms of a will. The best generic term is beneficiary, which avoids the old-fashioned distinctions between legatees taking legacies (personal property) and devisees taking devises (real property), terms which date from the Middle Ages. (See: **beneficiary, devise, devisee, legacy, will**)

legitimate: adj., adv.: 1) legal, proper, real. 2) referring to a child born to parents who are married. A baby born to parents who are not married is illegitimate, but can be made legitimate (legitimatized) by the subsequent marriage of the parents. 3) v. to make proper and/or legal.

lemon law: n. statutes adopted in some states to make it easier for a buyer of a new vehicle to sue for damages or replacement if the dealer or manufacturer cannot make it run properly after a reasonable number of attempts to fix the car. Without a "lemon law" auto makers have often demanded the buyer come back a dozen times and give up use of the car for lengthy periods while they test it, claiming they are "still trying" to make it run right.

lessee: n. the person renting property under a written lease from the owner (lessor). He/she/it is the tenant and the lessor is the landlord. (See: **landlord, landlord and tenant, lease, lessor, tenant**)

lesser crime: n. (See: **lesser-included offense**)

lesser-included offense: n. in criminal law, a crime which is proved by the same facts as a more serious crime. Example: Ignatz "Itchy" Fingers is charged with armed robbery, but the prosecution fails to prove Itchy used his pistol since the victims do not recall the gun, but does prove he took the jewels. Thus, he is convicted of larceny, which is a lesser form of theft and he will receive a lighter sentence. A common example is the so-called "wet reckless," which is the crime of driving recklessly after some drinking, but not necessarily while drunk. In plea bargains for first offenders in close cases the driver may plead guilty or "no contest" to this lesser-included offense instead of drunk driving, which carries a more severe penalty, including jail time. (See: **plea bargain**)

lessor: n. the owner of real property who rents it to a lessee pursuant to a written lease. Thus, he/she/it is the landlord and the lessee is the

tenant. (See: **landlord, landlord and tenant, lease, lessee, tenant**)

> *There is no country (like the United States) in the world in which the doing of justice is burdened by such heavy overhead charges or in which so great a force is maintained for a given amount of litigation.*
> *—Elihu root*

let: v. 1) to allow or permit. This is distinguished from "against one's will." The word can be very important legally, as in the statement "Lucy let Johnny have sexual relations with her," which can make a huge difference in a claim of rape. 2) to lease or rent real property, particularly a room or apartment, to another person. (See: **lease, rent, sublease**)

letter of credit: n. a document issued by a bank guaranteeing to provide a customer a line of credit (automatic loan up to a certain amount) for money or security for a loan. Such a letter is used primarily to facilitate long-distance business transactions.

letters: n. shorthand for letters testamentary or letters of administration. (See: **letters of administration, letters testamentary**)

letters of administration: n. a document issued by the court clerk which states the authority of the administrator of an estate of a person who has died, when there is no will or no available executor named by a will and an administrator has been appointed by the court. It is issued during probate of the estate as soon as the court approves the appointment of the administrator, who files a security bond if one is required. Certified copies of the letters are often required by banks and other financial institutions, the federal government, stock transfer agents or other courts before transfer of money or assets to the administrator of the estate. (See: **executor, probate**)

letters testamentary: n. a document issued by the court clerk which states the authority of the executor of an estate of a person who has died. It is issued during probate of the estate as soon as the court approves the appointment of the executor named in the will and the executor files a security bond if one is necessary (most well-drafted wills waive the need for a bond). Certified copies of the letters are often required by banks and other financial institutions, the federal government, stock transfer agents or other courts before transfer of money or assets to the executor of the estate. (See: **administrator, probate**)

leverage: 1) n. the use of borrowed money to purchase real estate or business assets, usually involving money equaling a high percentage of the value of the purchased property. 2) v. to borrow most of the funds necessary as a loan against real estate to buy other real estate or business assets. The dangers of high leverage are over-appraisal of the property to satisfy a lender, a decline in the value of the property (which may have been purchased during a period of high inflation), high carrying costs (interest, insurance, taxes, maintenance) which exceed income, vacancies and/or inability to finance improvements to increase profits. Too often the result is the collapse of "paper" real estate empires which have been created by risky leveraging.

levy: 1) v. to seize (take) property upon a writ of execution (an order to seize property) issued by the court to pay a money judgment granted in a lawsuit. The levy is actually made by a sheriff or other official at the request of the holder of the judgment (the winner in the lawsuit), and the property will be sold at a sheriff's sale to provide money to satisfy the unpaid judgment. 2) v. the act of a governmental legislative body, such as a board of supervisors or commissioners assessing a tax on all property, all sales, business licenses or any thing or transaction which may be taxed. Thus, the county "levies" a tax on businesses. 3) n. the seizure of property to satisfy a judgment. (See: **creditor's rights, sheriff's sale, tax, writ of execution**)

lewd and lascivious: adj., adv. references to conduct which includes people living together who are known not to be married, entertainment which aims at arousing the libido or primarily sexual sensation, open solicitation for prostitution or indecent exposure of genitalia (which is itself a crime). Due to the tendency of judges to be overly careful in writing about moral and/or sexual matters the definitions have been cloaked in old-fashioned modesty. Today the term usually applies to pornography, prostitution and indecent acts. (See: **indecent exposure, pornography, prostitution**)

liability: n. one of the most significant words in the field of law, liability means legal responsibility for one's acts or omissions. Failure of a person or entity to meet that responsibility leaves him/her/it open to a lawsuit for any resulting damages or a court order to perform (as in a breach of contract or violation of statute). In order to win a lawsuit the suing party (plaintiff) must prove the legal liability of the defendant if the plaintiff's allegations are shown to be true. This requires evidence of the duty to act, the failure to fulfill that duty and the connection (proximate cause) of that failure to some injury or harm to the plaintiff. Liability also applies to alleged criminal acts in which the defendant may be responsible for his/her acts which constitute a crime, thus making him/her subject to conviction and punishment. Example: Jack Jumpstart runs a stop sign in his car and hits Sarah Stepforth as she is crossing in the crosswalk. Jack has a duty of care to Sarah (and the public) which he breaches by his negligence, and therefore has liability for Sarah's injuries, giving her the right to bring a lawsuit against him. However, Jack's father owns the automobile and he, too, may have liability to Sarah based on a statute which makes a car owner liable for any damages caused by the vehicle he owns. The father's responsibility is based on "statutory liability" even though he personally breached no duty. A signer of a promissory note has liability for money due if it is not paid and so would a co-signer who guarantees it. A contractor who has agreed to complete a building has liability to the owner if he fails to complete on time. (See: **contract, joint liability, joint tortfeasors, negligence**)

liable: adj. responsible or obligated. Thus, a person or entity may be liable for damages due to negligence, liable to pay a debt, liable to perform an act which he/she/it contracted to do, or liable to punishment for commission of a crime. Failure to meet the responsibility or obligation opens one up to a lawsuit, and committing a crime can lead to a criminal prosecution. (See: **liability**)

libel: 1) n. to publish in print (including pictures), writing or broadcast through radio, television or film, an untruth about another which will do harm to that person or his/her reputation, by tending to bring the target into ridicule, hatred, scorn or contempt of others. Libel is the written or broadcast form of defamation, distinguished from slander, which is oral defamation. It is a tort (civil wrong) making the person or entity (like a newspaper, magazine or political organization) open to a lawsuit for damages by the person who can prove the statement about him/her was a lie. Publication need only be to one person, but it must be a statement which claims to be fact and is not clearly identified as an opinion. While it is sometimes said that the person making the libelous statement must have been intentional and malicious, actually it need only be obvious that the statement would do harm and is untrue. Proof of malice, however, does allow a party defamed to sue for general damages for damage to reputation, while an inadvertent libel limits the damages to actual harm (such as loss of business) called special damages. Libel per se involves statements so vicious that malice is assumed and does not require a proof of intent to get an award of general damages. Libel against the reputation of a person who has died will allow surviving members of the family to bring an action for damages. Most states provide for a party defamed by a periodical to demand a published retraction. If the correction is made, then there is no right to file a lawsuit. Governmental bodies are supposedly immune to actions for libel on the basis that there could be no intent by a non-personal entity, and further, public records are exempt from claims of libel. However, there is at least one known case in which there was a financial settlement as well as a published correction when a state government newsletter incorrectly stated that a dentist had been disciplined for illegal conduct. The rules covering libel against a "public figure" (particularly a political or governmental person) are special, based on U.S. Supreme Court decisions. The key is that to uphold the right to express opinions or fair comment on public figures, the libel must be malicious to constitute grounds for a lawsuit for damages. Minor errors in reporting are not libel, such as saying Mrs. Jones was 55 when she was only 48, or getting an address or title incorrect. 2) v. to broadcast or publish a written defamatory statement. (See: **defamation, libel per se, public figure, slander**)

libel per se: n. broadcast or written publication of a false statement about another which accuses him/her of a crime, immoral acts, inability to perform his/her profession, having a loathsome disease (like syphilis) or dishonesty in business. Such claims are considered so obviously harmful that malice need not be proved to obtain a judgment for "general damages," and not just specific losses. (See: **defamation, libel, slander**)

liberty: n. freedom from restraint and the power to follow one's own will to choose a course of conduct. Liberty, like freedom, has its inherent restraint to act without harm to others and within the accepted rules of conduct for the benefit of the general public.

license: 1) n. governmental permission to perform a particular act (like getting married), conduct a particular business or occupation, operate machinery or vehicles after proving ability to do so safely or use property for a certain purpose. 2) n. the certificate that proves one has been granted authority to do something under governmental license. 3) n. a private grant of right to use real property for a particular purpose, such as putting on a concert. 4) n. a private grant of the right to use some intellectual property such as a patent or musical composition. 5) v. to grant permission by governmental authority or private agreement. (See: **licensee, licensor**)

licensee: n. a person given a license by the government or under private agreement. (See: **license, licensor**)

licensor: n. a person who gives another a license, particularly a private party doing so, such as a business giving someone a license to sell its product. (See: **license, licensee**)

lie detector test: n. a popular name for a polygraph which tests the physiological reaction of a person to questions asked by a testing expert. A potential or actual criminal defendant or possible witness cannot be forced or ordered to take a lie detector test. Some habitual liars pass lie detector tests, and innocent, honest people fail them due to nervousness and other factors. However, law enforcement authorities usually believe the results, which occasionally exonerate (clear) a suspect. Since the results are sometimes unreliable, they are not admissible in a trial and may not be referred to. (See: **polygraph**)

lien: n. any official claim or charge against property or funds for payment of a debt or an amount owed for services rendered. A lien is usually a formal document signed by the party to whom money is owed and sometimes by the debtor who agrees to the amount due. A lien carries with it the right to sell property, if necessary, to obtain the money. A mortgage or a deed of trust is a form of lien, and any lien against real property must be recorded with the County Recorder to be enforceable, including an abstract of judgment which turns a judgment into a lien against the judgment debtor's property. There are numerous types of liens including: a mechanic's lien against the real property upon which a workman, contractor or supplier has provided work or materials, an attorney's lien for fees to be paid from funds recovered by his/her efforts, a medical lien for medical bills to be paid from funds recovered for an injury, a landlord's lien against a tenant's property for unpaid rent or damages, a tax lien to enforce the government's claim of unpaid taxes, or the security agreement (UCC-1) authorized by the Uniform Commercial Code. Most liens are enforceable in the order in which they were recorded or filed (in the case of security agreements), except tax liens, which have priority over the private citizen's claim. (See: **abstract of judgment, deed of trust, equitable lien, judgment debtor, landlord's lien, mechanic's lien, mortgage**)

lienor: n. a person who holds a lien on another's property or funds. (See: **lien**)

life estate: n. the right to use or occupy real property for one's life. Often this is given to a person (such as a family member) by deed or as a gift under a will with the idea that a younger person would then take the property upon the death of the one who receives the life estate. Title may also return to the person giving or deeding the property or to his/her surviving children or descendants upon the death of the life tenant—this is called "reversion." Example of creation of a life estate: "I grant to my mother, Molly McCree, the right to live in and/or receive rents from said real property, until her death," or "I give my daughter, Sadie Hawkins, said real property, subject to a life estate to my mother, Molly McCree." This means a woman's mother, Molly, gets to live in the house until she dies, then the woman's daughter, Sadie, will own the property.

life without possibility of parole: n. a sentence sometimes given for particularly vicious criminals in murder cases or to repeat felons, particularly if the crime is committed in a state which has no death penalty, the jury chooses not to impose the death penalty, or the judge feels it is simpler to lock the prisoner up and "throw away the key" rather than invite years of appeals while the prisoner languishes on death row. Opponents of capital punishment often advocate this penalty as a substitute for execution. It guarantees the criminal will not endanger the public, and the prospect of never being outside prison is severe punishment. Contrary arguments are that this penalty does not deter murderers, there is always the possibility of escape or killing a guard or fellow prisoner, or some soft-hearted Governor may someday reduce the sentence. (See: **three strikes, you're out**)

limitation of actions: n. the period of time in which a person has to file with the clerk of the court or appropriate agency what he/she believes is a valid lawsuit or claim. The period varies greatly depending on what type of case is involved, whether the suit is against the government, whether it is by a minor, and most importantly, in what state or federal jurisdiction the right to sue arose. This is more commonly called the statute of limitations, which are specific periods for various claims in each state. (See: **statute of limitations**)

limited jurisdiction: n. courts' authority over certain types of cases such as bankruptcy, claims against the government, probate, family matters, immigration and customs or limitations on courts' authority to try cases involving maximum amounts of money or value. (See: **court, jurisdiction**)

> *The ardor and stress of conflict are not favorable to abstract considerations of justice.*
> *— Chief Justice Harlan F. Stone*

limited liability: n. the maximum amount a person participating in a business can lose or be charged in case of claims against the company or its bankruptcy. A stockholder in a corporation can only lose his/her investment, and a limited partner can only lose his/her investment, but a general partner can be responsible for all the debts of the partnership. Parties to a contract can limit the amount each might owe the other, but cannot contract away the rights of a third party to make a claim. (See: **corporation, general partnership, limited partnership, liquidated damages, partnership, shareholder**)

limited partnership: n. a special type of partnership which is very common when people need funding for a business, or when they are putting together an investment in a real estate development. A limited partnership requires a written agreement between the business management, who is (are) general partner or partners, and all of the limited partners. Each limited partner makes an investment of funds into the partnership and is supposed to receive a pre-stated share of the profit, which is ordinarily greater than that of each of the general partners up to a point (such as return of the investment), and, thereafter, the limited partners will receive a lesser share than the general partner(s). The limited partners also will receive the tax benefit of a "passed through" loss (a personal income tax deduction for part of the loss) during the development stages of the partnership when the expenses exceed any receipts. Quite often there is also a provision for eventual buy-out of the limited partners by the general partner(s). The limited partners may not participate in the management decisions of the partnership or they will lose their limited partnership status. They do have the power to vote to remove the general partner(s), although usually the partnership agreement is structured so that such removal is virtually impossible unless the general partner in question has committed fraud. Since the limited investors have no control of the conduct over the partnership, they should make sure they have considerable knowledge about the reputation and record of the general partner(s) and the type of business. In fact, state laws require that there be some pre-existing acquaintanceship between the general and the limited partners or a detailed prospectus provided by the general partner(s) meeting very stringent and specific federal requirements of disclosure. The maximum number of limited partners is set by state law to prevent using interests in the limited partnership as if they were shares of stock

in a corporation. In addition to priority in profit, tax deductions, and potential share in the success of the enterprise, the limited partner is "limited" in potential loss, since all he/she can lose is his/her investment, and the general partners alone are subject to claims, debts in bankruptcy and lawsuits against the partnership. Limited partnerships must file their name and names and addresses of general partners with the Secretary of State or other designated officer in the state in which the partnership is created so the public can find out who the responsible parties are. Like a corporation, a limited partnership may not have a name which is too similar to another limited partnership or corporation. (See: **corporation, general partner, limited liability, partner, partnership**)

lineal descendant: n. a person who is in direct line to an ancestor, such as child, grandchild, great-grandchild and on forever. A lineal descendant is distinguished from a "collateral" descendant, which would be from the line of a brother, sister, aunt or uncle. (See: **descent and distribution**)

lineup: n. a law enforcement method used in an attempt to have a witness or victim identify a person suspected of committing a crime. The suspect is included in a line of people, including non-criminals and others (such as plainclothesmen, office clerks, etc.). Law enforcement officials ask each person in the lineup to speak and turn to profile, while the witness or victim studies each of them and then is asked which person in the lineup, if any, committed the crime in his/her presence. One danger with this system is that the officers will suggest by manner or tone which is the suspect, or that one person in the line-up appears, by dress or conduct, to seem more suspicious. This type of identification is precarious at best.

liquidate: v. to sell the assets of a business, paying bills and dividing the remainder among shareholders, partners or other investors. (See: **wind up**)

liquidated damages: n. an amount of money agreed upon by both parties to a contract which one will pay to the other upon breaching (breaking or backing out of) the agreement or if a lawsuit arises due to the breach. Sometimes the liquidated damages are the amount of a deposit or a down payment, or are based on a formula (such as 10% of the contract amount). The non-defaulting party may obtain a judgment for the amount of liquidated damages, often based on a stipulation (clear statement) contained in the contract, unless the party who has breached the contract can make a strong showing that the amount of liquidated damages was so "unconscionable" (far too high under the circumstances) that it appears there was fraud, misunderstanding or basic unfairness. (See: **contract, damages**)

lis pendens: (lease pen-dense) n. Latin for "a suit pending," a written notice that a lawsuit has been filed which concerns the title to real property or some interest in that real property. The *lis pendens* (or notice of pending action) is filed with the clerk of the court, certified that it has been filed, and then recorded with the County Recorder. This gives notice to the defendant who owns real estate that there is a claim on the property, and the recording informs the general public (and particularly anyone interested in buying or financing the property) that there is this potential claim against it. The *lis pendens* must include a legal description of the real property, and the lawsuit must involve the property. Otherwise, if there is a petition to remove the *lis pendens* from real property not involved in the lawsuit, the plaintiff who originally recorded a false *lis pendens* will be subject to payment of attorney's fees as a penalty. Example: Joe Plumbob provides work and materials to Smith's home, sues to enforce a mechanic's lien, but records a *lis pendens* describing three other properties owned by Smith; Plumbob can be penalized by court order.

literary property: n. the writings of an author which entitles him/her to the use of the work, including publication, and sale or license for a profit to others who will then have the right to publish it. Literary property includes books, articles, poetry, movie scripts, computer programs and any writing which lends itself to publication or use. A close question can arise when a professional writer sends letters to others: are they literary property? Probably not if they were intended to be just personal communications. J. D. Salinger, author of *The Catcher in the Rye*, thought otherwise and sued to prevent use of his letters sent to another writer. The case was compromised and settled. To protect any literary work and profits from it, the writer should mark it as copyrighted. (See: **copyright**)

litigant: n. any party to a lawsuit. This means plaintiff, defendant, petitioner, respondent, cross-complainant and cross-defendant, but not a witness or attorney.

litigation: n. any lawsuit or other resort to the courts to determine a legal question or matter.

litigious: adj. referring to a person who constantly brings or prolongs legal actions, particularly when the legal maneuvers are unnecessary or unfounded. Such persons often enjoy legal battles, controversy, the courtroom, the spotlight, use the courts to punish enemies, seek profit, and pursue minor matters which do not deserve judicial attention. Some of these people are called "professional plaintiffs."

living trust: n. sometimes called an *inter vivos* (Latin for "within one's life") trust, a trust created by a declaration of trust executed by the trustor or trustors (also called settlor or settlors) during his/her/their lifetime, as distinguished from a "testamentary trust," which is created by a will and only comes into force upon the death of the person who wrote the will. A living trust should not be confused with a "living will," which provides for medical care decisions when a person is terminally ill. While a living trust is a generic name for any trust which comes into existence during the lifetime of the person or persons creating the trust, most commonly it is a trust in which the trustor(s) or settlor(s) receive benefit(s) from the profits of the trust during their lifetimes, followed by a distribution upon the death of the last trustor (settlor) to die, or the trust continues on for the benefit of others (such as the next generation) with profits distributed to them. There are other types of living trusts including irrevocable trust, insurance trust, charitable remainder trust and some specialized trusts to manage some parts of the assets of a person or persons. (See: **beach bum trust provision, beneficiary, charitable remainder trust, *inter vivos*, living will, revocable trust, settlor, spendthrift clause, trust, trustee, trustor**)

living will: n. also called "a durable power of attorney," it is a document authorized by statutes in all states in which a person appoints someone as his/her proxy or representative to make decisions on maintaining extraordinary life-support if the person becomes too ill, is in a coma or is certain to die. In most states the basic language has been developed by medical associations or other experts and may provide various choices as to when such maintenance of life can be terminated. The decision must be made in consultation with the patient's doctor. The living will permits a terminal patient to die in dignity and protects the physician or hospital from liability for withdrawing or limiting life support. (See: **power of attorney**)

locus: (low-cuss) n. Latin for "place," it means "place which" this or that occurred.

loiter: v. to linger or hang around in a public place or business where one has no particular or legal purpose. In many states, cities and towns there are statutes or ordinances against loitering by which the police can arrest someone who refuses to "move along." There is a question as to whether such laws are constitutional. However, there is often another criminal statute or ordinance which can be applied specifically to control aggressive begging, soliciting prostitution, drug dealing, blocking entries to stores, public drunkenness or being a public nuisance.

long-arm statute: n. law which gives a local state court jurisdiction over an out-of-state company or individual whose actions caused damage locally or to a local resident. The legal test is whether the out-of-state defendant has contacts within the state which are "sufficiently substantial." An accident or injury within the state usually shows such a substantial contact. This is particularly important when a driver from one state is sued in another state for damages caused by his/her negligence there. It also can be employed if a product shipped from out-of-state fails, explodes or causes damage to a local person who sues in the state where he/she resides. The long-arm statute allows him/her to get local court jurisdiction over the defendant.

long cause: n. a lawsuit in which it is estimated that a trial will take more than one day. In many courts the so-called "short cause" cases will be scheduled more quickly than long cause cases, since "short cause" cases are easier to fit into busy court calendars. If a trial estimated as a "short cause" turns out to take longer than one day, the judge may declare a mistrial and force the parties to try the case over again from scratch at a later date as a "long cause." (See: **calendar call, court calendar, short cause**)

loss: n. 1) the value placed on injury or damages due to an accident caused by another's negligence, a breach of contract or other wrongdoing. The amount of monetary damages can be determined in a lawsuit. 2) when expenses are greater than profits, the difference between the amount of money spent and the income. (See: **damages**)

loss of bargain: n. the inability to complete a sale or other business deal, caused by another's breach of contract, intentional interference with one's business, negligence or some other wrongdoing. The amount of monetary damages resulting from this loss can be determined in a lawsuit. (See: **damages**)

loss of consortium: n. the inability of one's spouse to have normal marital relations, which is a euphemism for sexual intercourse. Such loss arises as a claim for damages when a spouse has been injured and cannot participate in sexual relations for a period of time or permanently due to the injury, or suffers from mental distress, due to a defendant's wrongdoing, which interferes with usual sexual activity. Thus, the uninjured spouse can join in the injured mate's lawsuit on a claim of loss of consortium, the value of which is speculative, but can be awarded if the jury (or judge sitting as trier of fact) is sufficiently impressed by the deprivation. (See: **consortium, damages**)

loss of use: n. the inability to use an automobile, premises or some equipment due to damage to the vehicle, premises or articles caused by the negligence or other wrongdoing of another. Examples: compensation for each day a car is out of commission during repairs or for the period of non-occupancy while a burned building is restored. A common standard of compensation (payment) is rental value of the automobile or premises, but the period of loss must be "reasonable," meaning the damages will be limited to a period in which a person would normally and promptly proceed to have the vehicle repaired or arrange reconstruction of the building or premises. (See: **damages**)

lower court: n. 1) any court of lesser rank, such as municipal or justice court below a superior or county court, a superior or county court below an appeals court, or a federal District Court of Appeals below the U.S. Supreme Court. 2) a reference in an appeal to the trial court which originally heard the case. Typical language in an appeals decision: "In the lower court, the judge ruled Defendant had no basis for...." (See: **courts**)

M

magistrate: n. 1) a generic term for any judge of a court, or anyone officially performing a judge's functions. 2) in a few states, an officer of the court at the lowest level who hears small claims lawsuits, serves as a judge for charges of minor crimes and/or conducts preliminary hearings in criminal cases to determine if there is enough evidence presented by the prosecution to hold the accused for trial. 3) in federal courts, an official who conducts routine hearings assigned by the federal judges, including preliminary hearings in criminal cases. (See: **judge, justice of the peace, preliminary hearing**)

Magna Carta: n. Latin for "Great Charter," it was a document delineating a series of laws establishing the rights of English barons and major landowners and limiting the absolute authority of the King of England. It became the basis for the rights of English citizens. It was signed reluctantly by King John on June 15, 1215, at Runnymede, at a table set up in a field under a canopy surrounded by the armed gentry. The Magna Carta was confirmed by John's son, Henry III, and in turn by Henry's son, Edward I. As John Cowell would write four centuries later: "although this charter consists of not above thirty seven Charters or Lawes yet it is of such extent, as all the Law wee have, is thought in some form to depend on it." Essentially a document for the nobility, it became the basis of individual rights as a part of the English Constitution, which is generally more custom than written documents. It is also spelled Magna Charta.

mail box rule: n. in contract law, making a written offer or acceptance of offer valid if sent in the mail, with postage, within the time in which the offer must be accepted, unless the offer requires acceptance by personal delivery on or before the specified date. The rule may also apply to mailing payments of insurance premiums when due. However, relying on this so-called "rule" can be dangerous, since the party awaiting the acceptance or payment may cancel the offer if there is no response in hand when the time runs out.

maim: v. to inflict a serious bodily injury, including mutilation or any harm which limits the victim's ability to function physically. Originally, in English common law it meant to cut off or permanently cripple a body part like an arm, leg, hand or foot. In criminal law, such serious harm becomes an "aggravated" assault, which is a felony subject to a prison term. (See: **mayhem**)

majority: n. 1) the age when a person can exercise all normal legal rights, including contracting and voting. It is 18 for most purposes, but there are rights such as drinking alcoholic beverages which is set at 21. 2) 50 percent, plus one of votes cast. (See: **child, infancy, minority**)

make: v. 1) to create something. 2) to sign a check, promissory note, bill of exchange or some other note which guarantees, promises or orders payment of money. (See: **bill of exchange, check, maker, promissory note**)

make one whole: v. to pay or award damages sufficient to put the party who was damaged back into the position he/she would have been in without the fault of another. (See: **damages**)

maker: n. 1) the person who signs a check or promissory note, which makes him/her responsible for payment. 2) a person who endorses a check or note over to another person before it is delivered, making the endorser obligated to pay until it is delivered. (See: **check, payee, payor, promissory note**)

malfeasance: n. intentionally doing something either legally or morally wrong which one had no right to do. It always involves dishonesty, illegality or knowingly exceeding authority for improper reasons. Malfeasance is distinguished from "misfeasance," which is committing a wrong or error by mistake, negligence or inadvertence, but not by intentional wrongdoing. Example: a city manager putting his indigent cousin on the city payroll at a wage the manager knows is above that allowed and/or letting him file false time cards is malfeasance; putting his able cousin on the payroll which, unknown to him, is a violation of an anti-nepotism statute is misfeasance. This distinction can apply to corporate officers, public officials, trustees and others cloaked with responsibility. (See: **misfeasance**)

malice: n. a conscious, intentional wrongdoing either of a civil wrong like libel (false written statement about another) or a criminal act like assault or murder, with the intention of doing harm to the victim. This intention includes ill-will, hatred or total disregard for the other's well-being. Often the mean nature of the act itself implies malice, without the party saying "I did it because I was mad at him, and I hated him," which would be express malice. Malice is an element in first degree murder. In a lawsuit for defamation (libel and slander) the existence of malice may increase the judgment to include general damages. Proof of malice is absolutely necessary for a "public figure" to win a lawsuit for defamation. (See: **defamation, libel, malice aforethought, malicious prosecution, murder, public figure, slander**)

malice aforethought: n. 1) the conscious intent to cause death or great bodily harm to another person before a person commits the crime. Such malice is a required element to prove first degree murder. 2) a general evil and depraved state of mind in which the person is unconcerned for the lives of others. Thus, if a person uses a gun to hold up a bank and an innocent bystander is killed in a shoot-out with police, there is malice aforethought. (See: **first degree murder, malice, murder**)

malicious prosecution: n. filing a lawsuit with the intention of creating problems for the defendant such as costs, attorneys' fees, anguish, or distraction when there is no substantial basis for the suit. If the defendant in the lawsuit wins and has evidence that the suit was filed out of spite and without any legal or factual foundation, he/she may, in turn, sue for damages against the person who filed the original action. If malice is clearly proved against the party who brought the original suit, punitive damages may be awarded along with special and general damages. In recent cases, courts have ruled that an attorney who knowingly assists a client in filing a worthless lawsuit out of malice or spite may be liable for damages along with the client. The suit by the victim to recover damages for a malicious prosecution cannot be filed until the original lawsuit is decided in favor of the victim. (See: **malice**)

malpractice: n. An act or continuing conduct of a professional which does not meet the standard of professional competence and results in provable damages to his/her client or patient. Such an error or omission may be through negligence, ignorance (when the professional should have known), or intentional wrongdoing. However, malpractice does not include the exercise of professional judgment even when the results are detrimental to the client or patient. Except in cases of extremely obvious or intentional wrongs, in order to prove malpractice there must be testimony of an expert as to the acceptable standard of care applied to the specific act or conduct which is claimed to be malpractice and testimony of the expert that the professional did not meet that standard. The defendant then can

produce his/her own expert to counter that testimony. Professions which are subject to lawsuits based on claims of malpractice include lawyers, physicians, dentists, hospitals, accountants, architects, engineers and real estate brokers. In some states in order to file an action for malpractice against a medical caregiver, there must be a written demand or notice which gives the physician or hospital a chance to settle the matter before a suit is filed. In actions against attorneys it is mandatory that the plaintiff prove that the error, if any, caused damages. This means that a lawsuit, claim or negotiation the attorney was handling would have resulted in a win or better recovery except for the malpractice. Thus, there is a requirement of proving the original "case within the case" during the trial of the malpractice claim. Contrary to public perception, substantial judgments in malpractice actions are rare, with studies showing that only a small percentage of the claims result in recovery for the allegedly aggrieved client or patient. The principal reason is that most cries of malpractice are unfounded and are based on unhappiness with the result of the original services no matter how well handled, a breakdown in communication between attorney or doctor and client or patient, anger with the professional, retaliation for attempts to collect unpaid fees or greed. (See: **errors and omissions**)

malum in se: (mal-uhm in say) adv. Latin referring to an act that is "wrong in itself," in its very nature being illegal because it violates the natural, moral or public principles of a civilized society. In criminal law it is one of the collection of crimes which are traditional and not just created by statute, which are "*malum prohibitum.*" Example: murder, rape, burglary and robbery are *malum in se*, while violations of the Securities and Exchange Act or most "white collar crimes" are *malum prohibitum*. (See: **malum prohibitum**)

> *Restraints upon those rights which in primitive and sparsely settled communities might well be regarded as arbitrary and unreasonable, may be indispensable to the safety and orderly life of the modern city.*
> —*Chief Justice Harlan F. Stone*

malum prohibitum: (mal-uhm prohibit-uhm) adj. Latin meaning "wrong due to being prohibited," which refers to crimes made so by statute, compared to crimes based on English common law and obvious violations of society's standards which are defined as *malum in se*. Statutory crimes include criminal violations of regulatory acts, "white collar crimes" such as improper use of insider information, issuance of stocks without a permit which are intentionally not supported by real assets and tax avoidance. (See: *malum in se*, **white collar crime**)

mandamus: (man-dame-us) n. Latin for "we order," a writ (more modernly called a "writ of mandate") which orders a public agency or governmental body to perform an act required by law when it has neglected or refused to do so. Examples: After petitions were filed with sufficient valid signatures to quali-

fy a proposition for the ballot, the city refuses to call the election, claiming it has a legal opinion that the proposal is unconstitutional. The backers of the proposition file a petition for a writ ordering the city to hold the election. The court will order a hearing on the writ and afterwards either issue the writ or deny the petition. Or a state agency refuses to release public information, a school district charges fees to a student in violation of state law, or a judge will not permit reporters entry at a public trial. All of these can be subject of petitions for a writ of *mandamus*. (See: **writ of mandate**)

mandate: n. 1) any mandatory order or requirement under statute, regulation, or by a public agency. 2) order of an appeals court to a lower court (usually the original trial court in the case) to comply with an appeals court's ruling, such as holding a new trial, dismissing the case or releasing a prisoner whose conviction has been overturned. 3) same as the writ of *mandamus*, which orders a public official or public body to comply with the law. (See: *mandamus*, **writ of mandate**)

mandatory: adj., adv. absolutely demanded or required.

mandatory joinder: n. the required inclusion of a party in a lawsuit whom the court finds is absolutely necessary to a resolution of all issues in the case. (See: **joinder**)

manifest: 1) adj., adv. completely obvious or evident. 2) n. a written list of goods in a shipment.

Mann Act: n. a federal statute making

it a crime to transport a woman across state lines for "immoral" purposes. The Mann Act was intended to prevent the movement of prostitutes from one state to another or in and out of the country in the so-called "white slave" trade. However, it also applies to a male taking his under-age girlfriend to a love-nest in a neighboring state, or a female transporting an under-age boy across the state line for such purposes. Maximum term is five years in a federal prison.

manslaughter: n. the unlawful killing of another person without premeditation or so-called "malice aforethought" (an evil intent prior to the killing). It is distinguished from murder (which brings greater penalties) by lack of any prior intention to kill anyone or create a deadly situation. There are two levels of manslaughter: voluntary and involuntary. Voluntary manslaughter includes killing in heat of passion or while committing a felony. Involuntary manslaughter occurs when a death is caused by a violation of a non-felony, such as reckless driving (called "vehicular manslaughter"). Examples: Eddy Hothead gets into a drunken argument in a saloon with his acquaintance Bob Bonehead, and Hothead hits Bonehead over the head with a beer bottle, causing internal bleeding and death. Brent Burgle sneaks into a warehouse intent on theft and is surprised by a security man, whom Burgle knocks down a flight of stairs, killing him. Both are voluntary manslaughter. However, if either man had used a gun, a murder charge is most likely since he brought a deadly weapon to use in the crime. The immediate rage in finding a loved one in bed with another followed by a killing before the passion cools usually limits the charge to voluntary manslaughter and not murder, but prior attacks could convince a District Attorney and a jury that the killing was not totally spontaneous. Lenny Leadfoot drives 70 miles per hour on a twisting mountain road, goes off a cliff and his passenger is killed in the crash. Leadfoot can be charged with involuntary manslaughter. (See: **homicide, murder**)

marital deduction: n. an estate tax deduction allowed a surviving spouse of half of the value of the estate of the deceased spouse. Thus, the minimum value of the estate before there is a possible federal estate tax rises from $600,000 (the level where estate tax begins to be calculated and charged) to $1,200,000 at the death of the first spouse to die. In trusts which a married couple creates, they can agree that on the death of the first to go, the amount of the property which is given to the survivor is limited to the amount which will not be subject to federal estate tax, thus delaying some or all estate tax until the death of the surviving spouse. Such trust provisions should be written only by an attorney and with consultation with an accountant or financial adviser. (See: **community property, estate tax, trust**)

marital rights: n. an old-fashioned expression for the rights of a husband (not rights of a wife) to sexual relations with his wife and to control her operation of the household. (See: **consortium, loss of consortium**)

maritime law: n. Also called "admiralty law" or "the law of admiralty," the laws and regulations, including international agreements and treaties, which exclusively govern activities at sea or in any navigable waters. In the United States, federal courts have jurisdiction over maritime law. (See: **admiralty**)

mark: n. an "X" made by a person who is illiterate or too weak to sign his/her full name, used in the expression "His Mark," or "Her Mark." On the rare occasion that this occurs, the "X" should be within or next to a notation such as "Theresa Testator, her mark." If the mark is intended as a signature to a will it should be formally witnessed (as signatures are) to make the will valid. (See: **will**)

marked for identification: adj. documents or objects presented during a trial before there has been testimony which confirms their authenticity and/or relevancy. Each item is given an exhibit identification letter or number and thus is marked for identification. The marked exhibits are actually introduced into evidence (made part of the official record) upon request of the lawyer offering the evidence and approval by the judge or by stipulation of both attorneys. Occasionally an exhibit marked for identification is rejected as evidence due to the judge agreeing (sustaining) with an opposing lawyer's objection such as for lack of relevancy or failure to show it is genuine or best evidence. (See: **best evidence rule, evidence, exhibit, lay a foundation, objection**)

marketable title: n. the title to real property which has no encumbrances (mortgage, deed of trust, lien or claim) and which is free of any reasonable objection (excluding minor mistakes in the description or typographical errors). A court will enforce a contract to buy and sell real estate if there is marketable title. (See: **contract, real property**)

market value: n. the price which a seller of property would receive in an open market by negotiation, as distinguished from a "distress" price on a forced or foreclosure sale, or from an auction. Market value of real property is normally determined by a professional appraiser who makes comparisons to similar property sales in the area, which are often called "comparables."

marriage: n. the joining of a male and female in matrimony by a person qualified by law to perform the ceremony (a minister, priest, judge, justice of the peace or some similar official), after having obtained a valid marriage license (which requires a blood test for venereal disease in about a third of the states and a waiting period from one to five days in several). The standard age for marriage without parental consent is 18 except for Georgia and Wyoming where it is 16, Rhode Island where women can marry at 16, and Mississippi in which it is 17 for boys and 15 for girls. More than half the states allow marriages at lesser ages with parental consent, going as low as 14 for both sexes in Alabama, Texas and Utah. Marriages in which the age requirements are not met can be annulled. Fourteen states recognize so-called "common law marriages" which establish a legal marriage for people who have lived together by agreement as husband and wife for a lengthy period of time without legal formalities. (See: **common law-marriage**)

marshal: 1) n. a federal court official who may serve papers and act as a law enforcement officer in keeping order in court, protecting federal officials, making arrests or participating in court-ordered police activities. Each district court has a federal marshal and a corps of deputies. 2) n. in several states, a law enforcement officer, similar to a sheriff or constable, who serves official documents and occasionally assists in police matters. 3) v. to collect the assets of the estate of a person who has died. This is a function of an executor or administrator of an estate. Sometimes the executor or administrator may ask the court to allow the sale or division of gifts in order to achieve the distribution the testator (writer of a will) desired. This is part of the marshaling process. 4) v. in bankruptcy, to establish priorities among creditors.

martial law: n. a system of complete control by a country's military over all activities, including civilian, in a theoretical or actual war zone, or during a period of emergency caused by a disaster such as an earthquake or flood, with the military commander having dictatorial powers. In the United States martial law must be ordered by the President as commander-in-chief and must be limited to the duration of the warfare or emergency. It cannot result in a long-term denial of constitutional rights, such as *habeas corpus,* the right to a trial, and to free press. Martial law was ordered in contested areas during the Civil War (but the Supreme Court ruled President Abraham Lincoln's suspension of the writ of *habeas corpus* was unconstitutional), and during the San Francisco earthquake and fire in 1906 when the city was in ruins, tens of thousands were homeless, and looting and disease posed great dangers to the public. Misuse of martial law, such as destruction of the veterans' encampment in Washington, D.C. under President Herbert Hoover, has proved unpopular in the United States. In many foreign countries martial law has become a method to establish and maintain dictatorships either by military leaders or politicians backed by the military. Martial law is not to be confused with "military law," which governs the conduct of the military services and applies only to service men and women. (See: **military law**)

Massachusetts Trust: n. a business in which the investors give management authority to a trustee and receive "trust certificates" representing their investments. Since they own only the certificates and do not participate in management, the investors can only lose their investment and are not personally liable for any debts of the trust. This is similar to a "limited partnership." A Massachusetts Trust is strictly a business entity and bears no relationship to a personal trust like living and testamentary trusts set up to manage and protect the assets of individuals and provide for eventual distribution.

master: n. 1) employer, in the area of

law known as "master and servant," which more properly should be called employer and employee. 2) a person, supposedly with special expertise, appointed by a judge to investigate a problem (such as whether a parent's home is appropriate for child visitation) and report back to the judge his/her findings and recommendations. (See: **employment, master and servant, *respondeat superior***)

master and servant: n. the body of law, including statutes and legal decisions which are precedents, which relates to the relationship of an employer and employee. (See: **employment, *respondeat superior*, servant agency**)

material: adj. relevant and significant. In a lawsuit, "material evidence" is distinguished from totally irrelevant or of such minor importance that the court will either ignore it, rule it immaterial if objected to, or not allow lengthy testimony upon such a matter. A "material breach" of a contract is a valid excuse by the other party not to perform. However, an insignificant divergence from the terms of the contract is not a material breach.

material representation: n. a convincing statement made to induce someone to enter into a contract to which the person would not have agreed without that assertion. Thus, if the material representation proves not to be true or to be misleading, the contract can be rescinded or cancelled without liability. (See: **contract, material**)

material witness: n. a person who apparently has information about the subject matter of a lawsuit or criminal prosecution which is significant enough to affect the outcome of the case or trial. Thus, the court must make every reasonable effort to allow such a witness to testify, including a continuance (delay in a trial) to accommodate him/her if late or temporarily unavailable. (See: **material, trial, witness**)

matter of record: n. anything, including testimony, evidence, rulings and sometimes arguments, which has been recorded by the court reporter or court clerk. It is an expression often heard in trials and legal arguments that "such and such is a matter of record" as distinguished from actions outside the court or discussions not written down or taped.

maturity: n. 1) the date when the payment of the principal amount owed under the terms of a promissory note or bill of exchange becomes due. Quite often a note states that failure to pay interest or installment payments when due "accelerates" the note, making the "maturity date" immediate if such payments are demanded and not paid. 2) the age when one becomes an adult, which is 18 for most purposes. (See: **acceleration, bill of exchange, legal age, promissory note**)

maxims: n. a collection of legal truisms which are used as "rules of thumb" by both judges and lawyers. They are listed in the codified statutes of most states, and include:
"When the reason of a rule ceases, so should the rule itself."

"He who consents to an act is not wronged by it."

"No one can take advantage of his own wrong."

"No one should suffer by the act of another."

"He who takes the benefit must bear the burden."

"For every wrong there is a remedy."

"Between rights otherwise equal, the earliest is preferred."

"No man is responsible for that which no man can control."

"The law helps the vigilant, before those who sleep on their rights."

"The law respects form less than substance."

"The law never requires impossibilities."

"The law neither does nor requires idle acts."

"The law disregards trifles."

"Particular expressions qualify those which are general."

"That is certain which can be made certain."

"Time does not confirm a void act."

"An interpretation which gives effect is preferred to one which makes void."

"Interpretation must be reasonable."

"Things happen according to the ordinary course of nature and the ordinary habits of life."

may: v. a choice to act or not, or a promise of a possibility, as distinguished from "shall," which makes it imperative. 2) in statutes, and sometimes in contracts, the word "may" must be read in context to determine if it means an act is optional or mandatory, for it may be an imperative. The same careful analysis must be made of the word "shall." Non-lawyers tend to see the word "may" and think they have a choice or are excused from complying with some statutory provision or regulation. (See: **shall**)

mayhem: 1) n. the criminal act of disabling, disfiguring or cutting off or making useless one of the members (leg, arm, hand, foot, eye) of another either intentionally or in a fight, called maiming. The serious nature of the injury makes mayhem a felony, which is called "aggravated assault" in most states. 2) v. to commit mayhem is to cause gross harm in an uncontrolled fashion. (See: **aggravated assault, assault, maim**)

McNabb-Mallory rule: n. a federal rule of evidence in criminal trials that prohibits the use of incriminating statements made by a defendant while he/she is detained beyond the legal period of time before being brought before a judge or magistrate (arraignment). This rule is seldom applied since the courts have become zealous about speedy arraignments and warnings to the accused about the right to remain silent and have a lawyer present. (See: **Miranda warning**)

mechanic's lien: n. the right of a craftsman, laborer, supplier, architect or other person who has worked upon improvements or delivered materials to a particular parcel of real estate (either as an employee of the owner or as a sub-contractor to a general contractor) to place a lien on that real property for the value of the services and/or materials if not paid. Numerous other technical laws surround mechanic's liens, including requirements of prompt written notice to the owner of the property (even before the general contractor has been tardy in making payment), limits on the amount collectable in some states, and various time limitations to enforce the lien. Ultimate, last-resort enforcement of the mechanic's lien is accomplished by filing a lawsuit to foreclose the lien and have the property sold in order to be paid. Property owners should make sure that their general contractors pay their employees or subcontractors to avoid a mechanic's lien, since the owner could be forced to pay the debts of a general contractor even though the owner has already paid the contractor. If the worker or supplier does not sue to enforce the mechanic's lien, he/she may still sue for the debt. (See: **lien**)

mediation: n. the attempt to settle a legal dispute through active participation of a third party (mediator) who works to find points of agreement and make those in conflict agree on a fair result. Mediation differs from arbitration, in which the third party (arbitrator) acts much like a judge in an out-of-court, less formal setting but does not actively participate in the discussion. Mediation has become very common in trying to resolve domestic relations disputes (divorce, child custody, visitation) and is often ordered by the judge in such cases. Mediation also has become more frequent in contract and civil damage cases. There are professional mediators or lawyers who do some mediation for substantial fees, but the financial cost is less than fighting the matter out in court and may achieve early settlement and an end to anxiety. However, mediation does not always result in a settlement. (See: **arbitration**)

mediator: n. a person who conducts mediation. A mediator is usually a lawyer or retired judge but can be a non-attorney specialist in the subject matter (like child custody) who tries to bring people and their disputes to early resolution through a conference. The mediator is an active participant in the discussions and attempts to work out a solution, unlike an arbitrator, who sits as a judge. (See: **arbitration, arbitrator, mediation**)

meet and confer: n. a requirement of courts that before certain types of motions and/or petitions will be heard by the judge, the lawyers (and sometimes their clients) must "meet and confer" to try to resolve the matter or at least determine the points of conflict. This has the beneficial effect of resolving many matters, reducing the time for arguments and making the lawyers and clients face up to the realities of their positions. On the other hand, it also can be a total waste of time for the parties and their attorneys. The meet and confer rule is particularly common (and useful) in domestic relations disputes over temporary support, custody, visitation and such issues which are freighted with emotion.

meeting of the minds: n. when two parties to an agreement (contract) both have the same understanding of the terms of the agreement. Such mutual comprehension is essential to a valid contract. It is provable by the express provisions of a written contract, without reference to any statements or hidden thoughts outside the writing. There would not be a meeting of the minds if Bill Buyer said, "I'll buy all your stock," and he meant shares in a corporation, and Sam Seller said, "I'll sell all my stock to you," and meant his cattle. (See: **contract**)

memorandum: n. 1) a brief writing, note, summary or outline. 2) A "memorandum of decision," or "memorandum opinion," is a brief statement by a judge announcing his/her ruling without detail or giving extensive reasons, which may or may not be followed by a more comprehensive written decision. Such memoranda (plural) are issued by appeals courts in language such as: "The petition of appellant is denied for the reasons stated in *Albini v. Younger*," or "The decision below is affirmed."

mens rea: (menz ray-ah) n. Latin for a "guilty mind," or criminal intent in committing the act. (See: **crime, intent**)

mental anguish: n. mental suffering which includes fright, feelings of distress, anxiety, depression, grief and/or psychosomatic physical symptoms. It is distinguished from physical pain due to an injury, but it may be considered in awarding damages for physical injury due to a defendant's negligence or intentional infliction of harm. Where there is no physical injury, damages can still be awarded for mental anguish if it is reasonable to presume such would naturally flow from the incident. Examples: holding a pistol to one's head, any threat of bodily harm when it appears it could be carried out, swinging with a scythe even though the assailant missed, or witnessing injury or death to a loved one. There are also situations in which the obvious result of the alleged wrongdoing would be mental distress due to embarrassment or damage to one's reputation through libel, and therefore damages can be awarded to the distressed party. However, there are limits: in general, breach of contract judgments cannot include damages for mental anguish due to the loss of a deal or employment. But then there is the case of the shop which failed to deliver the bridal gown in time for the wedding—mental anguish flows naturally (along with the bride's tears) from such a breach. (See: **damages, mental suffering**)

If law can be upheld only by enforcement officers, then our scheme of government is at an end. Every citizen has a personal duty in it—the duty to order his own actions, to so weigh the effect of his example, that his conduct shall be a positive force in his community with respect to the law.
—Herbert Hoover

mental competency: n. (See: **competent**)

mental cruelty: n. a term, rapidly going out of fashion and out of the statutes, which has been used to justify granting a divorce when the state laws required that some wrong had to be found in the defending spouse. In absence of actual physical cruelty (or unwillingness to discuss it) the person wanting the divorce could testify to a list of indignities ("he swore at me, he came home late, he humiliated me in front of friends, he read girlie magazines," or similar tales told about the wife) which would be verified by a relative or a friend to satisfy the judge that the petitioning spouse would suffer mental harm if the marriage continued and proved that there were grounds for a divorce. As "no-fault" divorce has gained favor, such charades have faded into legal history. (See: **cruelty, divorce**)

mental suffering: n. emotional pain synonymous with "mental anguish." (See: **mental anguish**)

mercantile law: n. that broad area of the law (also called commercial law), statutes, cases and customs which deal with trade, sales, buying, selling, transportation, contracts and all forms of business transactions. Much of the law of business transactions is covered by the *Uniform Commercial Code,* which has been adopted almost universally in the United States. (See: **commercial law, contract, corporation, seller,** *Uniform Commercial Code*)

merchantable: adj. a product of a high enough quality to make it fit for sale. To be merchantable an article for sale must be usable for the purpose it is made. It must be of average worth (not necessarily special) in the marketplace and must not be broken, unworkable, damaged, contaminated or flawed. (See: **sale**)

merger: n. 1) in corporate law, the joining together of two corporations in which one corporation transfers all of its assets to the other, which continues to exist. In effect one corporation "swallows" the other, but the shareholders of the swallowed company receive shares of the surviving corporation. A merger is distinguished from a "consolidation," in which both companies join together to create a new corporation. 2) in real property law, when an owner of an interest in property acquires a greater or lesser interest in the same property, the two interests become one. Examples: a person with a life estate is given the title to the property by inheritance, the life estate is merged with the titled interest. 3) another important form of merger occurs when a person acquires two parcels of land which were once a single lot that had been divided into two lots by a "lot split" granted by the city or county. If the minimum lot size has been increased by changes in local ordinances and the two lots are now sub-standard size, the buyer who acquires title in the two lots may find that they are "merged" into one lot and he or she has lost the right to build a house on each lot. To avoid this problem, the buyer should make sure title in each lot is obtained under a different name, i.e. husband taking one, and wife the other.

mesne: (mean, with a silent s) adj. from Norman French for intermediate, the middle point between two extremes. It is seldom used, except in reference to "mesne profits." (See: **mesne profits**)

mesne profits: n. profits which have accrued while there was a dispute over land ownership. If it is determined the party using the land did not have legal ownership, the true owner can sue for some or all of the profits made in the interim by the illegal tenant, which are thus called "mesne profits." (See: **mesne**)

metes and bounds: (meets and bounds) n. a surveyor's description of a parcel of real property, using carefully measured distances, angles and directions, which results in what is called a "legal description" of the land, as distinguished from merely a street address or parcel number. Such a metes and bounds description is required to be recorded in official county records on a subdivision map and in the deeds when the boundaries of a parcel or lot are first drawn.

military law: n. regulations governing the conduct of men and women in the armed services in relation to their military (not civilian) activities. (See: **court-martial, judge advocate**)

mining claim: n. a description by boundaries of real property in which metal ore and/or minerals may be located. A claim on public land must be filed with the Bureau of Land Management or other federal agency, and the claim must be "worked" by being mined or prepared for mining within a specific period of time.

ministerial act: n. an act, particularly of a governmental employee, which is performed according to statutes, legal authority, established procedures or instructions from a superior, without exercising any individual judgment.

minor: n. someone under legal age, which is generally 18, except for certain purposes such as drink-ing alcoholic beverages. (See: **legal age, maturity**)

minority: n. 1) in voting, a side with less than half the votes. 2) a term for people in a predominantly Caucasian country who are not Caucasian, such as the United States where Caucasians comprise the majority and the minorities include African Americans, Hispanics, Asians, indigenous Americans (Indians) and other so-called "people of color." This ironic term is used despite the fact that the majority of the world's population is not Caucasian. Sometimes the term is employed to include women and homosexuals. "Minority" carries with it a certain patronizing tone even when used to assert rights of peoples who have been discriminated against, either socially or by law. 3) the period of life under legal age. (See: **legal age, majority, minor**)

minutes: n. 1) the written record of meetings, particularly of boards of directors and/or shareholders of corporations, kept by the secretary of the corporation or organization. 2) the record of courtroom proceedings, such as the start and recess of hearings and trials, names of attorneys, witnesses and rulings of the court, kept by the clerk of the court or the judge. Such court minutes are not a transcript of everything that is said, which is taken down by the court reporter if recorded at all.

Miranda warning: n. the requirement, also called the Miranda rule, set by the U.S. Supreme Court in *Miranda v. Arizona* (1966) that prior to the time of arrest and any interrogation of a person suspected of a crime, he/she must be told that he/she has: the right to remain silent, the right to legal counsel, and the right to be told that anything he/she says can be used in court against him/her. The warnings are known as Miranda rights or just "rights." Further, if the accused person confesses to the authorities, the prosecution must prove to the judge that the defendant was informed of these rights and knowingly waived them, before the confession can be introduced in the defendant's criminal trial. The Miranda rule supposedly prevents self-incrimination in violation of the Fifth Amendment to the U.S. Constitution. Sometimes there is a question of admissibility of answers to questions made by the defendant *before* he/she was considered a prime suspect, raising a factual issue as to what is a *prime* suspect and when does a person become such a suspect? (See: **rights**)

"mirror" wills: n. the wills of a husband and wife which are identical except that each leaves the same gifts to the other, and each names the other as executor.

misadventure: n. a death due to unintentional accident without any violation of law or criminal negligence. Thus, there is no crime. (See: **homicide, manslaughter**)

misappropriation: n. the intentional, illegal use of the property or funds of another person for one's own use or other unauthorized purpose, particularly by a public official, a trustee of a trust, an executor or administrator of a dead person's estate or by any person with a responsibility to care for and protect another's assets (a fiduciary duty). It is a felony (a crime punishable by a prison sentence). (See: **embezzlement, fiduciary, larceny, theft**)

misdemeanor: n. a lesser crime punishable by a fine and/or county jail time for up to one year. Misdemeanors are distinguished from felonies, which can be punished by a state prison term. They are tried in the lowest local court such as municipal, police or justice courts. Typical misdemeanors include: petty theft, disturbing the peace, simple assault and battery, drunk driving without injury to others, drunkenness in public, various traffic violations, public nuisances and some crimes which can be charged either as a felony or misdemeanor depending on the circumstances and the discretion of the District Attorney. "High crimes and misdemeanors" referred to in the U.S. Constitution are felonies. (See: **felony**)

misfeasance: n. management of a business, public office or other responsibility in which there are errors and an unfortunate result through mistake or carelessness, but without evil intent and/or violation of law. Misfeasance is distinguished from "malfeasance," which is intentional conduct in violation of the law. (See: **malfeasance**)

misjoinder: n. the inclusion of parties (plaintiffs or defendants) or causes of action (legal claims) in a single lawsuit contrary to statute. Reasons for a court ruling that there is misjoinder include: a) the parties do not have the same rights to a judgment; b) they have conflicting interests; c) the situations in each claim (cause of action) are different or contradictory; or d) the defendants are not involved (even slightly) in the same transaction. In a criminal prosecution the most common cause for misjoinder is that the defendants were involved in different alleged crimes, or the charges are based on different transactions. (See: **joinder**)

misnomer: n. the wrong name.

misprision of a felony: n. the crime of concealing another's felony (serious crime) from law enforcement officers. (See: **accessory, aid and abet, felony**)

misrepresentation: n. the crime of misstating facts to obtain money, goods or benefits of another to which the accused is not entitled. Examples: a person a) falsely claims to represent a charity to obtain a donation which he/she keeps; b) says a painting is a genuine Jackson Pollock when it is a fake and thus is able to sell it for a price much greater than its true value. Misrepresentation is also called "false pretenses." (See: **false pretenses**)

mistake: n. 1) an error in comprehending facts, meaning of words or the law, which causes one party or both parties to enter into a contract without understanding the obligations or results. Such a mistake can entitle one party or both parties to a rescission (cancellation) of the contract. A mistaken understanding of the law (as distinguished from facts) by one party only is usually no basis for rescission since "ignorance of the law is no excuse." 2) an error discovered to be incorrect at a later time. (See: **contract, rescission**)

mistrial: n. the termination of a trial before its normal conclusion because of a procedural error, statements by a witness, judge or attorney which prejudice a jury, a deadlock by a jury without reaching a verdict after lengthy deliberation (a "hung" jury), or the failure to complete a trial within the time set by the court. When such situations arise, the judge, either on his own initiative or upon the motion (request) of one of the parties will "declare a mistrial," dismiss the jury if there is one and direct that the lawsuit or criminal prosecution be set for trial again, starting from the beginning. (See: **trial**)

mitigating circumstances: n. in criminal law, conditions or happenings which do not excuse or justify criminal conduct, but are considered out of mercy or fairness in deciding the degree of the offense the prosecutor charges or influencing reduction of the penalty upon conviction. Example: a young man shoots his father after years of being beaten, belittled, sworn at and treated without love. "Heat of passion" or "diminished capacity" are forms of such mitigating circumstances. (See: **diminished capacity, heat of passion, "Twinkie" defense**)

mitigation of damages: n. the requirement that someone injured by another's negligence or breach of contract must take reasonable steps to reduce the damages, injury or cost, and to prevent them from getting worse.

Thus, a person claiming to have been injured by another motorist should seek medical help and not let the problem worsen. If a tenant moves out before a lease has expired, a landlord must make reasonable attempts to re-let the property and take in some rents (which are credited against the amount remainder of the lease) to mitigate his/her loss.

M'Naughten rule: n. a traditional "right and wrong" test of legal insanity in criminal prosecutions. Under M'Naughten (its name comes from the trial of a notorious English assassin in the early 1800s), a defendant is legally insane if he/she cannot distinguish between right and wrong in regard to the crime with which he/she is charged. If the judge or the jury finds that the accused could not tell the difference, then there could not be criminal intent. Considering modern psychiatry and psychology, tests for lack of capacity to "think straight" (with lots of high-priced expert testimony) are used in most states either under the American Law Institute's Model Penal Code or the "Durham Rule." (See: **diminished capacity, insanity, temporary insanity, "Twinkie" defense**)

M. O.: n. slang for *modus operandi*, the way or pattern in which a repeat criminal usually commits his/her crime. (See: *modus operandi*)

modification: n. a change in an existing court order or judgment made necessary by a change in circumstances since the order or judgment was made or to cure an error. A motion (petition) to the court for modification is common after divorce judgments because the courts "retain jurisdiction" over matters concerning the children which may need changes such as terms of child support and custody.

modus operandi: (mode-us ah-purr-and-ee or ah-purr-and-eye) n. from Latin, a criminal investigation term for "way of operating," which may prove the accused has a pattern of repeating the same criminal acts using the same method. Examples: a repeat offender always wore a blue ski mask and used a sawed-off shotgun, climbed up trellises to burglarize, pretended to be a telephone repairman to gain entrance or set up phoney companies to disguise a fraudulent scheme.

moiety: (moy-et-tee) n. half. Generally a reference to interest in real property, moiety is seldom used today.

molestation: n. the crime of sexual acts with children up to the age of 18, including touching of private parts, exposure of genitalia, taking of pornographic pictures, rape, inducement of sexual acts with the molester or with other children and variations of these acts by pedophiles. Molestation also applies to incest by a relative with a minor family member and any unwanted sexual acts with adults short of rape. (See: **pedophilia, rape**)

monopoly: n. a business or inter-related group of businesses which controls so much of the production or sale of a product or kind of product as to control the market, including prices and distribution. Business practices, combinations and/or acquisitions which tend to create a monopoly may violate various federal statutes which regulate or prohibit business trusts and monopolies or prohibit restraint of trade. However, limited monopolies granted by a manufacturer to a wholesaler in a particular area are usually legal, since they are like "licenses." Public utilities such as electric, gas and water companies may also hold a monopoly in a particular geographic area since it is the only practical way to provide the public service, and they are regulated by state public utility commissions. (See: **antitrust laws, license, restraint of trade**)

month-to-month: adj. referring to a tenancy in which the tenant pays monthly rent and has no lease, and the tenancy can be terminated by the landlord at any time on thirty days notice. (See: **landlord and tenant, tenancy**)

monument: n. 1) an established landmark which a surveyor uses as part of a legal description of real property. 2) a building or other structure of historic importance, which may be recognized formally and marked by federal, state or local agencies, and therefore may not be torn down or substantially altered.

moot: adj. 1) unsettled, open to argument or debatable, specifically about a legal question which has not been determined by any decision of any court. 2) an issue only of academic interest. (See: **moot court, moot point**)

moot court: n. law school exercise in which students argue both sides of an appeal from a fictitious lawsuit in a mock court. There are also moot court contests between teams from different law schools. (See: **moot**)

moot point: n. 1) a legal question which no court has decided, so it is still debatable or unsettled. 2) an issue only of academic interest. (See: **moot**)

> *The complete independence of the courts of justice is peculiarly essential to a limited Constitution.*
> *—Alexander Hamilton, Federalist Papers*

moral certainty: n. in a criminal trial, the reasonable belief (but falling short of absolute certainty) of the trier of the fact (jury or judge sitting without a jury) that the evidence shows the defendant is guilty. Moral certainty is another way of saying "beyond a reasonable doubt." Since there is no exact measure of certainty it is always somewhat subjective and based on "reasonable" opinions of judge and/or jury. (See: **beyond a reasonable doubt, guilt, verdict**)

moral turpitude: n. gross violation of standards of moral conduct, vileness. An act involving moral turpitude is considered intentionally evil, making the act a crime. The existence of moral turpitude can bring a more severe criminal charge or penalty for a criminal defendant.

moratorium: n. 1) any suspension of activity, particularly voluntary suspension of collections of debts by a private enterprise or by government or pursuant to court order. 2) in bankruptcy, a halt to the right to collect a debt. In times of economic crisis or a natural disaster like a flood or earthquake, there may be a moratorium on foreclosures or mortgage payments until the public can get back to normal activities and earnings.

mortgage: n. a document in which the owner pledges his/her/its title to real property to a lender as security for a loan described in a promissory note. Mortgage is an old English term derived from two French words "mort" and "gage" meaning "dead pledge." To be enforceable the mortgage must be signed by the owner (borrower), acknowledged before a notary public, and recorded with the County Recorder or Recorder of Deeds. If the owner (mortgagor) fails to make payments on the promissory note (becomes delinquent) then the lender (mortgagee) can foreclose on the mortgage to force a sale of the real property to obtain payment from the proceeds, or obtain the property itself at a sheriff's sale upon foreclosure. However, catching up on delinquent payments and paying costs of foreclosure ("curing the default") can save the property. In some states the property can be redeemed by such payment even after foreclosure. Upon payment in full the mortgagee (lender) is required to execute a "satisfaction of mortgage" (sometimes called a "discharge of mortgage") and record it to clear the title to the property. A purchase-money mortgage is one given by a purchaser to a seller of real property as partial payment. A mortgagor may sell the property either "subject to a mortgage" in which the property is still security and the seller is still liable for payment, or the buyer "assumes the mortgage" and becomes personally responsible for payment of the loan. Under English common law a mortgage was an actual transfer of title to the lender, with the borrower having the right to occupy the property while it was in effect, but non-payment ended the right of occupation. Today only Connecticut, Maine, New Hampshire, North Carolina, Rhode Island and Vermont cling to the common law, and other states using mortgages treat them as liens on the property. More significantly, 14 states use a "deed of trust" (or "trust deed") as a mortgage. These states include: California, Illinois, Texas, Virginia, Colorado, Georgia, Alaska, Arizona, Idaho, Mississippi, Missouri, Montana, North Carolina and West Virginia. Under the deed of trust system title is technically given to a trustee to hold for the lender, who is called a beneficiary. (See: **deed of trust, foreclosure, judicial foreclosure, notice of default, trust deed**)

mortgagee: n. the person or business making a loan that is secured by the real property of the person (mortgagor) who owes him/her/it money. (See: **mortgage, mortgagor**)

mortgagor: n. the person who has borrowed money and pledged his/her real property as security for the money provided by the lender (mortgagee). (See: **mortgage, mortgagee**)

motion: n. a formal request made to a judge for an order or judgment. Motions are made in court all the time for many purposes: to continue (postpone) a trial to a later date, to get a modification of an order, for temporary child support, for a judgment, for dismissal of the opposing party's case, for a rehearing, for sanctions (payment of the moving party's costs or attorney's fees), or for dozens of other purposes. Most motions require a written petition, a written brief of legal reasons for granting the motion (often called "points and authorities"), written notice to the attorney for the opposing party and a hearing before a judge. However, during a trial or a hearing, an oral motion may be permitted.

motion for a new trial: n. a request made by the loser for the case to be tried again on the basis that there were significant legal errors in the way the trial was conducted and/or the jury or the judge sitting without a jury obviously came to an incorrect result. This motion must be made within a few days after the judgment is formally entered and is usually heard by the same judge who presided at the trial. Such a motion is seldom granted (particularly if the judge heard the case without a jury) unless there is some very clear error which any judge would recognize. Some lawyers feel the motion helps add to the record of argument leading to an appeal of the case to an appeals court. (See: **judgment notwithstanding the verdict, motion, N.O.V.**)

motion for dismissal (non-suit): n. application by a defendant in a lawsuit or criminal prosecution asking the judge to rule that the plaintiff (the party who filed the lawsuit) or the prosecution has not and cannot prove its case. Attorneys most often make this motion after the plaintiff or prosecutor has presented all the evidence they have, but they can make it at the end of the evidence presentation but before judgment or upon evidence being presented that proves to the judge that the defendant cannot lose. Quite often this is an oral motion, and arguments are made in the judge's chambers where the jury cannot hear. It is also sometimes called a motion for nonsuit. (See: **motion**)

motion for a summary judgment: n. a written request for a judgment in the moving party's favor before a lawsuit goes to trial and based on testimony recorded outside court, affidavits (declarations under penalty of perjury), depositions, admissions of fact and/or answers to written interrogatories, claiming that all factual and legal issues can be decided in the moving party's favor. These alleged facts are accompanied by a written legal brief (points and authorities) in support of the motion. The opposing party needs to show by affidavits, written declarations or points and authorities (written legal argument in support of the motion) that there are "triable issues of fact" and/or of law by points and authorities. If there are any triable issues the motion must be denied and the case can go to trial. Sometimes, if there are several claims (causes of action) such a motion may cause the judge to find (decide) that some causes of action can be decided under the motion, leaving fewer matters actually to be tried. The paperwork on both sides is complex, burdensome and in many states, based on strict procedures. (See: **motion**)

motion *in limine*: (lim-in-nay) n. Latin for "threshold," a motion made at the start of a trial requesting that the judge rule that certain evidence may not be introduced in trial. This is most common in criminal trials where evidence is subject to constitutional limitations, such as statements made without the Miranda warnings (reading the suspect his/her rights). (See: *in limine*, **Miranda warning, motion**)

motion to strike: n. a request for a judge's order to eliminate all or a portion of the legal pleading (complaint, answer) of the opposition on any one of several grounds. It is often used in an attempt to have an entire cause of action removed ("stricken") from the court record. A motion to strike is also made orally during trial to ask the judge to order "stricken" answers by a witness in violation of rules of evidence (laws covering what is admissible in trial). Even though the jury is admonished to ignore such an answer or some comment, the jury has heard it, and "a bell once rung, cannot be unrung." (See: **motion, strike**)

motion to suppress: n. a motion (usually on behalf of a criminal defendant) to disallow certain evidence in an upcoming trial. Example: a confession which the defendant alleges was signed while he was drunk or without the reading of his Miranda rights. Since the motion is made at the threshold of the trial, it is a motion *in limine*, which is Latin for "at the threshold." (See: **motion** *in limine*)

motive: n. in criminal investigation the probable reason a person committed a crime, such as jealousy, greed, revenge or part of a theft. While evidence of a motive may be admissible at trial, proof of motive is not necessary to prove a crime.

mouthpiece: n. old-fashioned slang for one's lawyer.

movant: n. the party in a lawsuit or other legal proceeding who makes a motion (application for a court order or judgment). (See: **motion, move**)

move: v. to make a motion in court applying for a court order or judgment. (See: **motion, movant**)

multifarious: adj., adv. reference to a lawsuit in which either party or various causes of action (claims based on different legal theories) are improperly joined together in the same suit. This is more commonly called misjoinder. (See: **misjoinder**)

multiplicity of suits: n. several actual or potential lawsuits which should be joined together in one suit and one trial. It is a basic principle of law that multiplicity is to be avoided when possible, practical and fair. Example: several suits are filed by different people against the same person or entity, based on the same set of facts and the same legal issues. On motion of either party or by the judge's own determination, the judge can order the cases consolidated.

municipal: adj. referring to an incorporated or chartered city or town.

municipal court: n. a lower court which usually tries criminal misdemeanors and civil lawsuits involving lesser amounts of money than superior, district or county courts. The authority, importance and geographical area covered differ from state to state. In California, municipal courts have county-wide jurisdiction, try misdemeanor criminal cases, conduct preliminary hearings of felonies and try cases up to $25,000, while in many states they only handle cases arising out of violations of city ordinances, traffic and/or small claims. (See: **court**)

muniment of title: n. documentary evidence of title to real property. A muniment could be a deed, a decree of distribution proving inheritance, or a contract of sale. (See: **deed, quiet title action, title**)

murder: n. the killing of a human being by a sane person, with intent, malice aforethought (prior intention to kill the particular victim or anyone who gets in the way) and with no legal excuse or authority. In those clear circumstances, this is first degree murder. By statute, many states consider a killing in which there is torture, movement of the person before the killing (kidnapping) or the death of a police officer or prison guard, or it was as an incident to another crime (as during a hold-up or rape), to be first degree murder, with or without premeditation and with malice presumed. Second degree murder is such a killing without premeditation, as in the heat of passion or in a sudden quarrel or fight. Malice in second degree murder may be implied from a death due to the reckless lack of concern for the life of others (such as firing a gun into a crowd or bashing someone with any deadly weapon). Depending on the circumstances and state laws, murder in the first or second degree may be chargeable to a person who did not actually kill, but was involved in a crime with a partner who actually did the killing or someone died as the result of the crime. Example: In a liquor store stick-up in which the clerk shoots back at the hold-up man and kills a bystander, the armed robber can be convicted of at least second degree murder. A charge of murder requires that the victim must die within a year of the attack. Death of an unborn child who is "quick" (fetus is moving) can be murder, provided there was premeditation, malice and no legal authority. Thus, abortion is not murder under the law. Example: Jack Violent shoots his pregnant girlfriend, killing the fetus. Manslaughter, both voluntary and involuntary, lacks the element of malice aforethought. (See: **first degree murder, homicide, malice aforethought, manslaughter, premeditation, second degree murder**)

mutual: adj., adv. referring to anything in which both parties have reciprocal rights, understanding or agreement.

mutual wills: n. wills made by two people (usually spouses, but could be "partners") in which each gives his/her estate to the other, or with dispositions they both agree upon. A later change by either is not invalid unless it can be proved that there was a contract in which each makes the will in the consideration for the other person making the will. (See: **mirror wills**)

National Labor Relations Board: n. an independent regulatory commission created in 1935 by the National Labor Relations Act (Wagner Act), with five members appointed by the President subject to confirmation by the Senate. The NLRB is intended to protect employees' rights to unionize, prevent abuses by employers or unions, and oversee union and organizing elections.

natural law: n. 1) standards of conduct derived from traditional moral principles (first mentioned by Roman jurists in the first century A.D.) and/or God's law and will. The biblical ten commandments, such as "thou shall not kill," are often included in those principles. Natural law assumes that all people believe in the same Judeo-Christian God and thus share an understanding of natural law premises. 2) the body of laws derived from nature and reason, embodied in the Declaration of Independence assertion that "all men are created equal, that they are endowed by their creator with certain inalienable Rights, that among these are Life, Liberty and the pursuit of happiness." 3) the opposite of "positive law," which is created by mankind through the state.

natural person: n. a real human being, as distinguished from a corporation, which is often treated at law as a fictitious person.

necessary: adj., adv. 1) essential. 2) less forcefully, it can mean convenient, useful or making good sense.

necessary inference: n. 1) a conclusion militated by reason and logic applied to known facts. 2) unavoidable meaning.

necessary party: n. a person or entity whose interests will be affected by the outcome of a lawsuit, whose absence as a party in the suit prevents a judgment on all issues, *but* who cannot be joined in the lawsuit because that would deny jurisdiction to the particular court (such as shifting jurisdiction from a state to federal court). In this rare technical situation, a necessary party who is not in the suit differs from an "indispensable party," who must be joined if the lawsuit is to proceed, and from a "proper party," who could be joined but is not essential. (See: **indispensable party, proper party**)

> *"If the law supposes that,"*
> *said Mr. Bumble, "the law is a*
> *ass—an idiot."*
> *—Charles Dickens, Oliver*
> *Twist*

negative declaration: n. a finding by a city council or other local government that a proposed development or project would have no effect on the environment and therefore the developer need not prepare and file an "environmental impact report." (See: **EIR, environmental impact report**)

negative pregnant: n. a denial of an

allegation in which a person actually admits more than he/she denies by denying only a part of the alleged fact. Example: Plaintiff alleges Defendant "misused more than a hundred thousand dollars placed in his trust in 1994." Defendant denies the amount was more than a hundred thousand, and denies it was given to him in 1994. Thus, he did not deny the misuse, just the amount and the date.

negligence: n. failure to exercise the care toward others which a reasonable or prudent person would do in the circumstances, or taking action which such a reasonable person would not. Negligence is accidental as distinguished from "intentional torts" (assault or trespass, for example) or from crimes, but a crime can also constitute negligence, such as reckless driving. Negligence can result in all types of accidents causing physical and/or property damage, but can also include business errors and miscalculations, such as a sloppy land survey. In making a claim for damages based on an allegation of another's negligence, the injured party (plaintiff) must prove: a) that the party alleged to be negligent had a duty to the injured party—specifically to the one injured or to the general public, b) that the defendant's action (or failure to act) was negligent—not what a reasonably prudent person would have done, c) that the damages were caused ("proximately caused") by the negligence. An added factor in the formula for determining negligence is whether the damages were "reasonably foreseeable" at the time of the alleged carelessness. If the injury is caused by something owned or controlled by the supposedly negligent party, but how the accident actually occurred is not known (like a ton of bricks falls from a construction job), negligence can be found based on the doctrine of *res ipsa loquitor* (Latin for "the thing speaks for itself"). Furthermore, in six states (Alabama, North Carolina, South Carolina, Tennessee, Virginia, Maryland) and the District of Columbia, an injured party will be denied any judgment (payment) if found to have been guilty of even slight "contributory negligence" in the accident. This archaic and unfair rule has been replaced by "comparative negligence" in the other 44 states, in which the negligence of the claimant is balanced with the percentage of blame placed on the other party or parties ("joint tortfeasors") causing the accident. In automobile accident cases in 16 states the head of the household is held liable for damages caused by any member of the family using the car under what is called the "family purpose" doctrine. Nine states (California, New York, Michigan, Florida, Idaho, Iowa, Minnesota, Nevada, Rhode Island) make the owner of the vehicle responsible for all damages caused by a driver given permission to use the car, whether or not the negligent driver has assets or insurance to pay a judgment. Eight states (Connecticut, Massachusetts, New Jersey, Oregon, Rhode Island, Tennessee, Virginia, West Virginia) allow the owner to rebut a presumption that the driver was authorized to use the car. Negligence is one of the greatest sources of litigation (along with contract and business disputes) in the United States. (See: **comparative negligence, contributory negligence, damages, family purpose doctrine, foreseeable risk, gross negligence, joint tortfeasors, liability, negligence *per se*, res ipsa loquitur, tort, tortfeasor**)

negligence *per se*: (purr say) n. negligence due to the violation of a public duty, such as high speed driving. (See: **negligence, *per se***)

negligent: adj., adv. careless in not fulfilling responsibility. (See: **negligence**)

negotiable instrument: n. check, promissory note, bill of exchange, security or any document representing money payable which can be transferred to another by handing it over (delivery) and/or endorsing it (signing one's name on the back either with no instructions or directing it to another, such as "pay to the order of Pamela Townsend"). (See: **bearer paper, bill of exchange, check, promissory note, security**)

negotiation: n. 1) the transfer of a check, promissory note, bill of exchange or other negotiable instrument to another for money, goods, services or other benefit. 2) give-and-take discussion or conference in an attempt to reach an agreement or settle a dispute. (See: **negotiable instrument**)

net: n., adj. the amount of money or value remaining after all costs, losses, taxes, depreciation of value and other expenses and deductions have been paid and/or subtracted. Thus the term is used in net profit, net income, net loss, net worth or net estate. (See: **net estate**)

net estate: n. the remaining estate of a person who has died, calculated by taking the value of all assets and subtracting all debts of the person who died, including funeral costs, expenses of administering the estate and any other allowable deductions. The federal estate tax (and/or state inheritance tax where it exists) is then based on the net estate value. (See: **estate tax, gift tax, inheritance tax**)

new matter: n. newly claimed facts or legal issues raised (brought up) by a defendant (the party being sued) to defend himself/herself/itself beyond just denying the allegations in the complaint filed by the person bringing the lawsuit (plaintiff). Such new matters are called "affirmative defenses." (See: **affirmative defense, answer**)

next friend: n. a person (often a relative) who voluntarily helps a minor or incompetent in legal matters, particularly by filing a lawsuit. However, this informal practice has been supplanted in almost all states by petitions for appointment of a guardian *ad litem* at the time the lawsuit is filed. (See: **guardian *ad litem***)

next of kin: n. 1) the nearest blood relatives of a person who has died, including the surviving spouse. 2) anyone who would receive a portion of the estate by the laws of descent and distribution if there is no will. (See: **descent and distribution**)

nihil: (ni [as in it]-hill) n. from Latin for nothing.

nil: n. from Latin *nihil*, nothing or zero.

nisi prius: (nee-see pree-us) adj. Latin for "unless first," in some jurisdictions it means the original trial court which heard a case as distinguished from a court of appeals, as in court *nisi prius*. "Court of original jurisdiction" is often substituted for the term *nisi prius*. (See: **original jurisdiction, trial court**)

> *The law holds that it is better that ten guilty persons escape, than one innocent suffer.*
> *—Sir William Blackstone, Commentaries on the Laws of England*

no contest: n. in criminal law, a defendant's plea in court that he/she will not contest the charge of a particular crime, also called *nolo contendere*. While technically not an admission of guilt for commission of the crime, the judge will treat a plea of "no contest" as such an admission and proceed to find the defendant guilty as charged. A "no contest" plea is often made in cases in which there is also a possible lawsuit for damages by a person injured by the criminal conduct (such as reckless driving, assault with a deadly weapon, aggravated assault), because it cannot be used in the civil lawsuit as an admission of fault. "No contest" is also used where there has been a "plea bargain" in which the defendant does not want to say he/she is guilty but accepts the sentence recommended by the prosecutor in exchange for not contesting the charge (which is often reduced to a lesser crime). It is standard practice for the judge to ask either the attorneys or the defendant, "Is there a factual basis for the plea?" before accepting it and finding the defendant guilty. (See: ***nolo contendere*, plea, plea bargain**)

no fault insurance: n: a type of automobile insurance required of car owners by law in 19 states (New York, Michigan, Massachusetts, Arkansas, Colorado, Connecticut, Delaware, Florida, Georgia, Hawaii, Kansas, Kentucky, Maryland, Minnesota, New Jersey, North Dakota, Oregon, South Carolina, South Dakota) and the District of Columbia, in which the persons injured in an accident are paid basic damages by the company that insured the vehicle in which they were riding or by which they were hit as a pedestrian. The amount of damages to be paid by the insurance is limited to actual medical and rehabilitation expenses, lost wages and necessary expenses (such as loss of use of the vehicle) with a low maximum and for a limited period. In addition, an injured person can sue the negligent driver for medical costs above the amount of the insurance, pain and suffering if the injuries required medical treatment or resulted in permanent injury, broken bones or disfigurement, or wrongful death. All registered automobiles must be insured. The benefits of no fault include rapid payment of all medical expenses in most cases; elimination of lawsuits except in cases involving lesser injuries, very serious injury or death; and elimination of extensive and costly investigation, proof of negligence, medical reports and depositions. The statutes vary in states requiring "no fault" insurance. There have been legal challenges to the statutes, primarily suggesting that limitations on the right to sue or establishment of narrow categories of injury for which a claim of "pain and suffering" may be included in a lawsuit are unconstitutional. State courts have struck down those restrictions which were arbitrary or prevented legitimate claims. The fight over no fault insurance laws continues state by state, with the insurance companies and some court reform advocates (who believe "no fault" alleviates a clogging of the courts) favoring it, and trial attorneys either opposing the proposal outright or wanting much more leeway for filing lawsuits. (See: **dissolution of marriage, negligence**)

no fault divorce: n. divorces (dissolutions) in which neither spouse is required to prove "fault" or marital misconduct on the part of the other. To obtain a divorce a spouse must merely assert incompatibility or irreconcilable differences, meaning the marriage has irretrievably broken down. This means there is no defense to a divorce petition (so a spouse cannot threaten to "fight" a divorce), there is no derogatory testimony, and marital misconduct cannot be used to achieve a division of property favorable to the "innocent" spouse. Increasingly popular since the 1960s, no fault divorce is in effect in every state except Illinois and South Dakota. (See: **dissolution of marriage, divorce**)

nolle prosequi: (no-lay pro-say-kwee) n. Latin for "we shall no longer prosecute," which is a declaration made to the judge by a prosecutor in a criminal case (or by a plaintiff in a civil lawsuit) either before or during trial, meaning the case against the defendant is being dropped. The statement is an admission that the charges cannot be proved, that evidence has demonstrated either innocence or a fatal flaw in the prosecution's claim or the district attorney has become convinced the accused is innocent. Understandably, usage of the phrase is rare. In the 1947 courtroom movie, *Boomerang*! the climactic moment arrived when the District Attorney himself proved the accused person innocent and declared *nolle prosequi*.

nolo contendere: (no-low kahn-ten-durr-ray) n. Latin for "I will not contest" the charges, which is a plea made by a defendant to a criminal charge, allowing the judge to then find him/her guilty, often called a "plea of no contest." (See: **no contest**)

nominal damages: n. a small amount of money awarded to a plaintiff in a lawsuit to show he/she was right but suffered no substantial harm. The most famous case of nominal damages was when Prime Minister Winston Churchill was awarded a shilling (about 25 cents) in a libel lawsuit he had brought against author Louis Adamic for writing that Churchill had been drunk during a dinner at the White House. The Prime Minister was vindicated, but the jury could not find that his towering reputation had been damaged. (See: **damages**)

nominal party: n. a defendant or a

plaintiff included in a lawsuit because of a technical connection with the matter in dispute, and necessary for the court to decide all issues and make a proper judgment, but with no responsibility, no fault and no right to recovery. Example: suing an escrow holder or trustee who is holding a title to real property or deposited funds but has no interest in the property, funds or the lawsuit. Thus the court can order the nominal defendant to transfer title or pay out the funds when the rights of the real parties are decided. (See: **necessary party, party**)

nominee: n. 1) a person or entity who is requested or named to act for another, such as an agent or trustee. 2) a potential successor to another's rights under a contract. Example: In a real estate purchase agreement, Bob Buyer agrees to purchase the property, but provides that title (legal ownership) will be granted to "Bob Buyer or nominee," so that Buyer can sell his rights to another person before the deal closes, or because Buyer is really acting for someone else. 3) the executor proposed by a person in a will is a nominee until officially appointed by the judge after the testator (will writer) has died, and the will is submitted for probate (administration of the estate). 4) a person chosen by convention, petition or primary election to be a candidate for public office. (See: **agent, executor**)

non compos mentis: (nahn com-pose meant-is) adj. referring to someone who is insane or not mentally competent to conduct one's affairs. (See: **competent, compos mentis**)

non-conforming use: n. the existing use (residential, commercial, agricultural, light industrial, etc.) of a parcel of real property which is zoned for a more limited or other use in the city or county's general plan. Usually such use is permitted only if the property was being so used before the adoption of the zoning ordinance which it violates. Example: a corner parcel has been used for a gasoline station for years, and now the city has zoned the entire area as residential (for homes only). The non-conforming use will be allowed as "grandfathered in," but if the station is torn down the only use would be residential. (See: **general plan, grandfathered in, zoning**)

non-contestability clause: n. an insurance policy provision which requires the insurance company to challenge any statement in the application for the insurance within a specific time. This prevents the company from denying coverage on the basis of fraud or error in the application when a claim is made by the policyholder.

non-contiguous: adj. referring to two or more parcels of real property which are not connected.

non-discretionary trust: n. a trust in which the trustee is directed to invest only in specifically named securities and to diversify the investments among certain types of securities. The trustee has no discretion or personal decision-making power in the matter. (See: **trust**)

non-feasance: n. the failure of an agent (employee) to perform a task he/she has agreed to do for his/her principal (employer), as distinguished from "misfeasance" (performing poorly) or "malfeasance" (performing illegally or wrongly). (See: **malfeasance, misfeasance**)

non-profit corporation: n. an organization incorporated under state laws and approved by both the state's Secretary of State and its taxing authority as operating for educational, charitable, social, religious, civic or humanitarian purposes. A non-profit corporation (also called "not for profit corporation") is formed by incorporators, has a board of directors and officers, but no shareholders. These incorporators, directors and officers may not receive a distribution of (any money from) profits, but officers and management may be paid reasonable salaries for services to the corporation. Upon dissolution of a nonprofit corporation its assets must be distributed to an organization existing for similar purposes under the "cy pres doctrine." In order for contributions to the corporation to be deductible as charitable gifts on federal income taxes, the corporation must submit a detailed application (with a substantial fee) for an Internal Revenue Service ruling that it is established for one of the specific nonprofit purposes spelled out in the Internal Revenue Code. Informational tax returns must be filed annually with the IRS and the state taxing body. In addition, the state Attorney General may have oversight powers to determine if the corporation is abiding by state laws by limiting its activities to its approved non-profit purposes and not milking the corporation for disguised profits. (See: **charity, corporation,** *cy pres* **doctrine**)

non sequitur: (nahn sek [as in heck]-kwit-her) n. Latin for "it does not follow." The term usually means that a conclusion does not logically follow from the facts or law, stated: "That's a *non sequitur*."

non-suit: n. a ruling by the judge in a lawsuit either when the plaintiff (the party who filed the suit) does not proceed to trial at the appointed time or has presented all his/her/its evidence and, in the judge's opinion, there is no evidence which could prove the plaintiff's case. A non-suit terminates the trial at that point and results in a dismissal of the plaintiff's case and judgment for the defendant. (See: **dismissal**)

no-par stock: n. shares in a corporation which are issued without a price per share stated on the stock certificate.

notary: (See: **notary public**)

notary public: n. a person authorized by the state in which the person resides to administer oaths (swearings to truth of a statement), take acknowledgments, certify documents and to take depositions if the notary is also a court reporter. The signature and seal or stamp of a notary public is necessary to attest to the oath of truth of a person making an affidavit and to attest that a person has acknowledged that he/she executed a deed, power of attorney or other document, and is required for recording in public records. The Secretary of State of each state appoints notaries public for a specified term of years. A notary public must see proof of identity (e.g. driver's license) of those swearing and keep an official journal of documents notarized. The authority is good only in the state which appoints the notary.

Why not put it out of the power of the vicious and the lawless to use us [women] with cruelty and indignity with impunity.
—Abigail Adams, letter to husband John Adams

note: n. a promissory note, a written statement of debt by one or more people to one or more people, with a statement of a specific amount owed or due, date it is due, interest (if any) on the amount, and other terms such as installments, penalty for late payment, full amount due if delinquent, how secured (as by real property), and attorneys' fees and costs if required to collect on the note. (See: **promissory note**)

not guilty: n. 1) plea of a person who claims not to have committed the crime of which he/she is accused, made in court when arraigned (first brought before a judge) or at a later time set by the court. The choices of what one can plea are: guilty, not guilty, no contest, not guilty by reason of insanity, or incompetent to stand trial. 2) verdict after trial by a judge sitting without a jury or by a jury (unanimous decision in all but two states, which allow a verdict by only 10 of 12 jurors), stating that the prosecution has not proved the defendant guilty of a crime or that it believes the accused person was insane at the time the crime was committed. The accused cannot be tried again for the crime charged. (See: **arraignment, not guilty by reason of insanity, plea**)

not guilty by reason of insanity: n. plea in court of a person charged with a crime who admits the criminal act, but whose attorney claims he/she was so mentally disturbed at the time of the crime that he/she lacked the capacity to have intended to commit a crime. Such a plea requires that the court set a trial on the issue of insanity alone either by a judge sitting without a jury or by a jury. A finding of insanity will result in a verdict of "not guilty," but, if the condition still exists, it may result in incarceration in a mental facility for the criminally insane or confinement in a mental hospital. If the insanity no longer exists (temporary insanity), the judge has the option to require some psychological therapy, but the treatment varies from state to state. This is not the same as insane at time of trial and thus incompetent to stand trial, which will postpone trial (in all likelihood forever) pending recovery while the defendant is confined to a mental facility. (See: **incompetent, insanity, insanity defense, not guilty, temporary insanity**)

notice: n. 1) information, usually in writing in all legal proceedings, of all documents filed, decisions, requests, motions, petitions, and upcoming dates. Notice is a vital principle of fairness and due process in legal procedure and must be given to both parties, to all those affected by a lawsuit or legal proceeding, to the opposing attorney and to the court. In short, neither a party nor the court can operate in secret, make private overtures or conceal actions. Notice of a lawsuit or petition for a court order begins with personal service on the defendants (delivery of notice to the person) of the complaint or petition, together with a summons or order to appear (or file an answer) in court. Thereafter, if a party is represented by an attorney, notice can usually be given to the attorney by mail. If there is a so-called *ex parte* hearing (an emergency session with a judge with only the requesting party or his/her attorney present) the party wanting the hearing must make a diligent attempt to give notice to the other party. A court may allow "constructive" notice by publication in an approved legal newspaper of a summons in a lawsuit. Examples: in a divorce action, publication gives constructive notice to a spouse known to have left the state or hiding to avoid service; in a quiet title action, notice by publication is given to alert unknown descendants of a dead person who may have had an interest in the real property which is the subject of a lawsuit. Recordation of deeds, mortgages, deeds of trust, easements, leases and other documents affecting real property title give "constructive" notice to the general public, and thus "constructive" notice to anyone interested in the property, without delivering notice to individuals. 2) a writing informing a party to a contract, promissory note, lease, rental agreement or other legal relationship of a delinquency in payment, default, intent to foreclose, notice to pay rent or quit (leave) or other notice required by the agreement, mortgage, deed of trust or statute. 3) information. 4) being informed of a fact, or should have known based on the circumstances, as "he had notice that the roof was not water-tight." (See: **constructive notice, notice to quit, 30-day notice, three-day notice**)

notice of default: n. a notice to a borrower with property as security under a mortgage or deed of trust that he/she is delinquent in payments. If the delinquency (money owed and late), plus costs of preparing the legal papers for the default, are not paid within a certain time, foreclosure proceedings may be commenced. Other people with funds secured by the same property are usually entitled to receive copies of the notice of default. (See: **notice**)

notice to quit: n. the notice given by a landlord (owner) to a tenant to leave the premises (quit) either by a certain date (usually 30 days) or to pay overdue rent or correct some other default (having pets, having caused damage, too many roommates, using the property for illegal purposes, etc.) within a short time (usually three days). A notice to quit must contain certain information, such as: names of the persons to leave, whether their tenancy is by written or oral agreement, an amount of any financial delinquency and the period it covers, and to whom they should surrender the premises. If the tenant is month-to-month, a notice to quit without reference to default usually requires no reason. Although state laws vary, generally the notice must be served personally on the tenant or posted in a prominent place like the front door with a copy sent by certified mail. Such notice and failure of the tenant to quit (leave) is a requirement to bring a lawsuit for unlawful detainer (often referred to as "eviction"). (See: **lease, month-to-month, notice, unlawful detainer**)

notorious possession: n. occupation of real property or holding personal property in a way which anyone can observe is as if the person is the owner.

N.O.V.: adj. shorthand acronym of Latin for *non obstante veredicto* (nahn ahb-stan-tuh very-dick-toe) meaning "notwithstanding the verdict," referring to a decision of a judge to set aside (reverse) a jury's decision in favor of one party in a lawsuit or a guilty verdict when the judge is convinced the judgment is not reasonably supported by the facts and/or the law. The result is called a "judgment N.O.V." Granting a motion for such a ruling means the court realizes it should have directed the jury to reach an opposite verdict in the first place. (See: **judgment notwithstanding the verdict, verdict**)

novation: n. agreement of parties to a contract to substitute a new contract for the old one. It extinguishes (cancels) the old agreement. A novation is often used when the parties find that payments or performance cannot be made under the terms of the original agreement, or the debtor will be forced to default or go into bankruptcy unless the debt is restructured. While voluntary, a novation is often the only way any funds can be paid. (See: **accord and satisfaction**)

noxious: adj. harmful to health, often referring to nuisances.

nugatory: adj. of no force or effect; invalid. Example: a statute which is unconstitutional is a nugatory law.

nuisance: n. the unreasonable, unwarranted and/or unlawful use of property, which causes inconvenience or damage to others, either to individuals and/or to the general public. Nuisances can include noxious smells, noise, burning, misdirection of water onto other property, illegal gambling, unauthorized collections of rusting autos, indecent signs and pictures on businesses and a host of bothersome activities. Where illegal they can be abated (changed, repaired or improved) by criminal or quasi-criminal charges. If a nuisance interferes with another person's quiet or peaceful or pleasant use of his/her property, it may be the basis for a lawsuit for damages and/or an injunction ordering the person or entity causing the nuisance to desist (stop) or limit the activity (such as closing down an activity in the evening). (See: **public nuisance**)

nullity: n. something which may be treated as nothing, as if it did not exist or never happened. This can occur by court ruling or enactment of a statute. The most common example is a nullity of a marriage by a court judgment. (See: **annulment**)

nunc pro tunc: (nuhnk proh tuhnk): adj. Latin for "now for then," this refers to changing back to an earlier date of an order, judgment or filing of a document. Such a retroactive redating requires a court order which can be obtained by a showing that the earlier date would have been legal, and there was error, accidental omission or neglect which has caused a problem or inconvenience which can be cured. Often the judge will grant the *nunc pro tunc* order *ex parte* (with only the applicant appearing and without notice). Examples: a court clerk fails to file an answer when he/she received it, and a *nunc pro tunc* date of filing is needed to meet the legal deadline (statute of limitations); a final divorce judgment is misdirected and, therefore, not signed and dated until the day after the re-marriage of one of the parties—the *nunc pro tunc* order will prevent the appearance or actuality of a bigamous marriage.

oath: n. 1) a swearing to tell the truth, the whole truth and nothing but the truth, which would subject the oath-taker to a prosecution for the crime of perjury if he/she knowingly lies in a statement either orally in a trial or deposition or in writing. Traditionally, the oath concludes "so help me God," but the approval of a supreme being is often omitted. Criminal perjury charges are rare, however, since the person stating the untruth will almost always claim error, mistake, loss of memory or opinion. At the beginning of any testimony by a witness, the clerk or court reporter administers an oath to the witness. 2) The "swearing in" of a person assuming a public office, sometimes called the "oath of office." 3) sworn commitment of allegiance, as to one's country. (See: **affidavit, perjury**)

obiter dicta: (oh-bitter dick-tah) n. remarks of a judge which are not necessary to reaching a decision, but are made as comments, illustrations or thoughts. Generally, *obiter dicta* is simply *dicta*. (See: ***dicta, dictum***)

object: 1) v. to ask the court not to allow a particular question asked of a witness by the opposing lawyer on the basis that it is either legally not permitted, confusing in its wording or improper in its "form." An attorney may also object to an answer to the question on the basis that it is not "responsive" since a witness is limited to answering a question as asked and is not allowed to make unsolicited comments. The trial attorney must be alert and quick in order to object before the witness answers. This is called an "objection" and must be based on a specific list of legal restrictions on questions. 2) n. a particular thing. 3) n. an aim or purpose, as "the object of the contract..." (See: **objection**)

objection: n. a lawyer's protest about the legal propriety of a question which has been asked of a witness by the opposing attorney, with the purpose of making the trial judge decide if the question can be asked. A proper objection must be based on one of the specific reasons for not allowing a question. These include: irrelevant, immaterial, incompetent (often stated together, which may mean the question is not about the issues in the trial or the witness is not qualified to answer), hearsay (the answer would be what someone told the witness rather than what he/she knew first-hand), leading (putting words in the mouth of one's own witness), calls for a conclusion (asking for opinion, not facts), compound question (two or more questions asked together), or lack of foundation (referring to a document lacking testimony as to authenticity or source). An objection must be made quickly and loudly to halt the witness before he/she answers. The judge will either "sustain" the objection (ruling out the question) or "overrule" it (allow the question). The judge may ask for an "offer of proof" in which the lawyer asking the question must explain to the court the reason the question is relevant, and what evidence his/her questions will bring out. Badly worded, confusing or compound questions are usually challenged by an objection to the form of the question, which is essentially a demand that the question be withdrawn and reworded. An attorney may "object" to a witness's answer as "non-responsive" to the question, but the proper request should be that the answer or a comment without a question be "stricken" from the record. (See: **compound question, lay a foundation, hearsay, immaterial, incompetent, irrelevant, leading question, object, overrule, sustain**)

obligation: n. a legal duty to pay or do something.

obligee: (ah-bluh-jee) n. the person or entity to whom an obligation is owed, like the one to be paid on a promissory note.

obligor: (ah-bluh-gore) n. the person or entity who owes an obligation to another, as one who must pay on a promissory note.

obscene: adj., adv. a highly subjective reference to material or acts which display or describe sexual activity in a manner appealing only to "prurient interest," with no legitimate artistic, literary or scientific purpose. Pictures, writings, film or public acts which are found to be obscene are not protected by the free speech guarantee of the First Amendment. However, the courts have had difficulty making a clear non-subjective definition since "one person's obscenity is another person's art," or, as one Supreme Court Justice stated, "I can't define it, but I know it when I see it." (See: **pornography**)

obstruction of justice: n. an attempt to interfere with the administration of the courts, the judicial system or law enforcement officers, including threatening witnesses, improper conversations with jurors, hiding evidence or interfering with an arrest. Such activity is a crime.

occupancy: n. 1) living in or using premises, as a tenant or owner. 2) taking possession of real property or a thing which has no known owner, with the intention of gaining ownership. (See: **occupant**)

occupant: n. 1) someone living in a residence or using premises, as a tenant or owner. 2) a person who takes possession of real property or a thing which has no known owner, intending to gain ownership. (See: **occupancy**)

occupation: n. 1) fairly permanent trade, profession, employment, business or means of livelihood. 2) possession of real property or use of a thing.

occupational disease: n. an illness resulting from long-term employment in a particular type of work, such as black lung disease among miners, or cancer among asbestos installers. If the chances of being afflicted by such an illness are significantly higher than the average in the population, then a former employee may receive benefits from Social Security or worker's compensation for a work-related disability.

occupational hazard: n. a danger or risk inherent in certain employments or workplaces, such as deep-sea diving, cutting timber, high-rise steel construction, high-voltage electrical wiring, use of pesticides, painting bridges and many factories. The risk factor may limit insurance coverage of death or injury while at work.

occupy the field: v. to preempt (monopolize) an area of statutory law by a higher authority, such as federal preemption of bankruptcy or interstate commerce over state legislation, and state statutes or state constitution prevailing over laws of cities and counties on certain topics. (See: **preemption**)

There is far too much law for those who can afford it, and far too little for those who cannot.
—Derek Bok, President of Harvard University

of counsel: adj. reference to an attorney who is not actively involved in the day-to-day work of a law firm, but may be available in particular matters or for consultation. This designation often identifies a semi-retired partner, an attorney who occasionally uses the office for a few clients or one who only consults on a particular case or on his/her specialty. Putting the name of the attorney "of counsel" on a law firm's stationery gives the office the prestige of the lawyer's name and reputation, without requiring his/her full-time presence.

off calendar: adj. refers to an order of the court to take a lawsuit, petition or motion off the list of pending cases or motions which are scheduled to be heard. A case or motion will be ordered off calendar if the lawyers agree (stipulate) to drop it, if the moving party's lawyer fails to appear, if a suit is settled pending final documentation or any number of procedural reasons for the judge to determine the case should not proceed at that time. A suit or motion can be put back "on calendar" by stipulation of the lawyers or upon motion of either party. (See: **calendar**)

offender: n. an accused defendant in a criminal case or one convicted of a crime. (See: **accused, defendant**)

offense: n. a crime or punishable violation of law of any type or magnitude. (See: **crime**)

offer: n. a specific proposal to enter into an agreement with another. An offer is essential to the formation of an enforceable contract. An offer and acceptance of the offer creates the contract. (See: **contract**)

offeree: n. a person or entity to whom an offer to enter into a contract is made by another (the offeror).

offer of proof: n. an explanation made by an attorney to a judge during trial to show why a question which has been objected to as immaterial or irrelevant will lead to evidence of value to proving the case of the lawyer's client. Often the judge will ask: "Where is this line of questions going?" and the offer of proof is the response. The offer provides the opposition a preview of the questions (and helps prevent surprise), but is essential to overcome the objections. (See: **evidence, immaterial, irrelevant, objection, testimony**)

offeror: n. a person or entity who makes a specific proposal to another (the offeree) to enter into a contract. (See: **contract, offer, offeree**)

officer: n. 1) a high-level management official of a corporation or an unincorporated business, hired by the board of directors of a corporation or the owner of a business, such as a president, vice president, secretary, financial officer or chief executive officer (CEO). Such officers have the actual or apparent authority to contract or otherwise act on behalf of the corporation or business. 2) a public official with executive authority ranging from city manager to governor. 3) a law enforcement person such as a policeman or woman, deputy sheriff or federal marshal.

officer of the court: n. any person who has an obligation to promote justice and effective operation of the judicial system, including judges, the attorneys who appear in court, bailiffs, clerks and other personnel. As officers of the court lawyers have an absolute ethical duty to tell judges the truth, including avoiding dishonesty or evasion about reasons the attorney or his/her client is not appearing, the location of documents and other matters related to conduct of the courts. (See: **attorney, bailiff, clerk, judge**)

official: 1) adj. referring to an act, document or anything sanctioned or authorized by a public official or public agency. The term can also apply to an organizational act or product which is authorized by the organization, such as an Official Boy Scout knife or emblem, an official warranty, membership card or set of rules. 2) n. a public officer or governmental employee who is empowered to exercise judgment. 3) n. an officer of a corporation or business. (See: **officer**)

official misconduct: n. improper and/or illegal acts by a public official which violate his/her duty to follow the law and act on behalf of the public good. Often such conduct is under the guise or "color" of official authority. (See: **color of law, official**)

officious intermeddler: n. a volunteer who assists and/or benefits another without contractual responsibility or legal duty to do so, but nevertheless wants compensation for his/her actions. The courts generally find that the intermeddler must rely on the equally voluntary gratitude of the recipient of the alleged benefit. (See: **Good Samaritan rule**)

offset: 1) n. also called a "setoff," the deduction by a debtor from a claim or demand of a debt or obligation. Such an offset is based upon a counterclaim against the party making the original claim. Example: Harry Hardhead makes a claim or files a lawsuit asking for $20,000 from Danny Debtor as the final payment in purchase of a restaurant; as part of his defense Debtor claims an offset of $10,000 for alleged funds owed by Hardhead for repairs Debtor made on property owned by Hardhead, thus reducing the claim of Hardhead to $10,000. 2) v. to counterclaim an alleged debt owed by a claimant to reduce the demand of that claimant. (See: **counter-claim, defense, setoff**)

offshore corporation: n. a corporation chartered under the laws of a country other than the United States. Some countries (particularly in the Caribbean) are popular nations of incorporation since they have little corporate regulation or taxes and only moderate management fees. Professional trustees and nominal officials in the country of incorporation perform routine contacts with the local government but take no active part in management. The reasons for the use of offshore corporations are best known to the incorporators, but may include avoidance of taxes, ease of international operations, freedom from state regulation and placement of funds in accounts out of the country.

omission: n. 1) failure to perform an act agreed to, where there is a duty to an individual or the public to act (including omitting to take care) or where it is required by law. Such an omission may give rise to a lawsuit in the same way as a negligent or improper act. 2) inadvertently leaving out a word, phrase or other language from a contract, deed, judgment or other document. If the parties agree that the omission was due to a mutual mistake, the document may be "reformed," but this may require a petition for a court order making the correction if it had been relied upon by government authorities or third parties. (See: **breach of contract, negligence, reformation**)

omnibus clause: n. 1) an automobile insurance policy clause which provides coverage no matter who is driving the car. 2) a provision in a judgment for distribution of an estate of a deceased person, giving "all other property" to the beneficiaries named in the will.

on all fours: adj. a reference to a lawsuit in which all the legal issues are identical (or so close as to make no difference) to another case, particularly an appeals decision which is a precedent in deciding the suit before the court. Thus, an attorney will argue that the prior case of, for example, *Steele v. Merritt* is "on all fours" with the case before the court, and so the court must reach the same conclusion. (See: **precedent**)

on demand: adj. in a promissory note, a requirement that the amount due must be paid when the person to whom the funds are owed demands payment (rather than upon a certain date or on installments). Such a note is called a "demand note." (See: **demand note**)

on file: prep. having been formally filed with the clerk of the court or the judge, such as a pleading is "on file." (See: **file**)

on or about: prep. a phrase referring to a date or place used in a complaint in a lawsuit or criminal charge if there is any uncertainty at all, in order to protect the person making the allegations of fact from being challenged as being inaccurate. Thus, a complaint will read "On or about July 11, 1994, Defendant drove his vehicle negligently and without due care on or about the cor-

ner of Sunset and Vine Streets...."
(See: **charge, complaint**)

on or before: prep. a phrase usually found in a contract or promissory note, designating performance
or payment by a particular date,
but which may be done prior to
that date.

on the merits: adj. referring to a
judgment, decision or ruling of a
court based upon the facts presented in evidence and the law applied
to that evidence. A judge decides a
case "on the merits" when he/she
bases the decision on the fundamental issues and considers technical and procedural defenses as either inconsequential or overcome.
Example: An attorney is two days
late in filing a set of legal points
and authorities in opposition to a
motion to dismiss. Rather than dismiss the case based on this technical procedural deficiency, the judge
considers the case "on the merits"
as if this mistake had not occurred.

on the stand: prep. testifying during
a trial, in which the witness almost
always sits in a chair beside the
judge's bench, often raised above the
floor level of the courtroom and behind a knee-high panel.

open court: n. the conduct of judicial
proceedings (trials, hearings and
routine matters such as trial settings) in which the public may be
present. Some hearings and discussions are held in the judge's chambers ("in camera") or with the courtroom cleared of non-participants
and/or the jury such as adoptions,
sanity hearings, juvenile criminal

charges and arguments over evidence
and motions which might prejudice
the jury. The Sixth Amendment to the
Constitution, later applied to the
states under the 14th Amendment,
guarantees criminal defendants a
"public trial," so all criminal proceedings are held in "open court." This
does not apply to pre-trial negotiations and procedural and motion discussions with the judge, which are
usually held in chambers.

opening statement: n. the explanation
by the attorneys for both sides at the
beginning of the trial of what will be
proved during the trial. The defendant's attorney may delay the opening
statement for the defense until the
plaintiff's evidence has been introduced. Unlike a "closing argument,"
the opening statement is supposed to
be a factual presentation and not an
argument. (See: **closing argument**)

operation of law: n. a change or transfer which occurs automatically due to
existing laws and not an agreement or
court order. Examples: a joint tenant
obtains full title to real property when
the other joint tenant dies; a spouse in
a community property state will take
title to all community property if the
spouse dies without a will that leaves
some of the dead mate's interest in the
community property to another; or a
guardianship of a minor *ad litem* (for
purposes of a lawsuit) ends automatically upon the child turning 18.

opinion: n. the explanation of a
court's judgment. When a trial court
judgment is appealed to a court of
appeals, the appeals judge's opinion
will be detailed, citing case precedents, analyzing the facts, the ap-

plicable law and the arguments of the attorneys for the parties. Those opinions considered by the court to be worthy of serving as a precedent or involving important legal issues will be published in the official reports available in most law libraries. Since appeals courts have anywhere from three to nine judges, there are often "dissenting opinions" which disagree with the majority opinion, and "concurring opinions" which agree with the result, but apply different emphasis, precedents or logic to reach the determination. Normally the majority opinion identifies the author, but some brief opinions are labeled "*in banc*" (by the bench) or "*per curiam*" (by the court) in which the author is not specified.

> *Man is a creature endowed with reason and free will; but when he goes to law as plaintiff, his reason seems to have left him; while, if he stands in the position of defendant, it is generally against his free will.*
> *—Gilbert Abbott A Beckett, The Comic Blackstone*

option: n. a right to purchase property or require another to perform upon agreed-upon terms. An option is paid for as part of a contract, but must be "exercised" in order for the property to be purchased or the performance of the other party to be required. "Exercise" of an option normally requires notice and payment of the contract price. Thus, a potential buyer of a tract of land might pay $5,000 for the option which gives him/her a period of time to decide if he/she wishes to purchase, tying up the property for that period, and then pay $500,000 for the property. If the time to exercise the option expires then the option terminates. The amount paid for the option itself is not refundable since the funds bought the option whether exercised or not. Often an option is the right to renew a contract such as a lease, broadcasting a television series, the employment of an actor or athlete, or some other existing business relationship. A "lease-option" contract provides for a lease of property with the right to purchase the property during or upon expiration of the lease.

or: conj. either; in the alternative. It is often vital to distinguish between "or" and "and." Example: Title to the Cadillac written "Mary or Bill Davidson" means either one could transfer the car, but if written "Mary and Bill Davidson," both must sign to change title.

O.R.: n. short for "own recognizance," meaning the judge allowed a person accused in a criminal case to go free pending trial without posting bail. A person so released is often referred to as having been "OR-ed." (See: **own recognizance**)

oral contract: n. an agreement made with spoken words and either no writing or only partially written. An oral contract is just as valid as a written agreement. The main problem with an oral contract is proving its existence or the terms. As one wag observed: "An oral contract is as good as the paper it's written on." An oral contract is often provable by action taken by one or both parties which is obviously in reliance on the existence of a contract. The other significant difference between oral and written contracts is that the time to sue for breach of an oral contract (the statute of limitations) is sometimes shorter. For example, California's limitation is two years for oral compared to four for written, Connecticut and Washington three for oral rather than six for written, and Georgia four for oral instead of 20 for written. (See: **agreement, contract**)

order: 1) n. every direction or mandate of a judge or a court which is not a judgment or legal opinion (although both may include an order) directing that something be done or that there is prohibition against some act. This can range from an order that a case will be tried on a certain date, to an order that a convicted defendant be executed at the state prison. 2) v. for a judge to direct that a party before the court perform a particular act or refrain from certain acts, or to direct a public official or court employee (like a sheriff) to take certain actions such as seizing property or arresting an AWOL defendant. (See: **judge, judgment**)

order to show cause: n. a judge's written mandate that a party appear in court on a certain date and give reasons, legal and/or factual, (show cause) why a particular order should not be made. This rather stringent method of making a party appear with proof and legal arguments is applied to cases of possible contempt for failure to pay child support, sanctions for failure to file necessary documents or appear previously, or to persuade the judge he/she should not grant a writ of mandate against a governmental agency. (See: **O.S.C.**)

ordinance: n. a statute enacted by a city or town.

ordinary: adj. regular, customary and continuing, and not unusual or extraordinary, as in ordinary expense, ordinary handling, ordinary risks or ordinary skill.

ordinary course of business: n. conduct of business within normal commercial customs and usages.

original jurisdiction: n. the authority of a court to hold a trial, as distinguished from appellate jurisdiction to hear appeals from trial judgments. (See: **jurisdiction**)

orphan: n. a child, particularly a minor, whose two natural parents are dead. In some cases, such as whether a child is eligible for public financial assistance to an orphan, "orphan" can mean a child who has lost one parent.

O.S.C.: n. short for order to show cause. (See: **order to show cause**)

ostensible agent: n. a person who has been given the appearance of being an employee or acting (an agent) for another (principal), which would make anyone dealing with the ostensible agent reasonably believe he/she was an employee or agent. This could include giving the ostensible agent stationery or forms of the company, letting him/her use the company truck, telephone or desk in the company office. Businesses should be careful not to allow such situations in which an ostensible agent could bind the business on a contract or make the apparent employer responsible for damages for an accident, libel or assault by the "agent." (See: **apparent authority, ostensible authority**)

ostensible authority: n. apparent authority to do something or represent another person or entity. (See: **apparent authority, ostensible agent**)

ouster: n. 1) the wrongful dispossession (putting out) of a rightful owner or tenant of real property, forcing the party pushed out of the premises to bring a lawsuit to regain possession. This often arises between partners (in a restaurant or store) or roommates, when one co-owner or co-tenant forces out the other, changes locks or makes occupancy intolerable. 2) removal of someone from a position or office against his/her expectations or will.

outbuilding: n. a structure not connected with the primary residence on a parcel of property. This may include a shed, garage, barn, cabana, pool house or cottage.

out of court: adj. referring to actions, including negotiations between parties and/or their attorneys, without any direct involvement of a judge or the judicial system. Most commonly it refers to an "out-of-court settlement" in which the parties work out a settlement agreement, which they may present to the court for inclusion in a judgment approving the agree-

ment so that the parties can request a court to enforce the settlement in case one of the parties reneges and fails to honor the terms of the settlement. Quite often a judgment approving an out-of-court settlement is held in abeyance and replaced by a dismissal if the terms are fulfilled. Some out-of-court settlements are kept confidential and the lawsuit is dismissed. (See: **settlement**)

outlaw: n. popularly, anyone who commits serious crimes and acts outside the law.

out-of-pocket expenses: n. moneys paid directly for necessary items by a contractor, trustee, executor, administrator or any person responsible to cover expenses not detailed by agreement. They may be recoverable from a defendant in a lawsuit for breach of contract; allowable for reimbursement by trustees, executors or administrators; or deductible by a landlord from a tenant's security deposit for damages beyond normal wear and tear.

You cannot change people's hearts merely by laws. Laws presumably express the conscience of a nation and its determination or will to do something.
—Dwight D. Eisenhower

output contract: n. an agreement in which a producer agrees to sell its entire production to the buyer, who in turn agrees to purchase the entire output, whatever that is. Example: an almond grower has a "home" for his output, and the packer of nuts is happy to have a sure-fire supply, even though it may have to store away a glut.

overcharge: v. 1) to charge more than a posted or advertised price. 2) to file a criminal complaint for crimes of greater degree than the known facts support, in an effort by the prosecutor to intimidate the accused.

overrule: v. 1) to reject an attorney's objection to a question to a witness or admission of evidence. By overruling the objection, the trial judge allows the question or evidence in court. If the judge agrees with the objection, he/she "sustains" the objection and does not allow the question or evidence. 2) to decide (by a court of appeals) that a prior appeals decision on a legal issue was not correct and is therefore no longer a valid precedent on that legal question. (See: **appellate court, objection, sustain**)

overt act: n. in criminal law, an action which might be innocent itself but if part of the preparation and active furtherance of a crime, can be introduced as evidence of a defendant's participation in a crime. Example: Rental of a van, purchase of explosives, obtaining a map of downtown New York City and going back and forth to the World Trade Center, could each be considered overt acts as part of the terrorist bombing of that building.

owe: v. to have a legal duty to pay funds to another. However, to owe does not make the amount "payable" if the date for payment has not yet arrived. (See: **debt, due, payable**)

own: v. to have legal title or right to something. Mere possession is not ownership.

owner: n. one who has legal title or right to something. Contrary to the cynical adage: "Possession is nine-tenths of the law," possession does not necessarily make one a legal owner. (See: **own**)

ownership: n. legal title coupled with exclusive legal right to possession. Co-ownership, however, means that more than one person has a legal interest in the same thing. (See: **own**)

own recognizance (O.R.): n. the basis for a judge allowing a person accused of a crime to be free while awaiting trial, without posting bail, on the defendant's own promise to appear and his/her reputation. The judge may consider the seriousness of the crime charged, the likelihood the defendant will always appear, the length of time the person has lived in the area, his/her reputation in the community, his/her employment, financial burdens and the demeanor of the accused. In minor crimes, traffic offenses and technical law violations such as leaky septic systems, judges routinely grant release on one's own recognizance. (See: **bail, O.R.**)

P

paid into court: adj. referring to money deposited with the clerk of the court by a person or entity who knows that the money is owed but does not know to whom they should pay it until the outcome of a lawsuit between two other parties is decided. In short, the party handing over the money is saying: "Here is the money. You two argue over it, but spare me the trouble and cost of the suit." Example: A contractor buys supplies from a hardware store on credit. The store is owned by two people who have dissolved their partnership and are fighting over who owns accounts receivable, including the funds owed by the contractor. The contractor knows he owes the money for his supplies, wants to meet his obligations, and wants to get rid of the debt. So the contractor gives what he thinks he owes the hardware store to the court to hold while the two former partners settle their differences. (See: **interpleader**)

pain and suffering: n. the physical and mental distress suffered from an injury, including actual broken bones and internal ruptures, but also the aches, pain, temporary and permanent limitations on activity, potential shortening of life, depression and embarrassment from scarring, all of which are part of the "general damages" recoverable by someone injured by another's negligence or intentional attack. The dollar value of damages for pain and suffering is subjective, as distinguished from medical bills, future medical costs and lost wages which can be calculated, called "special damages." (See: **damages, general damages, special damages, suffering**)

palimony: n. a substitute for alimony in cases in which the couple were not married but lived together for a long period and then terminated their relationship. The key issue is whether there was an agreement that one partner would support the other in return for the second making a home and performing other domestic duties beyond sexual pleasures. Written palimony contracts are rare, but the courts have found "implied" contracts, when a woman has given up her career, managed the household or assisted in the man's business for a lengthy period of time. In the past 20 years palimony suits have proliferated, particularly against celebrities and wealthy businessmen, but the earliest was the famous California case of Sarah Althea Hill v. Senator William Sharon in the 1880s, which Ms. Hill lost. The line between a mutual "affair" and a relationship warranting palimony is a difficult one which must be decided on a case by case basis. Palimony suits may be avoided by contracts written prior to or during the relationship. (See: **alimony**)

pander: 1) v. to solicit customers for a prostitute. 2) n. a pimp, who procures customers for a prostitute or lures a woman into prostitution, all for his own profit. 3) v. catering to special interests without any principles, such as a politician who says to whatever group he/she is addressing just what they want to hear to win their support, contributions or favors. (See: **prostitute**)

panderer: n. 1) a person who panders or solicits for a prostitute. 2) some politicians catering to special interests. (See: **pander**)

panel: n. the list of people selected to appear for jury duty. (See: **jury,** *venire*)

paper hanger: n. slang for a person who criminally writes and cashes "bad" checks on accounts he/she either does not have or which have no money in them. (See: **forgery, fraud**)

par: n. 1) an equal level. 2) the face value of a stock or bond, printed on the certificate, which is the amount the original purchaser paid the issuing corporation. However, most common stocks are issued as "no-par value," and the value reflects the current market for the stock. Preferred stocks state a par value upon which the dividends are calculated, and the par value of bonds establishes the final pay-off amount upon maturity, usually many years in the future. (See: **bond, common stock, preferred stock, stock**)

paralegal: n. a non-lawyer who performs routine tasks requiring some knowledge of the law and procedures and who is employed by a law office or works free-lance as an independent for various lawyers. Usually paralegals have taken a prescribed series of courses in law and legal processes, which is much less demanding than those required for a licensed attorney. Paralegals are increasingly popular, often handling much of the paperwork in probates of estates, divorce actions, bankruptcies, investigations, analyzing depositions, preparing and answering interrogatories and procedural motions and other specialized jobs. Clients should be sure that the hourly rate charged for paralegals is much less than that for the attorneys.

paramount title: n. a right to real property which prevails over any other person's claim of title. (See: **title**)

parcel: n. a defined piece of real estate, usually resulting from the division of a large area of land. It can range in size from a small lot to a gigantic ranch. 2) a package. (See: **real estate, real property**)

pardon: 1) v. to use the executive power of a Governor or President to forgive a person convicted of a crime, thus removing any remaining penalties or punishments and preventing any new prosecution of the person for the crime for which the pardon was given. A pardon strikes the conviction from the books as if it had never occurred, and the convicted person is treated as innocent. Sometimes pardons are given to an older rehabilitated person long after the sentence has been served to clear his/her record. However, a pardon can also terminate a sentence and free a prisoner when the chief executive is convinced there is doubt about the guilt or fairness of the trial, the party is rehabilitated and has performed worthy public service, or there are humanitarian reasons such as terminal illness. The most famous American pardon was the blanket pardon given by President Gerald Ford to ex-President Richard Nixon in the wake of the Watergate scandal and Nixon's resignation; that pardon closed the door to any future prosecution against Nixon for any crime before the pardon. A pardon is distinguished from "a commutation of sentence" which cuts short the term; "a reprieve," which is a temporary halt to punishment, particularly the death penalty, pending appeal or determination of whether the penalty should be reduced; "amnesty," which is a blanket "forgetting" of possible criminal charges due to a change in public circumstances (such as the end of a war or the draft system); or a "reduction in sentence," which shortens a sentence and can be granted by a judge or an executive. (See: **amnesty, commutation, reprieve**)

parens patriae: (paa-rens pat-tree-eye) n. Latin for "father of his country," the term for the doctrine that the government is the ultimate guardian of all people under a disability, especially children, whose care is only "entrusted" to their parents. Under this doctrine, in a divorce action or a guardianship application the court retains jurisdiction until the child is 18 years old, and a judge may change custody, child support or other rulings affecting the child's well-being, no matter what the parents may have

agreed or the court previously decided. (See: **child support, custody, divorce, guardian, ward**)

parent: n. the lawful and natural father or mother of a person. The word does not mean grandparent or ancestor, but can include an adoptive parent as a replacement for a natural parent. (See: **adoption**)

parental neglect: n. a crime consisting of acts or omissions of a parent (including a stepparent, adoptive parent or someone who, in practical terms, serves in a parent's role) which endangers the health and life of a child or fails to take steps necessary to the proper raising of a child. The neglect can include leaving a child alone when he or she needs protection; failure to provide food, clothing, medical attention or education to a child; or placing the child in dangerous or harmful circumstances, including exposing the child to a violent, abusive or sexually predatory person.

pari delicto: adj. equal fault. (See: ***in pari delicto***)

parish: n. 1) a geographic area served by a church (particularly Catholic) originally measured by whether people living in the area could walk to the church. 2) in Louisiana, the governmental equivalent of a county.

parody: n. the humorous use of an existing song, play, or writing which changes the words to give farcical and ironic meaning. Parodies have been challenged as copyright infringements on the original works, particularly since some have reaped terrific profits. Recent decisions favor the parodies and say they have an originality of their own and, thus, are not infringements. There is a free speech issue involved in these decisions since parodies traditionally have social and political significance. (See: **copyright**)

parol: adj. oral. (See: **parol evidence rule**)

parole: n. 1) the release of a convicted criminal defendant after he/she has completed part of his/her prison sentence, based on the concept that during the period of parole, the released criminal can prove he/she is rehabilitated and can "make good" in society. A parole generally has a specific period and terms such as reporting to a parole officer, not associating with other ex-convicts, and staying out of trouble. Violation of the terms may result in revocation of parole and a return to prison to complete his/her sentence. 2) a promise by a prisoner of war that if released he will not take up arms again.

parol evidence rule: n. if there is evidence in writing (such as a signed contract) the terms of the contract cannot be altered by evidence of oral (parol) agreements purporting to change, explain or contradict the written document.

partial: adj. not complete or entire. (See: **partial breach, partial disability**)

partial breach: n. the failure to meet a term of a contract which is so minimal that it does not cause the contract to fail or justify breach (breaking the contract) by the other contracting party. A partial breach can be remedied (made up) by a small reduction in payment or other adjustment. Example: a landlord promises to rent an apartment furnished, and when the tenants move in some furnishings are not there. The landlord may lower the rent temporarily until he/she can bring in the missing or expected items.

partial disability: n. the result of an injury which permanently reduces a person's ability to function, but still permits some working or other activity. In worker's compensation cases an injured worker is often awarded a percentage rating of permanent partial disability, which will entitle him/her to a money settlement. The percentage payoff is often based on a physician's evaluation of what part of the person's normal functioning is gone.

partial verdict: n. in a criminal trial, the result when the jury finds the defendant guilty of one or more charges but not guilty (or deadlocks) on one or more other charges. (See: **verdict**)

participate: v. to invest and then receive a part or share, as in business profits, payments on a promissory note, title to land, or as one of the beneficiaries of the estate of a person who has died.

partition: n. a lawsuit which one co-owner of real property can file to get a court order requiring the sale of the property and division of the profits, or division of the land between the co-owners, which is often a practical impossibility. Normally, a partition order provides for an appraisal of the total property, which sets the price for one of the parties to buy out the other's half.

Partition cases are common when co-owners differ on whether to sell, keep or divide the property.

partner: n. 1) one of the co-owners and investors in a "partnership" which is an on-going business enterprise entered into for profit. A "general partner" is responsible for the debts, contracts and actions of all the partners in the business, is an equal in management decisions unless there is an agreement establishing management duties and rights, and shares in the profits and losses based on the percentage of the investment (either in money or effort) in the partnership. A "limited partner" does not share responsibility for debts beyond his/her investment, cannot share in management, and shares in profits based on a written agreement. A "silent partner" is no different from any partner except he/she is not visible to the public and has no part in day-to-day management. 2) slang for "domestic partner," usually two people living together, either homosexual or heterosexual, sharing lives and possessions, and not married. (See: **domestic partners, general partner, limited partner, limited partnership, partnership**)

partnership: n. a business enterprise entered into for profit which is owned by more than one person, each of whom is a "partner." A partnership may be created by a formal written agreement, but may be based on an oral agreement or just a handshake. Each partner invests a certain amount (money, assets and/or effort) which establishes an agreed-upon percentage of ownership, is responsible for all the debts and contracts of the partnership even though another partner created the debt or entered into the contract, has a share in management decisions, and shares in profits and losses according to the percentage of the total investment. Often a partnership agreement may provide for certain division of management, shares of investment, profit and/or rights to buy out a partner upon leaving the partnership or death. Each partner owes the other partners a duty of full disclosure of information which affects the business and cannot commandeer for himself/herself business opportunities which rightfully belong to the partnership. A partnership which does business under a trade name must file with the county or state a certificate of "doing business under a fictitious name," which gives notice to the public of the names of partners and the business address. A "limited partnership" limits the responsibility for debts beyond the investment to the managing "general partners." The investing "limited partners" cannot participate in management and are limited to specific percentages of profit. A partnership differs from a "joint venture," which involves more than one investor for only a specific short-term project and prompt division of profits. Partnerships are traditionally the most fragile of business arrangements and are often dissolved and subject to disputes. But several million exist in the United States and, ironically, they are the favorite business entity for law firms. (See: **general partner, partner, limited partnership, silent partner**)

party: n. 1) one of the participants in a lawsuit or other legal proceeding who has an interest in the outcome. Parties include plaintiff (person filing suit), defendant (person sued or charged with a crime), petitioner (files a petition asking for a court ruling), respondent (usually in opposition to a petition or an appeal), cross-complainant (a defendant who sues someone else in the same lawsuit), or cross-defendant (a person sued by a cross-complainant). 2) a person or entity involved in an agreement. 3) a common reference by lawyers to people or entities involved in lawsuits, transactions, contracts or accidents, as in "both parties knew what was expected," "he is a party to the contract," "he was not a party to the criminal conspiracy...." (See: **contract, cross-complaint, defendant, indispensable party, necessary party, petitioner, plaintiff, proper party, real party in interest, respondent**)

party of the first part: n. reference in a written contract to identify one of the people entering into the agreement. The agreement would read "Mary McConnell (hereinafter called The Party of the First Part)." Better practice is to identify the parties by a short form of their name ("hereinafter referred to as McConnell") or as Buyer, Seller, Owner, Trustee or some other useful identification. Name use aids in following and understanding the contract and avoids confusion with "the party of the second part," which identifies another party to the agreement.

> It is not what a lawyer tells me I may do; but what humanity, reason, and justice tell me I ought to do.
> —*Edmund Burke*

party of the second part: n. a reference to a party to a written contract, as distinguished from "the party of the first part." (See: **party of the first part**)

party wall: n. a wall shared by two adjoining premises which is on the property line, such as in townhouses, condominiums, row houses or two units in a duplex. Both owners are responsible for maintaining structural integrity of the wall, even if the wall is entirely on the property of one of the parties.

passenger: n. a rider who has paid a fare on a train, bus, airline, taxi, ship, ferry, automobile or other carrier in the business of transporting people for a fee (a common carrier). A passenger is owed a duty of care by such a carrier and has a right to sue for damages for injuries suffered while being transported without proof of negligence. One tricky issue is whether a person who has entered the depot, station or airport, but not yet purchased a ticket or has not boarded, is entitled to the rights of a passenger to recover for damages. A passenger without payment of fare who is injured must prove the driver's negligence in a suit for damages. (See: **common carrier, guest statute**)

passion: n. (See: **heat of passion**)

passive: adj. referring to being inactive. A "passive trustee" is one who has no responsibilities other than to hold title or wait for an event which would activate the trust. "Passive income" for tax purposes includes any income in which there is no effort or active management, and is treated differently for some purposes, such as Social Security income limitations. It may include stock dividends, trust profits, rents with no management involvement and interest on bank accounts.

patent: 1) adj. obvious. Used in such expressions as a "patent defect" in an appliance. 2) n. an exclusive right to the benefits of an invention or improvement granted by the U.S. Patent Office, for a specific period of time, on the basis that it is novel (not previously known or described in a publication), "non-obvious" (a form which anyone in the field of expertise could identify), and useful. There are three types of patents: a) "utility patent" which includes a process, a machine (mechanism with moving parts), manufactured products, and compounds or mixtures (such as chemical formulas); b) "design patent" which is a new, original and ornamental design for a manufactured article; and c) "plant patent" which is a new variety of a cultivated asexually reproduced plant. Example: Secretary of Agriculture and later Vice President Henry A. Wallace developed hybrid corn which made him rich for life. A utility or plant patent lasts 17 years and a design patent lasts 14 years, but all types require payment of "maintenance" fees payable beginning 3 1/2 years after the issuance to keep them up. Patent law specialists can make a search of patents to determine if the proposed invention is truly unique, and if apparently so, can file an application, including detailed drawing and specifications. While awaiting issuance of the patent, products or designs should be marked "patent pending" or "pat. pending." Upon receiving the patent the product can be marked with the word "patent" and the number designated by the Patent Office. The rights can be transferred provided the assignment is signed and notarized to create a record or "licensed" for use. Manufacture of a product upon which there is an existing patent is "patent infringement" which can result in a lawsuit against the infringer with substantial damages granted. 3) n. a nearly obsolete expression for a grant of public land by the government to an individual. (See: **patent ambiguity, patent defect, patent infringement, patent pending**)

patent ambiguity: n. an obvious inconsistency in the language of a written document.

patent defect: n. an obvious flaw in a product or a document (such as leaving out the property description in a deed).

patent infringement: n. the manufacture and/or use of an invention or improvement for which someone else owns a patent issued by the government, without obtaining permission of the owner of the patent by contract, license or waiver. The infringing party will be liable to the owner of the patent for all profits made from the use of the invention, as well as any harm which can be shown by the inventor, whether the infringement was intentional or not. (See: **patent, infringement**)

patent pending: n. often abbreviated to "pat. pend." or "pat. pending," the term is printed on a product to inform others that an application for a patent has been filed with the U.S. Patent Office, but the patent has not yet been granted. (See: **patent**)

paternity suit: n. a lawsuit, usually by a mother, to prove that a named person is the father of her child (or the fetus she is carrying). Evidence of paternity may include blood tests (which can eliminate a man as a possible father), testimony about sexual relations between the woman and the alleged father, evidence of relationship of the couple during the time the woman became pregnant, admissions of fatherhood, comparison of child in looks, eye and hair color, race and, increasingly, DNA evidence. In addition to the desire to give the child a known natural father, proof of paternity will lead to the right to child support, birthing expenses and the child's inheritance from his father. The threat of a paternity suit against a man married to another may lead to a prompt and quiet settlement.

pawn: v. to pledge an item of personal property as security for a loan, with the property left with the pawnbroker. The interest rates are on the high side, the amount of the loan is well below the value of the pledged property, and the broker has the right to sell the item without further notice if the loan is not paid. Pawnbrokers are licensed by the state. (See: **pledge**)

pay: v. to deliver money owed.

payable: 1) adj. referring to a debt which is due. A debt may be owed, but not yet payable until a certain date or event. 2) n. a debt which is due. "Payables" are all the liabilities (debts) of a business.

payable on demand: adj. a debt on a promissory note or bill of exchange which must be paid when demanded by the payee (party to whom the debt is owed).

payee: n. the one named on a check or promissory note to receive payment.

payment in due course: n. the giving of funds to the holder of a promissory note or bill of exchange when due, without any knowledge that the document had been acquired by fraud or that the holder did not have valid title. The true owner of the bill or note cannot also demand payment, but must look to the recipient of the funds. (See: **holder in due course**)

payment in full: n. the giving of all funds due to another. This language is often inserted on the back of a check above the place for endorsement to prove that the payee accepts the payment as complete.

Common sense often makes good law.
—Justice William O. Douglas

payor (payer): n. the party who must make payment on a promissory note.

peaceable possession: n. in real estate, holding property without any adverse claim to possession or title by another.

peace bond: n. a bond required as part of a court order to guarantee that a person will stay away from another person he/she has threatened or bothered. The bond will be forfeit (given up) if the order is violated, but that is no consolation to a person injured, molested or murdered by the violator. (See: **injunction, stay away order**)

peculation: n. misappropriation of public (government) funds or property. (See: **misappropriation**)

pecuniary: adj. relating to money, as in "pecuniary loss."

pedophilia: n. an obsession with children as sex objects. Overt acts, including taking sexually explicit photographs, molesting children and exposing one's genitalia to children, are all crimes. The problem with these crimes is that pedophilia is also treated as a mental illness, and the pedophile is often released only to repeat the crimes or escalate the activity to the level of murder. (See: **molestation, pornography, rape**)

peeping tom: n. a person who stealthily peeks into windows, holes in restroom walls or other openings with the purpose of getting a sexual thrill from seeing women or girls undressed or couples making love. The term comes from the legendary Tom who was the one person who peeked when Lady Godiva rode her horse naked through the streets of Coventry to protest taxes. Being a peeping tom is treated as a crime based on sexual deviancy, with various names in different states. It forms the basis for a lawsuit by the victim on the basis of invasion of privacy.

peer: n. an equal. A "jury of one's peers," to which criminal defendants are constitutionally entitled, means an impartial group of citizens from the judicial district (e.g. county) in which the defendant lives. It does not mean a jury ethnically, educationally, economically or sexually the same as the defendant, although in some jurisdictions attempts are made to meet those criteria. (See: **jury of one's peers**)

peer review: n. an examination and evaluation of the performance of a professional or technician by a board or committee made up of people in the same occupation. This may arise in determining whether a person has been legitimately discharged, denied promotion or penalized by an employer, or is found to have failed to meet minimum standards of performance and is thus liable in a lawsuit claiming damages due to negligence.

penal: adj. referring to criminality, as in defining "penal code" (the laws specifying crimes and punishment), or "penal institution" (a state prison or penitentiary confining convicted felons).

penalty: n. 1) in criminal law, a money fine or forfeiture of property ordered by the judge after conviction for a crime. 2) an amount agreed in advance if payment or performance is not made on time, such as a "late payment" on a promissory note or lease, or a financial penalty for each day a building contractor fails to complete a job.

pendente lite: (pen-den-tay lee-tay) adj. Latin for awaiting the litigation (lawsuit). It is applied to court orders (such as temporary child support) which are in effect until the case is tried, or rights which cannot be enforced until the lawsuit is over.

pendent jurisdiction: n. in federal procedure, the policy that allows a federal court to decide a legal question normally tried in state courts because it is based on the same facts as a lawsuit which is under federal court jurisdiction. (It also may be spelled: pendant)

penitentiary: n. a state or federal prison in which convicts are held for commission of major crimes (felonies).

people: n. the designation for the prosecuting government in a criminal trial, as in *People v. Capone.* Such a case may also be captioned *State v. Davis* or in federal prosecutions, *United States v. Miller.*

per: prep. from Latin for "by means of" or simply, "by" as in "per day" (by day) or "*per capita*" (by head).

per capita: adj. Latin for "by head," meaning to be determined by the number of people. To find the *per capita* cost, the total number of persons are added up and the bill, tax or benefits are divided equally among those persons.

per curiam: adj. Latin for "by the court," defining a decision of an appeals court as a whole in which no judge is identified as the specific author.

per diem: adj. or n. Latin for "per

day," it is short for payment of daily expenses and/or fees of an employee or an agent.

peremptory: adj. absolute, final and not entitled to delay or reconsideration. The term is applied to writs, juror challenges or a date set for hearing.

peremptory challenge: n. the right of the plaintiff and the defendant in a jury trial to have a juror dismissed before trial without stating a reason. This challenge is distinguished from a "challenge for cause" (reason) based on the potential juror admitting bias, acquaintanceship with one of the parties or their attorney, personal knowledge about the facts, or some other basis for believing he/she might not be impartial. The number of peremptory challenges for each side will differ based on state law, the number of parties to a case, and whether it is a civil or criminal trial. The usual phrasing used by lawyers exercising the challenge is "Juror number seven may be excused." (See: **challenge for cause, jury,** *voir dire*)

peremptory writ of mandate (or mandamus): n. a final order of a court to any governmental body, government official or a lower court to perform an act the court finds is an official duty required by law. This is distinguished from an alternative writ of mandate (mandamus), which orders the governmental agency, court or officials to obey the order or show cause at a hearing why it should not. The usual practice is for anyone desiring such an order to file a petition for the alternative writ. If the officials do not comply with the order and fail to convince the court that the writ of mandate should be denied, then the court will issue the peremptory writ. In some emergency situations or when there is no conceivable reason for the government not to follow the law, then the peremptory writ will be issued after a notice of hearing without the alternative writ. (See: **mandamus, mandate**)

perfect: (with stress on the second syllable) v. 1) to complete; to take all required steps to achieve a result, such as obtaining a lien or other security by legal action or completing and filing all documents to present a case to a court of appeals. A mechanic's lien for labor and/or materials used to improve real property is "perfected" by filing a lawsuit and obtaining a judgment that the lien attaches to the property. 2) to make perfect. (See: **mechanic's lien**)

perfected: adj. having completed all necessary legal steps to achieve a result, such as perfected title to property. (See: **perfect**)

perform: v. 1) to fulfill one's obligations under a contract. 2) to comply with requirements of a court order. (See: **performance**)

performance: n. fulfillment of one's obligations required by contract. Specific performance of a contract may be demanded in a lawsuit. Partial performance is short of full performance spelled out in the contract, but if the contract provided for a series of acts or deliveries with payment for each of the series, there may be partial recovery for what has been performed or delivered even if there is not full performance. (See: **specific performance**)

perjurer: n. a person who intentionally lies while under an oath administered by a notary public, court clerk or other official, and thus commits the crime of perjury. A perjurer may commit perjury in oral testimony or by signing or acknowledging a written legal document (such as an affidavit, declaration under penalty of perjury, deed, license application, tax return) knowing the document contains false information. (See: **perjury**)

perjury: n. the crime of intentionally lying after being duly sworn (to tell the truth) by a notary public, court clerk or other official. This false statement may be made in testimony in court, administrative hearings, depositions, answers to interrogatories, as well as by signing or acknowledging a written legal document (such as affidavit, declaration under penalty of perjury, deed, license application, tax return) known to contain false information. Although it is a crime, prosecutions for perjury are rare, because a defendant will argue he/she merely made a mistake or misunderstood.

permanent disability: n. an injury which impairs the physical and/or mental ability of a person to perform his/her normal work or non-occupational activities supposedly for the remainder of his/her life. Under worker's compensation laws (covering on-the-job injuries) once the condition is stable, a degree of permanent disability is established even if the employee is able to work despite the physical problem. Permanent disability is also one basis for awarding general damages in a lawsuit for injury suffered due to the negligence or intentional attack of another. (See: **permanent injury, Workers' Compensation Acts**)

permanent injunction: n. a final order of a court that a person or entity refrain from certain activities permanently or take certain actions (usually to correct a nuisance) until completed. A permanent injunction is distinguished from a "preliminary" injunction which the court issues pending the outcome of a lawsuit or petition asking for the "permanent" injunction. (See: **injunction, preliminary injunction, temporary injunction**)

permanent injury: n. physical or mental damage which will restrict the employment and/or other activities of a person for the rest of his/her life. In a lawsuit to recover damages caused by the negligence or intentional wrongful act of another, a permanent injury can be a major element in an award of general damages. (See: **permanent disability**)

permissive: adj. 1) referring to any act which is allowed by court order, legal procedure, or agreement. 2) tolerant or allowing of others' behavior, suggesting contrary to others' standards.

permit: 1) v. to allow by silence, agreement or giving a license. 2) n. a license or other document given by an authorized public official or agency (building inspector, department of motor vehicles) to allow a person or business to perform certain acts. These can include building a structure, using a building, driving on the highway, conducting a retail business, and dozens of other activities. The purpose of permits is supposedly to guarantee that laws and regulations have been obeyed, but they also are a source of public revenue. (See: **license**)

perpetuity: n. forever. (See: **in perpetuity, rule against perpetuities**)

per se: (purr say) adj. Latin for "by itself," meaning inherently. Thus, a published writing which falsely accuses another of having a sexually transmitted disease or being a convicted felon is "libel *per se*," without further explanation of the meaning of the statement. (See: **libel per se, slander per se**)

person: n. 1) a human being. 2) a corporation treated as having the rights and obligations of a person. Counties and cities can be treated as a person in the same manner as a corporation. However, corporations, counties and cities cannot have the emotions of humans such as malice, and therefore are not liable for punitive damages unless there is a statute authorizing the award of punitive damages. (See: **corporation, party**)

personal effects: n. things which include clothes, cosmetics and items of adornment. This is not the same as "personalty" which means all tangible property which is not real property, money or investments. The expression is often found in wills ("I leave my personal effects to my niece, Susannah"). (See: **personalty**)

personal property: n. same as "personalty." (See: **personalty**)

311

personal service: n. delivering a summons, complaint, notice to quit tenancy or other legal document which must be served by handing it directly to the person named in the document. Personal service is distinguished from "constructive service," which includes posting the notice and then mailing a copy or publishing a summons on a person the court has found is hiding to avoid service, and from "substituted service," which is giving the document to someone else (another resident, a secretary or receptionist, or other responsible adult) at the address. (See: **constructive service, service of process, substituted service, summons**)

personal services: n. in contract law, the talents of a person which are unusual, special or unique and cannot be performed exactly the same by another. These can include the talents of an artist, an actor, a writer or professional services. The value of personal services is greater than general labor, so woodcarving is personal service and carpentry is not. Therefore, if an actor contracts to perform in a movie and fails to show, he/she will be liable for damages based on the difficulty to replace him. An artist who contracts to paint a picture cannot send a substitute, since he/she was retained for his/her unique ability and product.

personalty: n. movable assets (things, including animals) which are not real property, money or investments. (See: **real property, personal effects**)

per stirpes: (purr stir-peas) adj. Latin for "by roots," by representation. The term is commonly used in wills and trusts to describe the distribution when a beneficiary dies before the person whose estate is being divided. Example: "I leave $100,000 to my daughter, Eleanor, and if she shall predecease me, to her children, *per stirpes*." Thus, if Eleanor dies before her parent, then the $100,000 will be divided among her children equally. A way to make this more clear is to substitute for *per stirpes*: "...to her children, by right of representation, share and share alike," which is clear to the nonlawyer. If there is no provision for distribution to children of a predeceased child, then the gift will become part of the residue (what is left after specific gifts), and then the grandchildren may not share if there are surviving children of the giver. (See: **descent and distribution, trust, will**)

petition: 1) n. a formal written request to a court for an order of the court. It is distinguished from a complaint in a lawsuit which asks for damages and/or performance by the opposing party. Petitions include demands for writs, orders to show cause, modifications of prior orders, continuances, dismissal of a case, reduction of bail in criminal cases, a decree of distribution of an estate, appointment of a guardian, and a host of other matters arising in legal actions. 2) n. a general term for a writing signed by a number of people asking for a particular result from a private governing body (such as a homeowners association, a political party, or a club). 3) in public law, a writing signed by a number of people which is required to place a proposition or ordinance on the ballot, nominate a person for public office, or demand a recall election. Such petitions for official action must be signed by a specified number of registered voters (such as five percent). 4) v. to make a formal request of a court; to present a written request to an organization's governing body signed by one or more members. 5) n. a suit for divorce in some states, in which the parties are called petitioner and respondent. (See: **dissolution of marriage, divorce, motion, writ**)

petitioner: n. one who signs and/or files a petition. (See: **petition**)

petit jury: n. old-fashioned name for the jury sitting to hear a lawsuit or criminal prosecution, called "petit" (small) to distinguish it from a "grand" jury, which has other duties. (See: **Grand Jury, jury**)

petty larceny: n. a term used in many states for theft of a small amount of money or objects of little value (such as less than $500). It is distinguished from grand larceny, which is theft of property of greater worth and a felony punishable by a term in state prison. Petty larceny is a misdemeanor with a maximum punishment of a term in the county jail. States which only use the term "larceny" often treat theft of smaller amounts as a misdemeanor in charging and sentencing.

physician-patient privilege: n. the right and obligation of a physician to refuse to testify in a trial or other legal proceeding about any statement made to him/her by a patient on the basis that any communication between doctor and patient is confidential. A patient could sue the physician for damages if the doctor breaches the confidence by testifying. Of course, in most trials involving injuries the physician will testify with the plaintiff's permission. Note: when the defendant's physician examines the injured plaintiff, the plaintiff has given permission for that examination and potential testimony, so a plaintiff must be cautious in making statements. (See: **confidential communication, privilege**)

picketing: n. standing or parading near a business or government office usually with signs of protest or claims in labor disputes or public policy controversies (peace marches to pro- or anti-abortion advocates). Picketing is constitutionally guaranteed as free speech, but in some cases it may be limited by court order to prevent physical combat, blocking of entrances or threats to the public safety.

pierce the corporate veil: v. to prove that a corporation exists merely as a completely controlled front (alter ego) for an individual or management group, so that in a lawsuit the individual defendants can be held responsible (liable) for damages for actions of the corporation. If a corporation has issued stock and held regular meetings of shareholders and directors, it is unlikely a judge will "pierce" the veil and limit the liability to the corporation, unless there is proof that the corporation was created to accomplish a fraud on those dealing with it. (See: **corporation**)

pilferage: n. a crime of theft of little things, usually from shipments or baggage. (See: **theft**)

pimp: n. a person who procures a prostitute for customers or vice versa, sharing the profits of the person's activities. Supposedly he provides protection for the prostitutes, but quite often he will threaten, brutalize, rape, cheat and induce drug addiction of the prostitutes. A pimp commits the crime of pandering. (See: **pander, panderer, prostitution**)

pink slip: n. 1) slang for official automobile registration certificate, due to its color in some states. 2) slang for notice of being fired or laid off from a job.

piracy: n. the crime of robbery of ships or boats on the oceans. Accusation, trial and punishment of pirates may be under international agreement applicable anywhere, or under the laws of the particular nation where the accused has been captured.

plagiarism: n. taking the writings or literary concepts (a plot, characters, words) of another and selling and/or publishing them as one's own product. Quotes which are brief or are acknowledged as quotes do not constitute plagiarism. The actual author can bring a lawsuit for appropriation of his/her work against the plagiarist and recover the profits. Normally plagiarism is not a crime, but it can be used as the basis of a fraud charge or copyright infringement if prior creation can be proved. (See: **copyright, infringement**)

plain error: n. a mistake by the trial court found by a court of appeals to be very obvious and sufficient to require reversal of the trial decision.

plaintiff: n. the party who initiates a lawsuit by filing a complaint with the clerk of the court against the defendant(s) demanding damages, performance and/or court determination of rights. (See: **complaint, defendant, petitioner**)

plaintiff's attorney: n. the attorney who represents a plaintiff (the suing party) in a lawsuit. In lawyer parlance a "plaintiff's attorney" refers to a lawyer who regularly represents persons who are suing for damages, while a lawyer who is regularly chosen by an insurance company to represent its insureds is called a "defense attorney." (See: **defense attorney, plaintiff**)

plain view doctrine: n. the rule that a law enforcement officer may make a search and seizure without obtaining a search warrant *if* evidence of criminal activity or the product of a crime can be seen without entry or search. Example: a policeman stops a motorist for a minor traffic violation and can see in the car a pistol or a marijuana plant on the back seat, giving him "reasonable cause" to enter the vehicle to make a search. (See: **search and seizure, search warrant**)

plea: n. 1) in criminal law, the response by an accused defendant to each charge of the commission of a crime. Pleas normally are "not guilty," "guilty," "no contest" (admitting the facts, but unwilling to plead "guilty," thus resulting in the equivalent of a "guilty" verdict but without admitting the crime), or "not guilty by reason of insanity" (at the time of the criminal act). However, the accused may make a "dilatory plea" challenging the jurisdiction of the court or claiming that he/she is the wrong defendant, re-quiring a special hearing. He/she may admit the acts but have excuses to be considered (a "plea in abatement"), which may affect the judge's sentence. Pleas are entered orally at arraignment (first court appearance) or a continued (postponed) arraignment. If after a preliminary hearing the judge determines the defendant must face trial for a felony, he/she will have to enter a plea again before a judge of the trial court. 2) any written answer or other response filed by a defendant to a complaint or petition in a civil lawsuit. (See: **arraignment, plead, preliminary hearing**)

plea in abatement: n. (See: **plea**)

plea bargain: n. in criminal procedure, a negotiation between the defendant and his attorney on one side and the prosecutor on the other, in which the defendant agrees to plead "guilty" or "no contest" to some crimes, in return for reduction of the severity of the charges, dismissal of some of the charges, the prosecutor's willingness to recommend a particular sentence or some other benefit to the defendant. Sometimes one element of the bargain is that the defendant reveal information such as location of stolen goods, names of others participating in the crime or admission of other crimes (such as a string of burglaries). The judge must agree to the result of the plea bargain before accepting the plea. If he does not, then the bargain is cancelled. Reasons for the bargain include a desire to cut down on the number of trials, danger to the defendant of a long term in prison if convicted after trial and the ability to get information on criminal activity from the defendant. There are three dangers: a) an innocent defendant may be pressured into a confession and plea out of fear of a severe penalty if convicted; b) particularly vicious criminals will get lenient treatment and be back "on the street" in a short time; c) results in unequal treatment. Public antipathy to plea bargaining has led to some state statutes prohibiting the practice, but informal discussions can get around the ban. (See: **cop a plea, plea**)

plead: v. 1) in civil lawsuits and petitions, to file any document (pleading) including complaints, petitions, declarations, motions and memoranda of points and authorities. 2) in criminal law, to enter a plea of a defendant in response to each charge of criminal conduct. (See: **plea, pleading**)

pleading: n. 1) every legal document filed in a lawsuit, petition, motion and/or hearing, including complaint, petition, answer, demurrer, motion, declaration and memorandum of points and authorities (written argument citing precedents and statutes). Laypersons should be aware that, except possibly for petitions from prisoners, pleadings are required by state or federal statutes and/or court rules to be of a particular form and format: typed, signed, dated, with the name of the court, title and number of the case, name, address and telephone number of the attorney or person acting for himself/herself (*in pro per*) included. 2) the act of preparing and presenting legal documents and arguments. Good pleading is an art: clear, logical, well-organized and comprehensive. (See:

answer, complaint, demurrer, plea, plead)

pledge: v. to deposit personal property as security for a personal loan of money. If the loan is not repaid when due, the personal property pledged shall be forfeit to the lender. The property is known as collateral. To pledge is the same as to pawn. 2) to promise to do something. (See: **pawn**)

plenary: adj. full, complete, covering all matters, usually referring to an order, hearing or trial.

police court: n. in some states a type of municipal court which handles misdemeanors (minor crimes) and traffic violations, as well as conducting arraignments (first appearances) and preliminary hearings of those accused of felonies to decide if there is cause to send the defendant to a higher court for trial. Police courts only handle criminal cases-unlike those municipal courts which also have jurisdiction over some civil cases. (See: **arraignment, municipal court, preliminary hearing**)

police powers: n. from the 10th Amendment to the Constitution, which reserves to the states the rights and powers "not delegated to the United States," which include protection of the welfare, safety, health and even morals of the public. Police powers include licensing, inspection, zoning, safety regulations (which cover a lot of territory), quarantines, and working conditions as well as law enforcement. In short, police powers are the basis of a host of state regulatory statutes.

political question: n. the determination by a court (particularly the Supreme Court) that an issue raised about the conduct of public business is a "political" issue to be determined by the legislature (including Congress) or the executive branch and not by the courts. Since 1960 the U.S. Supreme Court has been willing to look at some questions previously considered "political," such as "one-man-one-vote," as constitutional issues.

polygamy: n. having more than one wife or husband at the same time, usually more than just two (which is "bigamy"). It is a crime in all states. (See: **bigamy**)

polygraph: n. a lie detector device, from Greek for "many" (poly) "message" (graph) since numerous physiological responses are tested when questions are answered. (See: **lie detector test**)

pornography: n. pictures and/or writings of sexual activity intended solely to excite lascivious feelings of a particularly blatant and aberrational kind, such as acts involving children, animals, orgies, and all types of sexual intercourse. The printing, publication, sale and distribution of "hard core" pornography is either a felony or misdemeanor in most states. Since determining what is pornography and what is "soft core" and "hard core" are subjective questions to judges, juries and law enforcement officials, it is difficult to define, since the law cases cannot print examples for the courts to follow. (See: **obscene**)

positive law: n. statutory man-made law, as compared to "natural law," which is purportedly based on universally accepted moral principles, "God's law," and/or derived from nature and reason. The term "positive law" was first used by Thomas Hobbes in *Leviathan* (1651). (See: **natural law, statute**)

posse comitatus: (pahs-see coh-mitt-tah-tus) n. from Latin for "possible force," the power of the sheriff to call upon any able-bodied adult men (and presumably women) in the county to assist him in apprehending a criminal. The assembled group is called a posse for short.

possess: v. to own, have title to, occupy, physically hold or have under exclusive control. In wills there is often the phrase "of which I die possessed," in describing the estate. (See: **possession**)

possession: n. 1) any article, object, asset or property which one owns, occupies, holds or has under control. 2) the act of owning, occupying, holding or having under control an article, object, asset or property. "Constructive possession" involves property which is not immediately held, but which one has the right to hold and the means to get (such as a key to a storeroom or safe deposit box). "Criminal possession" is the holding of property which it is illegal to possess such as controlled narcotics, stolen goods or liquor by a juvenile. The old adage "possession is nine-tenths of the law" is a rule of force and not of law, since ownership requires the right to possess as well as actual or constructive possession. (See: **possess**)

possession of stolen goods: n. the crime of possession of goods which one knows or which any reasonable person would realize were stolen. It is generally a felony. Innocent possession is not a crime, but the goods are generally returned to the legal owner. (See: **possession**)

possessory interest: n. in real estate, the intent and right of a person to occupy and/or exercise control over a particular plot of land. A possessory interest is distinguished from an interest in the title to property, which may not include the right to immediately occupy the property. Example: a long-term lease. (See: **possess, possession, real property**)

possibility of a reverter: n. the potential that the title to a real property interest will return to the original grantor or giver or to his/her lineal descendants. Examples of events which could cause the title to revert: A gift of property to a hospital on condition that it be used forever for health care, but if the building is no longer used for that purpose the property will revert to the family of the original grantor; the real property is given to a daughter and her children, but will revert to her brother's descendants if her line dies out without further issue. (See: **reversion**)

post: v. 1) to place a notice on the entrance or a prominent place on real property, such as a notice to quit (leave), pay rent or of intent to conduct a sheriff's sale, which requires mailing of a copy to the occupant to complete service of the notice. 2) to place a legal notice on a designated public place at the courthouse. 3) a commercial term for recording a payment. 4) to mail.

postdated check: n. a check delivered now with a written date in the future, so that it cannot be cashed until that date. The danger to the recipient is that such a check is legally only a promissory note due at the later date, and if the account is closed or short when the check is presented at the bank, the payee has no rights to demand payment by the bank or claim that the delivery of a bad check was criminal.

post mortem: n. Latin for "after death," an examination of a dead body to determine cause of death, generally called an autopsy. (See: **coroner**)

pot: n. slang for marijuana, an illegal narcotic.

pour over will: n. a will of a person who has already executed a trust in which all property is designated to be distributed or managed upon the death of the person whose possessions are in trust, leaving all property to the trust. A pour over will is a protection which is intended to guarantee that any assets which somehow were not included in the trust become assets of the trust upon the party's death. A pour over will often provides that if the trust is invalid in whole or in part, the distribution under the will must be made under the same terms as stated in the invalid trust. (See: **trust, will**)

power: n. the right, authority and ability to take some action or accomplish something, including demanding action, executing documents, contracting, taking title, transferring, exercising legal rights and many other acts.

power of acceptance: n. the ability to accept an offer and thus create a binding contract. In real estate an acceptance can only be made for a period specified in the offer, and the power is terminated permanently by the making of a counter-offer. Thus, one cannot make a counter-offer and then decide to accept the original offer.

power of appointment: n. the right to leave property by will, transfer, gift or distribution under a trust. Such a power is often found in a trust in which each of the trustors (the creators of the trust, usually a husband and wife) is empowered to write a will leaving his or her share (or some part) to someone. If the power of appointment is not used then it expires on the death of the person with the power.

power of attorney: n. a written document signed by a person giving another person the power to act in conducting the signer's business, including signing papers, checks, title documents, contracts, handling bank accounts and other activities in the name of the person granting the power. The person receiving the power of attorney (the agent) is "attorney in fact" for the person giving the power, and usually signs documents as "Melinda Hubbard, attorney in fact for Guilda Giver." There are two types of power of attorney: a) general power of attorney, which covers all activities, and b) special power of attorney, which grants powers limited to specific matters, such as selling a particular piece of real estate, handling some bank accounts or executing a limited partnership agreement. A power of attorney may expire on a date stated in the document or upon written cancellation. Usually the signer acknowledges before a notary public that he/she executed the power, so that it is recordable if necessary, as in a real estate transaction.

practicable: adj. when something can be done or performed.

practice: 1) n. custom or habit as shown by repeated action, as in "it is the practice in the industry to confirm orders before shipping." 2) n. the legal business, as in "law practice," or "the practice of the law." 3) v. to repeat an activity in order to maintain or improve skills, as "he practices the violin every evening." 4) v. to conduct a law business, as "she practices law in St. Louis."

pray: v. to formally request judicial judgment, relief and/or damages at the end of a complaint or petition. (See: **prayer**)

prayer: n. the specific request for judgment, relief and/or damages at the conclusion of a complaint or petition. A typical prayer would read: "The plaintiff prays for: 1) special damages in the sum of $17,500; 2) general damages according to proof [proved in trial]; 3) reasonable attorney's fees; 4) costs of suit; and 5) such other and further relief as the court shall deem proper." A prayer gives the judge an idea of what is sought, and may become the basis of a judgment if the defendant defaults (fails to file an answer). Sometimes a plaintiff will inflate damages in the prayer for publicity

or intimidation purposes, or because the plaintiff believes that a gigantic demand will be a better starting point in negotiations. However, the ridiculous multi-million prayers in smaller cases make plaintiffs look foolish and unrealistic. (See: **complaint, default judgment**)

precatory: adj. referring to a wish or advisory suggestion which does not have the force of a demand or a request which under the law must be obeyed. Thus "precatory words" in a will or trust would express a "hope that my daughter will keep the house in the family," but do not absolutely prevent her from selling it.

precedent: 1) n. a prior reported opinion of an appeals court which establishes the legal rule (authority) in the future on the same legal question decided in the prior judgment. Thus, "the rule in *Fishbeck v. Gladfelter* is precedent for the issue before the court in this case." The doctrine that a lower court must follow a precedent is called *stare decisis* 2) adj. before, as in the term "condition precedent," which is a situation which must exist before a party to a contract has to perform. (See: *stare decisis*)

predecease: v. to die before someone else, as "if my brother, Harry, should predecease me, his share of my estate I give to his son, Eugene."

preemption: n. the rule of law that if the federal government through Congress has enacted legislation on a subject matter it shall be controlling over state laws and/or preclude the state from enacting laws on the same subject if Congress has specifically stated it has "occupied the field." If Congress has not clearly claimed preemption, a federal or state court may decide the issue on the basis of history of the legislation (debate in Congress) and practice. Example: federal standards of meat or other products have preempted state laws. However, federal and state legislation on narcotics control may parallel each other.

preemptive right: n. the right of a shareholder in a corporation to have the first opportunity to purchase a new issue of stock of that corporation in proportion to the amount of stock already owned by the shareholder. (See: **corporation, shareholder, stock**)

preference: n. in bankruptcy, the payment of a debt to one creditor rather than dividing the assets equally among all those to whom he/she/it owes money, often by making a payment to a favored creditor just before filing a petition to be declared bankrupt. Such a preference is prohibited by law, and the favored creditor must pay the money to the bankruptcy trustee. However, the bankruptcy court may give secured creditors (with a judgment, lien, deed of trust, mortgage or collateralized loan) a legal preference over "general" creditors in distributing available funds or assets. (See: **bankruptcy**)

preferred dividend: n. a payment of a corporation's profits to holders of preferred shares of stock. (See: **preferred stock**)

preferred stock: n. a class of shares of stock in a corporation which gives the holders priority in payment of dividends (and distribution of assets in case of dissolution of the corporation) over owners of "common" stock at a fixed rate. While the assurance of first chance at profits is a psychological and real benefit, preferred stock shareholders do not participate in higher dividends if the corporation makes large profits, and usually cannot vote for directors. (See: **common stock, corporation, dividend, stock**)

> *Laws are made for men of common understanding, and should therefore be construed by the ordinary rules of common sense.*
> *—Thomas Jefferson*

preliminary hearing: n. in criminal law, a hearing to determine if a person charged with a felony (a serious crime punishable by a term in the state prison) should be tried for the crime charged, based on whether there is some substantial evidence that he/she committed the crime. A preliminary hearing is held in the lowest local court (municipal or police court), but only if the prosecutor has filed the charge without asking the Grand Jury for an indictment for the alleged crime. Such a hearing must be held within a few days after arraignment (presentation in court of the charges and the defendant's right to plead guilty or not guilty). Since neither side wants to reveal its trial strategy, the prosecution normally presents only enough evidence and testimony to show the probability of guilt, and defendants often put on no evidence at all at the preliminary hearing, unless there is a strong chance of getting the charges dismissed. If the judge finds sufficient evidence to try the defendant, the case is sent to the appropriate court (variously called superior, county, district, common pleas) for trial. If there is no such convincing evidence, the judge will dismiss the charges. In the "Perry Mason" television series, the courtroom scenes were almost always of preliminary hearings. (See: **arraignment, charge, Grand Jury, information**)

preliminary injunction: n. a court order made in the early stages of a lawsuit or petition which prohibits the parties from doing an act which is in dispute, thereby maintaining the status quo until there is a final judgment after trial. (See: **injunction, permanent injunction, temporary injunction**)

premeditation: n. planning, plotting or deliberating before doing something. Premeditation is an element in first degree murder and shows intent to commit that crime. (See: **first degree murder, malice aforethought, murder**)

premises: n. 1) in real estate, land and the improvements on it, a building, store, shop, apartment, or other designated structure. The exact premises may be important in determining if an outbuilding (shed, cabana, detached garage) is insured or whether a person accused of burglary has actually entered a structure. 2) in legal pleading, premises means "all that has hereinabove been stated," as in a

prayer (request) at the end of a complaint asking for "any further order deemed proper in the premises" (an order based on what has been stated in the complaint). (See: **real estate, structure**)

premium: n. 1) payment for insurance coverage either in a lump sum or by installments. 2) an extra payment for an act, option or priority.

prenuptial agreement: n. also called an antenuptial agreement, a written contract between two people who are about to marry, setting out the terms of possession of assets, treatment of future earnings, control of the property of each, and potential division if the marriage is later dissolved. These agreements are fairly common if either or both parties have substantial assets, children from a prior marriage, potential inheritances, high incomes, or have been "taken" by a previous spouse. (See: **antenuptial agreement**)

preponderance of the evidence: n. the greater weight of the evidence required in a civil (non-criminal) lawsuit for the trier of fact (jury or judge without a jury) to decide in favor of one side or the other. This preponderance is based on the more convincing evidence and its probable truth or accuracy, and not on the amount of evidence. Thus, one clearly knowledgeable witness may provide a preponderance of evidence over a dozen witnesses with hazy testimony, or a signed agreement with definite terms may outweigh opinions or speculation about what the parties intended. Preponderance of the evidence is required in a civil case and is contrasted with "beyond a reasonable doubt," which is the more severe test of evidence required to convict in a criminal trial. No matter what the definition stated in various legal opinions, the meaning is somewhat subjective. (See: **evidence**)

prerogative writ: n. an historic generic term for any writ (court order) directed to government agencies, public officials or another court. (See: **writ**)

prescription: n. the method of acquiring an easement upon another's real property by continued and regular use without permission of the property owner for a period of years required by the law of the state (commonly five years or more). Examples: Phillip Packer drives across the corner of Ralph Roundup's ranch to reach Packer's barn regularly for a period of ten years; for a decade Ronald Retailer uses the alley behind Marjorie Howard's house to reach his storeroom. In each case the result is a "prescriptive easement" for that specific use. It effectively gives the user an easement for use but not ownership of the property. (See: **prescriptive easement**)

prescriptive easement: n. an easement upon another's real property acquired by continued use without permission of the owner for a period provided by state law to establish the easement. The problems with prescriptive easements are that they do not show up on title reports, and the exact location and/or use of the easement is not always clear and occasionally moves by practice or erosion. (See: **easement, prescription**)

presentment: n. 1) making a demand for payment of a promissory note when it is due. 2) a report to a court by a Grand Jury, made on its own initiative without a request or presentation of evidence by the local prosecutor, that a "public" crime (illegal act by public officials or affecting the public good) has been committed. (See: **Grand Jury, promissory note**)

presiding judge: n. 1) in both state and federal appeals court, the judge who chairs the panel of three or more judges during hearings and supervises the business of the court. 2) in those counties or other jurisdictions with several judges, the one is chosen to direct the management of the courts, usually on an annual or other rotating basis. The presiding judge usually makes assignments of judges to specialized courts (juvenile, probate, criminal, law and motion, family law, etc.), oversees the calendar, and chairs meetings of the judges.

presumption: n. a rule of law which permits a court to assume a fact is true until such time as there is a preponderance (greater weight) of evidence which disproves or outweighs (rebuts) the presumption. Each presumption is based upon a particular set of apparent facts paired with established laws, logic, reasoning or individual rights. A presumption is rebuttable in that it can be refuted by factual evidence. One can present facts to persuade the judge that the presumption is not true. Examples: a child born of a husband and wife living together is presumed to be the natural child of the husband unless there is conclusive proof it is not; a person who has disappeared and not been heard from for seven years is presumed to be dead, but the presumption could be rebutted if he/she is found alive; an accused person is presumed innocent until proven guilty. These are sometimes called rebuttable presumptions to distinguish them from absolute, conclusive or irrebuttable presumptions in which rules of law and logic dictate that there is no possible way the presumption can be disproved. However, if a fact is absolute it is not truly a presumption at all, but a certainty.

presumption of innocence: n. a fundamental protection for a person accused of a crime, which requires the prosecution to prove its case against the defendant beyond a reasonable doubt. This is opposite from the criminal law in many countries, where the accused is considered guilty until he/she proves his/her innocence or the government completely fails to prove its case. (See: **beyond a reasonable doubt, presumption**)

pretermitted heir: n. the child of a person who has written a will in which the child is not left anything and is not mentioned at all. After the death of the parent, a pretermitted heir has the right to demand the share he/she would have received as an heir under the laws of distribution and descent. The reasoning is that the parent either inadvertently forgot the child or incorrectly believed the child was dead, and did not mean to leave him/her out. Thus, if someone wishes to disinherit a child or omit him/her from his/her will, that parent should specifically state in the will: "I leave nothing to my son,

Gordon," with or without a reason. Otherwise there may be unfair and unintended results. Example: Tommy Testator has three children, gives two of them $10,000 each, and the remainder (which turns out to be a million dollars) to set up a scholarship fund for orphans. His omitted child, who has not spoken to him for 20 years, is a pretermitted heir entitled to one-third of the estate, and will receive $340,000 compared to his siblings' specified $10,000 each. (See: **distribution and descent, heir**)

pretrial discovery: n. (See: **discovery**)

prevailing party: n. the winner in a lawsuit. Many contracts, leases, mortgages, deeds of trust or promissory notes provide that the "prevailing party" shall be entitled to recovery of attorney's fees and costs if legal action must be taken to enforce the agreement. Even if the plaintiff gets much less than the claim, he/she/it is the prevailing party entitled to include attorney's fees in the collectable costs. Usually there is no prevailing party when a complaint is voluntarily dismissed prior to trial or settled before or after trial has begun.

price fixing: n. a criminal violation of federal antitrust statutes in which several competing businesses reach a secret agreement (conspiracy) to set prices for their products to prevent real competition and keep the public from benefitting from price competition. Price fixing also includes secret setting of favorable prices between suppliers and favored manufacturers or distributors to beat the competition. (See: **antitrust law**)

323

prima facie: (pry-mah fay-shah) adj. Latin for "at first look," or "on its face," referring to a lawsuit or criminal prosecution in which the evidence before trial is sufficient to prove the case unless there is substantial contradictory evidence presented at trial. A *prima facie* case presented to a Grand Jury by the prosecution will result in an indictment. Example: in a charge of bad check writing, evidence of a half dozen checks written on a non-existent bank account makes it a *prima facie* case. However, proof that the bank had misprinted the account number on the checks might disprove the prosecution's apparent "open and shut" case. (See: ***prima facie* case**)

prima facie case: n. a plaintiff's lawsuit or a criminal charge which appears at first blush to be "open and shut." (See: ***prima facie***)

prime suspect: n. the one person law enforcement officers believe most probably committed a crime being investigated. Once a person is determined to be a prime suspect, the police must be careful to give the "Miranda warnings," or take the risk that any admissions (any evidence gained from the statements) by the suspect may be excluded in trial. (See: **Miranda warning**)

primogeniture: n. from Latin for "first born," the ancient rule from feudal England (except in the County of Kent) that the oldest son would inherit the entire estate of his parents (or nearest ancestor), and, if there was no male heir, the daughters would take (receive the property) in equal shares. The intent was to preserve larger properties from being broken up into small holdings, which might weaken the power of nobles. It does not exist in the United States. (See: **distribution and descent**)

principal: n. 1) main person in a business. 2) employer, the person hiring and directing employees (agents) to perform his/her/its business. It is particularly important to determine who is the principal since he/she/it is responsible for the acts of agents in the "scope of employment" under the doctrine of *respondeat superior*. 3) in criminal law, the main perpetrator (organizer and active committer) of a crime, as distinguished from an "accessory" who helps the principal in some fashion. The criminal principal is usually the person who originates the idea of committing the crime and/or directly carries it out, and is more likely to be charged with a higher degree of the crime, and receive a stiffer prison sentence. 4) adj. chief, leading, highest. (See: **accessory, agency, agent,** *respondeat superior*)

principal place of business: n. location of head office of a business where the books and records are kept and/or management works. In most states corporations must report their principal place of business to the Secretary of State.

prior(s): n. slang for a criminal defendant's previous record of criminal charges, convictions, or other judicial disposal of criminal cases (such as probation, dismissal or acquittal). Only previous felony convictions can be introduced into evidence. However, the record of "priors" can have an impact on sentencing, as with prior drunk driving convictions requiring mandatory jail sentences, and "three strikes, you're out," providing for extended sentences for the third felony conviction. (See: **three strikes, you're out**)

priority: n. the right to be first or ahead of the rights or claims of others. In bankruptcy law, the right to collect before other creditors is given to taxing authorities, judgment holders, secured creditors, bankruptcy trustees and attorneys. The right also can apply to mortgages, deeds of trusts or liens given priority in the order they were recorded (in the "race to the courthouse").

prior restraint: n. an attempt to prevent publication or broadcast of any statement, which is an unconstitutional restraint on free speech and free press (even in the guise of an anti-nuisance ordinance). Stemming from the First Amendment to the Constitution, the ban on prior restraint allows publication of libel, slander, obvious untruths, anti-government diatribes, racial and religious epithets, and almost any material, except if public security or public safety is endangered (false claim of poison in the reservoir or exhortation to commit a crime like a lynching) and some forms of pornography. The theory, articulated by the U.S. Supreme Court in *Near v. Minnesota* (1931) is that free speech and free press protections have priority, and lawsuits for libel and slander and prosecutions for criminal advocacy will curb the effect of defamation and untruths. Most other nations per-

mit prior restraint by court order or police action when the material appears to be defamatory (hurtful lies), salacious (nasty), or "improper, mischievous, or illegal" (in the words of Sir William Blackstone).

privacy: n. the right to be free of unnecessary public scrutiny or to be let alone. Once a person is a "public figure" or involved in newsworthy events, the right to privacy may evaporate. (See: **public figure, right to privacy**)

private carrier: n. one who provides transportation or delivery of goods for money, just for the particular instance, and not as a regular business. It is distinguished from a "common carrier" which is in the business, such as buses, railroads, trucking companies, airlines and taxis. However, a private carrier may be liable for injuries to anyone who pays or shares the cost of transport. (See: **common carrier, guest statute**)

private nuisance: n. the interference with an individual's peaceful enjoyment of one's property, which can be the basis for a lawsuit both for damages caused by the nuisance and an order (injunction) against continuing the noxious (offensive) activity or condition. Examples: fumes from a factory above the legal limit, loud noises well above the norm, directing rain water onto another person's property, operating an auto repair business in a neighborhood zoned residential, or numerous barking dogs. (See: **nuisance, public nuisance**)

private parts: n. men's or women's genitalia, excluding a woman's breasts, usually referred to in prosecutions for "indecent exposure" or production and/or sale of pornography.

private property: n. land not owned by the government or dedicated to public use.

private road: n. a road or driveway on privately owned property, limited to the use of the owner or a group of owners who share the use and maintain the road without help from a government agency. A private road has not been given to a government entity (like a county or city) and accepted by that entity for public use. Some private roads are used by the public, but should be closed off at least once a year to prove that an easement of use is not allowed and to prevent a prescriptive easement (taken by continued use) from arising. (See: **prescriptive easement**)

privilege: n. a special benefit, exemption from a duty, or immunity from penalty, given to a particular person, a group or a class of people.

privilege against self incrimination: n. a right to refuse to testify against oneself in a criminal prosecution or in any legal proceeding which might be used against the person. This privilege is guaranteed by the Fifth Amendment to the Constitution, which provides: "No person…shall be compelled in any criminal case to be a witness against himself…." Therefore, refusing to answer questions during a trial ("I refuse to answer on the ground it may tend to incriminate me") is called "taking the Fifth."

(See: **Bill of Rights, taking the Fifth**)

privileged communication: n. statements and conversations made under circumstances of assured confidentiality which must not be disclosed in court. These include communications between husband and wife, attorney and client, physician or therapist and patient, and minister or priest with anyone seeing them in their religious status. In some states the privilege is extended to reporters and informants. Thus, such people cannot be forced to testify or reveal the conversations to law enforcement or courts, even under threat of contempt of court, and if one should break the confidentiality he/she can be sued by the person who had confidence in him/her. The reason for the privilege is to allow people to speak with candor to spouse or professional counsellor, even though it may hinder a criminal prosecution. The extreme case is when a priest hears an admission of murder or other serious crime in the confessional and can do nothing about it. The privilege may be lost if the one who made the admission waives the privilege, or, in the case of an attorney, if the client sues the attorney claiming negligence in conduct of the case. (See: **attorney–client privilege, confidential physician–patient privilege**)

privileges and immunities: n. the fundamental rights that people enjoy in free governments, protected by the U.S. Constitution in Article IV: "The citizens of each state shall be entitled to all privileges and immunities in the several States," and specifically to be protected against state action by the Constitution's 14th Amendment

(1868): "No State shall make or enforce any law which shall abridge the privileges or immunities of citizens of the United States." The definition of "privileges and immunities" was first spelled out by Supreme Court Justice Bushrod Washington in 1823: "protection by the government, with the right to acquire and possess property of every kind, and to pursue and obtain happiness and safety, subject, nevertheless, to such restraints as the government may prescribe for the general good of the whole." However, the exact nature of privileges and immunities which the state governments could limit has long been in dispute, with the U.S. Supreme Court gradually tipping toward protecting the individual rights of citizens against state statutes that might impinge on constitutional rights.

privity: n. contact, connection or mutual interest between parties. The term is particularly important in the law of contracts, which requires that there be "privity" if one party to a contract can enforce the contract by a lawsuit against the other party. Thus, a tenant of a buyer of real property cannot sue the former owner (seller) of the property for failure to make repairs guaranteed by the land sales contract between seller and buyer since the tenant was not "in privity" with the seller. (See: **contract**)

probable cause: n. sufficient reason based upon known facts to believe a crime has been committed or that certain property is connected with a crime. Probable cause must exist for a law enforcement officer to make an arrest without a warrant, search without a warrant, or seize property in the belief the items were evidence of a crime. While some cases are easy (pistols and illicit drugs in plain sight, gunshots, a suspect running from a liquor store with a clerk screaming "help"), actions "typical" of drug dealers, burglars, prostitutes, thieves, or people with guilt "written across their faces," are more difficult to categorize. "Probable cause" is often subjective, but if the police officer's belief or even hunch was correct, finding stolen goods, the hidden weapon or drugs may be claimed as self-fulfilling proof of probable cause. Technically, probable cause has to exist prior to arrest, search or seizure. (See: **Bill of Rights, search, search and seizure**)

probate: 1) n. the process of proving a will is valid and thereafter administering the estate of a dead person according to the terms of the will. The first step is to file the purported will with the clerk of the appropriate court in the county where the deceased person lived, along with a petition to have the court approve the will and appoint the executor named in the will (or if none is available, an administrator) with a declaration of a person who had signed the will as a witness. If the court determines the will is valid, the court then "admits" the will to probate. 2) n. a general term for the entire process of administration of estates of dead persons, including those without wills, with court supervision. The means of "avoiding" probate exist, including creating trusts in which all possessions are handled by a trustee, making lifetime gifts or putting all substantial property in joint tenancy with an automatic right of survivorship in the joint owner. Even if there is a will, probate may not be necessary if the estate is small with no real estate title to be transferred or all of the estate is either jointly owned or community property. Reasons for avoiding probate are the fees set by statute and/or the court (depending on state laws) for attorneys, executors and administrators, the need to publish notices, court hearings, paperwork, the public nature of the proceedings and delays while waiting for creditors to file claims even when the deceased owed no one. 3) v. to prove a will in court and proceed with administration of a deceased's estate under court supervision. 4) adj. reference to the appropriate court for handling estate matters, as in "probate court." (See: **administrator, executor, will**)

probation: n. a chance to remain free (or serve only a short time) given by a judge to a person convicted of a crime instead of being sent to jail or prison, provided the person can be good. Probation is only given under specific court-ordered terms, such as performing public service work, staying away from liquor, paying a fine, maintaining good behavior, getting mental therapy and reporting regularly to a probation officer. Violation of probation terms will usually result in the person being sent to jail for the normal term. Repeat criminals are normally not eligible for probation. Probation is not the same as "parole," which is freedom under certain restrictions given to convicts at the end of their imprisonment. (See: **attorney-**

client privilege, physician-patient privilege, confidential communication**)

probative: adj. in evidence law, tending to prove something. Thus, testimony which is not probative (does not prove anything) is immaterial and not admissible or will be stricken from the record if objected to by opposing counsel. (See: **probative facts, probative value**)

probative facts: n. evidence which tends to prove something which is relative to the issues in a lawsuit or criminal prosecution. (See: **probative, probative value**)

probative value: n. evidence which is sufficiently useful to prove something important in a trial. However, probative value of proposed evidence must be weighed by the trial judge against prejudicing in the minds of jurors toward the opposing party or criminal defendant. A typical dispute arises when the prosecutor wishes to introduce the previous conduct of a defendant (particularly a criminal conviction) to show a tendency toward committing the crime charged, balanced against the right of the accused to be tried on the facts in the particular case and not prejudice him/her in the minds of the jury based on prior actions. (See: **probative**)

pro bono: adj. short for *pro bono publico,* Latin for "for the public good," legal work performed by lawyers without pay to help people with legal problems and limited or no funds, or provide legal assistance to organizations involved in social causes such as environmental, consumer, minority, youth, battered women and education organizations and charities.

procedure: n. the methods and mechanics of the legal process. These include filing complaints, answers and demurrers; serving documents on the opposition; setting hearings, depositions, motions, petitions, interrogatories; preparing orders; giving notice to the other parties; conduct of trials; and all the rules and laws governing that process. Every state has a set of procedural statutes (often called the Codes of Civil Procedure and Criminal Procedure), and courts have so-called "local rules," which govern times for filing documents, conduct of the courts and other technicalities. Law practice before the federal courts operates under the Federal Rules of Civil Procedure and the Federal Rules of Criminal Procedure. Procedural law is distinguished from "substantive" law, which involves the statutes and legal precedents upon which cases are tried and judgments made.

proceeding: n. any legal filing, hearing, trial and/or judgment in the ongoing conduct of a lawsuit or criminal prosecution. Collectively they are called "proceedings," as in "legal proceedings."

process: n. in law, the legal means by which a person is required to appear in court or a defendant is given notice of a legal action against him/her/it. When a complaint in a lawsuit is filed, it must be served on each defendant, together with a summons issued by the clerk of the court stating the amount of time (say, 30 days) in which the defendant has to file an answer or other legal pleading with the clerk of the court, and sent to the plaintiff. New York has an unusual system in which a summons may be served without a complaint. A subpena is similar to a summons but is a notice to a witness to appear at a deposition (testimony taken outside court), or at a trial. A subpena *duces tecum* is an order to deliver documents or other evidence either into court or to the attorney for a party to a lawsuit or criminal prosecution. An order to show cause is a court order to appear in court and give a reason why the court should not issue an order (such as paying temporary child support). The summons, complaint, subpena, subpena *duces tecum* and order to show cause must all be "served" on the defendant or person required to appear or produce, and this is called "service of process." Service of process is usually made by an officer of the court such as a deputy sheriff or marshal, or a professional process server, but can be performed by others in most jurisdictions. (See: **order to show cause, process server, service of process, subpena, summons**)

process server: n. a person who serves (delivers) legal papers in lawsuits, either as a profession or as a government official, such as a deputy sheriff, marshal or constable. (See: **service of process**)

proctor: n. 1) in admiralty (maritime) law, an attorney. 2) person who keeps order.

product liability: n. the responsibility of manufacturers, distributors and sellers of products to the public, to deliver products free of defects which harm an individual or numerous persons and to make good on that responsibility if their products are defective. These can include faulty auto brakes, contaminated baby food, exploding bottles of beer, flammable children's pajamas or lack of label warnings. Examples: Beauty Queen Hair Products makes a hair-permanent kit in which the formula will cause loss of hair to women with sensitive scalps, and Molly Makeup has her hair done at the Bon Ton Beauty Shop and suffers scalp burns and loss of hair. Molly has a claim for damages against Beauty Queen, the manufacturer. Big Boy Trucks makes a truck with a faulty steering gear, bought by Tom Holdtight. The gear fails and Holdtight runs off the road and breaks his back. Holdtight can sue Big Boy for the damages. The key element in product liability law is that a person who suffers harm need prove only the failure of the product to make the seller, distributor and/or manufacturer reliable for damages. An injured person usually need only sue the seller and let him/her/it bring the manufacturer or distributor into the lawsuit or require contribution toward a judgment. However, all those possibly responsible should be named in the suit as defendants if they are known. (See: **warrant, warranty**)

professional corporation: n. a corporation formed for the purpose of conducting a profession which requires a license to practice, including attorneys, physicians, dentists, certified public accountants, architects and real estate brokers. Most states provide for such corporations under special statutes which allow the corporation to operate with a single director, who is a professional. However, unlike other corporations, the organization does not provide a shield for liability for any professional negligence (malpractice) by the licensed professionals. (See: **corporation**)

professional negligence: n. (See: **malpractice**)

proffer: v. to offer evidence in a trial.

pro forma: 1) prep. Latin for "as a matter of form," the phrase refers to court rulings merely intended to facilitate the legal process (to move matters along). 2) n. an accountant's proposed financial statement for a business based on the assumption that certain events occurred, such as a 20% increase in annual sales or 6% inflation.

pro hac vice: (proh hock vee-chay) prep. Latin for "this time only," the phrase refers to the application of an out-of-state lawyer to appear in court for a particular trial, even though he/she is not licensed to practice in the state where the trial is being held. The application is usually granted, but sometimes the court requires association with a local attorney.

prohibition: n. forbidding an act or activity. A court order forbidding an act is a writ of prohibition, an injunction or a writ of mandate (mandamus) if against a public official. (See: **injunction, mandate**)

promise: 1) n. a firm agreement to

perform an act, refrain from acting or make a payment or delivery. In contract law, if the parties exchange promises, each promise is "consideration" (a valuable item) for the other promise. Failure to fulfill a promise in a contract is a breach of the contract, for which the other party may sue for performance and/or damages. 2) v. to make a firm agreement to act, refrain from acting or make a payment or delivery. (See: **consideration, contract, covenant**)

promissory estoppel: n. a false statement treated as a promise by a court when the listener had relied on what was told to him/her to his/her disadvantage. In order to see that justice is done a judge will preclude the maker of the statement from denying it. Thus, the legal inability of the person who made the false statement to deny it makes it an enforceable promise called "promissory estoppel," or an "equitable estoppel." Example: Bernie Blowhard tells Arthur Artist that Blowhard has a contract to make a movie and wants Artist to paint the background scenery in return for a percentage of the profits. Artist paints, and Blowhard then admits he needed the scenery to try to get a movie deal which fell through and there are no profits to share. Artist sues and the judge finds that Blowhard cannot deny a contract with Artist and gives Artist judgment for the value of his work. (See: **estoppel**)

promissory note: n. a written promise by a person (variously called maker, obligor, payor, promisor) to pay a specific amount of money (called "principal") to another (payee, obligee, promisee), usually to include a specified amount of interest on the unpaid principal amount (what he/she owes). The specified time of payment may be written as: a) whenever there is a demand, b) on a specific date, c) in installments with or without the interest included in each installment, d) installments with a final larger amount (balloon payment). A promissory note may contain other terms such as the right of the promisee to order payment be made to another person, penalties for late payments, a provision for attorney's fees and costs if there is a legal action to collect, the right to collect payment in full if the note is secured by real property and the property is sold ("due on sale" clause), and whether the note is secured by a mortgage or deed of trust or a financing statement (a filed security agreement for personal collateral called UCC-1). The promissory note is usually held by the party to whom the money is owed. There are legal limitations to the amount of interest which may be charged. Charging a rate in excess of the legal limit is called "usury," and this excess is legally uncollectible. When the amount due on the note, including interest and penalties (if any), is paid, the note must be cancelled and surrendered to the person(s) who signed it. A promissory note need only be signed and does not require an acknowledgement before a notary public to be valid. (See: **interest, obligee, obligor, usury**)

promoter: n. a person who puts together a business, particularly a corporation, including the financing. Usually the promoter is the principal shareholder or one of the management team and has a contract with the incorporators or makes a claim for shares of stock for his/her efforts in organization. Most states limit the amount of "promotional stock" since it is supported only by effort and not by assets or cash. (See: **promotional stock**)

promotional stock: n. stock issued in a newly formed corporation and given to a promoter (organizer) of the corporation in payment for his/her efforts in putting the company together and locating shareholders or other funding. Most states (and the federal Securities and Exchange Act) limit promotional stock to an amount reasonable for the effort since it is not backed by assets or money. (See: **promoter**)

proof: n. confirmation of a fact by evidence. In a trial, proof is what the trier of the fact (jury or judge without a jury) needs to become satisfied that there is "a preponderance of the evidence" in civil (non-criminal) cases and the defendant is guilty "beyond a reasonable doubt" in criminal prosecutions. However, each alleged fact must be proved separately, as must all the facts necessary to reach a judgment for the plaintiff (the person filing a lawsuit) or for the prosecution (the "people" or "state" represented by the prosecutor). The defendants in both civil suits and criminal trials need not provide absolute "proof" of non-responsibility in a civil case or innocence (in a criminal case), since the burden is on the plaintiff or prosecution to prove their cases (or prove the person guilty). (See: **beyond a reasonable doubt, preponderance of the evidence**)

pro per: adj. short for "*propria persona,*" which is Latin for "for oneself," usually applied to a person who represents himself/herself in a lawsuit rather than have an attorney. (See: *in pro per, in propria persona, propria persona*)

proper party: n. a person or entity who has an interest (financial or protection of some legal rights) in the subject matter of a lawsuit and, therefore, can join in the lawsuit as he/she/it wishes, or may be brought into the suit (as an unnecessary party) by one of the parties to the legal action. However, the judgment may leave some matters undecided. A proper party is distinguished from a "necessary party," which the court will order joined in (brought into) the suit if any judgment is to be reached. Example: Marianne Steel and Isaac Iron both own lots with vacation cabins up the hill from Allen Albright's ranch, and for years both Steel and Iron have driven up an old road across Albright's property to reach their cabins. Steel brings a quiet title action against Albright to establish a "prescriptive easement" over the roadway, but Iron does not. The court rules in favor of Steel, but says nothing about Iron. In this case Iron is a "proper party," but did not choose to participate, and it was not necessary for Steel to obtain a judgment for herself. (See: **necessary party, party**)

property: n. anything that is owned by a person or entity. Property is divided into two types: "real property," which is any interest in land, real estate, growing plants or the improvements on it, and "personal property" (sometimes called "personalty"), which is everything else. "Common property" is ownership by more than one person of the same possession. "Community property" is a form of joint ownership between husband and wife recognized in several states. "Separate property" is property owned by one spouse only in a community property state, or a married woman's sole ownership in some states. "Public property" refers to ownership by a governmental body such as the federal, state, county or city governments or their agencies (e.g. school or redevelopment districts). The government and the courts are obligated to protect property rights and to help clarify ownership. (See: **common property, community property, personal property, personalty, public property, real property, separate property**)

property damage: n. injury to real or personal property through another's negligence, willful destruction or by some act of nature. In lawsuits for damages caused by negligence or a willful act, property damage is distinguished from personal injury. Property damage may include harm to an automobile, a fence, a tree, a home or any other possession. The amount of recovery for property damage may be established by evidence of replacement value, cost of repairs, loss of use until repaired or replaced or, in the case of heirlooms or very personal items (e.g. wedding pictures), by subjective testimony as to sentimental value. (See: **damages, property**)

property tax: n. an annual governmental tax on real property or personal property based on a tax rate (so many dollars or cents per $100 value of the property). The value is usually established by an Assessor, a county official. In California the assessed value of real property is based on the amount of the last sale of the property, and the tax is limited to 1% of that figure (with a few minor exceptions) under the so-called "Proposition 13" state constitutional provision. In addition, there are special assessments for particular public property improvements such as sidewalks, tree planting, or storm drains which are charged to each property owner on the street in which the improvements are made. (See: **ad valorem, tax**)

propria persona: adj. from Latin, for oneself. (See: *in pro per, in propria persona, pro per*)

proprietary: adj. referring to ownership.

proprietary interest: n. a total or partial ownership.

proprietary rights: n. those rights which go with ownership of real property or a business.

proprietor: n. the owner of anything, but particularly the owner of a business operated by that individual.

pro rata: (proh rat-ah or proh ray-tah) adj. from Latin for "in proportion," referring to a share to be received or an amount to be paid based on the fractional share of ownership, responsibility or time used. Examples: an heir who receives one-quarter of an estate may be responsible for one-quarter of the estate taxes as his/her *pro rata* share. A buyer of a rental property will pay his/her *pro rata* share of the property taxes for that portion of the year in which he/she holds title.

pro se: (proh say) prep. Latin for "for himself." A party to a lawsuit who represents himself (acting *in propria persona*) is appearing in the case "*pro se.*" (See: ***in propria persona***)

prosecute: v. 1) in criminal law, to charge a person with a crime and thereafter pursue the case through trial on behalf of the government. This is normally the function of the District Attorney (called States Attorney or city prosecutor in some places) and the U.S. Attorney in federal criminal cases. A state Attorney General may prosecute in crimes of statewide importance, and the U.S. Attorney General, through the Solicitor General, may prosecute for crimes involving matters of national significance. 2) to conduct any legal action by a lawyer on behalf of a client, including both civil and criminal cases, but most commonly referring to prosecution for crimes. (See: **Attorney General, District Attorney, prosecution, prosecutor**)

prosecution: n. 1) in criminal law, the government attorney charging and trying the case against a person accused of a crime. 2) a common term for the government's side in a criminal case, as in "the prosecution will present five witnesses" or "the prosecution rests" (has completed its case). (See: **prosecute, prosecutor**)

prosecutor: n. generic term for the government's attorney in a criminal case, including District Attorney, States Attorney, U.S. Attorney, Attorney General, Solicitor General, or special prosecutor. A special prosecutor may be assigned to investigate as well as prosecute if necessary when a government official is involved directly or indirectly in the possible criminal activity. (See: **Attorney General, District Attorney, prosecute**)

prospectus: n. a detailed statement by a corporation required when there is an issuance of stock to the general public. A prospectus includes the financial status, the officers, the plans, contingent obligations (such as lawsuits) of the corporation, recent performance and other matters which would assist the potential investor or investment adviser to evaluate the stock and the prospects of the company for profit, loss or growth. The Federal Securities Act requires the filing of the prospectus with the Securities and Exchange Commission and the SEC's approval before any major stock issue. State laws generally require similar documentation for some issuances or offers of sales of stock within the state. Every potential purchaser of shares of a new stock shares must receive a copy of the prospectus, even though they are difficult to understand. Offerings to the public of limited partnership interests may require that a prospectus be prepared and delivered to each investor. (See: **blue sky laws, corporation, limited partnership, stock**)

prostitute: n. a person who receives payment for sexual intercourse or other sexual acts, generally as a regular occupation. Although usually a prostitute refers to a woman offering sexual favors to men, male prostitutes may perform homosexual acts for money or receive payment from women for sexual services. A woman prostitute who is sent on a "date" to the hotel room or residence of a male customer is commonly referred to as a "call girl." (See: **pander, panderer, prostitution**)

prostitution: n. the profession of performing sexual acts for money. Prostitution is a crime throughout the United States, except for a few counties in the state of Nevada, where it is allowed in licensed houses of prostitution. Soliciting acts of prostitution is also a crime, called pandering or simply, soliciting. Pandering on behalf of a prostitute is called pimping. (See: **pander, panderer, pimp, prostitute**)

The law embodies the story of a nation's development through many centuries, and it cannot be dealt with as if it contained only the axioms and corollaries of a book of numbers.
—Justice Oliver Wendell Holmes, Jr.

pro tanto: (proh tahn-toe) Latin for "only to that extent." Example: a judge gives an order for payments for one year, *pro tanto*.

protective custody: n. the act of law enforcement officials in placing a person in a government facility or foster home in order to protect him/her from a dangerous person or situation. Most commonly a child who has been neglected or battered or is in danger from a violent person is taken in as a temporary ward of the state and held in probation facilities or placed in a foster home until a court can decide the future placement of the child. Protective custody is sometimes used to help women threatened by a husband, boyfriend or a stalker, and also for witnesses who have been threatened with physical harm or death if they testify.

pro tem: 1) adj. short for the Latin *pro tempore*, temporarily or for the time being. In law, judge *pro tem* normally refers to a judge who is sitting temporarily for another judge or to an attorney who has been appointed to serve as a judge as a substitute for a regular judge. When an appeals justice is not available or there is a vacancy, a lower court judge is appointed Justice *Pro Tem* until a new Justice is appointed. Small claims cases are often heard by an attorney serving as Judge *Pro Tem*. 2) n. short for a temporary judge as "Sam Collins is *Pro Tem* today."

pro tempore: (proh temp-oh-ray): (See: *pro tem*)

protest: 1) v. to complain in some public way about any act already done or about to be done, such as adoption of a regulation by a county board, sending troops overseas, or use of the death penalty. 2) v. to dispute the amount of property taxes, the assessed evaluation of property for tax purposes or an import duty. 3) n. a written demand for payment of the amount owed on a promissory note which has not been paid when due or a check which has been dishonored (not paid by the bank).

prove: v. to present evidence and/or logic that makes a fact seem certain. A party must do this to convince a trier of fact (jury or judge sitting without a jury) as to facts claimed and to win a lawsuit or criminal case. (See: **proof**)

provisional remedy: n. a generic term for any temporary order of a court to protect a party from irreparable damage while a lawsuit or petition is pending. (See: **temporary injunction, temporary**)

proviso: n. a term or condition in a contract or title document.

proximate cause: n. a happening which results in an event, particularly injury due to negligence or an intentional wrongful act. In order to prevail (win) in a lawsuit for damages due to negligence or some other wrong, it is essential to claim (plead) proximate cause in the complaint and to prove in trial that the negligent act of the defendant was the proximate cause (and not some other reason) of the damages to the plaintiff (person filing the lawsuit). Sometimes there is an intervening cause which comes between the original negligence of the defendant and the injured plaintiff, which will either reduce the amount of responsibility or, if this intervening cause is the substantial reason for the injury, then the defendant will not be liable at all. In criminal law, the defendant's act must have been the proximate cause of the death of a victim to prove murder or manslaughter. (See: **intervening cause, negligence**)

proxy: n. 1) someone who is authorized to serve in one's place at a meeting, particularly with the right to cast votes. 2) the written authority given to someone to act or vote in someone's place. A proxy is commonly given to cast a stockholder's votes at a meeting of shareholders, and by board members and convention delegates.

prudent man rule: n. the requirement that a trustee, investment manager of pension funds, treasurer of a city or county, or any fiduciary (a trusted agent) must only invest funds entrusted to him/her as would a person of prudence, i.e. with discretion, care and intelligence. Thus solid "blue chip" securities, secured loans, federally guaranteed mortgages, treasury certificates and other conservative investments providing a reasonable return are within the prudent man rule. Some states have statutes which list the types of investments allowable under the rule. Unfortunately, the rule is subjective, and some financial managers have put funds into speculative investments to achieve higher rates of return, which has resulted in bankruptcy and disaster, as in the case of Orange County, California (1994). (See: **fiduciary, trustee**)

public: 1) n. the people of the nation, state, county, district or municipality which the government serves. 2) adj. referring to any agency, interest, property, or activity which is under the authority of the government or which belongs to the people. This distinguishes public from private interests as with public and private schools, public and private utilities, public and private hospitals, public and private lands and public and private roads.

public administrator: n. a county official with the responsibility to handle the affairs of someone who has died with no known or available relative, executor or friend. At times the public administrator may be instructed by a court to assume similar duties for a living person when no conservator or guardian is available. (See: **probate, administrative**)

publication: n. 1) anything made public by print (as in a newspaper, magazine, pamphlet, letter, telegram, computer modem or program, poster, brochure or pamphlet), orally, or by broadcast (radio, television). 2) placing a legal notice in an approved newspaper of general publication in the county or district in which the law requires such notice to be published. 3) in the law of defamation (libel and slander) publication of an untruth about another to at least one single person. Thus one letter can be the basis of a suit for libel, and telling one person is sufficient to show publication of slander. (See: **defamation, libel, notice, slander**)

public benefit corporation: n. a term used in some states for a nonprofit community service corporation. Typical examples are clubs like Kiwanis, Rotary, soroptimists and Lions. (See: **corporation, nonprofit corporation**)

public charge: n. a general term for an indigent, sick or severely handicapped person who must be taken care of at public expense.

public corporation: n. a corpora-

tion created to perform a governmental function or to operate under government control, such as a municipal water company or hospital. (See: **corporation**)

public defender: n. an elected or appointed public official (usually of a county), who is an attorney regularly assigned by the courts to defend people accused of crimes who cannot afford a private attorney. In larger counties the public defender has a large case load, numerous deputy public defenders and office staff. In each federal judicial district there is also a federal public defender, and some states have a state public defender to supervise the provision of attorneys to convicted indigents for appeals.

public domain: n. 1) in copyright law, the right of anyone to use literature, music or other previously copyrighted materials after the copyright period has expired. Although the copyright laws have been changed several times, a rule of thumb would be that the last possible date for copyright protection would be 50 years after the death of the author. Thus, the works of William Shakespeare, Mark Twain, Jack London and other classic writers are in the public domain and may be published by anyone without payment of a royalty. 2) all lands and waters owned by federal, state and local governments. (See: **copyright**)

public easement: n. the right of the general public to use certain streets, highways, paths or airspace. In most cases the easement came about through reservation of the right when land was deeded to individuals or by dedication of the land to the government. In some cases public easements come by prescription (use for many years) such as a pathway across private property down to the ocean. Beach access has been the source of controversy between government and private owners in many seaboard states. (See: **easement, prescriptive easement**)

public figure: n. in the law of defamation (libel and slander), a personage of great public interest or familiarity like a government official, politician, celebrity, business leader, movie star or sports hero. Incorrect harmful statements published about a public figure cannot be the basis of a lawsuit for defamation unless there is proof that the writer or publisher intentionally defamed the person with malice (hate). (See: **defamation, libel, slander**)

public nuisance: n. a nuisance which affects numerous members of the public or the public at large (how many people it takes to make a public is unknown), as distinguished from a nuisance which only does harm to a neighbor or a few private individuals. Example: a factory which spews out clouds of noxious fumes is a public nuisance but playing drums at three in the morning is a private nuisance bothering only the neighbors. (See: **nuisance**)

public property: n. property owned by the government or one of its agencies, divisions, or entities. Commonly a reference to parks, playgrounds, streets, sidewalks, schools, libraries and other property regularly used by the general public. (See: **common property**)

public record: n. any information, minutes, files, accounts or other records which a governmental body is required to maintain and which must be accessible to scrutiny by the public. This includes the files of most legal actions. A court will take "judicial notice" of a public record (including hearsay in the record) introduced as evidence. For example: a recorded deed to show transfer of title or a criminal judgment are both public records.

public trust doctrine: n. the principle that the government holds title to submerged land under navigable waters in trust for the benefit of the public. Thus, any use or sale of the land under water must be in the public interest. Nevertheless, there has been a great deal of use for offshore oil drilling, for landfill, and marine shoreline development, in which protection of the public interest has been dubious at best.

public use: n. the only purpose for which private property can be taken (condemned) by the government under its power of eminent domain. Public use includes: schools, streets, highways, hospitals, government buildings, parks, water reservoirs, flood control, slum clearance and redevelopment, public housing, public theaters and stadiums, safety facilities, harbors, bridges, railroads, airports, terminals, prisons, jails, public utilities, canals, and numerous other purposes designated as beneficial to the public. (See: **condemnation, eminent domain**)

public utility: n. any organization which provides services to the general public, although it may be privately owned. Public utilities include electric, gas, telephone, water and television cable systems, as well as streetcar and bus lines. They are allowed certain monopoly rights due to the practical need to service entire geographic areas with one system, but they are regulated by state, county and/or city public utility commissions under state laws. (See: **monopoly**)

publish: v. to make public to at least one other person by any means. (See: **publication**)

puffing: n. the exaggeration of the good points of a product, a business, real property and the prospects for future rise in value, profits and growth. Since a certain amount of "puffing" can be expected of any salesman, it cannot be the basis of a lawsuit for fraud or breach of contract unless the exaggeration exceeds the reality. However, if the puffery includes outright lies or has no basis in fact ("Sears Roebuck is building next door to your store site") a legal action for rescission of the contract or for fraud against the seller is possible. (See: **fraud**)

punitive damages: n. (synonymous with exemplary damages), damages awarded in a lawsuit as a punishment and example to others for malicious, evil or particularly fraudulent acts. (See: **exemplary damages**)

putative: adj. commonly believed, supposed or claimed. Thus a putative father is one believed to be the father unless proved otherwise, a putative marriage is one that is ac-

cepted as legal when in reality it was not lawful (e.g. due to failure to complete a prior divorce). A putative will is one that appears to be the final will but a later will is found that revokes it and shows that the putative will was not the last will of the deceased.

quantum meruit: (kwahn-tuhm mare-ooh-it) n. Latin for "as much as he deserved," the actual value of services performed. *Quantum meruit* determines the amount to be paid for services when no contract exists or when there is doubt as to the amount due for the work performed but done under circumstances when payment could be expected. This may include a physician's emergency aid, legal work when there was no contract, or evaluating the amount due when outside forces cause a job to be terminated unexpectedly. If a person sues for payment for services in such circumstances the judge or jury will calculate the amount due based on time and usual rate of pay or the customary charge, based on *quantum meruit* by implying a contract existed.

quash: v. to annul or set aside. In law, a motion to quash asks the judge for an order setting aside or nullifying an action, such as "quashing" service of a summons when the wrong person was served.

quasi: (kway-zeye, kwah-zee) adj., adv. from Latin for "as if," almost, somewhat, to a degree (always used in combination with another word). Quasi refers to things and actions which are not exactly or fully what they might appear, but have to be treated "as if" they were.

quasi community property: n. in community property states,

property acquired by a couple who have not been married, but have lived and purchased the property as if they were married. Often this includes property purchased or received by a couple shortly before marriage. (See: **community property, palimony, quasi**)

quasi contract: n. a situation in which there is an obligation as if there was a contract, although the technical requirements of a contract have not been fulfilled. (See: **contract, quasi**)

quasi corporation: n. a business which has operated as a corporation without completing the legal requirements, often in the period just before formal incorporation. (See: **corporation, quasi, de facto corporation**)

quasi-criminal: adj. a reference to a court's right to punish for actions or omissions as if they were criminal. The most common example is finding a parent who is delinquent in child support in contempt of court and penalizing him/her with a jail sentence. If a hearing is quasi-criminal the quasi-defendant is entitled to all due process protections afforded a criminal defendant. (See: **criminal, quasi**)

quasi *in rem*: adj. referring to a legal action which is primarily based on property rights, but includes personal rights as well. (See: ***in rem, in personam,* quasi**)

quasi-judicial: adj., adv. referring to the actions of an agency, boards or other government entity in which there are hearings, orders, judgments or other activities similar to those conducted by courts. Example: a public utilities hearing on setting telephone company rates is quasi-judicial. (See: **judicial, quasi**)

> *Judicial decrees may not change the heart, but they can restrain the heartless.*
> *—Martin Luther King, Jr.*

Queen's Bench: n. 1) the highest court in Great Britain during the reign of a Queen, so that opinions are identified as a volume of Queen's Bench (QB). 2) in the United States, organizations of women lawyers, dating from when women were a small minority of practicing attorneys and needed to encourage each other, urge employment of women attorneys, protect against discrimination and promote the cause of equality for women lawyers. Recent bar admissions now include close to 50 percent women.

query: n. common lawyer lingo for a question to be answered.

question of fact: n. in a lawsuit or criminal prosecution, an issue of fact in which the truth or falsity (or a mix of the two) must be determined by the "trier of fact" (the jury or the judge in a non-jury trial) in order to reach a decision in the case. A "question of fact" may also be raised in a motion for summary judgment which asks the court to determine whether there are any questions of fact to be tried, allowing the judge to rule on the case (usually to dismiss the complaint) at that point without a trial. "Questions of fact" are distinguished from "questions of law," which can only be decided by the judge. (See: **finding, judge, motion for summary judgment, question of law**)

question of law: n. an issue arising in a lawsuit or criminal prosecution which only relates to determination of what the law is, how it is applied to the facts in the case, and other purely legal points in contention. All "questions of law" arising before, during and sometimes after a trial are to be determined solely by the judge and not by the jury. "Questions of law" are differentiated from "questions of fact," which are decided by the jury and only by the judge if there is no jury. (See: **judge, question of fact, trier of fact**)

quid pro quo: (kwid proh kwoh) n. Latin for "something for something," to identify what each party to an agreement expects from the other, sometimes called mutual consideration. Example of its use: "What is the *quid pro quo* for my entering into this deal?" (See: **consideration**)

quiet enjoyment: n. the right to enjoy and use premises (particularly a residence) in peace and without interference. Quiet enjoyment is often a condition included in a lease. Thus, if the landlord interferes with quiet enjoyment, he/she may be sued for breach of contract. Disturbance of quiet enjoyment by another can be a "nuisance" for which a lawsuit may be brought to halt the interference or obtain damages for it. (See: **nuisance**)

quiet title action: n. a lawsuit to

establish a party's title to real property against anyone and everyone, and thus "quiet" any challenges or claims to the title. Such a suit usually arises when there is some question about clear title, there exists some recorded problem (such as an old lease or failure to clear title after payment of a mortgage), an error in description which casts doubt on the amount of property owned, or an easement used for years without a recorded description. An action for quiet title requires description of the property to be "quieted," naming as defendants anyone who might have an interest (including descendants—known or unknown—of prior owners), and the factual and legal basis for the claim of title. Notice must be given to all potentially interested parties, including known and unknown, by publication. If the court is convinced title is in the plaintiff (the plaintiff owns the title), a quiet title judgment will be granted which can be recorded and thus provide legal "good title." Quiet title actions are a common example of "friendly" lawsuits in which often there is no opposition. (See: **cloud on title, notice, title**)

quit: v. to leave, used in a written notice to a tenant to leave the premises (notice to quit). (See: **notice to quit, unlawful detainer**)

qui tam action: (kwee tam) n. from Latin for "who as well," a lawsuit brought by a private citizen (popularly called a "whistle blower") against a person or company who is believed to have violated the law in the performance of a contract with the government or in violation of a government regulation, when there is a statute which provides for a penalty for such violations. *Qui tam* suits are brought for "the government *as well as* the plaintiff." In a *qui tam* action the plaintiff (the person bringing the suit) will be entitled to a percentage of the recovery of the penalty (which may include large amounts for breach of contract) as a reward for exposing the wrongdoing and recovering funds for the government. Sometimes the federal or state government will intervene and become a party to the suit in order to guarantee success and be part of any negotiations and conduct of the case. This type of action is generally based on significant violations which involve fraudulent or criminal acts, and not technical violations and/or errors.

quitclaim deed: n. a real property deed which transfers (conveys) only that interest in the property in which the grantor has title. Commonly used in transfers of title or interests in title, quitclaims are often made to family members, divorcing spouses, or in other transactions between people well-known to each other. Quitclaim deeds are also used to clear up questions of full title when a person has a possible but unknown interest in the property. Grant deeds and warranty deeds guarantee (warrant) that the grantor has full title to the property or the interest the deed states is being conveyed, but quitclaim deeds do not warrant good title. (See: **convey, deed, grant deed, title**)

quorum: n. the number of people

required to be present before a meeting can conduct business. Unless stated differently in bylaws, articles, regulations or other rules established by the organization, a quorum is usually a majority of members. A quorum for meetings of corporate boards of directors, homeowners' associations, clubs and shareholders meetings are usually set in the bylaws. The quorum for meetings of governmental bodies such as commissions and boards are usually set by statute. (See: **bylaws**)

> *Government can exist without law, but law cannot exist without government.*
> *—John Locke*

quotient verdict: n. an award of money damages set by a jury in a lawsuit in which each juror states in writing his/her opinion of what the amount should be. Then the amounts are totalled and divided by the number of jurors to reach a figure for the award. A quotient verdict is illegal and improper since it is based on guesses and not a rational discussion of the facts. Such a judgment will be set aside on a motion for a new trial and a mistrial will be declared by the judge. (See: **award, damages, mistrial, motion for a new trial, verdict**)

quo warranto: (kwoh wahr-rahn-toe) n. the name for a writ (order) used to challenge another's right to either public or corporate office or challenge the legality of a corporation to its charter (articles). (See: **corporation, writ**)

race to the courthouse: n. slang for the rule that the first deed, deed of trust, mortgage, lien or judgment which is recorded with the County Recorder will have priority and prevail over later recordings no matter when the documents were dated. (See: **deed, judgment, lien, mortgage, recording**)

Racketeer Influenced Corrupt Organization (RICO) statute: n. a federal law which makes it a crime for organized criminal conspiracies to operate legitimate businesses.

racketeering: n. the federal crime of conspiring to organize to commit crimes, particularly as a regular business ("organized crime" or "the Mafia").

ransom: 1) n. money paid to a kidnapper in demand for the release of the person abducted. Ransom money can also be paid to return a valuable object such as a stolen painting. 2) v. to pay money to an abductor to return the person held captive. (See: **abduction, kidnapping**)

rape: 1) n. the crime of sexual intercourse (with actual penetration of a woman's vagina with the man's penis) without consent and accomplished through force, threat of violence or intimidation (such as a threat to harm a woman's child, husband or boyfriend). What constitutes lack of consent usually includes saying "no" or being too drunk or drug-influenced for the woman to be able to either resist or consent, but a recent Pennsylvania case ruled that a woman must do more than say "no" on the bizarre theory that "no" does not always mean "don't," but a flirtatious come-on. "Date rape" involves rape by an acquaintance who refuses to stop when told to. Defense attorneys often argue that there had to be physical resistance, but the modern view is that fear of harm and the relative strengths of the man and the woman are obvious deterrents to a woman fighting back. Any sexual intercourse with a child is rape and in most states sexual relations even with consent involving a girl 14 to 18 (with some variation on ages in a few states) is "statutory rape," on the basis that the female is unable to give consent. 2) v. to have sexual intercourse with a female without her consent through force, violence, threat or intimidation, or with a girl under age. Technically, a woman can be charged with rape by assisting a man in the rape of another woman. Dissatisfied with the typical prosecution of rape cases (in which the defense humiliates the accuser, and prosecutors are unable or unwilling to protect the woman from such tactics), women have been suing for civil damages for the physical and emotional damage caused by the rape, although too often the perpetrator has no funds. Protection services for rape victims have been developed by both public and private agencies. On the other side of the coin, there is the concern of law enforcement and prosecutors that women whose advances have been rejected by a man, or who have been caught in the act of consensual sexual intercourse may falsely cry "rape." (See: **date rape, statutory rape**)

ratable: adj. taxable according to value, such as an estate or property.

ratification: n. confirmation of an action which was not pre-approved and may not have been authorized, usually by a principal (employer) who adopts the acts of his/her agent (employee). (See: **agent, principal**)

ratify: v. to confirm and adopt the act of another even though it was not approved beforehand. Example: An employee for Holsinger's Hardware orders carpentry equipment from Phillips Screws and Nails although the employee was not authorized to buy anything. The president of Holsinger's ratifies the deal when Phillips delivers the order. A person under the legal age who makes a contract may ratify the contract when he/she reaches majority (usually 18) or may refuse to honor it without obligation. (See: **agent, principal**)

rational basis: n. a test of constitutionality of a statute, asking whether the law has a reasonable connection to achieving a legitimate and constitutional objective.

ready, willing and able: adj. fully prepared to act, as in performing a contract.

real estate: n. land, improvements and buildings thereon, including attached items and growing things. It is virtually the same as "real property," except real property includes

interests which are not physical such as a right to acquire the property in the future. (See: **real property**)

real estate investment trust: n. nicknamed REIT, a real estate investment organization which finds investors and buys real property and gives each investor either a percentage interest in the property itself or an interest in a loan secured by a mortgage or deed of trust on the property. Usually the loan is used to develop the property and build upon it, and then there is a division of profits upon sale—if there is a profit.

real party in interest: n. the person or entity who will benefit from a lawsuit or petition even though the plaintiff (the person filing the suit) is someone else, often called a "nominal" plaintiff. Example: a trustee files a suit against a person who damaged a building owned by the trust; the real party in the interest is the beneficiary of the trust.

real property: n. 1) all land, structures, firmly attached and integrated equipment (such as light fixtures or a well pump), anything growing on the land, and all "interests" in the property, which may include the right to future ownership (remainder), right to occupy for a period of time (tenancy or life estate), the right to drill for oil, the right to get the property back (a reversion) if it is no longer used for its current purpose (such as use for a hospital, school or city hall), use of airspace (condominium) or an easement across another's property. Real property should be thought of as a group of rights like a bundle of sticks which can be divided. It is distinguished from personal property which is made up of movable items. 2) one of the principal areas of law like contracts, negligence, probate, family law and criminal law. (See: **condominium, easement, life estate, personal property, real estate, reversion**)

realty: n. a short form of "real estate." (See: **real estate**)

reasonable: adj., adv. in law, just, rational, appropriate, ordinary or usual in the circumstances. It may refer to care, cause, compensation, doubt (in a criminal trial), and a host of other actions or activities.

reasonable care: n. the degree of caution and concern for the safety of himself/herself and others an ordinarily prudent and rational person would use in the circumstances. This is a subjective test of determining if a person is negligent, meaning he/she did not exercise reasonable care. (See: **duty of care, negligence**)

reasonable doubt: n. not being sure of a criminal defendant's guilt to a moral certainty. Thus, a juror (or judge sitting without a jury) must be convinced of guilt of a crime (or the degree of crime, as murder instead of manslaughter) "beyond a reasonable doubt," and the jury will be told so by the judge in the jury instructions. However, it is a subjective test since each juror will have to decide if his/her doubt is reasonable. It is more difficult to convict under that test, than "preponderance of the evidence" to decide for the plaintiff (party bringing the suit) in a civil (non-criminal) trial. (See: **preponderance of the evidence**)

reasonable reliance: n. particularly in contracts, what a prudent person would believe and act upon if told something by another. Typically, a person is promised a profit or other benefit, and in reliance takes steps in reliance on the promise, only to find the statements or promises were not true or were exaggerated. The one who relied can recover damages for the costs of his/her actions or demand performance if the reliance was "reasonable." If the promisor says he "owned the Brooklyn Bridge," reliance on that statement is not reasonable. In a complaint the language would read something like: "in reasonable reliance on defendant's statement (or promise), plaintiff did the following...." (See: **contract**)

reasonable speed: n. the speed of an automobile determined to be lower than the posted speed limit due to the circumstances, such as rain, icy road, heavy traffic, poor condition of the vehicle or gloom of night. Exceeding reasonable speed under the circumstances can result in being cited for speeding. In the law of negligence, exceeding reasonable speed in the prevailing conditions may be found to be negligent even though below the speed limit. (See: **negligence**)

reasonable time: n. in contracts, common custom in the business or under the circumstances will define "reasonable time" to perform or pay. It is bad practice to draft a contract using such a vague term.

reasonable wear and tear: n. commonly used in leases to limit the tenant's responsibility (and therefore liability to repair or repaint) upon leaving. It is subjective, but the considerations include the length of time of tenancy (the longer the occupancy the more wear and tear can be expected), the lack of unusual damage such as a hole in the wall or a broken window, and the condition of the premises when the tenant moved in. This is often a source of conflict between landlord and tenant, particularly when there is a deposit for any damages "beyond reasonable wear and tear." (See: **lease**)

> *Where-ever law ends, tyranny begins.*
> —*John Locke*

rebate: 1) n. a discount or deduction on sales price. A secret rebate given by a subcontractor to a contractor in return for getting the job is illegal, since it cheats the person hiring the contractor. 2) v. to give a discount or deduction.

rebuttable presumption: n. since a presumption is an assumption of fact accepted by the court until disproved, all presumptions are rebuttable. Thus rebuttable presumption is a redundancy. (See: **presumption**)

rebuttal: n. evidence introduced to counter, disprove or contradict the opposition's evidence or a presumption, or responsive legal argument.

recapture: n. in income tax, the requirement that upon sale of property the taxpayer pay the amount of tax savings from past years due to accelerated depreciation or deferred capital gains. (See: **income tax**)

receipt: n. a written and signed acknowledgment by the recipient of payment for goods, money in payment of a debt or receiving assets from the estate of someone who has died.

receiver: n. 1) a neutral person (often a professional trustee) appointed by a judge to take charge of the property and business of one of the parties to a lawsuit and receive his/her rents and profits while the right to the moneys has not been finally decided. Appointment of a receiver must be requested by petition of the other party to the suit, and will only be authorized if there is a strong showing that the moneys would not be available when a decision is made. The funds are held for the prevailing party. 2) a person appointed to receive rents and profits coming to a debtor either while a bankruptcy is being processed or while an arrangement is being worked out to pay creditors, so that funds will be paid for debts and possibly available for distribution to creditors. 3) shorthand for one who commits the crime of receiving stolen goods knowing they were obtained illegally.

receivership: n. the process of appointment by a court of a receiver to take custody of the property, business, rents and profits of a party to a lawsuit pending a final decision on disbursement or an agreement that a receiver control the financial receipts of a person who is deeply in debt (insolvent) for the benefit of creditors. Thus, the term "the business is in receivership." (See: **receiver**)

recess: n. a break in a trial or other court proceedings or a legislative session until a certain date and time. Recess is not to be confused with "adjournment," which winds up the proceedings.

recidivist: n. a repeat criminal offender, convicted of a crime after having been previously convicted. (See: **habitual criminal, three strikes, you're out**)

reciprocal discovery: n. the exchange of documents, lists of witnesses, and other information between the two sides of a lawsuit or criminal prosecution before trial. (See: **discovery**)

reciprocity: n. mutual exchange of privileges between states, nations, businesses or individuals. In regard to lawyers, reciprocity refers to recognizing the license of an attorney from another state without the necessity of taking the local state's bar examination. Such reciprocity is seldom granted now, since many large states refuse to give it.

reckless: adj. in both negligence and criminal cases, careless to the point of being heedless of the consequences ("grossly" negligent). Most commonly this refers to the traffic misdemeanor "reckless driving." It can also refer to use of firearms (shooting a gun in a public place), explosives or heavy equipment. (See: **careless, negligent, wet reckless**)

reckless disregard: n. gross negligence without concern for danger to others. Actually "reckless disregard" is redundant since reckless means there is a disregard for safety. (See: **reckless**)

reckless driving: n. operation of an automobile in a dangerous manner under the circumstances, including speeding (or going too fast for the conditions, even though within the posted speed limit), driving after drinking (but not drunk), having too many passengers in the car, cutting in and out of traffic, failing to yield to other vehicles and other negligent acts. It is a misdemeanor crime. A "wet reckless" is a plea in a drunk driving prosecution allowed to lessen the penalty when the blood alcohol level is close to the legal limit. (See: **reckless, wet reckless**)

reconveyance: n. in those states which use deeds of trust as a mortgage on real property to secure payment of a loan or other debt, the transfer of title by the trustee (which has been holding title to the real property) back to the borrower (on the written request of the borrower) when the secured debt is fully paid. Under the deed of trust the borrower transfers title in the real property to the trustee (often a title or escrow company) which holds it for the benefit of the lender (called "beneficiary"). The lender must surrender the promissory note to the trustee who cancels it and then reconveys title to the borrower and records the reconveyance. (See: **deed of trust**)

record: 1) v. (ree-cored) to put a document into the official records of a county at the office of the County Recorder or Recorder of Deeds. The process is that the document is taken or sent to the Recorder's office, a recording fee paid, the document is given a number (a document number, volume or reel number and page number), stamped with the date (and usually the time) of recording and then in most modern offices, microfilmed and the document returned a short time later. Normally recorded is any document affecting title to real property such as a deed, deed of trust, mortgage, reconveyance, release, declaration of homestead, easement, judgment, lien, request for notice of default, foreclosure, satisfaction of judgment, decree of distribution of a dead person's estates and sometimes long-term leases. These recordings provide a traceable chain of title to the property and give the public "constructive" notice of all interests in the property. In most states if there is more than one document affecting the property (such as two deeds, two mortgages, or a judgment and mortgage), the first one recorded has "seniority" and first claim on the property in what is called a "race to the courthouse." 2) v. to write down or tape the minutes, financial transactions, discussions and other happenings at meetings. 3) n. (reck-urred) in trials, hearings or other legal proceedings the total of the proceedings which are transcribed by a court reporter and included in the minutes of the clerk or judge, as well as all the documents filed in the case. On an appeal, the record includes everything that transpired before the appeal, upon which the written briefs (opposing legal arguments) and oral argument are based. On appeal the court can consider only the record, unless there is a claim of "newly discovered evidence." (See: **appeal, deed, deed of trust, hearing,** **mortgage, proceeding, race to the courthouse, trial**)

records: n. in business, particularly corporations, all the written business documents, especially about financial dealings. Thus, shareholders and partners are entitled to access to the "records" of the business.

recording acts: n. the statutes of each state which established the keeping of official records by County Recorders or Recorders of Deeds. (See: **record**)

recoupment: n. the right of a defendant in a lawsuit to demand deduction from the amount awarded to plaintiff (party bringing the suit) of a sum due the defendant from the plaintiff in the transaction which was the subject of the lawsuit. Example: Laura Landlord sues Tillie Tenant for nonpayment of rent, Tenant is entitled to deduct a deposit made at the commencement of the lease, or an amount Landlord received from re-renting the apartment before the lease expired. A recoupment is not the same as an "offset" (setoff), which can be money owed from any matter, including outside the lawsuit.

recourse: n. the right to demand payment to the writer of a check or bill of exchange. (See: **bill of exchange, check**)

recover: v. to receive a money judgment in a lawsuit.

recoverable: adj. referring to the amount of money to which a plaintiff (the party suing) is entitled in a lawsuit. Thus, a judge might rule "$12,500 is recoverable for lost wages, and $5,500 is recoverable for property damage to plaintiff's vehicle." (See: **damages, judgment**)

recovery: n. the amount of money and any other right or property received by a plaintiff in a lawsuit.

recusal: n. the act of a judge or prosecutor being removed or voluntarily stepping aside from a legal case due to conflict of interest or other good reason. (See: **recuse**)

recuse: v. to refuse to be a judge (or for a judge to agree to a request by one of the parties to step aside) in a lawsuit or appeal because of a conflict of interest or other good reason (acquaintanceship with one of the parties, for example). It also applies to a judge or prosecutor being removed or voluntarily removing himself/herself from a criminal case in which he/she has a conflict of interest, such as friendship or known enmity to the defendant. (See: **recusal**)

redeem: v. to buy back, as when an owner who had mortgaged his/her real property pays off the debt. The term also refers to paying the amount due and all charges after a foreclosure (because of failure to make payments when due) has begun. A person who has pawned a possession may redeem the item by paying the loan and interest to the pawnbroker. (See: **foreclosure, mortgage, redemption**)

redemption: n. the act of redeeming, buying back property by paying off a loan, interest and any costs of foreclosure. (See: **redeem**)

reentry: n. taking back possession and going into real property which one owns, particularly when a tenant has failed to pay rent or has abandoned the property, or possession has been restored to the owner by judgment in an unlawful detainer lawsuit. Reentry may also be allowed when a buyer defaults on payments on a contract of sale or upon foreclosure of a mortgage or deed of trust which secured a loan on the property. The right of reentry is usually written into leases and sometimes in mortgages. (See: **landlord and tenant**)

referee: n. a person to whom a judge refers a case to take testimony or acquire other evidence such as financial records and report to the court on such findings. (See: **master**)

referendum: n. the process by which the repeal or approval of an existing statute or state constitutional provision is voted upon. Many states provide for referenda (plural of referendum) which are placed on the ballot by a required number of voter signatures on a petition filed.

reformation: n. the correction or change of an existing document by court order upon petition of one of the parties to the document. Reformation will be ordered if there is proof that the parties did not intend the language as written or there was an omission due to mistake or misunderstanding. Quite often a party petitions for reformation when one or both parties realize the effect of the document as written is different from what was expected but it has already been recorded or filed with a governmental agency. Examples: a paragraph is omitted from a trust which results in the transfer to the trust being a gift subject to gift tax, and which needs to be corrected to keep the state taxing authority from demanding payment. The attorney writing the final draft of a limited partnership agreement writes in a calculation which would triple the profit to a limited partner above the amount discussed by the parties, and when the limited partner refuses to change the document, the general partner sues for reformation.

refresh one's memory: v. to use a document, exhibit or previous testimony in order to help a witness recall an event or prior statement when the witness has responded to a question that he/she could not remember. To attempt to "refresh" the memory of a forgetful or reluctant witness, the witness must have denied remembering and the attorney must have the witness identify the document, exhibit or prior statement (lay a foundation showing it is genuine). (See: **testimony**)

register: n. in corporations, the record of shareholders, and issuance and transfer of shares on the records of the corporation. (See: **corporation**)

registration statement: n. a detailed report to be filed with the Securities and Exchange Commission by a corporation making an issuance of shares to be advertised and sold to the general public in more than one state (in interstate commerce), which must be approved by the SEC before it will approve the stock issuance. (See: **blue sky laws, prospectus**)

registry of deeds: n. the records of land title documents kept by the County Recorder or Recorder of Deeds. These are usually kept on microfilm reels of copies of the original documents, which can be found by tracing the names of owners in the Grantor-Grantee index. These are public information but may require the assistance of an employee to locate. (See: **record**)

regulations: n. rules and administrative codes issued by governmental agencies at all levels, municipal, county, state and federal. Although they are not laws, regulations have the force of law, since they are adopted under authority granted by statutes, and often include penalties for violations. One problem is that regulations are not generally included in volumes containing state statutes or federal laws but often must be obtained from the agency or located in volumes in law libraries and not widely distributed. The regulation-making process involves hearings, publication in governmental journals which supposedly give public notice, and adoption by the agency. The process is best known to industries and special interests concerned with the subject matter, but only occasionally to the general public. Federal regulations are adopted in the manner designated in the Administrative Procedure Act (A.P.A.) and states usually have similar procedures.

rehearing: n. conducting a hearing again based on the motion of one of the parties to a lawsuit, petition or criminal prosecution, usually by the court or agency which originally heard the matter. Rehearings are usually requested due to newly discovered

351

evidence, an unfortunate and possibly unintended result of the original order, a change of circumstance or a simple claim that the judge or agency was just wrong.

rejection of claim: n. in probate law (administration of an estate of a person who died), a claim for a debt of the deceased denied (rejected) in total or in part by the executor or administrator of the estate. A claim is rejected in writing filed with the court, and a judge shall approve or disapprove the rejection if the claimant protests. If a claim is not acted upon it may be presumed to be approved in most states. There are other types of claims which may be rejected by agencies or individuals, which can be protested in a lawsuit if all administrative procedures are used first (under the rule called "exhaustion of administrative remedies").

release: 1) v. to give up a right as releasing one from his/her obligation to perform under a contract, or to relinquish a right to an interest in real property. 2) v. to give freedom, as letting out of prison. 3) n. the writing that grants a release.

release on one's own recognizance: v. for a judge to allow a criminal defendant pre-trial freedom without posting bail, based on the past history of the defendant, roots in the community, regular employment, the recommendation of the prosecutor, the type of crime, and in total the likelihood of making all appearances in court and the improbability that the defendant will commit another crime while awaiting trial. Often called "O.R." or "R.O.R," it is granted routinely in traffic matters, minor and technical crimes, and to people with no criminal record who display stability. It is called to be "ORed" in courtroom slang. (See: **bail, O.R.**)

relevancy: n. (See: **irrelevant, relevant**)

relevant: adj. having some reasonable connection with, and in regard to evidence in trial, having some value or tendency to prove a matter of fact significant to the case. Commonly, an objection to testimony or physical evidence is that it is "irrelevant." (See: **irrelevant, objection**)

reliance: n. acting upon another's statement of alleged fact, claim or promise. In contracts, if someone takes some steps ("changes his position" is the usual legal language) in reliance on the other's statement, claim or promise then the person upon whom the actor relied is entitled to contend there is a contract he/she can enforce. However, the reliance must be reasonable. (See: **reasonable reliance**)

reliction: n. gradual change of water line on real property which gives the owner more dry land. (See: **accretion**)

relief: n. generic term for all types of benefits which an order or judgment of court can give a party to a lawsuit, including money award, injunction, return of property, property title, alimony and dozens of other possibilities. (See: **judgment**)

remainder: n. in real property law, the interest in real property that is left after another interest in the property ends, such as full title after a life estate (the right to use the property until one dies). A remainder must be created by a deed or will. Example: Patricia Parent deeds Happy Acres Ranch to her sister Sally for life and upon Sally's death to Charla Childers, Sally's daughter, or Charla's children if she does not survive. Charla has a remainder, and her children have a "contingent remainder," which they will receive if Charla dies before title passes. A remainder is distinguished from a "reversion," which gives title back to the grantor of the property (upon Sally's death, in the example) or to the grantor's descendants; a reversion need not be spelled out in a deed or will, but can occur automatically by "operation of law." (See: **contingent remainder, deed, reversion, title, vested remainder**)

> *All are equal before the law and are entitled without any discrimination to equal protection of the law.*
> *—Article 7, International Declaration of Human Rights*

remainderman: n. the person who will receive a remainder in real property. (See: **remainder**)

remand: v. to send back. An appeals court may remand a case to the trial court for further action if it reverses the judgment of the lower court, or after a preliminary hearing a judge may remand into custody a person accused of a crime if the judge finds that a there is reason to hold the accused for trial. (See: **appeal, preliminary hearing**)

remedy: n. the means to achieve justice in any matter in which legal rights are involved. Remedies may be ordered by the court, granted by judgment after trial or hearing, by agreement (settlement) between the person claiming harm and the person he/she believes has caused it, and by the automatic operation of law. Some remedies require that certain acts be performed or prohibited (originally called "equity"); others involve payment of money to cover loss due to injury or breach of contract; and still others require a court's declaration of the rights of the parties and an order to honor them. An "extraordinary remedy" is a means employed by a judge to meet particular problems, such as appointment of a referee, master or receiver to investigate, report or take charge of property. A "provisional remedy" is a temporary solution to hold matters in status quo pending a final decision or an attempt to see if the remedy will work. (See: **equity, judgment, provisional remedy, settlement**)

remise: v. to give up something, sometimes used in quitclaim deeds. (See: **quitclaim deed**)

remittitur: n. 1) a judge's order reducing a judgment awarded by a jury when the award exceeds the amount asked for by the plaintiff (person who brought the suit). 2) an appeal's transmittal of a case back to the trial court so that the case can be retried, or an order entered consistent with the appeals court's decision (such as dismissing the plaintiff's case or awarding costs to the winning party on appeal). (See: **remand**)

remote: adj., adv. extremely far off or slight. Evidence may be so remote from the issues in a trial that it will not be allowed because it is "immaterial." An act which started the events which led to an accident may be too remote to be a cause, as distinguished from the "proximate cause." Example: While Doug Driver is passing a corner a friend calls out to him causing him to look away, and then Doug looks back and in the middle of the block is hit by a truck backing out of a driveway. The momentary inattention is not a cause of the injury, and is called a "remote cause." (See: **immaterial, proximate cause**)

removal: n. 1) the change of a legal case from one court to another, as from a state court to federal court or vice versa based on a motion by one of the parties stating that the other jurisdiction is more appropriate for the case. 2) taking away the position of a public official for cause, such as dishonesty, incompetence, conviction of a crime or successful impeachment.

renewal: n. keeping an existing arrangement in force for an additional period of time, such as a lease, a promissory note, insurance policy or any other contract. Renewal usually requires a writing or some action which evidences the new term.

rent: 1) v. to hire an object or real property for a period of time (or for an open-ended term) for specified payments. 2) n. the amount paid by the renter and received by the owner. Rent may be specified in a written lease, but also may be based on an oral agreement for either a short period or on a month-to-month basis in which the hiring may be terminated on a month's notice. (See: **lease, month-to-month**)

rental value: n. the amount which would be paid for rental of similar property in the same condition in the same area. Evidence of rental value becomes important in lawsuits in which loss of use of real property or equipment is an issue, and the rental value is the "measure of damages." In divorce cases in which one of the spouses stays in the family residence, the use of the property has rental value which is considered in balancing the income of the parties, determining division of property or setting the amount of alimony to be paid. (See: **rent**)

renunciation: n. 1) giving up a right, such as a right of inheritance, a gift under a will or abandoning the right to collect a debt on a note. 2) in criminal law, abandoning participation in a crime before it takes place, or an attempt to stop other participants from going ahead with the crime. A defendant may use renunciation as evidence of his/her innocence. Once the crime is underway, any claimed renunciation is factually too late.

reorganization: n. the implementation of a business plan to restructure a corporation, which may include transfers of stock between shareholders of two corporations in a merger. In bankruptcy, a corporation in deep financial trouble may be given time to reorganize while being protected from creditors by the bankruptcy court. The theory is that if the business is able to get on its feet the creditors will eventually collect. (See: **bankruptcy, corporation, merger**)

repair: v. to restore to former condition or in some contracts to operational soundness. Contracts should spell out the repairs to be made and what the final condition will be. Example: roof repairs should be more than a half-baked patching to temporarily halt leaking.

repeal: 1) v. to annul an existing law, by passage of a repealing statute, or by public vote on a referendum. Repeal of constitutional provisions requires an amendment, as with the repeal of prohibition in which the 21st Amendment repealed the 18th Amendment. 2) n. the act of annulling a statute.

replevin: n. under common law, the right to bring a lawsuit for recovery of goods improperly taken by another. In almost all states the term replevin in no longer used, since the states have adopted "one cause of action" for all civil wrongs.

reply brief: n. the written legal argument of the respondent (trial court winner) in answer to the "opening brief" of an appellant (a trial court loser who has appealed). (See: **appeal, appellee, respondent**)

reports: n. the published decisions of appeals courts in all states and federal courts, which are found in federal, state and regional series (called "reporters") which are constantly updated with pamphlets called "advance sheets" which are soon followed by bound volumes. There are also reports of specialized courts and particular subject matters such as taxes, bankruptcy and federal procedure. Thus there are Massachusetts Reports, Georgia Reports, Kansas Reports, California Supreme Court Reports, California Appellate Reports and similar series for every state. Regional reporters include Northeast, Atlantic, Southeast, Southern, Northwest, Pacific and so forth, and combine several states' decisions. For Supreme Court cases there are three major reporters, including U.S. Reports, Supreme Court Reporter, and Lawyer's Edition Supreme Court Reports. These reports are available in almost all law libraries.

repossess: v. to take back property through judicial processes, foreclosure, or self-help upon default in required payments.

represent: v. 1) to act as the agent for another. 2) to act as a client's attorney. 3) to state something as a fact, such as "I tell you this horse is only four years old." 4) to allege a fact in court, as "I represent to the court that we will present six witnesses," "We represent that this is the final contract between the parties." (See: **representation**)

representation: n. 1) the act of being another's agent. 2) acting as an attorney for a client. 3) a statement of alleged fact either in negotiations or in court. (See: **represent**)

representative: 1) n. an agent. 2) n. in probate law, a generic term for an executor or administrator of the estate of a person who has died, generally referred to as the "personal representative." 3) adj. typical, as "these pictures are representative of the conditions at the job site."

reprieve: n. a temporary delay in imposition of the death penalty (a punishment which cannot be reduced afterwards) by the executive order of the Governor of the state. Reasons for reprieves include the possibility of newly discovered evidence (another's involvement, evidence of mental impairment), awaiting the result of some last-minute appeal, or concern of the Governor that there may have been some error in the record which he/she should examine. On occasion a reprieve has saved a man found to be innocent. Upon the expiration of the reprieve the date for execution can be reset and the death penalty imposed. A reprieve is only a delay and is not a reduction of sentence, commutation of sentence or pardon.

repudiation: n. denial of the existence of a contract and/or refusal to perform a contract obligation. Repudiation is an anticipatory breach of a contract. (See: **anticipatory breach, contract**)

reputation: n. a person's good name, honor or what the community thinks of him/her. The quality and value of one's reputation is a key issue in suits for defamation (libel and slander) since the damage to one's reputation by published untruths may determine the amount of judgment against the defamer. Sometimes a person's favorable reputation is so great that most defamation cannot do him/her much harm. (See: **defamation, libel, slander**)

reputed: adj. referring to what is accepted by general public belief, whether or not correct.

request: 1) v. to ask or demand a judge to act (such as issuing a writ) or demanding something from the other party (such as production of documents), usually by a party to a lawsuit (usually the attorney). 2) n. the act of asking or demanding.

requirements contract: n. a contract between a supplier (or manufacturer) and a buyer, in which the supplier agrees to sell all the particular products that the buyer needs, and the buyer agrees to purchase the goods exclusively from the supplier. A requirements contract differs from an "an output contract," in which the buyer agrees to buy all the supplier produces. (See: **output contract**)

res: (rayz) n. Latin, "thing." In law lingo *res* is used in conjunction with other Latin words as "thing that."

res adjudicata: n. a thing (legal matter) already determined by a court, from Latin for "the thing has been judged." More properly *res judicata*. (See: *res judicata*)

resale: n. selling again, particularly at retail. 2) adj. referring to sales to the general public, as distinguished from wholesale, sales to retailers. In many states a "resale license" or "resale number" is required so that the state can monitor the collection of sales tax on retail sales.

rescind: v. to cancel a contract, putting the parties back to the position as if the contract had not existed. Both parties rescind a contract by mutual agreement, since a unilateral cancellation of a contract is a "breach" of the contract and could result in a lawsuit by the non-cancelling party. (See: **rescission**)

rescission: n. the cancellation of a contract by mutual agreement of the parties. (See: **rescind**)

rescue doctrine: n. the rule of law that if a rescuer of a person hurt or put in peril due to the negligence or intentional wrongdoing of another (the tortfeasor) is injured in the process of the rescue, the original wrongdoer is responsible in damages for the rescuer's injury. Example: Sydney Sparetire speeds on a mountain highway, and skids in front of Victor Victim, running Victim's car off the bank, trapping Victim in the vehicle. Raymond Rightguy stops, ties a rope to the grill of his car, slides down and extricates Victim, but on the way up slips and breaks his arm, and then finds the grill is badly bent. The negligent Sparetire is liable to Rightguy for his broken arm (including medical expenses, loss of wages and general damages for pain and suffering) as well as the property damage to the car grill. (See: **damages**)

reservation: n. a provision in a deed which keeps (reserves) to the grantor some right or portion of the property. The language might read: "Sarah Sims reserves to herself an easement of access to lots 6, 7 and 8," or "reserves mineral rights," or "except she reserves lot 5." (See: **reserve**)

reserve: v. to keep for oneself a right or a portion of the real property when transferring (conveying) a parcel of real estate to another. (See: **reservation**)

reserve fund: n. a fund of money created to take care of maintenance, repairs or unexpected expenses of a business or a multi-unit housing development (often condominiums or a housing cooperative) operated by a homeowners association or other governing body. Most states require that homeowners associations maintain such a fund.

res gestae: (rayz jest-tie) n. from Latin for "things done," it means all circumstances surrounding and connected with a happening. Thus, the *res gestae* of a crime includes the immediate area and all occurrences and statements immediately after the crime. Statements made within the *res gestae* of a crime or accident may be admitted in court even though they are "hearsay" on the basis that spontaneous statements in those circumstances are reliable.

residence: n. 1) the place where one makes his/her home. However, a person may have his/her state of "domicile" elsewhere for tax or other purposes, especially if the residence is for convenience or not of long standing. 2) in corporation law, the state of incorporation. (See: **resident**)

resident: n. a person who lives in a particular place. However, the term is vague depending on the permanence of the occupation. (See: **residence**)

residuary bequest: n. in a will, the gift of whatever is left (the residue) after specific gifts are given. It is also called a residuary legacy. (See: **residue**)

residue: n. in a will, the assets of the estate of a person who has died with a will (died testate) which are left after all specific gifts have been made. Typical language: "I leave the rest, residue and remainder [or just residue] of my estate to my grandchildren." If the residue is not given to any beneficiary it will be distributed pursuant to the laws of descent and distribution. (See: **descent and distribution, residuary bequest, will**)

res ipsa loquitur: (rayz ip-sah loh-quit-her) n. Latin for "the thing speaks for itself," a doctrine of law that one is presumed to be negligent if he/she/it had exclusive control of whatever caused the injury even though there is no specific evidence of an act of negligence, and without negligence the accident would not have happened. Examples: a) a load of bricks on the roof of a building being constructed by Highrise Construction Co. falls and injures Paul Pedestrian below, and Highrise is liable for Pedestrian's injury even though no one saw the load fall. b) While under anesthetic, Isabel Patient's nerve in her arm is damaged although it was not part of the surgical procedure, and she is unaware of which of a dozen medical people in the room caused the damage. Under *res ipsa loquitur* all those connected with the operation are liable for negligence. Lawyers often shorten the doctrine to "*res ips*," and find it a handy shorthand for a complex doctrine. (See: **negligence**)

resisting arrest: n. the crime of using physical force (no matter how slight in the eyes of most law enforcement officers) to prevent arrest, handcuffing and/or taking the accused to jail. It is also called "resisting an officer" (but that can include interfering with a peace officer's attempt to keep the peace) and is sometimes referred to merely as "resisting."

res judicata: (rayz judy-cot-ah) n. Latin for "the thing has been judged," meaning the issue before the court has already been decided by another court, between the same parties. Therefore, the court will dismiss the case before it as being useless. Example: an Ohio court determines that John is the father of Betty's child. John cannot raise the issue again in another state. Sometimes called *res adjudicata*. (See: **res adjudicata**)

resolution: n. a determination of policy of a corporation by the vote of its board of directors. Legislative bodies also pass resolutions, but they are often statements of policy, belief or appreciation, and not always enactment of statutes or ordinances.

respondeat superior: (rehs-pond-dee-at superior) n. Latin for "let the master answer," a key doctrine in the law of agency, which provides that a principal (employer) is responsible for the actions of his/her/its agent (employee) in the "course of employment." Thus, an agent who signs an agreement to purchase goods for his employer in the name of the employer can create a binding contract between the seller and the employer. Another example: if a delivery truck driver negligently hits a child in the street, the company for which the driver works will be liable for the injuries. (See: **agency, agent, negligence, principal**)

respondent: n. 1) the party who is required to answer a petition for a court order or writ requiring the respondent to take some action, halt an activity or obey a court's direction. In such matters the moving party (the one filing the petition) is usually called the "petitioner." Thus, the respondent is equivalent to a defendant in a lawsuit, but the potential result is a court order and not money damages. 2) on an appeal, the party who must respond to an appeal by the losing party in the trial court (called "appellant") in the appeals court.

responsible: adj. 1) legally liable or accountable. 2) having the ability to pay or perform.

Restatement of the Law: n. a series of detailed statements of the basic law in the United States on a variety of subjects written and updated by well-known legal scholars under the auspices of the American Law Institute since the 1930s. While not having the force of statutes or of decided precedents, the Restatement (as lawyers generally call it) has the prestige of the scholars who have studied the legal questions. Topics covered include agency, contracts, property, torts and trusts.

restitution: n. 1) returning to the proper owner property or the monetary value of loss. Sometimes restitution is made part of a judgment in negligence and/or contracts cases. 2)

in criminal cases, one of the penalties imposed is requiring return of stolen goods to the victim or payment to the victim for harm caused. Restitution may be a condition of granting a defendant probation or giving him/her a shorter sentence than normal.

restraining order: n. a temporary order of a court to keep conditions as they are (like not taking a child out of the county or not selling marital property) until there can be a hearing in which both parties are present. More properly it is called a temporary restraining order (shortened to TRO). (See: **injunction, permanent injunction**)

restraint on alienation: n. an attempt in a deed or will to prevent the sale or other transfer of real property either forever or for an extremely long period of time. Such a restraint on the freedom to transfer property is generally unlawful and therefore void or voidable (can be made void if an owner objects), since a present owner should not be able to tie the hands of future generations to deal with their property. This ban on a restraint on alienation (transfer) is called "the rule against perpetuities." Examples: Oliver Oldtimer sells his ranch to his son with the condition that title may never be transferred to anyone outside of the family. Martha Oldtimer in her will gives her home to her daughter Jacqueline on condition that "Jacqueline's descendants must never sell the place." However, one is generally allowed to limit transfer to a maximum period calculated by "lives in being, plus 21 years." Restraints on alienation (so-called restrictive covenants) based on race ("only

Caucasians may hold title") were declared unconstitutional in 1949. (See: **convey, deed, restrictive covenant, rule against perpetuities, use**)

restraint of trade: n. in antitrust law, any activity (including agreements among competitors or companies doing business with each other) which tends to limit trade, sales and transportation in interstate commerce or has a substantial impact on interstate commerce. Most of these actions are illegal under the various antitrust statutes. Some state laws also outlaw local restraints on competitive business activity. (See: a**ntitrust laws, monopoly, trust**)

restriction: n. any limitation on activity, by statute, regulation or contract provision. In multi-unit real estate developments, condominium and cooperative housing projects managed by homeowners' associations or similar organizations, such organizations are usually required by state law to impose restrictions on use. Thus, the restrictions are part of the "covenants, conditions and restrictions" intended to enhance the use of common facilities and property which are recorded and incorporated into the title of each owner. (See: **covenants conditions and restrictions**)

restrictive covenant: n. 1) an agreement included in a deed to real property that the buyer (grantee) will be limited as to the future use of the property. Example: no fence may be built on the property except of dark wood and not more than six feet high, no tennis court or swimming pool may be constructed within 30 feet of the property line, and no structure can be built within 20 feet of the frontage street. Commonly these covenants are written so that they can be enforced by the grantor and other owners in the subdivision, so that future owners will be bound by the covenant (called "covenant running with the land" if enforceable against future owners). All restrictive covenants based on race ("the property may be occupied only by Caucasians") were declared unconstitutional in 1949 and if they still show on deeds are null and void. (See: **covenant that runs with the land**)

restrictive endorsement: n. an endorsement signed on the back of a check, note or bill of exchange which restricts to whom the paper may be transferred. Example: "for transfer only to Frank Lowry, [signed] J. Ripps." Also spelled "indorsement." (See: **endorsement**)

result: n. common lawyer lingo for outcome of a lawsuit.

resulting trust: n. a trust implied by law (as determined by a court) that a person who holds title or possession was intended by agreement (implied by the circumstances) with the intended owner to hold the property for the intended owner. Thus, the holder is considered a trustee of a resulting trust for the proper owner as beneficiary. Although a legal fiction, the resulting trust forces the holder to honor the intention and prevents unjust enrichment. Example: Mahalia leaves $100,000 with her friend, Albert, while she is on a trip to Europe, asking him "to buy the old Barsallo place if it comes on the market." Albert buys the property, but has title put in his own name, which the court will find is held in a resulting trust for Mahalia. A resulting trust differs from a "constructive trust," which comes about when someone by accident, misunderstanding or dishonesty comes into possession of property belonging to another. (See: **constructive trust, trust**)

retainer: n. the advance payment to an attorney for services to be performed, intended to insure that the lawyer will represent the client and that the lawyer will be paid at least that amount. Commonly in matters which will involve extensive work there will be a retainer agreement signed by the attorney and client. Further payments for services can be expected as the time spent on the legal matter increases. Most lawyers do not want to be owed money and wish to be paid either in advance or promptly as the work is performed. One reason for the retainer, and the problem a lawyer faces, is that he/she does not want to abandon a client, but at the same time does not want to be stuck with extensive unpaid fees. (See: **attorney's fees**)

retire: v. 1) to stop working at one's occupation. 2) to pay off a promissory note and thus "retire" the loan. 3) for a jury to go into the jury room to decide on a verdict after all evi-dence, argument and jury instructions have been completed.

retraction: n. 1) to withdraw any legal document in a lawsuit or other legal proceeding, or withdraw a promise or offer of contract. 2) in defamation, particularly libel, the correction of any untruth published in a newspaper or magazine or broadcast on radio or television, usually upon the demand of the person about whom the damaging false statement was made. A clear and complete retraction will usually end the right of the defamed party to go forward with a lawsuit for damages for libel. In most states a retraction must be demanded before the suit is filed in order to cure the problem without litigation. (See: **defamation, libel**)

retrial: n. a new trial granted upon the motion of the losing party, based on obvious error, bias or newly discovered evidence, or after mistrial or reversed by an appeals court. (See: **motion for new trial**)

retroactive: adj. referring to a court's decision or a statute enacted by a legislative body which would result in application to past transactions and legal actions. In criminal law, statutes which would increase penalties or make criminal activities which had been previously legal are prohibited by the constitutional ban on *ex post facto* laws (Article I, Section 9). Most court decisions which change the elements necessary to prove a crime or the introduction of evidence such as confessions are usually made non-retroactive to prevent a flood of petitions of people convicted under prior rules. Nor can statutes or court decisions take away "vested" property rights or change contract rights. However, some decisions are so fundamental to justice they may have a retroactive effect, depending on the balance between stability of the law and the public good. Retroactive is also called "retrospective." (See: *ex post facto*)

return of service: n. written confirmation under oath by a process server declaring that there was service of legal documents (such as a summons and complaint). (See: **service, service of process**)

revenue ruling: n. a published opinion of the Internal Revenue Service stating what it would rule on future tax questions based on the same circumstances. These rulings are of general use to taxpayers, tax preparers, accountants and attorneys in anticipating tax treatment by the IRS. They have the force of law until otherwise determined by the federal tax court or a new revenue ruling. (See: **income tax**)

reversal: n. the decision of a court of appeal ruling that the judgment of a lower court was incorrect and is therefore reversed. The result is that the lower court which tried the case is instructed to dismiss the original action, retry the case or change its judgment. Examples: a court which denied a petition for writ of mandate is ordered to issue the writ. A lower court which gave judgment with no evidence of damages is ordered to dismiss.

reversible error: n. a legal mistake at the trial court level which is so significant (resulted in an improper judgment) that the judgment must be reversed by the appellate court. A reversible error is distinguished from an error which is minor or did not contribute to the judgment at the trial. (See: **reversal**)

reversion: n. in real property, the return to the grantor or his/her heirs of real property after all interests in the property given to others have terminated. Examples: a) George Generous deeded property to the local hospital district for "use for health facilities only," and the hospital is eventually torn down and the property is now vacant. The property reverts to George's descendants. b) George wills the property to his sister's children only, who later died without children. When the last grandchild dies the property reverts to George's descendants. Reversion is also called "reverter." (See: **reverter**)

reverter: n. synonymous with reversion. (See: **reversion**)

review: n. the judicial consideration of a lower court judgment by an appellate court, determining if there were legal errors sufficient to require reversal. The process requires notice of appeal, obtaining a transcript of the trial or hearing at the trial level, obtaining all the pleadings and other documents filed in the original trial, preparation of briefs citing precedents and arguing that there was reversible error. Then the respondent (winner at the trial court) may file a responsive brief, and the appellant (the one appealing the decision) has the chance to file a brief in response to the respondent. The next step is oral argument (if allowed) before the appellate court. Appeals on procedural issues normally do not include oral argument. If the appellate court denies the appeal a rehearing may be requested but is seldom granted. (See: **appeal, appellate court, reversal, reversible error**)

revival: n. 1) requesting a court to reinstate the force of an old judgment. 2) reinstating a contract or debt by a new agreement after the right to demand performance or collect has expired under the statute of limitations (the time to sue).

revocation: n. 1) mutual cancellation of a contract by the parties to it. 2) withdrawing an offer before it is accepted ("I revoke my offer"). 3) cancelling a document before it has come into legal effect or been acted upon, as revoking a will. 4) to recall a power or authority previously given, as cancelling a power of attorney or cancelling a driver's license due to traffic offenses. (See: **contract, will**)

revoke: v. to annul or cancel an act, particularly a statement, document or promise, as if it no longer existed. Thus, a person can revoke a will or revoke an offer to enter into a contract, and a government agency can revoke a license. (See: **revocation**)

RICO: n. (See: **Racketeer Influenced Corrupt Organization statute**)

rider: n. 1) an attachment to a document which adds to or amends it. Typical is an added provision to an insurance policy, such as additional coverage or temporary insurance to cover a public event. 2) in legislatures, an amendment tacked on to a bill which has little or no relevance to the main purpose of the legisla-

tion, but is a way to get the amendment passed if the basic bill has support. 3) passenger.

right: 1) n. an entitlement to something, whether to concepts like justice and due process or to ownership of property or some interest in property, real or personal. These rights include: various freedoms; protection against interference with enjoyment of life and property; civil rights enjoyed by citizens such as voting and access to the courts; natural rights accepted by civilized societies; human rights to protect people throughout the world from terror, torture, barbaric practices and deprivation of civil rights and profit from their labor; and such U.S. constitutional guarantees as the right to freedoms of speech, press, religion, assembly and petition. 2) adj. just, fair, correct. (See: **civil rights, marital rights, right privacy**)

rights: n. 1) plural of right, which is the collection of entitlements which a person may have and which are protected by the government and the courts or under an agreement (contract). 2) slang for the information which must be given by law enforcement officers to a person who is about to be arrested, is a prime suspect in a crime, or is officially accused of a crime. These "rights" are short for "Miranda rights," which the Supreme Court, in *Miranda v. Arizona* (1966), required be read to suspects, including the rights to remain silent and to have an attorney (and if the suspect cannot afford a lawyer, one will be provided), and warning that anything the suspect says can be used against him/her in court. Failure to recite these rights means that a confession may not be used as evidence. (See: **Miranda warning**)

> *Defiance of the law is the surest road to tyranny.*
> *—John F. Kennedy*

right of way: n. 1) a pathway or road with a specific description (e.g. "right to access and egress 20 feet wide along the northern line of Lot 7 of the Cobb subdivision in page 75 of maps"). 2) the right to cross property to go to and from another parcel. The right of way may be a specific grant of land or an "easement," which is a right to pass across another's land. The mere right to cross without a specific description is a "floating" easement. Some rights of way are for limited use such as repair of electric lines or for deliveries to the back door of a store. Railroads own title to a right of way upon which to build permanent tracks. 3) in traffic ordinances, a driver is entitled to the "right of way" to proceed first ahead of other vehicles or pedestrians, depending on certain rules of the road, such as the first to reach an intersection. Failure to yield the right of way to the vehicle or person entitled to it can result in a citation and fine, to say nothing of an accident. It can also be evidence of negligence in a lawsuit for injuries suffered in an accident. (See: **access, easement, egress, floating easement**)

right to privacy: n. the possible right to be let alone, in absence of some "reasonable" public interest in a person's activities, like those of celebrities or participants in newsworthy events. Invasion of the right to privacy can be the basis for a lawsuit for damages against the person or entity (such as a magazine or television show) violating the right. However, the right to privacy does not extend to prohibiting someone from taking another person's picture on the street. (See: **invasion of privacy, privacy**)

riot: n. 1) technically a turbulent and violent disturbance of peace by three or more people acting together. 2) an assemblage of people who are out of control, causing injury or endangering the physical safety of others and/or themselves, causing or threatening damage to property and often violating various laws both individually and as a group. The common thread is that the people in a riot have the power through violence to break the public peace and safety, requiring police action. Often a riot is declared after the crowd has been informed by police officers that the people constitute an "unlawful assembly" and are ordered to "disperse" immediately (historically in England called "reading the riot act"). If the crowd does not disperse, its members become subject to arrest for the crime of rioting, disturbing the peace, resisting arrest or other separate crimes ranging from assault to unlawful possession of firearms.

riparian: adj. referring to the banks of a river or stream. (See: **riparian rights**)

riparian rights: n. the right of the owner of the land forming the bank of a river or stream to use water from the waterway on the land, such as for drinking water or irrigation. State laws vary as to the extent of the rights, but controversy exists as to the extent of riparian rights for diversion of water to sell to others, for industrial purposes, to mine the land under the water for gravel or minerals or for docks and marinas. Consistent in these questions is that a riparian owner may not act to deny riparian rights to the owner of downstream properties along the waterway, meaning the water may not be dammed and channelled away from its natural course.

ripe: adj. in constitutional law, referring to a law case appealed from a state or federal court which is ready for consideration by the Supreme Court, meaning that all other avenues for determining the case have been exhausted, there is a real controversy and the law needs to be settled on one or more issues raised by the case.

risk: n. chances of danger or loss, particularly of property covered by an insurance policy or property being used or transported by another. Insurance companies assume the risk of loss and calculate their premiums by the value and the risk based on statistically determined chances. A trucking company assumes the risk of loss while carrying goods. (See: **assumption of risk, risk of loss**)

risk of loss: n. the responsibility a carrier, borrower or user of property or goods assumes or an insurance company agrees to cover if there is damage or loss. (See: **risk**)

roadside test: n. a preliminary test law enforcement officers use on a suspected drunk driver at the spot the driver has been pulled over. Essentially it is a test of equilibrium (balance), reflexes and mental acuity, consisting of standing on one foot and then the other, walking a straight line, touching one's nose with the forefinger of each hand, saying the alphabet backwards or counting by twos. Some tests include writing. Although sometimes a judgment call by the officers, a suspect's failure of the test is often obvious and may be supplemented by reports of slurred speech, bloodshot eyes, the smell of alcohol and answers to simple questions such as "How much did you have to drink?" or "Do you know where you are?" If the officer decides the driver is drunk, he/she will inform the driver he/she is being arrested for driving under the influence of alcohol, read the Miranda rights, arrest the driver and transport him/her to a nearby police facility, where the suspect is asked to submit to an alcohol blood test (breathalizer, blood or urine) which is more definitive than the subjective roadside test. If the driver refuses the blood alcohol test, the officer may testify in court on the roadside test results as proof of drunkenness if there is a trial of the accused. In cases in which the inability to drive effectively is due to use of narcotics or a combination of drugs and alcohol, the roadside test may provide crucial evidence of physical symptoms and mental confusion indicating inability to drive safely even though the alcohol level is below the legally drunk level. (See: **driving under the influence, driving while intoxicated, DUI, DWI, Miranda warning**)

robbery: n. 1) the direct taking of property (including money) from a person (victim) through force, threat or intimidation. Robbery is a felony (crime punishable by a term in state or federal prison). "Armed robbery" involves the use of a gun or other weapon which can do bodily harm, such as a knife or club, and under most state laws carries a stiffer penalty (longer possible term) than robbery by merely taking. 2) a term improperly used to describe thefts, including burglary (breaking and entering) and shoplifting (secret theft from the stock of a store), expressed: "We've been robbed." (See: **theft**)

rogatory letters: n. a written request by a judge to a judge in another state asking that a witness in the other state have his/her testimony taken in the other state's court for use in the local court case. (See: **deposition, testimony, witness**)

royalty: n. a percentage of gross or net profit or a fixed amount per sale to which a creator of a work is entitled which is determined by contract between the creator and the manufacturer, publisher, agent and/or distributor. Inventors, authors, movie makers, scriptwriters, music composers, musicians and other creators contract with the manufacturers, publishers, movie production companies and distributors, as well as producers and distributors for a license to manufacture and/or sell the product, who pay a royalty to the creator based on a percentage of funds received. Should someone use another person's creation either purposely or by mistake, the user could be found liable to the creator for all profits on the basis of copyright or patent infringement, which usually is far more than a royalty. However, a creator does not have to license his/her creation to anyone. (See: **copyright, infringement, patent**)

rule: 1) v. to decide a legal question, by a court, as in: "I rule that the plaintiff is entitled to the goods and damages for delay in the sum of $10,000." 2) v. to make a judicial command, such as: "I find that George Gonzo is the parent of Larry Gonzo and rule that he must pay support of $150 per month to the mother" for the support of Larry. 3) n. any regulation governing conduct. 4) n. one of the regulations of covering legal practice before a particular group of courts, collectively called "rules of court" adopted by local judges. 5) n. a legal principle set by the decision in an appellate case, as "the rule in the case of *Murray v. Crampton* is...." (See: **regulations, rules of court**)

rule against perpetuities: n. the legal prohibition against tying up property so that it cannot be transferred or vest title in another forever, for several future generations, or for a period of centuries. The maximum period in which real property title may be held without allowing title to vest in another is "lives in being plus 21 years." Therefore, a provision in a deed or will which reads, "Title shall be held by David Smith and, upon his death, title may only be held by his descendants until the year 2200, when it shall vest in the Trinity Episcopal Church," is invalid, but a provision that "the property will be held by my son George for his life, and thereafter by his son, Thomas, and for 20 years by his future children, before it may be conveyed (transferred) [or title shall then vest in the church]" is acceptable under the rule. (See: **restraint on alienation**)

rules of court: n. a set of procedural regulations adopted by courts which are mandatory upon parties and their lawyers on matters within the jurisdiction of those courts. Most states have statewide rules of court. Federal court rules are adopted by the district courts based on the Federal Rules of Procedure, and county, district and municipal court judges adopt what are called "local rules" of court. Local rules encompass the time allowed to file papers, the format of documents (including the paper colors of appeal court briefs), the number of copies to be filed, the procedure to file motions, the basis for calculating alimony and child support, fees for filing various documents and numerous other mundane but vital matters. These rules are violated or ignored at the peril of the client and his/her/its counsel. (See: **procedure, rule**)

ruling: n. court decision on a case or any legal question.

running with the land: adj. permanently part of the title (ownership) to real property. (See: **covenant running with the land**)

running at large: adj. 1) referring to cattle or other animals which have escaped from an enclosure and are wandering. The owner will be liable for damage caused by such animals. 2) political campaigning by a candidate running for an office from no specific district, but from an entire city, county or state.

S

said: adj. a reference back to a thing that was previously mentioned or identified, popular in legal documents, as "the said driver drove said automobile in a negligent manner."

sale: n. transfer of something (and title to it) in return for money (or other thing of value) on terms agreed upon between buyer and seller. The price paid may be based on a posted cost, established by negotiation between seller and buyer, or by auction with potential buyers bidding until the highest bid is accepted by the seller or his agent (auctioneer). (See: **contract, forced sale, sheriff's sale**)

salvage: 1) v. to save goods. 2) n. payment to a person or group which saves cargo from a shipwreck.

sanction: n. 1) a financial penalty imposed by a judge on a party or attorney for violation of a court rule, for receiving a special waiver of a rule, or as a fine for contempt of court. If a fine, the sanction may be paid to the court or to the opposing party to compensate the other side for inconvenience or added legal work due to the rule violation. Examples: a) under local rules Bagatelle's attorney is required to file a brief in response to the opposition's motion five days before the hearing, but is two days late. The judge accepts the documents, but imposes a $200 sanction on Bagatelle's attorney for the failure to file them on time. b) Campbell's lawyer wants to include a newly found expert in his list of witnesses, but the date for adding to the list has passed. The judge permits the added witness, but allows the opposition to take the expert's deposition, and imposes a sanction (fine) on Campbell to pay both sides' costs of the deposition and $500 attorney's fees to the opposing counsel. c) Defendant Danny Dipper says "you son-of-a-bitch" in court when the judge fines him $100 for jay-walking. The judge imposes a sanction of $200 and a day in jail for Danny's contempt of court. 2) v. to impose a fine or penalty as part of a judge's duty to maintain both order and fairness in court. 3) v. in international law, to impose economic constraints on trade against a country that violates international law or is guilty of human rights violations. 4) v. to allow or approve. This meaning is ironically in contrast to the other definitions of "sanction." (See: **contempt of court**)

satisfaction: n. receiving payment or performance of what is due. (See: **accord and satisfaction, contract, satisfaction of judgment**)

satisfaction of judgment: n. a document signed by a judgment creditor (the party owed the money judgment) stating that the full amount due on the judgment has been paid. The judgment creditor (the party who paid the judgment) is entitled to demand that the judgment creditor (the party to whom the money judgment is owed) sign the satisfaction of judgment, file it with the court clerk, acknowledge it before a notary public, and record the document with the County Recorder (or Recorder of Deeds) if there is an abstract of judgment (a document showing the amount of the judgment which is a lien on any real property belonging to the defendant) on record. (See: **abstract of judgment**)

satisfaction of mortgage: n. a document signed by a lender acknowledging that a mortgage has been fully paid. It must be recorded with the County Recorder (or Recorder of Deeds) to clear the title to the real property owned by the person who paid off the debt. (See: **mortgage**)

save harmless: v. 1) also called hold harmless, to indemnify (protect) another from harm or cost. 2) to agree to guarantee that any debt, lawsuit or claim which may arise as a result of a contract or contract performance will be paid or taken care of by the party making the guarantee. Example: the seller of a business agrees to "save harmless" the buyer from any unknown debts of the business. (See: **hold harmless, indemnify**)

savings and loan: n. a banking and lending institution, chartered either by a state or the federal government. Savings and loans only make loans secured by real property from deposits, upon which they pay interest slightly higher than that paid by most banks. In the early 1980s savings and loans were "de-regulated," allowing them to make loans for speculative land development, removing high reserve funds requirements, and allowing their funds to participate in competition with

banks. The result was use of many savings and loans for speculative and dishonest investments, lack of controls and tremendous losses to thousands of depositors. However, a properly managed, conservative savings and loan which concentrates on real estate loans guaranteed by the FHA (Federal Housing Administration) and/or sold in the secondary mortgage market can be safe, profitable and provide a valuable channel for savings into the home finance market.

scienter: n. Latin for "having knowledge." In criminal law, it refers to knowledge by a defendant that his/her acts were illegal or his/her statements were lies and thus fraudulent.

> *The Constitution does not provide for first and second class citizens.*
> *—Wendell L. Willkie*

scintilla: n. Latin for "spark." Scintilla is commonly used in reference to evidence, in the context that there must be a "scintilla of evidence" (at least a faint spark) upon which to base a judgment.

scope of employment: n. actions of an employee which further the business of the employer and are not personal business, which becomes the test as to whether an employer is liable for damages due to such actions under the doctrine of *respondeat superior* (make the master answer). Example: Dick Deliver drives a truck delivering groceries for Super-Duper Market. If Dick negligently runs the truck into Victor Victim's VW while making deliveries or on the way back from a delivery, then Super-Duper is liable since the accident was in the scope of employment. If Dick goes outside the delivery route to have lunch with his girlfriend and on the way hits Victim then there is a strong inference he was outside the scope of employment. (See: **master and servant,** *respondeat superior*)

scrivener: n. a person who writes a document for another, usually for a fee. If a lawyer merely writes out the terms of a lease or contract exactly as requested by the client, without giving legal advice, then the lawyer is just a scrivener and is probably not responsible for legal errors (unless they were so obvious as to warrant comment). A non-lawyer may act as a scrivener without getting in trouble for practicing law without a license.

seal: n. a device which creates an impression upon paper or melted wax, used by government agencies, corporations and notaries public to show that the document is validly executed, acknowledged or witnessed, since the seal is unique to the sealer. Corporate seals state the name, date and state of incorporation. Notaries increasingly use a rubber stamp instead of a seal since their print is easier to microfilm for official recording than is a faint embossed impression. Contracts used to be "sealed," but that is rare today.

sealed verdict: n. the decision of a jury when there is a delay in announcing the result, such as waiting for the judge, the parties and the attorneys to come back to court. The verdict is kept in a sealed envelope until handed to the judge when court reconvenes. (See: **jury, verdict**)

sealing of records: n. trial records and decisions which a judge orders kept secret. Usually these are the criminal records of under-age offenders which cannot be examined without a special court order or only by those connected with law enforcement. On occasion records in civil trials are sealed on the motion of a party claiming the need to protect inventions, business secrets or national security. Sometimes sealing is stipulated as part of a settlement to keep the terms from public scrutiny.

search: v. 1) to examine another's premises (including a vehicle) to look for evidence of criminal activity. It is unconstitutional under the 4th and 14th Amendments for law enforcement officers to conduct a search without a "search warrant" issued by a judge or without facts which give the officer "probable cause" to believe evidence of a specific crime is on the premises and there is not enough time to obtain a search warrant. 2) to trace the records of ownership of real property in what is commonly called a "title search." (See: **abstract, chain of title, probable cause, search and seizure, search warrant**)

search and seizure: n. examination of a person's premises (residence, business or vehicle) by law enforcement officers looking for evidence of the commission of a crime, and the taking (seizure and removal) of articles of evidence (such as controlled narcotics, a pistol, counterfeit bills, a blood-soaked blanket). The basic question is whether the search and seizure were "unreasonable" under the 4th

Amendment to the Constitution (applied to the states under the 14th Amendment), which provides: "The right of people to be secure in their persons, houses, papers, and effects, against unreasonable searches and seizures, shall not be violated." Thus, searches and seizures must be under the authority of a search warrant or when the officer has solid facts that give him/her "probable cause" to believe there was evidence of a specific crime on the premises but no time to get a warrant. Evidence obtained in violation of the Constitution is not admissible in court, nor is evidence traced through such illegal evidence. (See: **search, search warrant, probable cause, fruit of the poisonous tree**)

search warrant: n. a written order by a judge which permits a law enforcement officer to search a specific place (eg. 112 Magnolia Avenue, Apartment 3, or a 1991 Pontiac, Texas license number 123ABC) and identifies the persons (if known) and any articles intended to be seized (often specified by type, such as "weapons," "drugs and drug paraphernalia," "evidence of bodily harm"). Such a search warrant can only be issued upon a sworn written statement of a law enforcement officer (including a prosecutor). The 4th Amendment to the Constitution specifies: "...no warrants shall issue, but upon probable cause, supported by oath or affirmation, and particularly describing the place to be searched and the persons or things to be seized." The 14th Amendment applies the rule to the states. Evidence unconstitutionally seized cannot be used in court, nor

can evidence traced through such illegal evidence. (See: **fruit of the poisonous tree, probable cause, search, search and seizure**)

secondary boycott: n. an organized refusal to purchase the products of, do business with or perform services for (such as deliver goods) a company which is doing business with another company where the employees are on strike or in a labor dispute. Example: Big Basket Markets are being struck by the Retail Clerks Union, and Cupboard Canning and Wheato Bread are selling foodstuffs to Big Basket. The Teamsters Union then refuses to deliver to Cupboard and Wheato and asks all its members not to buy from those companies, although Cupboard and Wheato are not involved directly in the labor dispute. Such "secondary" boycotts are unfair labor practices under federal and many state laws and, thus, are illegal.

second degree murder: n. a non-premeditated killing, resulting from an assault in which death of the victim was a distinct possibility. Second degree murder is different from first degree murder, which is a premeditated, intentional killing or results from a vicious crime such as arson, rape or armed robbery. Exact distinctions on degree vary by state. (See: **first degree murder, manslaughter, murder**)

secret rebate: n. a kickback of money by a business to a "preferred" customer, not offered to the public or by a subcontractor to a contractor not shown on a job estimate. Both are illegal in most states as unfair business practices and may result in criminal penalties or refusal of a court to enforce a contract (written or oral) in which there is such a secret rebate. (See: **rebate**)

secured transaction: n. any loan or credit in which property is pledged as security in the event payment is not made. (See: **deed of trust, lien, mortgage, pawn, pawnshop, UCC-1**)

securities: n. generic term for shares of stock, bonds and debentures issued by corporations and governments to evidence ownership and terms of payment of dividends or final pay-off. They are called securities because the assets and/or the profits of the corporation or the credit of the government stand as security for payment. However, unlike secured transactions in which specific property is pledged, securities are only as good as the future profitability of the corporation or the management of the governmental agency. Most securities are traded on various stock or bond markets. (See: **bond, debenture, stock, share,**)

security deposit: n. a payment required by a landlord from a tenant to cover the expenses of any repairs of damages to the premises greater than normal "wear and tear." The security deposit must be returned within a short time (varying by states) after the tenant vacates, less the cost of repairing any unusual damage. Unfortunately for tenants, these damages are usually subject to the judgment of the landlord, who may desire to paint and refinish on the tenant's money, which results in many small claims suits. In a few

states the security deposit must be kept in a separate bank account, and some states require payment of interest on the amount held as a deposit. A security deposit is sometimes confused with a deposit of the "last month's rent," which may be credited to the tenant for the final month's rent. A security deposit cannot be used legally as a rent credit. (See: **landlord and tenant, lease, rent**)

security interest: n. generic term for the property rights of a lender or creditor whose right to collect a debt is secured by property. (See: **deed of trust, lien, mortgage, UCC-1**)

sedition: n. the federal crime of advocacy of insurrection against the government or support for an enemy of the nation during time of war, by speeches, publications and organization. Sedition usually involves actually conspiring to disrupt the legal operation of the government and is beyond expression of an opinion or protesting government policy. Sedition is a lesser crime than "treason," which requires actual betrayal of the government, or "espionage." Espionage involves spying on the government, trading state secrets (particularly military) to another country (even a friendly nation), or sabotaging governmental facilities, equipment or suppliers of the government, like an aircraft factory. During U.S. participation in World War II (1941–1945) several leaders of the German-American Bund, a pro-Nazi organization, were tried and convicted of sedition for actively interfering with the war effort. Since freedom of speech, press and assembly are guaranteed by the Bill of Rights and because treason and espionage charges can be made for overt acts against the nation's security, sedition charges are rare. (See: **espionage, treason**)

seduction: n. the use of charm, salesmanship, promises, gifts and flattery to induce another person to have sexual intercourse outside marriage, without any use of force or intimidation. At one time seduction was a crime in many states, but if the seducee (usually female) is of the age of consent and is not drugged, intoxicated or otherwise unable to consent, seduction is no longer criminal. However, just as adultery lingers in the criminal codes of some states, so does seduction. (See: **adultery, breach of promise, date rape, rape**)

seisin: (sees-in) n. an old feudal term for having both possession and title of real property. The word is found in some old deeds, meaning ownership in fee simple (full title to real property). (See: **fee simple, seized**)

seized (seised): n. 1) having ownership, commonly used in wills as "I give all the property of which I die seized as follows:...." 2) having taken possession of evidence for use in a criminal prosecution. 3) having taken property or a person by force. (See: **seisin, seizure**)

seizure: n. the taking by law enforcement officers of potential evidence in a criminal case. The constitutional limitations on seizure are the same as for search. Thus, evidence seized without a search warrant or without "probable cause" to believe a crime has been committed and

without time to get a search warrant, cannot be admitted in court, nor can evidence traced through the illegal seizure. (See: **search and seizure, search warrant, fruit of the poisonous tree**)

self-dealing: n. in the stock market, using secret "inside" information gained by being an official of a corporation (or from such an officer) to buy or sell stock (or real property wanted by the corporation) before the information becomes public (like a merger, poor profit report, striking oil). Self-dealing can also apply to general partners of a limited partnership who do not inform limited partners of business opportunities which should belong to the partnership. Self-dealing can result in a lawsuit for fraud by shareholders. Self-dealing with securities is a crime under the federal Securities and Exchange Act.

self-defense: n. the use of reasonable force to protect oneself or members of the family from bodily harm from the attack of an aggressor, if the defender has reason to believe he/she/they is/are in danger. Self-defense is a common defense by a person accused of assault, battery or homicide. The force used in self-defense may be sufficient for protection from apparent harm (not just an empty verbal threat) or to halt any danger from attack, but cannot be an excuse to continue the attack or use excessive force. Examples: an unarmed man punches Allen Alibi, who hits the attacker with a baseball bat. That is legitimate self-defense, but Alibi cannot chase after the attacker and shoot him or beat him senseless. If the attacker has a gun or a butcher knife and is verbally threatening, Alibi is probably warranted in shooting him. Basically, appropriate self-defense is judged on all the circumstances. Reasonable force can also be used to protect property from theft or destruction. Self-defense cannot include killing or great bodily harm to defend property, unless personal danger is also involved, as is the case in most burglaries, muggings or vandalism. (See: **assault, homicide**)

self-executing: adj. immediately effective without further action, legislation or legal steps. Some statutes are self-executing, as are some legal rights (such as when a person holds property as security and title passes automatically when payments are not made). Most judgments in lawsuits are not self-executing and are only documents giving the winning party the right to try to collect.

self-help: n. 1) obtaining relief or enforcing one's rights without resorting to legal action, such as repossessing a car when payments have not been made, retrieving borrowed or stolen goods, demanding and receiving payment or abating a nuisance (such as digging a ditch to divert flooding from another's property). Self-help is legal as long as it does not "break the public peace" or violate some other law (although brief trespass is common). 2) the maximizing of one's opportunities.

self-incrimination: n. making statements or producing evidence which tends to prove that one is guilty of a crime. The 5th Amendment to the U.S. Constitution guarantees that one cannot "be compelled in any

criminal case to be a witness against himself..." and the 14th Amendment applies that guarantee to state cases. Thus refusing to testify in court on the basis that the testimony may be self-incriminating is called "taking the Fifth." (See: **Miranda warning, rights, taking the Fifth**)

self-serving: adj. referring to a question asked of a party to a lawsuit or a statement by that person that serves no purpose and provides no evidence, but only argues or reinforces the legal position of that party. Example: Question asked by a lawyer of his own client: "Are you the sort of person who would never do anything dishonest?" Such a question may be objected to as "self-serving" by the opposing lawyer and will be disallowed by the judge, unless there is some evidentiary value. Some people add self-serving comments to their testimony, such as "I never tell lies," which can be stricken from the record as a self-serving declaration. (See: **objection**)

sell: v. to transfer possession and ownership of goods or other property for money or something of equivalent value. (See: **sale**)

seller: n. one who sells goods or other property to a buyer (purchaser). (See: **sale, sell**)

senior lien: n. the first security interest (lien or claim) placed upon property at a time before other liens, which are called "junior" liens. (See: **deed of trust, lien, race to the courthouse, mortgage, UCC-1**)

sentence: 1) n. the punishment given to a person convicted of a crime. A sentence is ordered by the judge, based on the verdict of the jury (or the judge's decision if there is no jury) within the possible punishments set by state law (or federal law in convictions for a federal crime). Popularly, "sentence" refers to the jail or prison time ordered after conviction, as in "his sentence was 10 years in state prison." Technically, a sentence includes all fines, community service, restitution or other punishment, or terms of probation. Defendants who are first offenders without a felony record may be entitled to a probation or pre-sentence report by a probation officer based on background information and circumstances of the crime, often resulting in a recommendation as to probation and amount of punishment. For misdemeanors (lesser crimes) the maximum sentence is usually one year in county jail, but for felonies (major crimes) the sentence can range from a year to the death penalty for murder in most states. Under some circumstances the defendant may receive a "suspended sentence," which means the punishment is not imposed if the defendant does not get into other trouble for the period he/she would have spent in jail or prison; "concurrent sentences," in which the prison time for more than one crime is served at the same time and only lasts as long as the longest term; "consecutive sentences," in which the terms for several crimes are served one after another; and "indeterminate" sentences, in which the actual release date is not set and will be based on review of prison conduct. 2) v. to impose a punishment on a person convicted of a crime. (See: **capital punishment, concurrent sentence, indeterminate sentence, restitution, suspended sentence**)

separate property: n. in community property states (California, Texas, Arizona, Idaho, Louisiana, New Mexico, Nevada and Washington), the property owned by one spouse which he/she acquired: a) before marriage, b) by inheritance, c) as a gift, d) assets traceable to other separate property such as money received from sale of a house owned before marriage, and e) property the spouses agree is separate property. State laws vary, but basically separate property can be controlled by the spouse owning it. The laws of descent applied to separate property and right to give separate property by will differ from the treatment of community property. Example: a child may inherit part of one spouse's separate property if there is no will, while community property would pass automatically to the spouse. Upon divorce community property is divided equally, while separate property is kept by the owner without division with the other spouse. (See: **community property**)

separation: n. married persons living apart, either informally by one leaving the home or agreeing to "separate" while sharing a residence without sexual relations, or formally by obtaining a "legal separation" or negotiating a "separation agreement" setting out the terms of separate living. (See: **legal separation, separation agreement**)

separation agreement: n. an agreement between two married people who have agreed to live apart for an unspecified period of time, perhaps forever. The agreement generally covers any alimony (money paid for spousal support), child support, custody arrangements if there are children, payment of bills and management of separate bank accounts. A separation agreement may determine division of property if the separation appears permanent. It cannot be enforced by court order unless one party files a petition for legal separation or files a lawsuit for specific performance of a contract. If the couple reconciles, the separation agreement is voidable (can be cancelled) by the parties. However, most separation agreements are interim agreements to serve between the time of separation and the eventual divorce of the parties. (See: **dissolution of marriage, divorce, legal separation, separation**)

sequester: v. to keep separate or apart. In so-called "high-profile" criminal prosecutions (involving major crimes, events or persons given wide publicity) the jury is sometimes "sequestered" in a hotel without access to news media, the general public or their families except under supervision, in order to prevent the jury from being "tainted" by information or opinions about the trial outside of the evidence in the courtroom. A witness may be sequestered from hearing the testimony of other witnesses, commonly called being "excluded," until after he/she has testified, supposedly to prevent that witness from being influenced by other evidence or tailoring his/her testimony to fit the stories of others. (See: **sequestration**)

sequestration: n. the act of a judge issuing an order that a jury or witness be sequestered (kept apart from outside contacts during trial). (See: **sequester**)

seriatim: (sear-ee-ah-tim) prep. Latin for "one after another" as in a series. Thus, issues or facts are discussed *seriatim* (or "*ad seriatim*"), meaning one by one in order. (See: **ad seriatim**)

servant: n. an employee of an employer, technically one who works for a master. A servant is distinguished from an "independent contractor" who operates his/her own business even though spending much time on the work of a particular person or entity. The servant has established hours or piece work, is under the direction of the employer even as to details, cannot work for competitors and acts for the benefit of the employer rather than for himself/herself. The employer of a servant must provide to the servant (employee) worker's compensation insurance, Social Security coverage, make income tax deductions, and provide benefit from various federal and state labor laws. An independent contractor is responsible for such payments and benefits himself/herself. (See: **employee, independent contractor, master and servant**)

service: n. 1) paid work by another person, either by contract or as an employee. "Personal services" is work that is either unique (such as an artist or actor) or based on a person's particular relationship to employer (such as a butler, nanny, traveling companion or live-in health care giver). 2) the domestic activities of a wife, including the marital relationship (consortium), are legally considered "services" for which a deprived husband may sue a person who has caused injury to his wife. 3) the official delivery of legal documents ("service of process") such as a summons, subpena, complaint, order to show cause (order to appear to show reasons why a judge should not make a particular order), writ (court order), or notice to quit the premises, as well as delivery by mail or in person of documents to opposing attorneys or parties, such as answers, motions, points and authorities, demands and responses. (See: **employment, loss of consortium, personal services, service of process**)

> *We cannot, as citizens, pick and choose the laws we will or will not obey.*
> *—Ronald Reagan*

service by FAX: n. delivery of legal documents required by statute to be "served" by transmitting through telecopier phone (FAX), followed by mailing an original ("hard copy"). Increasingly, the courts recognize this as legitimate service since it is instantaneous. (See: **service, service of process**)

service by mail: n. mailing legal pleadings to opposing attorneys or parties, while filing the original with the court clerk with a declaration stating that the copy was mailed to a particular person at a specific address. Once a party has responded by filing an answer, subsequent pleadings (except orders to show cause and orders of exami-

nation) can be served upon his/her/its attorney by mail. (See: **service**)

service by publication: n. serving a summons or other legal document in a lawsuit on a defendant by publishing the document in an advertisement in a newspaper of general circulation. Service by publication is used to give "constructive notice" to a defendant who is intentionally absent, in hiding, unknown (as a possible descendant of a former landowner), and only when allowed by a judge's order based on a sworn declaration of the inability to find the defendant after "due diligence" (trying hard). Service by publication is commonly used in a divorce action to serve a spouse who has disappeared without leaving a forwarding address or to give notice to people who might have a right to object to a "quiet title" action to clear title to real property. (See: **constructive notice-service, service of process**)

service of process: n. the delivery of copies of legal documents such as summons, complaint, subpena, order to show cause (order to appear and argue against a proposed order), writs, notice to quit the premises and certain other documents, usually by personal delivery to the defendant or other person to whom the documents are directed. So-called "substituted service" can be accomplished by leaving the documents with an adult resident of a home, with an employee with management duties at a business office or with a designated "agent for acceptance of service" (often with name and address filed with the state's Secretary of State), or, in some cases, by posting in a prominent place followed by mailing copies by certified mail to the opposing party. In certain cases of absent or unknown defendants, the court will allow service by publication in a newspaper. Once all parties have filed a complaint, answer or any pleading in a lawsuit, further documents usually can be served by mail or even FAX. (See: **personal service, service, service by FAX, service by mail, service by publication, substituted service**)

services: n. work performed for pay. (See: **personal services, service**)

servient estate: n. real property which has an easement or other use imposed upon it in favor of another property (called the "dominant estate"), such as right of way or use for access to an adjoining property or utility lines. The property giving usage is the servient estate, and the property holding usage of the easement is the dominant estate. (See: **covenant running with the land, dominant estate, easement**)

session: n. 1) a meeting (or "sitting") of a court for a particular period of time. "Session" technically means one day's business (as in "today's session"). 2) the term of an appeals court covering several months (as in the "Spring Term" or the "October Term").

set: v. to schedule, as to "set a case for trial."

set aside: v. to annul or negate a court order or judgment by another court order. Example: a court dismisses a complaint believing the case had been settled. Upon being informed by a lawyer's

motion that the lawsuit was not settled, the judge will issue an order to "set aside" the original dismissal.

setoff (offset): n. a claim by a defendant in a lawsuit that the plaintiff (party filing the original suit) owes the defendant money which should be subtracted from the amount of damages claimed by plaintiff. By claiming a setoff the defendant does not necessarily deny the plaintiff's original demand, but he/she claims the right to prove the plaintiff owes him/her an amount of money from some other transaction and that the amount should be deducted from the plaintiff's claim. (See: **affirmative defense, offset**)

setting: n. the action of a court, clerk or commissioner in scheduling a trial or hearing. (See: **set**)

settle: v. to resolve a lawsuit without a final court judgment by negotiation between the parties, usually with the assistance of attorneys and/or insurance adjusters, and sometimes prodding by a judge. Most legal disputes are settled prior to trial. (See: **settlement**)

settlement: n. the resolution of a lawsuit (or of a legal dispute prior to filing a complaint or petition) without going forward to a final court judgment. Most settlements are achieved by negotiation in which the attorneys (and sometimes an insurance adjuster with authority to pay a settlement amount on behalf of the company's insured defendant) and the parties agree to terms of settlement. Many states require a settlement conference a few weeks before trial in an effort to achieve settlement with a judge or assigned attorneys to facilitate the process. A settlement is sometimes reached based upon a final offer just prior to trial (proverbially "on the courthouse steps") or even after trial has begun. A settlement reached just before trial or after a trial or hearing has begun is often "read into the record" and approved by the court so that it can be enforced as a judgment if the terms of the settlement are not complied with. Most lawsuits result in settlement. (See: **settle**)

settlor: n. the person who creates a trust by a written trust declaration, called a "Trustor" in many (particularly western) states and sometimes referred to as the "Donor." The settlor usually transfers the original assets into the trust. (See: **trust, trustor**)

severable contract: n. an agreement which is made up of several separate contracts between the same parties, such as series of sales, shipments or different pieces of equipment. Therefore, breach of one of the separate (severable) contracts is not a breach of the remainder of the overall contract and is not an excuse for the other party to refuse to honor any divisable part of the contract which has not been breached. Example: Whitley Widget Company has contracted with Hardy Hardware to deliver a dozen wall heaters, one ton of nails, 100 rolls of linoleum and a truckload of roof tiles, with a price set for each type of product. Whitley no longer produces nails and cannot deliver them, but the other parts of the contract remain in force between Whitley and Hardy. (See: **breach of contract, contract**)

several liability: n. referring to responsibility of one party for the entire debt (as in "joint and several") or judgment when those who jointly agreed to pay the debt or are jointly ordered to pay a judgment do not do so. A person who is stuck with "several liability" because the others do not pay their part may sue the other joint debtors for contribution toward the payment he/she has made. (See: **contribution, joint and several, promissory note**)

severance: n. 1) a separating by court order, such as separate trials for criminal defendants who were charged with the same crime, or trying the negligence aspect of a lawsuit before a trial on the damages. Such division of issues in a trial is sometimes also called "bifurcation." Severance is granted when a joint trial might be unfair or reaching a decision on one issue (such as negligence) may save the trouble of hearing the other questions. 2) extra pay offered and made to a person to encourage him/her to resign, retire or settle a potential claim for discharge.

sex offender: n. generic term for all persons convicted of crimes involving sex, including rape, molestation, sexual harassment and pornography production or distribution. In most states convicted sex offenders are supposed to report to local police authorities, but many do not. (See: **molestation, pornography, rape, sexual harassment**)

sexual harassment: n. unwanted sexual approaches (including touching, feeling, groping) and/or repeated unpleasant, degrading and/or sexist remarks directed toward an employee with the implied suggestion that the target's employment status, promotion or favorable treatment depend upon a positive response and/or "cooperation." Sexual harassment is a private nuisance, unfair labor practice or, in some states, a civil wrong (tort) which may be the basis for a lawsuit against the individual who made the advances and against the employer who did not take steps to halt the harassment. A legal secretary recently won an award of more than $3 million against a prominent law firm in California for not controlling a partner notorious for his sexual harassment of female employees. (See: **nuisance**)

shall: v. 1) an imperative command as in "you shall not kill." 2) in some statutes, "shall" is a direction but does not mean mandatory, depending on the context.

share: n. 1) a portion of a benefit from a trust, estate, claim or business usually in equal division (or a specifically stated fraction) with others ("to my three daughters, in equal shares"). 2) a portion of ownership interest in a corporation, represented by a stock certificate stating the number of shares of an issue of the corporation's stock.

share and share alike: adj. referring to the equal division of a benefit from an estate, trust or gift, which includes the right of the survivors to divide the portion of any beneficiary who dies before receiving the gift. Example: Teal Testator wills her 2,000 shares of IBM stock "to my four nephews, Matthew, Mark, Luke and John, share and share alike." Luke dies before Testator, so the 2,000 shares will be divided among the three surviving nephews.

shareholder: n. the owner of one or more shares of stock in a corporation, commonly also called a "stockholder." The benefits of being a shareholder include receiving dividends for each share as determined by the board of directors, the right to vote (except for certain preferred shares) for members of the board of directors, to bring a derivative action (lawsuit) if the corporation is poorly managed, and to participate in the division of value of assets upon dissolution and winding up of the corporation, if there is any value. A shareholder should have his/her name registered with the corporation, but may hold a stock certificate which has been signed over to him/her. Before registration the new shareholder may not be able to cast votes represented by the shares. (See: **corporation, shareholders' meeting**)

shareholders' agreement: n. an employment agreement among the shareholders of a small corporation permitting a shareholder to take a management position with the corporation without any claim of conflict of interest or self-dealing against the shareholder/manager. Such agreements are common when there are only three or four shareholders.

shareholders' derivative action: n. a lawsuit by a corporation's shareholders, theoretically on behalf of the corporation, to protect and benefit all shareholders against the corporation for improper management. (See: **derivative action**)

shareholders' meeting: n. a meeting, usually annual, of all shareholders of a corporation (although in large corporations only a small percentage attend) to elect the board of directors and hear reports on the company's business situation. In larger corporations top management people hold the proxies signed over to them by many of the shareholders to vote for them. (See: **board of directors, corporation, proxy, shareholder**)

sharp practice: n. actions by a lawyer using misleading statements to opposing counsel or the court, denial of oral stipulations (agreements between attorneys) previously made, threats, improper use of process or tricky and/or dishonorable means barely within the law. A consistent pattern of sharp practice may lead to discipline by the state bar association or by the courts.

Shepardize: n. a method of locating reports of appeals decisions based on prior precedents from *Shepard's Citations*, books which list the volume and page number of published reports of every appeals court decision which cites a previously decided case or a statute. *Shepard's* exists for all sets of reports of appeals cases, and is updated every month with supplemental booklets. While it looks like a mathematician's book of tables, *Shepard's Citations* is an invaluable tool in finding appeals decisions which either follow, distinguish or deviate from prior case law. (See: **reports**)

sheriff: n. the top law enforcement officer for a county, usually elected and responsible for police protection outside of incorporated cities, management of the county jail, providing bailiffs for protection of the courts, and such civil activities as serving summonses, subpenas and writs, conducting judgment sales, and fulfilling various functions ordered by the courts. The office was brought to the United States from England and is unknown in most nations which use federal and state police. Canada, for example, has the highly professional Royal Canadian Mounted Police (and its Quebec equivalent) to serve for most non-municipal law enforcement. The position of sheriff has been criticized as lacking training standards, being overly political, not being coordinated with other jurisdictions, and being hampered by its lack of authority beyond the county line except when in "hot pursuit" of a suspect who crosses the county line. The sheriff's uniformed police are called "deputy sheriffs," with the number two person often entitled "under sheriff." (See: **bailiff, sheriff's sale**)

sheriff's sale: n. an auction sale of property held by the sheriff pursuant to a writ (court order) of execution (to seize and sell the property) to satisfy (pay) a judgment, after notice to the public. (See: **execution, forced sale, levy, writ**)

shield laws: n. statutes enacted in some states which declare that communications between news reporters and informants are confidential and privileged and thus cannot be testified to in court. This is similar to the doctor-patient, lawyer-client or priest-parishioner privilege. The concept is to allow a journalist to perform his/her function of gathering news without being ordered to reveal his/her sources and notes of conversations. In states which have no shield law, many judges have found reporters in contempt of court (and given them jail terms) for refusing to name informants or reveal information gathered on the promise of confidentiality. (See: **privileged communication**)

shifting the burden of proof: n. the result of the plaintiff in a lawsuit meeting its burden of proof in the case, in effect placing the burden with the defendant, at which time it presents a defense. There may be shifts of burden of proof on specific factual issues during a trial, which may impact the opposing parties and their need to produce evidence. (See: **burden of proof, *prima facie* case**)

short cause: n. a lawsuit which is estimated by the parties (usually their attorneys) and the trial setting judge to take no more than one day. Thus, a short cause may be called on the "short cause" calendar and get priority on the calendar since it can be fitted into the court's schedule and will not tie up a courtroom for a long period. Short causes may be treated differently from "long cause" cases, such as not requiring a settlement conference or having the cases tried by "pro tem" judges. However, if a supposed "short cause" lasts beyond one day the judge is authorized to declare a mistrial and the case will be reset later as a "long cause."

shortening time: n. an order of the court in response to the motion of a party to a lawsuit which allows setting a motion or other legal matter at a time shorter than provided by law or court rules. Shortening time is usually granted when the time for trial or some other court action is approaching and a hearing must be heard promptly by the judge. Example: the local rules require that a party give the other side 10 days' notice before a hearing. A hearing on adding a witness to the expert list would be useless unless heard in five days, since the trial is set to be called in nine days. The court may shorten the time to schedule the hearing to five days, provided the notice is served within 24 hours.

show cause order: n. an order of the court, also called an order to show cause or OSC, directing a party to a lawsuit to appear on a certain date to show cause why the judge should not issue a specific order or make a certain finding. Examples: an order to a husband directing that he show cause why the wife in a divorce action should not be awarded $1,000 a month alimony (spousal support) and $500 a month child support, why the husband should not be ordered to stay away, and why the wife should not have temporary custody of their child. (See: **order to show cause**)

sidebar: n. 1) physically, an area in front of or next to the judge's bench (the raised desk in front of the judge) away from the witness stand and the jury box, where lawyers are called to speak confidentially with the judge out of earshot of the jury. 2) a discussion between the judge and attorneys at the bench off the record and outside the hearing of the jurors or spectators. 3) in journalism, a brief story on a sidelight to a news story, such as a biographical sketch about a figure in the news or an anecdote related to the main story, and sometimes enclosed within a box. (See: **bench, approach the bench**)

sign: v. 1) to write one's signature on a document, including an "X" by an illiterate or physically impaired person, provided the mark is properly witnessed in writing as "Eddie Jones, his mark." An attorney-in-fact given authority to act for another person by a power of attorney may sign for the one giving the power but should identify the signature as "by his attorney-in-fact, George Goodman." 2) to communicate by sign language. (See: **mark, subscribe**)

silent partner: n. a non-legal term for an investor who puts money into a business, takes no part in management and is often unknown to customers. A "limited partner," who is prohibited from taking part in management and has no liability for debts beyond his/her investment, is a true silent partner. However, without a limited partnership agreement, a silent partner is responsible for the debts of the partnership as a general partner. (See: **general partner, limited partnership, partner**)

similarly situated: adj. with the same problems and circumstances, referring to the people represented by a plaintiff in a "class action," brought for the benefit of the party filing the suit as well as all those "similarly situated." To be similarly situated, the defendants, basic facts

and legal issues must be the same, and separate lawsuits would be impractical or burdensome. (See: **class action, multiplicity of suits**)

simple trust: n. a trust which requires that all income be distributed each year and not accumulated. (See: **trust**)

simultaneous death act: n. a statute in effect in most states which provides that if a husband and wife or siblings die in an accident in which they died at the same moment or it cannot be determined who died first, it is presumed that each died before the other for determining inheritance. (See: **descent and distribution**)

sine qua non: (see-nay kwah nahn) prep. Latin for "without which it could not be," an indispensable action or condition. Example: if Charlie Careless had not left the keys in the ignition, his 10-year-old son could not have started the car and backed it over Polly Playmate. So Charlie's act was the *sine qua non* of the injury to Playmate.

situs: n. Latin for "location," be it where the crime or accident took place or where the building stands.

slander: n. oral defamation, in which someone tells one or more persons an untruth about another, which untruth will harm the reputation of the person defamed. Slander is a civil wrong (tort) and can be the basis for a lawsuit. Damages (payoff for worth) for slander may be limited to actual (special) damages unless there is malicious intent, since such damages are usually difficult to specify and harder to prove. Some statements, such as an untrue accusation of having committed a crime, having a loathsome disease or being unable to perform one's occupation, are treated as slander *per se* since the harm and malice are obvious and therefore usually result in general and even punitive damage recovery by the person harmed. Words spoken over the air on television or radio are treated as libel (written defamation) and not slander on the theory that broadcasting reaches a large audience as much as if not more than printed publications. (See: **defamation, fair comment, libel. slander,**)

small claims court: n. a division of most municipal, city or other lowest local courts which hear cases involving relatively small amounts of money and without a request for court orders like eviction. The highest (jurisdictional) amount that can be considered in small claims court varies by state, but goes as high as $5,000 in California. In small claims court, attorneys may not represent clients, the filing fee is low, there is no jury, the procedure is fairly informal, each side has a short time to present his/her case and the right to appeal only permits a trial *de novo* (a new trial) at the next court level. Often the judge is an experienced lawyer sitting as a *pro tem* judge. Small claims court is a quick, inexpensive way to settle lesser legal disputes, although the controversies are often important to the participants. The well-known television program *People's Court* is intended to be a good example of a small claims court.

sodomy: n. anal copulation by a man inserting his penis in the anus either of another man or a woman. If accomplished by force, without consent or with someone incapable of consent, sodomy is a felony in all states in the same way that rape is. Homosexual (male to male) sodomy between consenting adults has also been found a felony but increasingly is either decriminalized or seldom prosecuted. Sodomy with a consenting adult female is virtually never prosecuted even in those states in which it remains on the books as a criminal offense. However, there have been a few cases, including one in Indiana, in which a now-estranged wife insisted that a husband be charged with sodomy for sexual acts while they were living together. Traditionally sodomy was called "a crime against nature." Sodomy does not include oral copulation or sexual acts with animals (bestiality). (See: **bestiality, rape**)

sole proprietorship: n. a business owned by one person, as distinguished from a partnership or corporation.

solicitation: n. the crime of encouraging or inducing another to commit a crime or join in the commission of a crime. Solicitation may refer to a prostitute's (or her pimp's) offer of sexual acts for pay. (See: **pander**)

solicitor: n. an English attorney who may perform all legal services except appear in court. Under the British system, the litigator or trial attorney takes special training in trial work and is called a "barrister." Occasionally a solicitor becomes a barrister, which is called "taking the silk." In the United States and Canada attorneys are referred to interchangeably as solicitors or barristers. (See: **attorney**)

Solicitor General: n. the chief trial attorney in the federal Department of Justice responsible for arguing cases before the Supreme Court and ranking second to the Attorney General in the Department.

solitary confinement: n. the placement of a prisoner in a federal or state prison in a cell away from other prisoners, usually as a form of internal penal discipline, but occasionally to protect the convict from other prisoners or to prevent the prisoner from causing trouble. Long-term solitary confinement may be found to be unconstitutional as "cruel and unusual punishment."

solvency: n. 1) having sufficient funds or other assets to pay debts. 2) having more assets than liabilities (debts). The contrast is "insolvency," which may be a basis for filing a petition in bankruptcy. (See: **bankruptcy, insolvency**)

sound mind and memory: n. having an understanding of one's actions and reasonable knowledge of one's family, possessions and surroundings. This is a phrase often included in the introductory paragraph of a will in which the testator (writer of the will) declares that he/she is "of sound mind and memory." The general test is whether the person making the will understood: a) the meaning and effect of the will, b) what the person owned (more or less), and c) the "natural objects of his/her bounty," meaning the immediate family and any other particularly close relatives or friends to whom he/she might

leave things. (See: **competent, incompetent, will**)

> *The laws, if they are to be observed, have need of good morals.*
> *—Niccolo Machiavelli*

sounds in: adj. referring to the underlying legal basis for a lawsuit or one of several causes of action in a suit, such as contract or tort (civil wrong). The phrasing might be: "Plaintiff's first cause of action against Defendant sounds in tort, and his second cause of action sounds in contract."

speaking demurrer: n. an attempt to introduce evidence during a hearing on a demurrer. A demurrer is a legal opposition to a complaint in a lawsuit (or to an answer), which says, in effect, that even if the factual claims (allegations) are true, there are legal flaws or failures in the lawsuit. Therefore, since the factual allegations are admitted for the sake of argument, introducing evidence is improper, and an attorney making a "speaking demurrer" will be halted, often in mid-argument. Example: Attorney Perry Pickwick files a demurrer to a complaint for damages due to medical malpractice, in which he argues that the suit was filed too late (after the time allowed by the statute of limitations) since the complaint itself stated the malpractice took place more than three years before the filing and the limitation by law is two years. However, the complaint also stated that the plaintiff Elsa Edwards did not discover the resulting problems until much later, and therefore, she had extra time. Faced with this counterargument, Pickwick attempts a "speaking demurrer" by arguing, "we have a letter in which plaintiff Edwards complained about pain right after the operation." (See: **demurrer**)

special: adj. referring to a particular purpose, person or happening. In law these include hearings, proceedings, administrator, master, orders and so forth.

special administrator: n. a person appointed by the court in a probate proceeding (management of the estate of a deceased person) to take charge of the assets and/or investigate the status of the estate and report to the court, usually when there is a dispute between beneficiaries (those who may receive from the estate) and the executor or administrator. (See: **probate**)

special appearance: n. the representation by an attorney of a person in court for: a) only that particular session of the court; b) on behalf of the client's regular attorney of record; c) as a favor for an unrepresented person; or d) pending a decision as to whether the attorney agrees to handle the person's case. A special appearance is different from a "general appearance" in which the attorney is committed to represent the client in all future matters, hearings and trial of the case unless he/she is allowed to withdraw or is substituted "out of" the case by the client. Quite often an attorney will make a "special appearance" to protect the interests of a potential client but before a fee has

been paid or arranged. (See: **general appearance**)

special circumstances: n. in criminal cases, particularly homicides, actions of the accused or the situation under which the crime was committed for which state statutes allow or require imposition of a more severe punishment. "Special circumstances" in murder cases may well result in the imposition of the death penalty for murder (in states with capital punishment) or life sentence without possibility of parole. Such circumstances may include: rape, kidnapping or maiming prior to the killing, multiple deaths, killing a police officer or prison guard, or actions showing wanton disregard for life, such as throwing a bomb into a restaurant. (See: **capital punishment**)

special damages: n. damages claimed and/or awarded in a lawsuit which were out-of-pocket costs directly as the result of the breach of contract, negligence or other wrongful act by the defendant. Special damages can include medical bills, repairs and replacement of property, loss of wages and other damages which are not speculative or subjective. They are distinguished from general damages, in which there is no evidence of a specific dollar figure. (See: **damages, general damages**)

special master: n. a person appointed by the court to carry out an order of the court, such as selling property or mediating child custody cases. A "special" master differs from a "master" in that he/she takes positive action rather than just investigating and reporting to the judge. (See: **master**)

special prosecutor: n. an attorney from outside of the government selected by the Attorney General or Congress to investigate and possibly prosecute a federal government official for wrongdoing in office. The theory behind appointing a special prosecutor is that there is a built-in conflict of interest between the Department of Justice and officials who may have political or governmental connections with that department. The most famous special prosecutor was law professor Archibald Cox, originally chosen to investigate White House (and President Richard Nixon's) involvement in the Watergate scandal. President Nixon demanded that Attorney General Elliot Richardson fire Cox, who was being aggressive in his investigation, and Richardson resigned rather than comply, as did Assistant Attorney General William Ruckelshaus. Deputy Attorney General Robert Bork finally discharged Cox.

special verdict: n. the jury's decisions or findings of fact with the application of the law to those facts left up to the judge, who will then render the final verdict. This type of limited verdict is used when the legal issues to be applied are complex or require difficult computation. (See: **specific finding**)

specific bequest: n. the gift in a will of a certain article to a certain person or persons. Example: "I give my diamond engagement ring to my niece, Sophie." (See: **bequest, will**)

specific devise: n. the gift in a will of a certain piece of real estate to a certain person or persons. Example: "I leave the Lazy Z Ranch to my brother, David." (See: **devise, will**)

specific finding: n. a decision on a fact made by a jury in its verdict and which the judge has requested the jury to determine as part of its deliberations. Often the judge gives a jury a list of decisions on findings of fact to be made to help the jurors focus on the issues. Example: Findings: Was defendant exceeding the speed limit?—yes; Was defendant negligent?—yes; If defendant was negligent, was the negligence a proximate cause of damages to defendant?—yes; and so forth. (See: **special verdict**)

specific legacy: n. a gift in a will of a certain article or property to a certain person or persons. (See: **legacy, specific bequest, specific devise, will**)

specific performance: n. the right of a party to a contract to demand that the defendant (the party who it is claimed breached the contract) be ordered in the judgment to perform the contract. Specific performance may be ordered instead of (or in addition to) a judgment for money if the contract can still be performed and money cannot sufficiently reward the plaintiff. Example: when a defendant was to deliver some unique item such as an artwork and did not, a judge may order the defendant to actually deliver the artwork. (See: **contract, prayer**)

speculative damages: n. possible financial loss or expenses claimed by a plaintiff (person filing a lawsuit) which are contingent upon a future occurrence, purely conjectural or highly improbable. Speculative damages should not be awarded, and jury instructions should so state. Examples: a) plaintiff believes that ten years hence, as he ages, he may begin to feel pain from a healed fracture although no physician has testified that this is likely to happen; b) plaintiff claims that defendant's failure to deliver products for sale may hurt plaintiff's reputation with future customers. (See: **damages**)

speedy trial: n. in criminal prosecutions, the right of a defendant to demand a trial within a short time since to be held in jail without trial is a violation of the "due process" provision of the 5th Amendment (applied to the states by the 14th Amendment). Each state has a statute or constitutional provision limiting the time an accused person may be held before trial (e.g. 45 days). Charges must be dismissed and the defendant released if the period expires without trial. However, defendants often waive the right to a speedy trial in order to prepare a stronger defense, and if the accused is free on bail he/she will not be hurt by the waiver. (See: **due process, trial**)

spendthrift clause: n. a provision in a trust or will that states that if a prospective beneficiary has pledged to turn over a gift he/she hopes to receive to a third party, the trustee or executor shall not honor such a pledge. The purpose is to prevent a "spendthrift" beneficiary from using a potential gift as security for credit on a speculative investment. Example: Junior Jones is talked into an investment in Florida swampland but has no money in hand to pay for it. So he tells the developer he will soon receive $50,000 from his aunt's trust and signs an assignment of the expected $50,000 to the developer. When the aunt dies, the trustee must ignore the developer's demand for payment based on the written assignment but may pay the funds directly to Junior. (See: **trust, will**)

spot zoning: n. a provision in a general plan which benefits a single parcel of land by creating a zone for use just for that parcel and different from the surrounding properties in the area. Example: in a residential neighborhood zoned for single-family dwellings with a minimum of 10,000 square feet, the corner service station property is zoned commercial. Spot zoning is not favored, since it smacks of favoritism and usually annoys neighbors. An existing commercial business can be accommodated by a "zoning variance" (allowing a nonconforming use for the time being) or a "grandfathered" right to continue a use existing when the zoning plan was adopted and which will terminate if the building is torn down. (See: **grandfathered in, zoning**)

spontaneous exclamation: n. a sudden statement caused by the speaker having seen a surprising, startling or shocking event (such as an accident or a death), or having suffered an injury. Even though the person who made the spontaneous exclamation is not available (such as he/she is dead or missing), a person who heard the exclamation may testify about it as an exception to the rule against "hearsay" evidence. The reason is that such an exclamation lacks planning and is assumed to have the ring of truth to it. Examples: "Chauncey shot him," "my leg is broken," "the blue Chevrolet hit the girl." (See: **hearsay**)

spousal support: n. payment for support of an ex-spouse (or a spouse while a divorce is pending) ordered by the court. More commonly called alimony, spousal support is the term used in California and a few other states as part of new non-confrontational language (such as "dissolution" instead of "divorce") now used since divorce is "no-fault" in all states but two. (See: **alimony, dissolution of marriage, divorce, no-fault**)

springing interest: n. a future right to title to real property created by a deed or will. Example: "I give title to my daughter Mabel for her lifetime, and, on her death, title to my grandson Rex." Rex has a springing interest in the property. (See: **future interest, interest, title**)

stakeholder: n. a person having in his/her possession (holding) money or property in which he/she has no interest, right or title, awaiting the outcome of a dispute between two or more claimants to the money or property. The stakeholder has a duty to deliver to the owner or owners the money or assets once the right to legal possession is established by judgment or agreement. (See: **escrow**)

standard of care: n. the watchfulness, attention, caution and prudence that a reasonable person in the circumstances would exercise. If a person's actions do not meet this standard of care, then his/her acts fail to meet the duty of care which all

people (supposedly) have toward others. Failure to meet the standard is negligence, and any damages resulting therefrom may be claimed in a lawsuit by the injured party. The problem is that the "standard" is often a subjective issue upon which reasonable people can differ. (See: **duty of care, foreseeable risk, negligence**)

standing: n. the right to file a lawsuit or file a petition under the circumstances. A plaintiff will have standing to sue in federal court if a) there is an actual controversy, b) a federal statute gives the federal court jurisdiction, and c) the parties are residents of different states or otherwise fit the constitutional requirements for federal court jurisdiction. A state court example: a trade association will have standing to file a petition for a writ of mandate to order a state government agency to enforce a regulation if the association represents businesses affected by the regulation, and it would be impractical for each business to file its own petition. (See: **actual controversy, jurisdiction**)

star chamber proceedings: n. any judicial or quasi-judicial action, trial or hearing which so grossly violates standards of "due process" that a party appearing in the proceedings (hearing or trial) is denied a fair hearing. The term comes from a large room with a ceiling decorated with stars in which secret hearings of the privy council and judges met to determine punishment for disobedience of the proclamations of King Henry VIII of Great Britain (1509–1547). The high-handed, unfair, predetermined judgments, which sent the accused to the Tower of London or to the chopping block, made "star chamber" synonymous with unfairness and illegality from the bench. In modern American history the best example of star chamber proceedings was the conduct of the House Un-American Activities Committee (1938–1975), which used its subpena power to intimidate citizens by asking them unconstitutional questions about their political beliefs and associations, and then charging them with contempt of Congress for refusing to answer. Another example was the conduct of criminal proceedings against black defendants in some southern states from 1876 until the late 1960s. (See: **due process, kangaroo court**)

stare decisis: (stah-ree duh-sigh-sis) n. Latin for "to stand by a decision," the doctrine that a trial court is bound by appellate court decisions (precedents) on a legal question which is raised in the lower court. Reliance on such precedents is required of trial courts until such time as an appellate court changes the rule, for the trial court cannot ignore the precedent (even when the trial judge believes it is "bad law"). (See: **appellate court, lower court, precedent**)

state: n. 1) the federal or state government and any of its departments, agencies or components (such as a city, county or board). 2) any of the 50 states comprising the United States. 3) a nation's government.

state action: n. in federal Civil Rights Acts, dating back to 1875, any activity by the government of a state, any of its components or employees (like a sheriff) who uses the "color of law" (claim of legal right) to violate an individual's civil rights. Such "state action" gives the person whose rights have been violated by a governmental body or official the right to sue that agency or person for damages. (See: **civil rights**)

state of domicile: n. the state in which a person has his/her permanent residence or intends to make his/her residence, as compared to where the person is living temporarily. Domicile depends on intent, location of a home where a person regularly sleeps and some conduct. A corporation's state of domicile is the state where the corporation is incorporated. (See: **domicile, resident**)

status conference: n. a pre-trial meeting of attorneys before a judge required under federal Rules of Procedure and in many states required to inform the court as to how the case is proceeding, what discovery has been conducted (depositions, interrogatories, production of documents), any settlement negotiations, probable length of trial and other matters relevant to moving the case toward trial. Court rules usually require the filing of a status conference statement prior to the conference. In federal courts the status conference is also the occasion for setting a trial date. (See: **discovery**)

statute: n. a federal or state written law enacted by the Congress or state legislature, respectively. Local statutes or laws are usually called "ordinances." Regulations, rulings, opinions, executive orders and proclamations are not statutes.

statute of frauds: n. law in every state which requires that certain documents be in writing, such as real property titles and transfers (conveyances), leases for more than a year, wills and some types of contracts. The original statute was enacted in England in 1677 to prevent fraudulent title claims. (See: **contracts, deeds, fraud, leases, wills**)

statute of limitations: n. a law which sets the maximum period which one can wait before filing a lawsuit, depending on the type of case or claim. The periods vary by state. Federal statutes set the limitations for suits filed in federal courts. If the lawsuit or claim is not filed before the statutory deadline, the right to sue or make a claim is forever dead (barred). The types of cases and statute of limitations periods are broken down among: personal injury from negligence or intentional wrongdoing, property damage from negligence or intentional wrongdoing, breach of an oral contract, breach of a written contract, professional malpractice, libel, slander, fraud, trespass, a claim against a governmental entity (usually a short time), and some other variations. In some instances a statute of limitations can be extended ("tolled") based on delay in discovery of the injury or on reasonable reliance on a trusted person (a fiduciary or confidential adviser who has hidden his/her own misuse of someone else's funds or failure to pay). A minor's right to bring an action for injuries due to negligence is tolled until the minor turns 18 (except for a claim against a governmental agency). There are also statutes of limitations on bringing criminal charges, but homicide generally has no time limitation on prosecution. The limitations (depending on the state) generally range from 1 to 6 years except for in Rhode Island, which uses 10 years for several causes of action. Louisiana has the strictest limitations, cutting off lawsuit rights at one year for almost all types of cases except contracts. California also has short periods, usually one year, with two years for most property damage and oral contracts and four years for written contracts. There are also statutes of limitations on the right to enforce a judgment, ranging from five to 25 years, depending on the state. Some states have special requirements before a lawsuit can be filed, such as a written warning to a physician in a claim of malpractice, making a demand upon a state agency and then waiting for the claim to be denied or ignored for a particular period, first demanding a retraction before filing a libel suit, and other variations. Vermont protects its ski resorts by allowing only one year for filing a lawsuit for injuries suffered in a skiing accident as an exception to that state's three-year statute of limitations for other personal injuries. (See: **demurrer, laches, toll**)

statutory offer of settlement: n. a written offer of a specific sum of money made by a defendant to a plaintiff, which will settle the lawsuit if accepted within a short time. The offer may be filed with the court, and if the eventual judgment for the plaintiff is less than the offer, the plaintiff will not be able to claim the court costs usually awarded to the prevailing party.

statutory rape: n. sexual intercourse with a female below the legal age of consent but above the age of a child, even if the female gave her consent, did not resist and/or mutually participated. In all but three states the age of consent is 18, and the age above which the female is no longer a child varies, although 14 is common. The theory of statutory rape is that the girl is incapable of giving consent, although marriage with a parent's consent is possible in many states at ages as low as 14. Intercourse with a female child (below 14 or whatever the state law provides) is rape, which is a felony. Increasingly statutory rape is not charged when there is clear consent by the female, particularly when the girl will not cooperate in a prosecution. Controversy continues over what constitutes "resistance" or "consent," particularly when some men insist a woman who said "no" really meant "yes." (See: **majority, minority, molestation, rape**)

stay: n. a court-ordered short-term delay in judicial proceedings to give a losing defendant time to arrange for payment of the judgment or move out of the premises in an unlawful detainer case. (See: **stay of execution**)

stay away order: n. a court order that a person may not come near and/or contact another. (See: **peace bond, restraining order**)

stay of execution: n. a court-ordered delay in inflicting the death penalty. (See: **stay**)

stipulation: n. an agreement, usually on a procedural matter, between the attorneys for the two sides in a legal action. Some stipulations are oral, but the courts often require that the stipulation be put in writing, signed and filed with the court.

stock: 1) n. inventory (goods) of a business meant for sale (as distinguished from equipment and facilities). 2) share in the ownership of a corporation (called "shares of stock" or simply "shares"). 3) cattle. 4) v. to keep goods ready for sale in a business. (See: **share, shareholder**)

stock certificate: n. printed document which states the name, incorporation state, date of incorporation, the registered number of the certificate, the number of shares of stock in a corporation the certificate represents, the name of the shareholder, the date of issuance and the number of shares authorized in the particular issue of stock, signed by the president and secretary of the corporation (or with facsimile signatures). On the reverse side of the certificate is a form for transfer of the certificate to another person. After transfer the new owner should register the change of ownership with the corporation. (See: **corporation, share, stock**)

stockholder: n. shareholder in a corporation. (See: **shareholder**)

stockholders' derivative action: n. (See: **derivative action, shareholders' derivative action**)

stock in trade: n. the inventory of merchandise held for sale.

stock option: n. the right to purchase

stock in the future at a price set at the time the option is granted (by sale or as compensation by the corporation). To actually obtain the shares of stock the owner of the option must "exercise" the option by paying the agreed upon price and requesting issuance of the shares. (See: **option, stock, share**)

stop and frisk: n. a law enforcement officer's search for a weapon confined to a suspect's outer clothing when either a bulge in the clothing or the outline of the weapon is visible. The search is commonly called a "pat down," and any further search requires either a search warrant or "probable cause" to believe the suspect will commit or has committed a crime (including carrying a concealed weapon, which itself is a crime). The limited right to "stop and frisk" is intended to halt the practice of random searches of people in hopes of finding evidence of criminal activity or merely for purposes of intimidation, particularly of minorities. (See: **probable cause, search, search and seizure, search warrant**)

straw man: n. 1) a person to whom title to property or a business interest is transferred for the sole purpose of concealing the true owner and/or the business machinations of the parties. Thus, the straw man has no real interest or participation but is merely a passive stand-in for a real participant who secretly controls activities. Sometimes a straw man is involved when the actual owner is not permitted to act, such as a person with a criminal record holding a liquor license. 2) an

argument which is intended to distract the other side from the real issues or waste the opponent's time and effort, sometimes called a "red herring" (for the belief that drawing a fish across a trail will mislead hunting dogs).

street: n. a roadway in an urban area, owned and maintained by the municipality for public use. A private road cannot be a street.

strict construction (narrow construction): n. interpreting the Constitution based on a literal and narrow definition of the language without reference to the differences in conditions when the Constitution was written and modern conditions, inventions and societal changes. By contrast "broad construction" looks to what someone thinks was the "intent" of the framers' language and expands and interprets the language extensively to meet current standards of human conduct and complexity of society. (See: **Constitution, construction**)

strict liability: n. automatic responsibility (without having to prove negligence) for damages due to possession and/or use of equipment, materials or possessions which are inherently dangerous, such as explosives, wild animals, poisonous snakes or assault weapons. This is analogous to the doctrine of *res ipsa loquitur* in which control, ownership and damages are sufficient to hold the owner liable. (See: **liability, negligence, *res ipsa loquitur***)

strike: 1) v. to remove a statement from the record of the court proceedings by order of the judge due to impropriety of a question, answer or comment to which there has been an objection. Often after a judge has stricken some comment or testimony (an answer made before an objection has stopped the witness), he/she admonishes (warns) the jury not to consider the stricken language, but the jury has a hard time forgetting since "a bell once rung cannot be unrung." 2) v. to order that language in a pleading (a complaint or an answer, for example) shall be removed or no longer be of any effect, usually after a motion by the opposing party and argument, on the basis that the language (which may be an entire cause of action) is not proper pleading, does not state a cause of action (a valid claim under the law) or is not in proper form. 3) n. the organized refusal of workers to remain on the job, usually accompanied by demands for a union contract, higher wages, better conditions or other employee desires, and possibly including a picket line to give voice to workers' demands and discourage or intimidate other workers and customers from entering the business, factory or store.

structure: n. anything built by man/woman, from a shed to a highrise or a bridge.

sua sponte: (sooh-uh spahn-tay) adj. Latin for "of one's own will," meaning on one's own volition, usually referring to a judge's order made without a request by any party to the case. These include an order transferring a case to another judge due to a conflict of interest or the judge's determination that his/her court does not have jurisdiction over the case.

subchapter S corporation: n. the choice by a small corporation to be treated under "subchapter S" by the Internal Revenue Service, which allows the corporation to be treated like a partnership for taxation purposes. This may provide the benefit of passing losses (particularly in the early development of the business) to the stockholders. Technically the term "subchapter S corporation" is a misnomer since it is a normal corporation except for the election (choice) which is filed on a form provided by the IRS normally immediately after incorporation, which election can be withdrawn before the beginning of a future taxable year. This election is usually prepared and filed with the IRS by the company's accountant and not the incorporating attorney. (See: **corporation**)

subcontractor: n. a person or business which has a contract (as an "independent contractor") and not an employee) with a contractor to provide some portion of the work or services on a project which the contractor has agreed to perform. In building construction, subcontractors may include such trades as plumbing, electrical, roofing, cement work and plastering. If a subcontractor is not paid for his/her work, he/she has the right to enforce a "mechanic' lien" on the real property upon which the work was done to collect. (See **contract, contractor, independent contractor, mechanic's lien**)

subject to: adj. referring to the acquisition of title to real property upon which there is an existing mortgage or deed of trust when the new owner agrees to take title with the responsibility to continue to make the payments on the promissory note secured by the mortgage or deed of trust. Thus, the new owner (grantee) buys the property "subject to" secured debt. However, should the new owner fail to pay, the original debtor will be liable for the payment, but the holder of the mortgage or beneficiary of the deed of trust may foreclose and the buyer could thus lose title. This differs from the new title holder "assuming" the mortgage or deed of trust by a written transfer of the obligation. Such a transfer must be approved by the lender, since the new owner's credit may or may not be as strong as the original owner/borrower's. (See: **assumption, deed of trust, mortgage, secured transactions**)

sublease: n. the lease to another of all or a portion of premises by a tenant who has leased the premises from the owner. A sublease may be prohibited by the original lease, or require written permission from the owner. In any event, the original tenant (lessee) is still responsible for paying the rent to the owner (landlord/lessor) through the term of the original lease and sublease. (See: **lease, rent**)

submitted: n. the conclusion of all evidence and argument in a hearing or trial, leaving the decision in the hands of the judge. Typically the judge will ask the attorneys after final arguments: "Is it submitted?" If so, no further argument is permitted.

subordination: n. allowing a debt or claim which has priority to take second position behind another debt, particularly a new loan. A property owner with a loan secured by the property who applies for another loan to make additions or repairs usually must get a subordination of the original loan so the new obligation is in first place. A declaration of homestead must always be subordinated to a loan. (See: **secured transactions, subordination agreement,**)

subordination agreement: n. a written contract in which a lender who has secured a loan by a mortgage or deed of trust agrees with the property owner to subordinate the first loan to a new loan (thus giving the new loan priority in any foreclosure or payoff). The agreement must be acknowledged by a notary so it can be recorded in the official county records. (See: **subordination**)

subornation of perjury: n. the crime of encouraging, inducing or assisting another in the commission of perjury, which is knowingly telling an untruth under oath. Example: lawyer Frank Foghorn is interviewing a witness in an accident case who tells Foghorn that Foghorn's client was jaywalking outside the crosswalk when struck by the defendant's car. Foghorn tells the witness to help his client by saying the accident occurred in the crosswalk and the witness so testifies in court. Foghorn is guilty of subornation of the witness's perjury. (See: **perjury**)

subpena (subpoena): (suh-pea-nah) n. an order of the court for a witness to appear at a particular time and place to testify and/or produce documents in the control of the witness (if a "subpena *duces tecum*"). A subpena is used to obtain testimony from a witness at both depositions (testimony under oath taken outside of court) and at trial. Subpenas are usually issued automatically by the court clerk but must be served personally on the party being summoned. Failure to appear as required by the subpena can be punished as contempt of court if it appears the absence was intentional or without cause. (See: **contempt of court, deposition, subpena** *duces tecum*, **subpoena, witness**)

subpena *duces tecum*: (suh-pea-nah dooh-chess-take-uhm or dooh-kess-take-uhm): a court order requiring a witness to bring documents in the possession or under the control of the witness to a certain place at a certain time. This subpena must be served personally on the person subpenaed. It is the common way to obtain potentially useful evidence, such as documents and business records, in the possession of a third party. A subpena *duces tecum* must specify the documents or types of documents (e.g. "profit and loss statements of ABC Corporation for years 1987 through 1995, all correspondence in regard to the contract between ABC Corporation and Merritt") or it will be subject to an objection that the request is "too broad and burdensome." To obtain documents from the opposing party, a "Request for Production of Documents" is more commonly used. Failure to respond to a subpena *duces tecum* may subject the party served with the subpena to punishment for contempt of court for disobeying a court order. (See: **contempt of court-subpena, witness**)

subpoena: n. the original spelling of subpena, still commonly used. (See: **subpena, subpena** *duces tecum*)

subrogation: n. assuming the legal rights of a person for whom expenses or a debt has been paid. Typically, subrogation occurs when an insurance company which pays its insured client for injuries and losses then sues the party which the injured person contends caused the damages to him/her. Example: Fred Farmer negligently builds a bonfire which gets out of control and starts a grass fire which spreads to Ned Neighbor's barn. Good Hands Insurance Co. has insured the barn, pays Neighbor his estimated cost of reconstruction of the barn, and then sues Farmer for that amount. Farmer will have all the "defenses" to the insurance company's suit that he would have had against Neighbor, including the contention that the cost of repairing the barn was less than Neighbor was paid or that Neighbor negligently got in the way of firefighters trying to put out the grass fire. (See: **negligence, subrogee, subrogor**)

subrogee: n. the person or entity that assumes the legal right to attempt to collect a claim of another (subrogor) in return for paying the other's expenses or debts which the other claims against a third party. A subrogee is usually the insurance company which has insured the party whose expenses were paid. Thus, the subrogee insurance company may file a lawsuit against a party which caused the damages to its insured which the subrogee paid. (See: **subrogation, subrogor**)

subrogor: n. a person or entity that

transfers his/her/its legal right to collect a claim to another (subrogee) in return for payment of the subrogor's expenses or debts which he/she/it claims. Thus, a person injured in an accident (subrogor) is paid by his/her/its own insurance company (subrogee) for the damages, and then the insurance company sues the party who apparently caused the damages. (See: **subrogation, subrogee**)

subscribe: v. 1) to sign at the end of a document. The courts have been flexible in recognizing signatures elsewhere on a contract or will, on the theory that a document should be found valid if possible. 2) to order and agree to pay for an issue of stock, bonds, limited partnership interest, investment or periodical magazine or newspaper.

substantial performance: n. in the law of contracts, fulfillment of the obligations agreed to in a contract, with only slight variances from the exact terms and/or unimportant omissions or minor defects. A simple test is whether the omission, variance or defect can be easily compensated for with money. Examples: a) the contract is for supplying 144 pumps for $14,400, and only 140 were delivered; b) the real property was supposed to be 80 acres and only contained 78 acres. This constitutes substantial performance unless the loss of two acres is crucial to the value of the property (e.g. reduced the number of lots able to be subdivided); c) the product was to be delivered on October 25 and did not arrive until November 5. This constitutes substantial performance

unless the product was required for a Halloween sale. (See: **contract, specific performance**)

substantive law: n. law which establishes principles and creates and defines rights limitations under which society is governed, as differentiated from "procedural law," which sets the rules and methods employed to obtain one's rights and, in particular, how the courts are conducted. (See: **procedure**)

substituted service: n. accomplishing service (delivery) of legal documents required to be served personally by leaving the documents with an adult resident of the home of the person to be served, with an employee with management duties at the office of an individual, with such an employee at corporate headquarters, with a designated "agent for acceptance of service" (often with name and address filed with the state's Secretary of State), or in some cases (like a notice to quit the premises) by posting in a prominent place followed by mailing copies by certified mail to the person to be served. (See: **service, service of process**)

substitute in: v. to take over a case from another lawyer, which must be confirmed by a written statement filed with the court. (See: **substitution of attorney**)

substitution: n. putting one person in place of another, in particular replacement of the attorney of record in a lawsuit with another attorney (or the party acting in *propria persona*). (See: **substitution of attorney**)

substitution of attorney: n. a

document in which the party to a lawsuit states that his/her attorney of record is being substituted for by another attorney or by the party acting for himself/herself (*in propria persona*). Normally the departing attorney and the replacement attorney will both sign the document, agreeing to the substitution, but only the new attorney need agree, since a party may replace counsel at any time. (See: **substitute in**)

succession: n. the statutory rules of inheritance of a dead person's estate when the property is not given by the terms of a will, also called laws of "descent and distribution." (See: **descent and distribution, inheritance**)

successive sentences: n. in criminal law, the imposition of the penalty for each of several crimes, one after the other, as compared to "concurrent sentences" (at the same time). Example: Carl Convict has been found guilty of manslaughter, assault with a deadly weapon and armed robbery, for which the maximum sentences are 15 years, 10 years and 10 years, respectively. By imposing successive sentences, the judge adds the terms together and sentences Convict to 35 years. Had the judge made the sentences concurrent, the maximum total would be 15 years. (See: **concurrent sentence, sentence**)

suffering: n. the pain, hurt, inconvenience, embarrassment and/or inability to perform normal activities as a result of injury, usually in the combination "pain and suffering,"

for which a person injured by another's negligence or wrongdoing may recover "general damages" (a money amount not based on specific calculation like medical bills but as compensation for the suffering which is subjective and based on the empathy of the trier of the facts—jury or judge sitting without a jury). (See: **damages, general damages, injury, negligence, pain and suffering**)

suicide: n. the intentional killing of oneself. Ironically, in most states suicide is a crime, but if successful there is no one to punish. However, attempted suicide can be a punishable crime (seldom charged against one surviving the attempt). "Assisted suicide" is usually treated as a crime, either specifically (as in Michigan) or as a form of homicide (second degree murder or manslaughter), even when done as a kindness to a loved one who is terminally ill and in great pain. (See: **homicide, manslaughter, second degree murder**)

sui generis: (sooh-ee jen-ur-iss) n. Latin for "one of a kind," unique.

suit: n. generic term for any filing of a complaint (or petition) asking for legal redress by judicial action, often called a "lawsuit." In common parlance a suit asking for a court order for action rather than a money judgment is often called a "petition," but technically it is a "suit in equity." (See: **lawsuit**)

sum certain: n. a specific amount stated in a contract or negotiable instrument (like a promissory note) at the time the document is written. A sum certain does not require future calculation or the awaiting of future happenings. Example: "Wanda Williams will pay Wilma Jackson $10,000 for redecorating her house, including all costs," is a sum certain as compared to "Williams will pay Jackson for time (at the rate of $50 an hour) and costs of materials for redecoration of Williams' house."

summation: n. the final argument of an attorney at the close of a trial in which he/she attempts to convince the judge and/or jury of the virtues of the client's case. (See: **closing argument**)

summary adjudication of issues: n. a court order ruling that certain factual issues are already determined prior to trial. This summary adjudication is based upon a motion by one of the parties contending that these issues are settled and need not be tried. The motion is supported by declarations under oath, excerpts from depositions which are under oath, admissions of fact by the opposing party and other discovery, as well as a legal argument (points and authorities). The other party may respond by counter-declarations and legal arguments attempting to show that these issues were "triable issues of fact." If there is any question as to whether there is conflict on the facts on an issue, the summary adjudication must be denied regarding that matter. The theory behind this summary process is to reduce the number of factual questions which will require evidence at trial and eliminate one or more causes of action in the complaint or conversely find a judgment for plaintiff. The motion for summary adjudication of issues often accompanies the broader motion for summary judgment, which can result in judgment on the entire complaint or some causes of action before the trial starts. The pleading procedures are extremely technical and complicated and are particularly dangerous to the party against whom such a motion is made. (See: **summary judgment**)

summary judgment: n. a court order ruling that no factual issues remain to be tried and therefore a cause of action or all causes of action in a complaint can be decided upon certain facts without trial. A summary judgment is based upon a motion by one of the parties that contends that *all* necessary factual issues are settled or so one-sided they need not be tried. The motion is supported by declarations under oath, excerpts from depositions which are under oath, admissions of fact and other discovery, as well as a legal argument (points and authorities), that argue that there are no triable issues of fact and that the settled facts require a summary judgment for the moving party. The opposing party will respond by counter-declarations and legal arguments attempting to show that there are "triable issues of fact." If it is unclear whether there is a triable issue of fact in any cause of action, then summary judgment must be denied as to that cause of action. The theory behind the summary judgment process is to eliminate the need to try settled factual issues and to decide without trial one or more causes of action in the complaint. The pleading procedures are extremely technical and complicated and are particularly dangerous to the party against whom the motion is made. (See:

cause of action, summary adjudication of issues)

summons: n. a document issued by the court at the time a lawsuit is filed, stating the name of both plaintiff and defendant, the title and file number of the case, the court and its address, the name and address of the plaintiff's attorney, and instructions as to the need to file a response to the complaint within a certain time (such as 30 days after service), usually with a form on the back on which information of service of summons and complaint is to be filled out and signed by the process server. A copy of the summons must be served on each defendant at the same time as the complaint to start the time running for the defendant to answer. Certain writs and orders to show cause are served instead of a summons since they contain the same information along with special orders of the court. After service to the defendants, the original summons, along with the "return of service" proving the summons and complaint were served, is filed with the court to show that each defendant was served. A summons differs from a subpena, which is an order to a witness to appear. (See: **complaint, order to show cause, service, service of process, writ**)

Superior Court: n. the name used in 16 states for the basic county trial court. (See: **court**)

supersedeas: (sooh-purr-said-ee-uhs) Latin for "you shall desist," an order (writ) by an appeals court commanding a lower court not to enforce or proceed with a judgment or sentence pending the decision on the appeal or until further order of the appeals court. (See: **appeal, court of appeals**)

superseding cause: n. the same as an "intervening cause" or "supervening cause," which is an event which occurs after the initial act leading to an accident and substantially causes the accident. The superseding cause relieves from responsibility (liability) the party whose act started the series of events which led to the accident, since the original negligence is no longer the proximate cause. (See: **intervening cause, proximate cause**)

supplemental: adj. referring to anything that is added to complete something, particularly a document, such as a supplemental declaration, supplemental complaint, supplemental answer, supplemental claim.

suppression of evidence: n. 1) a judge's determination not to allow evidence to be admitted in a criminal trial because it was illegally obtained or was discovered due to an illegal search. 2) the improper hiding of evidence by a prosecutor who is constitutionally required to reveal to the defense all evidence. Such suppression is a violation of the due process clause (5th Amendment, applied to states by the 14th Amendment) and may result in dismissal, mistrial or reversal on appeal, as well as contempt of court for the prosecutor. (See: **due process, evidence**)

supra: (sooh-prah) Latin for "above," in legal briefs and decisions it refers to the citation of a court decision which has been previously mentioned. Thus a case when first cited will be referred to as *Guinn v. United States*, (1915) 238 U.S. 347, meaning it can be found in volume 238 of the U.S. Reports (of the Supreme Court) at page 347 and was decided in 1915. The next time the case is cited as *Guinn v. United States*, *supra*.

supremacy clause: n. Article VI, section 2 of the U.S. Constitution, which reads: "This Constitution, and the Laws of the United States which shall be made in pursuance thereof; and all treaties made, or which shall be made, under the authority of the United States, shall be the supreme law of the land; and the judges in every state shall be bound thereby, any thing in the Constitution or laws of any state to the contrary notwithstanding." Thus a Supreme Court ruling can be binding on state courts if involving a constitutional issue.

Supreme Court: n. 1) the highest court in the United States, which has the ultimate power to decide constitutional questions and other appeals based on the jurisdiction granted by the Constitution, including cases based on federal statutes, between citizens of different states, and when the federal government is a party. The court is made up of nine members appointed for life by the President of the United States, with confirmation required by the Senate. One of the nine is the Chief Justice (appointed by the President if there is a vacancy), and the others are Associate Justices. 2) the ultimate appeals court in every state

except Maryland and New York (which call the highest court the Court of Appeals). 3) in New York a Supreme Court is a basic trial court much like a superior, county or district court in other states. (See: **court**)

surcharge: n. an additional charge of money made because it was omitted in the original calculation or as a penalty, such as for being late in making a payment.

surety: n. a guarantor of payment or performance if another fails to pay or perform, such as a bonding company which posts a bond for a guardian, an administrator or a building contractor. Most surety agreements require that a person looking to the surety (asking for payment) must first attempt to collect or obtain performance from the responsible person or entity. (See: **bond, guarantor**)

surplusage: n. a term used in analyzing legal documents and pleadings to refer to wording or statements which have no legal effect and, therefore, can be ignored.

surrebutal: n. in written or oral legal argument, the response to the other party's response (rebuttal) to the initial argument. In written briefs most courts will not allow more than a single surrebutal. The rule is usually the same for oral argument. However, occasionally the parties joust back and forth until the judge stops the debate.

surrender: v. 1) to turn over possession of real property, either voluntarily or upon demand, by tenant to landlord. 2) to give oneself up to law enforcement officials.

401

surrogate: n. 1) a person acting on behalf of another or a substitute, including a woman who gives birth to a baby of a mother who is unable to carry the child. 2) a judge in some states (notably New York) responsible only for probates, estates and adoptions.

surrogate court: n. a court in a few states (including New York) with jurisdiction over probates, estates and adoptions.

survivor: n. a person who outlives another, as in "to my sons, Arnold and Zeke, or the survivor." The survivor is determined at the time the asset or property is received, so if both sons are alive they are both survivors.

survivorship: n. the right to receive full title or ownership due to having survived another person. Survivorship is particularly applied to persons owning real property or other assets, such as bank accounts or stocks, in "joint tenancy." Joint tenancy includes the right of survivorship automatically, except that in some states joint tenancy of a bank account creates only a presumption of survivorship, which might be disproved by evidence that the joint tenancy was only for convenience. (See: **joint tenancy**)

suspended sentence: n. in criminal law, a penalty applied by a judge to a defendant convicted of a crime which the judge provides will not be enforced (is suspended) if the defendant performs certain services, makes restitution to persons harmed, stays out of trouble or meets other conditions. Should the sentenced party fail to follow these requirements, then the suspended sentence may be enforced. (See: **sentence**)

sustain: v. in trial practice, for a judge to agree that an attorney's objection, such as to a question, is valid. Thus, an attorney asks a witness a question, and the opposing lawyer objects, saying the question is "irrelevant, immaterial and incompetent," "leading," "argumentative," or some other objection. If the judge agrees he/she will rule "sustained," meaning the objection is approved and the question cannot be asked or answered. However, if the judge finds the question proper, he/she will "overrule" the objection.

swear: v. 1) to declare under oath that one will tell the truth (sometimes "the truth, the whole truth and nothing but the truth"). Failure to tell the truth and do so knowingly is the crime of perjury. 2) to administer an oath to a witness that he/she will tell the truth, which is done by a notary public, a court clerk, a court reporter or anyone authorized by law to administer oaths. 3) to install into office by administering an oath. 4) to use profanity. (See: **notary public, oath, perjury**)

swindle: v. to cheat through trick, device, false statements or other fraudulent methods with the intent to acquire money or property from another to which the swindler is not entitled. Swindling is a crime as one form of theft. (See: **fraud, theft**)

syndicate: n. a joint venture among

individuals and/or corporations to accomplish a particular business objective, such as the purchase, development and sale of a tract of real property, followed by division of the profits. A joint venture, and thus a syndicate, is much like a partnership, but has a specific objective or purpose, after the completion of which it will dissolve. (See: **joint venture**)

tainted evidence: n. in a criminal trial, information which has been obtained by illegal means or has been traced through evidence acquired by illegal search and/or seizure. This evidence is called "fruit of the poisonous tree" and is not admissible in court. (See: **fruit of the poisonous tree, probable cause, search and seizure, search warrant**)

take: v. to gain or obtain possession, including the receipt of a legacy from an estate, getting title to real property or stealing an object.

taking the Fifth: n. the refusal to testify on the ground that the testimony might tend to incriminate the witness in a crime, based on the Fifth Amendment to the Constitution, which provides that "No person...shall be compelled to be a witness against himself," applied to state courts by the 14th Amendment. The term became famous during televised Senate committee hearings on organized crime in 1951, when a series of crime bosses "took the Fifth." (See: **self-incrimination**)

tangible property: n. physical articles (things) as distinguished from "incorporeal" assets such as rights, patents, copyrights and franchises. Commonly tangible property is called "personalty." (See: **intangible property, personal property, personalty**)

tax: n. a governmental assessment (charge) upon property value, transactions (transfers and sales), licenses granting a right and/or income. These include federal and state income taxes, county and city taxes on real property, state and/or local sales tax based on a percentage of each retail transaction, duties on imports from foreign countries, business licenses, federal tax (and some states' taxes) on the estates of persons who have died, taxes on large gifts and a state "use" tax in lieu of sales tax imposed on certain goods bought outside of the state. (See: *ad valorem*, **capital gains, estate tax, franchise tax, gift tax, income tax, unified estate and gift tax, use tax**)

tax costs: n. a motion to contest a claim for court costs submitted by a prevailing party in a lawsuit. It is called a "Motion to Tax Costs" and asks the judge to deny or reduce claimed costs. Example: a winning party claims a right to have his/her attorneys' fees and telephone bills paid by the loser, even though they are not allowable as costs under state law or the contract which was the subject of the suit. So the loser makes a "Motion to Tax Costs" to avoid paying these charges.

Tax Court: n. a federal agency with courts in major cities which hear taxpayers' appeals from decisions of the Internal Revenue Service. Tax court hears the appeal *de novo* (as a trial rather than an appeal) and does not require payment of the amount claimed by the IRS before hearing the case. Tax court decisions may be appealed to the Federal District Court of Appeals. (See: **court, income tax**)

tax evasion: n. intentional and fraudulent attempt to escape payment of taxes in whole or in part. If proved to be intentional and not just an error or difference of opinion, tax evasion can be a chargeable federal crime. Evasion is distinguished from attempts to use interpretation of tax laws and/or imaginative accounting to reduce the amount of payable tax.

tax return: n. the form to be filed with a taxing authority by a taxpayer which details his/her/their income, expenses, exemptions, deductions and calculation of taxes which are chargeable to the taxpayer. (See: **tax**)

tax sale: n. an auction sale of a taxpayer's property conducted by the federal government to collect unpaid taxes.

temporary injunction: n. a court order prohibiting an action by a party to a lawsuit until there has been a trial or other court action. A temporary injunction differs from a "temporary restraining order" which is a short-term, stop-gap injunction issued pending a hearing, at which time a temporary injunction may be ordered to be in force until trial. The purpose of a temporary injunction is to maintain the status quo and prevent irreparable damage or change before the legal questions are determined. After the trial the court may issue a "permanent injunction" (making the temporary injunction a lasting rule) or "dissolve" (cancel) the temporary injunction. (See: **injunction, temporary restraining order**)

temporary insanity: n. in a criminal prosecution, a defense by the accused that he/she was briefly insane at the time the crime was committed and therefore was incapable of knowing the nature of his/her alleged criminal act. Temporary insanity is claimed as a defense whether or not the accused is mentally stable at the time of trial. One difficulty with a temporary insanity defense is the problem of proof, since any examination by psychiatrists had to be after the fact, so the only evidence must be the conduct of the accused immediately before or after the crime. It is similar to the defenses of "diminished capacity" to understand one's own actions, the so-called "Twinkie defense," the "abuse excuse," "heat of passion" and other claims of mental disturbance which raise the issue of criminal intent based on modern psychiatry and/or sociology. However, mental derangement at the time of an abrupt crime, such as a sudden attack or crime of passion, can be a valid defense or at least show lack of premeditation to reduce the degree of the crime. (See: **crime, defense, diminished capacity, insanity, intent, Twinkie defense**)

tenancy: n. the right to occupy real property permanently, for a time which may terminate upon a certain event, for a specific term, for a series of periods until cancelled (such as month-to-month), or at will (which may be terminated at any time). Some tenancy is for occupancy only as in a landlord–tenant situation, or a tenancy may also be based on ownership of title to the property. (See: **joint tenancy, landlord and tenant, tenancy at sufferance, tenancy at will, tenancy by the entirety, tenancy in common, tenant, title**)

tenancy at sufferance: n. a "holdover" tenancy after a lease has expired but before the landlord has demanded that the tenant quit (vacate) the premises. During a tenancy at sufferance the tenant is bound by the terms of the lease (including payment of rent) which existed before it expired. The only difference between a "tenancy at sufferance" and a "tenancy at will" is that the latter was created by agreement. (See: **landlord and tenant, tenancy, tenancy at will, unlawful detainer**)

tenancy at will: n. occupation of real property owned by another until such time as the landlord gives notice of termination of the tenancy (usually 30 days by state law or agreement), which may be given at any time. A tenancy at will is created by agreement between the tenant and the landlord, but it cannot be transferred by the tenant to someone else since the landlord controls the right to occupy. (See: **tenancy**)

tenancy by the entirety: n. joint ownership of title by husband and wife, in which both have the right to the entire property, and, upon the death of one, the other has title (right of survivorship). Tenancy by the entirety is used in many states and is analogous to "community property" in the seven states which recognize that type of property ownership. (See: **community property, tenancy**)

tenancy in common: n. title to property (usually real property, but it can apply to personal property) held by two or more persons, in which each has an "undivided interest" in the property and all have an equal right to use the property, even if the percentage of interests are not equal or the living spaces are different sizes. Unlike "joint tenancy," there is no "right of survivorship" if one of the tenants in common dies, and each interest may be separately sold, mortgaged or willed to another. Thus, unlike a joint tenancy interest, which passes automatically to the survivor, upon the death of a tenant in common there must be a probate (court supervised administration) of the estate of the deceased to transfer the interest (ownership) in the tenancy in common. (See: **joint tenancy, tenancy**)

tenant: n. a person who occupies real property owned by another based upon an agreement between the person and the landlord/owner, almost always for rental payments. (See: **tenancy**)

tender: 1) v. to present to another person an unconditional offer to enter into a contract. 2) v. to present payment to another. 3) n. delivery, except that the recipient has the choice not to accept the tender. However, the act of tender completes the responsibility of the person making the tender. (See: **delivery, offer**)

tenement: n. 1) a term found in older deeds or in boiler-plate deed language which means any structure on real property. 2) old run-down urban apartment buildings with several floors reached by stairways. (See: **structure**)

tentative trust: n. a bank account deposited in the name of the depositor "in trust for" someone else, which is a tentative trust until the death of the depositor since the money can be withdrawn at any time. (See: **trust**)

tenure: n. 1) in real property, the right to possess the property. 2) in employment contracts, particularly of public employees like school teachers or professors, a guaranteed right to a job (barring substantial inability to perform or some wrongful act) once a probationary period has passed.

term: n. 1) in contracts or leases, a period of time, such as five years, in which a contract or lease is in force. 2) in contracts, a specified condition or proviso. 3) a period for which a court sits or a legislature is in session. 4) a word or phrase for something, as "tenancy" is one term for "occupancy."

testacy: n. dying with a will (a testament). It is compared to "intestacy," which is dying without a will. (See: **intestacy**)

testamentary: adj. pertaining to a will.

testamentary capacity: n. having the mental competency to execute a will at the time the will was signed and witnessed. To have testamentary capacity, the author of the will must understand the nature of making a will, have a general idea of what he/she possesses, and know who are members of the immediate family or other "natural objects of his/her bounty." Inherent in that capacity is the ability to resist the pressures or domination of any person who may try to use undue influence on the distribution of the testator's (will writer's) estate. (See: **capacity, competent, undue influence, will**)

testamentary disposition: n. how the terms of a will divide the testator's (will writer's) estate, including specific gifts to named beneficiaries. (See: **will**)

testamentary trust: n. a trust created by the terms of a will. Example: "The residue of my estate shall form the corpus (body) of a trust, with the executor as trustee, for my children's health and education, which shall terminate when the last child attains the age of 25, when the remaining corpus and any accumulated profits shall be divided among my then living children." A testamentary trust differs from an "*inter vivos*" or "living" trust, which comes into being during the lifetime of the creator of the trust (called trustor, settlor or donor), usually from the time the declaration of trust is signed. (See: ***inter vivos* trust, living trust, trust, will**)

testator: n. a person who has written a will which is in effect at the time of his/her death. (See: **will**)

testatrix: n. female form of testator, although distinguishing between genders is falling out of fashion. (See: **testator**)

testify: v. to give oral evidence under oath in answer to questions posed by attorneys either at trial or at a deposition (testimony under oath outside of court), with the opportunity for opposing attorneys to cross-examine the witness in regard to answers given. (See: **deposition, evidence, testimony, trial**)

testimony: n. oral evidence given under oath by a witness in answer to questions posed by attorneys at trial or at a deposition (questioning under oath outside of court). (See: **deposition, evidence, testify, trial, witness**)

theft: n. the generic term for all crimes in which a person intentionally and fraudulently takes personal property of another without permission or consent and with the intent to convert it to the taker's use (including potential sale). In many states, if the value of the property taken is low (for example, less than $500) the crime is "petty theft," but it is "grand theft" for larger amounts, designated misdemeanor or felony, respectively. Theft is synonymous with "larceny." Although robbery (taking by force), burglary (taken by entering unlawfully) and embezzlement (stealing from an employer) are all commonly thought of as theft, they are distinguished by the means and methods used and are separately designated as those types of crimes in criminal charges and statutory punishments. (See: **burglary, embezzlement, larceny, robbery**)

third party: n. a person who is not a party to a contract or a transaction, but has an involvement (such as one who is a buyer from one of the parties, was present when the agreement was signed or made an offer that was rejected). The third party normally has no legal rights in the matter, unless the contract was made for the third party's benefit. (See: **beneficiary, third-party beneficiary**)

> *The police must obey the law while enforcing the law.*
> *—Chief Justice Earl Warren*

third-party beneficiary: n. a person who is not a party to a contract but has legal rights to enforce the contract or share in proceeds because the contract was made for the third party's benefit. Example: Grandma enters into a contract with Oldfield to purchase a Jaguar automobile to be given to grandchild as a graduation present. If Oldfield takes a down payment and then refuses to go through with the sale, grandchild may sue Oldfield for specific performance of the contract as a third-party beneficiary.

30-day notice: n. a notice by a landlord to a tenant on a month-to-month tenancy or a holdover tenant to leave the premises within 30 days. Such notice does not have to state any reason and is not based on failure to pay rent. The landlord's service of the notice and the tenant's failure to vacate at the end of 30 days provide the basis for a lawsuit for unlawful detainer (eviction) and a court judgment ordering the tenant to leave. While this is a common notice period, it does not apply in all states or all circumstances, such as local rent control ordinances. (See: **landlord**

and tenant, service, unlawful detainer)

three-day notice: n. a notice to pay
delinquent rent or quit (leave or vacate) the premises given by a landlord to a tenant, which in most
states gives the tenant three days to
pay or get out. Service of the notice
and failure of the tenant to pay or
vacate within three days provide the
basis for a lawsuit for unlawful detainer (eviction) for unpaid rent and
a court judgment ordering the tenant to leave. While the three-day notice period is common it does not
apply in all states or in all circumstances, such as local rent control ordinances. (See: **landlord and tenant, service, unlawful detainer**)

three strikes, you're out: n. recent
(beginning 1994) legislation enacted
in several states (and proposed in
many others, as well as possible federal law) which makes life terms (or
extremely long terms without parole)
mandatory for criminals who have
been convicted of a third felony (as in
California) or of three felonies involving violence, rape, use of a deadly
weapon or molestation. The impetus
for "three strikes, you're out" has
come from public outrage over murders, assaults, rapes and child mo-
lestations by released ex-convicts
with records of repeated violent
crimes. Concern has been expressed
about the provisions in some of the
bills which prohibit plea bargaining
of any charged felony down to a misdemeanor, deny any judicial discretion in sentencing and do not distinguish between violent felonies and
cases of non-violent crimes which involve small amounts of money.

tide lands: n. land between the high
and low tides, which is uncovered each
day by tidal action. This land belongs
to the owner of the land which fronts
on the sea at that point.

time is of the essence: n. a phrase
often used in contracts which in effect
says: the specified time and dates in
this agreement are vital and thus
mandatory, and "we mean it." Therefore any delay—reasonable or not,
slight or not—will be grounds for cancelling the agreement. (See: **contract**)

timely: adj. within the time required by
statute, court rules or contract. Example: a notice of appeal is required to be
filed within 60 days of the entry of
judgment, so a notice filed on the 61st
day is not "timely."

time served: n. the period a criminal
defendant has been in jail, often
while awaiting bail or awaiting trial.
Often a judge will give a defendant
"credit for time served," particularly
when sentencing for misdemeanors.
Example: Johnny Jumpstart was arrested for drunk driving and spent
the night in jail before he was released on his own recognizance. Since
the minimum sentence in his state
was 48 hours, the judge will sentence
him to that time, less 14 hours for
time served. After lengthy waits in
jail before trial, "time served" may
become very important to the defendant. (See: **sentence**)

title: n. 1) ownership of real property or
personal property, which stands
against the right of anyone else to
claim the property. In real property,
title is evidenced by a deed, judgment
of distribution from an estate or other

409

appropriate document recorded in the public records of the county. Title to personal property is generally shown by possession, particularly when no proof or strong evidence exists showing that the property belongs to another or that it has been stolen or known to be lost by another. In the case of automobiles and other vehicles, title is registered with the state's Department of Motor Vehicles, which issues a title document ("pink slip") to the owner. 2) the name for one's position in a business or organization, such as president, general manager, mayor, governor, duke. 3) the name for a legal case, such as *Eugene Chan v. Runabout Taxi Company, Inc.*, which is part of the "caption" of the case. (See: **caption, personal property, pink slip, real property, title search**)

title abstract: n. a history of the chain of title. (See: **abstract**)

title insurance: n. a policy issued by an insurance company guaranteeing that the title to a parcel of real property is clear and properly in the name of the title owner and that the owner has the right to deed the property (convey or sell) to another. Should a problem later arise with the title (such as an inaccurate description), the insurance company will pay the damages to the new title holder or secured lender or take steps to correct the problem. (See: **chain of title, title, title search**)

title report: n. the written analysis of the status of title to real property, including a property description, names of titleholders and how title is held (joint tenancy, etc.), tax rate, encumbrances (mortgages, liens, deeds of trusts, recorded judgments), and real property taxes due. A title report made when the report is ordered is called a "preliminary report," or a "prelim," and at time of recording an up-to-date report is issued which is the final title report. The history of the title is called an "abstract." A title report is prepared by a title company, an abstractor, an attorney or an escrow company, depending on local practice. Normally a title report's accuracy is insured by title insurance which will require the insurance company to either correct any error or pay damages resulting from a "cloud on title," encumbrance or title flaw in the title which was not reported. (See: **abstract, cloud on title, title, title company, title insurance**)

title search: n. the examination of county records for the property's title history by a title company, an abstractor, attorney or escrow officer to determine the "chain of title" and the current status of title, including owner, legal description, easements, property taxes due, encumbrances (mortgages or deeds of trust), long-term leases, judgments or other liens. When a title search is completed, a "preliminary report" on title will be issued by the searcher. On the recording date of any new transfer or encumbrance (such as a new secured loan), an updated "final title report" will be issued which will make it possible to obtain title insurance guaranteeing against any problems with the title. Sometimes the title search will turn up some "cloud on the title" which reveals something is wrong, such as a break in the chain of title, inaccurate property description in a previous deed or some old secured loan which has not been released. Such clouds can be a reason to cancel a contract for purchase of the real property. (See: **abstractor, chain of title, encumbrance, escrow, lien, title, title company, title insurance**)

toll: v. 1) to delay, suspend or hold off the effect of a statute. Examples: a) a minor is injured in an accident when he is 14 years old, and the state law (statute of limitations) allows a person hurt by negligence two years to file suit for damages. But for a minor the statute is "tolled" until he/she becomes 18 and decides whether or not to sue. Thus the minor has two years after 18 to file suit. b) state law allows 10 years to collect a judgment, but if the judgment debtor (party who owes the judgment amount) leaves the state, the time is "tolled," so the judgment creditor (party to whom judgment is owed) will have extra time to enforce the judgment equal to the time the debtor was out of state. 2) a charge to pass over land, use a toll road or turnpike, cross a bridge or take passage on a ferry.

tontine: n. a rare agreement among several persons who agree that each will invest in an annuity and the last to die will receive the remaining assets and profits.

tools of trade: n. in bankruptcy law, the equipment a person requires in order to pursue his occupation, which is exempt from claims of creditors. They are also generally exempt from attachment by judgment creditors since it is important

for a person to earn an income to support the family and pay creditors. (See: **bankruptcy**)

tort: n. from French for "wrong," a civil wrong or wrongful act, whether intentional or accidental, from which injury occurs to another. Torts include all negligence cases as well as intentional wrongs which result in harm. Therefore tort law is one of the major areas of law (along with contract, real property and criminal law) and results in more civil litigation than any other category. Some intentional torts may also be crimes, such as assault, battery, wrongful death, fraud, conversion (a euphemism for theft) and trespass on property and form the basis for a lawsuit for damages by the injured party. Defamation, including intentionally telling harmful untruths about another—either by print or broadcast (libel) or orally (slander)—is a tort and used to be a crime as well. (See: **assault, battery, conversion, damages, defamation, fraud, libel, negligence, slander, trespass, wrongful death**)

tort claims act: n. a federal or state act which, under certain conditions, waives governmental immunity and allows lawsuits by people who claim they have been harmed by torts (wrongful acts), including negligence, by government agencies or their employees. These acts also establish the procedure by which such claims are made. Before the enactment of tort claims acts, government bodies could not be sued without the specific permission of the government. The federal version is the Federal Tort Claims Act. (See: **Federal Tort Claims Act**)

tortfeasor: n. a person who commits a tort (civil wrong), either intentionally or through negligence. (See: **joint tortfeasors, tort**)

tortious: adj. referring to an act which is a tort (civil wrong). (See: **tort**)

to wit: prep. that is to say. Example: "the passengers in the vehicle, to wit: Arlene Jones, Betty Bumgartner and Sherry Younger."

trade: 1) n. a business or occupation for profit, particularly in retail or wholesale sales or requiring special mechanical skill. 2) v. to exchange one thing for another, which includes money for goods, goods for goods and favors for goods or money. (See: **trade fixture, trademark, trade secret**)

trade fixture: n. a piece of equipment on or attached to the real estate which is used in a trade or business. Trade fixtures differ from other fixtures in that they may be removed from the real estate (even if attached) at the end of the tenancy of the business, while ordinary fixtures attached to the real estate become part of the real estate. The business tenant must compensate the owner for any damages due to removal of trade fixtures or repair such damage. (See: **fixture, trade**)

trademark: n. a distinctive design, picture, emblem, logo or wording (or combination) affixed to goods for sale to identify the manufacturer as the source of the product. Words that merely name the maker (but without particular lettering) or a generic name for the product are not trademarks. Trademarks may be registered with the U.S. Patent Office to prove use and ownership. Use of another's trademark (or one that is confusingly similar) is infringement and the basis for a lawsuit for damages for unfair competition and/or a petition for an injunction against the use of the infringing trademark. (See: **trade name**)

trade name: n. a name of a business or one of its products which, by use of the name and public reputation, identifies the product as that of the business. A trade name belongs to the first business to use it, and the identification and reputation give it value and the right to protect the trade name against its use by others. Example: Sheaffer's is clearly identified as a fountain pen manufactured by the Sheaffer Company, and no one else can produce pens with that name. However, a motorcycle with the name Sheaffer would not be an infringement since the product is different. (See: **trademark**)

trader: in U.S. income tax law, a person who deals in property as a business, making several purchases and sales within a year as distinguished from a few sales of assets held for investment. Thus a trader will lose the right to defer capital gains by "exchanging" for another property. The exact details require consultation with a C.P.A. or attorney.

trade secret: n. a process, method, plan, formula or other information unique to a manufacturer, which gives it an advantage over competitors. Therefore the trade secret has value and may be protected by a court-ordered injunction against use or revelation of trade secrets by an employee, former employee or someone who comes into possession of the trade secret. The employer may seek damages against such a person for revealing the secret. In addition, the owner of a trade secret involved in a lawsuit may request a "protective order" from the judge to prohibit revelation of a trade secret or a sealing of the record in the case where references to the trade secret are made. A trade secret is a business process and not a patentable invention. (See: **patent, trade**)

transcript: n. the written record of all proceedings, including testimony, in a trial, hearing or deposition (out-of-court testimony under oath). Jurisdictions vary as to whether the attorneys' final arguments are recorded, with the Federal Court Reporter Act, but not all states, requiring inclusion. A copy of the transcript may be ordered from the court reporter and a fee paid for the transcription and first copy; if the opposing party also wants a copy, the cost will not include the transcription fee. In most appeals a copy of the transcript is required so that the court of appeals can review the entire proceedings in the trial court. Copies of depositions may be ordered for a fee from the court reporter who took down the testimony. Transcripts are not printed from the record unless transcription is requested.

transfer: n. 1) the movement of property from one person or entity to another. 2) passage of title to property from the owner to another person.

3) a piece of paper given to allow a person or shipment to continue travel.

transfer agent: n. a person or company retained by a corporation to process transfers and registration of shares of stock (stock certificates). One difficulty is that the stock certificates do not always include the name and address of the current transfer agent, but the information can be obtained from the corporation or a stockbroker. (See: **share, stock**)

transfer in contemplation of death: n. giving property under the belief of the giver that he/she is about to die or has a terminal illness. However, health recovery may result in cancellation of the gift. This is also called a "gift *causa mortis*." (See: **gift in contemplation of death**)

transferred intent: n. in both criminal and tort (civil wrong) law, when an intent to cause harm to one person results in harm to another person instead of the intended target, the law transfers the intent to the actual harm. Examples: a) with malice aforethought Nate Nogood intends to shoot his girlfriend and misses her, and the bullet hits a passerby, killing him. Nogood may be charged with first degree murder since the intent to commit murder is transferred to the actual crime. b) Steve Swinger takes a punch at Harvey Hasgood, his hated enemy, misses Hasgood and hits Hasgood's date, Teri Truehart, in the nose, breaking it. Truehart can not only sue Swinger for damages due to the assault but can claim punitive damages because the malice against Hasgood attaches to the hit upon Truehart. (See: **intent**)

treason: n. the crime of betraying one's country, defined in Article III, section 3 of the U.S. Constitution: "Treason against the United States shall consist only in levying war against them, or in adhering to their enemies, giving them aid and comfort." Treason requires overt acts and includes the giving of government security secrets to other countries, even if friendly, when the information could harm American security. Treason can include revealing to an antagonistic country secrets such as the design of a bomber being built by a private company for the Defense Department. Treason may include "espionage" (spying for a foreign power or doing damage to the operation of the government and its agencies, particularly those involved in security) but is separate and worse than "sedition," which involves a conspiracy to upset the operation of the government. (See: **espionage, sedition**)

treasury bill: n. a promissory note issued in multiples of $10,000 by the U.S. Treasury with a maturity date of not more than one year. (See: **treasury bond, treasury note**)

treasury bond: n. a long-term bond issued by the U.S. Treasury. (See: **treasury bill, treasury note**)

treasury note: n. a promissory note issued by the U.S. Treasury, for a period of one to five years. (See: **treasury bill, treasury bond**)

treasury stock: n. stock of a private corporation which was issued and then bought back by the corporation or otherwise reacquired by the corporation. Treasury stock held by a corporation earns dividends for the corporation, but the corporation may not cast votes in decision-making the way a regular shareholder would be entitled. (See: **share, stock**)

treaty: n. a pact between nations which, if entered into by the United States through its Executive Branch, must be approved by "two-thirds of the Senators present," under Article II, section 2 of the Constitution, to become effective. Presidents sometimes get around the Senate by entering into "Executive Agreements" with leaders of other countries which are a mode of cooperation and not enforceable treaties.

treble damages: n. tripling damages allowed by state statute in certain types of cases, such as not making good on a bad check or intentionally refusing to pay rent. Federal antitrust violations also carry treble damage penalties. (See: **damages**)

trespass: n. entering another person's property without permission of the owner or his/her agent and without lawful authority (like that given to a health inspector) and causing any damage, no matter how slight. Any interference with the owner's (or a legal tenant's) use of the property is a sufficient showing of damage and is a civil wrong (tort) sufficient to form the basis for a lawsuit against the trespasser by the owner or a tenant using the property. Trespass includes erecting a fence on another's property or a roof which overhangs a neighbor's property, swinging the boom of a crane with loads of building materials over another's property, or dumping debris on another's real estate. In addition to damages, a court may grant an injunction prohibiting any further continuing, repeated or permanent trespass. Trespass for an illegal purpose is a crime.

trial: n. the examination of facts and law presided over by a judge (or other magistrate, such as a commissioner or judge *pro tem*) with authority to hear the matter (jurisdiction). A trial begins with the calling of the parties to come and be heard and selection of a jury if one has been requested. Each party is entitled to an opening statement by his/her attorney (or the party if he/she is representing himself/herself), limited to an outline of what each side intends to prove (the defense may withhold the opening statement until the defense is ready to present evidence), followed by the presentation of evidence first by the plaintiff (in a civil case) or prosecution (in a criminal case), followed by the defense evidence, and then by rebuttal evidence by the plaintiff or prosecution to respond to the defense. At the conclusion of all evidence each attorney (plaintiff or prosecution first) can make a final argument which can include opinion and comment on evidence and legal questions. If it is a jury trial, the judge will give the jury a series of instructions as to the law of the case, based on "jury instructions" submitted by the attorneys and approved, rejected, modified and/or added to by the judge. Then the jury retires to the jury room, chooses a foreperson and decides the factual questions. If there is no jury, the judge will

determine legal issues and decide factual questions and render (give) a judgment. A jury will judge the factual issues and decide the verdict based on the law as given in the instructions by the judge. Final verdict or judgment usually concludes the trial, although in some criminal cases a further trial will be held to determine "special circumstances" (acts which will increase the punishment) or whether the death penalty should be imposed. Throughout a trial there may be various motions on legal issues, some of which may be argued in the judge's chambers. In most criminal cases the exact punishment will be determined by the judge at a hearing held at a later time.

trial court: n. the court which holds the original trial, as distinguished from a court of appeals. (See: **trial**)

trial *de novo*: n. a form of appeal in which the appeals court holds a trial as if no prior trial had been held. A trial *de novo* is common on appeals from small claims court judgments.

tribunal: n. any court, judicial body or board which has quasi-judicial functions, such as a public utilities board which sets rates or a planning commission which can allow variances from zoning regulations. (See: **court**)

trier of fact: n. the judge or jury responsible for deciding factual issues in a trial. If there is no jury the judge is the trier of fact as well as the trier of the law. In administrative hearings, an administrative law judge, a board, commission or referee may be the trier of fact.

triple net lease: n. a lease in which the

lessee's (tenant's) rent includes a share of real property taxes, insurance and maintenance as well as the basic rent. A "triple-net-lease" is standard in leases of commercial property in shopping centers and malls. (See: **lease, rent**)

T.R.O.: n. legal slang for temporary restraining order. (See: **restraining order**)

true bill: n. the written decision of a Grand Jury (signed by the Grand Jury foreperson) that it has heard sufficient evidence from the prosecution to believe that an accused person probably committed a crime and should be indicted. Thus, the indictment is sent to the court. (See: **indictment**)

trust: n. an entity created to hold assets for the benefit of certain persons or entities, with a trustee managing the trust (and often holding title on behalf of the trust). Most trusts are founded by the persons (called trustors, settlors and/or donors) who execute a written declaration of trust which establishes the trust and spells out the terms and conditions upon which it will be conducted. The declaration also names the original trustee or trustees, successor trustees or means to choose future trustees. The assets of the trust are usually given to the trust by the creators, although assets may be added by others. During the life of the trust, profits and, sometimes, a portion of the principal (called "corpus") may be distributed to the beneficiaries, and at some time in the future (such as the death of the last trustor or settlor) the remaining assets will be distributed to beneficiaries. A trust may take the place of a will and avoid probate (management of an estate with court supervision) by providing for distribution of all assets originally owned by the trustors or settlors upon their death. There are numerous types of trusts, including "revocable trusts" created to handle the trustors' assets (with the trustor acting as initial trustee), often called a "living trust" or "*inter vivos* trust" which only becomes irrevocable on the death of the first trustor; "irrevocable trust," which cannot be changed at any time; "charitable remainder unitrust," which provides for eventual guaranteed distribution of the corpus (assets) to charity, thus gaining a substantial tax benefit. There are also court-decreed "constructive" and "resulting" trusts over property held by someone for its owner. A "testamentary trust" can be created by a will to manage assets given to beneficiaries. (See: **charitable remainder trust, constructive trust, declaration of trust, *inter vivos* trust, living trust, resulting trust, settlor, testamentary trust, trustee, trustor**)

> *Justice should remove the bandage from her eyes long enough to distinguish between the vicious and the unfortunate.*
> *—Robert G. Ingersoll*

trust deed: n. another name for a deed of trust, a form of mortgage used in some states, in which title is transferred to a trustee to protect the lender (beneficiary) until the loan is paid back. (See: **deed of trust**)

trustee: n. a person or entity who holds the assets (corpus) of a trustee for the benefit of the beneficiaries and manages the trust and its assets under the terms of the trust stated in the declaration of trust which created it. In many "living trusts" the creator of the trust (trustor, settlor) names himself/herself (or themselves) as the original trustee who will manage the trust until his/her death when it is taken over by a successor trustee. In some trusts, such as a "charitable remainder unitrust," the trustee must be independent and therefore cannot be the creator of the trust. If a trustee has title to property, he/she/it holds title only for the benefit of the trust and its beneficiaries. (See: **settlor, trust, trustor**)

trustee in bankruptcy: n. a person appointed by a bankruptcy court to supervise the affairs of a person or business which is in bankruptcy, determine both assets and debts, marshal (gather) and manage the assets if necessary, and report to the court. Most trustees in bankruptcy are full-time professionals and are paid from the estates of the debtors. (See: **bankruptcy**)

trust fund: n. the principal (called the corpus) of a trust, made up of its assets and, sometimes, accumulated profits. (See: **trust**)

trustor: n. the creator of a trust (who normally places the original assets into the trust), called a "settlor" or "donor" in many states. Trustor is a title used primarily in western states. (See: **settlor, trust**)

Truth in Lending Act: n. a federal statute which requires a commercial lender (bank, savings and loan, mortgage broker) to give a borrower exact information on interest rates and a three-day period in which the borrower may compare and consider competitive terms and cancel the loan agreement.

turn states' evidence: v. for a person accused of a crime to decide to give the prosecutor evidence about the crime, including facts about other participants in the crime (or other crimes) in return for lenient treatment, a plea bargain and/or a recommendation of a light sentence.

"Twinkie" defense: n. a claim by a criminal defendant that at the time of the crime he/she was of diminished mental capacity due to intake of too much sugar, as from eating "Twinkies," sugar-rich snacks. The defense was argued successfully by a defense psychiatrist in the notorious case of former San Francisco County Supervisor Dan White, who shot and killed San Francisco Mayor George Moscone and County Supervisor Harvey Milk, resulting in White's conviction for only manslaughter instead of murder. (See: **diminished capacity**)

U

UCC-1: n. a financing agreement form for using personal property (e.g. equipment) to secure a loan under the provisions of the *Uniform Commercial Code (UCC)* adopted in almost all states.

ultimate fact: n. in a trial, a conclusion of fact which is logically deduced from evidence ("evidentiary facts"). Example: the evidentiary facts were that driver Larry Leadfoot a) exceeded the speed limit, b) drove over the double-line, c) skidded and lost control of his car; the ultimate fact was, therefore, Leadfoot was negligent. It is essential to introduce the evidentiary facts during the trial in order to prove the ultimate fact. A mere statement by a witness that "Leadfoot was negligent" is not sufficient, since it is an opinion of the witness and is not evidence. (See: **evidence**)

ultrahazardous activity: n. an action or process which is so inherently dangerous that the person or entity conducting the activity is "strictly liable" for any injury caused by the activity. Examples: working with high explosives or conducting a professional auto race on public streets.

ultra vires: (uhl-trah veye-rehz) adj. Latin for "beyond powers," in the law of corporations, referring to acts of a corporation and/or its officers outside the powers and/or authority allowed a corporation by law. Example: Directors of Highfliers, Inc. operate a small bank for its employees and friends, which corporate law does not permit without a bank charter, or sells shares of stock to the public before a permit is issued. (See: **corporation**)

unclean hands: n. a legal doctrine which is a defense to a complaint, which states that a party who is asking for a judgment cannot have the help of the court if he/she has done anything unethical in relation to the subject of the lawsuit. Thus, if a defendant can show the plaintiff had "unclean hands," the plaintiff's complaint will be dismissed or the plaintiff will be denied judgment. Unclean hands is a common "affirmative defense" pleaded by defendants and must be proved by the defendant. Example: Hank Hardnose sues Grace Goodenough for breach of contract for failure to pay the full amount for construction of an addition to her house. Goodenough proves that Hardnose had shown her faked estimates from subcontractors to justify his original bid to Goodenough. (See: **affirmative defense**)

unconscionable: adj. referring to a contract or bargain which is so unfair to a party that no reasonable or informed person would agree to it. In a suit for breach of contract, a court will not enforce an unconscionable contract (award damages or order specific performance) against the person unfairly treated, on the theory that he/she was misled, lacked information or signed under duress or misunderstanding. It is similar to an "adhesion contract," in which one party has taken advantage of a person dealing from weakness. (See: **adhesion contract, contract**)

unconstitutional: adj. referring to a statute, governmental conduct, court decision or private contract (such as a covenant which purports to limit transfer of real property only to Caucasians) which violate one or more provisions of the U.S. Constitution. The ultimate determination of constitutionality is the U.S. Supreme Court. Unconstitutional can also refer to violations of a state constitution. (See: **constitution, Supreme Court**)

under the influence: n. one of many phrases for being drunk on alcoholic beverages or high on drugs or a combination of alcohol and drugs. Driving a vehicle when "under the influence" of alcohol or drugs is a crime, as is "public drunkenness." (See: **driving under the influence, driving while intoxicated**)

underwrite: v. 1) to agree to pay an obligation which may arise from an insurance policy. 2) to guarantee purchase of all shares of stock or bonds being issued by a corporation, including an agreement to purchase by the underwriter if the public does not buy all the shares or bonds. 3) to guarantee by investment in a business or project. (See: **guarantee, guarantor, insurer, underwriter**)

underwriter: n. a company or person which/who underwrites an insurance policy, issue of corporate securities, business or project. (See: **underwrite**)

undisclosed principal: n. a person who uses an agent for his/her negotiations with a third party, often when the agent pretends to be acting for himself/herself. As a result, the third party does not know he/she can look to the real principal in any dispute. (See: **agent, principal**)

undivided interest: n. title to real property held by two or more persons without specifying the interests of each party by percentage or description of a portion of the real estate. Such interests are typical between joint tenants, tenants in common and tenants by the entirety. (See: **joint tenancy, real property, tenancy by the entirety, tenancy in common**)

> *Now, as always, the conflict over technicalities, mostly procedural, between judge and lawyers, takes more time than is occupied by the actual evidence.*
> *—Harold J. Laski*

undue influence: n. the amount of pressure which one uses to force someone to execute a will leaving assets in a particular way, to make a direct gift while alive or to sign a contract. The key element is that the influence was so great that the testator (will writer), donor (gift giver) or party to the contract had lost the ability to exercise his/her judgment and could not refuse to give in to the pressure. Evidence of such dominance of another's mind may result in invalidation of the will, gift or contract by a court if the will, gift or contract is challenged. Participation in preparation of the will, excluding other relatives being present when the testator and the attorney meet, are all evidence of undue pressure, and an imbalance or change in language which greatly favors the person exercising the influence is a factor in finding undue influence. Example: Pete Pounder constantly visits his aunt Agnes while she is ill and always urges her to leave her mansion to him instead of to her son. Pounder threatens to stop visiting the old lady, who is very lonely, tells her she is ungrateful for his attention, finally brings over an attorney who does not know Agnes and is present while she tells the attorney to write a new will in favor of Pounder. (See: **will, will contest**)

unfair competition: n. wrongful and/or fraudulent business methods to gain an unfair advantage over competitors, including: a) untrue or misleading advertising, b) misleading customers by imitative trademark, name or package, c) falsely disparaging another's product. Although state laws vary, unfair competition is the basis for a legal action (suit) for damages and/or an injunction to halt the deceptive practices against an unfair competitor if the practices tend to harm one's business.

unified estate and gift tax: n. in federal estate taxes, the value of the estate *plus* gifts upon which no gift tax has been paid are combined to determine the assets upon which the tax is calculated. The estate tax "kicks in" at $600,000 for each deceased person. In larger estates an experienced accountant is virtually mandatory to determine the estate

tax (if any) and prepare the tax return. (See: **estate tax, gift tax**)

Uniform Commercial Code: n. a set of statutes governing the conduct of business, sales, warranties, negotiable instruments, loans secured by personal property and other commercial matters, which has been adopted with minor variations by all states except Louisiana. (See: **UCC-1**)

unilateral contract: n. an agreement to pay in exchange for performance *if* the potential performer chooses to act. A "unilateral" contract is distinguished from a "bilateral" contract which is an exchange of one promise for another. Example of a unilateral contract: "I will pay you $1,000 if you bring my car from Cleveland to San Francisco." Bringing the car is acceptance. The difference is normally only of academic interest. (See: **bilateral contract, consideration, contract, performance**)

uninsured motorist clause: n. the clause in a policy of insurance on an automobile which provides that if the owner (or a passenger) of the automobile is injured by a negligent driver of another vehicle who does not have liability insurance, then the insurance company will pay its insured's actual damages.

unissued stock: n. a corporation's shares of stock which are authorized by its articles of incorporation but have never been issued (sold) to anyone. They differ from "treasury stock," which is stock that was issued and then reacquired by the corporation. (See: **corporation, share stock, treasury stock**)

unjust enrichment: n. a benefit by chance, mistake or another's misfortune for which the one enriched has not paid or worked and morally and ethically should not keep. If the money or property received rightly should have been delivered or belonged to another, then the party enriched must make restitution to the rightful owner. Usually a court will order such restitution if a lawsuit is brought by the party who should have the money or property. (See: **constructive trust**)

unlawful: adj. referring to any action which is in violation of a statute, federal or state constitution, or established legal precedents

unlawful assembly: n. the act of assembling for the purpose of starting a riot or breaching the peace or when such an assembly reasonably could be expected to cause a riot or endanger the public. Although freedom of assembly is guaranteed by the First Amendment to the Constitution, law enforcement has the right to require disbursement of such an assembly as part of the "police powers" of the state and the potential dangers of riot or breach of peace are subjective and decided on the spot by police officers or other public officials. Claims of "unlawful assembly" were often used to break up labor union picket lines until the late 1930s, against peaceful civil rights marches in the 1950s and 1960s, and by the police against anti-Vietnam War demonstrators in Los Angeles, Washington and Chicago in the late 1960s.

unlawful detainer: n. 1) keeping possession of real property without a right, such as after a lease has expired, after being served with a notice to quit (vacate, leave) for non-payment of rent or other breach of lease, or being a "squatter" on the property. Such possession entitles the owner to file a lawsuit for "unlawful detainer," asking for possession by court order, unpaid rent and damages. 2) a legal action to evict a tenant or other occupier of real property in possession, without a legal right, to declare a breach of lease, and/or a judgment for repossession, as well as unpaid rent and other damages. Such lawsuits have priority over most legal cases and therefore will be calendared for trial promptly. (See: **landlord and tenant, 30-day notice, three-day notice**)

unreasonable search and seizure: n. search of an individual or his/her premises (including an automobile) and/or seizure of evidence found in such a search by a law enforcement officer without a search warrant and without "probable cause" to believe evidence of a crime is present. Such a search and/or seizure is unconstitutional under the 4th Amendment (applied to the states by the 14th Amendment), and evidence obtained thereby may not be introduced in court. (See: **fruit of the poisonous tree, probable cause, search and seizure**)

use: n. the right to enjoy the benefits of real property or personal property (but primarily used in reference to real property), whether the owner of the right has ownership of title or not. Under English common law "use" of property became extremely important since title to real property could not be conveyed outside a family line due to "restraints on alienation," so "use" of the property was transferred instead. This is a simplification of the way "uses" were employed, but today it is only of academic interest.

use tax: n. a state tax on goods purchased in another state for use in the taxing state, to make up for local sales tax. Example: Bill Buyer, who lives in California (which has a sales tax), orders a freezer from a company in a state with no sales tax. California will attempt to charge a "use" tax equivalent to its sales tax.

usurious: adj. referring to the interest on a debt which exceeds the maximum interest rate allowed by law. (See: **usury**)

usury: n. a rate of interest on a debt which is exorbitant and in excess of the percentage allowed by law. Each state sets its own maximum interest rate. Courts will not enforce payment of interest on a loan if the rate is usurious, so a loan may result in being interest free. Charging usury as a practice is a crime, usually only charged if a person makes a business of usury, sometimes called "loan-sharking." Banks and other commercial lenders generally are not subject to anti-usury laws, but are governed by the marketplace and the competitive rates triggered by loan rates to institutions set by the Federal Reserve Bank. (See: **usurious**)

utter: v. 1) to issue a forged document. 2) to speak. (See: **forgery**)

uxor: n. Latin for "wife." In deeds and documents the term "*et ux.*" is sometimes used to mean "and wife," stemming from a time when a wife was a mere legal appendage of a man and not worthy of being named.

V

vacate: v. 1) for a judge to set aside or annul an order or judgment which he/she finds was improper. 2) to move out of real estate and cease occupancy.

vagrancy: n. moving about without a means to support oneself, without a permanent home, and relying on begging. Until recently it was considered a minor crime (misdemeanor) in many states. Constitutionally it is evident that being poor is not a crime. The same is true of "loitering." (See: **loiter**)

valuable consideration: n. a necessary element of a contract, which confers a benefit on the other party. Valuable consideration can include money, work, performance, assets, a promise or abstaining from an act. (See: **consideration, contract**)

variance: n. 1) an exception to a zoning ordinance, authorized by the appropriate governmental body such as a planning commission, zoning board, county commissioners or city council. Example: the zoning ordinance requires that no residences can be built within 10 feet of a property's back line, but due to the odd shape of May Matheson's property, she needs to build her dream house within five feet of the property line at one point. The local zoning board listens to her plea, finds that the neighbors do not object, and grants her a variance to build closer to the back line. 2) a difference between what the prosecution has charged and what it has proved against a criminal defendant. 3) a difference between what is alleged in a civil complaint and what is proved. A substantial variance may be fatal to the prosecution's case against the accused or fatal to a plaintiff's (the person who filed the suit) lawsuit. In each case the judge can dismiss the case as a matter of law, without sending the factual issues to the jury. In criminal cases the test of a fatal variance is somewhat stricter than in a civil lawsuit, since a minor difference between the charge and the proof may mislead the defendant and deny him/her "due process." (See: **dismissal, due process, proof**)

vehicular manslaughter: n. the crime of causing the death of a human being due to illegal driving of an automobile, including gross negligence, drunk driving, reckless driving or speeding. Vehicular manslaughter can be charged as a misdemeanor (minor crime with a maximum punishment of a year in county jail or only a fine) or a felony (punishable by a term in state prison) depending on the circumstances. Gross negligence or driving a few miles over the speed limit might be charged as a misdemeanor, but drunk driving resulting in a fatality is most likely treated as a felony. Death of a passenger, including a loved one or friend, can be vehicular manslaughter if due to illegal driving. (See: **gross negligence, manslaughter, reckless driving**)

vendee: n. a buyer, particularly of real property.

vendor: n. a seller, particularly of real property.

> *There is no distinctly native American criminal class except Congress.*
> *—Mark Twain*

venire: (ven-eer-ay) n. the list from which jurors may be selected. (See: **jury, panel**)

venue: n. 1) the proper or most convenient location for trial of a case. Normally, the venue in a criminal case is the judicial district or county where the crime was committed. For civil cases, venue is usually the district or county which is the residence of a principal defendant, where a contract was executed or is to be performed, or where an accident took place. However, the parties may agree to a different venue for convenience (such as where most witnesses are located). Sometimes a lawsuit is filed in a district or county which is not the proper venue, and if the defendant promptly objects (asks for a change of venue), the court will order transfer of the case to the proper venue. Example: a promissory note states that any suit for collection must be filed in Washington County, Indiana, and the case is filed in Lake County, Indiana. In high profile criminal cases the original venue may be considered not the best venue due to possible prejudice stemming from pre-trial publicity in the area or public sentiment about the case which might impact upon potential jurors. For these various reasons either party to a lawsuit or prosecution may move (ask) for a change of venue, which is up to the discretion of a judge in the court where the case or prosecution was originally filed. Venue is not to be confused with "jurisdiction," which establishes the right to bring a lawsuit (often anywhere within a state) whether or not it is the place which is the most convenient or appropriate location. (See: **forum *non conveniens***)

verdict: n. the decision of a jury after a trial, which must be accepted by the trial judge to be final. A judgment by a judge sitting without a jury is not a verdict. A "special verdict" is a decision by the jury on the factual questions in the case, leaving the application of the law to those facts to the judge, who makes the final judgment. A "directed verdict" is a decision following an instruction by the judge that the jury can only bring in a specific verdict ("based on the evidence you must bring in a verdict of 'not guilty'"). A "chance verdict" (decided by lot or the flip of a coin), a "compromise verdict" (based on some jurors voting against their beliefs to break a deadlock) and a "quotient verdict" (averaging the amount each juror wants to award) are all improper and will result in a mistrial (having the verdict thrown out by the judge) or be cause for reversal of the judgment on appeal. (See: **compromise verdict, directed verdict, judgment, quotient verdict, special verdict**)

verification: n. the declaration under oath or upon penalty of perjury that a statement or pleading is true, located at the end of a document. A typical verification reads: "I declare under penalty of perjury under the laws of the State of California, that I have read the above complaint and I know it is true of my own knowledge, except as to those things stated upon information and belief, and as to those I believe it to be true. Executed January 3, 1995, at Monrovia, California. (signed) Georgia Garner, declarant." If a complaint is verified then the answer to the complaint must be verified. (See: **answer, complaint, oath**)

vest: v. to give an absolute right to title or ownership, including real property and pension rights. (See: **vested, vested remainder**)

vested: adj. referring to having an absolute right or title, when previously the holder of the right or title only had an expectation. Example: after 20 years of employment Larry Loyal's pension rights are now vested. (See: **vest, vested remainder**)

vested remainder: n. the absolute right to receive title after a presently existing interest in real property terminates. A "vested remainder" is created by deed or by a decree of distribution of an estate given by will. Example: "Title to the Hard Luck Ranch to my son, Sean, subject to a life estate to my brother, Douglas." Sean has a "vested remainder" which is an absolute right, Sean could sell to another person at this time, with occupancy delayed until title would pass to him. (See: **vest, vested**)

vexatious litigation: n. filing a lawsuit with the knowledge that it has no legal basis, with its purpose to bother, annoy, embarrass and cause legal expenses to the defendant. Vexatious litigation includes continuing a lawsuit after discovery of the facts shows it has absolutely no merit. Upon judgment for the defendant, he/she has the right to file a suit for "malicious prosecution" against the original vexatious plaintiff. Moreover, most states allow a judge to penalize with sanctions a plaintiff and his/her attorney for filing or continuing a "frivolous" legal action (money award to the defendant for the trouble and/or attorney fees). (See: **frivolous, malicious prosecution, sanction**)

vicarious liability: n. sometimes called "imputed liability," attachment of responsibility to a person for harm or damages caused by another person in either a negligence lawsuit or criminal prosecution. Thus, an employer of an employee who injures someone through negligence while in the scope of employment (doing work for the employer) is vicariously liable for damages to the injured person. In most states a participant in a crime (like a hold-up) may be vicariously liable for murder if another member of the group shoots and kills a shopkeeper or policeman. (See: **felony murder, liability, imputed liability**)

vigilante: n. someone who takes the law into his/her own hands by trying and/or punishing another person without any legal authority. In the 1800s groups of vigilantes dispensed "frontier justice" by holding trials of accused horsethieves, rustlers and shooters, and then promptly hanging the accused if "convicted." A mother who shoots the alleged molester of her child is a vigilante.

viz: prep. to wit, or namely. Example:

"There were several problems, viz: leaky roof, dangerous electrical system and broken windows." (See: **to wit**)

void: adj. referring to a statute, contract, ruling or anything which is null and of no effect. A law or judgment found by an appeals court to be unconstitutional is void, a rescinded (mutually cancelled) contract is void, and a marriage which has been annulled by court judgment is void. (See: **voidable**)

voidable: adj. capable of being made void. Example: a contract entered into by a minor under 18 is voidable upon his/her reaching majority, but the minor may also affirm the contract at that time. "Voidable" is distinguished from "void" in that it means only that a thing can become void but is not necessarily void. (See: **void**)

void for vagueness: adj. referring to a statute defining a crime which is so vague that a reasonable person of at least average intelligence could not determine what elements constitute the crime. Such a vague statute is unconstitutional on the basis that a defendant could not defend against a charge of a crime which he/she could not understand, and thus would be denied "due process" mandated by the 5th Amendment, applied to the states by the 14th Amendment. (See: **due process**)

voir dire: (vwahr [with a near-silent "r"] deer) n. from French "to see to speak," the questioning of prospective jurors by a judge and attorneys in court. *Voir dire* is used to determine if any juror is biased and/or cannot deal with the issues fairly, or if there is cause not to allow a juror to serve (knowledge of the facts; acquaintanceship with parties, witnesses or attorneys; occupation which might lead to bias; prejudice against the death penalty; or previous experiences such as having been sued in a similar case). Actually one of the unspoken purposes of the *voir dire* is for the attorneys to get a feel for the personalities and likely views of the people on the jury panel. In some courts the judge asks most of the questions, while in others the lawyers are given substantial latitude and time to ask questions. Some jurors may be dismissed for cause by the judge, and the attorneys may excuse others in "peremptory" challenges without stating any reason. 2) questions asked to determine the competence of an alleged expert witness. 3) any hearing outside the presence of the jury held during trial. (See: **jury, peremptory challenge, expert witness**)

Judges must beware of hard constructions and strained inferences, for there is no worse torture than the torture of laws.
—Sir Francis Bacon

voluntary bankruptcy: n. the filing for bankruptcy by a debtor who believes he/she/it cannot pay bills and has more debts than assets. Voluntary bankruptcy differs from "involuntary bankruptcy" filed by creditors owed money to bring the debtor before the bankruptcy court. (See: **bankruptcy**)

voting trust: n. a trust which solicits vote proxies of shareholders of a corporation to elect a board of directors and vote on other matters at a shareholders' meeting. A voting trust is usually operated by current directors to insure continued control, but occasionally a voting trust represents a person or group trying to gain control of the corporation. (See: **corporation, proxy, shareholder, stockholder**)

waive: v. to voluntarily give up something, including not enforcing a term of a contract (such as insisting on payment on an exact date), or knowingly giving up a legal right such as a speedy trial, a jury trial or a hearing on extradition (the transfer to another state's jurisdiction of one accused of a crime in the other state). (See: **waiver**)

> *The common law is nothing else but reason.*
> *—Sir Edward Coke, Commentary on Littleton*

waiver: n. the intentional and voluntary giving up of something, such as a right, either by an express statement or by conduct (such as not enforcing a right). The problem which may arise is that a waiver may be interpreted as giving up the right to enforce the same right in the future. Example: the holder of a promissory note who several times allows the debtor to pay many weeks late does not agree to waive the due date on future payments. A waiver of a legal right in court must be expressed on the record. (See: **waive**)

wanton: adj. 1) grossly negligent to the extent of being recklessly unconcerned with the safety of people or property. Examples: speeding by a school while it is letting out students or firing a shotgun in a public park. 2) sexually immoral and unrestrained.

ward: n. 1) a person (usually a minor) who has a guardian appointed by the court to care for and take responsibility for that person. A governmental agency may take temporary custody of a minor for his/her protection and care if the child is suffering from parental neglect or abuse, or has been in trouble with the law. Such a child is a "ward of the court" (if the custody is court-ordered) or a "ward of the state." 2) a political division of a city, much like a council district. (See: **guardian**)

warrant: 1) n. an order (writ) of a court which directs a law enforcement officer (usually a sheriff) to arrest and bring a person before the judge, such as a person who is charged with a crime, convicted of a crime but failed to appear for sentencing, owes a fine or is in contempt of court. A "bench warrant" is an order to appear issued by the court when a person does not appear for a hearing, which can be resolved by posting bail or appearing. A "search warrant" is an order permitting a law enforcement officer to search a particular premises and/or person for certain types of evidence, based on a declaration by a law enforcement official, including a district attorney. 2) v. to claim to a purchaser that merchandise is sound, of good quality or will perform as it should, or that title to real property belongs to the seller. (See: **guarantee, search and seizure, search warrant**)

warranty: n. a written statement of good quality of merchandise, clear title to real estate or that a fact stated in a contract is true. An "express warranty" is a definite written statement and "implied warranty" is based on the circumstances surrounding the sale or the creation of the contract. (See: **warrant**)

warranty deed: n. a deed to real property which guarantees that the seller owns clear title which can be transferred (conveyed). A "grant deed" generally is a warranty deed, while a "quitclaim deed" is not. (See: **grant deed, quitclaim deed, warrant**)

waste: n. 1) any damage to real property by a tenant which lessens its value to the landlord, owner or future owner. An owner can sue for damages for waste, terminate a lease of one committing waste and/or obtain an injunction against further waste. 2) garbage, which may include poisonous effluents.

watered stock: n. shares of stock of a corporation which have been issued at a price far greater than true value. In this case, the actual value of all shares is less than the value carried on the books of the corporation. (See: **corporation, share, stock**)

weight of evidence: n. the strength, value and believability of evidence presented on a factual issue by one side as compared to evidence introduced by the other side. (See: **evidence, preponderance of the evidence**)

wet reckless: n. a plea to a charge of reckless driving which was "alcohol related." A wet reckless results from a plea bargain to reduce a charge of drunk driving when the amount of blood alcohol was borderline illegal, there was no accident and no prior record. The result is a lower fine, no jail time and no record of a drunk driving conviction, but if there is a subsequent drunk driving conviction the "wet reckless" will be considered a "prior" drunk driving conviction and result in a heavier sentence required for a second conviction. (See: **driving under the influence, DUI, DWI, plea bargain**)

whiplash: n. a common neck and/or back injury suffered in automobile accidents (particularly from being hit from the rear) in which the head and/or upper back is snapped back and forth suddenly and violently by the impact. The injury is to the "soft tissues" and sometimes to the vertebrae, does not always evidence itself for a day or two, and can cause pain and disability for periods up to a year. The degree of injury and the pain and suffering from whiplash are often in dispute in claims and lawsuits for damages due to negligent driving.

white collar crime: n. a generic term for crimes involving commercial fraud, cheating consumers, swindles, insider trading on the stock market, embezzlement and other forms of dishonest business schemes. The term comes from the out-of-date assumption that business executives wear white shirts with ties. It also theoretically distinguishes these crimes and criminals from physical crimes, supposedly likely to be committed by "blue collar" workers.

widow: n. a woman whose husband died while she was married to him and who has not since remarried. A divorced woman whose ex-husband dies is not a widow, except for the purpose of certain Social Security benefits traceable to the ex-husband.

widower: n. a man whose wife died while he was married to her and who has not remarried.

widow's election: n. the choice a widow makes between accepting what her husband left her in his will and what she would receive by the laws of succession. Example: the state law in which the husband died would give his widow one-half of his estate by the law of succession (the other half going to the children) if there were no will, but in his will the late husband left his widow only one-quarter of his estate. She can elect to take the one-half. (See: **community property, descent and distribution, succession, will**)

will: n. a written document which leaves the estate of the person who signed the will to named persons or entities (beneficiaries, legatees, divisees) including portions or percentages of the estate, specific gifts, creation of trusts for management and future distribution of all or a portion of the estate (a testamentary trust). A will usually names an executor (and possibly substitute executors) to manage the estate, states the authority and obligations of the executor in the management and distribution of the estate, sometimes gives funeral and/or burial instructions, nominates guardians of minor children and spells out other terms. To be valid the will must be signed by the person who made it (testator) be dated (but an incorrect date will not invalidate the will) and witnessed by two people (except in Vermont which requires three). In some states the witnesses must be disinterested, or in some states, a gift to a witness is void but the will is valid. A will totally in the handwriting of the testator, signed and dated (a "holographic will") but without witnesses, is valid in many but not all, states. If the will (also called a Last Will and Testament) is still in force at the time of the death of the testator (will writer), and there is a substantial estate and/or real estate, then the will must be probated (approved by the court, managed and distributed by the executor under court supervision). If there is no executor named or the executor is dead or unable or unwilling to serve, an administrator ("with will annexed") will be appointed by the court. A written amendment or addition to a will is called a "codicil" and must be signed, dated and witnessed just as is a will, and must refer to the original will it amends. If there is no estate, including the situation in which the assets have all been placed in a trust, then the will need not be probated. (See: **codicil, estate, executor, guardian, holographic will, last will and testament, probate, testator**)

will contest: n. a lawsuit challenging the validity of a will and/or its terms. Bases for contesting a will include the competency of the maker of the will (testator) at the time the will was signed, the "undue influence" of someone who used pressure to force the testator to give him/her substantial gifts in the will, the existence of another will or trust, challenging il legal terms or technical faults in the execution of the will, such as not having been validly witnessed. A trial of the will contest must be held before the will can be probated, since if the will is invalid, it cannot be probated. (See: *in terrorem* **clause, probate, will**)

> *The right to be left alone—the most comprehensive of rights and the right most valued by civilized men.*
> **—Justice Louis D. Brandeis**

willful: adj. referring to acts which are intentional, conscious and directed toward achieving a purpose. Some willful conduct which has wrongful or unfortunate results is considered "hardheaded," "stubborn" and even "malicious." Example: "The defendant's attack on his neighbor was willful." (See: **willfully**)

willfully: adv. referring to doing something intentionally, purposefully and stubbornly. Examples: "He drove the car willfully into the crowd on the sidewalk." "She willfully left the dangerous substances on the property." (See: **willful**)

wind up: v. to liquidate (sell or dispose of) assets of a corporation or partnership. (See: **winding up**)

winding up: n. liquidating the assets of a corporation or partnership, settling accounts, paying bills, distributing remaining assets to shareholders or partners, and then dissolving the business. Winding up a non-profit corpora-

tion requires a plan for distribution of assets to some charitable or other non-profit entity under the *cy pres* doctrine. (See: **corporation, *cy pres* doctrine, partnership**)

wiretap: n. using an electronic device to listen in on telephone lines, which is illegal unless allowed by court order based upon a showing by law enforcement of "probable cause" to believe the communications are part of criminal activities. Use of wiretap is also a wrongful act for which the party whose telephones were tapped may sue the party performing the act and/or listening in as an invasion of privacy or for theft of information. A wiretap differs from a "bug," which is a radio device secretly placed in one's premises to listen in on conversations or to tape incoming calls without notice to the caller. The same rules of illegality and tort liability apply to "bugging." (See: **invasion of privacy, probable cause**)

withdrawal: n. 1) in criminal law, leaving a conspiracy to commit a crime before the actual crime is committed, which is similar to "renunciation." If the withdrawal is before any overt criminal act the withdrawer may escape prosecution. 2) the removal of money from a bank account. (See: **check, renunciation**)

witness: 1) n. a person who testifies under oath in a trial (or a deposition which may be used in a trial if the witness is not available) with first-hand or expert evidence useful in a lawsuit. A party to the lawsuit (plaintiff or defendant) may be a witness. 2) n. a person who sees an event. 3) n. a person who observes the signing of a document like a will or a contract and signs as a witness on the document attesting that the document was signed in the presence of the witness. 4) v. to sign a document verifying that he/she observed the execution of the document such as a will. (See: **deposition, evidence, trial, will**)

witness stand: n. a chair at the end of the judge's bench on the jury box side, usually with a low "modesty screen," where a witness sits and gives testimony after he/she has sworn to tell the truth. When called to testify the witness "takes the stand." Most witness stands are equipped with a microphone linked to an amplifying system so that judge, attorneys and jury can hear the testimony clearly. (See: **witness**)

words of art: n. 1) specialized language with meaning peculiar to a particular profession, art, technical work, science or other field of endeavor. 2) jargon known only to people who specialize in a particular occupation.

Workers' Compensation Acts: n. state statutes which establish liability of employers for injuries to workers while on the job or illnesses due to the employment, and requiring insurance to protect the workers. Worker's compensation is not based on negligence of the employer, but is absolute liability for medical coverage, a percentage of lost wages or salary, costs of rehabilitation and retraining, and payment for any permanent injury (usually based on an evaluation of limitation). Worker's

Compensation Acts provide for a system of hearings and quasi-judicial determinations by administrative law judges and appeal boards. However, if worker's' compensation is granted, it becomes the only remedy against an employer and does not include general damages for pain and suffering. Thus, an injured worker may waive workers' compensation and sue the employer for damages caused by the employer's negligence. If a third party contributed to the damages, the injured worker may sue that party for damages even though he/she receives worker's' compensation, but recovery may be subject to a lien for moneys paid out by the workers' compensation insurance company.

Workmen's Compensation: n. a former name for worker's compensation before the unisex title of the acts was adopted. (See: **Worker's Compensation Acts**)

work product: n. the writings, notes, memoranda, reports on conversations with the client or witness, research and confidential materials which an attorney has developed while representing a client, particularly in preparation for trial. A "work product" may not be demanded or subpenaed by the opposing party, as are documents, letters by and from third parties and other evidence, since the work product reflects the confidential strategy, tactics and theories to be employed by the attorney.

World Court: n. the Court of International Justice, founded by the United Nations in 1945, which hears international disputes, but only when the parties (usually governments) agree to have the issue heard and to be bound by the decision.

writ: n. a written order of a judge requiring specific action by the person or entity to whom the writ is directed.

writ of attachment: n. a court order directing a sheriff (or other law enforcement officer) to seize property of a defendant which would satisfy a judgment against that defendant. (See: **attachment**)

writ of *coram nobis*: (writ of core-uhm noh-bis) n. from Latin for "in our presence," an order by a court of appeals to a court which rendered judgment requiring that trial court to consider facts not on the trial record which might have resulted in a different judgment if known at the time of trial.

writ of execution: n. a court order to a sheriff to enforce a judgment by levying on real or personal property of a judgment debtor to obtain funds to satisfy the judgment amount (pay the winning plaintiff). (See: **execution**)

writ of mandate (mandamus): n. a court order to a government agency, including another court, to follow the law by correcting its prior actions or ceasing illegal acts. (See: *mandamus,* **mandate**)

You [should] recognize in any society that the individual must have rights that are guarded.
—Eleanor Roosevelt

wrongful death: n. the death of a human being as the result of a wrongful act of another person. Such wrongful acts include: negligence (like careless driving), an intentional attack such as assault and/or battery, a death in the course of another crime, vehicular manslaughter, manslaughter or murder. Wrongful death is the basis for a lawsuit (wrongful death action) against the party or parties who caused the death filed on behalf of the members of the family who have lost the company and support of the deceased. Thus, a child might be entitled to compensation for the personal loss of a father as well as the amount of financial support the child would have received from the now-dead parent while a minor, a wife would recover damages for loss of her husband's love and companionship and a lifetime of expected support, while a parent would be limited to damages for loss of companionship but not support. A lawsuit for wrongful death may be filed by the executor or administrator of the estate of the deceased or by the individual beneficiaries (family members).

wrongful termination: n. a right of an employee to sue his/her employer for damages (loss of wage and "fringe" benefits, and, if against "public policy," for punitive damages). To bring such a suit the discharge of the employee must have been without "cause," and the employee a) had an express contract of continued employment or there was an "implied" contract based on the circumstances of his/her hiring or legitimate reasons to believe the employment would be permanent, b) there is a violation of statutory prohibitions against discrimination due to race, gender, sexual preference or age, or c) the discharge was contrary to "public policy" such as in retribution for exposing dishonest acts of the employer. An employee who believes he/she has been wrongfully terminated may bring an action (file a suit) for damages for discharge, as well as for breach of contract, but the court decisions have become increasingly strict in limiting an employee's grounds for suit.

your honor: n. the proper way to address a judge in court.

youthful offenders: n. under-age people accused of crimes who are processed through a juvenile court and juvenile detention or prison facilities. In most states a youth-ful offender is under the age of 18. Often a court has the latitude to try some young defendants as adults, particularly for repeat offenders who appear to be beyond rehabilitation and are involved in major crimes like murder, manslaughter, armed robbery, rape or aggravated assault. A youthful offender has certain advantages: he/she will be kept in a juvenile prison instead of a penitentiary, is more likely than an adult to get probation, can only receive a maximum prison sentence not to exceed a 25th birthday or some other limitation and cannot get the death penalty. (See: **juvenile delinquent**)

zoning: n. a system of developing a city or county plan in which various geographic areas (zones) are restricted to certain uses and development, such as industrial, light industrial, commercial, light-commercial, agricultural, single-family residential, multi-unit residential, parks, schools and other purposes. Zoning is the chief planning tool of local government to guide the future development of a community, protect neighborhoods, concentrate retail business and industry, channel traffic and play a major role in the enhancement of urban as well as small-town life. In 1926, zoning was declared constitutional by the U.S. Supreme Court in *Village of Euclid v. Ambler Realty Co.*

The constitution is what the judges say it is.
—Chief Justice Charles Evans Hughes (said before he was on the Supreme Court)

APPENDICES

THE CONSTITUTION OF THE UNITED STATES OF AMERICA

Appendix I

We the people of the United States, in order to form a more perfect union, establish justice, insure domestic tranquility, provide for the common defense, promote the general welfare, and secure the blessings of liberty to ourselves and our posterity, do ordain and establish this Constitution for the United States of America.

ARTICLE I.

Section 1—Legislative powers; in whom vested:

All legislative powers herein granted shall be vested in a Congress of the United States, which shall consist of a Senate and House of Representatives.

Section 2—House of Representatives, how and by whom chosen. Qualifications of a Representative. Representatives and direct taxes, how apportioned. Enumeration. Vacancies to be filled. Power of choosing officers, and of impeachment.

1. The House of Representatives shall be composed of members chosen every second year by the people of the several States, and the electors in each State shall have the qualifications requisite for electors of the most numerous branch of the State Legislature.

2. No person shall be a Representative who shall not have attained to the age of twenty-five years, and been seven years a citizen of the United States, and who shall not, when elected, be an inhabitant of that State in which he shall be chosen.

3. *Representatives and direct taxes shall be apportioned among the several States which may be included within this Union, according to their respective numbers, which shall be determined by adding to the whole number of free persons, including those bound to service for a term of years, and excluding Indians not taxed, three-fifths of all other persons. (The previous sentence in italics was superseded by Amendment IV, section 2.)* The actual enumeration shall be made within three years after the first meeting of the Congress of the United States, and within every subsequent term of ten years, in such manner as they shall by law direct. The number of Representatives shall not exceed one for every thirty thousand, but each State shall have at least one Representative; and until such enumeration shall be made, the state of New Hampshire shall be entitled to choose three, Massachusetts eight, Rhode Island and Providence Plantations one, Connecticut five, New York six, New Jersey four, Pennsylvania eight, Delaware one, Maryland six, Virginia ten, North Carolina five, South Carolina five, and Georgia three.

4. When vacancies happen in the representation from any State, the Executive Authority thereof shall issue writs of election to fill such vacancies.

5. The House of Representatives shall choose their Speaker and other officers; and shall have the sole power of impeachment.

Section 3—Senators, how and by whom chosen. How classified. Qualifications of a Senator. President of the Senate, his right to vote. President pro tem., and other officers of the Senate, how chosen. Power to try impeachments. When President is tried, Chief Justice to preside. Sentence.

1. The Senate of the United States shall be composed of two Senators from each State, *chosen by the Legislature thereof (The preceding words in italics were superseded by Amendment XVII, section 1.)* for six years; and each Senator shall have one vote.

2. Immediately after they shall be assembled in consequence of the first election, they shall be divided as equally as may be into three classes. The seats of the Senators of the first class shall be vacated at the expiration of the second year, of the second class at the expiration of the fourth year, and the third class at the expiration of the sixth year, so that one third may be chosen every second year; *and if vacancies happen by resignation, or otherwise, during the recess of the Legislature of any State, the Executive thereof may make temporary appointments until the next meeting of the Legislature, which shall then fill such vacancies. (The preceding words in italics were superseded by Amendment XVII, section 2.)*

3. No person shall be a Senator who shall not have attained to the age of thirty years, and been nine years a citizen of the United States, and who shall not, when elected, be an inhabitant of that State for which he shall be chosen.

4. The Vice President of the United States shall be President of the Senate, but shall have no vote, unless they be equally divided.

5. The Senate shall choose their other officers, and also a President pro tempore, in the absence of the Vice President, or when he shall exercise the office of President of the United States.

6. The Senate shall have the sole power to try all impeachments. When sitting for that purpose, they shall be on oath or affirmation. When the President of the United States is tried, the Chief Justice shall preside: and no person shall be convicted without the concurrence of two-thirds of the members present.

7. Judgment in cases of impeachment shall not extend further than to removal from office, and disqualification to hold and enjoy any office of honor, trust or profit under the United States: but the party convicted shall nevertheless be liable and subject to indictment, trial, judgment and punishment, according to law.

Section 4—Times, etc., of holding elections, how prescribed. One session each year.

1. The times, places and manner of holding elections for Senators and Representatives, shall be prescribed in each State by the Legislature thereof; but the Congress may at any time by law make or alter such regulations, except as to the places of choosing Senators.

2. The Congress shall assemble at least once in every year, and such meeting shall *be on the first Monday in December, (The preceding words in italics were superseded by Amendement XX, section 2.)* unless they shall by law appoint a different day.

Section 5—Membership, quorum, adjournments, rules. Power to punish or expel. Journal. Time of adjournments, how limited, etc.

1. Each House shall be the judge of the elections, returns and qualifications of its own members, and a majority of each shall constitute a quorum to do business; but a smaller number may adjourn from day to day, and may be authorized to compel the attendance of absent members, in such manner, and under such penalties as each House may provide.

2. Each House may determine the rules of its proceedings, punish its members for disorderly behavior, and, with the concurrence of two-thirds, expel a member.

3. Each House shall keep a journal of its proceedings, and from time to time publish the same, excepting such parts as may in their judgment require secrecy; and the yeas and nays of the members of either House on any question shall, at the desire of one-fifth of those present, be entered on the journal.

4. Neither House, during the session of Congress, shall, without the consent of the other, adjourn for more than three days, nor to any other place than that in which the two Houses shall be sitting.

Section 6—Compensation, privileges, disqualifications in certain cases.

1. The Senators and Representatives shall receive a compensation for their services, to be ascertained by law, and paid out of the Treasury of the United States. They shall in all cases, except treason, felony and breach of the peace, be privileged from arrest during their attendance at the session of their respective Houses, and in going to and returning from the same; and for any speech or debate in either House, they shall not be questioned in any other place.

2. No Senator or Representative shall, during the time for which he was elected, be appointed to any civil office under the authority of the United States, which shall have been created, or the emoluments whereof shall have been increased during such time; and no person holding any office under the United States, shall be a member of either House during his continuance in office.

Section 7—House to originate all revenue bills. Veto. Bill may be passed by two-thirds of each House, notwithstanding, etc. Bill, not returned in ten days, to become a law. Provisions as to orders, concurrent resolutions, etc.

1. All bills for raising revenue shall originate in the House of Representatives; but the Senate may propose or concur with amendments as on other bills.

2. Every bill which shall have passed the House of Representatives and the Senate, shall, before it becomes a law, be presented to the President of the United States; if he approves he shall sign it, but if not he shall return it, with his objections to that House in which it shall have originated, who shall enter the objections at large on their journal, and proceed to reconsider it. If after such reconsideration two-thirds of that House shall agree to pass the bill, it shall be sent, together with the objections, to the other House, by which it shall likewise be reconsidered, and if approved by

two-thirds of that House, it shall become a law. But in all such cases the votes of both Houses shall be determined by yeas and nays, and the names of the persons voting for and against the bill shall be entered on the journal of each House respectively. If any bill shall not be returned by the President within ten days (Sundays excepted) after it shall have been presented to him, the same shall be a law, in like manner as if he had signed it, unless the Congress by their adjournment prevent its return, in which case it shall not be a law.

3. Every order, resolution, or vote to which the concurrence of the Senate and House of Representatives may be necessary (except on a question of adjournment) shall be presented to the President of the United States; and before the same shall take effect, shall be approved by him, or being disapproved by him, shall be repassed by two-thirds of the Senate and House of Representatives, according to the rules and limitations prescribed in the case of a bill.

Section 8—Powers of Congress.

The Congress shall have power

1. To lay and collect taxes, duties, imposts and excises, to pay the debts and provide for the common defense and general welfare of the United States; but all duties, imposts and excises shall be uniform throughout the United States;

2. To borrow money on the credit of the United States;

3. To regulate commerce with foreign nations, and among the several States, and with the Indian tribes;

4. To establish a uniform rule of naturalization, and uniform laws on the subject of bankruptcies throughout the United States;

5. To coin money, regulate the value thereof, and of foreign coin, and fix the standard of weights and measures;

6. To provide for the punishment of counterfeiting the securities and current coin of the United States;

7. To establish post-offices and post-roads;

8. To promote the progress of science and useful arts, by securing for limited times to authors and inventors the exclusive right to their respective writings and discoveries;

9. To constitute tribunals inferior to the Supreme Court;

10. To define and punish piracies and felonies committed on the high seas, and offenses against the law of nations;

11. To declare war, grant letters of marque and reprisal, and make rules concerning captures on land and water;

12. To raise and support armies, but no appropriation of money to that use shall be for a longer term than two years;

13. To provide and maintain a navy;

14. To make rules for the government and regulation of the land and naval forces;

15. To provide for calling forth the militia to execute the laws of the Union, suppress insurrections and repel invasions;

16. To provide for organizing, arming, and disciplining the militia, and for governing such part of them as may be employed in the service of the United States, reserving to the States

respectively, the appointment of the officers, and the authority of training the militia according to the discipline prescribed by Congress;

17. To exercise exclusive legislation in all cases whatsoever, over such district (not exceeding ten miles square) as may, by cession of particular States, and the acceptance of Congress, become the seat of the Government of the United States, and to exercise like authority over all places purchased by the consent of the Legislature of the State in which the same shall be, for the erection of forts, magazines, arsenals, dockyards, and other needful buildings;—And

18. To make all laws which shall be necessary and proper for carrying into execution the foregoing powers, and all other powers vested by this Constitution in the Government of the United States, or in any department or officer thereof.

Section 9—Provision as to migration or importation of certain persons. Habeas corpus, bills of attainder, etc. Taxes, how apportioned. No export duty. No commercial preference. Money, how drawn from Treasury, etc. No titular nobility. Officers not to receive presents, etc.

1. The migration or importation of such persons as any of the states now existing shall think proper to admit, shall not be prohibited by the Congress prior to the year one thousand eight hundred and eight, but a tax or duty may be imposed on such importation, not exceeding ten dollars for each person.

2. The privilege of the writ of habeas corpus shall not be suspended, unless when in cases of rebellion or invasion the public safety may require it.

3. No bill of attainder or ex post facto law shall be passed.

4. No capitation, or other direct, tax shall be laid, unless in proportion to the census or enumeration herein before directed to be taken. *(Modified by Amendment XVI.)*

5. No tax or duty shall be laid on articles exported from any State.

6. No preference shall be given by any regulation of commerce or revenue to the ports of one State over those of another: nor shall vessels bound to, or from, one state, be obliged to enter, clear, or pay duties in another.

7. No money shall be drawn from the Treasury, but in consequence of appropriations made by law; and a regular statement and account of receipts and expenditures of all public money shall be published from time to time.

8. No title of nobility shall be granted by the United States: and no person holding any office of profit or trust under them, shall, without the consent of the Congress, accept of any present, emolument, office, or title, of any kind whatever, from any king, prince, or foreign state.

Section 10—States prohibited from the exercise of certain powers.

1. No State shall enter into any treaty, alliance, or confederation; grant letters of marque and reprisal; coin money; emit bills of credit; make anything but gold and silver coin a tender in payment of debts; pass any bill of attainder, ex post facto law, or law impairing the obligation of contracts, or grant any title of nobility.

2. No state shall, without the consent of the Congress, lay any

imposts or duties on imports or exports, except what may be absolutely necessary for executing its inspection laws: and the net produce of all duties and imposts, laid by any State on imports or exports, shall be for the use of the Treasury of the United States; and all such laws shall be subject to the revision and control of the Congress.

3. No State shall, without the consent of Congress, lay any duty of tonnage, keep troops, or ships of war in time of peace, enter into any agreement or compact with another State, or with a foreign power, or engage in war, unless actually invaded, or in such imminent danger as will not admit of delay.

ARTICLE II

Section 1—President: his term of office. Electors of President; number and how appointed. Electors to vote on same day. Qualification of President. On whom his duties devolve in case of removal, death, etc. President's compensation. His oath of office.

1. The Executive power shall be vested in a President of the United States of America. He shall hold his office during the term of four years, and, together with the Vice President, chosen for the same term, be elected, as follows:

2. Each State shall appoint, in such manner as the Legislature thereof may direct, a number of electors, equal to the whole number of Senators and Representatives to which the State may be entitled in the Congress: but no Senator or Representative, or person holding an office of trust or profit under the United States, shall be appointed an elector.

The electors shall meet in their respective states, and vote by ballot for two persons, of whom one at least shall not be an inhabitant of the same state with themselves. And they shall make a list of all the persons voted for, and of the number of votes for each; which list they shall sign and certify, and transmit sealed to the seat of the government of the United States, directed to the President of the Senate. The President of the Senate shall, in the presence of the Senate and House of Representatives, open all the certificates, and the votes shall then be counted. The person having the greatest number of votes shall be the President, if such number be a majority of the whole number of electors appointed; and if there be more than one who have such majority, and have an equal number of votes, then the House of Representatives shall immediately choose by ballot one of them for President; and if no person have a majority, then from the five highest on the list the said House shall in like manner choose the President. But in choosing the President, the votes shall be taken by States, the representation from each state having one vote; a quorum for this purpose shall consist of a member or members from two thirds of the states, and a majority of all the states shall be necessary to a choice. In every case, after the choice of the President, the person having the greatest number of votes of the electors shall be the Vice President. But if there should remain two or more who have equal votes, the Senate shall choose from them by ballot the Vice President. (This clause was superseded by Amendment XII.)

3. The Congress may determine the time of choosing the electors, and

the day on which they shall give their votes; which day shall be the same throughout the United States.

4. No person except a natural born citizen, or a citizen of the United States, at the time of the adoption of this Constitution, shall be eligible to the office of President; neither shall any person be eligible to that office who shall not have attained to the age of thirty five years, and been fourteen years a resident within the United States. *(For qualification of the Vice President, see Amendment XII.)*

5. *In case of the removal of the President from office, or of his death, resignation, or inability to discharge the powers and duties of the said office, the same shall devolve on the Vice President, and the Congress may by law provide for the case of removal, death, resignation or inability, both of the President and Vice President, declaring what officer shall then act as President, and such officer shall act accordingly, until the disability be removed, or a President shall be elected. (This clause was modified by Amendments XX and XXV.)*

6. The President shall, at stated times, receive for his services, a compensation, which shall neither be increased nor diminished during the period for which he shall have been elected, and he shall not receive within that period any other emolument from the United States, or any of them.

7. Before he enter on the execution of his office, he shall take the following oath or affirmation:

I do solemnly swear (or affirm) that I will faithfully execute the office of President of the United States, and will to the best of my ability, preserve, protect and defend the Constitution of the United States.

Section 2—President to be Commander-in-Chief. He may require opinions of cabinet officers, etc., may pardon. Treaty-making power. Nomination of certain officers. When President may fill vacancies.

1. The President shall be commander in chief of the Army and Navy of the United States, and of the militia of the several States, when called into the actual service of the United States; he may require the opinion, in writing, of the principal officer in each of the executive departments, upon any subject relating to the duties of their respective offices, and he shall have power to grant reprieves and pardons for offenses against the United States, except in cases of impeachment.

2. He shall have power, by and with the advice and consent of the Senate, to make treaties, provided two-thirds of the Senators present concur; and he shall nominate, and by and with the advice and consent of the Senate, shall appoint ambassadors, other public ministers and consuls, judges of the Supreme Court, and all other officers of the United States, whose appointments are not herein otherwise provided for, and which shall be established by law: but the Congress may by law vest the appointment of such inferior officers, as they think proper, in the President alone, in the courts of law, or in the heads of departments.

3. The President shall have power to fill up all vacancies that may happen during the recess of the Senate, by granting commissions, which shall expire at the end of their next session.

Section 3—President shall communicate to Congress. He may convene and adjourn Congress, in case of disagreement, etc. Shall receive ambassadors, execute laws, and commission officers.

He shall from time to time give to the Congress information of the state of the union, and recommend to their consideration such measures as he shall judge necessary and expedient; he may, on extraordinary occasions, convene both Houses, or either of them, and in case of disagreement between them, with respect to the time of adjournment, he may adjourn them to such time as he shall think proper; he shall receive ambassadors and other public ministers; he shall take care that the laws be faithfully executed, and shall commission all the officers of the United States.

Section 4—All civil offices forfeited for certain crimes.

The President, Vice President, and all civil officers of the United States, shall be removed from office on impeachment for, and conviction of, treason, bribery, or other high crimes and misdemeanors.

ARTICLE III

Section 1—Judicial powers, Tenure. Compensation.

The judicial power of the United States, shall be vested in one Supreme Court, and in such inferior courts as the Congress may from time to time ordain and establish. The judges, both of the Supreme and inferior courts, shall hold their offices during good behavior, and shall, at stated times, receive for their services, a compensation, which shall not be diminished during their continuance in office.

Section 2—Judicial power; to what cases it extends. Original jurisdiction of Supreme Court; appellate jurisdiction. Trial by jury, etc. Trial, where.

1. *The judicial power shall extend to all cases, in law and equity, arising under this Constitution, the laws of the United States, and treaties made, or which shall be made, under their authority; to all cases affecting ambassadors, other public ministers and consuls; to all cases of admiralty and maritime jurisdiction; to controversies to which the United States shall be a party; to controversies between two or more States; between a State and citizens of another State; between citizens of different States; between citizens of the same State claiming lands under grants of different States, and between a State, or the citizens thereof, and foreign states, citizens or subjects. (This section was modified by Amendment XI.)*

2. In all cases affecting ambassadors, other public ministers and consuls, and those in which a State shall be party, the Supreme Court shall have original jurisdiction. In all the other cases before mentioned, the Supreme Court shall have appellate jurisdiction, both as to law and fact, with such exceptions, and under such regulations as the Congress shall make.

3. The trial of all crimes, except in cases of impeachment, shall be by jury; and such trial shall be held in the State where the said crimes shall have been committed; but when not committed within any State, the trial shall be at such place or places as the Congress may by law have directed.

Section 3—Treason Defined, Proof of, Punishment of.

1. Treason against the United States, shall consist only in levying war against them, or in adhering to their enemies, giving them aid and comfort. No person shall be convicted of treason unless on the testimony of two witnesses to the same overt act, or on confession in open court.

2. The Congress shall have power to declare the punishment of treason, but no attainder of treason shall work corruption of blood, or forfeiture except during the life of the person attainted.

ARTICLE IV

Section 1—Each State to give credit to the public acts, etc., of every other State.

Full faith and credit shall be given in each State to the public acts, records, and judicial proceedings of every other State. And the Congress may by general laws prescribe the manner in which such acts, records, and proceedings shall be proved, and the effect thereof.

Section 2—Privileges of citizens of each State. Fugitives from justice to be delivered up. Persons held to service having escaped, to be delivered up.

1. The citizens of each State shall be entitled to all privileges and immunities of citizens in the several States.

2. A person charged in any State with treason, felony, or other crime, who shall flee from justice, and be found in another State, shall on demand of the Executive authority of the State from which he fled, be delivered up, to be removed to the State having jurisdiction of the crime.

3. *No person held to service or labor in one State, under the laws thereof, escaping into another, shall, in consequence of any law or regulation therein, be discharged from such service or labor, but shall be delivered up on claim of the party to whom such service or labor may be due. (This clause was superseded by Amendment XIII.)*

Section 3—Admission of new States. Power of Congress over territory and other property.

1. New States may be admitted by the Congress into this union; but no new State shall be formed or erected within the jurisdiction of any other State; nor any State be formed by the junction of two or more States, or parts of States, without the consent of the Legislatures of the States concerned as well as of the Congress.

2. The Congress shall have power to dispose of and make all needful rules and regulations respecting the territory or other property belonging to the United States; and nothing in this Constitution shall be so construed as to prejudice any claims of the United States, or of any particular State.

Section 4—Republican form of government guaranteed. Each state to be protected.

The United States shall guarantee to every State in this Union a Republican form of government, and shall protect each of them against invasion; and on application of the Legislature, or of the Executive (when the Legislature cannot be convened) against domestic violence.

ARTICLE V

Constitution: how amended; proviso.

The Congress, whenever two-thirds of both Houses shall deem it necessary, shall propose amendments to this Constitution, or, on the application of the Legislatures of two-thirds of the several States, shall call a convention for proposing amendments, which, in either case, shall be valid to all intents and purposes, as part of this Constitution, when ratified by the Legislatures of three-fourths of the several States, or by conventions in three-fourths thereof, as the one or the other mode of ratification may be proposed by the Congress; provided that no amendment which may be made prior to the year one thousand eight hundred and eight shall in any manner affect the first and fourth clauses in the Ninth Section of the First Article; and that no State, without its consent, shall be deprived of its equal suffrage in the Senate.

ARTICLE VI

Certain debts, etc., declared valid. Supremacy of Constitution, treaties, and law of the United States. Oath to support Constitution, by whom taken. No religious test.

1. All debts contracted and engagements entered into, before the adoption of this Constitution, shall be as valid against the United States under this Constitution, as under the Confederation.

2. This Constitution, and the laws of the United States which shall be made in pursuance thereof; and all treaties made, or which shall be made, under the authority of the United States, shall be the supreme law of the land; and the judges in every State shall be bound thereby, any thing in the Constitution or laws of any State to the contrary notwithstanding.

3. The Senators and Representatives before mentioned, and the members of the several State Legislatures, and all executive and judicial officers, both of the United States and of the several States, shall be bound by oath or affirmation, to support this Constitution; but no religious test shall ever be required as a qualification to any office or public trust under the United States.

ARTICLE VII

What ratification shall establish Constitution.

The ratification of the Conventions of nine States, shall be sufficient for the establishment of this Constitution between the States so ratifying the same.

Done in convention by the unanimous consent of the States present the Seventeenth day of September in the year of our Lord one thousand seven hundred and eighty seven, and of the independence of the United States of America the Twelfth. In witness whereof we have hereunto subscribed our Names,

George Washington-President and deputy from Virginia

New Hampshire—John Langdon, Nicholas Gilman

Massachusetts—Nathaniel Gorham, Rufus King

Connecticut—Wm. Saml. Johnson, Roger Sherman

New York—Alexander Hamilton

New Jersey—Wil. Livingston, David Brearly, Wm. Paterson, Jona. Dayton

Pennsylvania—B. Franklin, Thomas Mifflin, Robt. Morris, Geo. Clymer, Thos. FitzSimons, Jared Ingersoll, James Wilson, Gouv. Morris

Delaware—Geo. Read, Gunning Bedford Jun., John Dickinson, Richard Bassett, Jaco. Broom

Maryland—James McHenry, Dan of Saint Thomas' Jenifer, Danl. Carroll

Virginia—John Blair, James Madison Jr.

North Carolina: Wm. Blount, Rich'd. Dobbs Spaight, Hugh Williamson

South Carolina: J. Rutledge, Charles Cotesworth Pinckney, Charles Pinckney, Pierce Butler

Georgia: William Few, Abr. Baldwin

Attest: William Jackson, Secretary.

AMENDMENTS TO THE CONSTITUTION OF THE UNITED STATES

(The first ten amendments known as the Bill of Rights were passed by Congress on September 25, 1789, and ratified by sufficient states on December 15, 1791)

Amendment I (1791)

Religious establishment prohibited. Freedom of speech, of the press, and right to petition.

Congress shall make no law respecting an establishment of religion, or prohibiting the free exercise thereof; or abridging the freedom of speech, or of the press; or the right of the people peaceably to assemble, and to petition the Government for a redress of grievances.

Amendment II (1791)

Right to keep and bear arms.

A well-regulated militia, being necessary to the security of a free State, the right of the people to keep and bear arms, shall not be infringed.

Amendment III (1791)

Conditions for quarters for soldiers.

No soldier shall, in time of peace be quartered in any house, without the consent of the owner, nor in time of war, but in a manner to be prescribed by law.

Amendment IV (1791)

Right of search and seizure regulated.

The right of the people to be secure in their persons, houses, papers, and effects, against unreasonable searches and seizures, shall not be violated, and no warrants shall issue, but upon probable cause, supported by oath or affirmation, and particularly describing the place to be searched, and the persons or things to be seized.

Amendment V (1791)

Provisions concerning prosecution. Trial and punishment—private property not to be taken for public use without compensation.

No person shall be held to answer for a capital, or otherwise infamous crime, unless on a presentment or indictment of a Grand Jury, except in cases arising in the land or naval forces, or in the militia, when in actual service in time of war or public danger; nor shall any person be subject for the same offense to be twice put in jeopardy of life or limb; nor shall be compelled in any criminal case to be a witness against himself, nor be deprived of life, liberty, or property, without due process of law; nor shall private property be taken for public use without just compensation.

Amendment VI (1791)

Right to speedy trial, witnesses, etc.

In all criminal prosecutions, the accused shall enjoy the right to a speedy and public trial, by an impartial jury of the State and district wherein the crime shall have been committed, which district shall have been previously ascertained by law, and to be informed of the nature and cause of the accusation; to be confronted with the witnesses against him; to have compulsory process for obtaining witnesses in his favor, and to have the assistance of counsel for his defense.

Amendment VII (1791)

Right of trial by jury.

In suits at common law, where the value in controversy shall exceed twenty dollars, the right of trial by jury shall be preserved, and no fact tried by a jury shall be otherwise reexamined in any court of the United States, than according to the rules of the common law.

Amendment VIII (1791)

Excessive bail or fines and cruel punishment prohibited.

Excessive bail shall not be required, nor excessive fines imposed, nor cruel and unusual punishments inflicted.

Amendment IX (1791)

Rule of construction of Constitution.

The enumeration in the Constitution, of certain rights, shall not be construed to deny or disparage others retained by the people.

Amendment X (1791)

Rights of States under Constitution

The powers not delegated to the United States by the Constitution, nor prohibited by it to the States, are reserved to the States respectively, or to the people.

Amendment XI (1798)

Judicial powers construed.

The judicial power of the United States shall not be construed to extend to any suit in law or equity, commenced or prosecuted against one of the United States by citizens of another State, or by citizens or subjects of any foreign state.

Amendment XII (1804)

Manner of choosing President and Vice-President.

The Electors shall meet in their respective States and vote by ballot for President and Vice-President, one of whom, at least, shall not be an inhabitant of the same State with themselves; they shall name in their ballots the person voted for as President, and in distinct ballots the person voted for as Vice-President, and they shall make distinct lists of all persons voted for as President, and of all persons voted for as Vice-President, and of the number of votes for each, which lists they shall sign and certify, and transmit sealed to the seat of the Government of the United States, directed to the President of the Senate; the President of the Senate shall, in the presence of the Senate and House of Representatives, open all the certificates and the votes shall then be counted; the person having the greatest number of votes for President, shall be the President, if such number be a majority of the whole number of Electors appointed; and if no person have such majority, then from the persons having the highest numbers not exceeding three on the list of those voted for as President, the House of Representatives shall choose immediately, by ballot, the President. But in choosing the President, the votes shall be taken by States, the representation from each State having one vote; a quorum for this purpose shall consist of a member or members from two-thirds of the States, and a majority of all the States shall be necessary to a choice. *And if the House of Representatives shall not choose a President whenever the right of choice shall devolve upon them, before the fourth day of March next following, then the Vice-President shall act as President, as in the case of the death or other constitutional disability of the President. (The preceding sentence in italics was superseded by Amendment XX, section 3.)* The person having the greatest number of votes as Vice-President, shall be the Vice-President, if such number be a majority of the whole number of Electors appointed, and if no person have a majority, then from the two highest numbers on the list, the Senate shall choose the Vice-President; a quorum for the purpose shall consist of two-thirds of the whole number of Senators, and a majority of the whole number shall be necessary to a choice. But no person constitutionally ineligible to the office of President shall be eligible to that of Vice-President of the United States.

Amendment XIII (1865)

Slavery abolished.

1. Neither slavery nor involuntary servitude, except as a punishment for crime whereof the party shall have been duly convicted, shall exist within the United States, or any place subject to their jurisdiction.

2. Congress shall have power to enforce this article by appropriate legislation.

Amendment XIV (1868)

Citizenship rights not to be abridged.

1. All persons born or naturalized in the United States, and subject to the jurisdiction thereof, are citizens of the United States and of the State wherein

they reside. No State shall make or enforce any law which shall abridge the privileges or immunities of citizens of the United States; nor shall any State deprive any person of life, liberty, or property, without due process of law; nor deny to any person within its jurisdiction the equal protection of the laws.

2. Representatives shall be apportioned among the several States according to their respective numbers, counting the whole number of persons in each State, excluding Indians not taxed. But when the right to vote at any election for the choice of Electors for President and Vice President of the United States, Representatives in Congress, the executive and judicial officers of a State, or the members of the Legislature thereof, is denied to any of the male inhabitants of such State, being twenty-one years of age, and citizens of the United States, or in any way abridged, except for participation in rebellion, or other crime, the basis of representation therein shall be reduced in the proportion which the number of such male citizens shall bear to the whole number of male citizens twenty-one years of age in such State.

3. No person shall be a Senator or Representative in Congress, or Elector of President and Vice-President, or hold any office, civil or military, under the United States, or under any State, who, having previously taken an oath, as a member of Congress, or as an officer of the United States, or as a member of any State Legislature, or as an executive or judicial officer of any State, to support the Constitution of the United States, shall have engaged in insurrection or rebellion against the same, or given aid or comfort to the enemies thereof. But Congress may by a vote of two-thirds of each House, remove such disability.

4. The validity of the public debt of the United States, authorized by law, including debts incurred for payment of pensions and bounties for services in suppressing insurrection or rebellion, shall not be questioned. But neither the United States nor any State shall assume or pay any debt or obligation incurred in aid of insurrection or rebellion against the United States, or any claim for the loss or emancipation of any slave; but all such debts, obligations and claims shall be held illegal and void.

5. The Congress shall have power to enforce, by appropriate legislation, the provisions of this article.

Amendment XV (1870)

Race no bar on voting rights.

1. The right of citizens of the United States to vote shall not be denied or abridged by the United States or by any State on account of race, color, or previous condition of servitude.

2. The Congress shall have power to enforce this article by appropriate legislation.

Amendment XVI (1913)

Income taxes authorized.

The Congress shall have power to lay and collect taxes on incomes, from whatever source derived, without apportionment among the several States, and without regard to any census of enumeration.

Amendment XVII (1913)

United States Senators to be elected by direct popular vote.

The Senate of the United States shall be composed of two Senators from each State, elected by the people thereof, for six years; and each Senator shall have one vote. The electors in each State shall have the qualifications requisite for electors of the most numerous branch of the State Legislatures.

When vacancies happen in the representation of any State in the Senate, the executive authority of such State shall issue writs of election to fill such vacancies: Provided, That the Legislature of any State may empower the Executive thereof to make temporary appointments until the people fill the vacancies by election as the Legislature may direct.

This amendment shall not be so construed as to affect the election or term of any Senator chosen before it becomes valid as part of the Constitution.

Amendment XVIII (1919)

Liquor prohibition amendment.

1. After one year from the ratification of this article the manufacture, sale, or transportation of intoxicating liquors within, the importation thereof into, or the exportation thereof from the United States and all territory subject to the jurisdiction thereof for beverage purposes is hereby prohibited.

2. The Congress and the several States shall have concurrent power to enforce this article by appropriate legislation.

3. This article shall be inoperative unless it shall have been ratified as an amendment to the Constitution by the Legislatures of the several States, as provided in the Constitution, within seven years from the date of the submission hereof to the States by the Congress.

Amendment XIX (1920)

Giving nationwide suffrage to women.

The right of citizens of the United States to vote shall not be denied or abridged by the United States or by any State on account of sex.

Congress shall have power to enforce this Article by appropriate legislation.

Amendment XX (1933)

Terms of President and Vice President to begin on January 20; those of Senators, Representatives, January 3.

1. The terms of the President and Vice President shall end at noon on the 20th day of January, and the terms of Senators and Representatives at noon on the 3d day of January, of the years in which such terms would have ended if this article had not been ratified; and the terms of their successors shall then begin.

2. The Congress shall assemble at least once in every year, and such meeting shall begin at noon on the 3d day of January, unless they shall by law appoint a different day.

3. If, at the time fixed for the beginning of the term of the President, the President elect shall have died, the Vice President elect shall become

President. If a President shall not have been chosen before the time fixed for the beginning of his term, or if the President elect shall have failed to qualify, then the Vice President elect shall act as President until a President shall have qualified; and the Congress may by law provide for the case wherein neither a President elect nor a Vice President elect shall have qualified, declaring who shall then act as President, or the manner in which one who is to act shall be selected, and such person shall act accordingly until a President or Vice President shall have qualified.

4. The Congress may by law provide for the case of the death of any of the persons from whom the House of Representatives may choose a President whenever the right of choice shall have devolved upon them, and for the case of the death of any of the persons from whom the Senate may choose a Vice President whenever the right of choice shall have devolved upon them.

5. Sections 1 and 2 shall take effect on the 15th day of October following the ratification of this article.

6. This article shall be inoperative unless it shall have been ratified as an amendment to the Constitution by the Legislatures of three-fourths of the several States with-in seven years from the date of its submission.

Amendment XXI (1933)

Repeal of Amendment XVIII.

1. The eighteenth article of amendment to the Constitution of the United States is here-by repealed.

2. The transportation or importation into any State, Territory, or Possession of the United States for delivery or use therein of intoxicating liquors, in violation of the laws thereof, is hereby prohibited.

3. This article shall be inoperative unless it shall have been ratified as an amendment to the Constitution by conventions in the several States, as provided in the Constitution, within seven years from the date of the submission hereof to the States by the Congress.

Amendment XXII (1951)

Limiting Presidential terms of office.

1. No person shall be elected to the office of the President more than twice, and no person who has held the office of President, or acted as President, for more than two years of a term to which some other person was elected President shall be elected to the office of the President more than once. But this article shall not apply to any person holding the office of President when this article was proposed by the Congress, and shall not prevent any person who may be holding the office of President, or acting as President, during the term within which this article becomes operative from holding the office of President or acting as President during the remainder of such term.

2. This article shall be inoperative unless it shall have been ratified as an amendment to the Constitution by the Legislatures of three-fourths of the several States within seven years from the date of its submission to the States by the Congress.

Amendment XXIII (1961)

Presidential vote for District of Columbia.

1. The District constituting the seat of Government of the United States shall appoint in such manner as the Congress may direct:

A number of electors of President and Vice President equal to the whole number of Senators and Representatives in Congress to which the District would be entitled if it were a state, but in no event more than the least populous State; they shall be in addition to those appointed by the States, but they shall be considered, for the purposes of the election of President and Vice President, to be electors appointed by a State; and they shall meet in the District and perform such duties as provided by the twelfth article of amendment.

2. The Congress shall have power to enforce this article by appropriate legislation.

Amendment XXIV (1964)

Barring poll tax in federal elections.

1. The right of citizens of the United States to vote in any primary or other election for President or Vice President, for electors for President or Vice President, or for Senator or Representative in Congress, shall not be denied or abridged by the United States or any State by reason of failure to pay any poll tax or other tax.

2. The Congress shall have power to enforce this article by appropriate legislation.

Amendment XXV (1967)

Presidential disability and succession.

1. In case of the removal of the President from office or of his death or resignation, the Vice President shall become President.

2. Whenever there is a vacancy in the office of the Vice President, the President shall nominate a Vice President who shall take office upon confirmation by a majority vote of both houses of Congress.

3. Whenever the President transmits to the President pro tempore of the Senate and the Speaker of the House of Representatives his written declaration that he is unable to discharge the powers and duties of his office, and until he transmits to them a written declaration to the contrary, such powers and duties shall be discharged by the Vice President as Acting President.

4. Whenever the Vice President and a majority of either the principal officers of the executive departments or of such other body as Congress may by law provide, transmit to the President pro tempore of the Senate and the Speaker of the House of Representatives their written declaration that the President is unable to discharge the powers and duties of his office, the Vice President shall immediately assume the powers and duties of the office as Acting President.

Thereafter, when the President transmits to the President pro tempore of the Senate and the Speaker of the House of Representatives his written declaration that no inability exists, he shall resume the powers and duties of his office unless the Vice President and a majority of either the principal officers of the executive department or of such other body as Congress may by law provide, transmit within four days to the President pro tempore of the Senate and the Speaker of the House of Representatives their written declaration that the President is unable to discharge the powers and duties of his office. Thereupon Congress shall decide the issue, assembling within forty-eight hours for that purpose if not in session.

If the Congress, within twenty-one days after receipt of the latter written declaration, or, if Congress is not in session, within twenty-one days after Congress is required to assemble, determines by two-thirds vote of both houses that the President is unable to discharge the powers and duties of his office, the Vice President shall continue to discharge the same as Acting President; otherwise, the President shall resume the powers and duties of his office.

Amendment XXVI (1971)

Lowering voting age to 18 years.
1. The right of citizens of the United States, who are 18 years of age or older, to vote shall not be denied or abridged by the United States or any state on account of age.
2. The Congress shall have the power to enforce this article by appropriate legislation.

Amendment XXVII (Passed Sept. 25, 1789; ratified May 7, 1992)

Congressional pay.
No law, varying the compensation for the services of the Senators and Representatives, shall take effect, until an election of Representatives shall have intervened.

Appendix II

UNITED STATES SUPREME COURT

The U. S. Supreme Court is located at United States Supreme Court Building, One First Street NE, Washington, D.C. 20543. Telephone: (202) 479-3000 for the clerk's office. There are nine justices, including the Chief Justice, appointed for life (unless convicted under an impeachment) by the President, with confirmation by the Senate. The Chief Justice is paid $171,500 a year, and the Associate Justices, $164,100 per year. The annual term, when the Court sits as a full court, begins the first week of October, and continues until the Court decides to adjourn.

The current members of the court are: Chief Justice William H. Rehnquist, Arizona, appointed to the court by President Richard M. Nixon in 1972 and appointed Chief Justice by President Ronald Reagan in 1986; John Paul Stevens, Illinois, appointed by President Gerald R. Ford, 1975; Sandra Day O'Connor (the first woman on the Supreme Court), Arizona, appointed by President Reagan, 1981; Antonin Scalia, Virginia, appointed by President Reagan, 1986; Anthony M. Kennedy, California, appointed by President Reagan, 1988; David H. Souter, New Hampshire, appointed by President George Bush, 1990; Clarence Thomas, Virginia, appointed by President Bush, 1991; Ruth Bader Ginsburg, District of Columbia, appointed by President Bill Clinton, 1993; Stephen Breyer, Massachusetts, appointed by President Clinton, 1994. The Supreme Court considers as many as 6,500 cases a year, but in most cases confirms without comment the ruling below. Less than 200 cases are argued before the court each year, and opinions signed by the court average about 140 a year.

UNITED STATES COURTS OF APPEALS

There are 11 Courts of Appeals for "circuits" comprising several states, plus a Federal circuit based in Washington, D.C. to hear customs, patent and court of claims appeals and an Appeals Court for Washington, D.C. which is under federal law only. Appeals judges are paid $141,700 annually. The term "circuit" comes from the original practice of having members of the Supreme Court go on circuit to hear appeals, which was discontinued in 1891 when the Courts of Appeal were established. Each member of the Supreme Court is assigned a circuit to oversee, or to hear special matters such as a stay of execution. Over 40,000 appeals are heard each year.

First Circuit: Maine, Massachusetts, New Hampshire, Rhode Island, Puerto Rico, at Boston, Massachusetts 02109.

Second Circuit: Connecticut, New York, Vermont, at New York City, New York 10007.

Third Circuit: Delaware, New Jersey, Pennsylvania, Virgin Islands, at Philadelphia, Pennsylvania 19106.

Fourth Circuit: Maryland, North Carolina, South Carolina, Virginia, West Virginia, at Richmond, Virginia 23219.

Fifth Circuit: Louisiana, Mississippi, Texas, at New Orleans, Louisiana 70103.

Sixth Circuit: Kentucky, Michigan, Ohio, Tennessee, at Cincinnati, Ohio 45202.

Seventh Circuit: Illinois, Indiana, Wisconsin, at Chicago, Illinois 60604.

Eighth Circuit: Arkansas, Iowa, Minnesota, Missouri, Nebraska, North Dakota, South Dakota, at St. Louis, Missouri 63101.

Ninth Circuit: Alaska, Arizona, California, Hawaii, Idaho, Montana, Nevada, Oregon, Washington, Guam, North Mariana Islands, at San Francisco, California 94119.

Tenth Circuit: Colorado, Kansas, New Mexico, Oklahoma, Utah, Wyoming, at Denver, Colorado 80294.

Eleventh Circuit: Alabama, Florida, Georgia, at Atlanta, Georgia 30303.

Federal Circuit: at Washington, D.C. 20439.

District of Columbia: at Washington, D.C. 20001.

UNITED STATES DISTRICT COURTS

The District Courts are the trial courts for most federal cases, and there are one or more districts in each state. District Court judges are paid $133,600 per year.

Alabama: Northern District at Birmingham, Middle District at Montgomery, Southern District at Mobile.

Alaska: at Anchorage.

Arizona: at Phoenix.

Arkansas: Eastern District at Little Rock, Western District at Fort Smith.

California: Northern District at San Francisco, Eastern District at Sacramento, Central District at Los Angeles, Southern District at San Diego.

Colorado: at Denver.

Connecticut: at New Haven.

Delaware: at Wilmington.

District of Columbia: at Washington, D.C.

Florida: Northern District at Tallahassee, Middle District at Jacksonville, Southern District at Miami.

Georgia: Northern District at Atlanta, Middle District at Macon, Southern District at Savannah.

Hawaii: at Honolulu.

Idaho: at Boise.

Illinois: Northern District at Chicago, Central District at Springfield, Southern District at East St Louis.

Indiana: Northern District at South Bend, Southern District at Indianapolis.

Iowa: Northern District at Cedar Rapids, Southern District at Des Moines.

Kansas: at Wichita.

Kentucky: Eastern District at Lexington, Western District at Louisville.

Louisiana: Eastern District at New Orleans, Middle District at Baton Rouge, Western District at Shreveport

Maine: at Portland.

Maryland: at Baltimore.

Massachusetts: at Boston.

Michigan: Eastern District at Detroit, Western District at Grand Rapids.

Minnesota: at St. Paul.

Mississippi: Northern District at Oxford, Southern District at Jackson.

Missouri: Eastern District at St Louis, Western District at Kansas City.

Montana: at Billings.

Nebraska: at Omaha.

Nevada: at Reno.

New Hampshire: at Concord.

New Jersey: at Newark.

New Mexico: at Albuquerque.

New York: Northern District at Syracuse, Eastern District at Brooklyn, Southern District at New York City, Western District at Buffalo.

North Carolina: Eastern District at Raleigh, Middle District at Greensboro, Western District at Asheville.

North Dakota: at Bismarck.

Ohio: Northern District at Cleveland, Southern District at Columbus.

Oklahoma: Northern District at Tulsa, Eastern District at Muskogee, Western District at Oklahoma City.

Oregon: at Portland.

Pennsylvania: Eastern District at Philadelphia, Middle District at Scranton, Western District at Pittsburgh.

Rhode Island: at Providence.

South Carolina: at Columbia.

South Dakota: at Sioux Falls.

Tennessee: Eastern District at Knoxville, Middle District at Nashville, Western District at Memphis.

Texas: Northern District at Dallas, Southern District at Houston, Eastern District at Tyler, Western District at San Antonio.

Utah: at Salt Lake City.

Vermont: at Burlington.

Virginia: Eastern District at Alexandria, Western District at Roanoke.

Washington: Eastern District at Spokane, Western District at Seattle.

West Virginia: Northern District at Elkins, Southern District at Charleston.

Wisconsin: Eastern District at Milwaukee, Western District at Madison.

Wyoming: at Cheyenne.

TERRITORIAL DISTRICT COURTS: Guam at Agana, Puerto Rico at Hato Rex, and Virgin Islands at St. Croix.

UNITED STATES COURT OF INTERNATIONAL TRADE: New York City, New York 10007.

UNITED STATES COURT OF FEDERAL CLAIMS: Washington, D.C. 20005.

UNITED STATES TAX COURT: Washington, D.C. 20217.

UNITED STATES COURT OF VETERANS APPEALS: Washington, D.C. 20004.

STATE SUPREME AND APPEALS COURTS

Every state has a state court appeals system, in which the highest court is called the State Supreme Court except in Maryland and New York, where that court is called the Court of Appeals. Many states have interim appeals courts which hear the appeals from trial courts, and from those appeals courts the decisions may be appealed to the highest court, but in most cases only if the State Supreme Court (state appeals court in New York and Maryland) wishes to hear the case, usually because the case requires legal clarification of conflicting decisions or the establishment of a precedent.

An appeal from a state court ruling may be made to the U. S. Supreme Court only if there is a U. S. Constitutional issue involved.

State Supreme Courts (not to be confused with Supreme Court in New York, which is a trial court) generally sit at the state capital, although there are exceptions such as California, where the court is headquartered in San Francisco.

MAJOR SUPREME COURT DECISIONS

Appendix III

Marbury v. Madison (1803): Chief Justice John Marshall used a dispute over judicial appointments to declare a judiciary act unconstitutional, in order to establish the power of the Supreme Court to decide the constitutionality of statutes.

Martin v. Hunter's Lessee (1816): In a decision by Justice Joseph Story the Supreme Court extended its right of judicial review on constitutionality to appeals from state and federal courts.

McCulloch v. Maryland (1819): In ruling that the federal government could charter a bank and a state could not tax that bank, Chief Justice John Marshall established that the federal government has "implied powers" to carry out any and all powers given by the Constitution without state interference.

Gibbons v. Ogden (1824): Chief Justice John Marshall's decision struck down state barriers to interstate commerce. The case involved a steamboat operator who was denied a license by one of the states he serviced.

Dred Scott v. Sanford (1857): The ruling that a slave taken to a free state was still a slave, helped trigger the Civil War.

Slaughter House Cases (1873): In upholding the contract rights to an owner of a monopoly on slaughter houses granted by the "carpet bagger" government of Louisiana, by a vote of 5-4, the court ruled that the "privileges and immunities" protections of the Constitution now applied to the states through the 14th Amendment.

Plessy v. Ferguson (1896): Despite a vigorous dissent by Justice John Harlan, the court ruled that "separate but equal" facilities for blacks were constitutional, which remained the rule until Brown v. Board of Education (1954).

Muller v. Oregon (1908): A state law setting a maximum of working hours for women was upheld, with future Justice Louis D. Brandeis arguing for the state.

Standard Oil Co. of New Jersey v. United States (1911): The court confirmed the dissolution of the Standard Oil Trust, because its monopoly position was an unreasonable restraint on trade under the Sherman Antitrust Act.

Schenk v. United States (1919): In sustaining the Espionage Act of 1917 enacted during World War I, the court ruled that freedom of speech and freedom of press could be limited if the words in the circumstances were such that created "a clear and present danger."

Gitlow v. New York (1925): The court ruled that the First Amendment right to free speech applied to state laws under the 14th Amendment.

Village of Euclid v. Amber Realty (1926): The court ruled that zoning ordinances are a legitimate exercise of the states' police powers.

Near v. Minnesota (1931): "Prior restraint" on publications is a violation of free speech and free press, the court ruled in striking down a state law that allowed the police to confiscate publications that were "malicious, scandalous or obscene." The case involved a virulently anti-Semitic pamphlet.

Norris v. Alabama (1935): The "Scottsboro" case, in which several young black men were falsely charged with the rape of a young white woman, was overturned on the basis that organized exclusion of blacks from jury panels (the pool of potential jurors) was a violation of the defendants' constitutional right to due process.

Schecter Poultry Corp. v. United States (1935): The court struck down the National Industrial Recovery Act (a key measure of the New Deal) on the basis that the government had improperly delegated authority to make rules governing industries in interstate commerce. The decision by an aging court (called "nine old men" by its critics) and other rulings that New Deal legislation was unconstitutional prompted President Franklin D. Roosevelt to launch his ill-fated effort to "pack" the Supreme Court by adding an additional justice for each one who would not retire at 70. Death and resignation soon gave Roosevelt vacancies to fill on the court.

Darby v. United States (1941): In a decision by Justice Harlan Stone the court sustained that portion of the 1938 Fair Labor Standards Act prohibiting child labor and regulating wages and hours, on the basis that the federal government's power to regulate interstate commerce included the authority to "promote" commerce as well as prohibit it, a position argued in a dissent by Oliver Wendell Holmes in 1916.

Brown v. Board of Education of Topeka (1954): Chief Justice Earl Warren ruled for a unanimous court that separate educational facilities for blacks and whites are inherently unequal and equal conditions for all races must be provided with "all deliberate speed," overturning Plessy v. Ferguson.

Roth v. United States (1957): The court denied free speech and free press protection to obscene material which was "utterly without redeeming social value."

Mapp v. Ohio (1961): Evidence obtained by illegal search and seizure could not be introduced in state or federal trials.

Engel v. Vitale (1962): School prayers, even though voluntary and nondenominational, were found to violate the constitutional prohibition against laws which tend toward the establishment of a religion (separation of church and state).

Baker v. Carr (1962): In the first "one-man-one-vote" decision, the court ruled that districts which were malapportioned (varied substantially in population) denied the voters "equal protection" and were therefore unconstitutional.

Gideon v. Wainwright (1963): The court extended the original constitutional right to an attorney in federal criminal cases for those who could not afford representation to indigent defendants in state prosecutions under the due process clause of the 14th Amendment. This meant that an attorney had to be appointed to represent criminal defendants, greatly expanding the use of public defenders. The case for the poor defendant was carried for free by future Supreme Court Justice Abe Fortas.

New York Times v. Sullivan (1964): A landmark decision in the field of libel, which ruled that the commercial press was shielded from lawsuits by public officials (later extended to "public figures") for libel unless the public official could show the defamatory statement (even though false) was motivated by "malice," meaning the defamer knew it was false or made it with "reckless disregard of whether it was false or not." The theory was that otherwise potential libel suits would put a chill on the reporting on public officials by the media.

Reynolds v. Sims (1964): The second "one-man-one-vote" landmark decision, which ruled that both houses of state legislatures had to be apportioned with districts of approximately equal populations. The result was reapportionment of upper houses (state senates) and some lower houses throughout the nation for the 1966 elections.

Griswold v. Connecticut (1965): The court struck down laws against the sale or use of contraceptives as an invasion of personal privacy.

Miranda v. Arizona (1966): The court established the rights of a criminal suspect to remain silent, to be told he/she can have legal counsel and that anything he/she says can be used in court. Furthermore, to use a confession or admission in court the prosecution must prove the suspect knowingly waived those rights, and thus the "rights" should be read or recited to the suspect. These became known as the "Miranda rights."

Roe v. Wade (1973): The court ruled that abortions (previously limited to those necessary to save a woman's life) were legal, and any state law which denied the right of a woman to have an abortion in the first trimester (three months) of pregnancy was a denial of her right to privacy under the due process guarantee in the 14th Amendment. Until that ruling every state had statutes making an elective abortion a crime.

Gregg v. Georgia (1976): The death penalty for murder was found not to be in and of itself a "cruel and unusual punishment" prohibited by the 8th Amendment, but the character of the defendant was to be considered in deciding whether to impose the death penalty.

Woodson v. North Carolina (1976) A "mandatory" death penalty for first-degree murder was ruled unconstitutional since a defendant had the right to individual consideration of the facts in his/her case.

Regents of the University of California v. Bakke (1978): The "reverse discrimination case" which found that a white applicant for a medical school which received federal funding could not be excluded due to his race (a limited quota for whites under the school's admission plan) due to the non-discrimination provisions of the 1964 Civil Rights Act.

United Steelworkers of America v. Weber (1979): The 1964 Civil Rights Act provisions for "affirmative action" programs to encourage minority hiring for jobs in which the minorities were previously underrepresented were ruled constitutional.

STATE BAR ASSOCIATIONS

Appendix IV

Alabama State Bar: 415 Dexter Avenue, P. O. Box 671, Montgomery, AL 36101 Tel.: (205) 269-1515

Alaska Bar Association: 310 K Street, Suite 602, Anchorage, AK 99510 Tel.: (907) 272-7469

State Bar of Arizona: 363 North First Avenue, Suite 858, Phoenix, AZ 85003 Tel.: (602) 252-4804

Arkansas Bar Association: 400 West Markham, Little Rock, AR 72201 Tel.: (501) 375-4605

State Bar of California: 555 Franklin Street, San Francisco, CA 94102 Tel.: (415) 561-8200

Colorado Bar Association: 1900 Grant Street, Suite 950, Denver, CO 80203-4309 Tel.: (303) 860-1112

Connecticut Bar Association: 101 Corporate Place, Rocky Hill, CT 06067 Tel.: (203) 721-0025

Delaware Bar Association: 1225 King Street, 10th Floor, P. O. Box 1709, Wilmington, DE 19899 Tel.: (302) 658-2579

The District of Columbia Bar: 1707 L Street, N.W., 6th Floor, Washington, D. C. 20036 Tel.: (202) 331-3883

The Florida Bar: 650 Apalachee Parkway, Tallahassee, FL 32399-2300 Tel.: (904) 561-5600

State Bar of Georgia: 800 The Hurt Building, Atlanta, GA 30303 Tel.: (800) 334-6865

Hawaii State Bar Association: P. O. Box 26, Honolulu, HI 96810 Tel.: (808) 537-1868 FAX: (808) 521-7936

Idaho State Bar: 204 West State Street, P. O. Box 895, Boise, ID 83701-0895 Tel.: (208) 342-8958 FAX: (208) 342-3799

Illinois State Bar Association: Illinois Bar Center, 424 South 2nd Street, Springfield, IL 62701-1779 Tel.: (217) 525-1760 FAX: (217) 525-0712

Indiana State Bar Association: 230 East Ohio Street, 6th Floor, Indianapolis, IN 46204 Tel.: (317) 639-5465

Iowa State Bar Association: 521 East Locust Street, Des Moines, IA 50309 Tel.: (515) 243-3179

Kansas Bar Association: 1200 Harrison Street, Topeka, KS 66601 Tel.: (913) 234-5696 FAX: (913) 234-3813

Kentucky Bar Association: 514 West Main Street, Frankfort, KY 40601-1883 Tel.: (502) 564-3795 FAX: (502) 564-3225

Louisiana State Bar Association: 601 St. Charles Avenue, New Orleans, LA 70130 Tel.: (504) 566-1600

Maine State Bar Association: 124 State Street, P. O. Box 788, Augusta, ME 04332-0788 Tel.: (207) 622-7523 FAX: (207) 623-4140

Maryland Bar Association, Inc.: The Maryland Bar Center, 520 West Fayette Street, Baltimore, MD 21201 Tel.: (410) 685-7878 FAX: (410) 837-0518

Massachusetts Bar Association: 20 West Street, Boston, MA 02111-1204 Tel.: (617) 542-3602 FAX: (617) 426-4344

State Bar of Michigan: 306 Townsend Street, Lansing, MI 48933-2083 Tel.: (517) 372-9030

Minnesota State Bar Association: 514 Nicollet Avenue, Suite 300, Minneapolis, MN 55402 Tel.: (612) 333-1183 FAX: (612) 333-4927

Mississippi State Bar: 643 North State Street, P. O. Box 2168, Jackson, MS 39225 Tel.: (601) 948-4471

The Missouri Bar: 326 Monroe Street, P. O. Box 119, Jefferson City, MO 65102 Tel.: (314) 635-4128 FAX: (314) 635-2811

State Bar of Montana: 46 North Last Chance Gulch, Suite 2A, P. O. Box 577, Helena, MT 59624 Tel.: (406) 442-7660 FAX: (406) 442-7663

Nebraska State Bar Association: 635 South 14th Street, P. O. Box 81809, Lincoln, NE 68501 Tel.: (402) 475-7091 FAX: (402) 475-7098

State Bar of Nevada: 201 Las Vegas Blvd. South, Suite 200, Las Vegas, NV 89101-6579 Tel.: (702) 382-2200 FAX: (702) 385-2878

New Hampshire Bar Association: 112 Pleasant Street, Concord, NH 03301 Tel.: (603) 224-6942

New Jersey State Bar Association: One Constitution Square, New Brunswick, NJ 08901-1500 Tel.: (908) 249-5000 FAX: (908) 249-2815

State Bar of New Mexico: 121 Tijeres N. E., Garden Level, P. O. Box 25883, Albuquerque, NM 87125 Tel.: (505) 842-6132 FAX: (505) 843-8765

New York State Bar Association: One Elk Street, Albany, NY 12207 Tel.: (518) 463-3200

North Carolina State Bar: 208 Fayetteville Street Mall, P. O. Box 25908, Raleigh, NC 27611 Tel.: (919) 828-4620

State Bar Association of North Dakota: 515-1/2 East Broadway, Suite 101, P. O. Box 2136, Bismarck, ND 58502 Tel.: (701) 255-1404

Ohio State Bar Association: 1700 Lake Shore Drive, P. O. Box 16562, Columbus, OH 43216 Tel.: (614) 487-2050 FAX: (614) 487-1008

Oklahoma Bar Association: 1901 North Lincoln Blvd., P. O. Box 53036, State Capitol Station, Oklahoma City, OK 73152 Tel.: (405) 524-2365

Oregon State Bar: 5200 S. W. Meadows Road, P. O. Box 1689, Lake Oswego, OR 97035-0889 Tel.: (503) 620-0222

Pennsylvania Bar Association: 100 South Street, P. O. Box 186, Harrisburg, PA 17108 Tel.: (717) 238-6715

Rhode Island Bar Association: 115 Cedar Street, Providence, RI 02903 Tel.: (401) 421-5740

South Carolina Bar: 950 Taylor Street, P. O. Box 608, Columbia, SC 29202-0608 Tel.: (803) 799-6653 FAX: (803) 799-4118

State Bar of South Dakota: 222 East Capitol, Pierre, SD 57501 Tel.: (605) 224-7554

Tennessee Bar Association: 3622 West End Avenue, Nashville, TN 37205 Tel.: (615) 383-7421

State Bar of Texas: P. O. Box 12487, State Capitol Station, Austin, TX 78711 Tel.: (512) 463-1463

Utah State Bar: 645 South 200 East, Salt Lake City, UT 84111-3834 Tel.: (801) 531-9077

Vermont Bar Association: 35-37 Court Street, P. O. Box 100, Montpelier, VT 05602 Tel.: (802) 223-2020 FAX: (802) 223-1573

Virginia State Bar: Eighth and Main Building, Suite 1500, 707 East Main Street, Richmond, VA 23219-2803 Tel.: (804) 775-0500 FAX: (804)775-0501

Washington State Bar Association: 500 Westin Bldg., 2001 6th Avenue, Seattle, WA 98121-2599 Tel.: (206) 448-0441

West Virginia State Bar: 2006 Kanawha Blvd. East, Charleston, WV 25311 Tel.: (304) 558-2456

State Bar of Wisconsin: 402 West Wilson Street, P. O. Box 7158, Madison, WI 53707-7158 Tel.: (608) 257-3838

Wyoming State Bar: 500 Randall Avenue, P. O. Box 109, Cheyenne, WY 92003-0109 Tel.: (307) 632-9061

Guam Bar Association: 141 San Ramon Road, Agana, Guam 96910 Tel.: 641-477-7623

Puerto Rico Bar Association: P. O. Box 1900, San Juan, PR 00903 Tel.: (809) 721-3358 FAX: (809) 725-0330

Virgin Islands Bar Association: P. O. Box 4108, Christiansted, Virgin Islands, 00822 Tel.: (809) 778-7497 FAX: (809) 778-7497

When future President John Adams came to court in Boston to be sworn in as an attorney he forgot to bring his lawyer sponsor to attest to his skill and honesty. Another attorney stepped forward and swore to Adams' talent, saving the young man further embarrassment.

San Francisco 49ers' quarterback Steve Young is an attorney, as is Oakland A's manager Tony LaRussa. Other sports figure attorneys include announcers Mel Allen and Howard Cosell, as well as Miller Huggins, who managed the "Murderers' Row" New York Yankees in the 1920s.

Canada's first two women judges, appointed in 1916 and 1917, were not lawyers but writers of legislation and advocates of the legal rights of women and children.

Francis Bacon, the British essayist and philosopher, was sacked as the Crown's Attorney General for taking bribes.

President Franklin D. Roosevelt never graduated from law school, because he failed courses at Columbia in his final semester and did not bother to make them up. He satisfied the courts by oral examination that he was qualified.

Famous trial attorney Clarence Darrow planted a spy on the staff of the District Attorney, from whom he learned that the prosecution had absolute proof that his clients, the McNamara brothers, were guilty of setting off the bomb at the Los Angeles Times in 1911 which killed 20 people.

Swift justice was meted out to Giuseppe Zangara, who tried to shoot President-elect Franklin D. Roosevelt in Florida on February 15, 1933, but mortally wounded Chicago Mayor Anton Cermak instead. Cermak died March 6. The murder trial began the next day, Zanagara was convicted in a brief trial, and was electrocuted March 20, just 33 days after the shooting.

The so-called "Field Codes," used as the model for basic laws of California and several western states, were written by attorney David Dudley Field for New York, but were never fully adopted by that state. However, his brother, Stephen Field, came to California in the Gold Rush, became a member of the California state legislature and had the codes adopted there. Soon they were copied by several other states. Stephen Field was later appointed to the U.S. Supreme Court. Other Field brothers were Cyrus, who laid the Atlantic Cable, and Henry, a noted writer and theologian.

Hoagy Carmichael, songwriter, singer and actor, who wrote "Stardust" and other popular songs, was a lawyer.

Under early English common law, a potential juror would not be disqualified because he knew the circumstances of the case, and, in fact, such knowledge was considered an advantage.

It was widely reported that Sir William Blackstone, who wrote the *Commentaries on the Law of England,* the bible on the common law, sipped from a bottle of port while writing. When the bottle was empty the day's work was done.

After World War II many states waived the bar examination for servicemen who had been in their final year of law school or had graduated without taking the state examination when they went into the armed forces.

Lizzie Borden, known in song and story for hatcheting her parents to death ("Lizzie Borden took an ax, and gave her mother 40 whacks, and when she saw what she had done, she gave her father 41.") was actually acquitted of murder charges.

America's first woman admitted to the bar was Arabella Mansfield of Iowa on June 15, 1869, when the admitting judge ruled that the word "men" in the state law meant men and/or women. However, Mrs. Mansfield never actively practiced, but served as a professor at Iowa Wesleyan and later DePauw.

The Supreme Court ruled in 1873 that the question of whether a woman could be admitted to the bar was a matter of state jurisdiction and refused to apply the 14th Amendment. For example, Myra Colby Bradwell, owner of the *Chicago Legal News,* had been turned down in 1869, but in 1872

was made an "honorary" member of the Illinois Bar Association. Mrs. Bradwell was eventually admitted, as was her daughter, who was first in her class at Union College of the Law (now Northwestern).

Until 1878, California law limited lawyers to "white males" only, but Clara Shortridge Foltz lobbied through an amendment to the state codes striking that provision, and became California's first woman lawyer in 1878. She and Laura De Force Gordon also successfully sued to overturn the prohibition against women students at Hastings College of the Law, the only public law college in California, after they had been kicked out after two days of classes. Mrs. Foltz later had a 54-year career as an active lawyer and legal reformer.

Vice President Aaron Burr shot and killed former Secretary of Treasury Alexander Hamilton in a duel on July 11, 1804, despite the fact that these two lawyers had been co-counsel on several lawsuits.

In 1859 David Terry, Chief Justice of the California Supreme Court, resigned in order to fight a duel with U. S. Senator David C. Broderick, whom Terry shot and killed. Terry was later shot to death by a U. S. marshal when Terry threatened to attack Supreme Court Justice Stephen Field in a railroad station.

Three current members of the U. S. Supreme Court, Antonin Scalia, Anthony M. Kennedy and David H. Souter, graduated from Harvard Law School, while Chief Justice William H. Rehnquist and Sandra

Day O'Connor received degrees from Stanford Law School. Justice Kennedy received his undergraduate degree from Stanford.

William O. Douglas served the longest on the Supreme Court, 36 years, from 1939-1975.

In the Federal Courts of Appeal, Puerto Rico is included in the same circuit court with Maine, Massachusetts, New Hampshire and Rhode Island, while the Virgin Islands are lumped together with Delaware, New Jersey and Pennsylvania. More rationally, Guam is included with the West Coast states.

Byron "Whizzer" White from the University of Colorado was the only All-American football player to serve on the Supreme Court.

Seven states allow people to take the bar examination without a law degree if they have studied law with a lawyer, usually for four years. These are California (four years), Maine (one year of law school and two with a lawyer), Vermont (three years of undergraduate study and four years in a law office), New York (one year of law school and two of tutoring), Virginia (undergraduate degree and four years study with a lawyer), Washington (same), and Wyoming (one year of law school and two years with a lawyer). Very few attempt this route and the pass rate on the bar examination is very low.

This advertisement for legal quizzes appeared in 1897. The required subjects in law schools today would be very much the same except for the addition of conflicts of laws (between federal and state statutes and cases), taxation (the income tax was legalized in 1913), ethics (which gained favor in the 1960s), and such specialties as labor and environmental law.

CAPITAL PUNISHMENT, BY STATE

Appendix VI

Thirty-seven states and the federal government all provide for capital punishment (the death penalty) for certain crimes.

Alabama: Crimes punishable: murder during commission of a felony; murder of a peace officer, guard or public official; contract murder, murder while serving a life sentence or with a prior murder conviction; murder of a child or a witness; and drive-by shooting resulting in death. The minimum age for the death sentence is 16 years. At the beginning of 1994, 120 were on death row, four of whom were women. There were 10 executions between 1977-93, all by electrocution.

Arizona: Crimes punishable: first-degree murder with aggravating factor. No age limitation. At the beginning of 1994, 112 were on death row, including one woman. There were three executions since 1977 (two in 1993). Means: gas or lethal injection.

Arkansas: Crimes punishable: capital murder, felony murder, killing a law enforcement officer, teacher, public official or candidate, guard or military personnel, multiple murders, killing while under life sentence, contract murder. Minimum age is 14 years. On death row: 33, including one woman. Four executions since 1977, none in 1983. Means: lethal injection or gas.

California: Crimes punishable: first-degree murder with special circumstances (including kidnapping), killing by life-term prisoner, treason, train wrecking, perjury resulting in another's execution. There were 363 on death row, including four women. Minimum age is 18. Two executions since 1977, both by gas. Means: lethal injection or gas.

Colorado: Crimes punishable: first-degree murder, death during kidnapping, felony murder. Mentally retarded are exempted. Minimum age: 18. Three men on death row. There have been no executions since 1977. Means: lethal injection or gas.

Connecticut: Crimes punishable: felony murder, murder with a prior killing, contract murder, killing a peace officer or guard, murder while serving life term, death during a kidnapping or sexual assault, multiple murders, death caused by sale of heroin or cocaine, killing with an assault weapon. Minimum age: 18. Five men on death row with no executions since 1977. Means: electrocution.

Delaware: Crimes punishable: first-degree murder with aggravating circumstances. Minimum age: 16. Fifteen men on death row. Three executions since 1977. Means: lethal injection.

Florida: Crimes punishable: first-degree murder and other specified felonies, including drug trafficking. No age limitation. Death row inmates number 324, including 30 women. Thirty-two executions (second only to Texas in number) since 1977. Means: electrocution.

Georgia: Crimes punishable: murder, death in kidnapping, aircraft hijacking, treason. Minimum age: 17. On death row: 96 men. Since 1977, 17 executions. Means: electrocution.

Idaho: Crimes punishable: first-degree murder, aggravated kidnapping. No minimum age. Twenty-one men and one woman (all white) on death row. No executions since 1977. Means: lethal injection or firing squad.

Illinois: Crimes punishable: first-degree murder with aggravating factor. Age minimum: 18. On death row: 152, including nine women. One execution since 1977. Means: lethal injection.

Indiana: Crimes punishable: murder with aggravating circumstances. Minimum age: 16. On death row: 47 men. Two executions since 1977. Means: electrocution.

Kentucky: Crimes punishable: murder with aggravating circumstances, death during kidnap. Minimum age: 16. On death row: 30 men. No executions since 1977. Means: electrocution.

Louisiana: Crimes punishable: first-degree murder, treason. Minimum age: 15. On death row: 45 men. Twenty-one executions since 1977. Means: lethal injection.

Maryland: Crimes punishable: first-degree murder, felony murder. Minimum age: 18. On death row: 15 men. No executions since 1977. Means: gas.

Mississippi: Crimes punishable: felony murder, murder while under life sentence, killing police officer or guard, contract murder, murder by explosive, killing elected official, rape of child under 14 by adult even without death of victim, skyjacking. Minimum age: 16. On death row: 49 men and one woman. Four executions since 1977. Means: lethal injection.

Missouri: Crimes punishable: first-degree murder. Minimum age: 16. On death row: 58 men and two women. Eleven executions since 1977. Means: lethal injection, gas.

Montana: Crimes punishable: deliberate killing, death during kidnap (including death of rescuer), aggravated assault or kidnapping by prison inmate who has been previously convicted of homicide or is an habitual criminal. No age minimum. On death row: eight men. No executions since 1977. Means: lethal injection, hanging.

Nebraska: Crimes punishable: first-degree murder. Minimum age: 18. On death row: 11 men. No executions since 1977. Means: electrocution.

New Hampshire: Crimes punishable: contract murder, killing law enforcement officer or kidnap victim, or murder while under life sentence without possibility of parole. Minimum age: 17. On death row: none. No executions since 1977; in fact only one since 1930. Means: lethal injection.

Nevada: Crimes punishable: first degree murder with any one of nine aggravating circumstances. On death row: 65. Five executions since 1977. Means: lethal injection.

New Jersey: Crimes punishable: intentional murder, contract murder. Minimum age: 18. On death row: seven men. No executions since 1977. Means: lethal injection.

New Mexico: Crimes punishable: first-degree murder, felony murder with aggravating circumstances. Minimum age: 18. On death row: one. No executions since 1977. Means: lethal injection.

New York: A bill reinstating capital punishment was enacted by the state legislature and signed by Governor George Pataki in March, 1995, to take effect in September. Similar legislation had been vetoed 18 times by former Governors Mario Cuomo and Hugh Carey, and there had been no executions since 1963. Crimes punishable: intentional murders during rape, robbery or kidnapping, serial killings, murders of judges, police officers and guards, contract murder, and deaths resulting from torture. The mentally retarded (except those killing while in prison) and pregnant women could not be executed. There are no persons on death row. Between 1930 and 1963 New York had led the nation in number of executions.

North Carolina: Crimes punishable: first-degree murder. Minimum age: 17. On death row: 65, including two women. Five executions since 1977. Means: lethal injection, gas.

Ohio: Crimes punishable: felony murder, contract murder, murder during escape, assassination, killing of police officer or witness, murder with prior homicide conviction, murder while in prison. Minimum age: 18. On death row: 129 men. No executions since 1977. Means: lethal injection, electrocution.

Oklahoma: Crimes punishable: premeditated murder, felony murder, murder of a child who has been tortured. Minimum age: 16. On death row: 118 men and four women. Three executions since 1977. Means: lethal injection.

Oregon: Crimes punishable: aggravated murder. Minimum age: 18. On death row: 13 men. No executions since 1977. Means: lethal injection.

Pennsylvania: Crimes punishable: first-degree murder. No minimum age. On death row: 169, including three women. No executions since 1977. Means: lethal injection.

South Carolina: Crimes punishable: murder with aggravating circumstances. No minimum age. On death row: 47 men. Four executions since 1977. Means: electrocution.

South Dakota: Crimes punishable: first-degree murder, felony murder, gross physical injury to kidnap victim even if victim lives. No minimum age. On death row: two. No executions since 1977, and only one since 1930. Means: lethal injection.

Tennessee: Crimes punishable: first-degree murder. Minimum age: 18. On death row: 97 men and one woman. No executions since 1977. Means: electrocution.

Texas: Crimes punishable: murder of public safety officer including fireman or guard, felony murder, contract murder, multiple killings, murder by prisoner, murder of a child under six. Minimum age: 17. On death row: 357, including three women. Executions since 1977: 71, most in the nation. Means: lethal injection.

Utah: Crimes punishable: aggravated murder. No minimum age. On death row: three men. Four executions since 1977. Means: lethal injection, firing squad.

Virginia: Crimes punishable: felony murder, contract murder, murder of law enforcement officer, murder by a prisoner, multiple killings, murder arising from drug crime, killing of child under 12. Minimum age: 15. On death row: 49 men. Since 1977, 22 executions. Means: electrocution.

Washington: Crimes punishable: aggravated first-degree murder. No minimum age. On death row: 10 men. One execution since 1977. Means: lethal injection, hanging.

Wyoming: Crimes punishable: first-degree murder, felony murder. Minimum age: 16. No one on death row. Means: lethal injection.

Federal: Crimes punishable: first-degree murder, killing any law enforcement officer, espionage, death due to airjacking, murder of federal official, treason, death during bank robbery, train wrecking resulting in death, murder while a member of the armed forces. There were six under penalty of death in 1994, but there have been no federal executions since early 1950s.

No death penalty in Alaska, Hawaii, Iowa, Kansas, Maine, Massachusetts, Michigan, Minnesota, North Dakota, Rhode Island, Vermont, West Virginia, Wisconsin, Washington, D.C.

Source: *Capital Punishment* 1993, Bureau of Justice Statistics.

Since this official report there have been more executions in 1994 and 1995 and the number awaiting death sentences has increased.

The Accused: (1988) A victim of gang rape caught in the law enforcement/judicial system convinces female prosecutor to press for conviction instead of settling for a plea bargain. Jodie Foster won Academy Award. Also Kelly McGillis, Bernie Coulson, Leo Rossi.

Adam's Rib: (1949) Husband and wife attorneys argue two sides of a murder case with great wit. Spencer Tracy, who played several lawyer roles, and Katharine Hepburn.

Anatomy of a Murder: (1959) Classic courtroom thriller (and good law research) written by a justice of Michigan Supreme Court. Jimmy Stewart, Lee Remick, Ben Gazzara, Arthur O'Connell, Eve Arden, George C. Scott.

And Justice for All: (1979) Al Pacino fights corruption in the legal system, with climactic courtroom explosion at crooked judge. Jack Warden, John Forsythe, Lee Strasberg, Christine Lahti, Craig T. Nelson.

Boomerang!: (1947) Dramatic tale of legal ethics when D.A. realizes defendant is not guilty, based on actual case tried by future Attorney General Homer Cummings. Dana Andrews, Lee J. Cobb, Arthur Kennedy, Ed Begley, Sr., Karl Malden.

The Caine Mutiny: (1954) Tension-filled military trial in which Captain Queeg (with ball bearings rolling in nervous fingers) claims his crew mutinied. Humphrey Bogart, Van Johnson, Fred MacMurray, Robert Francis, E. G. Marshall, Lee Marvin.

Class Action: (1990) Father and daughter lawyers battle in court in fair flick made better by two leads, Gene Hackman and Mary Elizabeth Mastrantonio.

Compulsion: (1959) Based on the Loeb-Leopold 1920s thrill killing by spoiled rich young men, highlight is Orson Welles in 15-minute capsulized version of Clarence Darrow's argument against the death penalty. With . Dean Stockwell, Diane Varsi, E. G. Marshall.

A Few Good Men: (1992) Tom Cruise, assisted by Demi Moore, defends young Marines charged with murder. Also Jack Nicholson.

The Firm: (1993) Tale of top-of-class neophyte attorney caught in a law firm fronting for crooks with deadly results. Tom Cruise, Gene Hackman, Jeanne Tripplehorn, Holly Hunter, Hal Holbrook.

Inherit the Wind: (1960) The 1920s Scopes "Monkey Trial" is fought out between Spencer Tracy as Clarence Darrow and Fredric March as William Jennings Bryan, arguing over teaching evolution. Also Gene Kelly, Florence Eldridge, Dick York, Harry Morgan.

In the Name of the Father: (1993) A determined woman attorney wins exoneration for a young Irishman and his family framed for a terrorist bombing. Oscar nominations for Emma Thompson, Daniel Day-Lewis and Pete Postlethwait.

Judge Priest: (1934) Legendary Will Rogers plays folksy southern judge based on Irvin S. Cobb stories. Compare to *To Kill a Mockingbird* three decades later as racial attitudes changed. With Tom Brown, Anita Louise, Stepin Fetchit.

Judgment at Nuremberg: (1961) War crimes trial of Nazis after World War II with Academy Award-winning screenplay. With Spencer Tracy, Burt Lancaster, Maximilian Schell (also an Oscar), Marlene Dietrich, Judy Garland, Richard Widmark, Montgomery Clift.

Kramer v. Kramer: (1979) Ultimate child custody film which won Best Picture Academy Award, also Best Actor, Director, Supporting Actress, and Screenplay. Dustin Hoffman, Meryl Streep, Jane Alexander, Justin Henry.

Legal Eagles: (1986) Opposing lawyers in murder case, Robert Redford and Debra Winger fall in love. Also Daryl Hannah, Brian Dennehy, Terence Stamp.

The Mouthpiece: (1932) Prosecutor becomes criminal defense lawyer representing mobsters for the big bucks. Warren William, Sidney Fox, Mae Madison, Aline MacMahon, John Wray, Guy Kibbee.

Music Box: (1989) Jessica Lange as lawyer daughter of accused war criminal defends him without being sure he is innocent. Also Armin Mueller-Stahl, Frederic Forrest, Donald Moffat.

Paradine Case: (1947) An Alfred Hitchcock mystery with Gregory Peck as lawyer defending Alida Valli on murder charge. With Ann Todd, Charles Laughton, Charles Coburn, Ethel Barrymore.

The People v. O'Hara: (1951) Lawyer with shady past has to clean up his act to save a client. Spencer Tracy, Pat O'Brien, Diana Lynn, John Hodiak.

Presumed Innocent: (1990) Scott Turow's bestseller in which attorney is under suspicion for murder of woman lawyer with whom he had affair. Harrison Ford, Brian Dennehy, Raul Julia, Bonnie Bedelia, Paul Winfield, Greta Scacchi.

State's Attorney: (1931) John Barrymore stars as flashy district attorney defending a mobster, who was his childhood friend. Also Helen Twelvetrees, William Boyd, Ralph Ince.

Suspect: (1987) Public Defender Cher represents deaf homeless vet Liam Neeson and gets help from juror Dennis Quaid with more fun than logic. Also John Mahoney, Philip Bosco.

To Kill a Mockingbird: (1962) Small-town southern lawyer defends black man accused of rape during Depression, fighting racism and unfair judicial system while trying to prove his client's innocence. Adapted from Harper Lee's novel, screenplay won Academy Award as did star Gregory Peck. Also Mary Badham, Philip Alford, Brock Peters, Robert Duvall.

The Trial: (1963) A French adaptation of Kafka's eerie novel, well directed by Orson Welles. Anthony Perkins plays the accused, with Jeanne Moreau, Romy Schneider, Elsa Martinelli and Welles himself.

Trial of Mary Dugan: (1929) The first courtroom movie in sound, a woman is accused of murdering her lover, is deserted by attorney, and saved by new counsel. Norma Shearer, Lewis Stone, H. B. Warner, Raymond Hackett.

True Believer: (1989) Lawyer who has shed radical ideals for high-paying law career, takes on appeal of Asian convict at urging of young law clerk. James Woods, Robert Downey, Jr., Yuji Okumoto, Margaret Colin.

Twelve Angry Men: (1957) "The" jury movie, in which the arguments and emotions of the jurors make viewer feel sequestered with them. Henry Fonda, Lee J. Cobb, Ed Begley, Sr., Martin Balsam, E. G. Marshall, Jack Klugman and Jack Warden head a stellar panel.

The Verdict: (1982) Broken-down alcoholic storefront lawyer takes on powerful defendants in negligence case to gain final redemption for wasted career. Paul Newman in the lead backed by Charlotte Rampling, Jack Warden, James Mason, Milo O'Shea, Edward Binns, Lindsay Crouse.

Witness for the Prosecution: (1957) An Agatha Christie legal thriller with Charles Laughton as defense barrister fighting back from disastrous testimony by Marlene Dietrich against his client (Tyrone Power) accused of killing an old lady. Also Elsa Lanchester, Una O'Connor, Ian Wolfe.